GUIDE TO RURAL SCOTLAND

By James Gracie

D0302707

Published by:
Travel Publishing Ltd
7a Apollo House, Calleva Park
Aldermaston, Berks, RG7 8TN
ISBN 1-902-00796-4
© Travel Publishing Ltd

Country Living is a registered trademark of The National
Magazine Company Limited.

First Published:

COUNTRY LIVING GUIDES:

East Anglia
Heart of England
Ireland
Scotland

PLEASE NOTE:

All advertisements in this publication have been accepted in good faith by Travel
Publishing and they have not necessarily been endorsed by *Country Living*
Magazine.

All information is included by the publishers in good faith and is believed to be
correct at the time of going to press. No responsibility can be accepted for errors.

Editor: James Gracie

Printing by: Scotprint, Haddington

Location Maps:© Maps in Minutes ™ (2003)   © Crown Copyright, Ordnance Survey 2003

Walks: Walks have been reproduced from the Jarrold Pathfinder Guides
                 © Jarrold Publishing

Walk Maps: Reproduced from Ordnance Survey mapping on behalf of the
                 Controller of Her Majesty's Stationery Office, © Crown Copyright.
                 Licence Number MC 100035812

Cover Design: Lines & Words, Aldermaston

Cover Photo: The River Dee, Braemar, Grampian © www.britainonview.com

Text Photos: Text photos have been kindly supplied by the Britain on View photo library
                 and the author, James Gracie   © www.britainonview.com © James Gracie

Foreword

Scotland has some of Britain's most spectacular scenery. In the Highlands, there are mountains, steep-sided glens and deep lochs while further south the scenery is gentler with flowing rivers and rolling farmland. It is also a country steeped in history and culture - with castles, cathedrals and universities throughout. So whether you want to spend time walking in the wilderness or exploring some of the most romantic ruins in the country, Scotland will not disappoint.

Each month *Country Living Magazine* celebrates the richness and diversity of our countryside with features on rural Britain and Ireland and the traditions that have their roots there. So it is with great pleasure that I introduce you to the latest in our series of *Rural Guides*.

This book will help you explore Scotland and all that it has to offer with its directory of places to stay, eat and drink, its fascinating insights into local history and heritage, and its comprehensive range of Scottish producers of food, arts and crafts. So if you're heading north across the border for the first time or are already a frequent visitor to Scotland then I hope this book will inform and entertain you. Above all, I hope that it will help you enjoy your trip and all that Scotland has to offer.

Susy Smith

Susy Smith

P.S. To subscribe to *Country Living Magazine* every month, call 01858 438844

Introduction

James Gracie is a full time writer who has written many books on Scotland. His articles have appeared in numerous UK newspapers and magazines and he has also broadcast with *Radio Scotland*. Although he has visited and written about many parts of the world, James, who lives in Scotland, finds that writing about the UK is still the most stimulating and rewarding experience. He has used this experience to excellent effect in the first edition of *The Country Living Magazine Guide to* Rural *Scotland* which is packed with vivid descriptions, historical stories, amusing anecdotes and interesting facts on hundreds of places in this wild and often wonderful country.

Scotland is endowed with some of the most beautiful and stunning scenery in the British Isles from the desolate peaks of the Highlands and rugged coastlines of the mainland and off-shore islands, to the peaceful and fertile valleys of the Scottish Borders. But the visitor can also find quiet villages, cosy market towns, neat fishing ports as well as the history and culture of the larger cities such as Edinburgh. Scotland is definitely a country worth exploring!

The coloured advertising panels within each chapter provide further information on places to see, stay, eat, drink, shop and even exercise! We have also selected a number of walks from *Jarrold's Pathfinder Guides* which we highly recommend if you wish to appreciate fully the beauty and charm of the varied rural landscapes of Scotland.

The guide however is not simply an "armchair tour". Its prime aim is to encourage the reader to visit the places described and discover much more about the wonderful towns, villages and countryside of Scotland. Whether you decide to explore this country by wheeled transport or by foot we are sure you will find it a very uplifting experience.

We are always interested in receiving comments on places covered (or not covered) in our guides so please do not hesitate to use the reader reaction form provided at the rear of this guide to give us your considered comments. This will help us refine and improve the content of the next edition. We also welcome any general comments which will help improve the overall presentation of the guides themselves.

Finally, for more information on the full range of travel guides published by Travel Publishing please refer to the details and order form at the rear of this guide or log on to our website at www.travelpublishing.co.uk

Travel Publishing

Locator Map

Chapter 13

Chapter 12

Chapter 11

Chapter 10

Chapter 9

Chapter 8

Chapter 7

Chapter 6

Chapter 5

Chapter 4

Chapter 3

Chapter 1

Chapter 2

Contents

SELF-CATERING HOLIDAYS IN SCOTLAND

Tel: 08705 168571 for a brochure or visit website: www.assc.co.uk for details of all the properties and late availability

A self-catering holiday is the perfect way to discover the dramatic natural beauty of Scotland, to meet the friendly Scottish people, to make the most of the excellent produce of land and sea and to feel 'at home' while enjoying true value for money and total freedom.

Quality accommodation, including houses, cottages, apartments, chalets, castles and lodges,

is available all over Scotland, catering for couples, families large and small and groups of friends. Many of the establishments provide facilities for children and many are happy to accept pets. Non-smoking properties are available.

All the properties belong to an owner or operator who is a member of the **Association of Scotland's Self-Caterers**, the only trade association working exclusively for the self catering in Scotland, and are committed to the Association's principles of Comfort, Cleanliness, Courtesy and Efficiency. Those principles apply

across the board, from the fairly basic to the luxurious, ensuring that guests have the best possible holiday experience. The ASSC, formed in 1978, is closely involved in the operation of VisitScotland Quality Assurance, which ensures that quality is maintained by annual inspection of all the properties.

Some of the members' individual properties are registered under the National Accessibility Scheme with identified criteria meeting the needs of visitors with disabilities. The categories range

from the ability to walk a few paces and up 3 steps to full unassisted wheelchair access.

Many of the properties are members of various other schemes. Among these are the Walkers & Cyclists Scheme and the Green Tourism Scheme working for exceptional environmental standards in areas such as energy, water, waste, pollution and transport.

A large number of the properties offer short breaks as well as the usual weekly bookings; some take credit cards, and all accept payment by cheque.

1 THE BORDERS

The area known as the Scottish Borders stretches from the boundaries of Dumfriesshire in the west to the shores of the North Sea in the east. Tourists who drive north tend to pass right through it on their way to the Highlands, dismissing it airily as "not the real Scotland". This is a mistake. The Borders are as beautiful in their own way as any other part of the country, and have every bit as much history as the lochs, glens and high mountains of the north. Certainly the scenery is less rugged, and the hills are rounder with green, fertile valleys which cut through high, lonely moorland, cosy market towns, picturesque villages, stately homes, castles and - the area's crowning glory - ruined abbeys aplenty.

St Abb's Head

This is where Scotland's nationhood was forged. During the Wars of Independence English troops passed through the area time and time again, raping and pillaging as they went. And the Scots were not slow in seeking revenge. They crossed over the border and caused just as much bloodshed in northern England. This eventually led - even in quieter times - to bands of men (both Scottish and English) known as reivers or moss troopers, who killed, burned and rustled at will, then escaped back to their own country to avoid retribution. Over the years their escapades have been romanticised, but at best they were no more than thugs and bullies who only respected the gun and the sword.

But for all that, the Scottish Borders is a place of high chivalry and romantic border ballads, some of them based on the bloodthirsty incidents that once scarred the area. Sir Walter Scott, though he was born in Edinburgh in 1771, was at heart a Borders man, and collected the ballads. This resulted in the *Border Minstrelsy*, published between 1802 and 1803 in three volumes. His later books, almost single-handedly, created the modern image of Scotland as a mist-shrouded land of heather, bagpipes and Highland chieftains in kilts. When George IV visited Scotland in 1822, he also created what people now call "Scotland's national costume" of kilt, plaid, knitted socks and Highland bonnet, based on the simple everyday wear of Highlanders. The dignitaries who awaited George's ship at Leith had to wear the outfit, much to their embarrassment, and so too did the king, though he

LOCATOR MAP

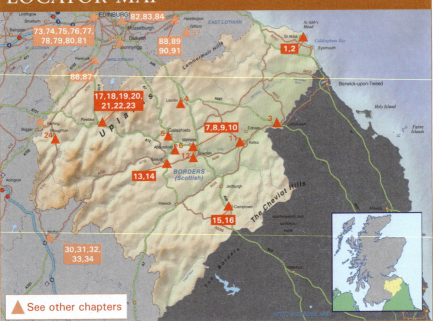

Linlithgow
Broxburn
EDINBURGH! 82,83,84
Haddington
EAST LOTHIAN
St Abb's Head
Bathgate
73,74,75,76,77,
78,79,80,81
Musselburgh
Gifford
Dalkeith
Bonnyrigg
88,89,
90,91
St Abbs
Coldingham Bay
Eyemouth
1,2
LOTHIAN
Penicuik
MIDLOTHIAN
Lammermuir Hills
Berwick-upon-Tweed
86,87
Lauder
Holy Island
17,18,19,20,
21,22,23
U p l a n d s
Peebles
Stirling
Bigger
Broughton
24
Galashiels
7,8,9,10
Ednam
3
Coldstream
Farne Islands
5
Melrose
1
Kelso
Abbotsford
6
BORDERS
(Scottish)
12
Bowden
13,14
Jedburgh
Abington
Hawick
Camptown
The Cheviot Hills
15,16
NORTHUMBERLAND NATIONAL PARK
30,31,32,
33,34
The Borders
NORTHUMBERLAND

⚠ See other chapters

ADVERTISERS AND PLACES OF INTEREST

had the added indignity of pink tights! And this was despite the fact that Scott once boasted that he had never worn a kilt in his life because "...thank God, my ancestors could always afford trousers." But his literary efforts did give Scotland a much needed identity, and put it firmly on the European map.

Scott was not the only literary figure associated with the Scottish Borders. James Hogg, nicknamed the "Ettrick Shepherd", was born in the Ettrick Valley, and is best known for his *Confessions of a Justified Sinner*. And John Buchan, whose most famous book was undoubtedly *The Thirty Nine Steps*, has associations with Broughton in Peeblesshire. It was here that his father (a clergyman) and mother were married, and it was here that his maternal grandparents farmed.

River Tweed, Elibank

The Scottish Borders, however, are most famous for their abbeys. Melrose, Kelso, Jedburgh and Dryburgh are romantic ruins nowadays, but at their height they were powerful and rich, even establishing sheep farming in the area, something which remains to this day. They all sat on the main routes north, so were constantly attacked and despoiled by the invading English armies. The monks patiently rebuilt them, until, at least in Melrose's case, the abbey was abandoned after an English attack and the monks converted to Protestantism. Now the abbeys don't echo to the chanting of monks, but to the tramp of tourists' feet and the click of cameras.

The River Tweed flows through the Borders. For part of its way, it forms the boundary between Scotland and England before becoming wholly Scottish near Kelso. In some ways, it defines the area, and most of its towns, from Coldstream to Peebles, sit on its banks. It was once a mighty salmon river, but this has declined in recent years. However, its beauty has never changed, and it still flows through fresh green valleys and rich countryside.

There are a series of themed trails that can be followed in the Scottish Borders. The Berwickshire Car Trail (72 miles) takes you through that area called "The Merse", which is one of the richest and most attractive farming areas in Britain; The Ballads Trail (103 miles) which explores the areas associated with the great Borders ballads; and the Poets of the Scottish Borders Trail (118 miles), which takes you to places of literary interest. There are also three further trails which deal with individual writers - the Sir Walter Scott Trail (66 miles); the James Hogg Trail (62 miles); and the John Buchan Trail (77 miles).

DUNS

From 1853 until 1975, Duns was the county town of Berwickshire, a county which is unusual in that Berwick itself is in England, and has been since 1482. Before that, Greenlaw was the county town.

Duns is a small, picturesque place with a wide market place and many old buildings. On the outskirts of the town is **Duns Law**, and on its west side is a cairn which marks where the town originally stood. You get a magnificent view of the surrounding countryside from the top. On clear days you can also see the Lammermuir Hills to the north, the Cheviots to the south, and the North Sea, 12 miles to the east. A Covenanting army, which opposed the appointment of bishops in the Church of Scotland, set up camp here under General Leslie in the 17th century. A **Covenantors Stone** commemorates the event.

It was close to Duns that **Johannes Scotus Duns** was born in about 1265. He became a Franciscan monk, and was also known as the "subtle doctor". He became one of the greatest theologians and philosophers of the 13th and 14th centuries, and taught at Oxford, Paris and Cologne, where he died. His influence is still felt within the Roman Catholic Church today, though when he was alive some of his opponents had an unflattering name for his followers - "Dunses", from which we get the word dunce. In 1991 he was made "venerable", the first stage on the way to sainthood. Duns Public Park has a statue of him, and the Franciscan order of monks erected a cairn to his memory in 1966 within the grounds of **Duns Castle**. Also within the castle grounds is the 32 acre **Duns Castle Nature Reserve**, the focal point of which is a pond with the quaint name of Hen Poo. The castle itself incorporates an old

tower built in the 14th century for Randolph, Earl of Moray.

Jim Clark the racing driver was born in Fife, but lived from the age of six in a farm near Duns. He was world champion in 1963 and 1965, but in 1968 was killed in Germany. The **Jim Clark Memorial Trophy Room** in Newton Street has mementos of the great man, including the two world championship trophies. He lies buried at Chirnside, five miles from Duns.

The **Tolbooth House**, on the west side of the market square, was once the town house of the area's leading 17th century landowner, Sir James Cockburn. Much grander, however, is **Manderston House**, a mile east of the town. It was the last great stately home to be built in Britain, and dates from the early 1900s. Its great silver staircase is the only one in existence, though it has a more unusual feature that also delights visitors - a comprehensive collection of biscuit tins. This is because it is the home of the Palmer family, of Huntly and Palmer biscuits fame. It is open to the public.

AROUND DUNS

Abbey St. Bathans

5 miles N of Duns on a minor road off the B6355

Abbey St. Bathans is a picturesque village lying in the valley of the Whiteadder Water, deep in the Lammermuir Hills. It sits on the **Southern Upland Way**, a footpath that runs from Portpartick on the west coast of Scotland to Cockburnspath on the east coast. In 1170 a small priory was set up here by Ada, Countess of Dunbar, and its scant remains are incorporated into the present **Parish Church**. It contains the tombstone of a former prioress, with a carving showing her and her pet dog.

On **Cockburn Law**, to the south of the village, is the **Edinshall Broch**, dating from the Iron Age. It is one of the few Lowland examples of a fortified stone tower which is more commonly found in the Highlands. Its name derives from a legendary three-headed giant who once terrorised the area in olden times.

Storm Clouds, St Abb's Head

COCKBURNSPATH

11 miles N of Duns just off the A1

This small village is the eastern terminal of the Southern Upland Way. The ruined **Cockburnspath Tower** dates from the 15th and 16th centuries, and was owned by the Dunbars, the Holmes, the Sinclairs and the Douglases. **Pease Dean**, a Scottish Wildlife Trust nature reserve, is nearby. **Pease Bridge**, built in 1783, was at one time the highest stone bridge in Europe. The **Parish Church** dates partly from the 14th century.

COLDINGHAM

11 miles NE of Duns on the A1107

Coldingham Priory was founded in 1098 by King Edgar (1072-1107), son of King Malcolm Canmore of Scotland, and he gifted it to the monks of Durham Cathedral. Like the better known abbeys to the west, it fared badly during the

Wars of Independence in the 13th and 14th centuries. In 1648 it suffered the humiliation of being blown up by Cromwell's troops. However, the ruins were restored in 1854, and it became the village's parish church.

ST. ABBS

12 miles NE of Duns, on the B6438

This lovely fishing village sits on the coast, a mile east of Coldingham. The coastline here is rugged and spectacular, with tall cliffs that plunge down to the sea. **St. Abb's Head** (National Trust for Scotland - see panel on page 6) is to the north of the village, and is 300 feet above the shoreline. It is riddled with caves which were once the haunt of smugglers. The place is named after St. Ebba, a 7th

---

CASTLE ROCK

Murrayfield, St. Abbs, Berwickshire TD14 5PP
Tel: 01890 771715   e-mail: boowood@compuserve.com
Fax: 01890 771520   website: www.castlerockbandb.co.uk

Castle Rock is a superior B&B establishment offering wonderful hospitality in a beautiful area steeped in history. All the rooms are extremely comfortable, with a double and a single bed and en suite facilities. One bedroom boasts a four poster, while another has a spa bath! There are telephones, hospitality trays, electric blankets, colour satellite TVs and clock-radios. The owner, Barbara Wood, offers evening meals in the spacious dining room, using only the finest and freshest of local produce, and there is a carefully selected wine list. Castle Rock is such a friendly place that people always want to return!

ST ABBS HEAD NATIONAL NATURE RESERVE

Ranger's Cottage, Northfield, St Abbs, Eyemouth,
Borders TD14 5QF
Tel: 018907 71443   Fax: 018907 71606.
website: www.nts.org.uk

Formed by an extinct volcano, **The Head** is the best known landmark along the magnificent Berwickshire coast. Home to thousands of nesting seabirds in summer, the Head also has a wealth of other wildlife and fine views along the coast. In recognition of its importance to both wildlife and people, the Head was declared a National Nature Reserve in 1983. The offshore waters lie within a Special Area of Conservation and form part of Scotland's only

Voluntary Marine Nature Reserve. A new remote camera link to Nature Reserve Centre allows visitors to observe seabirds during nesting season (recorded footage out of season). Exhibition, toilets.

century nun who was the sister of Oswy, King of Northumbria. On the cliff top she founded a monastery, though it later fell into disrepute due to a lack of austerity and discipline. An old legend recounts how the nuns spent their days eating, drinking and gossiping instead of praying and doing good works.

The whole area is now a National Nature Reserve, owned by the National Trust for Scotland. And it's not just the cliff tops that are popular with visitors - the offshore waters have some of the best diving in Scotland.

EDROM

3 miles E of Duns on the A6105

This small village is visited mainly for its fine **Parish Church** of 1732, which has some earlier Norman details. Within it you'll find the Blackadder Aisle, containing a tomb from 1553. In the kirkyard is a mausoleum which incorporates a Norman arch. It originally came from a church built in the early 12th century.

CHIRNSIDE

5 miles E of Duns just off the A6105

The village's **Parish Church** has an impressive Norman doorway at its west end, and in the kirkyard is the grave of Jim Clark the racing driver, who was killed in 1968. Though it looks peaceful nowadays, it did have one frightening moment during World War 1, when it was accidentally bombed by the Germans from a Zeppelin.

It sits on a low hill, among some lovely countryside, close to where the Blackadder Water and Whiteadder Water meet, and there are some wonderful views to be had.

HUTTON

8 miles E of Duns on a minor road off the B6460

The village's **Parish Church** dates from 1835, and has a fine old bell of 1661. **Hutton Castle** was the home of Sir William Burrell, the millionaire shipping magnate and art collector who donated his vast collection to the city of Glasgow.

AYTON

9 miles E of Duns on the B6355

Ayton sits on the wonderfully named River Eye, half a mile west of the A1, the main trunk road connecting Edinburgh with the south. **Ayton Castle** dates from the 19th century, and is reckoned to be one of the finest examples in the country of a style of architecture called "Scottish Baronial", which took as its inspiration the castles built in Scotland during medieval times. Though no Scottish

Ayton Castle

castle of the medieval period ever looked like this, the place does have a distinctly Scottish feel, with its turrets and pinnacles. It is sometimes open on Saturday afternoons, or by appointment.

PAXTON

9 miles E of Duns just off the B6461

This small village sits just north of the banks of the Tweed. The 480-feet long **Union Suspension Bridge** crosses the river here, connecting Scotland and England. It was built in 1820, and was Britain's first major suspension bridge designed to carry traffic. The designer was Sir Samuel Browne, who also designed the innovative wrought iron chain links used in its construction.

Paxton House sits just to the south of the village, close to the river. It was built in 1758 by Patrick Home, 13th Laird of Wedderburn, who, while on the Continent, had wooed and won the illegitimate daughter of Frederik the Great of Prussia. After their marriage he hoped to make this gracious country

house their home. The marriage, however, never took place, and all that is left to remind future generations of his love affair - apart from the house itself - is a pair of the young lady's gloves, which are still on display.

The house was designed by John and James Adam, with plaster work designed by their more famous brother Robert. It is said to be the finest Palladian mansion in Britain, with a magnificent collection of Chippendale furniture on show. One of the outposts of the National Galleries of Scotland is located here, and you can also see a fine international collection of paintings.

FOULDEN

9 miles E of Duns, on the A6105

Foulden's main claim to fame is its magnificent **Tithe Barn**, which has two storeys and typically Scottish crow-stepped gables. It dates from medieval times, though it was considerably altered in the 18th and 19th centuries. In olden days, farming communities gave one tenth, or "tithe" of their produce to the church, and this was where it was stored.

EYEMOUTH

12 miles E of Duns on the A1107

Eyemouth owes its existence to fishing. As its name suggests, it stands at the mouth of the River Eye, and an old

Eyemouth

document dated 1298 links its foundation as a fishing port with Coldingham Priory. At one time it was a centre for smuggling, and many of the old quayside buildings still have tunnels and cellars where smuggled goods were stored. **Gungreen House** which lies to the south of the harbour, was the centre for the "trade".

Every year in July the town has its traditional **Herring Queen Festival**, when local fishing boats - suitably dressed up for the occasion - escort a boat carrying the newly declared "herring queen" into Eyemouth Harbour. **Eyemouth Museum** has displays about the history of the town and its fishing industry. It opened in 1981, exactly one hundred years after an infamous tragedy, when 189 fishermen (129 of whom were from Eyemouth) perished at sea in a raging storm well in sight of shore.

LADYKIRK

7 miles SE of Duns, on a minor road off the B6470

The small village is named after the **Parish Church of St. Mary**, which dates from 1500. It was built by James IV as an act of thanksgiving after he nearly perished while crossing the nearby River Tweed. It is made entirely of stone (even its roof has stone slabs instead of tiles) in case it was ever set alight by marauding English troops.

COLDSTREAM

9 miles S of Duns on the A697

It was here, in 1660, that General Monck founded one of Britain's most famous regiments - the **Coldstream Guards**. In 1659, a year after Cromwell's death, Monck had established his headquarters in Coldstream. He feared that Cromwell's son Richard (who had been made

CRAFT HOUSE GALLERY

Coldstream, Berwickshire TD12 4LW
Tel: 01890 882965

Coldstream is a small town on the banks of the Tweed, which at this point is the border between Scotland and England. Within the Hirsel Country Park, a mile north of the town, you'll find the **Craft House Gallery**, housed in a cosy, picturesque listed building. It is owned and run by Wilma Bannink, and you are sure to find art and craft items that would make lovely memories of your time in the area. There are wonderful ranges of jewellery, wooden bowls and ornaments, prints, walking sticks, paintings, furniture, sculpture, wrought iron work, glass, ceramics and a host of other items in all price ranges. The staff are attentive and knowledgeable, and always on hand to offer informed and friendly advice.

Everything in the shop is made locally, so Wilma knows each craft worker personally, and chooses only the finest items to display in the shop. Each item of jewellery is individually made, and therefore unique, using gold, silver, beadwork and stone settings that show off the craftsmanship to perfection. The paintings are in oils, watercolour or acrylic, and cover a wide range of themes, from animals to local landscapes. Artists and craftpersons sometimes give demonstrations on the premises, so if you're lucky you could actually see them making the pieces that are on sale. This is a wonderful place to visit, full of fascinating items. You're sure to find something to your taste at the Craft House Gallery. Open daily throughout the year from 10.30am-5pm.

Protector) and his Commonwealth generals were too weak to run Britain, so he raised a regiment of men who had formerly been in the Commonwealth army, and marched them to London in order to restore Charles II to the throne. A memorial within Henderson Park commemorates the raising of the regiment, and the

THIRLESTANE CASTLE

By Lauder, Borders
Tel: 01578 722430 Fax: 01578 722761
e-mail: admin@thirlestanecastle.co.uk
website: www.thirlestanecastle.co.uk

Thirlestane, one of the oldest and finest castles in Scotland is set in lovely Border hills at Lauder, 28 miles south of Edinburgh and 68 miles north of Newcastle, on the A68. Built originally as a defensive fort in the 13th century it was rebuilt in the 16th century as the home of the Maitlands. As the seat of the Earls and Duke of Lauderdale it was enlarged and embellished over the centuries but it still remains home to the Maitland family. The Duke's ghost is said to haunt the castle.

See the Panelled Room and the Library with their defensive walls up to 13 feet thick. Absorb the atmosphere of the Billiard Room with its fascinating salmon fly screen. Climb the ancient turnpike stair to the Duke's Suite, where there are incomparable 17th century plasterwork ceilings. Relish the splendour of the Green Drawing Room and the Ante Drawing Room with their exquisite ceilings and joinery. Sink into nostalgia as you enter the Family Nurseries with their unique collection of historic toys. Some are in replica form for children to use, and dipping into the dressing up chest can create some memorable moments on a family holiday.

Coldstream Museum in the market square has extensive displays on its history, as well as that of the town.

The **Coldstream Bridge** across the Tweed was built in 1766, and links Scotland and England. It replaced an old ford which had been used as a crossing point for centuries. In 1786 Robert Burns entered England by the bridge, and a plaque commemorates the event. In the 19th century, Coldstream was as famous as Gretna Green for runaway marriages. At the Scottish end of the bridge is the **Old Toll House** where, in one 13 year period, 1,466 marriages were conducted.

The Hirsal lies one mile north of the town. It has been the home of the Earls of Home since 1611, and Sir Alec Douglas Home, Britain's prime minister in the 1960s, had his home here. The grounds can be visited, though the house isn't open to the public.

GREENLAW

6 miles W of Duns on the A697

From 1696 until 1853, this village was the county town of Berwickshire. The **Parish Church** has a fine tower which dates from 1712, and which was originally the town jail. The ruins of **Hume Castle** lies three miles south of the town. It was captured by Cromwellian troops in 1651, and partly restored in 1794. As the ruins of the castle sit 600 feet above sea level, there are marvellous views to be had of the surrounding countryside.

LAUDER

16 miles W of Duns on the A68

The A68 trunk road is one of the main highways south from Edinburgh to England. The picturesque town of Lauder, with its sturdy 17th, 18th and 19th century cottages, straddles the road, its most distinctive feature being the 17th century Parish Church, shaped like a Greek cross.

The original church stood further to the east, close to where **Thirlestane Castle** (see panel on page 9) now stands. This impressive castle - which looks more French than Scottish - was originally built in the 13th century, but was extended and refurbished for the Maitland family in the 16th century. The most famous member of the family was John Maitland, second Earl, and, from 1672, first Duke of Lauderdale. From 1660 until 1680 he was Secretary of Scottish Affairs, and was a close friend of Charles II. He was a member of the king's famous group of advisers called the "Cabal Cabinet", the name being taken from the surnames and titles of its members (Maitland was the "L"). So powerful did he become that people soon referred to him as the "uncrowned king of Scotland". His ghost is said to haunt the Castle.

It was he who had the medieval parish church moved from its old site in front of the castle to its present one, to open up the view from the his home. Legend says that he told one of his bowmen to fire an arrow westwards from the castle steps, and wherever it fell there would he build a new church. The bowman did as he was instructed, and that is why the present parish church is within the town.

GALASHIELS

Galashiels is the centre of the Scottish Borders woollen industry. At one time the place had many woollen and tweed mills, though the industry declined in the latter part of the 20th century due to cheap imports. It sits on the Gala Water (in fact, locals refer to the town simply as "Gala"), and so important was the textile industry to the town that the motto of its Manufacturer's Corporation was "We dye to live and live to die".

Being close to the border, the town has a bloody history. Every year in July the town holds the **Braw Lads Gathering**, which celebrates this history. On the town's coat-of-arms are the words "soor plooms" ("sour plums"), which commemorates an incident which is said to have taken place in 1337. Some English troops were passing through the area, and stole some plums from a local orchard. So incensed were the citizens of the town that they killed every one of the soldiers.

The town's **Mercat Cross** ("market cross") dates from 1695. It was at its predecessor that the betrothal of James IV and Margaret Tudor, Henry VII's daughter, took place. The town's oldest building is **Old Gala House**, which dates from the 15th century. It was the town house of a local family called the Pringles, who were Lairds of Gala, and

GLENELLWYN

89 Melrose Road, Galashiels, Scottish Borders TD1 2BX
Tel: 01896 752964

Gwen Young has owned and managed the **Glenellwyn** B&B for the last seven years, and during that time has established it as one of the best and most comfortable B&Bs in the Scottish Borders. She has three extremely comfortable rooms - a double and two singles, all with colour TV and tea and coffee making facilities. This handsome, red sandstone house has a lovely, mature garden where visitors can relax with views of the lovely Eildon Hills. People are assured of a warm, Scottish welcome here.

now it houses a museum and art gallery. It is surrounded by well kept and colourful gardens. The town's **War Memorial** has been called one of the finest in Britain, and is a bronze statue of a border reiver on horseback. Both the Southern Upland Way and the **Tweed Cycleway** pass close to the town.

Abbotsford

AROUND GALASHIELS

ABBOTSFORD

2 miles S of Galashiels, on the B6860

The Scottish Borders most famous son (even though he was born in Edinburgh) was undoubtedly **Sir Walter Scott**. Almost single-handedly, through his books, he forged a national identity for Scotland, and has been called the country's greatest ambassador for tourism. He was born in 1771, and called to the bar in 1792. Seven years later he was appointed Sheriff-Depute at Selkirk Sheriff court. His first work of fiction was *The Lay of the Last Minstrel*, written in verse form. It was published in 1805. His first true novel was *Waverley*, which was published anonymously.

Such was his eventual fame that he was able to buy an old farmstead called "Clartyhole" ("clarty" is an old Scots word for "dirty", so you imagine the state it was in), which he pulled down. Between 1817 and 1822 he built his new home on the site, and called it **Abbotsford** (see panel on page 12) after an old monastic ford which once crossed the nearby Tweed.

It is in the Scots Baronial style, and is crammed with mementos and objects that show Scott's passion for Scottish history. Here you can see a lock of

Charles Edward Stuart's hair, a piece of oatcake found within the sporran of a Jacobite killed at Culloden and a glass tumbler on which Burns has etched some verses. The hallway is Gothic, with dark wood panelling that formerly adorned an old kirk, and above the fireplace is a carriage clock that once belonged to Marie Antoinette.

Scott's study is a workroom rather than a place of comfort. Here, after his wife's death in 1826, he worked himself into an early grave, writing novel after novel to pay off his huge debts. At five every morning he rose and went to his study to write before setting out for the courtroom at Selkirk. When he returned in the evening, he wrote late into the night. And through all this punishing schedule, he still found time to travel and keep up a correspondence with many influential people.

But it eventually took its toll, and on September 21st 1832 he died, aged just 61 and tired out from overwork. He had just returned from a trip abroad, and a bed was set up by the window in Abbotsford's dining room so that he could see out towards the river Tweed. He was buried beside his wife in Dryburgh Abbey.

ABBOTSFORD

Abbotsford, Near Melrose TD6 9BQ
Tel: 01896 752043 Fax: 01896 752916
e-mail: abbotsford@melrose.bordernet.co.uk

Sir Walter Scott and Scotland are inseparable. Though born in Edinburgh, he was a Borders man through and through, and steeped in the old ballads of the area. He spent much of his childhood in the Borders, and loved every inch of them. In 1799 he was appointed Sheriff-depute for Selkirkshire - something that pleased him greatly - and in 1804 rented the property of Ashiestiel on the River Tweed near Selkirk. He was now writing seriously, with *Marmion*, and *The Lady of the Lake* under his belt. In 1811 he bought a property near Galashiels called Clartyhole, and it was here he built **Abbotsford**, which was to be his home until he died in 1832. It was here also that he wrote all of his great novels, such as *Waverley*, *A Legend of Montrose*, *Ivanhoe*, *Kenilworth*, *Redgauntlet* and *Quentin Durward*.

It is a wonderful place - full, not only of memorabilia connected with the great man, but of treasures connected with the history of Scotland itself. Sir Walter was a magpie in this respect, and all the objects he collected are still within the house to be seen and admired. As you enter the main door, you are confronted with an entrance hall panelled with the original panelling from Dunfermline's Old Parish Kirk and the Palace of Holyrood in Edinburgh. The huge stone fireplace is partly copied from

one of the original stalls in Melrose Abbey, and above it is a clock once owned by Marie Antoinette.

You could spend all day in the entrance hall alone, but there is much to see elsewhere as well. A door to your right takes you into Sir Walter's study, where he did his writing. It is obviously a workroom, and not a place of comfort. On top of his writing desk is a small, portable bureau which he used when not at home. It is made of wood from the ships of the Spanish Armada. Every morning at 5 am Sir Walter came down the circular staircase from his bedroom above to begin work here. In the same year that his wife died, the publishing firm in which he was a partner went bankrupt, and Sir Walter worked until his death to pay off its massive debts.

The library is a large, airy room, and here you will find the writer's collection of over 9,000 books, some of them very precious indeed. And in the showcases are further examples of his magpie ways. Here you can see Rob Roy's purse, a piece of oatcake taken from the sporran of a Jacobite killed at Culloden and a lock of Charles Edward Stuart's hair. Then go through into the drawing room, hung with hand-painted Chinese paper, and see Sir Henry Raeburn's famous portrait of Sir Walter painted in 1809 when he was 38 years old, as well as portraits of his mother and father.

You will be fascinated by the urn filled with old bones found in Athens and given to Sir Walter by Lord Byron in 1811, and the pieces of silver given to the great man by his many admirers. There is also a roll top desk presented by George IV, one of Scott's greatest admirers. But perhaps the most poignant room is the dining room, where Sir Walter died in 1832, worn out by hard work. He had come back from a trip to the Continent that had not, as intended, reinvigorated him. His bed was set up at the window so that he could see the grounds he loved, and here he died on September 21st 1832, aged just 61.

And you can also explore the grounds, and see the small chapel erected after his death. Abbotsford is truly a magical place to visit, and you will not come away unaffected by its atmosphere.

CLOVENFORD

3 miles W of Galashiels on the A72

This small, attractive village sits a mile north of the Tweed, and, in keeping with the river's reputation for fine fishing, is home to the **School of Casting, Salmon and Trout Fishing**.

STOW

7 miles N of Galashiels on the A7

This delightful village (sometimes also known as Stow-in-Wedale) sits on the **Gala Water**. It's most imposing feature is the magnificent **St. Mary of Wedal Parish Church**, which has a 140-feet high spire. To the west are the **Moorfoot Hills**, and to the east is a stretch of lonely moorland which separates it from Lauderdale. The B6362 passes over the moorland rising to over 1100 feet as it does so and connects stow with Lauder. It makes an attractive five mile drive.

GORDON

11 miles NE of Galashiels on the A6105

Clan Gordon originated in the lands surrounding this quiet village, which sits on a crossroads. In the 14th century it moved north to Aberdeenshire, and is now looked upon as a Highland clan. The well preserved ruins of **Greenknowe Tower** lie to the north of the village. It has a typically Scottish L-shaped layout, and was built in 1581 by James Seton of

Touch and his wife Jane Edmonstone. It was later owned by the Pringles, one of the great Borders families.

MELLERSTAIN

10 miles E of Galashiels, on an unmarked road between the A6089 and the B6397

This gracious stately home was designed by William Adam in the 1720s, with later work being done by his son Robert. It is reckoned to be one of the finest Georgian mansions in Britain, and has fine collections of furniture and paintings, including works by Gainsborough, Van Dyck and Allan Ramsay. The grounds also have many attractions, not least of which are the Italian terraces, laid out in 1909 by Sir Reginald Blomfield. There are wonderful views towards the Cheviot Hills.

MELROSE

3 miles E of Galashiels on the B6361, just off the A6091

Legend states that King Arthur and his court lie buried under the triple peaks of the **Eildon Hills**, which overlook this small, attractive town. There is a waymarked path leading to the summit, which makes an excellent climb if you're reasonably fit and healthy. From the top the views are superb.

Melrose sits on the Southern Upland Way, and is visited mainly to view the

ORMISTON & RENWICK

High Street, Melrose, Scottish Borders TD6 9PB
Tel: 01896 822163 e-mail: info@ormistonrenwick.co.uk
Fax: 01896 823660 website: www.ormistonrenwick.co.uk

While you're in the historic town of Melrose, with its wonderful abbey ruins, why not visit one of the Scottish Border's best garden centres, **Ormiston & Renwick**. Here you will find the very best in flowers, shrubs and trees, garden furniture and seeds (including 27 varieties of seed potatoes!).
Owned and managed by Sheila and Martin Cox, it has been in existence since 1804. At the rear is a conservatory which carries a wide range of indoor plants, and there is sure to be something to fit everyone's taste! So make this your number one stop in Melrose.

ruins of **Melrose Abbey**
(Historic Scotland), which
are acknowledged to be the
loveliest in the Borders. The
abbey was founded in 1136
by David I, and soon rose to
become one of the most
important in the country.
The present ruins date from
rebuildings in the 14th and
15th centuries after attacks
by the troops of Richard III
of England. It was in Melrose
Abbey that the heart of
Robert I (also known as

Melrose Abbey

Robert the Bruce), Scotland's great king
and leader during part of the Wars of
Independence, was buried. After his
death it had been removed from his body
and placed in a casket so that Sir James
Douglas might take it to the Holy Land
for burial. But Sir James was killed en
route, and the casket was brought back
to Melrose. In the 1990s, during
restoration work on the abbey, the lead
casket containing his heart was
discovered and reburied. The spot is now
marked by a cross.

Close to the abbey ruins is **Priorwood
Gardens** (National Trust for Scotland -
see panel opposite). It specialises in
growing and drying flowers and plants
used in flower arranging, and classes are
available which teach the basic
techniques involved. The Trust also owns

and manages **Harmony Garden**
(National Trust for Scotland - see panel
opposite), set in the grounds of a 19th
century house, which is not open to
the public.

The remains of **Trimontium Roman
Fort** lies a mile east of Melrose. It is
named after the three peaks of the Eildon
Hills, and covers 15 acres. It once housed
1,500 Roman soldiers, and supported a
large town of civilians which covered a
further 200 acres. In Melrose's main
square is the **Three Hills Roman
Heritage Centre**, with displays and
artifacts that illustrate what life was like
in Scotland's largest Roman fort. On
Thursday afternoons (also on Tuesday in
July and August) a guided five mile, four
hour walk to the fort takes place, leaving
from the Centre.

PYROCANTHUS

32 Market Square, Melrose, Roxburghshire TD6 9PP
Tel: 01896 822590
e-mail: pyrocanthus@btopenworld.com
website: www.pyrocanthus.co.uk

Situated at the heart of one of the most picturesque small towns
in the Borders, **Pyrocanthus** is a shop that sells quality objects
and works of art influenced by the best in contemporary Scottish
and Scandinavian design. There is a fine range of ceramics and glass, contemporary wood design,
candles, candlesticks, hand-made Scottish cards and small items of furniture. The shop is spacious
and well laid out, with staff that are friendly and knowledgeable. This is the ideal place to buy a
souvenir of your visit to one of the loveliest parts of Scotland.

HARMONY GARDEN

St Mary's Road, Melrose, Borders TD6 9LJ
website: www.nts.org.uk

A delightfully tranquil walled garden comprising lawns, herbaceous and mixed borders, vegetable and fruit areas, and a rich display of spring bulbs. The garden is set around an early 19th century house (not open to the public), built by Melrose joiner Robert Waugh, who named it "Harmony" after the Jamaican pimento plantation where he had made his fortune, **Harmony Garden** has excellent views of Melrose Abbey and the Eildon Hills and is situated near Priorwood Garden (see below).

PRIORWOOD GARDEN & DRIED FLOWER SHOP

Melrose, Borders, TD6 9PX
Tel : 01896 822493 Fax: 01896 823181 Shop: Tel: 01896 822965
e-mail priorwooddriedflowers@nts.org.uk
website: www.nts.org.uk

A specialist garden where most of the plants grown are suitable for drying. The colourful and imaginative selection ensures variety for the dried flower arrangements made here. Visitors can enjoy a stroll through the orchard which includes historic varieties of apples that are organically grown. Enjoy the different blossoms in spring, a picnic here in the summer, and catch a glimpse of the impressive ruins of Melrose Abbey which overlook the garden. **Priorwood Garden** is a short walk from Harmony Garden (see above). For information on day courses throughout the year, please contact the property.

Two miles outside the town, on a bend in the Tweed, is the site of **Old Melrose**. In about AD650 Celtic monks from Iona founded a monastery here. It was close by, a year later, that **St. Cuthbert** was born. He became a shepherd among the local hills, but after a vision entered the monastery to train as a monk. Though he was an unassuming, quiet man who prized prayer and solitude, he eventually rose to become prior of Lindisfarne. He now lies buried in Durham Cathedral, where his tomb was, in medieval times, a place of pilgrimage. The 62-mile long walking route called **St. Cuthbert's Way** now links Melrose and Lindisfarne. And the 55 mile long **Abbey Cycle Route** connects Melrose with the three other great abbeys of the Borders - Kelso, Dryburgh and Jedburgh.

The whole of the Scottish Borders is a rugby playing area, and it was in Melrose that the version of the game known as **Rugby Sevens** was invented.

EARLSTON

5 miles E of Galashiels on the A68

Black Hill dominates this small Lauderdale town, and it gives good views of the surrounding countryside. Earlston was the birthplace, in about 1220, of one of Scotland's earliest poets, **Thomas Learmont of Earlston**, also known as Thomas the Rhymer, Thomas of Erceldoune or True Thomas. He was also a seer, and legend says he foretold of many events in Scottish history, including the death of Alexander III in 1285 and the Battle of Bannockburn in 1314. Even during his lifetime, he attained an almost mythical status. It was said, for instance, that he regularly went off to live with the fairies in the fairy kingdom beneath the Eildon Hills.

But Thomas regularly travelled abroad, and this no doubt accounted for his absences.

SMAILHOLM

9 miles E of Galashiels on the B6397

The gaunt **Smailholm Tower** (Historic Scotland) sits on top of a low, rocky outcrop. Sir Walter Scott, while a boy, spent many holidays at Sandyknowe, his paternal grandparent's home nearby, and was influenced by the history and romance of the place. It now houses a collection of costumed figures and tapestries connected with the writer and his works.

KELSO

14 miles E of Galashiels on the A698

Kelso's **Market Square**, said to be the largest in Scotland, would not look out of place in a French or Belgian town. It is surrounded by imposing 18th and 19th century buildings, the most important of which is the elegant **Town House** of 1816, which now houses the local tourism office.

The town sits at the junction of the Tweed and Teviot, and perhaps its most important attraction for tourists are the ruins of **Kelso Abbey** (Historic Scotland).

It was founded in 1128 by David I, who had earlier founded a monastery at Selkirk, but moved it to Kelso before work could get underway. It was the largest of the Borders abbeys, and was finally destroyed in 1545 by the English during that period of Scottish history known as the **Rough Wooing**, when Henry VIII was trying to coerce the Scots into letting Mary Stuart (better known as "Mary Queen of Scots") marry his son Edward. Fifteen years later the Reformation arrived in Scotland, and the abbey was never rebuilt. All that remains of the church nowadays are the church transepts, part of the tower, two bays of the nave and the west end.

The **Kelso Civic Week** is held every year in July, one of the many similar ceremonies that take place in other Borders towns to celebrate their history and heritage.

Kelso sits in the former county of Roxburghshire, and three miles south west of the town is the site of the once-proud **Royal Burgh of Roxburgh**. This was a thriving, walled town in medieval times, but nothing now remains of it apart from a few bumps in a field, thanks to repeated raids by the English.

The site of **Roxburgh Castle** stands at the confluence of the Tweed and Teviot. It is no more than a high mound nowadays, though at one time it was one of the most important Castles in the Borders. It was during a siege of the castle that James II was killed when a cannon accidentally blew up in his face. Roxburgh Castle has now been suggested as yet another site for King Arthur's fabled Camelot.

Kelso

To the west of Kelso, and across the river from the Castle, stands one of the most magnificent stately homes in the country - **Floors Castle**, the home of the Duke and Duchess of Roxburgh. It is Scotland's largest inhabited house, and sits on the "floors", or flat lands, adjoining the Tweed. It has a large collection of works or art, furniture, tapestries and ceramics. A holly tree in the deer park supposedly marks the spot where James II was killed by a cannon.

Floors Castle

EDNAM

15 miles E of Galashiels on the B6461

Ednam has a double claim to fame - it was the birthplace of two men who wrote the words to two of the most famous songs in Britain. **James Thomson** was born in 1700, and wrote the words of *Rule Britannia*, while **Henry Francis Lyte** wrote the words of *Abide with Me*. To the south of the village, at Ferniehill, is a memorial to Thomson, while the bridge over the river has a plaque commemorating Lyte.

DRYBURGH

6 miles SE of Galashiels off the B6356

The ruins of **Dryburgh Abbey** (Historic Scotland) sit within a lop of the River Tweed, and must be the most romantically situated of any of the great Border abbeys. Very little remains of the great abbey church apart from the transepts and the west door, though the other buildings grouped round the cloister can still be explored.

The abbey was founded in 1150 for the Premonstratensian order of monks by Hugh de Morville, Constable of Scotland, and built on a site that was already sacred. A Celtic monk called St. Modan had already established a monastery

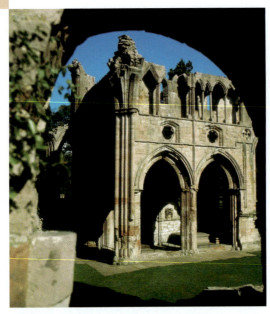

Dryburgh Abbey

that of **Field Marshall Earl Haig of Bemersyde**. He was Commander-in-Chief of the British Expeditionary Forces in France and Flanders during World War I.

A short walk from the ruins is the 22-feet high **William Wallace Statue**. Scotland's military leader during the Wars of Independence, he spent a lot of time hiding from the English in the surrounding countryside and in Ettrick Forest. And north of the abbey is the famous **Scott's View**, which gives a superb view towards the Eildon Hills. The spot is so called because it was one of Sir Walter Scott's favourite places, and he often came up here on horseback seeking inspiration. A poignant story is told of how Sir Walter's horses, while pulling the hearse with his coffin on it to Dryburgh Abbey, stopped here of their own accord, as they had always done when he was alive. The best way to get to the site is from the A68, where it is signposted from the Leadfoot Viaduct spanning the Tweed.

there in the 6th or 7th century, though this would have been a simple affair of wooden churches, store houses and drystone beehive cells where the monks lived, all surrounded by a low earth wall. In 1322, while retreating from Scotland, Edward II's army attacked the abbey, destroying and looting it, the first of many such attacks over the years.

Within the south transept are the graves of Sir Walter Scott and his French wife Charlotte Charpontier, as well as

Mertoun House and Gardens are close by. The house is closed to the public, but the 26 acre gardens can be visited on Saturdays, Sundays and Bank Holiday Mondays. In the grounds of the house

stands **Mertoun Kirk**, which is open for Sunday services.

ST. BOSWELLS

6 miles SE of Galashiels on the A68

St. Boisal, after whom the village is named, was a 7th century Celtic monk who was abbot of the monastery at Old Melrose. On St. Boisal's Day (July 18) each year the village's green is given over to a fair. In olden times, it was one of the largest fairs in the Borders, and attracted many people - especially gypsies - from all over Scotland and Northern England.

SELKIRK

5 miles S of Galashiels on the A7

Selkirk is a small, quiet royal burgh on the edge of the Ettrick Forest. It was once the county town of Selkirkshire, and it was here, in 1113, that David I founded

an abbey. However, before one stone was laid on top of another, David changed his mind, and 15 years later he moved the monks to Kelso. The Ettrick Water, a tributary of the Tweed, flows to the west of the town. Here it is joined from the west by the Yarrow Water, which flows down through the Vale of Yarrow, one of the most scenic valleys in the Borders.

Selkirk is where Sir Walter was Sheriff-Depute (a judge in a sheriff court) until his death in 1832. A statue of him stands outside the **Old Courthouse** in the High street, and inside there is an audio-visual display explaining his work (both legal and literary) and his associations with the town. Also in the High Street is a statue of **Mungo Park**, the great African explorer and surgeon, who was born in Yarrow in 1771. He was killed along with all his men by natives at Boussa in Africa

ROB ELLIOT FURNITURE AND SUE ELLIOT CREATIVE SILKS AND VELVETS

River Cottage, Riverside Road, Selkirk, Selkirkshire TD7 5DU
Tel/Fax: 01750 722243   website: www.robelliotfurniture.com
e-mail: rob.elliot@ic24.net e-mail: sueelliotselkirk@yahoo.co.uk

Rob Elliot has been in the furniture making business for over 15 years, while his wife Sue has worked with silks and silk velvets for over five years. Their premises are adjacent to each other on the banks of the River Ettrick, and together they form **Rob Elliot Furniture and Sue Elliot Creative Silks and Velvets**. Rob works in burr elm, a wood renowned for its rich colour and grain. Bringing his skills to the natural beauty of the wood, Rob Elliot has succeeded in producing furniture to be treasured; furniture sought out by householder and connoisseur alike. It is difficult to stand beside a piece of Rob Elliot's warm, inviting furniture and not touch it! Over the years clients have commissioned Rob to make beds, tables, desks, chairs, bookcases, dressers and a host of other items of furniture that have earned him a fine reputation. Pieces are usually on display in his riverside workshop, and to preserve the beauty of the countryside, he uses only wood from trees that have died naturally.

Sue designs and produces individually crafted silk and silk velvet gifts and accessories such as scarves and wraps, sarongs, cushions, jewellery rolls, bags, decorative mirrors and silk-covered books and photograph albums. Her work has grown from her love of colour and texture and results in finished items that are highly sought after. Like her husband, she accepts commissions, and can make items of any size or colour to complement an outfit or colour scheme. Her work is on display and can be purchased from her studio shop. When you're in Selkirk, why not visit Rob and Sue's studio workshops and see their beautifully crafted works.

in 1806, though news of his gruesome fate didn't reach Britain until 1812.

The oldest building in Selkirk is **Halliwell's House**, where there is a small museum and art gallery. **Robert D. Clapperton Photographic** is a working museum and photography archive. Here, in days gone by, the citizens of Selkirk posed stiffly while their photographs were taken. At **Selkirk Glass**, just off the A7, you can see glass paperweights being made.

Selkirk's **Common Riding Ceremony** - one of those civic occasions that are common in the Scottish Borders - takes place each year in June. In days gone by, it was very important to delineate the marches, or boundaries of burghs, towns and their common lands, so they were inspected each year to make sure no one was encroaching on them. Over 500 riders take part in today's ceremony,

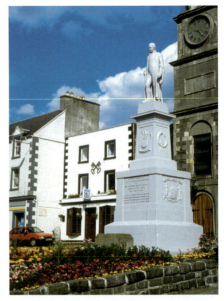

Scott's Monument, Market Square, Selkirk

GLEN HOTEL

Yarrow Terrace, Selkirk, Selkirkshire TD7 5AS
Tel/Fax: 01750 20259
website: www.glenhotel.co.uk

The **Glen Hotel** is a lovely old stone built Victorian house standing only a few yards from Ettrick Water. It is owned and run by Catherine McDonald and Derek Johnson, who are determined to make any stay in their establishment a comfortable and memorable one. The eight bedrooms are superbly furnished and decorated and extremely comfortable, with one of them even boasting a four-poster bed. As you would expect in a hotel of this standard, all have private facilities, as well as colour TV sets and tea and coffee making facilities. The welcoming and cosy bar opens out into the hotel's manicured gardens, perfect for a relaxing drink in the evening after a hard day's sightseeing, fishing, walking or golfing!

The dining room is spacious and elegant, and serves superb food. The cuisine is a blend of Scottish and French, and uses only the finest and freshest local produce wherever possible. These include salmon, smoked fish, beef, lamb, pork and vegetables, all prepared in an imaginative way so dining

here is an experience to be savoured. There is a fine, select range of à la carte meals at both lunchtime and dinner, and the wine list has been carefully chosen to complement the food. The Glen Hotel offers a traditional full Scottish breakfast, or a lighter alternative such as a Continental breakfast. There is a shoe cleaning service, as well as ironing facilities and hair dryers on request. Small private parties and business meetings can also be arranged. Staying at the Glen is a real pleasure!

which commemorates the old custom. However, it also commemorates the darkest day in the town's history. In 1513, 80 of Selkirk's bravest men left the town to fight alongside James IV at Flodden in Northumberland. The battle was a complete rout, and on that day Scotland lost the flower of its manhood. The king himself was killed, along with nobles, bishops and ordinary soldiers. Only one Selkirk man - named Fletcher - returned alive to the town. The Selkirk flag had been lost, but he had managed to capture a bloodstained English one. The **Flodden Memorial** , built in 1913, can be seen outside the Victoria Halls in the High street.

YARROW

10 miles W of Galashiels on the A708

Within the tiny hamlet of Yarrow, seven miles west of Selkirk, is the small **Yarrow Parish Church**, a picturesque building where Sir Walter Scott's great-grandfather was once minister.

BOWHILL

7 miles W of Galashiels, off the A708

This stately Georgian mansion is the Borders home of the Duke and Duchess of Queensberry and Buccleuch, the largest landowners in Southern Scotland. In its grounds is the splendid **Bowhill Little Theatre**, where many professional and amateur plays are performed. Close to Bowhill is **Aikwood Tower**, now the home of Sir David Steel. It was once the home of the legendary medieval wizard, Michael Scott, who lived between 1175 and 1234. He studied at

Oxford, and for a while was the official astrologer to Emperor Frederick II. Inside the tower there is a small exhibition about James Hogg the writer.

ST. MARY'S LOCH

18 miles SW of Galashiels on the A708

The praises of St. Mary's Loch have been sung by both Scott and Wordsworth. It is in a truly delightful situation, surrounded by low, rounded green hills. Its sister loch, the **Loch o' the Lowes**, is separated from it by a narrow tongue of land, where you will find **Tibbie Shiel's Inn**, now a favourite haunt of fishermen. It is named after Isabella Shiels, the woman who ran the establishment from its opening in 1824 until her death in 1878. The inn's visitors' book records such names as R.L. Stevenson, Thomas Carlyle and William Gladstone. The Southern Upland Way passes close by, making it a favourite stopping-off point for walkers.

James Hogg, the "Ettrick Shepherd", was born in the vicinity in 1770. He, too, visited the inn, and was a great friend of Sir Walter Scott. Perhaps his best remembered book nowadays is *Confessions of a Justified Sinner*.

St. Mary's Loch

HAWICK

With a population of over 16,000 people, Hawick is the largest town in the Scottish Borders. It sits in Teviotdale, and is famous for the quality of its knitwear. Names like Pringle, Lyle and Scott are recognised worldwide.

The attractive **St. Mary's Parish Church** dates from 1763, and replaces an earlier 13th century building. The town's oldest building is **Drumlanrig Tower**. In 1570 a raid by English troops destroyed most of Hawick, apart from the church and the tower. It was once moated, and, in typical Scottish fashion, L-shaped before the area between the two legs of the "L" was filled in. It belonged to the Douglas family of Drumlanrig, and it was here that Anna, Duchess of Queensberry and Buccleuch, and widow of the executed Duke of Monmouth, occasionally stayed. The basement was later used as a prison, and when the tower became a hotel, it was used as a wine cellar. The tower has been restored, and now houses displays and artifacts about the history of the Scottish Borders.

The **Hawick Common Riding** takes place every year in June, and involves, as most civic occasions in the Borders do, horses and riders. It commemorates yet another skirmish between the Scots and the English, this time one that took place in 1514. Some English troops were camped near the town, and a few young men attacked them and captured their flag. In the 1990s the Common Riding was embroiled in a different kind of altercation. Up until then, only male horse riders participated. This was all thrown into confusion when two women tried to join the troop. This provoked an uproar in the town, and soon it was divided into two camps - those who wanted to preserve the status quo and those who wanted change. Even some women in the town didn't want women participating.

The whole thing was settled in a court of law, which decided that women should be allowed to take part. But even today this decision rankles with a lot of Hawick citizens, and in some quarters women participants are merely tolerated.

On the banks of the Teviot is **Wilton Lodge Park**, which has 107 acres of riverside walks and gardens. Here you will find the **Hawick Museum and Art Gallery**, which explains the history of the town and its industries. Also in the town is the **Jimmy Guthrie Statue**, which commemorates one of its most illustrious sons, a TT rider who won the world championship in 1930.

Many of the local mills, such as **Peter Scott and Company** in Buccleuch street and **Wrights of Trowmill** have visitors centres and guided tours. At Trinity Mills you'll also find **The Hawick Cashmere Company**, which has a viewing gallery and shop.

AROUND HAWICK

DENHOLM
5 miles NE of Hawick on the A698

This pleasant village was the birthplace in 1775 of John Leyden, a poet, essayist and doctor who was a friend of Sir Walter Scott. He was a fluent speaker of many Eastern languages, and eventually settled in Calcutta, where he published a series of essays on the languages spoken on the sub-continent. The **John Leyden Memorial**, on the village green, commemorates him. Another literary figure born in the village was **Sir James Murray**. Before moving to London he was the headmaster of Hawick Subscription School. He was then editor of the *Oxford English Dictionary*, and died in 1915.

JEDBURGH

9 miles NE of Hawick on the A68

The present day A68 was at one time the main route between Scotland and England. For this reason, both English and Scottish armies marched backwards and forwards along it when the two countries were at war. It passes over the Cheviots, and at **Carter Bar**, nine miles south of Jedburgh and right on the border,

Jedburgh Abbey

there are splendid views to be had. It sits 1,370 feet above sea level, and it almost seems that the whole of Southern Scotland is spread out before you as you look northwards. In the 18th and early 19th centuries great herds of cattle and sheep were driven south over this route to the markets of Northern England.

Jedburgh is an attractive small town with many gaily painted houses and cottages which regularly wins awards in the "Beautiful Scotland in Bloom" contests. The ruins of **Jedburgh Abbey** (Historic Scotland) sit on the banks of the Jed Water, It was founded in 1138 by David I, who founded so many of the great abbeys in the Borders. It was destroyed at least nine times by the English, and every time the monks patiently got on with rebuilding it afterwards. A visitor centre explains its story.

Mary Stuart visited the town in 1566 to preside over local courts, and stayed in what is now called **Mary Queen of Scots House**, which is now a museum and visitor centre. While held in captivity in England by Elizabeth I, she once declared that she would have preferred to have died in Jedburgh.

JEDFOREST DEER AND FARM PARK

Mervinslaw Estate, Camptown, Jedburgh TD8 6PL
Tel: 01835 840364 Fax: 01835 840362
e-mail: hopedate@gtobalnet.co.uk
website: www.aboutscottand.com/jedforest/

The Jedforest Deer and Farm Park is located just off the main A68 Edinburgh to Newcastle road some 5 miles south of Jedburgh. There are magnificent herds of deer and you can find out more about farming today. You can see how they look after the animals and protect the countryside and watch the farm in action on our special demonstration days. In addition explore the farm animals of yesteryear within the large conservation collection of rare breeds of sheep, pigs, cattle, chickens, ducks and others.

There is a coffee shop, barbecue area, picnic area as well as both indoor and outdoor adventure areas. Rangers offer walks through the lovely Scottish Borders' countryside and allow you to discover more about the environment, nature and wildlife.

JEDFOREST HOTEL

Camptown, Jedburgh, Roxburghshire TD8 6PJ
Tel: 01835 840222   Fax: 01835 840226
e-mail: mail@jedforest.freeserve.co.uk
website: www.jedforesthotel.freeserve.co.uk

Ideally situated on the A68 road to Edinburgh, the **Jedforest Hotel** is only seven miles from the border. It sits in 35 acres of grounds, with private fishing in the Jed Water. The rooms are fully en suite, and have hospitality trays, telephones, colour TVs and many other features you would associate with a four star establishment. Some even boast king-sized beds! The food in the Bardoulets Restaurant is famed throughout Scotland, and is served in an intimate yet spacious dining room with a continental ambience. Use the hotel as a base from which to explore the area, or as a stop-over as you drive up or down the A68.

Jedburgh Castle Jail is in Castlegate, and was once a 19th century Howard Reform prison. It now recreates the conditions inside such a prison, and has displays on the history of the town.

The **Jedforest Deer and Farm Park** (see panel on page 23) is situated on the A68 five miles south of the town, and is a modern working farm with a herd of deer and rare breeds. There are also birds of prey demonstations, using eagles, owls and hawks. Five miles north east of Jedburgh town are the **Teviot Water Gardens**, which cascade down towards the River Teviot.

ANCRUM

10 miles NE of Hawick on the B6400

To the north of Ancrum the **Battle of Ancrum Moor** was fought in 1545. It was during the period known as the "Rough Wooing" when Henry VIII was trying to persuade the Scots to allow the young Mary Stuart to marry his son. Three thousand English and - surpisingingly - Scottish troops were ambushed by a hastily assembled army of Borderers. During the battle the Scots changed sides, resulting in a resounding victory for the Borderers.

Two miles west of the village, on a low hill called Peniel Heugh, is the **Waterloo Monument**, which can be seen for miles around. It was built in 1815 by the Marquis of Lothian to celebrate Britain's victory at the Battle of Waterloo. **Harestanes Countryside Visitor Centre** lies close to the village, and has various organised walks and activities. It is possible to walk from the Visitor Centre to the Waterloo Monument in just over an hour if you are reasonably fit.

MOREBATTLE

17 miles NE of Hawick on the B6401

The countryside surrounding Morebattle was once a hiding place for Covenantors, those people who opposed the imposition of bishops on the Church of Scotland by Charles II. It sits on the Kale Water, and to the north is **Linton Church**, which is partly Norman. It has a fine Norman font and a belfry dating from 1697.

The ruins of Cessford Castle, which surrendered to the English in 1545, is two miles to the south west.

KIRK YETHOLM

21 miles NE of Hawick on the B6352

Kirk Yetholm is the northern "terminus" of the **Pennine Way**, and St. Cuthbert's Way passes close by as well. Both it and its twin village of Town Yetholm were where the Scottish "kings and queens of the gypsies" lived. The most famous was Esther Faa Blyth, who lived in the 19th century.

In 1898 her son, Charles Faa Blyth was crowned king at Yetholm, and though the ceremony had lost much of its significance by this time, it was still attended by over 10,000 gypsies from all over Britain. A small cottage is still pointed out as his "palace".

HERMITAGE CASTLE
10 miles N of Hawick on a minor road off the B6399

Hermitage Castle (Historic Scotland) dates from the 14th century. It is a gaunt, imposing building with thick stone walls and stout defences - testimony to the bloody warfare and lawlessness that was rife here before the union of Scotland and England. While staying at Jedburgh, Mary Stuart rode the 50 miles to Hermitage Castle and back again in one day to visit the Earl of Bothwell, who later became her husband. A story grew up that during the journey she lost her watch. It was finally confirmed as being true when it was recovered in the 19th century.

NEWCASTLETON
15 miles S of Hawick, on the B6357

Newcastleton sits on the Liddel Water in Liddesdale, and is a relatively new village, having been planned and laid out by the Duke of Queensberry and Buccleuch in 1793 as a hand loom weaving centre. The **Liddesdale Heritage Centre Museum** in the old Townfoot Kirk in South Hermitage Street has displays about the history of the area and its old industries. This is the heartland of the great Borders families of Kerr, Elliot and Armstrong. The whole area was always a place of great unrest when Scotland and England were separate countries.

KERSHOPEFOOT
18 miles S of Hawick, on a minor road just off the B6357

The border between Scotland and England follows the line of the Kershope Burn in a south westerly direction for a few miles until it reaches the Liddel Water at Kershopefoot. There the border becomes the Liddel Water itself. This point - where the two rivers meet - was very important in the days when Scotland and England were separate countries. Here the Wardens of the Marches of both Scotland and England would meet regularly to discuss matters of mutual importance and seek redress for crimes committed by both sides. A jury of 12 men was appointed, with the English choosing the six Scottish jurists and the Scots choosing the six English jurists. However, the meetings were not always civilised affairs, and some even ended in violence. Many of the Wardens and their men were chased deep into their own territory if redress wasn't forthcoming.

PEEBLES

This prosperous town, which sits on the banks of the Tweed, looks peaceful enough nowadays, but it has a history every bit as bloodthirsty as the other towns in the Scottish Borders. The English burnt and destroyed it in 1545 during the Rough Wooing, it was occupied by Cromwell in 1649, and finally Charles Edward Stuart occupied it in 1745. At one time it had a large, well defended castle, but every trace of it has gone now.

Beltane Week is held every year in July, when the Beltane Queen is crowned. Though it is an ancient ceremony which may go back into the mists of time, the present one dates only

D.M. DIAMONDS

61 High Street, Peebles, Peeblesshire EH45 8AN
Tel: 01721 724228

DM Diamonds, on Peebles High Street, clearly shows that diamonds are more than just a girl's best friend! For here you will see a wealth of fabulous jewellery in the shop's spacious and fascinating gallery, most of it crafted from sparkling, precious gems by Derrick Marwick, a craftsman who brings years of experience to creating works of art that are timeless in their beauty. Derrick is originally from the Orkneys, and you can view him as he carefully works his magic on items of gold and silver, set with diamonds and other stones. He can also reshape, remount or refurbish existing pieces of jewellery you may own to the highest of standards. He will even design and create new items especially for you.

The shop also sells a wide range of other jewellery, under the caring eye of Derrick's wife Theresa. She and her husband are both a mine of information on all kinds of jewellery, and will offer friendly, impartial advice about anything in the shop. There is plenty of free parking in Peebles's High Street, so park your car there and come in for a good browse. The displays are full of rings, brooches, pendants, earrings, gold chains - all competitively priced so that you can buy that perfect gift or souvenir of your holiday in the Scottish borders. There is jewellery by well-known designer Sheila Fleet on show as well, and items by Stewart Moar, an Orcadian designer who has a fine reputation. And on the walls international and local artists display their oils, water colours and prints, giving the whole shop a colourful and warm aspect. If you're in Peebles, this is a place you can't afford to miss.

THE GIFT BOX

29 High Street, Peebles EH45 8AN
Tel: 01721 721283 Fax: 01721 723913

Owned and managed by Stephanie Morrison, **The Gift Box** is the place to go to in Peebles for that special gift. It sits right on the High Street, and you can't miss its smart, blue exterior. There is plenty of on street parking close by, and the town itself is full of history, and well worth exploring. The interior of the shop is bright and spacious, and has a wonderful range of gifts, ranging from candles and cards to glassware and jewellery. The range of cards includes traditional and contemporary cards for all occasions, and the sparkling glassware would grace any room. Another gift range is the modern jewellery. Everything from rings, necklaces and earrings are on sale, made from the finest sterling silver. There is also beaded, hand made jewellery by Carrie Elspeth - an unusual line that has become a very popular gift.

One of the more unusual gift items on sale are ceramic cows from the well known 'Cow Parade' series. They stem from an art exhibition held in the United States some time ago, and now these wacky animals are much collected both here and abroad. Or why not buy a scented candle from the Yankee range? They are extremely beautiful, and come in a wide range of scents that add a certain something to a living room or parlour when lit. The staff at The Gift Box are friendly and knowledgeable, and can offer you helpful advice when choosing a gift. The prices are remarkably reasonable, and Stephanie also sells gift wrapping paper and lovely boxes to make any gift you buy just that wee bit special! The Gift Box is a unique, fresh and bright shop, with an eye for new, innovative ideas that are sure to please. It is open six days a week from 9.30 am to 5 pm, and over the Christmas period is also open on Sundays.

from Queen Victoria's Jubilee, when it was revived as a holiday and celebration for the people of the town. The **Chambers Institute** (which incorporates part of the Queensberry Lodging of 1644) is named after the Chambers Brothers of publishing fame who were born in the town, and it houses a small museum and art gallery. It was in the Queensberry Lodging that William Douglas, the **4th Duke of Queensberry**, known as "Old Q" was born in 1725. He was Vice Admiral for Scotland, a close friend of the then Prince of Wales, and was notorious for his extravagance, huge debts and dissolute life. His ambition in

Cross Kirk Ruins, Peebles

life, it is said, was to turn horse racing into an exact science. Another museum - this time a more unusual one - is to be found in Innerleithen Road - the **Cornice Museum**, which is dedicated to ornate plasterwork.

MOSHULU CLASSIC SHOES

27 High Street, Peebles, Peeblesshire EH45 8AN
Tel: 01721 722211

In the High Street in Peebles you will find **Moshulu Classic Shoes**, a colourful and fascinating shop that sells a wide range of men's and women's high quality footwear under the Moshulu label. The name originates from a tribe of North American Indians, and was then given to a merchant trading ship, the S.S. Moshulu. The shop is owned by husband and wife team, June and Trevor Swan, who also own similar shops in Kelso, Edinburgh and St. Andrews. Moshulu is a comparatively new name in shoe manufacture and design, but has already gained a good reputation for quality and value for money. Most of the shoe models are made in Italy but the company itself is British, being based in Exeter. The emphasis is on comfort, and the smart, colourful models on offer in the shop certainly reflect this!

There's everything from carpet slippers and leisure shoes to walking boots, moccasins and casual shoes. Slippers include the comfortable 'Weston' and the 'Arlon' models for men, or the ultra lightweight

'Wengen' for women, with their simulated animal skin look. The beautifully styled 'Limerick' and 'Rhodes' models are for wearing at those smart but casual events, and the sturdy 'Pembroke' and 'Hexham' walking boots are in supple suede or leather, with a breathable waterproof membrane on a rugged, cleated outsole. The prices are remarkably reasonable, and you can browse for as long as you like, with absolutely no obligation to buy. The staff have an in depth knowledge of all the shoes on sale, and is always on hand to offer friendly, impartial advice.

THE PUMPKIN PATCH

The Old coach House, 9 Bridgegate, Peebles, Peeblesshire EH45 8RZ
Tel: 01721 729458 e-mail: pumpkinpatchmail@aol.com
Fax: 01721 724218   websites: www.ivycottagecrafts.com or
www.pumpkinpatchonline.co.uk

The Pumpkin Patch is more that just a gift shop. It is an
establishment that is inspired by the country stores of the United
States and Canada. It sells a wide range of handmade crafts, cards,
candles, home fragrances and so much more. It also, for instance, carries a wide range of craft supplies
for crafts such as etching, painting, and candle and soap making. Walk in, and you're immediately
struck by the subtle fragrances. This is the perfect place to buy a souvenir of your stay in the Scottish
Borders, so when you're in Peebles, why not call in and see for yourself? You won't be disappointed.

WOODLANDS B&B

Venlaw Farm Road, Peebles, Peeblesshire EH45 8QY

Set within an acre of land that was originally an old orchard,
the four star **Woodlands B&B** is one of the best guest houses
in the quaint Borders town of Peebles. It has three extremely
comfortable and well-decorated rooms - two en suite doubles
and one twin with a private bathroom - and the breakfasts
are hearty and beautifully cooked from local fresh produce
wherever possible. Owners Janette and Ian Fawcett will go
out of their way to make your stay with them so much of
an enjoyable experience that you'll want to return.

ANTIQUES & ANTIQUE CLOCKS

3 High Street, Pennels Close, Peebles EH45 8AG
Tel: 01721 723599

Jurgen Tübbecke, the owner of **Antiques & Antique
Clocks**, is an internationally acclaimed clockmaker and
craftsman.

Within his spacious and fascinating shop, situated
in an old alleyway off Peebles High Street, you will find
a fabulous range of
Timepieces, Scientific
Instruments, Cameras,
small antique furnishings and paintings old and new, some by local
artists. The list is endless.

Should you have visited the
National Museum of Scotland,
you cannot fail to have noticed
the awe-inspiring Millennium
Clock, on which Jurgen had
the honour of working as part
of the team.

Come and visit this
friendly shop, in the beautiful
Borders Town of Peebles, and
see (and hear) for yourself.

HEAD TO TOE

43 High Street, Peebles EH45 8AN
Tel: 01721 722752
website: www.headtoe.co.uk

'Bath, Bed and Beyond' painted above the door of this attractive, traditonally fronted shop gives a taste of what lies within, with its wonderful array of gifts. It is owned and run by Freda

McCulloch who has spent many years in retail management. Freda knows the value of good service and has an in-depth knowledge of the items she has on display.

This is a deceptively large shop, selling a wide range of luxury gifts, cards, bath and beauty products, silver jewellery and hand woven country clothes from Ireland.

Borders Country Pine Furniture is on show at the rear of the shop and provides an attractive backdrop for a beautiful range of quilts, bedlinen and nightwear. Of particular note is a large choice of unusual gifts for babies and young children, featuring brand names such as Kaloo and Kitted Out. The shop is open Monday to Saturday 9.30am - 5pm.

Just off the Neidpath Road is the tower of the former **St. Andrew's Church**. The present Parish Church was built in Victorian times, and occupies a prominent site at the west end of the High Street, near the **Cuddy Bridge** over the Eddleston Water, a tributary of the Tweed. To the north of the town are the remains of the **Cross Kirk**, a Trinitarian friary founded in 1261. The **Cross Keys Inn** dates from the 17th century, and is said to be the original of the "Cleikum Inn" in Scott's St. Ronan's Well.

AROUND PEEBLES

NEIDPATH CASTLE
1 mile W of Peebles off the A72

This tall, sturdy tower house on the banks of the Tweed is the epitome of Scottish Castles. It was built by the Hays in the 14th century, and originally consisted of three great vaulted halls, one above the other, reached by winding stone staircases. The top hall was eventually removed, and replaced by a timber roof. Beneath what was the guardroom there is a dungeon. Prisoners were lowered into it by rope, and in some cases, promptly forgotten about. In the 16th century, the Hay family rose to prominence in Scotland, and the castle was visited by both Mary Stuart and her son James VI.

KAILZIE GARDENS
3 miles E of Peebles, on the B7062

The gardens extend to over 14 acres, and are open to the public. The main part is contained within an old walled garden.

INNERLEITHEN
6 miles E of Peebles on the A72

Innerleithen is a small, sturdy spa town of stone cottages, and was the original for Sir Walter Scott's St. Ronan's Well. The well is real enough, and the **St. Ronan's Well Interpretive Centre** at Wells Brae explains its history. The waters from it were full of sulphur and other supposedly curative minerals.

The most visited tourtist attraction in the town is the **Robert Smail's Printing Works** (National Trust for Scotland) in the High street. It is a genuine small-town printing works that was taken over - complete with all the machinery - by the National Trust in 1987, soon after it closed down. Now you can see how type was set and printed in the early 20th century, and even have a go yourself. There is also a small office, a paper store and a reconstructed lovely water wheel.

TRAQUAIR

6 miles SE of Pebbles on the B709

Traquair is visited for one thing - **Traquair House**, one of the most fascinating buildings in Scotland. It is reputed to be the oldest continuously inhabited house in the country, and began life in about AD950 as a royal hunting lodge on the banks of the Tweed. Over 27 kings and queens have visited the place, including Alexander I in the 11th century, Edward I of England (known as "The Hammer of the Scots" because of his ultimately unsuccessful attempts to conquer Scotland) in the 13th century and Mary Stuart in the 16th century.

One laird of Traquair fell at Flodden with James IV, and in the 18th century the then laird was an ardent Jacobite, supporting the exiled Stuart's claim to the throne of Britain. Charles Edward Stuart visited in 1745, and when he left, the laird closed the main gates to his estate, called the **Bear Gates**, vowing they would never be opened again until a Stuart ascended the British throne once more. They have remained closed

to this day.

Traquair is not an elegant house. Rather it is sturdy and solid, looking for all the world like a fusion of Scottish and French architecture. Inside it has a bed once slept in by Mary Stuart, secret passages and priest's holes. Throughout the Scottish Reformation the lairds of Traquair remained staunchly Catholic, and even today there is a Catholic chapel in one of the wings.

Beneath the chapel is a brewhouse, which the then laird renovated in 1965. It is said that Charles Edward Stuart sampled the Traquair ale on his visit in 1745, and now you can do the same, as the **Traquair House Brewery** produces a range of fine strong ales.

DRUMELZIER

8 miles SW of Peebles, on the B712

The Drumelzier Burn joins the Tweed near the village, and it is said to be the burial place of one of King Arthur's knights. **Drumelzier Castle** once stood close to the spot, though little of it now remains. The kirkyard of **Drumelzier Parish Church** contains an interesting old burial vault of the Tweedie family.

STOBO

5 miles SW of Peebles on the B712

Stobo Parish Church is one of the oldest churches in the Scottish Borders, and has a Norman tower, nave and chancel, with some later features added. The south doorway is 13th century, and is reached through a sturdy barrel-vaulted porch. Nearby is **Stobo Castle**, now one of the country's leading health farms and spas, set in some lovely grounds.

DAWYCK

6 miles SW of Peebles on the B712

The **Dawyck Botanic Garden and Arboretum** covers 62 ares, and is an outpost of the National Botanic Garden

BROUGHTON GALLERY

Broughton, near Biggar ML12 6HJ
Tel: 01899 830234

The mansion house of Broughton Place is the epitome of a 17th century Scottish tower house. In fact, it was built in the 1930s by the architect Sir Basil Spence, and stands on the site of a much older house once owned by John Murray of Broughton, secretary to Charles Edward Stuart. And it is here that you will find the **Broughton Gallery**, one of the best exhibition spaces in the whole of Scotland. Owned by Jane and Graham Buchanan-Dunlop, it features and sells paintings by living artists (mostly Scottish) who have earned a good reputation, but which are still not beyond the pockets of most people. It also exhibits sculpture, ceramics, glass, wood and jewellery from makers all over Britain. Certain craft items are continuously in stock, while exhibitions by individual artists are held on a regular basis.

The entrance to the gallery is by a massive door of weathered oak, and the main part of the gallery is the house's old drawing room, with a polished oak floor and fine moulded plasterwork. It is lit by five huge windows - ideal to display both paintings and three-dimensional work. The gallery's aim is to sell crafts which are well-designed, well-made and reasonably priced, and in this it has succeeded admirably. Graham himself is a painter of note, and sometimes exhibits in the gallery. He and his wife are always on hand to offer friendly, thoughtful advice, and guide you to something that is just right for you. You can phone or write for the latest programme of exhibitions.

of Scotland. It sits on the Scrape Burn, a tributary of the Tweed, and has a unique collection of conifers, rhododendrons and other tree species.

BROUGHTON

10 miles W of Peebles on the A701

Broughton has associations with one of Scotland's greatest writers, John Buchan, Governor General of Canada and author of, among other things, *The Thirty Nine Steps*. He was born in Perth, though his maternal grandparents had a farm near Broughton. Buchan's father, a free church minister, and his mother, married in the village. The former Free Kirk now houses the **John Buchan Centre**, which has displays about his life and writing.

WEST LINTON

9 miles NW of Peebles just off the A702

West Linton is a delightful village, though it has seen a lot of expansion

over the last few years, due to the fact that it lies only 16 miles south of Edinburgh city centre, making it ideal commuting territory. However, it has lost none of its charm, and it remains a typical Scottish country village. At its heart is the whitewashed **St. Andrew's Parish Church**, which dates from 1781, and in its kirkyard are the graves of many stone carvers, testimony to a rural industry that once flourished here. **Lady Gifford's Well**, in the main street, has some wonderful stone carvings dating from 1666 on one of its sides.

Each year in June the local **Whipman** ceremonies take place. They date from 1803, when some local agricultural workers decided to form a benevolent society, which they called "The Whipmen of Linton" (a "whipman" was a carter). The festivities now last a full week, and include honouring the Whipman and his Lass.

LOCATOR MAP

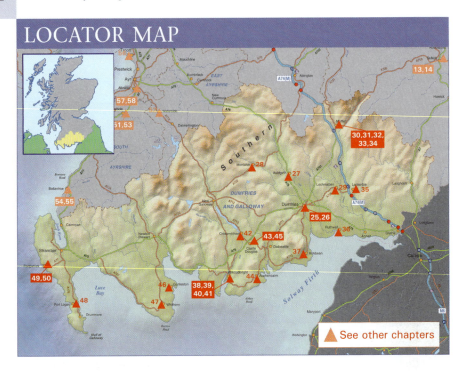

13,14

30,31,32,
33,34

28

27

29

35

57,58

51,53

54,55

25,26

42

43,45

36

37

49,50

46

38,39,
40,41

47

48

44

🔺 See other chapters

ADVERTISERS AND PLACES OF INTEREST

2 DUMFRIES AND GALLOWAY

Dumfries and Galloway would appear to be the forgotten area of Scotland when it comes to tourism. Visitors driving up from England on the M6 pass through the eastern edge of it, hell bent on experiencing the "real Scotland", which is perceived to be the high mountains, lochs, kilts. sporrans and bagpipes of the Highlands.

This has been both a blessing and a curse for South West Scotland. It remains relatively quiet and unexplored, but at the same time the local

River Nith, nr Thornhill

tourism chiefs have had to work just that wee bit harder to bring the charms of the area to the public. Though tourists are now gradually discovering that Dumfries and Galloway is every bit as rich in history and scenery as Northern Scotland, it still remains "Scotland's best kept secret".

There are over 200 miles of coastline, with small coves, sandy beaches, fishing villages and soaring cliffs. There are old abbeys, country villages, market towns, stately homes and castles galore, and scenery that ranges from high hills and moorland to rich pasture and soft, verdant dales. Country roads and lanes meander through it all, just crying out to be explored, and the high inland areas are ideal for walking. In the fields you are likely to see herds of the region's own cattle - the Belted Galloways, so called because they have a wide white belt running running round their black bodies.

The towns are full of history, and well worth exploring. Dumfries - full of old red sandstone buildings - is the largest and is often called the "Queen of the South". Though its population is no more than 30,000, it feels like a much larger place, and has a wonderful shopping centre where you'll find common High Street names as well as smaller, more intimate shops. Kirkcudbright, on the banks of the Dee, is a fishing town and royal burgh. Because of the quality of light found here, it has always had a thriving artistic community, which is reflected in its many galleries. Stranraer is one of Scotland's main ferry ports for Ireland, and the market town of Lockerbie, just off the M74 (the main road north to Glasgow) is forever associated with the plane disaster of 1988.

The area contains the three former counties of Dumfriesshire, Kirkcudbrightshire and Wigtownshire. Each one has its own particular charm and historical associations. Dumfriesshire, for instance, has associations with Robert Burns, while Kirkcudbrightshire was the birthplace of John Paul Jones, founder of the US Navy. And Wigtownshire can lay fair claim to be be the cradle of Scottish Christianity, as it was here, in the 5th century, that St. Ninian founded a monastery - the first in Scotland.

Surrounding the low lying coastal areas are high hills and moorland which cut off the area from the rest of Scotland.

Sweetheart Abbey, New Abbey

For this reason it was almost independent of the Scottish king in medieval times, and was ruled by a succession of families that cocked a snoop at Edinburgh, from the mighty Lords of Galloway to the later Douglas family. All have left their mark in stone, and Devorgilla's Bridge in Dumfries, built by the Lady of Galloway in the 13th century, and Threave Castle, stronghold of the Douglases, bear witness to their power.

This was an area much favoured by monks, so there are many abbey ruins

Isle of Whithorn

to be explored, from Sweetheart Abbey (which gave the name "sweetheart" to the English language) to Dundrennan and Glenluce, which means "valley of light". The Castles are equally impressive. Drumlanrig, Threave, Cardoness, Caerlaverock - they all played their part in Scotland's turbulent history.

One thing which surprises and impresses first time visitors is the mildness of the climate in this part of Scotland. It is washed by the Gulf Stream, and palm trees flourish quite happily in cottage gardens. Because of this, the coastline is sometimes called the "Scottish Riviera", and it abounds with lush, formal gardens such as the Logan Botanic Garden in Wigtownshire.

DUMFRIES

The Royal Burgh of Dumfries was once the county town of Dumfriesshire, and is today the adminstrative capital of Dumfries and Galloway. Its nickname is "Queen of the South", and its warm, red sandstone buildings make it live up to this apt description. It sits on the banks of the Nith, and was once voted the town with the best quality of life in Britain.

Its roots go deep into Scottish history. It played an important part in the Wars of Independence, and it was here, in 1306, that Robert I (also known as Robert the Bruce) murdered the Red Comyn, who was a rival claimant to the throne of Scotland. The murder was committedt before the high altar of the Greyfriar's Monastery. It earned Bruce an excommunication from the Pope, though it didn't seem to worry him all that much, as he immediately had himself crowned king of Scotland at Scone in the presence of the Scottish bishops. They were equally unimpressed by the Pope's pronouncement, as they continued to give him communion. The friary is gone now, and the red sandstone **Greyfriar's Kirk**, with its soaring steeple, stands close to where it once stood.

In the High street is the **Midsteeple**, built in 1707. It was formerly the town hall and jail, and on its south face there is a carving of an "ell", an old Scots measurement of about 37 inches. There is also a table of distances from Dumfries to various Scottish towns, and to one town in England - Huntingdon. This is because three medieval Scottish kings were also Earls of Huntingdon, and it was one of the main places where Scottish drovers took cattle to market in the 17th and 18th centuries. The **Theatre Royal**, one of the oldest theatres in Scotland, stands in Shakespeare Street.

River Nith and Dumfries Town

It dates from 1792, and Robert Burns used to attend performances there.

Dumfries proper sits on the east bank of the Nith. On the west bank, up until 1929, when it was amalgamated with Dumfries, was the separate burgh of Maxwelltown. It became a burgh in 1810, and actually stood in Kirkcudbrightshire, as the Nith, at this point, was the boundary between it and Dumfriesshire. Connecting the two towns is **Devorgilla's Bridge**. Though the present one dates from around 1431, the original bridge was built in the 13th century by Devorgilla, Lady of Galloway. Her husband was **John Balliol**, who founded Balliol College in Oxford. At the Maxwelltown end of the bridge is the **Old Bridge House**, which has a small museum illustrating everyday life in the area in times past. Also on the

Robert Burns Statue

Maxwelltown side of the river, on a prominent hill, is **Dumfries Museum**, housed in an 18th century windmill. It's most famous "exhibit" is a working **Camera Obscura**, which gives marvellous view over the town.

On the northern outskirts of Dumfries, next to the modern houses of a council estate, stand the impressive ruins of **Lincluden College**. It was built in 1164 as a Benedictine nunnery by Uchtred, Lord of Galloway. However it was suppressed in the 14th century by the fourth Earl of Douglas, nicknamed **Archibald the Grim**, with the building being taken over as a collegiate church. The present red sandstone ruins date from that time. One of its treasures is the elaborate tomb of **Princess Margaret of Scotland**, daughter of Robert III. Close to the site is the **Lincluden Motte**, a low, artificial hill which was later terraced and incorporated into a garden.

At Heathhall, on the eastern outskirts of the town, is the **Dumfries and Galloway Aviation Museum**. It covers three floors in an old RAF airfield, and has a good collection of military aircraft, both jet and propeller driven, as well as engines, photographs and other memorabilia. The **Crichton Royal Museum** is within what was the Crichton Royal Hospital, and documents the history of mental health care in Scotland. For those interested in genealogy, the **Dumfries and Galloway Family History Research Centre** in Glasgow street should be visited. There are archives, fiches and books about local history and families. For a modest fee, you can use the extensive facilities.

Dumfries Academy, a handsome building in Academy Street, once had J.M. Barrie as a pupil. Though born in

Kirriemuir in Angus, he spend part of his childhood in Dumfries, and he and his school friends used to play pirates in the garden of **Moat Brae House** (not open to the public). He later admitted that it gave him the original idea for Peter Pan and Captain Hook.

Burns' House

But the writer most associated with Dumfries is Robert Burns. Though born in Alloway in Ayrshire, he died here in 1796, and now lies, along with his wife Jean Armour and five of his family, in the dignified Grecian-style **Burns Mausoleum** in the kirkyard of **St. Michael's Parish Church**. The mausoleum was built in 1815, and in that year his remains were transferred there, though he suffered the indignity of having his coffin opened so that people could gaze one last time at Scotland's national poet. The church was built in the 1740s, and is normally open to the public. A plaque marks the poet's family pew, and long after his death his wife Jean was a regular attender. Also in the kirkyard are the graves of many of Burns's friends.

Robert lived in what was then called Mill Vennel but is now called Burns Street. **Burns's House** still stands, and is open to the public. Though not a grand dwelling, it is substantial, and shows that, just before his death, Robert had at last achieved financial stability through his work as an exciseman. He lived here for the last three years of his life, and on display are letters, books and manuscripts, as well as the pistol he kept with him at all times as he carried out his work, and the chair he sat in as he wrote his last poems.

The **Robert Burns Centre** sits on the west bank of the Nith, and tells the full story of the poet and his many connections with the town. Included is a model of Dumfries as Burns would have known it in the 18th century. There is also a cinema with a full programme of popular films.

TORBAY LODGE

31/33 Lover's walk, Dumfries, Dumfriesshire DG1 1LR
Tel/Fax: 01387 253922
e-mail: enquiries@torbaylodge.co.uk website: www.topbaylodge.co.uk

Housed in a red sandstone listed building, **Torbay Lodge** is only a few minutes from the centre of the historic town of Dumfries. Many of the comfortable bedrooms have en suite facilities, and bathrooms and toilets are all fitted to the highest standards. Hosts Colin and Amanda McQueen offer the very best in Scottish hospitality at this fine establishment. The breakfasts are exceptional - try the traditional Scottish, or something lighter, such as fresh fruit and muesli or fresh strawberries in season. Once you visit, you're sure to come back.

ALEXANDER AND MARGARET ROBB

Windsover Cottage, Auldgirth,
Dumfriesshire DG2 0UB
Tel: 01387 740502. e-mail: info@arrobb.co.uk
website: www.arrobb.co.uk

Auldgirth set amid the glorious scenery of Nithsdale, eight miles north of Dumfries, is where you'll find the studio of **Alexander and Margaret Robb**. They are both professional artists. Alexander specialises in landscape, still life and portraiture and exhibits his work in a number of galleries throughout Britian. Purchasers of his work include HRH the Duke of Edinburgh, the Dumfriesshire Educational Trust and the Dumfries & Galloway Regional Council. Margaret has been concentrating

on a series of life-size pastel portraits direct from sitters for the past two years and recently, together with Alexander and six other artists, successfully held a major exhibition of portraits called "Face to Face" in Gracefield Arts Centre in Dumfries. People are very welcome to visit the studio to see new works by both Alexander and Margaret, but it is best to telephone beforehand to obtain simple directions and to arrange a suitable date and time.

In addition to his own painting, Alexander has been a tutor of summer schools for a number of years, mainly in Southwest Scotland but also in Canada, and now runs two summer school courses in July and August each year, conveniently centred in the new custom built studio adjoining their cottage at Auldgirth. The two, six-day courses, with six to eight students in each, are highly enjoyable for both the beginner and the more experienced artist and are a pleasant way of meeting people with a mutual interest in drawing and painting. Subjects include still-life and portraits (when wet) and landscape painting amongst the varied but always beautiful scenery of Nithsdale when the weather is fine. In addition to the lovely views there are many special things of historic and artistic interest to see in the surrounding area - for example, stately Drumlanrig Castle which contains paintings by Leonardo da Vinci and Holbein and the famous *Portrait of an Old Woman Reading* by Rembrandt.

As well as providing specific information concerning their summer school courses, Alexander and Margaret can supply a list of convenient accommodation nearby for course students and offer help with booking if required. The courses are remarkably good value and popular with people from all over Britian and abroad. Why not contact Alexander and Margaret and arrange a visit to see their work or book onto one of the courses? You won't be disappointed.

HOLYWOOD

2 miles N of Dumfries on the A76

This small hamlet was once the setting for **Holywood Abbey**, a great medieval structure that has completely disappeared. The present Parish Church was partly built in 1779 from the stones of the abbey. Nearby is a stone circle called the **Twelve Apostles**, though one massive stone is now missing.

DALSWINTON

6 miles N of Dumfries on a minor road off the A76

Dalswinton is no more that a row of cottages on either side of the road. However, it is attractive enough, and was built to house workers from the nearby estate, also called Dalswinton. In the late 18th century, Robert Burns lived across the River Nith in Ellisland Farm, and visited the estate's then owner, Patrick Millar, on many occasions. In the policies (not open to the public) is **Dalswinton Loch**, where Patrick encouraged William Symington to experiment with a steam-driven boat. It is thought that Burns may have been a passenger on one of its first sailings, though he never wrote about it.

ELLISLAND

6 miles N of Dumfries off the A76

In June 1788 Robert Burns brought his family south from Mauchline in Ayrshire to farm at Ellisland, which he leased from Patrick Millar of Dalswinton. The soil, however, proved to be stony and infertile, and by 1791 he had packed up and moved to Dumfries. Nowadays the farm gives no hint of those hard times, and sits on a beautiful spot beside the River Nith. It was this romantic location which made Burns lease it in the first place.

Here he wrote some of his best poetry, including *Auld Lang Syne* and that masterpiece of the comic/macabre, *Tam*

O' Shanter. Burns himself used to recount how the story of Tam's drunken ride from Ayr to Alloway was composed as he walked the banks of the Nith, where he chuckled out loud as he dreamed up his hero's adventures with the witches. The farm is now a museum dedicated to his memory. To the north is the small **Hermitage Cottage**, where Burns used to muse and write poetry.

AE

8 miles N of Dumfries on a minor road between the A701 and the A76

This small forestry village is famous for having the shortest name of any place in Britain. It has the added distinction of being the only place whose name has no consonants. It was founded as late as 1947 to house the workers who worked among the conifers of the **Forest of Ae**.

CLOSEBURN

11 miles NE of Dumfries on the A76

Closeburn is situated in the heart of Nithsdale, one of the most beautiful parts of Dumfriesshire. To the north the land closes in to form a narrow dale that is thick with trees (and which looks wonderful in autumn). At Closeburn, however, it gradually opens out to form a broad, fertile expanse of farmland that is dotted with hedgerows and whitewashed farmhouses. The Parish Church sits across some fields from the main village, and beside it are the ruins of the **Old Parish Church**, which date from 1741. **Closeburn Castle** (not open to the public) is an old stronghold of the Kirkpatricks, who were closely associated with Robert the Bruce.

THORNHILL

13 miles N of Dumfries on the A76

Thornhill has a wide main street with pollarded trees marching down each side, bringing a distinctly French feel to

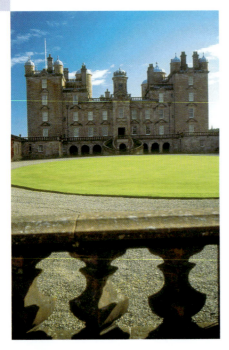

Drumlanrig Castle

the place. It was laid out in 1714 by the Duke of Queensberry, whose residence, Drumlanrig Castle, still lies three miles to the north. At the crossroads in the middle of the village is a monument surmounted by a winged horse, a symbol of the Dukes of Queensberry. In a field to the west of the village, on the other side of the Nith, is the **Boatford Cross**, associated with a ferry and ford that preceded the present day bridge.

DRUMLANRIG CASTLE
16 miles N of Dumfries on a minor road off the A76

This is the sumptuous Dumfriesshire home of the Duke and Duchess of Queensberry and Buccleuch. It was built in the late 17th century on the site of an earlier castle, and has a collection of fine paintings by such artists as Rembrandt, Gainsborough and Hans Holbein.

Surrounding it is a country park and gardens, with a small "village" of craftsmen housed in some of the old outbuildings.

DURISDEER
19 miles N of Dumfries on a minor road off the A702

Durisdeer is no more than a huddle of stone houses and a **Parish Church** of 1699. Attached to the church, unusually, is the former parish school. The church, however, has a delightful secret. The **Durisdeer Marbles** is an elaborate funerary monument to the second Duke of Queensberry and his wife, erected above their burial vault behind the pulpit. The marbles were sculpted by a Flemish sculptor called Jan Nost, and are said to be the best of their kind in the country.

Durisdeer Marbles

DUNSCORE

8 miles NW of Dumfries on the B729

This pretty little village has a neat, whitewashed **Parish Church** dating from 1823. It was in the previous church that Robert Burns and his family used to worship when he stayed at nearby Ellisland Farm.

Within the Parish of Dunscore is Lochenhead Farm, where, in 1897, **Jane Haining** was born. She is famous as being the only British person to have perished at Auschwitz Concentration Camp during World War II. While still young, she joined the Church of Scotland's Jewish Mission Service, and eventually became matron of the Jewish Mission in Budapest in 1932. In 1944 she was arrested by the Germans, purportedly because she had been listening to BBC broadcasts, but actually because she was working among Jews. She was taken to Auschwitz, and on July 17 died there. Her death certificate said she died of cachexia, a wasting disease, but there is little doubt that she was gassed.

Also close to Dunscore is **Craigenputtock Farm**, where Thomas Carlyle wrote *Sartor Resartus*. It was on Templand Hill on the farm that an unusual - and farcical - event took place in July 1786. It concerned a religious sect called the Buchanites, named after its founder, Elspeth Buchan. She was better known as **Mother Buchan**, daughter of an innkeeper from North East Scotland (see also Crocketford and Irvine).

Her story begins in the Ayrshire town of Irvine, where she founded her sect. She promised people immortality by breathing on them, and told them that she herself was immortal, and would be bodily transported to heaven on a set date. She attracted a Church of Scotland clergyman called Hugh Whyte, and together they began seeking converts.

But the dignitaries of the town took exception to their beliefs, and the Rev'd Whyte was deposed from his church. So, together with 46 followers, Mother Buchan and the minister set out on the road, heading south into Dumfriesshire.

Eventually in July 1786 Mother Buchan declared that there would be a 40 day fast (from which both she and the minister would be exempt!) before she ascended to heaven, taking all her converts with her. A rough wooden platform was erected on Templand Hill, and there the Buchanites stood, waiting to be taken up into heaven. But as soon as all the converts had mounted the steps to the platform, a great gust of wind caught it and blew it over, with all the people landing ingnominiously on the muddy ground. The sect lasted for a few more years, but eventually petered out when Mother Buchan had the effrontery to die a natural death.

PENPONT

13 miles N of Dumfries, on the A702

There is nothing particularly special about Penpont. It is just a lovely wee village, where, in the summer months, the gardens are a riot of colourful flowers. The cathedralesque **Parish Church** dates from Victorian times, and seems far too large for such a small place.

KEIR

12 miles N of Dumfries on a minor road off the A702

This small hamlet was the birthplace of **Kirkpatrick Macmillan**, the inventor of the bicycle as we know it today. He was born in 1813, and while all his brothers pursued successful careers away from the village, Kirkpatrick was content to stay at home and be a blacksmith.

Hobby horses, which relied on riders pushing themselves forward with their feet, had been around for some time, but Kirkpatrick's bicycle was the first to incorporate pedals. On June 6 1842, to publicise his invention, he set out on a 70-mile trip to Glasgow, pedalling as he went. News soon spread of his epic journey, and when he arrived in the city he was greeted by cheering crowds. However, as he had passed through the Gorbals, then a village on the edge of the city, he knocked down a young girl, and even though she wasn't badly injured, he was fined five shillings by the city magistrates. This is the world's first instance of a cyclist being prosecuted for a traffic offence. One of the magistrates, however, offered to pay his fine if he could have a go on the bicycle.

TYNRON

15 miles N of Dumfries on minor road off the A702

This small, remote conservation village has only one building dating from after

1900. The **Parish Church**, which looks too big for such a small place, dates from 1837, and was one of the last in Scotland to be lit by oil lamps. In the early 20th century there was a small distillery in the village which supplied whisky to the Houses of Parliament in London.

MONIAIVE

16 miles NW of Dumfries on the A702

This pleasant village sits at the head of Glencairn, through which the Cairn Water, a tributary of the Nith, flows. It is actually two villages - **Dunreggan** on one side of the narrow river and Moniaive proper on the other. The **James Renwick Monument** commemorates a Covenanting martyr who died in 1688.

James Paterson was a member of that group of painters known as the "Glasgow Boys". In 1882 he settled in the village with his wife, and lived there until 1906, when he moved to Edinburgh. The **James**

WOODLEA HOTEL

by Moniaive, Dumfriesshire DG3 4EN
Tel: 01848 200209 Fax: 01848 200114
e-mail: mike_horley@msn.com
website: www.woodlea-hotel.ndo.co.uk

Moniaive is a picturesque and historic village set among the rolling green hills of Dumfriesshire. Close to the edge of the village is a wonderful award winning country house hotel called the **Woodlea Hotel**, owned and run by Pam and Mike Horley. They've been here since 2002, and during that time have made many improvements and additions to what already was one of the most select and popular establishments in the area. The building itself is over 300 years old, and this, coupled with all the modern amenities you would expect from a quality hotel, means that its reputation remains high as a place offering the very best in Scottish hospitality.

It is open daily for bar lunches, dinners and Sunday lunches, and relaxing three-day weekend breaks throughout the year can be arranged at remarkably low prices. The turreted 50 seat restaurant area, with its chandeliers, has recently been completely refurbished, and is both inviting and spacious, with outstanding food. Only the finest and freshest local produce is used wherever possible, and among the range of wines, beer and spirits in the bar, which can seat up to 60, there is sure to be something to appeal to everyone's palate. The resident's lounge has a log fire, which is always welcoming and cosy in the winter months. In the summer, you can relax by the hotel's "tropical" indoor pool, or in the sauna area. There is ample car parking, eight caravan sites(with all facilities) and four acres of beautiful grounds. The hotel is open to non- residents, so this is the ideal place to have lunch while exploring Dumfriesshire, or that intimate candlelit dinner in the evening.

Moniaive Village

Paterson Museum is housed in a small cottage in North Street, and has displays about the great man. It was founded by his granddaughter Anne Paterson-Wallace, herself a painter of some note.

KIRKLAND

13 miles NW of Dumfries on the A702

Maxwelton House (not open to the public) was the birthplace in 1682 of Anna Laurie, better known in song as *Bonnie Annie Laurie*. The original words to the song were written by William Douglas of Finland, though he later jilted her to become a Jacobite soldier. The words were later modified and added to by a sister-in-law of the Duke of Queensberry and Buccleuch, who also set it to a tune of her own composition. Anna herself went on to marry Alexander Fergusson, 14th Laird of Craigdarroch. She is thought

Annie Laurie in Later Life

to be buried in the kirkyard of **Kirkland Parish Church**, though no one knows for certain.

KIRKCONNEL (UPPER NITHSDALE)

31 miles N of Dumfries on the A76

This former mining village is not to be confused with Kirkconnell House near New Abbey or Kirkconnel graveyard in Annandale. The fine old **St. Connel's Parish Church** dates from 1729, though high among the hills to the north of the village is the site of the original church. It was in Kirkconnel, in 1845, that the poet **Alexander Anderson** (better known as "The Surfaceman") was born. Though brought up in humble circumstances, he went on to become Assistant Librarian at Edinburgh University. A memorial next to the kirkyard commemorates him.

SANQUHAR

28 miles N of Dumfries on the A76

This small royal burgh (it was given this status in 1598) sits in Upper Nithsdale. The name (which is pronounced "San-kar") comes from Old Welsh, the language spoken by the Britons who lived here long ago, and means "old fort". The site of this fort was on a small hillock to the north of the town, behind the present-day Sanquhar Academy. Close to it is **St. Bride's Parish Church**, built in 1824 on the site of a much earlier church.

The handsome **Sanquhar Tolbooth** on the main street was designed by William Adam and built in 1735 as a town hall, school and jail. It now houses a small museum with displays about the town's history. Also in Main street is the **Sanquhar Post Office**. It dates from 1712 and is the oldest continuously used post office in the world.

The town sits on the Southern Upland Way, so is a popular stopping off point for walkers and hikers. A shorter walk - the **Sanquhar Historic Walk** - takes you round many of the town's historic attractions.

To the south of the town are the ruins of **Sanquhar Castle**, an old Douglas stronghold. William Douglas, who wrote the original version of *Bonnie Annie Laurie*, was born here in 1672. The castle was originally built in the 11th century, though what you see now dates from much later.

In the 17th century, Sanquhar was a great centre for the Covenantors, those people who opposed the imposing of bishops on the Church of Scotland by Charles II. The period was known as the "Killing Times", as many men (and women) were put to the sword because they adhered to their religious principles. One of the most militant Covenantors was a man called **Richard Cameron**, whose followers were called Cameronians, and who also indirectly gave his name to the former Scottish regiment called The Cameronians (Scottish Rifles). In 1680 he rode into Sanquhar and attached what became known as the **Sanquhar Declaration** to the town's market cross. This disowned Charles II, and effectively declared war on him. Later in the same year he was killed at the Battle of Airds Moss in Ayrshire.

During the 18th century, Sanquhar was a centre for hand knitting, using intricate patterns that made the garments popular throughout Scotland. Up until the 1950s these patterns had never been properly published, but since then it has been possible to buy both hand and machine knitted garments featuring them.

ELIOCK HOUSE

25 miles N of Dumfries on a minor road running parallel to the A76

Though Eliock House is not open to the public, it has an interesting story attached to it. It was the birthplace, in 1560, of **James Crichton**, also known as "The Admirable Crichton". He was the son of the then Lord Advocate of Scotland, and by all accounts was a brilliant young man. He was educated at St. Andrews University before travelling extensively through Europe, where he became a soldier and university lecturer. He could speak 12 languages fluently, and was a fine swordsman. He eventually became a lecturer at the University of Mantua in Italy, where one of his pupils was Vinciento di Gonzaga, son of the city's ruler, the Duke of Mantua.

The story goes that he was returning home one evening from a party, and was set upon by a gang of muggers. Using his sword, he defeated each one. However, he recognised one of the muggers as Vinciento, and rather than run him through, handed him his sword in humility. However, Vinciento was not as honourable a man as James, and when he took the sword he stabbed James in the heart, killing him outright. This was in 1582, when James was only 22 years old.

WANLOCKHEAD

25 miles N of Dumfries on the B797

People are usually surprised to find that Scotland's highest village is not in the Highlands. but in the Lowlands. Wanlockhead, in the Lowther Hills, sits at a mean height of 1,531 feet above sea level, and is a former lead mining village which was founded in the early 18th century. Here you'll find the **Museum of Leadmining**, which explains the industry, and gives you the opportunity

Beam Engine, Wanlockhead

to go down a real lead mine - the **Lochnell Mine**. In a small cottage above the museum is the **Miners' Library**, founded in 1756, making it the second oldest subscription library in Scotland (the oldest is in Leadhills, Wanlockhead's sister village, across the county boundary in Lanarkshire).

Within the village you'll also find an old water-powered **Beam Engine**, which, appropriately enough, used to pump water from the mines. **The Leadhills and Wanlockhead Light Railway** is Britain's highest adhesion railway, with a two foot gauge rack, and connects Wanlockhead to Leadhills. At its highest point, the track reaches 1,498 feet above sea level. It was originally built (using a

conventional gauge track) to take refined lead to Scotland's industrial heartland in Lanarkshire, but finally closed in 1938. Trips are available on the re-opened two-mile section.

Lead was not the only metal mined in the surrounding hills. In olden days, the whole area was known as "God's Treasure House in Scotland", because of the gold found there. The Scottish Regalia (known as "The Honours of Scotland") incorporated gold found in the surrounding hills. It is said that over 5000 men were employed to mine it. The largest nugget of gold ever discovered in Britain was found in the area. It weighed two pounds and was as large as a cricket ball. Gold panning is still a popular activity here, and Wanlockhead is a popular venue for the annual UK **National Gold Panning Championships**.

LOCHMABEN

8 miles NE of Dumfries on the A709

Lochmaben is a small royal burgh in Annandale. In the vicinity are many small lochs, and in some of them you

BEECHWOOD COUNTRY HOUSE HOTEL

Harthope Place, Moffat, Dumfriesshire DG10 9HX
Tel: 01683 220210 e-mail: enquiries@beechwoodcountryhousehotel.co.uk
Fax: 01683 220889 website: www.beechwoodcountryhousehotel.co.uk

Beechwood Country House Hotel is a graceful country house that sits on the green slopes overlooking the picturesque and historic town of Moffat. Originally built in 1848 by the Hope-Johnstone family,

it later became "Miss Thomson's Private Adventure Boarding Establishment and School for Young Ladies". Now it is an elegant yet comfortable country house hotel owned and run by Cheryl and Stavros Michaelides that offers the very best in Scottish hospitality. Many of the original features have been retained, and these, coupled with the high levels of service and value for money, have created a haven for those people wishing to have a relaxing holiday or short break amid some wonderful scenery. Or it can be used as a base while exploring the Borders of Southwest Scotland, with their wealth of stately homes, old ruined abbeys and quaint villages. The house sits in a charming garden, itself set in 12 acres of beech wood. These provide an ever changing panorama of colour as the seasons blend into each other - fresh and green in the summer months, and warm golds and oranges when autumn follows.

There is so much to do in the immediate area. You can go for strolls through the hotel grounds, for instance, or play golf on the nearby 18-hole golf course. The hotel can even arrange fishing, riding, pony trekking and rough shooting. Or you can go further afield and explore the Borders or Dumfries and Galloway, which brim over with history and heritage.

All the public rooms overlook the garden. There are two sitting rooms - one with a small cocktail bar - which are cosy and welcoming. Here you can relax with a quiet drink or a coffee as you read the papers, play chess (one of the pastimes provided) or read a book from the hotel's small but select library. As you would expect, the rooms are all en suite, and have those little extras that make you feel right at home - colour TV, clock/radio, hair dryer, mending box, tea and coffee facilities, electric underblankets, bathrobes, direct dial phone, and so on.

The cuisine is outstanding. The hotel's kitchens use only the finest and freshest local produce wherever possible for the table d'hôte menu. So eating here in the elegant but informal dining room is an experience not to be missed. And there is a select range of fine wines to accompany your meal, as well as aperitifs, malt whiskies, brandies and liqueurs.

The breakfasts too are exceptional. You can choose the full traditional Scottish breakfast or a light Continental breakfast. If you're heading off to do some sightseeing in the area, or indeed if you're driving home when your holiday has ended, the hotel can prepare a gourmet packed lunch to order.

The Beechwood is an exceptional hotel, set in an exceptional area. If it's pampering you're after, and a memorable and happy holiday experience, then this is the place for you.

find vendace, a rare species of fish. Near the Castle Loch stands the scant remains of **Lochmaben Castle**, which originally covered 16 acres. An earlier castle on the site belonged to the Bruce family, Lords of Annandale, and it is said to be the birthplace of Robert the Bruce (who later became Robert I of Scotland). Turnberry in Ayrshire makes a similar, and more likely, claim.

Skipmyre, to the south west of the town, was the birthplace in 1658 of **William Paterson**, founder of the Bank of England in 1694. He was the chief instigator of a less successful venture - the Darien Scheme of 1698, the purpose of which was to found a Scottish colony in modern-day Panama. Many Scots who made the voyage to Central America perished there from disease and starvation.

MOFFAT

20 miles NE of Dumfries on the A701 just off the M74

Sheep farming has always been important in this upland part of Dumfriesshire, and in the centre of the town's broad main street is the **Colvin Fountain**, surmounted by the statue of a ram. Moffat is in a fertile bowl surrounded by low, green hills, and was at one time a thriving spa, thanks to mineral springs that were discovered on the outskirts of the town in in the 17th century. By 1827 the sulphurous waters were being pumped into town, and it later became a fashionable place for Victorians who wished to "take the waters".

In 1882 **Air Chief Marshall Lord Dowding**, who oversaw the Battle of

LOTHLORIEN EMPORIUM

22 Well Street, Moffat DG10 9DP
Tel: 01683 221144 or 07802 419563
e-mail: linda@lothlorien-emporium.fsnet.co.uk
website:www.lothlorien97.co.uk

Looking for that perfect souvenir to take home with you to remind you of a great holiday in Scotland? Then head for the **Lothlorien Emporium** in Moffat. Here you'll find an amazing display of antiques and collectable items at prices to suit every pocket. The selection within this wonderful shop has been carefully chosen by the owner, Linda Payne, to reflect the best that is available in pottery, porcelain, small items of furniture, fashion jewellery, metal ware, framed prints, silver, dressing table sets and exquisite dolls. There are also antiques toys related to films and TV programmes such as Dr Who, Star Wars and Gerry Anderson, as well as games such as Kerplunk, Monopoly and Mousetrap. So it's ideal for buying something for the younger members of the family as well.

This is the kind of shop where you should take your time and browse carefully, as you're surely

spoiled for choice. The range on offer is enormous, and it has been tastefully and thoughtfully laid out so that shopping here is a positive pleasure. Plus, of course, the owner is always on hand to offer advice. Moffat is just off the M74, the main motorway north from Carlisle, so stopping off at this picturesque little market town - once famous for its spa - is so easy to do. Why not spend a few hours here, possibly looking round the shops and having a meal? Then head for the Lothlorien Emporium to make your visit complete.

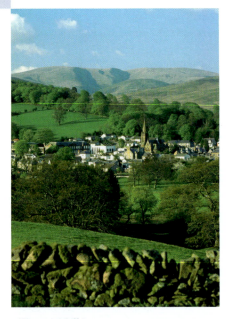

View over Moffat

Britain,was born here. In the old kirkyard to the south of the main street is the grave of **John Louden McAdam**, the great road builder, and after whom Tarmacadam is named. He died in 1836, and though born in Ayr, he lived in Dumcrieff House outside Moffat.

The **Moffat Museum** at The Neuk, Church Gate, charts the history of the town. The **Black Bull Inn**, dating from 1568, had Robert Burns as a regular visitor as he carried out his duties as an exciseman. While hunting Covenantors in the area, Graham of Claverhouse (known as "Bonnie Dundee" or "Bloody Clavers" depending on how you view the history of the time), used it as his headquarters. A hostelry with a unique claim to fame is the **Star Hotel** on the east side of the main street. At only 20 feet wide, it is the narrowest fully-functioning hotel in Britain. On the other side of the street is the former

BUCHAN GUEST HOUSE

13 Beechgrove, Moffat, Dumfriesshire DG10 9RS
Tel/Fax: 01683 220378 e-mail: buchanhouse220@aol.com
website: www.buchanguesthouse.co.uk

Buchan Guest House is one of the most attractive guest houses in Dumfriesshire, and sits in the small town of Moffat, just off the M74 motorway between Carlisle and Glasgow. It is a grade B listed building, and in the summer months positively froths with colour as the many hanging baskets and borders come alive with flowers. There are four en suite rooms, a family suite of two rooms and a large shower room, and another two rooms with private bathrooms. The family suite can sleep up to eight people. These rooms are all extremely comfortable and cosy, with colour TVs and tea and coffee making facilities.

The breakfasts here are hearty and filling, and always beautifully cooked. You can have a traditional Scottish breakfast or two fish options and three vegetarian options, and Continental breakfasts are available. You can also order evening meals, though the B&B's owner, Brenda Wallace, likes to discuss

the menu with you beforehand so that you can have a meal of your choice that takes into account food allergies or dietary constraints. There is also a large residents' lounge overlooking a bowling green, where you can relax after a day's sightseeing. Though the Buchan Guest House isn't licensed, there are plenty of glasses on hand should you bring in your own bottle. And Brenda will be more than willing to chill a bottle of wine for you beforehand. Parking at this first rate B&B is easy - its car park can take up to eight cars, and the road immediately outside is completely free from yellow lines.

MARVIG GUEST HOUSE

Academy Road, Moffat, Dumfriesshire DG10 9HW
Tel: 01683 220628 e-mail: marvig.moffat@telco4u.net

Situated in the lovely lowland Scottish town of Moffat, just off the M74, **Marvig Guest House** is the perfect place either for a peaceful stopover on the road north or south, or as a base from which to explore the local area, which is not only very beautiful, but also offers places of historical interest, craft shops, galleries and activities for all ages. Marvig has four comfortable rooms, two being fully en suite, and all rooms have TVs, central heating, wash hand basins and tea making facilities; private car-parking is also available. Awarded three stars by the Scottish Tourist Board, Marvig is owned and run by Carolyn and Jeremy Fox, who will give you the warmest of welcomes in this neat and tidy guest house.

CLAUDIO'S

The Old Police Station, Burnside,Moffat DG10 9DX
Tel: 01683 220958
e-mail: fcapriglione@hotmail.com
website: www.claudios.co.uk

Claudio's is a family-run restaurant in the small market town of Moffat, just off the M74. As its address suggests, it is housed in the town's old police station, and uses only the finest local produce wherever possible. It has gained an enviable reputation not only for the food, but for the friendly, helpful service and value for money. The restaurant's fish dishes are renowned, as are its pizzas and pastas. This is traditional Italian cuisine at its best, and the place makes an ideal stop for dinner on the road north to Glasgow and beyond.

Moffat House, dating from the 1750s. It too is now a hotel.

One of the finest drives in the area is to take the A708 north eastwards to Selkirk for 30 miles, passing St. Mary's Loch on the way.

GREY MARE'S TAIL

28 miles NE of Dumfries just off the A708

The Grey Mare's Tail (National Trust for Scotland) is a spectacular 200 feet high waterfall which is fed by the waters of Loch Skeen, high in the hills. There is a car park and visitors centre, where you can watch, by CCTV, a peregrine falcon's nest site. The area is particularly rich in wild flora and fauna, including a herd of wild goats. There is a programme of guided walks in the summer months. The area surrounding the falls has changed little since it was a favourite hiding place for Covenantors in the 17th century.

TWEEDSWELL

26 miles NE of Dumfries, well off the A701

This area - the source of the River Tweed - is a good mile from the road. It seems strange that within the space of a few miles, three of Scotland's main rivers rise, yet flow in different directions. The source of the Clyde, which flows north, is close by, as is the source of the Annan, which flows south towards the Solway Firth. The Tweed flows north east before turning east and going through the Scottish Borders region until it reaches the North Sea

Close by is a great hollowed out area among the hills known as the **Devil's Beeftub**. Here the Border reivers of old hid the cattle they had rustled south of the border. And to the east is **Hartfell**, supposedly the home of **Merlin the Magician** in the days of King Arthur.

ESKDALEMUIR

23 miles NE of Dumfries on the B709

The **Samye Ling Centre** is one of Dumfriesshire's most unusual tourist attractions, and is a true hidden gem. It is the largest Tibetan Buddhist monastery in Western Europe, and sits among the high hills of Eskdalemuir, just off the main road. As well as being a monastery and temple, it is a place where Tibetan culture, customs and art is preserved. Its colourful Eastern-style buildings have fluttering flags and whirling prayer wheels, which seem totally incongruous in a typically Scottish moorland setting. Close by is **Eskdalemuir Observatory**, which opened in 1908. In June 1953 it recorded the highest short-term rainfall ever experienced in Scotland - 3.15 inches in half an hour. This represents about 15 per cent of the annual rainfall in some areas of Scotland.

Bentpath Library, Westerkirk

LANGHOLM

24 miles NE of Dumfries on the A7

Though within Dumfriesshire, the "muckle toon" of Langholm in Eskdale has the feel of the Scottish Borders to it. Christopher Grieve, better known as **Hugh McDairmid**, was born here in 1892, though it took many years for the good people of the town to even acknowledge the existence of Scotland's greatest 20th century poet, never mind his undoubted contribution to Scottish literature. The town is situated in Armstrong country, and the **Armstrong Clan Museum** in Lodge Walk in Castleholm traces the history of this great Borders family. On the last Friday in July the annual **Common Riding Ceremony** takes place.

WESTERKIRK

29 miles NE of Dumfries, on the B709

This lonely parish in Eskdale was the birthplace, in 1757, of **Thomas Telford**, the great civil engineer. He is famous for designing and constructing the Caledonian Canal and the Menai Straits Bridge in Wales. The new town of Telford in Shropshire is named after him, as at one time he was the surveyor of public works for the county. He died in 1834 and was buried in Westminster Abbey. Within the parish is **Bentpath Library**, founded in 1792 for the use of antimony miners who worked in the Meggat Valley.

LOCKERBIE

10 miles NE of Dumfries off the M74

The quiet market town of Lockerbie, which has a population of no more than 4.000, is remembered for one thing - the **Lockerbie Disaster** of 1988. On the evening of December 21st, a terrorist bomb exploded on Pan Am flight 101 as it flew high over the town. It's cockpit crashed into a field at **Tundergarth** to the east of the town and its fuselage crashed into the town itself, killing all the passengers and crew as well as 11 people on the ground. **The Remembrance**

CAFE 91 RESTAURANT

91-93 High Street, Lockerbie DG11 2DA
Tel: 01576 202379
e-mail: scottscafe91@aol.com

The **Café 91 Restaurant** calls itself "the best in town", and this is no idle boast. It is spacious and spotlessly clean, with seating for 50. It's position on the town's main road makes it an ideal stopping off place for people travelling north or south on the nearby M74 motorway. It has a grading from Taste of Scotland, meaning that the food is beautifully cooked from only the freshest local produce wherever possible. From juicy steaks to pasta penne and tasty home made soups, Caf é 91 Restaurant has it all.

Garden is in the town cemetery on the A709, to the west of the town beyond the M74. It is a peaceful spot, though there is still an air of raw emotion about the place, and no one visits without a lump in the throat.

In 1593, the **Battle of Dryfe Sands** took place near Lockerbie. Two great Borders families in the area - the Maxwells and the Johnstones - were forever fighting and bickering, and eventually they met in battle. The Maxwells, with 2,000 men, looked the likeliest victors, though the Johnstones, with a mere 400 men, won the day. Over 700 Maxwells were killed.

ECCLEFECHAN

14 miles E of Dumfries on the B7976

This small village's rather curious name means "The Church of Fechan", an Irish saint that lived in the 7th century. Thomas Carlyle the author was born here him 1795, in a house in the main street. Called the Arched House, it was built by Thomas's father and uncle, who were stonemasons. It is now officially called **Carlyle's Birthplace** (National Trust for Scotland), and within it are displays and artifacts that explain the man's life and works.

KIRKCONNEL (KIRTLEBRIDGE)

16 miles E of Dumfriesshire off the M74

In the kirkyard of the ruined Kirkconnel

Church are the graves of **Fair Helen of Kirkconnel Lea** and her lover Adam Fleming. Their story is a romantic one, and a famous ballad was written about it.

Helen, one of the great beauties of the area, was loved by two men, Adam Fleming and a man named Bell, whose first name isn't known. Helen found herself falling in love with Fleming, and Bell was consumed with jealousy. He therefore hatched a plot to murder his rival. If he couldn't have Helen, then neither could Fleming. He waylaid the couple as they were courting near the kirkyard, and drew out a pistol, which he aimed at Fleming's heart. But as he fired, Helen threw herself in front of her lover, and was instantly killed.

There are two versions of what happened next. One version says that Fleming killed Bell where he stood, and another says that Bell fled. Fleming pursued him to Madrid, where he killed him. Either way, he was heartbroken, and joined the army to try and forget about Helen. But he couldn't, and eventually returned to Kirkconnel. He lay down on her grave, and there died of a broken heart. A few days later he was buried beside her. However, there is no conclusive proof that the events ever happened at all, and no records have ever been unearthed proving or disproving them. It is not even known when the tragic events are supposed to have taken place.

This Kirkconnel should not be confused with Kirkconnel in Upper Nithsdale, or Kirkconnell House near New Abbey in Kirkcudbrightshire.

KIRKPATRICK FLEMING

19 miles E of Dumfries off the M74

This pleasant little village is famous as being the supposed site of **Robert the Bruce's Cave**, where William Irving hid him from the English for three months while he was

Marriage Room, Gretna Green

on the run. It was also where he is supposed to have seen the spider that inspired him to try again in his efforts to free Scotland. However, there are other caves in Scotland, and even Ireland, that also make the same claim.

GRETNA GREEN

23 miles E of Dumfries off the M74

This small village, before it was bypassed by the M74, was the weary traveller's first introduction to Scotland if they had travelled north through Carlisle. Up until a short while ago, it was a decidedly tacky and money-making introduction, and did nothing to enhance Scotland's reputation as a tourist destination. In recent years, however, efforts have been made to clean it up and make it more welcoming, though there is still some way to go yet.

As it was the first village in Scotland if you were travelling up the west coast, it became a favourite place for runaways couples from England to get married. In 1754 irregular marriages, as they were called, were made illegal in England, with the legal age at which people could get married without parental consent being raised to 21. This didn't apply in Scotland, so a " marriage industry" grew

up in Gretna Green. The actual border between Scotland and England is the River Sark just south of the village, and on the Scottish side of the bridge is the **Old Toll House**, where many marriages took place. Another favourite location was **Gretna Hall** though the most popular place was the **Old Blacksmith's Shop** in the centre of the village. Here the "Anvil Priests" charged anything from a dram of whisky to a guinea for conducting what was a perfectly legal ceremony over the anvil.

By 1856 the industry came to an end, due to what was called the "Brougham Act", an Act of Parliament which stipulated that at least one of the parties had to have been resident in Scotland for 21 days before the ceremony took place. This act was only repealed as late as 1979. However, a further Act of Parliament of 1940 was passed which stated that all marriages had to take place either in a church or registry office.

Couples still come from all over the world to get married across the anvil in Gretna Green, though the ceremony is no more that a confirmation of vows taken earlier in the village's registry office. The Old Blacksmith's Shop is still open, and within it is an exhibition about the old marriage trade.

Gretna Green is within an area that was once known as the **Debatable Lands**, so called because both Scotland and England claimed them before the 16th century. It was a lawless place, and a safe haven for the Border reivers. The **Lochmaben Stone**, a mile to the south west of the village, is where representatives of both countries used to meet to settle disputes, though more often than not they were settled by swords rather than words.

CANONBIE

26 miles E of Dumfries off the A7

The village of Canonbie sits just on the Scottish side of the border, and was once the site of a priory - the only Scottish monastery suppressed by the English King Henry VIII in the 16th century. The name means "the town of the canons", and some of the priory's stones may have gone into building **Hollow's Bridge** across the Esk, said to be Scotland's fastest flowing river. A stone and plaque beyond the bridge marks the site of **Gilnockie Castle**, once the home of **Johnnie Armstrong**, one of the greatest reivers of all. In 1530 Johnnie was invited to a great gathering at Carlanrig in Teviotdale by James V, who had

promised him safe conduct, even though he was one of the most wanted men in the kingdom. James, however, went back on his word and had Johnnie and his men strung up on the spot. Perhaps the most amazing aspect of this story is that James was no more than 18 years old at the time. Some of the stones of Gilnockie Castle may also have gone into the building of Hollows Bridge.

Close by, but not open to the public, is **Hollows Tower**, a typical Borders castle, which dates from the 16th century.

ANNAN

14 miles E of Dumfries on the A75

Annan was granted royal burgh status in the 13th century, and is a pleasant, quiet place on the River Annan. **Annan Parish Church** on the High Street dates from 1786, and is built of the local red sandstone, as are many buildings in the town. In Bank Street is the **Historic Resources Centre**, a small museum with a programme of displays and exhibitions on the history of the town and its people.

Though it sits a mile from the sea, Annan was once an important seaport with a boat building yard, and vestiges of the old harbour, now sadly silted up, can still be seen. From April to August each year **Haaf Net Fishing**, which dates back to Viking times, is still carried out at the mouth of the River Annan. The fishermen stand chest deep in the middle of the river wielding haaf nets, which are attached to long wooden frames, and wait until fish - usually salmon - swim into the nets. In 1538 James V granted the fishermen of the time a royal charter, and in 1992 the owners of a time share development further up the river challenged the charter in court.

Kershopefoot, nr Canonbie

They claimed that the haaf nets were "fixed engines", which were forbidden. However, the judge took the view that they weren't, and that the charter was still in force today.

At one time the **Solway Viaduct Bridge** linked Scotland and England by rail. It stood to the south of the town, and crossed the Solway Firth. It opened in 1870, and took both goods and passenger trains between Dumfriesshire and Cumbria. At that time it was the longest railway bridge across water in Britain. In the winter of 1881 it was damaged when great ice flows smashed into its piers, which were sunk deep into the Solway sands. The then keeper of the bridge, John Welch, plus two of his colleagues, remained in their small cabin on the bridge as the lumps of ice - some as big as 27 feet across - smashed against the supports. At 3.30am they were ordered to leave their posts. And it was just in the nick of time, as two lengths of the bridge, one 50 feet long and one 300 feet long, collapsed into the Firth, taking down 37 girders and 45 pillars. No one was injured in the disaster, though the bridge was never used again to take trains. In 1934 it was dismantled, and all that is left nowadays are the shore approaches and the stump of a pillar in the middle of the water.

Annan was the birthplace, in 1792, of **Edward Irving**, whose followers were called Irvingites, and who founded the **Catholic Apostolic Church**. For many years it was a popular movement, and relied on elaborate church services, full of ritual and colour, and a complicated hierarchy of priests, ministers and deacons. It was also the birthplace, in

SAVINGS BANK MUSEUM

Ruthwell, Dumfries DG1 4NN
Tel: 01387 870640
e-mail: tsbmuseum@btinternet.com

Dr Henry Duncan was an accomplished artist and some of his work is displayed in the museum, but he is best remembered as the man who identified the first fossil footprints in Britain. Minister of the Ruthwell parish church for 50 years, he opened the world's first commercial savings bank in 1810. The museum also houses a large collection of early home savings boxes, coins and bank notes from many parts of the world. Open daily 10am to 1pm and 2pm to 5pm except Sundays and Bank Holidays from 1st October until Easter.

1721, of **Thomas Blacklock**, the first blind Church of Scotland minister.

RUTHWELL

10 miles SE of Dumfries off the B724

The 18 feet high **Ruthwell Cross**, which dates from about AD800, is within the Parish Church. At the time it was carved, this part of Scotland was within the Anglo Saxon kingdom of Northumbria. It shows scenes from the Gospels, entwining vines and verses from an old poem called *The Dream of the Rood*, written, it is thought, by Caedmon, who lived in St. Hilda's monastery in Whitby. The **Rev'd Henry Duncan**, the parish minister, founded the world's first savings bank in Ruthwell in 1810, and the achievement is remembered in the small **Savings Bank Museum** (see panel above).

POWFOOT

13 miles SE of Dumfries on a minor road off the B724

Though it is a small, quiet village on the Solway coast, plans were once laid to make Powfoot one of the biggest holiday resorts in Dumfries and Galloway. In the

Powfoot

late 19th and early 20th centuries there were grandiose schemes to build hotels, gardens, bowling greens, a promenade and pier and golf courses. Most of them were never realised, though the Pow Burn did eventually trickle down through a series of ornamental lakes towards the Firth, and some terraces of red brick houses were built. These terraces are now listed buildings, though they would look more at home in Lancashire they do on the Solway coast.

The main instigators of the scheme were two Merseyside builders called Bell and Burnie, who began building the houses in 1891. For a short while Powfoot did become a fashionable place for a holiday, though lacked a promenade and pier - two must-haves if the place was to be a long term success. So it was decided to build them. However, local fishermen objected, saying that a promenade and its associated sea wall would interfere with their livelihood. The matter went to court, the fishermen won, and the plans for Powfoot were abandoned.

CAERLAVEROCK
7 miles S of Dumfries on the B725

Caerlaverock Castle Historic Scotland) is one of the most romantic ruins in Scotland. It is everyone's idea of a medieval castle, with a moat, twin-towered gatehouse and strong, thick walls. Unusually, it is triangular in plan, and was built as the chief seat of the mighty Maxwell family, one of the most powerful in Dumfriesshire. It was attacked in 1300 by English troops under Edward I, the "Hammer of the Scots", when Lord Maxwell and his garrison were forced to surrender. Until the Union of the Crowns in 1603, it was fought over time and time again. Anticipating years of peace after this event, in the early 1600s Lord Nithsdale had some fine Renaissance buildings erected in the courtyard. However, the castle saw action once again in 1640, when Royalist forces defending it

Caerlaverock Castle

surrendered to a Covenanting army. Thereafter it fell into ruin. Nowadays it is one of Dumfries and Galloway's premier tourist attractions, and has a siege warfare exhibition, a children's adventure park and a nature trail.

The 1,350-acre **Caerlaverock Wildfowl and Wetlands Trust** lies about three miles west of the Castle. A wide variety of wildlife can be observed at this nature reserve, including swans and barnacle geese. The extremely rare natterjack toad can also be seen. There are three observation towers, 20 hides and a swan observatory linked by nature trails. Other visitor facilities include a shop, refreshments and binocular hire. Some parts of the site are wheelchair friendly.

The **Solway Coast Heritage Trail** passes through the nature reserve. It is well signposted, and stretches from Gretna in the east to Stranraer in the west, a total of 80 miles, and covers many important historical sites and buildings.

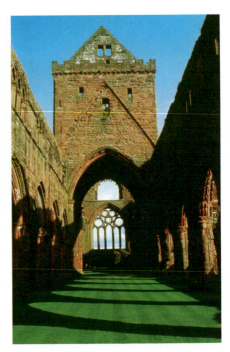

Sweetheart Abbey

NEW ABBEY

6 miles S of Dumfries on the A710

New Abbey sits in the shadow of **The Criffel**, which, at 1,866 feet high, is the highest peak in the area. The hauntingly beautiful ruins of of **Sweetheart Abbey** (Historic Scotland) dominate the village's neat cottages. The story of its founding in 1273 by Devorgilla, Lady of Galloway, is a poignant one. Her husband had been John Balliol of Barnard Castle in County Durham (the man who founded Oxford's Balliol College), and it seems to have been a true love match. When he died, she was devastated, and carried his embalmed heart around with her in a small casket. She also founded the abbey in his memory, and it became known as the "Abbey of the Dolce Cor", or

"Sweetheart Abbey". When she died both she and her husband's heart were buried before the high altar. Parts of her tomb were recovered after the Reformation and reassembled, and it can still be seen. Her effigy shows her clutching her husband's heart. In its kirkyard lies William Paterson, founder of the Bank of England.

Also in the village is the **New Abbey Corn Mill** (Historic Scotland). It dates from the 18th century, and is in full working order. There are regular demonstations of how water powered the mill. It is thought to stand on the site of the original abbey mill.

Shambellie House, on the northern approaches to New Abbey, houses the **Shambellie House Museum of Costume**, part of the Royal Museums. It was donated in 1977 by Charles Stewart, with the costumes dating from early Victorian times up until the 1930s. They are now displayed in appropriate settings which show them off to perfection.

KIRKBEAN

10 miles S of Dumfries on the A710

On the estate of Arbigland, two miles south of the village, is the cottage where John Paul Jones, founder of the American Navy, was born in 1747. It is now a small museum. Kirkbean has one further American connection - it was the birthplace of Dr James Craik, George Washington's personal physician. Kirkbean Parish Church dates from 1776.

CROCKETFORD

9 miles W of Dumfries on the A75

This small village, though it looks unprepossessing enough nowadays, has a macabre tale to tell. It concerns Mother Buchan, who founded a sect called the Buchanites (see also Dunscore and Irvine). Her real name was Elspeth Buchan, and she claimed to confer immortality on people merely by breathing on them. She also claimed that she herself was immortal. Having been driven out of Irvine in Ayrshire, where the sect was founded, she and her followers went south into Dumfriesshire. In July 1786 she announced that there would be a 40-day fast, after which all the sect members would ascend to heaven. This was to take place at Dunscore, in Dumfriesshire.

Alas, the ascent never happened, and some of her followers deserted her. However, some remained staunch after Mother Buchan declared that it was a lack of faith among her followers that prevented the ascent from taking place. However, an even bigger disappointment

CAVENS HOTEL

Kirkbean, Dumfries & Galloway DG2 8AA
Tel:01387 880234 Fax: 01387 880467
e-mail: enquiries@cavens.com website: www.cavens.com

Cavens Hotel was originally built in 1752 by Sir Richard Oswald, a tobacco baron, as the centrepiece of his vast estates in South West Scotland. Now it has been turned into an extremely comfortable country house hotel that offers all that is best in Scottish hospitality. Owners Jane and Angus Fordyce, who have owned and managed the hotel for over three years, have gone out of their way to create a place that is sumptuous, spacious and welcoming. The hotel boasts seven fully en suite rooms, each one generously proportioned, individually furnished and decorated to a high standard.

The Oswald Room has a verandah overlooking the carefully tended gardens, and one of the other rooms has a six-foot bed! Angus has worked for over 20 years in top London hotels, and personally takes care of the cuisine, which is of the highest standard. Only the finest and freshest local produce

is used wherever possible, and includes smoked salmon, venison, Galloway beef and delicious local cheeses. Cavens makes the ideal base to explore the Solway coast, or the nearby Burns Country, and there are opportunities for golf (internationally renowned Southerness course one mile away), shooting, ornithology, nature study and observing wildlife. Or perhaps you're looking for a place where you can relax and recharge your batteries? Then the Cavens Hotel is the ideal place for this as well. Go for leisurely walks among the beautiful scenery of this part of Scotland and return to a roaring log fire and a glass of single malt.

was to beset the followers when, in 1791, she died. On her deathbed she announced that she was going up to heaven to prepare the way, and that she would return in six days. However, if a lack of faith was shown, it might take ten years to make all the arrangements in heaven. If she didn't return in ten years, then she would in 50 years time. She then died peacefully.

Amazingly, some people still believed in her. One was a man named Andrew Innes, and he made off with Mother Buchan's body. It was soon recovered, but alas she showed no signs of life after six days. The body was eventually buried in a kirkyard, and then, amazingly, dug back up again and buried beneath a kitchen hearth, where it lay for many years.

All of the Buchanites had by now dispersed, but Andrew Innes remained true. He dug her body up for a second time, and took it off to his cottage in Crocketford, where he placed it in a specially built outhouse. By 1841, Andrew was an old man, and he eagerly anticipated Mother Buchan's return after 50 years. He gave away his life savings in anticipation of ascending to heaven, and sat beside the body looking for signs of life. Of course, nothing happened, and he blamed himself and his lack of faith for her non-return. He lived for a further four years, and was eventually buried beside Mother Buchan in the same grave behind his cottage.

KIRKCUDBRIGHT

Kirkcudbright (pronounced "Kirk-coo-bree") is one of the true hidden gems of Scotland. It is a royal burgh and fishing port sitting close to the mouth of the River Dee, and its tongue-twister of a name simply means "the kirk of St.

HIGH STREET GALLERY

84 High Street, Kirkcudbright, Kirkcudbrightshire DG6 4JL
Tel: 01557 331660
e-mail: contact@highstgallery.co.uk
website: www.highstgallery.co.uk

Kirkcudbright is a small seaport close to the Solway Firth that is famous for the quality of its light, and this has attracted many famous artists to settle here over the years. It is also famous for its intimate art galleries that sell original works of art. One of the best is the **High Street Gallery**, owned and run by graduates of Glasgow School of Art Maureen Briggs and Richard Ross. Here you'll find paintings, sculpture, ceramics and prints by modern Scottish artists such as Peter Howson, Archie Sutter Watt, Moira and Stuart Beaty, James Macaulay, Davy Brown, Richard Coley and so on. Plus there are fine works by Kirkcudbright artists of the past, such as Jessie M. King, E.A. Taylor, William Miles Johnston, Anna Hotchkis, Anne Dallas and David Sassoon.

Both Maureen and Richard are still practising artists, and bring a wealth of experience to the choosing of the works of art to hang in their gallery. They can offer friendly and knowledgeable advice to prospective purchasers about style and price, and are always on hand to advise on the selling of

high quality individual works of art or collections. The gallery is in a listed 18th century building in the High Street, which is full of elegant Georgian and Victorian buildings, close to the old Tolbooth and jail, where John Paul Jones, founder of the American navy, was once a prisoner. If you are looking for a distinctive gift while holidaying in this picturesque and historic part of Scotland, then the High Street Gallery is the place for you.

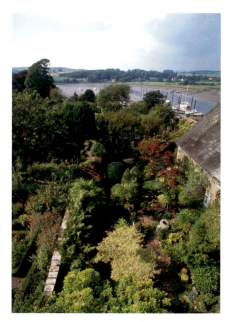

View over Kirkcudbright

Dumfries and Galloway has an exceptionally mild climate, thanks to the Gulf Stream, and this, coupled with the excellent light, led to the founding of an artists' colony here in the early 20th century.

St Cuthbert is supposed to have founded the first church in the area, in the present town cemetery. Grave diggers, it is claimed, have often dug up carved stones from various buildings that have stood on the site since then. The present **St Cuthbert's Parish Church** is nearer the centre of the town, and dates from 1838. Within the old graveyard is the well-known **Billy Marshall's Grave**. Billy was known as the "King of Galloway Tinkers", and he died in 1792 when he was 120 years old.

The **Greyfriar's Kirk** is all that remains of a Franciscan friary that once stood in the town. It dates from the 16th century, though was originally founded by Alan, Lord of Galloway, father of Devorgilla, in 1224. The church stands on a slight rise called **Moat's Brae**, suggesting that this was a meeting place of some kind in medieval times. It has been altered over the years, and it is now an Episcopalian place of worship. Within it is the ornate tomb of **Sir Thomas MacLellan of Bombie** and his wife Grizzell Maxwell. It was erected in 1597, but it hides a secret. Sir Thomas's son salvaged effigies from an earlier tomb and placed them on top

Cuthbert". It was in existence in at least the 11th century, though it didn't receive its royal charter until 1455. It is the former county town of Kirkcudbrightshire, which is also known as the "Stewartry of Kirkcudbright".

Here you will find brightly painted houses dating from Georgian, Regency and Victorian times, and it makes a wonderful backdrop to all the history that is associated with the place.

GLADSTONE HOUSE

48 High Street, Kirkcudbright, Kirkcudbrightshire DG6 4JX
Tel/Fax: 01557 3311734 e-mail: hilarygladstone@aol.com

Gladstone House, one of Kirkcudbright's finest houses, is Grade II listed and retains many of its distinctive Georgian features. Gordon and Hilary Cowan offer traditional hospitality to their guests and use produce which is locally sourced.The Guest House has three extremely comfortable en suite bedrooms offering panoramic views of the town. It also features an elegant residents lounge sympathetically furnished with fine antiques and pictures. Service and hospitality combine to ensure a memorable visit.

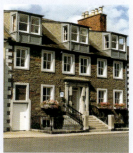

of his parents' one, which is essentially a Renaissance structure.

Sir Thomas's home was the nearby **MacLellan's Castle** (Historic Scotland), thought to have been built from stone from the friary. It isn't really a castle, but a fine town house for a man who became provost (the Scottish equivalent of mayor) of Kirkcudbright. It is open to the public.

If you walk up Castle Bank past the whitewashed **Harbour Cottage Gallery** you will reach the High Street. It runs parallel to Castle Street for some distance, then takes a 90 degree turn to the left. It must be one of the most charming and elegant streets in Scotland, full of Georgian and Regency houses that are painted in bright uncompromising colours such as green

MacLellan's Castle

and yellow. **Auchingool House** is the oldest, and dates from 1617. It was built for the McCullochs of Auchengool.

Broughton House (National Trust for Scotland) dates from the 18th century, and was the home of **A.E. Hornel** the artist. He was one of the Glasgow boys, and died in 1933. Behind it is the

THE BLUE BARN

8 Castle Street, Kirkcudbright,
Kirkcudbrightshire DG6 4JA
Tel/Fax: 01557 339189

The Royal Burgh of Kirkcudbright is famous for its artistic connections, as well as its Georgian and Regency architecture. Dominating the place are the romantic ruins of MacLellan's Castle, which are open to the public. And in Castle Street, named after the town's most prominent feature, you'll find **The Blue Barn**, a shop with a wonderful range of contemporary craft items and gifts. In keeping with its name, it has been painted in lively shades of blue, which blend in perfectly with the other buildings in this historic area of the town. In keeping with its promotion of the area's crafts, the interior of the shop was built by local craftsmen, and the individually built display benches in solid wood now sets off the many gift items to perfection.

The basement - known as the Barn Basement - has been turned into another display area. Everything on sale here has been carefully chosen, though the prices remain competitive and surprisingly low.

From colourful cards to toys and bowls, the Blue Barn is sure to have something to take your fancy. After a day exploring the castle, the delightful harbour, the numerous art galleries and the colourful streets in Kirkcudbright, head for the Blue Barn for all your souvenir needs. Lindsay Picken, who owns and runs it, is always ready to offer expert and friendly advice. If you just want to browse, however, you can do so to your heart's content - though be warned - you'll inevitably see something in the shop's range of goods that you just have to buy.

marvellous **Japanese Garden**, influenced by trips that Hornel made to the Far East in search of inspiration. Further along is **Greengates House** (not open to the public), former home of **Jessie M. King**, another famous artist. At the High Street's dog leg stands the early 17th century **Tolbooth**, once the centre for the town's civil affairs. Now it is a museum and art gallery, and tells the story of the town and its artists' colony. It was opened by the Queen in 1993. The town jail was also housed within the Tolbooth, and John Paul Jones, founder of the American Navy, was imprisoned here for murder before leaving Scotland. He got his revenge when he returned to the town aboard an American ship in April 1778 and shelled nearby **St. Mary's Isle** (not an island, but a peninsula), where the Earl of Selkirk's grand house was situated, and where a medieval nunnery once stood. It is said that Jones also landed with about 40 men and set out to capture the Earl. However, he was not at home, so they took the silver plate instead. Six years later Jones returned the plate, full of apologies.

If St. Mary's Isle is a peninsula, then **Manxman's Lake** is even more peculiar. For not only is it one of Scotland's genuine "lakes" (as opposed to lochs) it is also a a small inlet of Kirkcudbright Bay, and not a lake at all.

A walk up St. Mary's Wynd beside the Tolbooth takes you to **Castledykes**, where once stood a mighty royal castle. Edward I stayed here during the Wars of Independence, as did Henry VI of England after his defeat at the Battle of Towton in 1461. James IV also used it as a convenient stopping off point on his many pilgrimages to St. Ninian's shrine at Whithorn.

Broughton House Gardens

The town also has its literary associations. **Dorothy L. Sayers** spent many holidays here, and set her Lord Peter Wimsey whodunit *Five Red Herrings* among the artists' colony. It is not her best work, as the solution to the mystery over-relies on a knowledge of the colours on an artist's palette and train times between Kirkcudbright and Ayrshire. Ronald Searle also knew the town, and he based his St. Trinian's School on St. Trinian's in Edinburgh, attended by the daughters of another Kirkcudbright artist, W. Miles Johnston.

If you wish to learn more about the town and its people, make your way to the **Stewartry Museum** in St. Mary's Street, which has many displays and artifacts.

AROUND KIRKCUDBRIGHT

TONGLAND
2 miles N of Kirkcudbright on the A711

The magnificent **Tongland Abbey** once stood here, and in the kirkyard are its scant remains - a length of wall pierced by a small medieval archway. **Tongland Power Station** (see panel on page 62) is part of the Galloway hydro-electric scheme of the 1930s, and conducted

GALLOWAY HYDROS VISITOR CENTRE

Tongland Power Station, Kirkudbright
Tel: 01557 330114

A guided tour of Galloway Hydros will give you an insight into the force of nature that is captured, channelled and released back into the environment, enabling Scottish Power to produce pure, clean energy. The Visitor Centre tells the story of the construction of the Galloway Hydros in the 1930s and the tour takes you into the power station, the control room and the turbine hall. You will learn about the operation of the power stations and how they contribute to the national electricity grid system. Close by is the impressive Tongland Dam and Reservoir - the power source. Here, you might catch a glimpse of a migrating salmon. A picnic area and refreshments room allow you to relax and enjoy the tranquility.

Tongland Bridge

LOCH KEN

9 miles N of Kirkcudbright between the A713 and the A762

This narrow, nine-mile long stretch of water was created in 1930s during the construction of the Galloway hydro-electric scheme, with the turbines being housed in the power house at Tongland. Other schemes were built at Clatteringshaws and Loch Doon. Loch Ken, which is no more than a mile wide at its widest, is now a favourite spot for bird watching and watersports.

NEW GALLOWAY

17 miles N of Kirkcudbright on the A762

Though no bigger than a village, New Galloway is a proud royal burgh which received its royal charter in 1630. It is a picturesque place, and part of that area of Kirkcudbrightshire known as the **Glenkens**, which consists of high

tours are available. **Tongland Bridge** is a graceful, single-arched structure across the Dee. It was designed by Thomas Telford and built in 1805.

PLUMED HORSE RESTAURANT

Crossmichael, Castle Douglas, Kirkcudbrightshire DG7 3AU
Tel: 01556 670333 Mobile: 07736 807333
e-mail: plumedhorse@aol.com

The **Plumed Horse Restaurant** is a small, rural restaurant with one Michelin star that is well worth seeking out. Owned and run by chef Tony Borthwick, it is set in a whitewashed barn conversion in the middle of the village, and has a stylish, warm yellow interior over two floors. It has developed an enviable

reputation for its food, which is based on fresh local produce, such as seafood, beef and lamb, cooked with flare and imagination. Simplicity is the watchword here, and the Plumed Horse Restaurant was voted Scottish Newcomer of the Year in 2002.

moorland and green, fertile dales. The grave of a Covenantor shot in 1685 is to be found in **Kells Churchyard**, north of the town.

Each year the town hosts the **Scottish Alternative Games**, where sports such as gird and cleek racing (hoop and stick racing), hurlin' the curlin' stane (throwing the curling stone), flingin' the herd's bunnet (throwing the herdman's bonnet) and tossin' the sheaf (throwing a sheaf of corn) are popular events.

BALMACLELLAN

18 miles N of Kirkcudbright off the A712

This picturesque village was the home of **Robert Paterson**, a stonemason who was the original for Old Mortality in Scott's book of the same name. He travelled the country in the 18th century cleaning up Covenanting memorials and monuments, and eventually he left home for good to concentrate on this work, leaving behind a no doubt angry wife and several children. He finally died in 1800, and up until then he continued to travel throughout Scotland on an old grey pony.

In the village is the **Clog and Shoe Workshop**, where 18 styles of traditional footwear are manufactured. Visitors can look round and see the shoes being made.

ST. JOHN'S TOWN OF DALRY

19 miles N of Kirkcudbright on the A713

This small, attractive village is sometimes referred to simply as Dalry, though it mustn't be confused with another, larger Dalry in Ayrshire. It sits on the Southern Upland Way, and is a favourite stopping off point for wakers and hikers. Within the village is a curious, chair-shaped rock commonly known as **St. John's Chair**. Local tradition states that John the Baptist rested in it, though quite what he was doing in the Glenkens area of Kirkcudbrightshire has never been adequately explained.

When a reservoir was created at **Lochinvar** near Dalry some time ago, the scant remains of Lochinvar tower house were submerged beneath the waters. This was the home of Young Lochinvar, written about by Sir Walter Scott in the famous lines:

O, young Lochinvar is come out of the west,
Through all the wide border his steed was the best.....

CARSPHAIRN

27 miles N of Kirkcudbright on the A713

The main industry in the area used to be lead mining, though all traces have now disappeared, apart from a few depressions in the ground. It was close to Carsphairn that John Louden McAdam, after whom Tarmacadam is named, experimented with his road surfaces. His father had a small estate here. If you want to find out more about the village and its people, go to the **Carsphairn Heritage Centre**.

CASTLE DOUGLAS

9 miles NE of Kirkcudbright off the A75

Castle Douglas was given its burgh charter in 1791. It was founded by William Douglas, a local merchant who made his money trading with Virginia and the West Indies. Before that, it had been a small hamlet called Carlingwark. Douglas intended building a thriving manufacturing town that relied on the woollen industry, though he was only partially successful. However, he did lay the foundations of a charming and picturesque town where some of his original 18th century buildings can still be seen. **Carlingwark Loch** lies on the edge of the town, and one of Douglas's grandiose plans was to connect it to the

THE POSTHORN

26/30 St. Andrew Street, Castle Douglas,
Kirkcudbrightshire DG7 1DE
Tel: 01556 502531 Fax: 01556 503330

The Posthorn, in the picturesque and historic town of Castle Douglas, has earned an enviable international reputation, and is recognised as the leading supplier in Scotland of Border Fine Arts and Moorcroft Pottery and Enamels. It really is a dream come true for collectors, and the shop is crammed with all sorts of fine sculptures, bowls, vases and fine porcelain dinner, tea and coffee sets. Founded in 1974, the shop owes most of its success to the personal service it offers, and high standards it has set over the years.

Border Fine Arts was founded in Langholm in Dumfriesshire the same year that the Posthorn was founded, and the countryside surrounding the town has inspired the many delightful items it has modelled and manufactured over the years. The Posthorn has an in-depth knowledge of the range that is second to none, and so you are assured of knowledgeable, friendly advice whenever you visit the shop. Some pieces have even been

developed exclusively for The Posthorn, such as the four sculptures in the *Urban* series, which are now much sought after and collectable. The shop also stocks the wonderful Border Fine Arts Gold Edition pieces, where the first in an edition size are offered exclusively to special retailers,such as the five sculptures in the Haymaking Series. The fifth and final piece "Hay Bogie" will be available from late 2003 and some of the earlier pieces in the series are still available.

In 1998 W. Moorcroft, manufacturers of the fine Moorcoft Pottery, acquired Kingsley Enamels, a company specialising in decorative metal work, and now make and market enamel ware along with its original fine pottery. The Posthorn not only sells its current range of products, it also sells retired pieces, both pottery and enamels. Visit The Posthorn and you could be the proud owner of a limited edition enamel or one of the Prestige Pottery pieces, such as *Parramore,* which was only produced in small numbers. An exclusive run of just 75 pairs of enamel vases called *The Harrowers* was produced exclusively for The Posthorn. Editions such as this are in great demand from collectors, and can increase dramatically in value over the years.

The shop also retails quality china ware, pottery and porcelain from other manufacturers, such as Royal Doulton, Wedgwood, Coalport, Spode, Portmeirion, Lladro, Royal Worcester, Lorna Bailey and Waterford, to name but a few. There is also Edinburgh Crystal and the Royal Crown Derby range of fine paperweights. You are free to browse and the shop also offers a reliable mail order service. Why not visit their website on www.posthorn.co.uk for more information such as events and shows as well as pieces for sale.

sea by a canal so that ships could sail right into the heart of the settlement, which lies five miles from the coast.

In Market street is the **Castle Douglas Art Gallery**, gifted to the town in 1938 by the artist Ethel Bristow. There is a continuously changing exhibition of paintings, sculpture and crafts. The **Sulworth Brewery** is in King Street, and you can look round it and see the brewing process in action, from barley to beer, and enjoy a complementary half pint of Galloway real ale.

THREAVE GARDENS AND ESTATE
1 mile W of Castle Douglas off the A75

The Threave Gardens and Estate (National Trust for Scotland - see panel on page 67) cover 62 acres, and

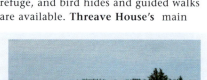

Threave Gardens

surrounds a house built in 1872 by a Liverpool businessman. It is home to the Trust's School of Practical Gardening, where the principles of nature conservation, forestry and agriculture are taught. The estate also has a wildfowl refuge, and bird hides and guided walks are available. **Threave House's** main

BALCARY BAY COUNTRY HOUSE HOTEL

Auchencairn, near Castle Douglas,
Kirkcudbrightshire DG7 1QZ
Tel: 01556 640217/640311 Fax: 01556 640272
e-mail: reservations@balcary-bay-hotel.co.uk
website: www.balcary-bay-hotel.co.uk

The beautiful, four star **Balcary Bay Country House Hotel** sits right on the coast in an area of Galloway that is romantic in its isolation, and full of the old intrigues of the smuggling trade that was carried out here in the 17th and 18th centuries. Originally owned

by a shipping firm, it was known to harbour illegal loot in its secret underground passages. The house still retains much of its original character., but has married this to the modern concepts of comfort, relaxation and style. There are twenty well-appointed bedrooms, all fully en suite and all decorated to an extremely high standard. Each one has a colour TV, radio, telephone, tea and coffee making facilities and a hair dryer. Many of the rooms enjoy magnificent views across the bay, with the remainder overlooking the lovely gardens.

The award winning cuisine is sure to delight the most discerning of palates, and is based on fresh, local produce such as Galloway beef, lamb, lobsters, prawns and, of course, Balcary Bay salmon. The wine list is comprehensive, and there is sure to be something that makes the perfect accompaniment to a meal. After dinner, you can relax in the cocktail bar, and enjoy one of the many malt whiskies that are on offer. Galloway is a beautiful but relatively unexplored area of Scotland, and enjoys a mild climate thanks to the Gulf Stream.

rooms are open to the public. They have been restored to how they looked in the 1930s. There is a plant centre and a countryside centre in the converted stables.

THREAVE CASTLE

8 miles NE of Kirkcudbright off the A75

The magnificent ruins of Threave Castle (Historic Scotland) stands on an island in the River Dee, reached by a small ferry that answers the call of a bell on the riverbank jetty. The castle was built by Archibald Douglas, 4th Earl of Douglas, known as Archibald the Grim (because of the dark and ugly set of his face) soon after the Lordship of Galloway was bestowed on him in 1369 by Robert III. He died at Threave in 1400, one of the most powerful men in Scotland. During his Lordship he consistently ignored the commands of his king, instead going his own way. His descendants were no better, and James II finally laid siege to the castle in 1455 in a bid to end their power. So strong was it that it held out for two months before its surrender ended the influence of the Douglas family.

Threave Castle

DALBEATTIE

11 miles NE of Kirkcudbright on the A711

Dalbeattie is a small, neat burgh which stands to the east of the furthermost point of navigation on the Water of Urr, and was at one time a small port. Ships of up to 60 tons regularly docked here, after making the four mile trip upstream from the sea, pulled by teams of horses. The "Pool of Dalbeattie", as the harbour area was called, is now derelict, and the river has silted up.

Dalbeattie was a planned community, founded in the 1790s as a textile centre and quarrying town, working the deposits of granite in the area. About a mile from the town, on the west bank of the Urr, is the site of **Buittle Castle and Bailey**. It was the home of John Balliol, Edward I's puppet king of Scotland and son of Devorgilla, Lady of Galloway. Robert I founded a royal burgh in the bailey of the castle, and a recent archaeological dig has unearthed much information about its layout. A later tower house stands close by.

In the centre of the town, on the wall of the former town hall, is the **Murdoch Memorial**, a large plaque which commemorates William Murdoch, who was First Officer aboard the ill-fated Titanic, which sank in 1912. History has never dealt kindly with the man, as he has been unfairly accused over the years of being a coward who attempted to shoot passengers who tried to leave the ship, not allowing third class passengers near the lifeboats, and of accepting bribes from first class passengers so that they could get access to lifeboats to which they were not entitled.

Witness statements presented at the Board of Enquiry showed that he acted

THREAVE

Castle Douglas, Dumfries & Galloway, DG7 I R
Tel: 01556 502575 Fax: 01556 502683
Ranger/naturalist: tel (01556) 502575
e-mail threave@nts.org.uk website: www.nts.org.uk

Threave Garden is delightful in all seasons. At 26 hectares (64 acres), it is best known for its spectacular springtime daffodils (nearly 200 varieties), but herbaceous beds are colourful in summer and trees and heather garden are striking in autumn. The Victorian house is home to the Trust's School of Practical Gardening. The principal rooms in **Threave House** opened to the public for the first time in 2002 and have attracted great interest. The interiors have been restored to their appearance in the 1930s, and from the house visitors can enjoy impressive vistas of the Galloway countryside. Guided walks. Maxwelton Collection of local bygones in the Visitor Centre on show for the first time in 2003. Plant Centre.

Threave Estate is a wildfowl refuge and is designated a Special Protection Area for its breeding waders and wintering wildfowl. The important wetlands are designated an Area of Special Scientific Interest. Threave provides a good example of integrated management of the land, taking account of agriculture, forestry and nature conservation. Marked walks include a 2.5km estate trail through this variety of landscapes, and hides provide good cover to observe bird activity. A Countryside Centre in the old stables highlights nature conservation, forestry and agriculture at Threave.

correctly and fairly at all times, and he was officially cleared of any wrong doing. The later film, however, still showed him in a bad light.

MOAT OF URR

13 miles NE of Kirkcudbright off the B794

This is a 12th century motte-hill. It still remains the largest man-made hill in Scotland, and at one time had a wooden castle on its summit, which was supposedly built by William de Berkeley. An old legend recounts how Robert the Bruce, later to become Robert I of Scotland, was resting at the motte-hill when he was surprised by an English knight, Sir Walter Selby. They began fighting, with Sir Walter gaining the upper hand until a peasant woman

called Dame Sprotte emerged from a nearby cottage to see what all the noise was about. She immediately took matters into her own hands, and lunged at the the Englishman, pulling his hair. He lost his balance and fell over, whereupon Robert I disarmed him. The old woman was enraged to see that the king didn't kill Sir Walter there and then. Instead he suggested that the three of them take porridge in the cottage.

Dame Sprotte immediately protested, saying that an Englishman wasn't welcome in her home. But Robert the Bruce insisted, and with a bad grace she let them sit at her table. However, she refused to give the Englishman a spoon. Robert the Bruce then said that, for saving his life, he would grant her as

much land as she could run round when he became king. So Dame Sprotte left the cottage and began running round in ever increasing circles.

It's an intriguing and entertaining legend, but whether it ever happened or not is another matter. What is not in doubt, however, is that when Robert eventually became king, he inexplicably granted 20 Scottish acres of land at Urr to a family of peasants called Sprotte, and in payment the Sprotte descendants had to give a bowl of porridge to the then King of Scotland whenever he came by that way.

ROCKCLIFFE

10 miles E of Kirkcudbright off the A710

This village was at one time a great smuggling centre, but is now a quiet resort. **Rough Island** (National Trust for Scotland) is a 20 acre bird sanctuary just off the coastline, and the **Moat of Mark** (also National Trust for Scotland) lies just to the north of the village. The moat is an ancient hill fort. Between Rockcliffe and the village of Kippford, two miles away, is the **Muckle Lands and Jubilee Path** (National Trust for Scotland), 51 acres of rough, attractive coastline.

KIPPFORD

10 miles NE of Kirkcudbright off the A710

The Solway tides are among the fastest in Britain, but this hasn't prevented Kippford from becoming a yachting resort. Like Rockcliffe, it was once a thriving centre for smuggling, bringing in contraband from Ireland and the Isle of Man.

PALNACKIE

10 miles NE of Kirkcudbright on the A711

Though this attractive little village sits a mile from the sea on the Urr Water, it was at one time

a thriving little port. Each year, in summer, it hosts the **World Flounder Tramping Championships**. People come from all over the world to go out onto the mud flats south of the village and search for flounders hiding beneath the mud, using their bare feet. The person who collects the largest poundage is declared the winner. It may appear to be a harmless and eccentric pastime, but flounder tramping was a recognised way of catching the fish in olden times.

In the village is the **North Glen Gallery**, which features glass blowing plus interior and exterior design. Advice on local walks and wildlife is also available.

ORCHARDTON TOWER

8 miles NE of Kirkcudbright off the A711

This small tower house is the only circular castle in Scotland, and dates from the middle of the 15th century. It was built by a man called John Cairns. It is not open to the public, but can be viewed from the road.

DUNDRENNAN

4 miles SE of Kirkcudbright on the A711

Within the village are the substantial ruins of **Dundrennan Abbey** (Historic Scotland). The abbey was founded in 1142 by David I and Fergus, Lord of Galloway. Though there are only scant

Dundrennan Abbey

remains of the church, the chapter house and some of the other buildings are well worth exploring. It was at Dundrennan Abbey that Mary Stuart spent her last night on Scottish soil before setting sail across the Solway to England and her eventual execution.

CAIRNHOLY

11 miles W of Kirkcudbright off the A75

Cairnholy comprises two chambered burial cairns dating from between 2000 and 3000BC. Their most remarkable feature are the huge stones that went into their construction, and no one has yet worked out how they were raised and manoeuvred into place. A mile north are the ruins of **Carsluith Castle**, built by the Browns of Carsluith in the 16th century.

CREETOWN

15 miles NW of Kirkcudbright on the A75

The neat and picturesque village of Creetown sits at the mouth of the River Cree, and was once a granite mining centre. The **Creetown Gem Rock Museum**, within a former school, was established in 1971, and has amassed a huge collection of gemstones and minerals from all over the world. There are also exhibitions and displays on geology, and the formation of the earth from earliest times. It even has an "erupting volcano". In St. John Street is the **Creetown Exhibition Centre**, which features local history and wildlife, as well as occasional exhibitions of paintings by local artists. The **Creetown Country Weekend** is held every year in September, and features country and western music.

TWYNHOLM

3 miles NW of Kirkcudbright on the A75

Twynholm is the home village of David Coulthard the racing driver. The **David Coulthard Museum** in the main street celebrates his life and achievements.

GATEHOUSE OF FLEET

7 miles NW of Kirkcudbright on the A75

This small town was the original for the "Kippletringan" of *Guy Mannering* by Sir Walter Scott. It sits on the Water of Fleet, and was once a small seaport, though it sits half a mile from the open sea. The Fleet was canalised in 1823 by Alexander Murray of Cally House, and the port area of the town was called **Port MacAdam**, though the site has now been grassed over.

The town was laid out in the 1760s by James Murray of Broughton, who wished to create a great industrial town. Thankfully, he never succeeded, and the town remains more or less as it was in the mid-18th century. Within one of the old cotton mills is a museum called **Mill on the Fleet**, which explains the history of the town's former weaving industry.

It was within the **Murray Arms** that Burns is supposed to have set down the words for *Scots Wha Hae*. A mile west of the town you'll find the substantial ruins of **Cardonness Castle** (Historic Scotland) perched above the A75. This six-storey tower house was built in the 15th century as the home of the powerful McCulloch of Galloway family.

STRANRAER

Stranraer sits at the head of Loch Ryan, and on the edge of that hammer-shaped peninsula jutting out into the Irish Sea called the **Rhinns of Galloway**. It is a royal burgh, having been given its charter in 1617, and is now one of the main ports for Northern Ireland. The town has narrow streets and alleyways, and in the centre you will find the **Castle of St. John**, a tower house dating from the 16th century. Claverhouse based himself in it as he hunted down Covenantors in the area, and it was later

used as the town jail. Now it is a small museum. Within the **Old Town Hall** is another museum which explains the history of Stranraer and the former county of Wigtownshire.

Stranraer was home to **Sir John Ross** (1777-1856) who explored the North West Passage between the Atlantic and the Pacific. He lived in **North West Castle**, which is now a hotel. He was born near Kirkcolm in the Rhinns of Galloway, the son of a minister. During his travels, he discovered the Boothia Peninsula, North America's most northerly point.

On the town's sea front is the **Princess Victoria Monument**, which commemorates the tragic sinking of the car ferry Princess Victoria on January 31 1953. It was bound for Larne in Northern Ireland with 127 passengers and 49 of a crew, but when it left the shelter of Loch Ryan it encountered the full force of a horrific gale. Lifeboats were launched, but the ferry eventually sank with the loss of 134 lives.

AROUND STRANRAER

CASTLE KENNEDY GARDENS
3 miles E of Stranraer off the A75

These magnificent gardens cover 75 acres between the small Black and White Lochs, and are laid out around the romantic ivy-clad ruins of Castle Kennedy, which was destroyed by fire in 1710. They were created in 1733 by the 2nd Earl of Stair, and being a field marshal under the Duke of Marlborough, he managed to get troops to help with the work of laying some of them out. **Lochinch Castle** is fairly modern, and sits within the gardens. It is the home of the Earl and Countess of Stair, and is not open to the public.

SOULSEAT LOCH
3 miles E off Stranraer on a minor road off the A75

A narrow peninsula juts out into the waters of the loch, and it was here that **Soulseat Abbey** once stood. Though a few hillocks and indentations remain, nothing of the abbey survives above ground.

DUNRAGIT
6 miles E of Stranraer on the A75

In this small village you will find **Glenwhan Gardens**, overlooking the beautiful Glenluce Bay. They were started from scratch in 1979, and now cover 12 acres.

CAIRNRYAN
5 miles N of Stranraer on the A77

This village straggles along the shores of Loch Ryan. Between the road and the shoreline is a complex of car parks, piers and jetties - the Scottish terminus of the P&O ferry to Northern Ireland. It was here that the famous aircraft carrier **HMS Ark Royal** was scrapped.

GLENTROOL
20 miles NE of Stranraer on a minor road off the A714 at Bargrennan

It was here, close to the lovely Loch Trool, that Robert I defeated an English army in March 1307, soon after landing on the Scottish mainland to begin his campaign to free Scotland of its English conquerors. His small army had hidden itself among the hills above the loch, and when the English troops went past, they opened proceedings by rolling great boulders down on them. It was a turning point in the Wars of Independence, not because it was a magnificent victory that crippled Edward I's army, but because it gave the Scots great heart to go on fighting. **Bruce's Stone** commemorates the victory.

A few miles to the north is **The Merrick**, at 2,784 the highest hill in the Lowlands of Scotland.

GLENLUCE
10 miles E of Stranraer off the A75

This attractive little village has been bypassed by the A75, the main route from Northern England and the Borders to the ferry ports at Stranraer and Cairnryan. At one time it was home to **Alexander Agnew**, nicknamed the "Devil of Luce", who was hanged for blasphemy in the 17th century. A mile to the north west are the lovely ruins of **Glenluce Abbey** (Historic Scotland), founded in 1192 by Roland, Lord of Galloway, for the Cistercians. Mary Stuart visited the abbey, as did Robert I and James IV as he made his way to St. Ninian's Shrine at Whithorn. There is a particularly fine chapter house, and an exhibition of objects excavated on the site. **Castle of Park** is close by, and is an imposing mansion built in about 1590 for Thomas Hay, son of the last Abbot of Glenluce.

Immediately after the Reformation of 1560, the then Earl of Cassillis, head of the Kennedy family, claimed the property and lands of Glenluce Abbey. He persuaded one of the monks to forge the abbot's signature on a document which granted him the lands, then ordered some of his men to kill the monk. He then put the men who had carried out the foul deed on his behalf on trial, found them guilty, and had them executed.

NEWTON STEWART
22 miles E of Stranraer on the A75

This handsome and well laid out town received its burgh charter in 1677. It sits on the River Cree, close to where it enters Wigtown Bay, and makes the perfect centre for a fishing or walking holiday. **Newton Stewart Museum** is to be found in York Road, and has displays and exhibits which tell the history of the town and its people.

Sophie's Puppetstube and Doll's House is a small, unusual museum with a reputation that goes far beyond Scotland. It sits in Queen Street, and has over 50 exquisitely made doll's houses and room settings at a scale of 1:12, all behind glass. There is also a collection of over 200 dressed dolls.

Four miles south of the town is the **Wigtown Bay Local Nature Reserve**, the largest local nature reserve in Britain. There is a bird sanctuary and a ranger service. Four miles north is the **Woods of Cree**, run by the Royal Society for the Protection of Birds. The reserve is rich in song birds.

KIRKCOWAN
17 miles E of Stranraer on the B733, off the A75

This small picturesque village has a **Parish Church** dating from 1834 which has external stairs to the upper galleries.

River Cree, Newton Stewart

WALK 1

Loch Trool

Start	Caldons Campsite, 1½miles (2.4km) east of Glen Trool Visitor Centre at Stroan Bridge
Distance	5½ miles (8.9km)
Approximate time	3 hours
Parking	Forestry Commission car parks at Caldons Campsite. There are two car parks for day visitors either side of the bridge over Water of Trool
Refreshments	None
Ordnance Survey maps	Landranger 77 (Dalmellington to New Galloway), Pathfinder 526 (Glentrool Village & Bargrennan), Outdoor Leisure Map 32 (Galloway Forest Park)

This is arguably the finest short walk in Dumfries and Galloway. For a modest distance and moderate effort, you enjoy the most outstanding views across Loch Trool to the surrounding peaks from many different angles as you circuit the loch. The route is well waymarked and easy to follow but there is likely to be some muddy and rough stretches. It is worth choosing a fine day and taking your time over this walk.

The area around Loch Trool is associated with some of the most momentous events in Scottish history. A short distance (and signposted) from the start is the Martyr's Tomb, marking the place where six Covenanters were executed in 1685 for refusing to accept Charles II as head of the Church of Scotland. The route later passes the site of a battle between the Scots and English in 1307, and the Bruce Stone which commemorates Robert the Bruce's victory in that battle.

Start at the bridge over the Water of Trool and bear left, following for the first half of the walk both Southern Upland Way marker posts and green-topped Loch Trool Trail posts. Turn left to cross a footbridge over Caldons Burn, continue

along a path beside it and pass the toilet block to reach a tarmac drive. Turn left through the campsite and by the shop on the right, turn left again. Continue along the tarmac drive which curves to the right. Turn left along a track, following the waymarks, cross a burn and shortly bear right along a path through woodland. The path curves uphill to a kissing-gate . Go through to enter conifer plantations.

The next part of the walk is particularly attractive as you follow a switchback route – with some quite steep climbs at times – through woodland above Loch Trool. The views across the water to the hills on the north side, including a striking view of Merrick at one point, are magnificent.

WALK 1

Near the end of the loch the path passes the location of the Battle of Glentrool in 1307 where the Scots, under Robert the Bruce, ambushed an English army and defeated it by rolling boulders down the steep slopes on to the English cavalry.

Eventually the path descends to Glenhead Burn . Cross the footbridge ahead, here leaving the Southern Upland Way, turn left alongside the tree-lined burn and bear right away from it, following green-topped posts, to a track. Turn left and now comes another attractive part of the walk as you proceed through delightful deciduous woodland. After crossing Gairland Burn the track ascends to a gate. Go through, keep ahead to cross a bridge over Buchan Burn and follow the track uphill. Just after a right bend, turn left along an uphill path to Bruce's Stone **B** , a fine viewpoint

overlooking Loch Trool and the scene of the king's victory in 1307.

Turn right to rejoin the track by a car park and turn left along a lane, passing through a second car park. Continue along the lane for 1 mile (1.6km) and look out for where a green-topped post directs you to turn left into conifer woodland **C** .

Cross a footbridge over a burn and then follow a winding and undulating path back through the trees to the start.

If the last part of the walk – between point **C** *and the start – is closed for felling operations, simply continue along the lane to the entrance to Caldons Campsite and turn left along the tarmac drive to return to the start.* ●

WIGTOWN

23 miles E of Stranraer on the A714

Wigtown is a small royal burgh which received its royal charter in 1457, though it has been in existence since at least the 13th century. It is now officially **Scotland's Book Town**, and has many bookshops and small publishing houses. In the kirkyard of the local church are the **Martyr's Graves**. In 1685, two Covenantors, Margaret McLachlan (aged

Martyr's Graves

63) and Margaret Wilson (aged 18) were executed for adhering to the Covenant, which, simply put, opposed bishops in the Church of Scotland. The two women were tied to posts sunk in the sands at the mouth of the River Bladnoch, and were drowned as the tide rose over their heads. McLachlan died first, as her stake was further from the shore, and it was hoped that when Wilson saw this, she would recant. But she didn't, and she drowned also. The river has changed course since the 1680s, and the area where the executions took place is now salt marsh. The **Martyr's Monument** stands on the spot. Another monument, the **Covenantors Monument**, stands on a hill behind the town. It is a tall, slender column, and from the top of the hill there are views over Wigtown Bay.

One mile south west of the town is **Bladnoch Distillery**, Scotland's most southerly whisky distillery. There is a visitors centre and guided tours.

CHAPEL FINIAN

16 miles SE of Stranraer on the A747

The A747 hugs the coastline of Luce Bay for most of its length. The ruins of Chapel Finian sits on the landward side of the road, though in truth all there is to see are low foundations. It's their age which make them interesting, as they date from the 10th century. From then until the Reformation the chapel was probably used as a stopping off point for pilgrims making their way to St Ninian's Shrine at Whithorn, 12 miles to the south east. St. Finian of Moville lived during the 6th century, and was the

STABLES HOUSE

Home Farm, Garlieston, near Newton Stewart, Wigtownshire DG8 8HF
Tel: 01988 600694 Fax: 01988 600695

Set amid the splendid scenery and heritage of Galloway House Estate, **The Stables** comprise two beautifully restored self-catering cottages within a 1750's stables block with garden. The cottages which sleep 2 to 4 and 6 to 8 people have extremely comfortable bedrooms, fully fitted kitchens

and sitting rooms with real fires and sofa beds. It is very near a safe sandy beach, historic walled garden and arboretum. It makes an ideal base for exploring an area rich in history and natural beauty.

founder of a great monastic school in Northern Ireland where St. Columba once studied.

WHITHORN

27 miles SE of Stranraer on the A746

This small royal burgh, which is really no more than a village, is one of the most important places in Scottish history. It has often been called "The Cradle of Scottish Christianity", as, long before St. Columba came to Iona, **St. Ninian** had set up a great monastery here. It would have been a complex of chapels, monks' cells and workshops, surrounded by a rath, or low wall. However, it had one unusual building - the main chapel was built of stone, rather than the more usual wood, and it was painted white. For this reason it became known as the **Candida Casa**, or "White House". When this part of Scotland was absorbed into the Anglian kingdom of Northumbria for a short while, the name was translated into Anglo-Saxon as "Hwit Aerne", which in turn became Whithorn.

Whithorn was always an important ecclesiastical centre, as archeological digs in the 1980s and 90s confirmed. In the 12th century Fergus, Lord of Galloway, founded a **Whithorn Priory** (Historic Scotland) here, and it subsequently

Whithorn Priory

became the cathedral for the diocese of Galloway. One unusual aspect of the diocese was that for many years it came under the archdiocese of York, even though it was in Scotland.

All that is left of the great priory church and cathedral is its nave and crypt. To the west of the crypt are the scant remains of foundations, thought to be those of the original Candida Casa. The priory contained the shrine of St. Ninian, and in medieval times became a place of pilgrimage. Many Scottish monarchs, including James IV (who was a frequent visitor) and Mary Stuart visited. Close to the priory is the **Priory Museum** (Historic Scotland), with a collection of stones with Christian

---

PRIORY ANTIQUES

29 George Street, Whithorn, Wigtownshire DG8 8NS
Tel: 01988 500517

Priory Antiques is located in a quaint old courtyard behind a well-proportioned Georgian house on Whithorn's main street. Owned and run by Mary Arnott for over 15 years, it specialises in fine quality antiques such as furniture, silver, paintings, ceramics and jewellery, all at surprisingly affordable prices. Whithorn  is where Christianity first came to Scotland, and any visit to the town should also include a visit to this fascinating shop, where you are free to browse and admire the range of fine antiques on show. You're are sure to find something to suit your taste and pocket.

Isle of Whithorn

from the main street towards the abbey precincts. Also on the main street is the **Whithorn Visitors Centre**. Archaeological excavations took place close to the priory, showing that even in the Dark Ages the town was a thriving centre of trade as well as an ecclesiastical town. The centre explains the artifacts and discoveries made, and shows what the place looked like all those years ago.

symbols carved on them. The most famous is the **Latinus Stone**, dating from the 5th century, and it may be the earliest known carved stone in Scotland.

The town's main street is wide and spacious, with many small Georgian, Regency and Victorian buildings. **The Pend** dates from about 1500, and leads

ISLE OF WHITHORN

30 miles SE of Stranraer on the B7004

This is a small fishing village which, rather confusingly, isn't an island. It is very attractive, and on a headland near the shoreline are the ruins of the tiny **St. Ninian's Chapel**. At one time people thought that this was the site of Candida Casa, but it was probably built for

LOGAN FISH POND

Port Logan, Stranraer
Tel/Fax: 01776 860300
e-mail: ian.whitehead6@btinternet.com
website: www.loganfishpond.co.uk

The first time visitor to **Logan Fish Pond** is often amazed and surprised by what they see. Not until they enter through the original Fish Keepers Cottage and have their first glimpse of the pond below do they have any idea of what this unique and historic attraction holds.

In 1788 Andrew McDouall Laird of Logan decided to create a Fish Larder for storing live sea fish by adapting a natural rock formation in the form of a blow hole, formed during the last ice-age. The work took 12 years and was finished in 1800. Many visitors return year after year and indeed some have

been doing so for 50 or 60 years, feeding the fish today as they remember doing so as children. In the springtime, the area around the Pond is a carpet of daffodils, primroses and bluebells and later in the year these are replaced with an abundance of wild flowers, including thrift and sea campion.

On the rocks next to the Fish Pond is a restored Victorian Bathing Hut which adjoins a Bathing Pool. Recent additions to the original pond include Touch Pools, Cave Aquarium and Gift Shop. Open 1st March to 30th September 12 noon to 5pm and 1st October to 31st October 12 noon to 4pm. Some disabled access.

pilgrims coming to St. Ninian's Shrine by sea. At nearby Glasserton, on the shore, is **St. Ninain's Cave**, where the saint is supposed to have spent may lonely hours praying and fasting. Whether he actually did or not has never been established, but it does have ancient crosses carved on its walls.

KIRKMADRINE

8 miles S of Stranraer on a minor road off the A716

In the porch of what was the tiny medieval parish church of Toskerton are some old carved stones called the **Kirkmadrine Stones**, thought to be the oldest such stones in Scotland after Whithorn. They were discovered when the ruins of the church were being refurbished and converted into a burial place by a local family.

ARDWELL

10 miles S of Stranraer on the A716

Ardwell Gardens surround the 18th century Ardwell House on the Rhinns of Galloway. They feature both a woodland and formal garden, as well as good views out over Luce Bay.

PORT LOGAN

12 miles S of Stranraer on the B7065

Port Logan is a small fishing village situated on Port Logan Bay. Close by is the **Port Logan Fish Pond** (see panel opposite), a remarkable tidal pool carved out of solid rock and famous for its tame sea fish, which can be fed by hand. It was constructed in about 1800 as a source of fresh fish for the larders of nearby Logan House.

If anywhere testifies to the mildness of the climate in these parts, it is the **Logan Botanical Garden**, an outpost of the

National Botanic Gardens of Scotland. Exotic plants from all over the world, such as the tree fern (which can normally only survive in glass houses in Britain), grow quite freely out of doors here. There are also magnolias, eucalyptus, palm trees and passion flowers. Over 40 per cent of all the plants in the garden come from the Southern Hemisphere.

This whole area has now found fame for a different reason. It is here that the popular TV series 2000 Acres of Sky is filmed, though the action is supposed to be taking place on a Hebridean island.

KIRKMAIDEN

15 miles S of Stranraer on the B7065

Kirkmaiden is Scotland's most southerly parish. Four miles south of the village is the **Mull of Galloway**, Scotland's most southerly point. People are sometimes surprised to find that is further south than Durham or Hartlepool. The lighthouse was built in 1828 to the designs of Robert Stevenson, father of R.L. Stevenson, and sits on massive cliffs 270 feet above sea level.

PORTPATRICK

6 miles SW of Stranraer on the A77

This lovely little seaside village is the

Portpatrick

KNOCKINAAM LODGE

Portpatrick, Wigtownshire DG9 9AD
Tel: 01776 810471 Fax: 01776 810435

Knockinaam Lodge is a secret haven of peace and tranquillity, concealed from the world by thickly wooded hills. Here, where the lawns are spacious and well tended, a guest can relax knowing that the worries of the world are miles away. And here as well, you will be amazed to discover that records show there can be 130 days of sunshine each year! The rooms at this select and exclusive country house hotel are comfortable and elegant, with crisp, white sheets, a wealth of lilies in vases, and stunning views of the sea from the windows. All, of course, are en suite, with fluffy, luxurious towels, brass taps and scented toiletries as standard. Imagine wakening up in the morning with the sun streaming in through the windows and the smell of the sea in your nostrils before hot coffee and Scottish pastries assault your senses!

Food is taken very seriously in Knockinaam and the cuisine is imaginative and contemporary, with extensive use of fresh local ingredients. Dinner here is an adventure, a journey of anticipation, and the wine list must be lingered over, covering 200 French wines and a further 200 Italian, Australian

and Californian wines. The hotel bar is cosy and welcoming, and after dinner you can relax here with a fine brandy or, as you are in Scotland, dram of rare old Scottish malt whisky. There are over 100 to choose from, each one to be savoured and idled over as the logs on the open fire crackle, sending shadows over the warm wood panelling. This is an old shooting lodge built in 1869, and John Buchan describes it in his book *The Thirty Nine Steps*. It was here too, in Knockinaam, that Churchill and Eisenhower met in secret to plan the D Day landings.

DUNSKEY COUNTRY HOLIDAY COTTAGES

Dunskey House, Portpatrick, Stranraer,
Wigtownshire DG9 8TJ
Tel: 01776 810211 Fax: 01776 810581
e-mail: info@dunskey.com website: www.dunskey.com

Portpartick is one of the most picturesque seaside villages in Scotland, and a mile and a half from it is the Dunskey Estate, where you will find three delightful **Country Holiday Cottages**. This superior self catering accommodation consists of traditional, stone built cottages, all within half a mile of each other, and all offering the peace and tranquillity of glorious countryside while still being within easy reach of good pubs, restaurants and other amenities. The whole area is rich in history and heritage, and there are opportunities for fishing, golf, birdwatching, walking and viewing wonderful gardens benefiting from the gulf stream.

DUNSKEY GARDENS, LICENSED TEAROOM WITH TERRACE.

The Walled Garden is one of Dumfries and Galloway's hidden gardens. Many people visiting get no further than the Seasons Tearoom, the delicious smells of home cooking are just too irresistible. This

is a pity because at Dunskey Gardens enthusiasts will find plants that are considered to be familiar old friends, as well as many rare and unusual specimens. The McKenzie and Moncur Greenhouses although unheated contain many tender plants. The woodland gardens provide a change of scenery and a chance to see the local flora and fauna, especially in the spring months, when the woods are carpeted with first snowdrops then bluebells. Loch Fishing. Fly only from boat and bank.

western "terminus" for the Southern Upland Way, a footpath which snakes across Southern Scotland to the North Sea. At one time the village was Scotland's main port for Ireland, but was in such an exposed position (even though its harbour is sheltered) that Stranraer gradually took over.

It sits round a little harbour, and has become a holiday resort, giving rise to many craft shops and galleries. The ruins of the former **Parish Church**, dating from the 17th century, sit just off the main street, and have a curious round tower instead of the more common square one. To the south are the ruins of **Dunskey Castle**, built in the early 16th century by the Adair family. Also to the south of the village is **Knockinaam Lodge** (not open to the public - see panel opposite), where Churchill and Eisenhower met over several months to plan the D-Day Landings of World War II.

LOCATOR MAP

ADVERTISERS AND PLACES OF INTEREST

3 AYRSHIRE AND ARRAN

Before 1975, when local government was reorganised in Scotland, Ayrshire was Scotland's largest Lowland county. It stretches along the Firth of Clyde for over 65 miles, with a rich, broad agricultural area to the west that merges into a more rugged area of moorland and low hills the further inland you go. This is Burns country, and when the poet Keats made his pilgrimage to Burns's birthplace, he compared the county to Devon.

It was anciently divided into three parts, Cunningham, Kyle and Carrick. Cunningham is the most northerly, and is the most industrialised area, though it managed this without losing too much of its rural aspect. Kyle is the central portion, between the Rivers Irvine and Doon. It is perhaps the richest area in terms of agriculture, with many dairy farms, and the distinctive Ayrshire cattle can be seen dotting the fields. It is divided yet again by the River Ayr into two further areas: Kyle Regal and Kyle Stewart, reflecting the fact that the king owned one area, while the stewards of the royal household (who later went on to become the Stewart monarchs) owned the other. Carrick is the southern part, and is the least "developed" of the areas, though even here there used to be small coal mines in the valley of the Water of Girvan. There are areas of rich farmland here, though there are areas

Culzean Castle

of high moorland as well, cut into by fertile glens, where small, hidden villages seem to hide until you come upon the suddenly as you drive along.

Ayrshire and Rabbie (never, ever, "Robbie"!) Burns are inextricably linked. He was born in Alloway, now a prosperous suburb of the holiday resort of Ayr, and spent most of his life in the county before moving south to Dumfriesshire when he was 29 years old. His life is well documented, and all over the county you will see places where he stayed, visited, drank or courted. Most are well signposted, and you could easily spend a week motoring through quiet country lanes to visit them all. Ayr - Alloway - Irvine - Kilmarnock - Mauchline - Kirkoswald - they all have Burns associations.

Ailsa Craig

The three main towns in the county are Ayr, Irvine and Kilmarnock. Irvine is the largest, though it wasn't always so. In the 1960s it was designated a new town, and took an overspill population from Glasgow. New housing was built, the town centre was redeveloped and industrial estates opened. Though it lost some of its character, the central core is still worth exploring. Kilmarnock, traditionally the county's industrial hub, is next in size. In the early 1970s its town centre underwent a disastrous re-development, and many of its Edwardian, Victorian and earlier buildings were swept away to be replaced by what must be one of the dreariest and least-needed shopping malls in Scotland. However, a few yards away from all of this, the historical area round the Laigh Kirk was untouched, and it has been sympathetically restored. Ayr is the former county town of Ayrshire, and before local government was the commercial and administrative centre of the area. It is still prosperous, and has possibly the best shopping in the county.

Before Glaswegians were lured away to the beaches of Spain and the sunshine of Florida, the Ayrshire coast was their main holiday destination, and for a short while it earned the nickname the "Costa Clyde". The main resorts included Largs, Saltcoats, Troon, Prestwick, Ayr and Girvan. These halcyon days have gone, and now the whole coastline has earned a different nickname - the "Costa Geriatrica", because of the number of people who retire there.

As well as Burns, you can't get far away from golf in Ayrshire. Both Troon and Turnberry regularly host the British Open, and the very first Open Championship was held at Prestwick in 1860. These are all links courses, close to the coastline. And the coast once "hosted" another activity - smuggling. It is said that even the caves beneath Culzean Castle were once storage places for brandy, tobacco and fine silks that were smuggled in from the Isle of Man and Ireland.

The whole area seems to be awash with castles, from spectacular Culzean Castle , perched on a cliff above the Firth of Clyde, to Kelburn Castle near Largs, the substantial ruins of Loudoun Castle in the Irvine Valley and Dean Castle in Kilmarnock, with its fine collection of armour and rare musical instruments.

The Ayrshire coalfields used to employ thousands of miners, but now not one coal mine remains open, and most vestiges of the industry have gone. It didn't scar the landscape to the same extent as the South Yorkshire or South Wales coalfields did, and in some of the areas where coal mining was once king, you would never know that the industry existed at all.

Twenty miles offshore is the island of Arran. At one time it formed part of the county of Bute, but now comes under Ayrshire. It has been called "Scotland in Miniature", and is a wonderful blend of wild scenery, pastoral views, mountains and rocky coastlines. Its

Sunset over Arran

history stretches right back into the mists of time, as witnessed by its mysterious burial cairns, standing stones and stone circles. As recently as the 18th century Gaelic was spoken by its inhabitants. There are two other, smaller islands within the area - Great and Little Cumbrae, off the coast near Largs. Little Cumbrae only has one or two houses and no ferry, but Great Cumbrae has the small town of Millport - a holiday resort - on its southern shore. The town should really be a city, as the Cathedral of the Isles is located here. It dates from Victorian times, and though some people mistakenly call it the smallest cathedral in Europe (this honour in fact goes to a tiny cathedral in Greece) it is still the smallest in Britain. It is one of the true hidden gems of Scotland, and is well worth seeking out.

MAYBOLE

This quiet town is traditionally the capital of Carrick. It sits on a hillside about four miles from the sea, and it was here, in 1756, that Burns's parents William Burnes (he later dropped the "e") and Agnes Broun met. William actually came from the North East of Scotland, and had moved some time earlier to the South West. Agnes, however, was a native of Ayrshire, and had lived in Maybole since the age of 13.

In 1562, one of the most famous incidents of the Scottish Reformation took place in Maybole. The actual date of the Reformation is given as 1560, though for a good many years after this there were still important vestiges of Roman Catholicism remaining. The monks and canons of the various abbeys, for instance, if they hadn't converted to Protestantism, were left alone in their buildings, though they were not allowed to take in novices. Quintin Kennedy (son of the 2nd Earl of Cassillis), was still Abbot of Crossraguel Abbey in 1562, two years after the Reformation was officially espoused by Parliament. And the Collegiate Church in Maybole was still offering up Mass to congregations of up to 200 people in 1563, when it was

finally declared illegal. In view of this, both Kennedy and John Knox agreed to meet in Maybole and openly debate the significance and doctrine of the Mass.

The meeting duly took place in the small room of a house in Back Vennel where the provost of Maybole Collegiate church lived. Forty people from either side were allowed into the room to hear the debate, which lasted three days. The house was still standing in the early 20th century, and people who saw the room were amazed that it could accommodate 80 people, so small was it. The people of the town crowded round the house, trying to hear what was going on, or having the information relayed to them. The arguments went one way, and then the other, with neither Knox or Kennedy giving an inch. Finally, when the town ran out of food to feed the 80 people, it came to an end with no firm conclusion.

Though the Provost's House has gone, the ruins of **Maybole Collegiate Church** can still be viewed from the outside. It was founded in 1371 by Sir John Kennedy of Dunure "for the purpose of celebrating daily Divine Service for the happy state of himself, his wife Mary and their seven children", and dedicated to the Virgin Mary.

There are two "castles" in Maybole. One, now part of the former **Town Hall**,

was the 17th century town house of the lairds of Blairquhan Castle about five miles west of the town. The other one, now called simply **Maybole Castle**, was the town house of the Earls of Cassillis, head of the powerful Kennedy family. There is a curious legend attached to this building. The 6th Earl, John Kennedy, had married Lady Jean Hamilton, daughter of the Earl of Haddington. However, it was a marriage of convenience, as she was already in love with Sir John Faa of Dunbar, nicknamed the "King of the Gypsies". Therefore she went unwillingly to Ayrshire, where she never forgot her true love. One day, while the Earl was in London, Sir John Faa arrived in Maybole and carried away his true love.

However, the Earl returned unexpectedly, and set off in pursuit. He caught Sir John Faa, and in front of his wife, had him and his men hanged within the grounds of Cassillis Castle. The Countess was then incarcerated in Maybole Castle, where she spent the rest of her life in one small room making tapestries. A window high in the castle is supposed to belong to the room, and above it are some curious carvings of heads, supposed to be those of Sir John and his men. The 6th earl lived from about 1595 to 1668, so the events must have taken place in the 17th century.

However, it is completely untrue. The basic tale is told in many guises throughout Europe, and certainly no gypsy would have been a "sir". And letters written by both the Earl and the Countess shows that they were actually a close and loving couple.

AROUND MAYBOLE

Electric Brae

3 miles NW of Maybole, signposted on the A719

Stop your car in a convenient layby at the side of the road here, put it out of gear and let off the handbrake, and the car will slowly roll uphill. Better still, lay a football on the surface of the layby and watch it do the same (though footballs have a nasty habit of rolling into the ditch at the side of the road). The phenomenon has nothing to do with electricity. It's an optical illusion - one of the best there is. The surrounding landscape makes you think that the road runs uphill when in fact it goes downhill. If seen from a distance (and one of the best viewpoints is about half a mile south of the spot) the illusion still holds good.

Kirkmichael

3 miles E of Maybole on the B7045

Like its near neighbour Crosshill, Kirkmichael is a former weaving village. However, unlike Crosshill, its roots go deep into Scottish history. The **Parish Church** dates form 1790, and the

Kirkmichael Village

picturesque lychgate from about 1700. Within the old kirkyard is the grave of a Covenantor called Gilbert MacAdam, killed in 1686.

Every May the **Kirkmichael International Guitar Festival** takes place. It was founded by Martin Taylor, the world famous jazz guitarist who lives locally, and people come from all over the world to participate. It covers everything from jazz and pop to country and classical. Huge marquees are set up, and local pubs usually have impromptu jamming sessions and folk concerts.

CROSSHILL
3 miles SE of Maybole on the B7023

This former weaving village was founded in about 1808, and has many small, single-storey cottages where the weavers once lived and worked. Most were Irish, attracted to the place by the prospect of work. There are no outstanding buildings, nor does it have much history attached to it, but it is a picturesque conservation village, and it's well worth a visit for this alone.

STRAITON
6 miles SE of Maybole on the B741

This is one of the most attractive villages in Ayrshire, and sits on the Water of Girvan. It is a planned village, with rose-covered cottages on either side of a broad main street. The local pub, the **Black Bull**, dates from 1766, and some parts of **St. Cuthbert's Parish Church** date from 1510. To the north west of the village is **Blairquhan**, a Tudor-Gothic mansion that sits on the site of an earlier tower house once owned by the Kennedy family. It is now the home of the Hunter Blairs, and on a hill above the village stands the **Hunter Blair Monument**, built in 1856 to commemorate James Hunter Blair, killed at the battle of

Inkerman. The house is sometimes open to the public in the summer months.

A narrow road heads south from here called the **Nick o' Balloch**, and goes over high, wild hills and moorland until it drops down into Glentrool. It makes a wonderful drive, as the scenery, though lonely and windswept in places, is hauntingly beautiful.

DALMELLINGTON
11 miles E of Maybole on the A713

This large, isolated village on the banks of the River Doon was once a centre for coal mining and ironmaking. Over the last few years, it has exploited its rich industrial past, and created visitor centres and museums that explain this heritage. The **Dunaskin Open Air Museum** (see panel opposite) covers 110 acres, and has many facets, each one well worth exploring. The **Iron Works**, which first opened in the 1840s to take advantage of the rich seams of coal hereabouts, are the largest restored 19th century ironworks in Europe. There are also the **Brickworks** and the **Scottish Industrial Railway Centre**, where steam trains occasionally run on a restored track. Within the village you will find the **Cathcartson Centre**, housed in 18th century weaving cottages, which show how weavers lived long ago.

LOCH DOON
11 miles E of Maybole on a minor road off the A713

This lovely loch, deep among the hills, is the source of the River Doon, made famous by Robert Burns. When a hydroelectric scheme raised the level of the water in the loch in the 1930s, the ruins of **Loch Doon Castle**, which stood on an island, were dismantled stone by stone and rebuilt on the shoreline. At the beginning of the 13th century, it withstood a siege by the invading

THE DUNASKIN HERITAGE CENTRE

Dalmellington Road, Waterside, Patna, Ayrshire
Tel: 01292 531144
e-mail: Dunaskin@btconnect.com website: www.dunaskin.org.uk

The Dalmellington Iron Company was founded in 1848, at the height of the Industrial Revolution. At its zenith, the company's eight furnaces worked day and night, providing employment for around 1,400 people, until the last furnace was blown out in 1921. The company produced coal and, later, bricks, up until 1976, when the kilns were finally extinguished. Today, the site has been preserved as Europe's best remaining example of a Victorian Ironworks, with over half its 110 acres listed as a Scheduled Ancient Monument.

Dunaskin is a visitor attraction for all the family. The Dunaskin Experience lets you explore the past as it was actually lived by Ayrshire people. An open air, living museum set amidst beautiful rolling countryside, it follows the story of the people and places of the Doon Valley through the Industrial Revolution, two World Wars and right up to modern times. There's the Mary Gallagher Experience: an audio visual which recreates Ayrshire life in the 19th and early 20th centuries. For younger children there's the new Furnace Play Tower. Teenagers can interact with Billy the Brick Computer Quiz.

Everyone will enjoy the delightful walks, including Dunaskin Glen which is a designated Site of Special Scientific Interest. There's a period cottage and industrial machinery. You can even feel what it was like to work in a coal mine. Finally you can break your visit and meet the welcoming staff at Chimneys Restaurant and Coffee Shop and browse in the Gift Shop.

English army for three years before surrendering. Its keeper, Sir Christopher Seton, (Robert I's brother-in-law) was later executed at Dumfries.

During World War I, there were plans to set up a **School of Aerial Gunnery** at the loch. The plan was to have the aircraft take off from the waters of the loch and fire at specially built moving targets on the steep hills going down to the loch's shores. After spending many millions of pounds, the idea was abandoned when it was discovered that the ground surrounding the loch was too soggy to allow building, and that the loch invariably froze over in winter.

In the late 1970s a scheme was announced to bore 32 tunnels in the surrounding hills to store Britain's radioactive waste, but after many protests by local people, the idea was abandoned.

OLD DAILLY

9 miles S of Maybole on the B734

The ruins of **Old Dailly Parish Church**, dating from the 16th century, stand by the side of the road. Within the kirkyard are two hefty stones called the **Charter Stones**, which people tried to lift as a trial of strength in olden days. Within the kirkyard lies **William Bell Scott**, the pre-Raphaelite artist and poet. He died at nearby **Penkill Castle** (not open to the public) in 1890. Many of the pre-Raphaelite Brotherhood stayed at the place, including **Dante Gabriel Rosetti**. The castle was built in about 1490 by Adam Boyd, grandson of Lord Boyd of Kilmarnock, and is a picture-postcard building with a tower and turrets.

Close by is **Bargany House**, a former Kennedy stronghold, with its marvellous gardens.

New Dailly

5 miles S of Maybole on the B741

This is a former mining village, successor to Old Dailly three miles away after that settlement was abandoned. The **Parish Church** is T-shaped, and was built in 1766.

Barr

11 miles S of Maybole on the B734

Barr is one of the most beautiful villages in Ayrshire, and lies tucked in a fold of the Carrick Hills. It was once the site of the wonderfully named **Kirkdandie Fair**, one of the largest such fairs in Southern Scotland in the 18th and 19th centuries. It was held on a strip of land south west of the village, in the valley of the River Stinchar, and close to the old Kirkdandie Church, of which not a stone now remains. Here farmers would hire labour for the following six months or a year. It was also a day of entertainment for those attending, with ale tents, peddlers, fisticuff contests, fire and brimstone preachers, jugglers and musicians all in attendance. It's main claim to fame, however, was not its size (and it was an enormous fair) but the fighting that took place there. It became known as the "Donnybrook of Scotland", and gangs of youths from as far away as Ireland and Northern England came to take part in the pitched battles.

On the hills above Barr is the estate of Changue (pronounced "Shang"), to which an old legend is attached. It seems that the **Laird of Changue** was a spendthrift who was always in debt, even though he indulged in a little smuggling on the side. One evening, when returning home from a smuggling assignation, he was confronted by Satan, who promised him riches if he would sell his soul. The laird agreed, and he became rich beyond his dreams. However, as he

Barr Village

grew older, he began to regret the bargain. Eventually the Devil appeared to him once more, this time demanding his soul. The Laird drew a large circle round himself on the ground, and invited the Devil to enter it. If Satan could force the Laird out of the circle, he could have his soul. If the Laird forced the Devil out of the circle, the laird could keep it. Battle ensued, and the Laird won. Up until the 19th century a great bare circle on some grassland was pointed out as the place where the battle took place.

Dunure

5 miles NW of Maybole off the A719

Dunure is a small, attractive fishing village that would not look out of place in Cornwall. If arriving by car, you get a good view of the small cottages and pubs surrounding the harbour. The gaunt ruins of **Dunure Castle** (not open to the public) are on the southern outskirts of the village, and present a daunting prospect, especially as they are unsafe and crumbling into the sea. It was within the walls of the castle (an old Kennedy stronghold) that a famous incident called the **Roasting of the Abbot** took place in 1570. The Kennedys were at the height of their powers - kings in all but name of southern Ayrshire and Galloway. Gilbert, the 4th Earl, owned vast tracks of land, but was greedy for more, and turned his attention to the rich lands of Crossraguel Abbey nearby. Since the Reformation in 1560, they had been looked after by Allan Stewart, Commendator (lay abbot) of the abbey. Gilbert invited Allan to a huge feast at his castle of Dunure, and Allan, suspecting nothing, accepted. Instead of dining, he was stripped and placed in the Black Vault. He was asked to sign over the abbey lands, but refused. A great fire was lit, and he was placed over it on a spit until he eventually agreed.

The Old Parish Church of St. Oswald

However, when he was released he protested to the king, who ordered Kennedy to pay the going rate for the lands. But so powerful was Kennedy that he ignored the command, and he got away with both his crimes and the land.

KIRKOSWALD

4 miles SW of Maybole on the A77

It was to Kirkoswald, in 1775, that Burns came for a short while to learn surveying. Though his poem Tam O' Shanter is set in Alloway, all the characters in it come from the parish of Kirkoswald, which was where his maternal grandparents came from. **Kirkoswald Parish Church**, above the village, dates from 1777, and was designed by Robert Adam at the same time as he was working on Culzean Castle, which sits two miles to the north west.

Dwight D. Eisenhower, the President of the United States, worshipped here twice in the 1950s, once when he was actually in office. This was because he had holiday accommodation at Culzean Castle. Another visitor to the church was Randolph Fields, who, with his business partner Richard Branson, founded Virgin Airlines. Fields loved this part of Scotland, and holidayed here regularly. He died in 1997, leaving some money in his will for the restoration of the church. Later, his widow presented the church with a small table and plaque.

The ruins of the **Old Parish Church of St. Oswald** sit in the heart of the village. Within its kirkyard are the graves of many people associated with Robert Burns, including David Graham of Shanter Farm, the original of Tam O' Shanter. The ruins contain an interesting relic, known as **Robert the Bruce's Baptismal Font**. Both Lochmaben and Turnberry claim to be the birthplace of Robert I, though Turnberry seems the more likely. This because it was the ancestral home of the Countess of Carrick, who was Robert's mother, and who was known to be living there around the time her son was born. The story goes that the baby was premature, and that he was rushed to Crossraguel

CULZEAN CASTLE AND COUNTRY PARK

Maybole, South Ayrshire, KA19 8LE
Functions, events and Eisenhower Apartment:
Tel: 01655 884455 Fax 01655 884503
Group/school bookings, ranger service, Country Park
information:
Tel: 01655 884400 Fax 01655 884522.
e-mail: culzean@nts.org.uk
website: www.culzeancastle.net

Robert Adam converted a rather ordinary fortified tower house into this elegant bachelor residence for David Kennedy, 10th Earl of Cassillis, between 1777 and 1792. He also built a "Roman" viaduct and Ruined Arch to add drama to this Italianate castle in its spectacular cliff top setting. Both the exterior stonework and the interior of the castle have been restored by the National Trust for Scotland. It contains a fine collection of paintings and furniture, and a display of weapons in the Armoury. The Circular Saloon has a superb panoramic view over the Firth of Clyde and the beautiful Oval Staircase is Robert Adam's final masterpiece of interior design.

In 1945 the top floor was given to General Eisenhower as a token of Scotland's recognition of his role during World War II. His apartment is now run as a small country house hotel, and an Eisenhower Exhibition in the castle tells something of Ike the man and his visits to Culzean. The Georgian Kitchen gives a glimpse of life below stairs 200 years ago. Educational programmes and tours are available. Through the Clocktower Courtyard, a coach house and stables have been converted into the Castle Shop and Old Stables Coffee House.

The Country Park - Scotland's first country park, created in 1969 and consisting of 228 hectares (563 acres) contains a wealth of natural and historical interest. Miles of woodland walks take the visitor to the Deer Park, along the Cliff Walk or to the many restored estate buildings, such as the Ruined Arch and Viaduct, beautiful Camellia House and unique Pagoda. Garden areas include the terraced Fountain Court and the Walled Garden with its redesigned pleasure garden and impressive reconstructed Victorian Vinery. The exciting adventure playground introduces children to the wildlife of the park and the Swan Pond is a perfect spot for a family picnic.

The Visitor Centre, formerly the Home Farm, is the focus for the main visitor facilities. These include the Home Farm Restaurant, the Home Farm Shop, the Country Park Shop and Plant Centre. The new auditorium and exhibition at the Visitor Centre explain the history of Culzean and the

Trust's conservation work, and there are smaller interpretive centres at the Gas House, Ice House and Swan Pond. Three miles of coastline provide panoramic views across the Firth of Clyde and improved facilities have been provided at Croy Shore - 1½ miles of beach - accessed from the A719. The ranger service provides an extensive environmental education service and interpretive programme.

Culzean Castle

Abbey for baptism in case he died. The abbey's font was used, and when Crossraguel was abandoned at the Reformation, the font found its way to Kirkoswald.

Soutar Johnnie's Cottage (National Trust for Scotland) sits on the main street, and is a low, thatched cottage where John Davidson, a "soutar", or cobbler, lived. He featured in *Tam O' Shanter*.

In the vicinity of the village a great battle was once fought. St Oswald was a Northumbrian prince who fled to Iona on the death of his father in the 7th century. When he attained manhood, he decided to return to Northumbria and reclaim his throne. On his way south, he met his enemies at Kirkoswald and defeated them. It is said that over 1,000 soldiers were killed. Oswald built a church on the site in thanksgiving for the victory.

CULZEAN CASTLE
4 miles W of Maybole off the A719

Culzean Castle (National Trust for Scotland - see panel opposite) is the Trust's most visited property, and for good reason. It is perched spectacularly on high cliffs above the Firth of Clyde, and was designed by Robert Adam in 1777. It is universally acclaimed as his finest work, and was built round an old Kennedy tower house for the 10th Earl of Cassillis, head of the Kennedy family. It has some wonderful features, including the Oval Staircase and the Circular Salon, which has views over the Firth of Clyde. Surrounding the castle is Culzean Castle Country Park, with formal gardens, woodland walks, a swan pond, a deer park and a wonderful fountain court. An apartment in the castle was given to Dwight D. Eisenhower, President of the United States, in gratitude for his efforts during World War II. Eisenhower subsequently spent a few golfing holidays there. Now the **Eisenhower Presentation**, within the castle, explains his connections with the area, and has exhibits about D-Day.

On the shoreline are the **Gasworks**, which at one time produced gas to light and heat the castle, and the former **Home Farm** has been turned into a visitor centre, shop, interpretation centre and restaurant. Like the Solway coast, this area has a mild climate, and palm trees flourish in the castle grounds.

WALK 2

Culzean Castle and Country Park

Start	Culzean Country Park Visitor Centre
Distance	3½ miles (5.6km)
Approximate time	2 hours
Parking	Car park next to the visitor centre
Refreshments	Café at the visitor centre, kiosks throughout the park
Ordnance Survey maps	Landranger 70 (Ayr and Kilmarnock), Pathfinders 479, NS21/31 (Dunure & Dalrymple) and 491, NS 20/30 (Maybole[South] & Dailly)

Although only a short walk, there is so much to see in the grounds of Culzean Castle, now a country park maintained by the National Trust for Scotland, that you could well devote most of the day to it. As well as the castle itself, there are many ancillary buildings plus such attractions as a Deer Park, Walled Garden and Swan Pond, all set amidst beautiful woodlands. Many would agree that the highlight of the route is the walk along the cliff path near the end. This winds through trees on the top of the cliffs, providing a series of magnificent views of the castle, along the wild and rugged Ayrshire coastline and across the Firth of Clyde to the mountains of Arran.

The walk begins in the circular courtyard of the visitor centre, imaginatively created from what was the Home Farm of the estate. Facing the sea, go through an archway on the left and walk along a path to a tarmac drive. Cross it and continue along the path, signposted "Castle", which initially keeps parallel to the drive and emerges on to another drive by the Ruined Arch and Viaduct. This was designed by Robert Adam to form a romantic and imposing entrance to Culzean Castle. The castle is just to the right but is best left to near the end of the walk.

Walk along the drive – or along the parallel path to the right of it – to the Walled Garden. To the left is the Deer Park, originally much larger than at present, and a brief detour to the right brings you to the Camellia House, designed as an orangery in 1818. In front of the Walled Garden – well worth an exploration – take the tarmac drive which turns left Ⓐ and heads gently uphill through woodland, keeping on the main drive all the

while. On reaching a long, low white building, formerly a mill, the drive turns first left and then right around the end of the building. Keep ahead along a rough track gently downhill into woodland, bending right and continuing under a disused railway bridge.

Immediately turn right on to a path to join the tree-lined track of the disused railway Ⓑ , operational between 1906 and 1955, and keep along it as far as a bridge. To the right are grand views across the Firth of Clyde to Arran. Climb the steps to the right of the bridge, turn right Ⓒ along a track and head gently downhill, under an impressive beech-lined canopy, to pass through the Cat Gates, one of the entrances to the estate and guarded by stone cats.

Pass through the gates and at a fork about 50yds (46m) ahead, take the left-hand path to reach a crossroads. Turn left, beside a burn on the right, cross a drive and continue along the path to the Swan Pond, a most attractive and popular part of the park. Turn left alongside the pond, continue across grass to pick up a path again and at a sign to Port Carrick and Barwhin Hill turn left for a brief detour, descending steps to the fine beach at Port Carrick.

Return to the path beside the pond, turn left along it, cross a footbridge and continue along the uphill path ahead. Take the first path on the left **D** – this is the Cliff Walk – and follow a winding, undulating path through woodlands on top of the cliffs. This is a most memorable part of the walk, with magnificent views along the Ayrshire coast and across the sea to the mountains of Arran and the long line of the Kintyre peninsula beyond. At a T-junction, turn left to continue above the sea for some impressive views of Culzean Castle ahead. Take the left-hand path at a fork and continue across grass towards the castle. Turn right through a gate, go down steps and turn left to walk across the Fountain Court in front of the castle.

Splendidly situated on a precipitous cliff above the Firth of Clyde, Culzean Castle was originally a tower-house belonging to the Kennedys of Carrick, later the earls of Cassillis, of nearby Dunure. After Dunure Castle fell into ruin, it became their principal residence and, in keeping with its new status, it was completely reconstructed for the 10th earl by the renowned Scottish architect Robert Adam between 1777 and 1792. It is basically an elegant Georgian country house but Adam included some medieval-looking towers and turrets to give it a more castle-like appearance. In 1946 General Eisenhower was given a flat on the top floor in gratitude for his role in the Allied victory in World War II; this flat is now an Eisenhower museum.

At the far end of the Fountain Court, turn right across grass and pass under the arch of the viaduct seen earlier. Keep walking ahead to join a tarmac drive and follow it back to the visitor centre. ●

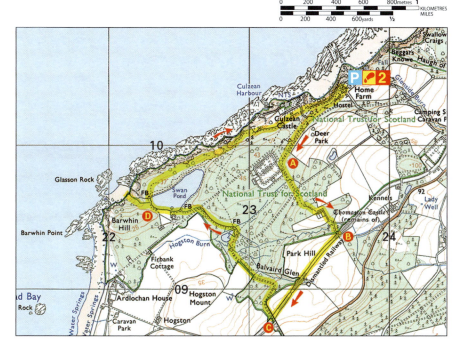

Ailsa Golf Course, Turnberry

TURNBERRY

7 miles SW of Maybole on the A719

Very little survives of **Turnberry Castle**, the supposed birthplace of Robert I, better known as Robert the Bruce. It sits close to the shore, on what is now Turnberry Golf Course (where the British Open Golf Championship is occasionally played), with a lighthouse occupying the site. The story of how Bruce's parents met is an unusual one. It seems that the Countess of Turnberry, a young widow, was staring out from a castle window when she saw a young knight and his entourage ride by. She immediately became infatuated by the handsome young man, and ordered her men to kidnap him and bring him to the castle.

This they did, and he turned out to be Robert de Brus, Lord of Annandale, who lived in Lochmaben Castle. She persuaded him to marry her, and the result of the marriage was Robert the Bruce, who became Earl of Carrick on his mother's death. To this day, the heir to the British throne carries the title.

The elegant **Turnberry Hotel** is one of the country's premier hotels. It even has its own small runway for light aircraft and helicopters. During World War II this whole area had been a huge allied airfield, and some of the runways still exist.

CROSSRAGUEL ABBEY

2 miles SW of Maybole, on the A77

Crossraguel Abbey (Historic Scotland) was founded in 1244 for the Clunaic order of monks by Duncan, Earl of Carrick. The romantic ruins sit beside the busy A77, and are extremely well preserved. You get a good idea of how a medieval monastery was laid out by exploring them, and some of the stone carving, especially that in the almost complete chapter house, is well worth seeking out. The ruins as you see them now date from the 13th century, though there were later additions as the abbey prospered. It became one of the most important ecclesiastical centres in South West Scotland, and even had its own mint.

To the north are the ruins of **Baltersan Castle**, an old fortified tower house built in 1584 by John Kennedy of Pennyglen

Crossraguel Abbey

and his wife Margaret Cathcart. Two hundred years ago it was described as a fine house with gardens, parks and orchards surrounding it. Now it is a roofless ruin.

GIRVAN

10 miles SW of Maybole on the A77

Ailsa Craig

This pleasant little town is the main holiday resort in Carrick. It is a thriving fishing port, and sits at the mouth of the Water of Girvan. Though there is a long sandy beach, a boating pond and a small amusement park, it is a quiet place, still popular with retired people. To the south is **Byne Hill**, and from the top there is a fine view of the Firth of Clyde. On a fine day Northern Ireland can clearly be seen.

Out in the Firth, the magnificent bulk of **Ailsa Craig** rises sheer from the water. It is the plug of an old volcano which is now a bird sanctuary, and boat trips leave from Girvan harbour to give you a closer look.

On Knockcushan Street in the town is a small, curious spired building with the nickname **Auld Stumpy**. It dates from the 18th century, and at one time was part of the McMaster Hall, which burnt down in 1939. Behind Knockcushan House, nearer the harbour, are **Knockcushan Gardens**, the site of a court held in 1328 by Robert I. **The McKechnie Institute** in Dalrymple Street sometimes hosts art and craft exhibitions.

COLMONELL

19 miles S of Maybole on the B734

The River Stinchar is the most southerly of Ayrshire's rivers, and flows through a lovely glen bordered on each side by high moorland and hills. Colmonell, a quiet village of small neat cottages, sits four miles from the mouth of the river. Close by are the romantic ruins of **Kirkhill Castle**, and two miles west sits **Knockdollan Hill**, at one time called the "false Ailsa Craig", because of its resemblance to the volcanic island in the Firth of Clyde.

BALLANTRAE

23 miles S of Maybole on the A77

When on a walking tour of Carrick in 1876, R.L. Stevenson spent a night in this small fishing village. However, the reception he got was hostile because of his avant garde clothes. He later got his revenge by writing a book called *The Master of Ballantrae* which has nothing to do with Ballantrae in Ayrshire, but which has caused confusion ever since.

In the churchyard, across the road from the undistinguished parish church, is the old kirkyard of the former church. Within it is the **Bargany Aisle**, containing the ornate tomb of Gilbert Kennedy, laird of of Bargany and Ardstinchar. There were two main branches of the great Kennedy family in

COSSES COUNTRY HOUSE

Nr. Ballantrae, Ayrshire KA26 0LR
Tel: 01465 831363; Fax: 01465 831598
e-mail: cosses@compuserve.com
website: www.cossescountryhouse.com

For a "little bit of heaven" there is no finer place
than **Cosses Country House**, set in 12 acres of
mature garden and woodland. It dates from 1606,
when it was a shooting lodge, and now offers three comfortable en suite bedrooms, superbly furnished
to make any stay a memorable one. The food here is magnificent, using fresh local produce, and
dinner is always an enjoyable experience, with drinks served beforehand in the sitting room. If you
want to be cosseted, then Cosses Country House is the place for you.

the 16th century, and they fought
constantly to decide who was the most
powerful. This fighting involved
everyone in the area, whether they were
Kennedys or not, and it was not a safe
time to be living in South Ayrshire. One
of the branches was the Kennedys of
Cassillis, whose chief was the Earl of
Cassillis, and the other was the Kennedys
of Bargany, with the Laird of Bargany
and Ardstinchar being the chief. No
quarter was given or taken during the
fighting, and the whole thing came to a
head in 1601, when the two branches
met in battle near Ayr. Bargany was
killed, and the power of the Bargany
Kennedys was broken forever. It is said
that the Laird's funeral was the largest
ever witnessed in the area, with
thousands of mourners following
the coffin.

The ruins of **Ardstinchar Castle**,
Bargany's main residence, can be seen
beside the river to the south of the village.

LENDALFOOT

18 miles S of Maybole on the A77

Near Lendalfoot are the ruins of
Carleton Castle, which have an
intriguing legend attached. It was home
to Sir John Carleton, who, the story
goes, earned his living in a particularly
gruesome fashion. He married ladies of
wealth and enticed them to a spot called
Gamesloup, where he pushed them to
their deaths and inherited their wealth.
Sir John went through seven or eight
such wives before meeting his match.
She was the daughter of Kennedy of
Culzean, a cadet branch of the powerful
Kennedys. After he married her, Sir John
duly took her to Gamesloup. However,

BALKISSOCK LODGE

Ballantrae, near Girvan, Ayrshire KA26 0LP
Tel: 01465 831537
website: www.balkissocklodge.co.uk

Situated in the beautiful hills behind Ballantrae,
Balkissock Lodge is a gracious Georgian house that has
been converted into an extremely comfortable guest house.
The three rooms - a double, a twin and a single - have
recently been refurbished to a high standard, and boast
colour TVs and hospitality trays. The hosts, Fran and
Dennis Sweeney, are both accomplished cooks, and use fresh local produce wherever possible in their
breakfasts and three course dinners. Vegetarian and other diets can be catered for by arrangement.

rumours were abounding by this time, and the lady was extremely wary. So much so that instead of her being thrown to her death, she threw Sir John over the cliff, and lived happily ever after on his inherited wealth.

However, the story is not as gruesome as that of another man who lived locally. His name was Sawney Bean, and he lived down on the shore at Bennane Head south of

Bridge over River Ayr

Lendalfoot in a cave that is now known as **Sawney Bean's Cave**. It is easily reached by a footpath from the layby on the road above, and it was here that Sawney and his large family lived. They were a family of cannibals who waylaid travellers in Carrick and carried their bodies back to the cave, where they pickled the flesh before eating it. They evaded capture for many years, and eventually James VI intervened. At the head of a troop of men, he captured the Beans in the cave and marched them off the Edinburgh, where they were executed. It's a wonderful story, though there is only one thing wrong with it - it isn't true. No record has ever been uncovered about their trial or execution during James VI's reign, or indeed the reign of any other king.

AYR

Ayr was at one time the main holiday resort on Scotland's west coast. It stands on the banks of the River Ayr, and is an important fishing and trading port. It is the former county town of Ayrshire, with the headquarters being the beautiful **County Buildings** in Wellington Square. It is an important royal burgh, and was

granted its royal charter in about 1203. The most distinctive building in the town is the **Town House** with its tall slender steeple, built to a design of Thomas Hamilton between 1827 and 1832. Seen from the north, across the River Ayr, it blends in beautifully with a range of Georgian buildings,

After the Battle of Bannockburn, Bruce held his first parliament in the town, in the ancient St John's Kirk. The kirk has gone now, pulled down by Cromwell's troops so that the stone could be used to build **Ayr Citadel**, which itself has largely gone apart from a few walls. But the kirk's tower, now called **St. John's Tower**, still stands among some Edwardian villas near the shore.

In place of the old kirk, Oliver Cromwell built the **Auld Parish Kirk**, which dates from the mid 1600s. It stands on the site of a medieval friary close to the river, and is a T-shaped building surrounded by old gravestones and tombs, some very ornate. Within the **Kirkyard Lychgate** can be seen a couple of mortsafes, which at one time were placed over fresh graves to prevent grave robbing.

Ayr was the staring off point for Tam O' Shanter's drunken and macabre ride homewards after a night drinking at an inn. He is supposed to have left from the thatched **Tam O'Shanter Inn** in the High Street. At one time it was a small museum, but now it has reverted to its original purpose, and you can enjoy a drink there once more.

Robert Burns and Ayr are inseparable. He was born in a village on the southern outskirts of the town, and knew the place well. Off the High Street is the **Auld Brig o' Ayr**, which dates from the 14th century, and a few yards down river is the **New Bridge** of 1878, successor to an older "New Bridge". In his poem *The Twa Brigs* Burns predicts that the old bridge will outlast the new one, and he was proved right when the predecessor of today's New Bridge was swept away in a flood, leaving the old one intact.

The oldest secular building in the town is **Loudoun Hall**, which dates from 1513. It sits close to the New Bridge and the Town Hall, and was built as a fine town house for the Campbells of Loudoun, hereditary Sheriffs of Ayr, who lived in Loudoun Castle further to the north. It was going to be demolished just after World War II, but was saved when its importance was realised. Another old building is **Lady Cathcart's House**, in the Sandgate. It is a tenement building dating from the 17th century, and it was here, in 1756, that John Louden McAdam, the road engineer after whom Tarmacadam is named, was born.

The New Bridge takes you north across the river to **Newton-upon-Ayr**, once a separate burgh with its own council and provost. It was certainly in existence in the 13th century, though it didn't receive its burgh charter until some time in the 14th. Part of its old tolbooth, or town house, survives as **Newton Tower**, now on a traffic island off the main street.

South of the town, perched on a cliff overlooking the Firth of Clyde, is

Greenan Castle, which dates from the 17th century. As a building it has no great claim to fame, though it always looks like it is in imminent danger of falling into the sea. However, some historians have suggested that this might be yet another possible site of King Arthur's **Camelot**.

AROUND AYR

MONKTON
4 miles N of Ayr on the A79

Traffic between Glasgow and Ayr used to thunder through Monkton, but now it is bypassed. It sits on the edge of Prestwick Airport, and at one time the main road even cut across the airport's main runway, meaning that traffic was held up as an aircraft came in or took off. The ruins of 13th century **St Cuthbert's Parish Church** sit in the heart of the village, and at one time the Rev'd Thomas Burns, Robert Burns' nephew, was minister here. William Wallace, it is said, once fell asleep in the church, and had a dream in which an old man presented him with a sword and a young woman presented him with a wand. He took it to mean that he must continue his struggle for Scotland's freedom.

To the north of the village is a curious monument known as **MacRae's Monument**, which sits on a slight rise. It commemorates a local man who was born into poverty but rose to become the Governor of Madras in India. The estate of Ladykirk is a few miles east of Monkton. It was here, in **Ladykirk Chapel**, which has all but vanished, that Robert II, the first Stewart king, married Elizabeth Muir of Rowallan.

TROON
5 miles N of Ayr on the A759

This quiet seaside resort is synonymous with golf, and the British Open has been

TIGH DEARG

31 Victoria Drive, Troon, Ayrshire KA10 6JF
Tel: 01292 311552
e-mail: alan_norma_31@hotmail.com

Set in Troon on the beautiful Ayrshire coast, **Tigh Dearg** is a friendly
and comfortable B&B with superior en suite rooms that offer all
that is best in Scottish hospitality. This detached red sandstone
house has luxurious fittings and a visitor's lounge that offers a
colour TV and luxury fittings. and fixtures. The rooms - a double, twin and single - have hospitality
trays in each one. The full Scottish breakfasts are filling and hearty, though lighter options are available
if required. Troon is a small, gracious town noted for its golf courses and ferry connections, and a stay
at the Tigh Dearg mustn't be missed if you're in the area.

played here several times. It is a young
town, laid out in the early 1800s by the
4th Duke of Portland, who wished to
create a harbour from which to export
the coal from his Ayrshire coal mines. It
formed the western terminus of
Scotland's earliest rail line, the **Troon
and Kilmarnock Railway**, opened in
1812. In 1816 the Duke introduced a
steam locomotive to it, which soon
started pulling passenger trains.

The town now forms one of the main
ferry ports linking Scotland and Ireland.
On the shore is the **Ballast Bank**, created
over the years as ships discharged their
ballast before taking on coal for Ireland.
Behind the town a narrow road runs up
from the hamlet of Loans onto the
Dumdonald Hills, from where there is
a marvellous view out over the Firth
of Clyde.

SYMINGTON
6 miles N of Ayr off the A77

Symington is a pleasant village of old
cottages somewhat spoiled by a large
estate of council houses on its northern
edge. However, the core of the village is
still picturesque, and has one gem -
Symington Parish Church, Ayrshire's
oldest church still in use. This Norman
building was erected in the 12th century,
and has on its east wall a trio of
delightful round-arched windows dating

from that time.

On a hillside to the west of the village,
across the busy A77 at Barnweil, is the
Wallace Monument. It marks the spot
where William Wallace stood and
watched the "barns o' Ayr burn weil"
after he set fire to them when they were
garrisoned by English troops. Close to it
are the scant remains of **Barnweil
Church**, where John Knox once
preached. And in a field nearby are the
outlines of a curious square-shaped fort
that dates from ancient times.

DUNDONALD
8 miles N of Ayr on the B730

The impressive ruins of **Dundonald
Castle** (Historic Scotland) sit on a hill
overlooking this pleasant village. The site
has been occupied for thousands of
years, and the present castle is the
second or third that has stood here. It
was built by Robert II, the first Stewart
king of Scotland, when he ascended the
throne in 1371, and was his favourite
residence. He also died here in 1390.
When Boswell and Dr. Johnson visited
the castle in 1773, Johnson was much
amused by the humble home of "Good
King Bob", not realising that the remains
he saw were a fraction of what was built
originally. Since then it has been owned
by the Wallaces and the Cochranes, who
became Earls of Dundonald.

The **Parish Church** dates from 1804, and is the third church to have stood on the site. To the north of the village is the hamlet of **Drybridge**, so-called because it grew up around a bridge built in the early 1800s over the Duke of Portland's railway line linking Troon and Kilmarnock. It was the first bridge in the county not to cross water, hence "dry bridge".

TARBOLTON

7 miles NE of Ayr on the B744

When Burns stayed at nearby **Lochlee Farm** (not open to the public) both he and his brother Gilbert looked to Tarbolton for their leisure activities, such as they were. They founded a debating society which met in a thatched house in the village, and this house is now the **Bachelor's Club** (National Trust for Scotland). It was here that Burns took dancing lessons, something of which his father disapproved. Round the fireplace in the upper room is a helical pattern drawn in chalk - an old Ayrshire custom which was supposed to have prevented the Devil (known as "Aul' Nick" in these parts) from entering the house via the chimney.

Tarbolton Parish Church is an impressive building dating from 1821 with an elegant spire. A mile west of the village is the tiny hamlet of **Fail** (not to be confused with Failford). At one time a Trinitarian monastery stood here, of which not a stone survives above ground.

MAUCHLINE

10 miles NE of Ayr on the A76

When Burns's father died at Lochlee near Tarbolton, the Burns family moved to **Mossgeil Farm** (not open to

the public) to the north of the village of Mauchline. The farm buildings that Burns knew are no more, but its successor still stands among fields that are considerably more fertile than they were in the poet's day.

It was in Mauchline that Burns was to meet his future wife, Jean Armour, and it was here that they settled down after marriage. Their home in Castle Street still stands, and is now the **Burns House Museum**. The red sandstone building actually had four families living in it in the 18th century, but it has now been converted so that various exhibitions can be accommodated. Robert and Jean's apartment has been furnished much as it would have been when they moved in in 1788. Across from it, but now a private house, stood **Nance Tannock's Inn**, Burns' favourite "howff", or drinking place.

Mauchline Parish Church is not the one Burns knew. It was built in 1826 to replace the Norman church, which by that time was in a sad state of repair. The kirkyard, however, still has many graves associated with the poet. Four of his children are buried here, as is **William Fisher**, immortalised as Holy Willie in *Holy Willie's Prayer*. He was an elder of the kirk, and Burns used him to attack

Burns House Museum

the cant and hypocrisy prevalent at the time. In the "prayer", Holy Willie asks for divine retribution for all those people who have sinned, while at the same time asking forgiveness of his own, understandable sins. He was actually rebuked by the kirk for drunkenness at one point, so no doubt excessive drinking was one of the sins he found understandable. He was eventually found in a ditch during a snowstorm in 1809, frozen to death. The kirkyard also contains the grave of **Rev'd William Auld**, the kirk minister, whom Burns referred to as "Daddy" Auld. A chart on the church wall gives the burial spot of all these people. Opposite the church is **Poosie Nancy's Inn**. Though not a great frequenter of this establishment, Burns drank there occasionally, and people can still drink there today.

Poosie Nancy's Inn

To the north of the village is the **Burns Memorial**, built in 1897 of red sandstone. Inside there is a small museum, and from the top there is a good view of the surrounding rich farmlands. Beside the memorial, and forming part of it, are some picturesque almshouses for old people.

Gavin Hamilton was Burns' best friend and also his landlord. His house can still be seen, though it is not open to the public. Attached to it is a curious 15th century tower house built of the local red sandstone. This is popularly known as **Abbot Hunter's Tower**, and was at one time the headquarters of the vast estates that the monks of Melrose Abbey owned in this part of Ayrshire.

To the south of the village is to be found the **Mauchline Viaduct**, which carries the Glasgow-Dumfries rail line across the River Ayr. It cannot be seen from the main road, but a detour down the former road which has now been bypassed gives a good view of what is considered to be one of the finest and most elegant railway bridges in the world. Work started on building it in 1843, and it is still Britain's highest stone and brick built railway bridge, being 163 feet above the bed of the river. It has three smaller arches at each end, and a graceful arch in the middle that spans 181 feet.

FAILFORD
7 miles E of Ayr on the B743

Failford is no more than a small hamlet with picturesque old cottages and an inn. Near here, in 1786, Burns took his farewell of Highland Mary before she set off for her home in Argyllshire. He had asked her to accompany him to Jamaica as his wife, and she had accepted, and was going home to make the final arrangements. However, she died at Greenock , and Burns never emigrated. The **Failford Monument**, on a slight rise, commemorates the event.

A mile east of Failford, in a field, are the slight remains of a burial cairn, and legend tells us that this was the burial place of the legendary **Old King Cole** of nursery rhyme fame. He was supposed to have been a real person - a British king

called Coel or Coilus, to give him his
Latin name. In the Dark Ages, he fought
a great battle in Ayrshire against the
Scots of Argyllshire, whose king was
Fergus. Coel's army was heavily defeated,
and Coel himself had to flee the
battlefield. Eventually he was captured
and killed, and his subjects later buried
him and his immediate entourage with
some pomp at the spot where he had
been slain.

At one time the nearby stream was
called the "Bloody Burn", and one field
beside the burn was known as "Dead
Men's Holm", where the dead were
supposed to have been buried. Tales were
often told of farmers' ploughs turning up
pieces of human bone and armour in the
past. The tumulus was opened in 1837,
and some cremated bones within clay
pots were discovered, suggesting the
burial of someone important.

COYLTON
6 miles E of Ayr on the A70

Coylton is said to be named after Old
King Cole, as is that district of Ayrshire
called Kyle. The ruins of the ancient
Coylton Parish Church are to be found
at Old Coylton, to the south of the
present village. At one time it was
thought that Old King Cole was buried
within its kirkyard.

OCHILTREE
11 miles E of Ayr on the A70

Ochiltree was the birthplace, in 1869, of
George Douglas Brown the writer. His
most famous book was *The House with the
Green Shutters*, which was set in the
township of Barbie, a thinly disguised
Ochiltree. It was a direct challenge to
Scottish writers known as the "Kailyard
School", who wrote about the Scottish
countryside, villages and people in a
cosy, innocent manner. Not many of the
characters in Brown's book have

redeeming features, and it caused a
sensation when published. The cottage
where he was born (not open to the
public) is now known as "The House
with the Green Shutters", and indeed
someone has added green shutters to the
house front to make it look authentic.

AUCHINLECK
13 miles E of Ayr on the A76

Though it is a former mining village,
Auchinleck is an ancient place. **James
Boswell**, Samuel Johnson's biographer,
though born in Edinburgh, was an
Auchinleck man, his family seat being
the 18th century **Auchinleck House** (not
open to the public) to the west of the
village. His father Lord Auchinleck, a
High Court judge, was sorely tried by his
son's errant ways, and when Boswell
brought Johnson here when the pair
were doing their Scottish tour, his
father was not enamoured of the
great Englishman.

Boswell himself is buried in a small
mausoleum attached to the former
Auchinleck Parish Church, which is no
longer used for worship. It now houses a
small museum dedicated to the man.

SORN
14 miles E of Ayr on the B743

Sorn is one of the most picturesque
villages in Ayrshire. It sits on the River
Ayr, with an ancient bridge spanning it,
and has many delightful cottages with
colourful gardens. Sorn Parish Church
dates from 1658, and the lofts, or
galleries, are reached by outside
staircases, due to the lack of space inside.
Near the village is **Sorn Castle** (not open
to the public), which dates from the 14th
century. James V or VI (no one is quite
sure which one) visited the castle on
horseback in the depths of winter to
attend a wedding there.

Alexander Peden was born at

Auchinleck in 1625, and was a Covenantor who held conventicles - illegal prayer meetings - at lonely spots all over central Ayrshire, especially around Sorn. He was also known as **Prophet Peden**, and the area abounds with places named after him, such as Peden's Pulpit and Peden's Table. There is even a field called Preaching Peden.

CUMNOCK

15 miles E of Ayr on the A76

This small industrial town was granted its burgh charter in 1509. In the middle of its square sits **Cumnock Old Parish Church**, a building which seems to sprout transepts, apses and porches all over the place. The village of Lugar sits two miles west of the town, and here you will find **Bello Mill** (not open to the public), birthplace in 1754 of **William Murdoch**, the pioneer of gas lighting. He conducted his experiments in a cave on the banks of the Lugar Water upstream from the mill.

Dumfries House (not open to the public), lies west of Cumnock, and was designed for the 4th Earl of Dumfries in the mid 1700s by Robert and John Adam.

MUIRKIRK

23 miles E of Ayr on the A70

This former mining village is surrounded by bleak but lovely moorland. To the south, on an unmarked road, is the **John Louden McAdam Monument**, erected where tar works owned by him once stood. To the west is the site of the Battle of Airds Moss, where a Covenanting army was heavily defeated by Government troops. A memorial marks the site.

NEW CUMNOCK

19 miles SE of Ayr on the A76

It was near New Cumnock that the **Knockshinnoch Mining Disaster** took

place in 1950. 129 miners were trapped underground when a slurry of mud and peat filled some mine workings that were too near the surface. 116 were eventually brought out alive, and the rescuers showed great bravery in doing so. A feature film was later made about the disaster.

To the south of the village lies **Glen Afton**, through which flows the Afton Water. A cairn marks the spot where Burns was inspired to write *Flow Gently Sweet Afton*. An unmarked road follows the river for some of the way, and it makes a pleasant short drive.

DALRYMPLE

5 miles SE of Ayr on the B7034

It was in this quiet village of weavers' cottages that Robert Burns first received an education. While staying at Mount Oliphant Farm he and his brother Gilbert attended the parish school on alternate weeks. The village sits on the River Doon, and has a small Parish

Cassillis Castle

Church built in 1849. Two miles south lies **Cassillis Castle** (not open to the public), home to the Earl of Cassillis and Marquis of Ailsa, head of the Kennedy family. It is a grand tower house with pepper pot turrets, and can be seen from the road. It was built in the 14th century, though has been added to over the years.

PRESTWICK
2 miles S of Ayr on the A79

Prestwick is one of the oldest towns in Scotland, having attained its first burgh charter sometime in the 12th century. It was granted a further charter in 1600. It was one of the most popular Clyde coast resorts until foreign holidays took over, and it was here, in 1860, that the first **British Open Golf Championship** was played. Some men met in the **Red Lion** (which still exists) in 1851 and formed the Prestwick Golf Club. Nine years later they formed a championship that was open to anyone, not just members of the club, and thus the British Open was inaugurated. Eight players took part in that first competition.

Prestwick International Airport stands to the north of the town. At one time it was Scotland's transAtlantic gateway, and though it has now lost this status it is still a busy place, being the main starting point for package holidays. On March 2nd 1960 the airport had its most famous visitor - **Elvis Presley**. He

was returning home from Germany after doing his national service, and stopped off at the American airbase (now gone) at the airport for refuelling. It was the only time that he ever set foot on British soil, and in later years, when asked which country he would most like to visit in the world, he replied that he would love to come back to Scotland. A plaque near the "Graceland Bar" in the airport recalls the event, and fans still turn up from all over the world to look at it.

The name Prestwick means the "priest's burgh", and the ruins of the ancient **Parish Church of St Nicholas** can be seen near the coastline. At **Kingcase** there was once a lazar house which Robert I visited on many occasions seeking a cure form leprosy. **Bruce's Well** can still be seen there.

ALLOWAY
2 miles S of Ayr on the B7024

In this quiet village stands **Burns' Cottage**, where the poet Robert Burns was born in 1759. It is a simple, thatched, single storey cottage built by Robert's own father, and is open to the public. Robert Burns was not the "heaven-taught ploughman" of legend, but, for his time, a highly educated man who could speak French, knew his history, philosophy and classics, and could read and write music. He could

DOONBRAE

Alloway, Ayrshire KA7 4PQ
Tel/ Fax: 01292 442511 e-mail: doonbrae@aol.com
website: www.aboutscotland.com/ayrshire/doonbrae

Doonbrae is an elegant Georgian House dating from 1810, and set in over two acres of beautiful gardens next to the famous "Brig o' Doon". It offers three extremely comfortable rooms (one double and two twin, with one of the twins being fully en suite) on a B&B basis. The furnishings speak of country living in a bygone age, though the service and attention to detail is definitely 21st century. Guests can relax in a light, airy drawing room which has magnificent views over the River Doon, and even make tea or coffee in the "Butler's Pantry" if they wish.

also play the fiddle, and, surprisingly, the guitar. He was probably better educated than some of the aristocrats who lionised him when he went to Edinburgh in later life.

This was all thanks to his father William. He valued learning highly, and sent both Robert and his brother Gilbert to school. Nor was Robert a peasant. Though poor, William was a tenant farmer, and employed both farm workers and servants to work on his farm. To illustrate this point, two of Robert Burns' sons entered the British army, one achieving the rank of Lt. Colonel and the other Colonel. And one of Gilbert's sons became a minister in the Church of Scotland.

At one time Alloway was a country village, but now it is an affluent suburb of Ayr, full of large impressive houses and villas. Burns's Cottage has become a place of pilgrimage, and people from all over the world come to pay their respects. Within the grounds of the cottage is the **Burns Museum**, with a priceless collection of manuscripts, letters and personal possessions.

Spanning the River Doon is the

Brig o' Doon

graceful **Brig o' Doon**, a single arched structure dating from the 15th century. It was across this bridge that Tam O' Shanter was chased by witches after disturbing their revelries in Alloway kirk. He managed to reach the keystone of the bridge, and therefore safety, just in time, as witches cannot cross running water. However, his horse Meg lost its tail in the encounter. In Burns's day it lay on the main road south to Maybole, but now it has been bypassed by a later, wider bridge.

The **Burns Memorial**, a handsome Grecian temple, stands among the beautiful memorial gardens. It was built in the 1820s, barely 30 years after Burns died, and houses a small display. **Alloway Kirk** lies on the other side of

WHITELEY'S FARM

By Alloway, Ayr, Ayrshire KA7 4EG
Tel: 01292 443968; Fax: 01292 442876
e-mail: millerint@btinternet.com

Two miles from Alloway, birthplace of Robert Burns, you'll find **Whiteley's Farm**, owned and run by Bill and Brenda Miller. Stable Cottage is a superior, four-star self-catering cottage that offers the highest standards in comfort and convenience. It has a double bedroom, a sitting room with radio, TV and telephone, a fully equipped kitchen and a bathroom with separate bath and shower. The place is centrally heated, and all linen, crockery and towels are supplied. This is the perfect base to explore an area of Scotland that is rich in history and heritage.

the road, and is where the witches in Tam O' Shanter met on that wild night. In the kirkyard is the grave of William Burnes (the "e" was eventually dropped from the name), Robert's father. The church dates from medieval times, but even in Burns' day was a ruin.

The **Tam O' Shanter Experience** is a visitors centre which shows two audio visual presentations within its large auditorium. One illustrates Burns' life, and the other recreates Tam O' Shanter's fateful ride south from Ayr. East of the village is **Mount Oliphant Farm** (not open to the public) where Burns and his family moved to when he was seven years old.

KILMARNOCK

This large town is the capital of the northern portion of Ayrshire called Cunningham. Though it is largely an industrial town, it is still an ancient place, and may date back to the 7th century when St. Marnock, a Celtic missionary, set up a small church here. The present **Laigh Kirk**, the town's parish church, was rebuilt in 1810 after 21 members of the congregation were killed in a stampede to get out of the previous building when they thought it was collapsing. The tower dates from the 17th century, though a date stone on it incorrectly says "1410".

The town's other old church is the **Old High Kirk**, which was built in 1732. A pillar called the **Soulis Stone** built into its kirkyard wall commemorates an English knight called Soulis, though no one, surprisingly, is quite sure who he was.

Kilmarnock has many Burns associations, and it was here that his first book of poems - the **Kilmarnock Edition** - was published in 1786. The printing works owned by John Wilson stood in Star Inn Close (now gone) and a plaque in the modern shopping mall marks the spot where it once stood. Wilson's grave is within the High Kirk graveyard. A copy of the Kilmarnock Edition is now worth many thousands of pounds. Also in the Mall is a stone marking the spot where **John Nesbit**, a Covenantor, was executed in 1683. His grave can be seen within the Laigh Kirk graveyard.

A **Burns Statue** was unveiled at Kilmarnock Cross in the 1990s by the Princess Royal, and in Kay Park is the **Burns Memorial** (no longer open to the public). It is an impressive red sandstone building with a statue of the poet by W.G. Stevenson.

It was in a shop in King Street (now gone) that Johnnie Walker first began blending and bottling whisky in 1820. A statue of Walker stands in The Strand, outside the Laigh Kirk, and the **Johnnie Walker Bottling Plant** in Hill Street is one of the largest plants of its kind in the world.

The **Dick Institute**, a museum and art

The Dick Institute

gallery, is in Elmbank Avenue. It is housed in a grand classical building, and has impressive collections connected with geology, archaeology, biology and local history. The gallery is also impressive, and has paintings by Corot, Constable, Turner and Kilmarnock's own internationally acclaimed painter, **Robert Colquhoun**. The area around the museum is particularly attractive, with a war memorial and the ornate facade of the town's former technical college. Also in Elmbank Avenue is a statue of **James Shaw** (known affectionately in the town as "Jimmy Shaw"), who became Lord Mayor of London in 1805.

Dean Castle

The impressive **Dean Castle** stands north east of the town centre. It is the oldest building in the town, and was the home of the Earls of Kilmarnock, the last one of which, the 4th Earl, was beheaded in London for his part in the Jacobite Uprising of 1745 and 1746. The Boyd family, who became the Earls of Kilmarnock, was one of the most important families in Scotland in the 15th century, and eventually became Regents for a short while. One of them even married a sister of the Scottish king, though he was later stripped of his titles.

There are, in fact, two castles - a tower house dating from at least the 14th century and a later "palace". Both are enclosed in a curtain wall. Within the castle is a wonderful collection of armour and a collection of rare musical instruments. Surrounding it all is the **Dean Castle Country Park**, with woodland walks and a small zoo.

While the 4th Earl was in London awaiting execution, his wife stayed at Kilmarnock House (now gone) which stood in the middle of the town. Daily she walked the grounds, awaiting news of his fate. The grounds have now become Howard Park, within which is still to be found **Lady's Walk**. Today the wooded path is said to be haunted by her ghost.

Across from the new courthouse, on the site now occupied by the **Old Sheriff Court**, was where the Kilmarnock terminus of the Troon/Kilmarnock Railway, Scotland's oldest rail line, once stood. Two miles west of the town is the **Gatehead Viaduct**, which carried it across the River Irvine. It is Scotland's oldest railway bridge.

Riccarton, a suburb of the town, is pointed out as a possible birthplace of **William Wallace**, though Elderslie in Renfrewshire seems a more likely location. The place was named after Sir Richard Wallace, William's uncle, who had a castle in the vicinity. However, William probably had his first encounter with English troops here, when English soldiers tried to steal some fish he had caught in the River Irvine.

At **Crosshouse**, a former mining village to the west of the town, **Andrew Fisher** was born in 1862. He rose to become prime minister of Australia on three separate occasions.

AROUND KILMARNOCK

FENWICK
4 miles N of Kilmarnock off the A77

Fenwick (pronounced "Finnick") is really two villages - High Fenwick and Low Fenwick. They lie on the edge of the Fenwick Moors, which separate the farmlands of Ayrshire from the southern outskirts of the Glasgow conurbation. They were originally weaving villages, and some of the weavers' cottages can still be seen, with one large window on one side of the front door which gave light to the weaving room, and a smaller window on the other, giving light to the living quarters. Nowadays they have been refurbished and extended, and house well-off Glasgow and Kilmarnock commuters.

Fenwick Parish Church dates from 1643, and is an attractive, whitewashed building in the shape of a Greek cross. On one outside wall still hang the **Jougs** - a metal collar which was placed round the neck of wrongdoers as a punishment in days gone by. Five miles to the north

of the village is **Lochgoin Farm**, which has a small Covenanting museum

MOSCOW
4 miles NE of Kilmarnock on the A719

There is nothing unusual about this small hamlet of neat cottages, but it is famous for its name, though the correct pronunciation is Moss-cow, with the emphasis on the "cow". It actually stands on a small stream which some wag in the past named the Volga. The name stuck, and it is now called that on maps.

STEWARTON
5 miles N of Kilmarnock on the A735

Stewarton is a small burgh which received its burgh charter in 1623. It is famous as being the home of bonnet making, and was the birthplace, in 1739, of **David Dale**, the industrialist and social reformer who founded New Lanark. The **Parish Church of St. Columba** dates from 1697, though it has been much altered since.

DUNLOP
7 miles N of Kilmarnock on the A735

This is a delightful village of small weaver's cottages. The **Parish Church** dates from 1835, though it incorporates fragments in the north aisle from an earlier building. In the kirkyard is the ornate **Hans Hamilton Tomb**, containing a memorial to Dunlop's first Protestant minister. James VI later made him Viscount Clandeboyes, and the 17th century **Clandeboyes Hall** beside the mausoleum was named after him, and was the first village school.

Fenwick Parish Church

GALSTON

4 miles E of Kilmarnock on the A71

This pleasant little burgh in the Irvine Valley has a splendid Parish Church of 1808 on a slight rise above its main street. Another, later, church not to be missed is **St. Sophia's R.C. Church**, modelled on the Hagia St. Sophia in Istanbul. **Barr Castle** is a solid tower house in the middle of the town in which John Knox preached in 1556. An ancient game of handball used to be played against its walls by locals.

North of the town are the impressive ruins of **Loudoun Castle**, ancestral home of the Campbells, Earls of Loudoun. Before it was burnt down in 1941, it was called the "Windsor of the North", so lavish was the entertainment and hospitality laid on there. Three ghosts reputedly haunt the ruins - a Grey Lady, a Phantom Piper and a Benevolent Monk. At one time William Wallace's great sword was kept here, but it was sold in 1930. Beside its walls is the **Auld Yew Tree**, under which Hugh, the third Earl, drafted the Treaty of Union of 1707 which did away with the Scottish parliament.

Loudoun Castle was the home of one of the most tragic women in Victorian times. **Lady Flora Hastings** shook the monarchy and government in 1839 when people turned against the 20-year old Queen Victoria and espoused Lady Flora's cause instead. Flora was a Lady of the Bedchamber in Victoria's household who contracted a disease which so swelled her stomach that she looked pregnant. Gossip raged through the court, and she was eventually shunned by everyone, even though doctors confirmed that she was ill. Neither the young queen nor the government of the day did anything to dispel the rumours, and soon people were turning against Victoria. It was her turn to be shunned, and instead of doing something about it, she decided to ride out the storm.

But to no avail. While out riding in her carriage in London, people turned their backs on her, which shocked her to the core. However, she still did nothing about it, neither seeking a reconciliation with Flora or denying the rumours. It was only when Flora was on her deathbed that Victoria visited her, and after she died, many people still wouldn't forgive their young queen.

Flora's body was brought back to Loudoun Castle and buried in the medieval **Loudoun Kirk**, whose ruins can be seen a couples of miles west of the castle. People now think that she had a wasting liver disease or ovarian cancer.

Today the **Loudoun Castle Theme Park** is located within the castle grounds, with fairground rides and woodland walks.

NEWMILNS

7 miles E of Kilmarnock on the A71

This is a small lace making town which received its burgh charter in 1490,

Loudoun Castle

making it the oldest inland burgh in Ayrshire. The small crow-step gabled **Town House** dates from the 1730s, and behind the **Loudoun Arms**, which itself dates form the early 18th century, is **Newmilns Tower**, an early 16th century tower house built by the Campbells of Loudoun.

During the American Civil War the weavers of Newmilns sent a message of support to Abraham Lincoln, who in turn sent back an American flag. This was later lost, and a replacement was given to the town in 1949. It is now on display in the early 19th century Parish Church in the main street.

DARVEL
7 miles W of Kilmarnock on the A71

Like Newmilns, this small burgh was a former lace making centre, the skills having been brought here by the Dutch in the 17th century. It was laid out in the late 18th and early 19th centuries as a new town, and its original layout has altered little since then. It was in the farm of Lochfield, near the town, that **Sir Alexander Fleming**, the discoverer of penicillin, was born in 1881. To the east of the town is the immense bulk of **Loudoun Hill**, the plug of an extinct volcano. Both William Wallace and Robert I fought battles here against the English in 1297 and 1307 respectively. South of the town is the highest hill in the area (1,258 feet),the curiously named **Distinkhorn**.

IRVINE
7 miles W of Kilmarnock on the A71

Though it was designated as Britain's first seaside new town in the mid 1960s, Irvine is an ancient seaport and royal burgh sitting at the mouth of the River Irvine. It is a mixture of old and new, and is surrounded by many industrial estates and new housing areas. Robert

Burns came here in 1781 to learn flax dressing, and stayed in a cottage in the cobbled **Glasgow Vennel**, once the town's main road north. A small museum is now housed in the cottage and the heckling shop behind.

But Irvine's literary associations don't stop with Burns. **John Galt**, the author of *Annals of the Parish*, was born here, as was **Alexander McMillan**, who founded the great London publishing house. And there is one further, more unusual, literary connection. In 1815 **Edgar Allan Poe**, the American author of macabre tales, was brought to the town by his guardian, a Virginian merchant called John Allan, who had been born in Irvine. Edgar spent two months in the town, and attended the local school before going on to London. It is said that part of his studies while at the Irvine school was copying the epitaphs on the gravestones in the local kirkyard, something which would have prepared him for his later literary efforts.

The ruins of **Seagate Castle** date from the 16th century. It is said that Mary Stewart lodged here briefly in 1563. Every year in August the town has its **Marymas Week**, which celebrates it's links with the queen. However, Marymas Week goes back long before Mary Stewart visited Irvine. There is little doubt that it was originally a pre-Reformation religious festival to do with the Virgin Mary, as the local church was dedicated to her.

It was in Irvine, in the 18th century, that a curious cult called the Buchanites (see also Dunscore and Crocketford) was founded by Elspeth Buchan, an innkeeper's daughter from North East Scotland. She promised her followers eternal life by breathing on them, and told them that she herself was immortal. She attracted many followers, including a gullible Church of Scotland minister called Hugh Whyte. She and her followers were hounded from town, and they set out for Dumfriesshire, where Mother Buchan, as she was nicknamed, eventually had the effrontery to die a natural death, causing the cult to break up.

Down by the harbour is the **Magnum Centre**, one of the largest leisure centres in Scotland. On the other side of the river is the **Big Idea**, which calls itself the world's first inventors' centre. It's a combination of exhibition, display centre, laboratory, discovery centre and workshop.

Scottish Maritime Museum

One of the three **Scottish Maritime Museum** sites is to be found in Irvine's harbour area (the others being in Glasgow and Dumbarton). It has a wide collection of ships, most of which you can board and explore. There's also the Linthouse Engine Works housing a vast collection of maritime related machinery, such as winding gear, engines and so on. The Shipworker's Tenement Flat shows what life was like for shipyard workers in a typical "room and kitchen" of the 1920s.

In 1839, Irvine's Eglinton Castle was the venue for the **Eglinton Tournament**, organised by the 13th Earl of Eglinton in the form of a great medieval tournament, with jousting, horse riding and other knightly pursuits. Aristocracy from all over Europe came to the castle, and the whole three-day event promised to be a colourful and chivalrous affair. However, the weather had other ideas, and such was the ferocity of the rain that the jousting area, and indeed most of the land surrounding Eglinton Castle, was turned into a quagmire, reducing everything to a farce. The castle is no

more, but the grounds have been turned into the **Eglinton Country Park**.

Dreghorn lies to the east of Irvine, and it was here, in 1840, that yet another famous Ayrshireman was born. His name was **John Boyd Dunlop**, who invented the pneumatic tyre. **Dreghorn Parish Church** is a curious octagonal building which was built in 1780.

ARDROSSAN, STEVENSTON AND SALTCOATS
11 miles W of Kilmarnock on the A78

These three former holiday resorts sit on the Ayrshire coast north of Irvine. Ardrossan is the most industrialised of the three, and is the Calmac ferry terminal for Arran. It was laid out in the early 19th century by the 12th Earl of Eglinton, though the ruins of **Ardrossan Castle** date back to the 1400s. It was once a stronghold of the Montgomery family, and sits on a low hill overlooking the main street. Cromwell used its stones to build the Citadel at Ayr. Beside the ruins is **The Obelisk**, which commemorates a local doctor. **St. Peter in Chains** was built in 1938, and is said to be one of the finest modern churches in Ayrshire.

The **North Ayrshire Museum** in Saltcoats is housed in the former

Saltcoats Parish Church, and has an interesting local history section, plus a graveslab that may have marked the grave of an ancestor of Edgar Allan Poe. It has a fine beach, though its immediate environs consist of dull council flats. The name of the town is a reminder that there were once salt pans here, where sea water was boiled off and the salt collected and sold as a preservative. **Saltcoats Harbour** dates from the 17th century, and at low tide fossilised trees can be seen on the harbour floor. **Betsy Miller**, the only woman ever to become a registered ship's captain in the 19th century, was born in the town.

Stevenston is an unprepossessing town. However, it has a fine **Parish Church** which dates from 1832. In 1873 the British Dynamite Company established a factory at Ardeer, close to the town. It later became Nobel's Explosive Company, and in 1926 became part of ICI.

KILMAURS

2 miles NW of Kilmarnock on the A735

This is a pleasant village no more than a couple of fields away from the outskirts of Kilmarnock. However, it is a self-contained community which received a burgh charter in 1527, and has a picturesque 17th century **Tolbooth**, still with its jougs attached to one wall. This was a metal collar which was placed round the neck of offenders. The Parish Church dates from 1888, and replaced an earlier medieval church which was collegiate. Attached to it is the **Glencairn Aisle**, a 16th century structure with a magnificently ornate monument to the 8th Earl of Glencairn and his family, who lie in a vault beneath it.

John Boyd Orr, the first Director of the United Nations Food and Agriculture Organisation, was born in the village in 1880.

KILWINNING

9 miles NW of Kilmarnock on the A737

The ruins of **Kilwinning Abbey** dominate the town. It was built for the Tironensian order of monks in the 12th century, though it was rebuilt and altered over the yars. The remains are not as extensive as those at Crossraguel, and the tower now attached to them dates only from 1815. It replaced the original medieval tower which collapsed. It is here that the **Papingo Shoot** is held every year, when archers shoot directly upwards at a target (the "papingo") held from a window of the tower. Shoots like this were once common throughout Britain, and in Kilwinning's case the target is a wooden pigeon. Within the ruins is the plain Kilwinning Parish Church, with nothing much to commend by way of architecture.

DALGARVEN MILL

10 miles NW of Kilmarnock on the A737

The **Mill** (see panel below) dates from

DALGARVEN MILL

nr Dalry, Glasgow
Tel: 01294 552448

There has been a mill on the site since the 14th century, set up by the monks of Kilwinning Abbey. The present mill was erected in 1640 and rebuilt in 1880 after being damaged by fire. The Garnock waters power a six metre diameter breast shot wheel that drives the French millstones through cast iron gearing. With ongoing restoration, it is hoped that demonstration milling will soon be possible. The three storey grain store has been converted to house an extensive collection of Ayrshire farming and domestic memorabilia and there is an exhibition drawn from a collection of over 600 Victorian and Edwardian costumes. There are delightful walks by the river and a coffee shop and museum to complete your visit.

about 1620, and sits in a picturesque location close to the main road. It now houses a museum dedicated to country life in Ayrshire, and has a small tea room.

DALRY

11 miles NW of Kilmarnock on the A737

The square of this small industrial town is dominated by **St. Margaret's Parish Church**, built in the 1870s. The name comes from the Gaelic "dal righe", meaning the "field of the king", though who the king in question was has never been established. A large mansion called **Blair** (not open to the public) sits to the south east of the town, built round what was a typical Scottish fortified tower. The parkland surrounding it was laid out by William Blair in the 1760.

BEITH

12 miles NW of Kilmarnock off the A737

This is a small, attractive town sitting in the Garnock Valley. The ruins of the **Auld Kirk** date from the late 16th century, while the impressive **High Church** dates from the early 19th century. Though not a beautiful town, Beith's **Eglinton Street** is well worth seeking out, as it is full of neat two-storey buildings of the 18th and 19th centuries.

KILBIRNIE

13 miles NW of Kilmarnock on the A760

This small industrial town has one of the most interesting churches in Ayrshire. The **Barony Parish Church** dates originally from the 15th century, and inside is some wonderful 17th and 18th century woodwork, including the exuberant Crawford Loft and the Cunningham Aisle, where the wealthy families of the area once sat during church services. The ruins of **Kilbirnie Place** (the word being a corruption of

"palace") sit next to the golf course, and date from the 15th century.

WEST KILBRIDE

16 miles NW of Kilmarnock off the A78

This prosperous and sedate village sits inland from **Seamill**, and is home to many Glasgow commuters. When Thomas Boyd, son of Lord Kilmarnock, and later created Earl of Arran, married Princess Mary of Scotland in the 15th century, he built **Law Castle** as a grand family home. However, he later had to flee the country, and the marriage was annulled. Portencross is a small hamlet on a headland to the north of West Kilbride, and here stand the substantial ruins of yet another Boyd stronghold - **Portencross Castle**, which date from the 14th century. Also on the headland is **Hunterston Castle** (not open to the public) and **Hunterston Nuclear Power Station**.

CUMBRAES

19 miles NW of Kilmarnock, in the Firth of Clyde

These two islands once formed part of the County of Bute, but since the local government reorganisation of 1975, they have come under Ayrshire. **Little Cumbrae** is privately owned, and cannot be visited, but a ferry from Largs connects **Great Cumbrae** to the mainland. The only town on Great Cumbrae is **Millport**, where stands the Collegiate Church of the Holy Spirit, better known as **Cathedral of the Isles**. It is the smallest cathedral in Britain (some people say the smallest in Europe, but this isn't so), and is one of Scotland's gems. Its nave is 40 feet by 20 feet, and can only seat 100 people. However, it is a genuine cathedral, as it has the *cathedra*, or throne, of the Scottish Episcopalian Church's Bishop of the Isles. It was designed by William Butterfield, who also designed Keble College, Oxford, for the 6th Earl of Glasgow, who lived at Kelburn Castle on the mainland. Built in 1851, it formed part of a theological complex and community which flourished for some time in the 19th century. The church ceiling is decorated with all the wild flowers found on the island in the mid-19th century.

Largs Town

On the eastern shore of the island, facing the mainland, is the **University Marine Biological Station**, an institution of both Glasgow and London Universities. It offers research facilities for students of marine life, as well as tuition in diving, and there is a small museum which is open to the public.

LARGS

19 miles NW of Kilmarnock on the A78

Largs is the epitome of the Clyde coast holiday resort. During the last fortnight in July, hordes of holiday makers would descend on the Clyde coast towns by train and coach for a fortnight away from the work and smoke of Glasgow. The great days are gone now, as Glaswegians now prefer Spain or Florida, but the place still caters for day trippers and retired people.

The **Battle of Largs** took place in 1263, and a tall thin monument (known locally as **The Pencil**) to the south of the town commemorates the event. Alexander III defeated an armada commanded by Haakan IV of Norway, and Scotland was at last free of the Viking yolk. Within the town is **Vikingar**, an interpretation centre and museum that explains the links between Scotland and the Vikings all those years ago. **Largs Museum**, which has local collections, is also worth a visit, as is the **Skelmorlie Aisle**, situated in a small

graveyard just off the main street. It is a former transept of the medieval parish church of Largs, and contains the magnificent tomb of Sir Robert Montgomery of Skelmorlie and his wife. It is in the Renaissance style and dates from 1634. The present **St. Columba's Parish Church** sits on the sea front, and is of red sandstone. It was built in 1892 and has a tall slender spire.

Within the local cemetery is buried Sir William Burrell, the shipping millionaire who gave the Burrell Collection to Glasgow, and to the south of the town is **Kelburn Castle**, ancestral home of the Boyles, Earls of Glasgow. Within the grounds are a country park with craft shops, adventure playgrounds and woodland walks.

ARRAN

The Isle of Arran sits 13 miles off the coast of Ayrshire. It has been called "Scotland in Miniature", as it is mountainous to the north, low lying in the middle, and hilly in the south. It is 19 miles long by 10 miles wide, and within its 165 square miles there is plenty of history and some spectacular scenery. This is an island of Celtic saints, standing stones, stone circles, castles and ancient burial cairns. Up until the early 19th century, Gaelic was spoken here, even though most of the island is further south than Berwick-upon-Tweed.

Isle of Arran

The northern portion is every bit as spectacular as the Highlands, as anyone who has driven from Brodick to Lochranza will testify. For those with the stamina, the island's highest point, Goatfell (2,866 feet) can be climbed. **Brodick** is the ferry port, the crossing from Ardrossan taking 55 minutes. It is strung out along Brodick Bay, and was once a resort for holidaying Glaswegians. Just north is the **Arran Brewery**, where you can see the processes that go into making ales and beers. And at Home Farm are the premises of **Arran Aromatics**, which makes body care products and scented candles. Again, you can watch the manufacturing processes.

The **Isle of Arran Heritage Museum**,

THE BURNSIDE

Auchrannie road, Brodick, Isle of Arran KA27 8B
Tel/Fax: 01770 303888
e-mail: mas@theburnside.com
website: www.theburnside.com

The Burnside is a very special art gallery in Brodick, the main ferry port on the beautiful Isle of Arran. It opened in 2002, as the fulfilment of a dream by it's owner Mhairi-Aileen, who came to Arran as a child. Now it is probably the largest gallery on the west coast of Scotland, with various exhibitions held throughout the year, and a continual winter textile exhibition. Ten artists and craftspeople regularly exhibit at the Burnside, now known as the "Burnsiders". Their work is original and exciting, and ranges from sculpture and porcelain to weaving and textiles all at realistic prices. Other artists from the island, the mainland and even abroad exhibit occasionally as well.

Occasionally a professional spinner gives demonstrations using wool from local sheep using a traditional spinning wheel, and other artists will sometimes work within the gallery, explaining the techniques they use. The spacious gallery has two display areas and coffee is served as you browse. One of the main features of the Burnside is the work of Scottish sculptor Tim Pomeroy, who works mainly in stone, and whose inspiration is the human figure and human relationships. Another feature is a collection of miniatures in fine porcelain, none more that three inches tall. The Burnside is a fascinating place, and if you are looking for a unique gift, you should pay a visit when you're on Arran.

north of the village, shows the history of the island and its people. Further on is the entrance to **Brodick Castle** (National Trust for Scotland). This former Hamilton stronghold (the Hamiltons were created Earls of Arran when the Boyds of Kilmarnock forfeited the title) sits on a hillside high above Brodick Bay, and has wonderful views. There has been a castle or fort on the site since at least the Dark Ages, though the present building dates from the 16th century. Inside is a fine collection of paintings and furniture.

Brodick Bay

The road north from Brodick takes you to the former fishing village of **Corrie**, which is quaint and picturesque. It has neat, whitewashed cottages whose gardens flame with colour in the summer months, and an old harbour. The A841 continues on through the bleak but hauntingly beautiful **Glen Chalmadale** before reaching **Lochranza**, on the northern shore of the island.

GLENASHDALE PROPERTIES

Pier Buildings, Brodick, Isle of Arran KA27 8AX
Tel: 01770 302121 Fax: 01770 302123
e-mail: ukfilter@lineone.net

The Isle of Arran is often called "Scotland in Miniature", and sits in the Firth of Clyde. With its frequent ferry services, short distance from Glasgow and excellent road links to the south, getting there is no problem. The current owners of **Glenashdale Properties** have been letting Point House and Cottages for two decades, and are continually upgrading the properties to achieve top quality accommodation. The properties are reached by a private road, and with seven acres of mixed lawns and woodlands, house guests are assured of seclusion. The grounds lead directly to the beach, with magnificent views to the Goat Fell mountain range and Holy Isle. There is ample car parking and safe play areas for children.

Point House has four bedrooms - two doubles, a twin and a single - comfortable lounge, dining room with a small sunroom extension, bathroom, toilet and kitchen. Heating is electric, with an open fire in the dining room and an oil fired Rayburn in the kitchen.

Point House Cottage has two double bedrooms (one en-suite) and a bunk room, lounge, bathroom and fitted kitchen with a small dining room off. Heating is electric, with a wood burning stove in the lounge. Garden Cottage has one double en-suite bedroom, one bunk room, shower room/toilet, fitted kitchen and lounge/dining room incorporating a conservatory leading to a patio. All kitchens have electric cookers, washing machines, fridge/freezers and microwaves, while Garden Cottage also has a dishwasher. All lounges have colour TVs. Pets are welcome in two of the properties.

The name means "loch of the rowan tree river", and it is the terminus for a ferry which runs to the Mull of Kintyre in the summer months. Here you will find the **Isle of Arran Whisky Distillery**, one of the newest distilleries in Scotland. It has conducted tours and a visitors centre. **Lochranza Castle** (Historic Scotland) was built in the 16th century on the site of an earlier castle, which had been a hunting lodge of the Scottish kings. The present building belonged to several families over the years, including the Campbells and Montgomeries.

Catacol is a small hamlet beyond Lochranza which sits opposite the Mull of Kintyre, only four miles away. The row of identical cottages on the landward side of the road is known as the **Twelve Apostles**, and was built in the 19th century to accommodate those people cleared from Glen Catacol in favour of deer.

Inland from Machrie Bay, a few miles down the coast, is **Auchagallon Stone Circle**. It is in fact a Bronze Age burial cairn with a circle of standing stones surrounding it. It is one of several such monuments in the area, with the **Machrie Moore Stone Circle** and the **Moss Farm Road Stone Circle** being other good examples.

The high, dramatic cliffs at **Drumadoon** stand, not above the shoreline, but a raised beach. The **King's Cave** is close to the shoreline and is one of several caves in Scotland where Robert I is supposed to have seen the spider. From the village of **Blackwaterfoot** the B880 road, also known as The String, cuts across the centre of the island towards Brodick. The village of **Shiskine** sits on the road, and has the small **Parish Church of St. Molas**, with an ancient carved stone of a saint embedded in its wall. St Molas was

THE LAGG INN

Lagg, Kilmory. Isle of Arran KA27 8PQ
Tel: 01770 870255 Fax: 01770 870250
e-mail:thelagginn@connectfree.co.uk
website: www.arran.net/lagg/inn

Arran's most historic inn, **The Lagg Inn**, has been offering the very best in hospitality since 1791. It is the perfect place for a quiet holiday away from the stresses of modern living, and has a great reputation for its food, its drink and its wonderful accommodation. The inn has an attractive range of extremely comfortable rooms on offer - double, family, twin and single - and all have colour TVs with satellite channels and hospitality trays. The rooms are fully en suite, and some have direct dial phones. There is a charming and spacious residents' lounge, with smart, traditional furniture, wall lighting and fully fitted carpets. Just the place in which to relax with a book or newspaper.

Good food is important at the Lagg Inn, and the Burnside Restaurant has a cosy and intimate atmosphere where you can enjoy meals prepared from fresh local produce. Rack of lamb - trout -

venison - medallions of pork - are all cooked in an imaginative way, offering guests a real culinary experience. And there is a superb range of wines to go with the meals. The attractive lounge bar has a wide range of drinks, from single malts to local beers, as well as teas and coffees. In the public bar you can play pool or darts, and meet the locals. Arran is a wonderful island, and the Lagg Inn is the prefect base from which to explore it. Why not ask about the inn's car ferry packages, or a golf break, playing over the island's seven challenging golf courses? Great value for money!

a Celtic saint who lived a life of austerity on Holy Island, off the coast at Lamlash. Also worth visiting is the **Balmichael Visitor Centre**, which is also on The String road.

South of Blackwaterfoot, the coast road continues towards **Lagg**, on Arran's southern coast. If you need convincing about the mildness of the climate in these parts, you need look no further than the palm trees in the garden of the Lagg Inn. The **Torrylinn Creamery**, which makes traditional Dunlop cheese in the old-fashioned way, can be visited. About a mile from the coast at Kildonan (which is on an unmarked road off the main road) is the tiny island of **Pladda**, which has a lighthouse built in 1820 by the father of R.L. Stevenson. The scant ruins of **Kildonan Castle** mark a castle given to Robert III's illegitimate son John in 1406.

The road swings north once more, making for **Whiting Bay**, another popular holiday resort in times gone by. At one time it was a fishing port, and takes its name from the whiting that

Lochranza

were caught off its shores. A good walk starts from just south of the village, and takes you up to **Glenashdale Falls** and the prehistoric burial cairns known as the **Giant's Caves**.

Lamlash sits on Lamlash Bay. Having the local high school and the hospital, the village could be said to be the island's capital. In Lamlash Bay sits the huge bulk of **Holy Island**, once the home of St. Molas, and now home to a Tibetan monastery. **Arran Provisions**, the island's largest employer, makes a wide range of preserves, mustards and jams, and has a visitor's centre.

Continuing on northwards from Lamlash brings you back to Brodick.

4 GLASGOW AND WEST CENTRAL SCOTLAND

It was here, in Glasgow, Lanarkshire, Renfrewshire and Dunbartonshire, that Scotland was forged as a great industrial nation. It is the most populous area in the country, though visitors are surprised to learn that it still contains places of great beauty. Much of Scotland's history was played out here as well, and it was the birthplace of such people as John Logie Baird the inventor of television, David Livingstone the explorer and William Smellie the father of modern midwifery.

Though the Clyde is better known as an industrial river, its upper reaches pass through some beautiful areas of moorland and hills which are ideal for walking. And its lower reaches, just before they become the Firth of Clyde, are beautiful as well. Then there's Loch Lomond, the largest stretch of water in Britain and the most beautiful in Scotland.

Glasgow from the Clyde

Dominating the area is Glasgow. It was once nicknamed "the second city of the Empire", as it was Britain's second largest city, with a population of well over one million. Now, thanks to an overspill policy which saw many of its inhabitants decanted to other towns, the population is closer to 700,000. Since its founding, it has gone through many changes. It was firstly an ecclesiastical centre which grew round its cathedral. It next became a place of learning because of its university. Then it became a place of trade and commerce, thanks to the Clyde, and after that a place of industry. Now it has reinvented itself once more, this time as a cosmopolitan, European city with a burgeoning café society full of poets, artists, writers, journalists and TV people. If you go to Glasgow, at least once during your visit do what many Glaswegians do - sit at a pavement café and watch people as they watch you.

There are art galleries, museums and theatres galore, and it has the reputation of being the second best shopping centre in Britain. The shopping

LOCATOR MAP

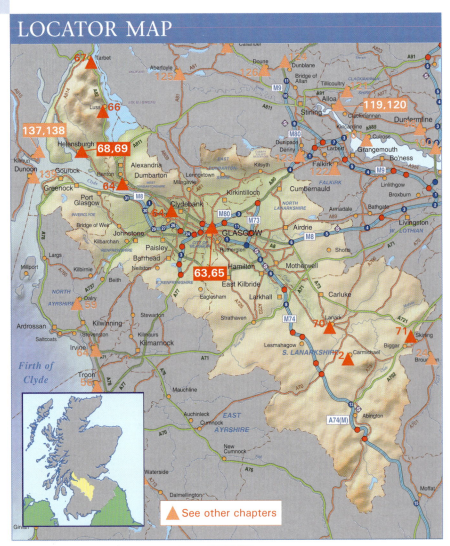

See other chapters

ADVERTISERS AND PLACES OF INTEREST

malls range from the huge, such as the St. Enoch's Centre and the Buchanan Galleries, to the more exclusive and intimate, such as the Italian Centre and Princess Square. And, of course, at weekends, there's "The Barras", Glasgow's own market, selling everything from fruit and vegetables to clothing, antiques and books.

The city has many glitzy restaurants, nightclubs and cafés (with a new one, it would seem, opening up every day), and is home to The Royal Scottish National Orchestra, the BBC Scottish Symphony Orchestra, Scottish Opera and Scottish Ballet. It is also reckoned that it is one of Britain's best dressed cities, with more Armani, Gucchi and Versace outfits worn here that anywhere else in Britain outside London.

It's also an easy place to get out of. An hour on a train from Central Station takes you to the banks of Loch Lomond, the cosy market town of Lanark, deep in the Clyde Valley, or the beaches of the Firth of Clyde. Thousands of Glaswegians make the trips each year. And, what with the city's bustle, it's easy to forget that the Highland Boundary Fault, which separates the Highlands from the Lowlands, is not all that far to the north, and indeed runs through the middle of Loch Lomond.

"The Clyde made Glasgow", runs an old saying, "and Glasgow made the Clyde". And it's true. Up until the 18th century, Glasgow was reckoned to be an inland city sitting on a shallow, fordable river. Then the Clyde was canalised, and Glasgow took off. But in the Clyde Valley you would never even suspect that the great city was only a few miles to the north. This is a place of bucolic scenery - of green, wooded hillsides running down to the river, and of orchards and quiet villages with even quieter pubs. It is said that the monks of Lesmahagow Priory brought the growing of apples to the area, though the greenhouses full of tomatoes no doubt came a lot later. Near the river's source, the scenery is altogether sterner, with lonely moorland that has a gaunt but haunting beauty.

The towns in the area are also worth exploring, from Dumbarton and Helensburgh at the mouth of the Clyde to Hamilton, Lanark and East Kilbride further inland. There are towns where the excesses of coal mining and steel-making blighted the landscape, but these industries provided money and employment at one time, so should not be dismissed or glossed over. And a huge cleaning up operation has been going on for years, turning this industrial heritage into tourist attractions such as Summerlee in Coatbridge.

The days of heavy industry have long gone, and now the main employers in the area are light engineering, electronics (Scotland is the main microchip manufacturing centre in Europe), banking and the media. But the area's industrial past should be looked back on with pride. This was the powerhouse of Scotland, and led the way during the Industrial Revolution.

GLASGOW

At one time, Glasgow was synonymous with poverty, crime, gang fights, dirt and drunkenness. It was not an image it deserved, but it stuck. Now the city has made a concerted effort to create a new image - one of a forward looking, inventive city full of creative energy. Glitzy restaurants, theatres, concert halls, museums, night clubs, trendy cafés and welcoming pubs now proliferate.

The River Clyde, Glasgow

But Glasgow has changed its image more than once over the years. It began as an ecclesiastical centre grouped round its cathedral, then reinvented itself as a place of learning when its university was founded in 1451. The deepening and widening of the Clyde next made it a place of trade. It dealt mainly with the Americas, in such commodities as tobacco and cotton. Then, in the 19th century, it became a place of industry, with shipbuilding yards dotted along the Clyde and many factories serving them situated throughout the city. Now it relies on tourism, the media, service industries and banking for employment.

The **Cathedral of St. Mungo** (Historic Scotland) sits on the site of a monastery founded by St. Kentigern in the 6th century. The present building dates from the 12th century and later, and was founded by David I. In its crypt is **St. Mungo's Tomb**, once a place of pilgrimage. The **Blackadder Aisle** was added to the main building in about 1500 by Bishop Blackadder, and is an elegant, late Gothic structure which was to be part of a new southern transept that was never built.

Glasgow Necropolis sits on a hill behind the cathedral, separated by a road which lies within a deep gully. This is the course of the ancient **Molindinar Burn**, which is still there, covered over and piped in beneath the ground. The Necropolis was the main burial ground for the great and good of Glasgow, and has many splendid monuments from Victorian times and earlier.

The **St. Mungo Museum of Religious Life and Art** is situated in the square in front of the

Cathedral of St. Mungo

THE TALL SHIP AT GLASGOW HARBOUR

100 Stobcross Road, Glasgow G3 8QQ
Tel: 0141 222 2513
e-mail: info@thetallship.com website: www.thetallship.com

Sail through 100 years of maritime history at the Tall Ship at Glasgow Harbour. Follow the remarkable restoration of the Glenlee from an abandoned hulk in Seville harbour to her fully rigged splendour today and learn about the living conditions aboard a deep sea trading ship. Explore the cargo hold where you will see what goods she carried, the deck house where the crew lived, the poop deck and the galley. Also in the harbour is the Pier 17 restaurant, a gift shop and various exhibitions and events. Phone for details.

Golborne began canalising it so that large ships could sail up into the city, and it became a great seaport. The **Tall Ship at Glasgow Harbour** (see panel opposite) in Stobcross Road tells the story of the river and its effect on the city, as well as the industries it spawned. The tall ship itself, the **S.V. Glenlee**, was built in 1869. At Braehead, further down the Clyde, is another museum, **Clydebuilt**, which is part of the **Scottish Maritime Museum** (see panel on page 124). It tells the story of the river from about 1700 to the present day.

cathedral. It looks like an ancient building, but actually dates from the late 20th century. It explores all the main religious traditions in the world, from Christianity and Judaism to Islam and Hinduism.

Across the square from it is the city's **Royal Infirmary**. The original infirmary was built between 1792 and 1794 to designs by James Adam. It was demolished in 1907 and rebuilt over the next seven year to the designs of James Miller, and was in its day Britain's largest non-governmental building. Across the High Street is the city's oldest secular building, **Provand's Lordship**. It was built in 1471 as a manse for the former St. Nicholas Hospital.

In the 17th century the Clyde was so shallow at Glasgow that people could wade across it. In 1768 a man called John

Close to the Tall Ship is the **Scottish Exhibition and Conference Centre**, with exhibition areas and conference halls. It has nothing to commend it architecturally, being rather plain. However, right next to it is a structure which has become one of Glasgow's signature buildings - **The Armadillo**, a huge conference hall whose shape owes a lot to the Sydney Opera House.

The Armadillo

Glaswegians gave it this nickname because it does indeed look like a huge metallic armadillo. Across the river from it is the **Glasgow Science Centre**, built on the site of the former Glasgow Garden Festival. It is a combination of museum, laboratory and hands-on exhibition. It has four floors covering most areas of science and discovery. The accompanying **Glasgow Tower** is Scotland's largest free standing structure, and was built as a local landmark, with views over the city from the top. Unfortunately, due to problems, it is more often closed than open. Also in the complex is an IMAX Theatre.

Even before Glasgow reinvented itself in the 1980s and 1990s, it had always been a city that took its art seriously, and had many art galleries and museums. Like many large cities, the **West End** was where the well-off lived, as the prevailing winds carried the smells of the city away from it. It is still the trendiest area in the city, and is close to the old university and the BBC studios. Here you'll find the **Kelvingrove Art Gallery and Museum**, with large international collections covering history, botany, zoology and geology. It also has an internationally renowned collection of paintings and sculpture - possibly the most comprehensive civic collection in Europe.

Behind it, and across the River Kelvin, are the impressive buildings of **Glasgow**

SCOTTISH MARITIME MUSEUM

Harbourside, Irvine KA12 8QE
Tel: 01294 278283 Fax: 01294 313211

The museum is sited in three locations - the Scottish Maritime Museum at Irvine, Clydebuilt at Braehead and the Denny Ship Model Experiment at Dumbarton. At Irvine you will have the opportunity for a guided tour which includes a restored 1920's shipyard worker's 'Tenement Flat' and a collection of moored vessels in the harbour, some of which can be boarded. Trips are occasionally available for visitors. The museum shop stocks a wide selection of souvenirs and light meals, snacks and drinks are served at the Puffers Coffee Shop on the wharf. Open every day 10am to 5pm.

University, founded in 1451, and one of three universities in the city. The "yooni", as it is called in Glasgow, originally stood in the High Street, but moved here in the 19th century. It has Britain's largest school of medicine.

The **Glasgow Museum of Transport** is across the road from the Kelvingrove Museum. It has collections of cars, buses, trains and other forms of transport, plus a marvellous collection of model ships, most of which were built by the old shipbuilding yards on the Clyde. Perhaps its most distinctive exhibit is a recreation of an old station on Glasgow's underground railway system, which was upgraded in the late 1970s, though its proper name is the **Glasgow Subway** rather than "underground" or "metro". The present subway layout is a simple double circular track linking the centre of the city with the West End, and that, coupled with the carriages' orange livery, has given it the nickname of "The Clockwork Orange".

Also in the West End are the **Hunterian Museum** and the **Hunterian**

Art Gallery, both named after the Hunter Brothers, who pioneered surgery both in Glasgow and London in the 18th century. The museum has fine collections covering many subjects, while the gallery has paintings, furniture and examples of interior design by Mackintosh and Whistler. At the top of Byres Road is the **Glasgow Botanic Garden**, which has as its centrepiece the huge **Kibble Palace,** a greenhouse with plants from all over the world.

Glasgow Botanic Garden

The heart of the city is now **George Square**, a large open area surrounded by fine Victorian buildings. The most impressive are the dignified and confident **City Chambers**, and conducted tours are available round a building which more than any signifies the wealth and importance of Glasgow in the 19th century. The Square also has statues galore, and once a year a huge marquee houses an art exhibition where paintings can be bought.

Round the corner from George Square is **Hutcheson's Hall** (National Trust for Scotland), founded in 1641 as a hospital by brothers George and Thomas Hutcheson. The present building was designed by David Hamilton and dates from 1802-1805. Inside are portraits of famous Glaswegians, a gallery for exhibitions and a National Trust for Scotland gift shop.

It sits next to that area of the city known as the **Merchant City**. It once housed the homes and offices of the rich merchants who made their money from trading with the colonies, and is now a smart area full expensive apartment

blocks, trendy pubs, cafés and wine bars. The merchants who traded in tobacco were called the **Tobacco Barons**, and they became immensely rich, eventually building fine mansions on the outskirts of the city to show off their new found wealth and status.

In Queen Street is the **Gallery of Modern Art**, housed in what was one of the Tobacco Baron's fine town houses. It has been much altered since then, but is still an elegant building, with four floors of paintings and sculpture by such people as Sean Reid, Beryl Cook and Peter Howson.

A more modest home is to be found in Buccleuch Street, near Charing Cross. It is now called the **Tenement House** (National Trust for Scotland), and recreates a genteel first-floor tenement flat lived in by the city's lower middle classes in the early 20th century. The building dates from the late 19th century, and was lived in for over 50 years by Miss Agnes Toward. It is her personal possessions which you can see.

Charles Rennie Mackintosh is the city's most famous architect. He was born in 1868, the son of a policeman, and designed many buildings in the city. The most famous is the **Glasgow School of Art**, in Refrew Street, not far from the Tenement House. It is still a working art college, and conducted tours are available. Note the fine wrought iron railings around the windows. They aren't just there for show - Mackintosh designed them so that window cleaners could rest their ladders on them. **Martyr's School** in Parson Street is another example of Mackintosh's work, and is to be found close to the Royal Infirmary.

The **Lighthouse** is Scotland's "centre for architecture, design and the city". It is in Mitchell Lane in the city centre, in a building Mackintosh designed early in his career. There is a Mackintosh Room, a programme of exhibitions and a conference suite. On the south side of the river is **Scotland Street School**, another of his buildings. It is now a museum of education. Also on the south side is the **House for an Art Lover**, within Bellahouston Park. Mackintosh

submitted the design for this house to a competition in a German magazine, but it was never built during his lifetime. In the Hunterian Museum is the **Mackintosh House**, featuring the principle rooms from his own house, together with a collection of original sketches and water colours.

Another Glasgow architect who is now widely admired is Alexander Thomson, better known as **Greek Thomson** because of the Greek influences on his work. His best known building is **Holmwood House** (National Trust for Scotland) in Cathcart, south of the river. **St. Vincent Street Church** was also designed by him.

Glasgow, it is reckoned, has more parkland per head of population than any other British city, and there are many areas which have a distinctly rural aspect. **Pollok Country Park** lies on the south side of the city, and within it you will find Pollok House (National Trust for Scotland - see panel below). This

POLLOK HOUSE

Pollok Country Park, 2060 Pollokshaws Road, Glasgow G43 1AT
Tel: 0141 616 6410 Fax: 014) 616 6521
e-mail pollokhouse@nts.org.uk
website: www.nts.org.uk

Visit **Pollok House** and capture the flavour of one of Scotland's grandest Edwardian country houses. It is the ancestral home of the Maxwells of Pollok, who have lived on this site for 700 years. The present house, which

replaced three earlier structures, was begun in 1747. It was extended from 1890 by Sir John Stirling Maxwell, a founder member of The National Trust for Scotland.

The house contains much original furniture as well as some of the finest Spanish paintings in Britain. A rare survival is the magnificent suite of servants' quarters, which shows the scale of country house life around 1900. These contain the popular Edwardian Kitchen Restaurant, renowned for its lunch menu and home baking, and the shop in the Housekeeper's Room. At weekends, visitors can see a reconstruction, of the way the house might have been run at the turn of the last century. Pollok House is set amid formal and walled gardens at the heart of **Pollok Country Park**.

Georgian mansion belonged to the Stirling Maxwells, and now houses a collection of decorative arts. Also in the park is the **Burrell Collection**, housed in a purpose-built complex of galleries. William Burrell gifted a huge collection of objects to the City of Glasgow, and now over 8,000 of them are on display.

Glasgow Green has been called "Glasgow's lung", and it is here, near the city's east end, that you'll find the **People's Palace**. Using artifacts and displays it takes you through the history of the city. Close by is the former **Templeton's Carpet Factory**, based on a Venetian design, and now housing a business centre. In the genteel West End is another huge open area - **Kelvingrove Park**.

Glasgow is Britain's second largest shopping centre, the main shopping streets being Argyll Street, Buchanan Street and Sauchiehall Street. There are also huge malls. The **St. Enoch Centre** and the **Buchanan Galleries** are in the centre of the city, and have most of the large High Street names. At Braehead, to the west of the city, is the **Braehead Shopping Centre**, while The Forge is in Parkhead, near the east end.

Perhaps the trendiest and most exclusive retail developments are Princes Square, just off Buchanan Street, and the Italian Centre in the Merchant City, where Versace and Armani both have their outlets.

AROUND GLASGOW

KIRKINTILLOCH

7 miles NE of Glasgow city centre on the A803

Kirkintilloch sits on the **Forth and Clyde Canal**, which has recently been restored and reopened. The former parish church dates from 1644, and now houses the **Auld Kirk Museum**. In Peel Park are some slight remains of the **Antonine Wall**, built by the Romans.

CUMBERNAULD

12 miles NE of Glasgow city centre off the A80

The new town of Cumbernauld was founded to take some of the overspill population of Glasgow after World War II. The centre of the town sits on a hill above the A80, and was the setting for the early 1980s film *Gregory's Girl*. To the south east is **Palacecraigs Country Park**. It covers 750 acres, and was developed in the 1970s. Along with Kirkintilloch, the town was located in a detached part of Dunbartonshire up until local government reorganisation in the mid 1970s.

KILSYTH

11 miles NE of Glasgow city centre on the A803

This former mining town sits at the foot of the Kilsyth Hills. The **Battle of Kilsyth** battle took place here in 1645, when Montrose defeated a Covenanting army.

RUTHERGLEN

2 miles SE of Glasgow city centre on the A749

Rutherglen is one of the oldest royal burghs in Scotland, having been granted its charter in the 12th century by David I. For a short while it was incorporated into the city of Glasgow, something most of its fiercely independent inhabitants resented, but now it has become part of South Lanarkshire. The modern parish church sits in Main Street, and in its kirkyard is all that is left of the medieval **Parish Church** -the gable. The Town Hall, next to the kirkyard, dates from 1861.

NEWTON MEARNS

7 miles S of Glasgow city centre on the A77

Newton Mearns is a small, desirable suburb of Glasgow full of prosperous

Paisley Abbey

Abbey Church of Saints Mary the Virgin, James the Greater of Compostella, Mirin and Milburga, otherwise known as **Paisley Abbey**. It was founded in the 12th century by Walter FitzAlan, the first High Steward of Scotland, and ancestor of the great Stewart dynasty that ruled Scotland and latterly Britain. All the non-royal stewards are buried within its walls, as well as Robert III and Marjory, daughter of Robert I. It was Marjory who married the sixth High Steward of Scotland, and who died in childbirth giving birth to Robert II, the first Stewart king, in 1316. He was actually born in the abbey, so this great building can legitimately claim to be the cradle of the Stewarts.

bungalows and villas. **Mearns Parish Church**, a square, whitewashed building, dates from 1755. **Greenbank House** (National Trust for Scotland) is surrounded by beautiful gardens, though the elegant Georgian house itself is closed to the public. Gardening demonstrations are sometimes held.

CLYDEBANK

5 miles E of Glasgow city centre on the A814

In early 1941, the **Clydebank Blitz** flattened the centre of this shipbuilding town, and caused many deaths. In fact the town suffered more damage from air raids than any other place in Britain in proportion to its size. Now the centre has been redeveloped, though it is largely unattractive and sparse. The **Clydebank Museum** in the Town Hall has exhibits devoted to the Blitz, as well as to the Singer sewing machine factory that once stood here.

PAISLEY

5 miles W of Glasgow city centre on the A761

Paisley is often called the "largest town in Scotland". This is because the other, larger settlements of Glasgow, Edinburgh, Aberdeen and Dundee are cities. Its main building is the great

The building as you see it now dates from the 12th century onwards, though most of it comes from the 15th century. The ruined choir was rebuilt in the early 1900s, and the building is now the town's Parish Church. It contains a memorial to the Rev'd John Witherspoon, a former minister of the abbey, who was one of the signatories of the American Declaration of Independence. The burial place of Robert III is marked by a graveslab given to the abbey by Queen Victoria.

Another grand church in Paisley is the **Thomas Coats Memorial Baptist Church**, sometimes known as the "Baptist Cathedral of Europe" because of its size. It was built in 1894 in memory of Thomas Coats, of the J. & P. Coats thread making firm. The same Thomas gifted the **Coats Observatory** to the town's Philosophical Institution in 1883, and it is now open to the public. Adjacent is **Paisley Museum and Art Galleries**, with a display of Paisley shawls and other memorabilia.

At the corner of George Street and Shuttle Street are the small 18th century weavers' cottages known as the **Sma' Shot Cottages**. They house an interpretation centre which highlights the Paisley weavers of the past, especially their lives and living conditions. **Paisley Arts Centre** is in nearby New Street, in the former Laigh Kirk of 1878.

In 1774, Robert Tannahill the poet was born in **Tannahill Cottage** in Queen Street. He was a silk weaver who wrote the words to such beautiful songs as *Jessie the Flower o' Dunblane* and *The Braes o' Gleniffer*. The actual braes now form part of the **Gleniffer Braes Country Park**, just outside the town.

RENFREW

5 miles W of Glasgow city centre on the A741

This ancient royal burgh was granted its royal charter in 1143, making it one of the oldest in Scotland. The **Battle of Renfrew** was fought here in 1164 between the army of Somerled, Lord of the Isles, and that of Malcolm IV, king of Scots. The royal army was commanded by Walter FitzAlan, founder of Paisley Abbey, and Somerled was defeated. This defeat at last brought the Western Isles fully into the kingdom of Scotland.

BEARSDEN AND MILNGAVIE

6 miles NW of Glasgow city centre on the A809 and the A81

These two prosperous towns belong to Glasgow's commuting belt. They are full of large Edwardian villas and bungalows dating from the 1930s. The line of the Antonine Wall (named after Roman Emperor Antoninus

Pius) passes close by. It was built of turf in the 2nd century to keep out the warring tribesmen of the north, whom the Romans called Picts, and stretched for 37 miles from the Firth of Clyde to the Firth of Forth. In Bearsden there are also the remains of a **Roman Bathhouse**.

Mugdock Country Park sits off the A81 north of Milngavie (pronounced "Mul-guy"), and is the southern starting point for the 95-mile long **West Highland Way**, a long distance footpath which connects the Glasgow conurbation with Fort William.

DUMBARTON

This ancient royal burgh is dominated by an old volcanic plug on the shores of the Clyde which is over 240 feet high. On it sits **Dumbarton Castle** (Historic Scotland). It is one of the oldest fortified sites in Britain, and at one time was the capital of Strathclyde, a British kingdom that was absorbed into Scotland in the 11th century.

The name means the "fort of the Britons", and though the town is "Dumbarton", the former county was always "Dunbartonshire", with an "n". The castle consists mainly of barracks

Dumbarton Catsle and River Clyde

nowadays, but there is still plenty to see, including a fine 12th century gateway, a dungeon and a small museum. From the top of the hill there is a splendid view out over the Clyde, which widens out at this point into the Firth of Clyde.

The **Denny Tank Museum** forms part of the Scottish Maritime Museum, and is the oldest experimental water tank in the world. It is the length of a football field, and was built in 1882 to test models of the hull shapes of ships being built in Denny's shipyard in the town. On display are many of the models that were actually tested here.

In Church Street is an old archway called the **College Bow**, all that is left of the former Collegiate Church of St. Mary. **Overtoun Estate** is at the foot of the Kilpatrick Hills, and has many attractions, including historic gardens, wooded glens and gorges. Guided walks are available in the summer.

AROUND DUMBARTON

ALEXANDRIA
3 miles N of Dumbarton off the A82

This small, rather plain industrial town, in the valley of the Leven just south of Loch Lomond, is home to the **Antartex Village Visitor Centre**. It incorporates a factory making sheepskin coats (with tours available), a mill shop and a small craft village. Nearby is the **Lomond Factory Outlets and Motoring Memories Museum**, housed in the former Argyll factory, where "Argyll" motor cars - one of several makes of car once manufactured in Scotland - were assembled.

OLD KILPATRICK
2 miles E of Dumbarton off the A82

This small village, some people claim, is the birthplace of **St. Patrick**, patron saint of Ireland, though Wales may have a stronger claim. The village marked the western end of the Antonine Wall. The **Erskine Bridge** over the Clyde was opened in 1971 by Princess Anne.

BALLOCH
4 miles N of Dumbarton on the A811

The River Leven leaves **Loch Lomond** here and heads towards Dumbarton and the Clyde, four miles away. The loch, which covers 27 square miles, is Scotland's largest expanse of water, and some people reckon it is the most beautiful in Britain. **The Loch Lomond and Trossachs National Park** is the first such park in Scotland, and the **Loch Lomond Shores**, opened in 2002, includes the National Park Gateway.

The loch is at its widest at the south, then gradually gets narrower and deeper the further north it goes. At some points it reaches a depth of over 600 feet, making it the third deepest loch in Scotland. Many songs have been written about it, the most famous undoubtedly being *The Bonnie, Bonnie Banks o' Loch Lomond*. It was supposedly written by a Jacobite prisoner held in Carlisle Castle who was due to be executed. He is telling a fellow Jacobite prisoner, whose life has been spared, that he will take the "low road" (i.e. the road of death) to Scotland, while his colleague will take the "high road" (i.e. the overland road while still alive). The road of death will take him home sooner.

At the nearby village of **Gartocharn** is **Duncryne Hill**, nicknamed "The Dumpling" because of its shape, and you get a wonderful view from the top, not just of the loch, but of the surrounding countryside.

A line drawn across the loch from Glen Fruin to Balmaha follows the **Highland**

Boundary Fault, which separates the Highlands from the Lowlands. The Balloch Castle Country Park, north east of Balloch, has walks and gardens. The Leven Valley Heritage Trail takes you southwards from Balloch towards Dumbarton, passing through such small industrial towns as Renton and Alexandria. Renton has one unusual claim to fame. In 1888 its football team (now gone) beat West Bromwich Albion at Hampden Park to become football champions of the world.

Loch Lomond from Luss

Luss

11 miles N of Dumbarton off the A82

Luss is one of the most beautiful villages in Scotland, and for years has been the setting for Scotland's longest running soap opera, *High Road*, in which it is called Glendarroch. It was built as an estate village by the Colquhouns (pronounced "Ca-hoons") who owned the land, and sits right on the banks of

INVERBEG INN

Luss, Loch Lomondside, Dunbartonshire G83 8PD
Tel: 01436 860678 Fax: 01436 860686
e-mail: inverbeginn.co.uk
website: www.scottish.selection.co.uk

The **Inverbeg Inn** is one of the best known and best loved small hotels in Scotland. It sits on the banks of beautiful Loch Lomond, and has an enviable reputation for its hospitality and food. It dates back to 1814, and from it you get stunning views east towards Ben Lomond and Ben Vrackie. The accommodation is either within the hotel itself or in the newer Lodge, situated right by the loch side. There is a range of light, airy accommodation that goes from comfy individuality to sheer luxury, and in the Lodge there are three suites that are perfect for that special occasion. All the rooms and suites are, of course, fully en suite, and have everything you need for a relaxing and enjoyable stay - colour TV, courtesy tray with home made shortbread, trouser press, hair dryer, and direct dial telephone.

And the food is every bit as good as the accommodation. In fact, the hotel is well known for the high standards it sets in its kitchen. Only the finest and freshest of local produce is used, such as

scallops, beef, venison, salmon and mussels. Eat in the traditional, spacious dining room or have a tasty snack in the Caledonian Bar, where there is also a fine range of real Scottish ales and malt whiskies. The Inverbeg Inn is three miles north of Luss (where the TV soap *High Road* is filmed), and firmly in the Highlands. Yet it is easily accessible from Glasgow, with its airport being no more that a 40 minute drive away. For this reason, it makes an ideal touring base from which to explore Argyllshire, Glasgow, the Trossachs and Loch Lomondside.

WALK 3

Doune Hill

Start	Glenmollachan, at head of Glen Luss
Distance	7½ miles (12.1km)
Approximate time	5 hours
Parking	Very limited parking at Glenmollachan
Refreshments	None
Ordnance Survey maps	Outdoor Leisure 39 (Loch Lomond), Landranger 56 (Loch Lomond and Inveraray)

Although Doune Hill is officially 100ft or so below being a Corbett, its ascent, with that of Beinn Eich, makes an invigorating day out. Few summits achieve such a superlative 360° view, and after the usual initial hard slog of an hour or so the going is easy. Hills like this (its top is at 2,408ft/734m) are not to be despised and climbing this one will make the walker look forward to more days on the Luss hills. This is very much a hill for sheep, and dogs are unwelcome.

There are only about five or six parking spaces at Glenmollochan in Glen Luss, and if these are already occupied the only alternative is to use the car park in Luss village and stride the 2½miles (4km) up the glen. From Glenmollochan go up the lane to Edentaggart, taking in the view up Glen Mollochan at the second bridge.

After the farm (its yard can be bypassed through a sheepfold) continue up the track and pass through the gate. Here there is also a gate on the right **A** which gives access to the lower slopes of Beinn Eich. Go through this and climb up with the wall to the right; as you climb note the fine corrie (Coire Cann) on the other side of Glen Luss and the view of Loch Lomond which opens up to the east. Another gate ahead gives access to the open hill through a sheep fence. Continue to climb directly up to reach the ridge leading to the summit of Beinn Eich **B** (you will find several false summits en route). The path to this first objective runs on the top of a rocky causeway (with a low cliff to the left). Ben Lomond is well seen from here, as is the Cobbler. The summit proves to be a very narrow ridge with precipitous views down the glens on each side. The square-topped hill ahead is Cruach an t-Sidhein, though the ridge bends to the right of this towards Doune Hill. Peat banks are frequent obstacles before the start of the climb up Beinn Lochain.

Another short descent follows after you reach the summit **C** . Now Loch Long can be seen beyond Glen Douglas, as can the summits of the Arrochar Alps.

The short ascent to the triangulation pillar on Doune Hill **D** seems effortless after what has gone before. Few hills of such modest height can boast such a superb all-round view.

Climb down eastwards from the summit, taking care as the ground is steep and rough in places. The unnamed hill on the other side of Bealach an Duin looks a promising viewpoint but offers little that cannot be seen from Doune Hill. The bealach is criss-crossed by the tyre-marks of shepherds' trial bikes; follow the headwaters of the Mollochan Burn down to the glen. The way down is steep and tussocky and lacks an obvious path although old fencing posts to the right of the burn may be useful as rough guides. In spring and summer a wealth of wild flowers adorn the lower parts of the valley, amongst them several species of orchid.

At the bottom of the glen there is the vestige of a path in places but the way close to the burn is quite wet and difficult, and it is probably easiest to walk a little above the stream on the drier, north-eastern side of the glen. The Land Rover track begins (or ends) at what looks like the remains of a bothy **E**, and leads to the lane just above Glenmollochan, the starting point ●

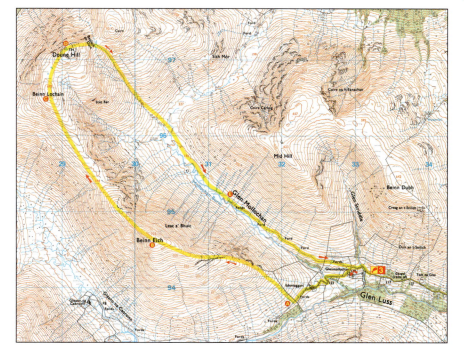

LOMONDBANK HOUSE

Tarbet, by Arrochar, Argyll, G83 7DG
Tel/Fax: 01301 702258
e-mail: brown-rebus@supanet.com

A warm welcome awaits you at **Lomondbank House**, a B&B establishment that combines all modern conveniences with good, old-fashioned Scottish hospitality. There are three individually decorated and furnished rooms on offer, all en suite and all with TVs and hospitality trays. The house sits on an elevated position, and the views out over Loch Lomond are stunning. The cooking is superb, and the breakfasts, whether full Scottish or something a wee bit lighter, are sure to set you up for a day's sightseeing in one of the most beautiful areas of Scotland.

Loch Lomond. **The Parish Church of St. Mackessog** is well worth a visit.

On the opposite side of the loch is the majestic bulk of Ben Lomond, the most southerly of Scotland's "Munros", or mountains over 3,000 feet high. It is a comfortable climb if you are reasonably fit and healthy. The loch itself has a number of islands, the chief one being **Inchmurrin**. A small ferry leaves from Midross on the mainland to take you across in 15 minutes. There is a hotel and a ruined castle. The island opposite Luss is **Inchlonaig**, the "island of the yew trees". Robert I's archers used the yew wood from the island to construct their bows.

HELENSBURGH

8 miles W of Dumbarton on the A814

This town is now within Argyllshire, though prior to local government reorganisation is was in Dunbartonshire. It is a planned town, laid out in the 18th

THE HILL HOUSE

Upper Colquhoun Street, Helensburgh G84 9AJ
Tel: 01436 673900 Fax: 01436 674685
website: www.nts.org.uk

The finest of Charles Rennie Mackintosh's domestic creations, **The Hill House** sits high above the Clyde, commanding fine views over the river estuary. Walter Blackie, director of the well known Glasgow publishers, commissioned not only the house and garden but much of the furniture and all the interior fittings and decorative schemes. Mackintosh's wife, Margaret MacDonald, contributed fabric designs and a unique gesso overmantel. The overall effect is daring, but restrained in its elegance: the result, timeless rooms, as modern today as they must have been in 1904 when the Blackie family moved in.

An information room interprets the special relationship between architect and patron and provides a historical context for Inspirations, a dazzling exhibition in the upper east wing and the gardens. It brings together exceptional pieces of domestic design by great living designers, all of whom, in some way, pay homage to Mackintosh's elegance and invention. Inspiring comparisons may be drawn between the work of Mackintosh, now recognised as one of the geniuses of the early 20th century, and pieces that themselves have become 21st century icons.

The gardens have been restored to their former glory, and reflect features common to Mackintosh's architectural designs. They also contain a kinetic sculpture given to the house by the artist George Rickey.

century by Sir James Colquhoun of Luss, and named after his wife. It is now a small holiday resort, and is one of the ports of call in July and August for the **PS Waverley**, the world's last ocean going paddle steamer, which plies the Clyde.

It was in Helensburgh, in 1888, that **John Logie Baird**, the inventor of television, was born. He was the first man to transmit TV pictures across the Atlantic, and also developed colour television. He first experimented with mechanical scanning, but moved over to electronic scanning - the system used today - when he saw its possibilities.

In Upper Colquhoun Street you will find one of the most significant buildings in Scotland - **The Hill House** (National Trust for Scotland - see panel opposite). It was designed by Charles Rennie Mackintosh for Walter Blackie the publisher in 1902, and is one of his finest achievements. He not only designed the building, he designed the interior decoration, some of the soft furnishings, the fittings and the furniture.

North of the town is **Glen Fruin**, which takes you via a narrow road to Loch Lomond. It was the scene of a battle in 1603 when the MacGregors defeated the Colquhouns with much loss of life.

CARDROSS

4 miles W of Dumbarton on the A814

Geilston Gardens (National Trust for Scotland) surround a late 17th century house (not open to the public). Its many attractive features include a fruit and vegetable garden, a walled garden and a burn winding through a small wooded glen. **St. Mahew's Chapel**, dates originally from 1294, but was restored in 1955. It was in the former **Cardross**

Castle that Robert I died from leprosy in 1329.

GARELOCHHEAD
14 miles NW of Dumbarton on the A814

This village sits at the head of the beautiful **Gare Loch**, which stretches inland from the Firth of Clyde for seven miles. It is a good centre for walking or sailing. At **Cove**, five miles south on the Rosneath Peninsula, are the **Linn Botanical Gardens**, which has over 200 species of rhododendron.

Greenock from Lyle Hill

GREENOCK

Greenock is a large industrial town and port on the south bank of the Clyde, near that point known as the **Tail of The Bank**, where the Firth turns south and widens out towards the open sea. In 1736 **James Watt**, who perfected the steam engine, was born here.

On a hill behind the town stands a huge **Cross of Lorraine**, mounted on an anchor. It dates from 1946, and commemorates the Free French sailors who lost their lives on the Atlantic during World War II. Many Scottish emigrants left their native land bound for America in the 19th century, and **Customhouse Quay** was a major point of departure. **The Custom House**, dating form 1810, reflects the fact that this was once a significant port. It now houses a small museum. Another museum is in the **McLean Museum and Art Gallery** on Kelly Street. It has displays and exhibits about local history, and paintings by such well known artists as Boudin, Courbin and the Scottish Colourists.

In Greenock Cemetery is the grave of **Highland Mary**, Burns' lover. Her full name was Mary Campbell, and she had agreed to accompany him when he planned to emigrate to Jamaica. Unfortunately, on her was home to Dunoon to make arrangements, she died. She was formerly buried in the kirkyard of the Old West Kirk, but was reburied in 1920. This church, which dated from the late 16th century, was dismantled in 1926, with some of the stones being used to build the **New West Kirk**, on the Esplanade. It contains some good stained glass and wood carving.

McLean Museum and Art Gallery

AROUND GREENOCK

Port Glasgow

3 miles E of Greenock on the A8

Before the River Clyde was deepened in the 18th century, this town, as its name implies, was the main port for the City of Glasgow. Situated on the shore, and once surrounded by uncompromising industrial buildings, stands **Newark Castle** (Historic Scotland). It was originally built in the 15th century by George Maxwell, and enlarged by his descendant, Patrick. He gained notoriety by murdering two neighbours and beating his wife, to whom he had been married for 44 years, and who bore him 16 children.

Finlaystone Estate

5 miles E of Greenock off the A8

This estate is open to the public, and is the home of the present head of Clan MacMillan. There are gardens and 140 acres of woodland. Finlaystone House, at the heart of the estate, dates back to the 14th century, though it has been enlarged and altered over the years. Tours are possible by prior arrangement.

Kilbarchan

11 miles SE of Greenock, off the A761

Kilbarchan is undoubtedly the most picturesque village in Renfrewshire, and is a huddle of 18th century weaving cottages. The **Weaver's Cottage** (National Trust for Scotland) dates from 1723, and shows what a weaver's cottage would have looked like in the early 18th century. It has a working loom, where demonstrations are sometimes given.

Lochwinnoch, which was also a weaving village, lies a few miles south, with the **Clyde Muirshiel Regional Park** close by. There are nature trails,

moorland walks and watersports on Castle Semple Loch.

Gourock

2 miles W of Greenock on the A770

When Glaswegians took their holidays in Firth of Clyde resorts, Gourock was one of the most popular. It is now joined on to Greenock, though it was once a separate, proud burgh. It sits on the south bank of the Clyde, at a point where the scenery is particularly attractive. On the north bank can be seen the Rosneath Peninsula, the Gare Loch and the entrance to Loch Long, and behind these the majestic hills of Argyllshire.

The Firth of Clyde is famous as being a centre for yachting, and Gourock is the home of the **Royal Gourock Yacht Club**, situated near the Promenade. Between Kempock Street and Castle Gardens is the famous **Granny Kempock's Stone**, which dates from prehistoric times. It gets its name because it is shaped like a cloaked figure, and to walk around it is said to bring good luck. At Cloch Point, four miles south west of the town, is the **Cloch Lighthouse**, built in 1797. It is a famous landmark for ships sailing up the Firth towards Glasgow or Greenock.

HAMILTON

Hamilton is a large, bustling town that was once the county town of Lanarkshire. It was created a royal burgh in 1548, though it lost its royal status in 1669. One of the most prominent landmarks in the town is the **County Buildings** in Almada Street, a skyscraper that was once the headquarters of Lanarkshire County Council, but is now occupied by South Lanarkshire Council. They were built in the early 1960s, and are modelled on the United Nations building in New York.

Chatelherault and the Avon Gorge

Start	Chatelherault Country Park, off A72 near Ferniegair to the south of Hamilton
Distance	5 miles (8km) - shorter version 3½mile (5.6km)
Approximate time	2½ hours (1½ hours for shorter walk)
Parking	Chatelherault Country Park
Refreshments	Café at the visitor centre
Ordnance Survey maps	Landranger 64 (Glasgow, Motherwell & Airdriek), Pathfinder 431, NS65/75 (Hamilton)

Almost the whole of this highly attractive walk is either along the edge of, or through, the beautiful woodlands that clothe the sides of the Avon Gorge, sometimes above and sometimes below the river. The country park is based around Chatelherault, a former hunting-lodge of the dukes of Hamilton, and there is plenty of historic interest in the restored lodge itself, the nearby scanty ruins of Cadzow Castle and the Duke's Monument. All the paths are clear, well surfaced and well signposted. The shorter version of the walk omits the detour to the Duke's Monument.

There is nothing Scottish sounding about Chatelherault. The name is that of a French duchy, a gift from the French king to the Hamilton family for helping to arrange the betrothal of Mary, Queen of Scots to the dauphin in 1548. The house was built in the 18th century as a hunting lodge and summerhouse for the 5th duke of Hamilton and was part of an overall design, linked to Hamilton Palace by a Grand Avenue of trees. Mining subsidence led to the demolition of Hamilton Palace in the 1920s, and Chatelherault fell into ruin after World War II. It was restored as a museum in the 1980s, and part of the High Parks estate, formerly a royal and later a ducal hunting forest, became a country park. Although the palace has gone, the view from the front of the lodge is still impressive, stretching northwards across the park to Hamilton and the 18th century mausoleum, and beyond that to the urbanised Clyde Valley on the fringes of Glasgow.

The walk begins in front of the visitor centre, which was once the kennels for the hunting dogs. Facing the building, turn left along a tarmac path, signposted "Riverside Walks". The path heads gently downhill, does a U-bend to the left, continues down and bends right to cross the Duke's Bridge high above the River Avon. From here there are fine views both up and down the river. Head uphill and bend right to pass to the left of the scanty remains of Cadzow Castle, believed to have been built in the early 16th century by James Hamilton, who also built the nearby Craignethan Castle.

After passing the castle, follow the tarmac path around a left bend to a T-junction of paths in front of a gate Ⓐ.

For the short walk, turn left here in the "Cadzow Oaks and White Bridge" direction.

WALK 4

The full version of the walk makes a detour to the Duke's Monument. Turn right at the T-junction on to a path which twists and turns, keeping along the top-left inside edge of woodland for most of the time. To the left are fine views across the pastures of High Parks, dotted with some of the ancient Cadzow Oaks. On reaching a sign to the Duke's Monument, bear right along a tarmac drive to the Grecian-style memorial, **B** erected in honour of the 11th duke of Hamilton. After his death in 1863, £1,500 was raised by friends and tenants and the dramatic site above the Avon Gorge was chosen by his wife because it commanded a view of both Chatelherault and the former ducal palace. The bronze bust of the duke was moved to the courtyard of the visitor centre for safety.

Walk back along the drive and at the first sign to Chatelherault and Cadzow Castle – where the drive curves right – keep ahead along a path through woodland to a T-junction **C**. Turn left – here picking up the earlier route – and re-trace your steps to the T-junction where you rejoin the shorter walk **A**.

Keep ahead along an enclosed path to a T-junction and turn right to join the Avon Walkway. Follow an attractive and well-surfaced path which twists and turns along the top-right edge of woodland above the Avon Gorge for nearly 1½ miles (2.4km). The path passes through mixed broad-leaved and conifer woodland and there are more fine views to the right of some of the ancient Cadzow Oaks.

At a sign "White Bridge and Chatelherault", turn left **D** on to a path into the trees and at a fork, continue along the left-hand path which descends, via steps and more twists and turns, to cross the White Bridge over the River Avon. This is another delightful spot, with more grand views both up and downstream. On the other side the path turns left to keep alongside or just above the river through more beautiful mixed woodland.

Later the path ascends to a fork by a stand of Douglas Fir. At this point continue along the right-hand upper path, heading gently uphill through dark conifers to a gate. Pass beside it and turn right to return to the start.●

Chatelherault Country Park

The town has close connections with the Dukes of Hamilton, Scotland's premier peers, who nowadays live in East Lothian. Up until the 1920s, the immense **Hamilton Palace** stood to the north east of the town, close to the River Clyde. Then, in one of the grossest acts of vandalism ever to be perpetrated in Scotland, it was pulled down. It was said to be the grandest non-royal residence in Britain, and the official reason for its demolition was given as subsidence from coal mines worked beneath it by the Duke himself. But though there were coal mines in the area, the Duke had instructed that no mines were to be driven beneath the Palace.

Not a stone of it now remains above ground, though the grandiose **Hamilton Mausoleum** still stands. It is a curious, circular building topped with an immense dome, and is full of Masonic symbolism. There is a chapel above and a crypt below, and was built by Alexander, the tenth Duke, in the mid-19th century as a burial place both for himself and his ancestors. The upper chapel is said to have one of the longest echoes of any building in Britain. Alexander had his ancestors removed from a burial vault in

the old Collegiate Church of St. Mary (now demolished) and reinterred in the crypt. When he himself died in 1852 he was laid in the sarcophagus of an ancient Egyptian princess and placed in the upper chapel.

All the bodies, however, were removed in 1921 and buried in the town's Bent Cemetery, the Duke still inside the sarcophagus. Near the grave is the burial place of one of Scotland's most popular entertainers - **Sir Harry Lauder**. The mausoleum is now open to the public, and visitors should look out for the doors of the crypt, which lock from the inside as well as the outside. The reason is simple - when the bodies and their coffins reposed there, a servant from Hamilton Palace was sent once a month to dust them down and sweep the floor. The doors were locked from the inside to prevent ghoulish sightseers from peering inside, though a policeman always stood on guard when the maid was carrying out her task.

An avenue of trees once stretched the two miles from Hamilton Palace to the hunting lodge of **Chatelherault**, east of the town. Most of the avenue is gone now, though Chatelherault (pronounced "Shattley-Row") is still standing. It was designed by William Adam and built in the 1730s as a hunting lodge and kennels for the Dukes of Hamilton. Indeed it was known at the time as the "dog kennels". The building looks imposing, but is no more than one room deep throughout. It was completely refurbished in the 1980s, and is now the centrepiece of a huge country park called **Chatelherault**

Country Park. It got its name because at one time the Dukes of Hamilton were also the Dukes of Chatellerault (note the different spelling) near Poitou in France. The title was bestowed on them in 1548 by Henry II of France for their help in arranging the marriage of Mary Stuart to the young Dauphin, heir to the French throne.

The park has over ten miles of woodland walks, plus the ruins of **Cadzow Castle**, once visited by Mary Stuart. This was the original home of the Hamiltons until they moved into what was to become Hamilton Palace. At the time they moved, they changed the name of the town from Cadzow to Hamilton. There are also the remains of an Iron Age Fort and the **Cadzow Oaks**, which are said to be over 500 years old. In a field is a small heard of White Cattle, descendants of the original wild cattle that once roamed the country.

Hamilton Parish Church was built at the same time as Chatelherault, and was also designed by William Adam. It is in the shape of a Greek cross, with a cupola over the crossing. In front of the church stands the pre-Norman **Netherton Cross**, and in the kirkyard is the **Heads Monument**, commemorating four Covenantors beheaded in Edinburgh after the Pentland Uprising of 1666.

The **Low Parks Museum** is housed in a former coaching inn dating from the 18th century. It has exhibits and displays about local history, and has a special display about Lanarkshire's own regiment - **The Cameronians (Scottish Rifles)**. Raised as a Covenanting force in the 17th century, it choose to disband itself in 1966 rather than amalgamate with another regiment.

Hamilton is the start of a tourist trail called the **Clyde Valley Tourist Route**, which follows the Clyde Valley south to Abington and the M74 motorway.

AROUND HAMILTON

MOTHERWELL AND WISHAW
3 miles E of Hamilton on the A721

Though they are separate towns, these two industrial settlements were, until 1975, classed as one burgh. Steel making was the main industry here, though all vestiges of the famous Ravenscraig works have now gone. The award-winning **Motherwell Heritage Centre** on High Road tells the story of the towns and their industries. To the west of Motherwell is **Strathclyde Park**, which covers 1,100 acres. It was laid out on waste ground in the 1970s, and its artificial loch (created by diverting the course of the Clyde) hosted the rowing events during the 1986 Commonwealth Games, held in Edinburgh. On its banks are the remains of a **Roman Bathhouse**, and there are guided walks as well as nature trails and a camping and caravan park.

DALSERF
6 miles E of Hamilton off the A72

This tiny Clyde Valley hamlet was once a sizable village, with inns and a ferry across the Clyde. Now it has no more than a few old, picturesque cottages and **Dalserf Parish Church**. It was built in 1655, though an old chapel dedicated to St. Serf once stood on the site. With its whitewashed walls and its rectangular windows, it looks more like a small house than a church, and while not being a thing of beauty, it has a quiet charm about it. In the kirkyard is a pre-Norman "hogs back" graveslab, which was dug up in 1897.

The **Rev'd John Macmillan** was known as the "last of the Covenantors", and a memorial to him can be seen in the kirkyard. His followers were called Macmillanites, and he died in 1753.

STRATHAVEN

7 miles S of Hamilton on the A726

As the name suggests, Strathaven (pronounced "Stray-ven") sits in the valley of the River Avon, a tributary of the Clyde. It is a pleasant little country town, and has the ruins of **Strathaven Castle**, all that is left of a once large and powerful 14th century stronghold. It was built by the Stewarts, and then fell into the hands of the powerful Hamiltons. A legend says that, before the Reformation, one of the castle's owners had his wife walled up alive in the castle, and when parts of a wall fell down in the 19th century, human bones were discovered among the rubble.

The **John Hastie Museum** sits at the edge of the John Hastie Park, and has collections to do with local history. To the west of the town is the site of the **Battle of Drumclog**, fought in 1679 between Government troops and a Covenanting army. A small memorial on a minor road off the A71 commemorates the event.

EAST KILBRIDE

5 miles W of Hamilton on the A726

Since the small village of East Kilbride was designated as Scotland's first post-war new town in 1947, it has gown into a large and thriving town with a population of just under 70,000 people. Its main claim to fame is its shopping facilities. There are three under-cover malls, **Princes Mall**, the **Olympia Centre** and **The Plaza**, and all offer the usual High Street names. A new mall recently opened, which means that the town has one of the largest under-cover shopping centres in Britain.

In the Calderwood area of the town is the **Hunter Museum**, housed in the farmhouse of Long Calderwood, where the Hunter Brothers were born in the

18th century. They were pioneers of surgery, and worked both in London and Glasgow, and a small display highlights their lives and achievements. The Hunterian Museum in Glasgow is named after them.

On the outskirts of the town is **Calderwood Country Park**, based around Torrance House (not open to the public). It has play areas, a small zoo, nature trails and riverside walks. To the north of the town is the **James Hamilton Heritage Park**, with a 16-acre boating loch. Behind it is the restored 15th century **Mains Castle** (not open to the public). Close by is the **Scottish Museum of Country Life**, run jointly by the National Trust for Scotland and the Royal Museums. It is based around Wester Kittochside Farm, which had been home to the Reid family since the 16th century. In 1992 it was gifted to the National Trust or Scotland by Margaret Reid, the last of the family. The museum houses Scotland's national collection of agricultural implements and machinery, and the elegant farmhouse of Wester Kittochside, which dates from 1783, is also open to the public.

EAGLESHAM

9 miles W of Hamilton on the B764

This picturesque village was planned and laid out by the 10th Earl of Eglinton in the mid 1700s. It has a plan like a huge latter "A", with the point facing moorland behind the village. The horizontal bar of the "A" passes through an enormous village green known as **The Orry**, on which at one time stood a cotton mill. The period cottages and houses, all smartly painted, give a perfect picture of Scottish rural life, though the village now owes more to business people who have snapped up properties here and who commute northwards into Glasgow each day. The **Parish Church** dates from 1788, and has an Alpine look about it. This isn't surprising, as the Earl was an admirer of the many small villages in Northern Italy.

Eaglesham came to the world's attention in 1941 when **Rudolph Hess**, Hitler's deputy, landed in a field in a nearby farm, after flying from Germany in an ME 110. He parachuted from the plane (while it was upside down) and was taken by farmer David McLean to his house, where he was treated fairly and firmly. He gave his name as Alfred Horn, but his real identity was soon established. He said he was on a secret mission to the Duke of Hamilton, and had been aiming to land near Dungavel House, a Hamilton hunting lodge some miles away.

He was then taken to Maryhill Barracks in Glasgow, where he was sometimes in the custody of William Ross, then a corporal, but later the Secretary of State for Scotland. Hess was later moved to Buchanan Castle near Drymen in Stirlingshire, where he was interrogated.

BOTHWELL

2 miles NW of Hamilton off the M74

In the centre of this small, prosperous town is **St. Bride's Parish Church**, which has a chancel dating from 1398 and a nave and tower dating from 1833. The chancel was built as part of a grand collegiate church founded by Archibald the Grim, 3rd Earl of Douglas, and has a roof made entirely of stone slabs. Outside the west end of the nave is a memorial to **Joanna Bailey**, a poet and playwright born in the Manse of Bothwell in 1762. She was much admired in her time, and Sir Walter Scott praised her as being one of the finest writers of the late 18th century.

Some distance from the town are the extensive ruins of **Bothwell Castle** (Historic Scotland). Historians have

called it one of the finest surviving secular medieval buildings in Scotland. It was originally built in the 13th century by Walter de Moravia, and its thick, red sandstone walls still look impressive. The mighty Donjon, or tower, is one of the finest in Scotland.

Upstream from the castle is **Bothwell Bridge**, site of a famous battle in 1679 between Covenantors and Royalist forces commanded by the Duke of Monmouth. The Covenantors were heavily defeated, with over 500 being killed and 1,200 taken prisoner. A memorial commemorates the event. The bridge you see today is basically the same structure, though it has been altered and widened over the years.

BLANTYRE

3 miles NW of Hamilton on the A724

This plain, former mining town is visited mainly for the **David Livingstone Centre** (National Trust for Scotland), which sits close to the banks of the Clyde. Here, in a tenement block called Shuttle Row, the famous African explorer, missionary and doctor was born in 1813. The birth room is, in fact, a one-room flat, though the whole of the building has been given over to displays and exhibits. It was built to house the workers in a great cotton mill which one stood on the banks of the river. Livingstone himself worked in it for a while.

LANARK

Set above the valley of the River Clyde at its upper reaches, Lanark has its roots deep in Scotland's history. Every year, in June, the town celebrates Lanimer Day, which originated as a ceremony of riding the boundaries of the burgh and its common lands.

High on a wall of the 18th century **St. Nicholas Church** is a statue of William

Wallace the Scottish freedom fighter. It recalls that when the town's castle (now gone) was garrisoned by English troops, he was taken captive and imprisoned within it. With the help of his "lenman" or sweetheart, he managed to escape. For this, she was publicly executed by the English sheriff. To avenge her death, Wallace returned and personally killed the sheriff himself. In the Westport you'll find the **Royal Burgh of Lanark Museum**, which explains the incident, as well as other aspects of the town's history.

The ruins of **St. Kentigern's Church** lie near the centre of the town. This was the original parish church, and in its kirkyard is the grave of **William Smellie** (pronounced "Smillie"), the father of modern midwifery, who died in 1763.

New Lanark lies in the Clyde Valley proper, on the banks of the river. It is a World Heritage Site, and it was here, in

1785, that David Dale founded a new cotton mill village of 2,500 people than was to become a model for social reform. Under his son-in-law Robert Owen, who was the mill manager, there were good working conditions, decent homes, fair wages, schools and health care. The mills were still in production as late as 1968, but now the whole village has been turned into one great museum and interpretation centre. It is under the care of the New Lanark Conservation Trust, and has become one of the most popular tourist destinations in Britain, even though most of the tenements are still occupied by families.

Attractions include a **Visitor Centre**, where there is a New Millennium Ride and a Textile Machinery Exhibition, a Millworker's House, the Village Store Exhibition and Robert Owen's House. A 3-D show called Annie McLeod's Story is shown in Robert Owen's School, and uses

New Lanark

BIGGAR

10 miles SE of Lanark on the A702

This small, pleasant country town was once a place of great importance, and was granted burgh status in 1451. There must be more museums per head of population in it than any other comparable town in Britain.

The **Biggar Gas Works Museum**, housed in the town's former gas works, explains the processes involved in producing gas from coal, and the **Moat Heritage Centre** has displays which explains the history of the area from millions of years ago up until the present day. **Greenhill Covenantors House** explains more recent history - that of the Covenantors in the 17th century, when people resisted the attempts of Charles II to make the Church of Scotland Episcopalian, and sometimes paid with their lives. The house originally stood at Wiston, 10 miles away, but was dismantled and taken stone by stone to Biggar. It now celebrates the struggles and hardships of the Covenanting movement.

the latest digital technology. Also in the village is a **Scottish Wildlife Trust Visitors Centre**.

The mills were powered by the waters of the Clyde, and close by are the **Falls of Clyde** waterfalls, the most famous being Cora Lynn and Bonnington. However, a hydroelectric electric scheme now harnesses the power of the water, which bypasses the Falls and goes through turbines in the power station. The Falls are therefore only seen at their most spectacular at certain times of the year, when the turbines are undergoing maintenance.

AROUND LANARK

CARLUKE

9 miles SE of Hamilton on the A73

This small, unremarkable town stands above the Clyde Valley, which at one time was noted for its orchards. The bell tower of the former Parish Church, dating from 1715, still stands near the centre of the town.

Biggar

The **Gladstone Court Museum** has a recreated Victorian street, with dressmakers, boot makers and even a schoolroom. And the Albion Building houses the **Albion Motor Archives**, which are the records of the famous Albion Motor Company, which was founded locally in 1899. It grew to be the largest manufacturer of commercial vehicles in the British Empire, and is now part of Leyland DAF. **Brownsbank Cottage**, a mile and a half from town, was the home of the Scottish poet Christopher Grieve, better known as Hugh McDiarmid. He died in 1978, and his widow Velda continued to live there until she too died in 1989. It has now been restored to exactly how it was when McDiarmid lived there, and is home to a writer-in-residence. It can be visited by appointment only.

The **Biggar Puppet Theatre** is a professional company of puppeteers who work out of a small, Victorian theatre that seats 100 people. It is Scotland's largest puppet company, and regularly tours Britain.

To the west of the town are the villages of **Abington** and **Crawford**. They sit just off the M74, and make good stopping off points as you head north or south from Glasgow or Carlisle.

CARMICHAEL

4 miles S of Lanark on a minor road W of the A73

The **Discover Carmichael Visitors Centre** is situated on the Carmichael Estate, and has a display of waxwork models that depict famous charters and events in Scotland's history, such as the execution of Mary Stuart. There is also a small display about wind energy.

Carmichael Parish Church dates from 1750, and has a laird's loft, where the local laird and his family worshipped away from the prying eyes of the main

SKIRLING HOUSE

Skirling, by Biggar, Lanarkshire ML12 6HD
Tel: 01899 860274 Fax: 01899 860255
e-mail: enquiry@skirlinghouse.com.
website: www.skirlinghouse.com

Skirling House provides high quality accommodation and fine dining amid luxurious surroundings of beautiful paintings, rich fabrics and antiques. The house was designed by the Arts & Crafts architect Ramsay Traquair in, in 1908 for Lord Charmichael, a prominent art collector at the time. Used as his country retreat, it contained his art collection, inlcuing a magnificent 16th century Florentine carved wooden ceiling, which can now be seen in the drawing room. The Arts & Crafts influence can also be seen in the ornate wrought ironwork and the decorative carvings.

Bob Hunter is the proprietor and chef of this house, set amid lovely Borders scenery, and is helped by his wife, Isobel when she is not at work in Edinburgh. The five en-suite bedrooms are large and

comfortable with TV's and hospitality trays, and the breakfasts are delicious, including dishes such as scrambled eggs with smoked salmon. The dinner menu is imaginative and beautifully presented, with the emphasis on fresh local produce including meat, fish and cheese. The vegetables, as much as possible, are grown in the house garden. A good wine list ensures the perfect accompaniment to your meal. In summer drinks can be taken in the garden and in winter, afternoon tea can be taken in the drawing room with its comfortable sofas and open log fire, making this a perfect place to relax, take a stroll in the countryside or explore the local historic attractions.

CROSSRIDGE COUNTRY COTTAGES

Crossridge House, Carmichael, near Biggar,
South Lanarkshire ML12 6NG
Tel: 01555 880455/880589 e-mail: crossridge.house@amserve.net
Fax: 01555 880493 website: www.crossridgeholidaycottages.co.uk

Crossridge Country Cottages are located between Edinburgh and Glasgow, and amidst beautiful countryside. Here you will find superior self catering accommodation in cottages over 200 years old, which have been tastefully converted to offer all modern amenities and can sleep up to four people. The lounges are comfortable, with two single sofa beds, the kitchens are well equipped and the double bedrooms are beautifully decorated and furnished with pine furniture. The bathrooms have bath/shower, toilet and wash hand basin.

congregation. One of the lairds of old, the Earl of Hyndford, left a sum of money called the Hyndford Mortification to provide a yearly pair of trousers and a supply of whisky for the local schoolmaster.

LEADHILLS

18 miles S of Lanark on the B797

Like its sister village of Wanlockhead in Dumfriesshire, Leadhills is a former lead mining village high in the Lowther Hills. It has the highest golf course in Scotland, and is full of 18th and 19th century cottages that once housed the lead miners. Here you will find the main station for the Leadhills and Wanlockhead Light Railway, which runs on a narrow gauge track, and is the highest adhesion railway in Britain. The **Allan Ramsay Library** is the oldest subscription library in Scotland, and is named after the famous poet, who was born in the village in 1684. In the graveyard is the tomb of John Taylor, who died so the headstone says, when he was 137 years old. Next to the cemetery is a monument to **William Symington**, who was born in the village in 1764. He worked as an engineer in the local lead mines, and was a pioneer of steam driven ships. His paddle boat the Charlotte Dundas was launched at Grangemouth in Stirlingshire in 1802.

DOUGLAS

8 miles SW of Lanark on the A70

Though it is a former mining village, there is much history in Douglas. In 1968 the disbandment of the Scottish regiment The Cameronians (Scottish Rifles) took place in the grounds of **Castle Dangerous**, ancestral home of the Douglases, of which only a tower now survives. It was here that the regiment was first raised in 1689 by **James, Earl of Angus**, whose statue stands in the centre of the village.

The centre of the village is a conservation area, with many old cottages and houses. The **Sun Inn** of 1621 was once the village tolbooth, where justice was dispensed. **Old St Bride's** is the choir of the former parish church, and dates from the 14th century. Within it are memorials and funerary monuments to members of the Douglas family, including Archibald, the 5th Earl of Angus, who was killed at Flodden, and whose nickname was Bell the Cat. There is also a memorial to the **Good Sir James of Douglas**, killed by the Moors in Spain while taking Robert I's heart to the Holy Land for burial.

The clock in the clock tower was a gifted to the church by Mary Queen of Scots in 1565, and is the oldest working clock in Scotland.

LOCATOR MAP

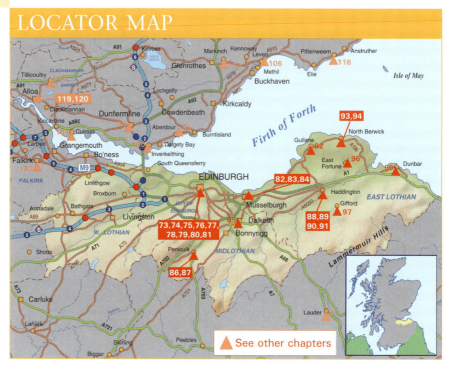

See other chapters

ADVERTISERS AND PLACES OF INTEREST

5 EDINBURGH AND THE LOTHIANS

The area consists of three former counties - West Lothian, Midlothian and East Lothian. At one time they were called, respectively, Linlithgowshire. Edinburghshire and Haddingtonshire, after their main towns. Towards the shores of the Firth of Forth, the land is generally low lying and fertile, with higher ground the further south you go. Both West Lothian and Midlothian were once coal mining areas, but now all vestiges of the industry have disappeared, while East Lothian is largely agricultural, though there were small pockets of industry where it bordered with Midlothian.

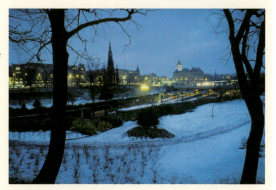

Princes Street, Edinburgh

The whole area is at the heart of Scottish history, and it is full of quiet pastoral villages, marvellous scenery, castles, churches and grand houses. There was certainly industry here, but it never intruded in the way that it did in West Central Scotland, though Bathgate, Dalkeith and the new town of

Seals, Newhaven

Livingston are largely industrial towns. And the hills to the south of the Lothians- the Pentlands and the Moorfoots - are well worth exploring. They are not as rugged or grand as, say, the Highlands, or some parts of the Borders, but their high, bleak moorland and their hidden glens have a lonely beauty.

The Pentland Hills are to the south west of the city, and stretch towards Lanarkshire. They are gloriously austere, rising to an area of moorland that is gaunt without being forbidding. The Moorfoots are to the south, and stretch

Tantallon Castle

down into the Borders. To the south east are the Lammermuirs, which also stretch down into the Borders, and which provide a wonderful backdrop for the soft, verdant scenery of East Lothian. Here you will find Haddington, a gem of a place, and one of the loveliest towns in Scotland. There is also a varied coastline, which takes in such former holiday resorts as Dunbar and North Berwick, and many golf courses. The countryside is particularly attractive, with old villages, ancient churches, woodland and quiet country lanes.

West Lothian has a history of mining shale and coal, though most vestiges of these industries have now disappeared, apart from a few red shale waste heaps (known as "bings" in Scotland). Linlithgow, while not its largest town, is certainly its most important historically speaking. Within its royal palace Mary Stuart was born in 1542.

Midlothian also had coal mines at one time, though they have now all disappeared as well. There is still history here, however, and Rosslyn Chapel, Crichton Castle and the Scottish Mining Museum at Newtongrange should not be missed.

Dominating the area, of course, is the City of Edinburgh, Scotland's capital. It's an ancient place, and probably has more history attached to it than any other comparable city in the world. Some people have even claimed that it is the standard against which we should judge other cities. A fortnight is not enough to take in all that it has to offer. St. Giles Cathedral -

Craigmiller Castle

the Palace of Holyroodhouse - Edinburgh Castle - the museums and art galleries - the Royal Mile - the Scott Monument - the New Town - all are household names, and all have a fascination and a story that goes deep into Scottish history.

EDINBURGH

Edinburgh has rightly earned its nickname of the "Athens of the North", as it brims with beautiful buildings and positively overflows with history. It is Scotland's capital city, an honour it has held since medieval times. Whereas Glasgow has had to work hard on its image, Edinburgh has not, though this has meant that the place has become complacent on occasions.

But because of the new Scottish Parliament, Edinburgh has rediscovered itself, and the world has rediscovered it as well. There is a buzz about the place, and it has become one of the most desirable cities in which to live in Britain. But even before it had the new parliament, it still played a vital part in the life of modern Scotland, as the Church of Scotland's headquarters are here, as well as the country's chief law courts. And it is important in a European context as well - it is the sixth most important financial centre in Europe, with millions of pounds passing through its financial institutions each week.

Edinburgh's crowning glory is **Edinburgh Castle**, which sits high on a volcanic plug overlooking the city. Though there has been a fortification of some kind on the site for thousands of years, the first stone castle was built by Malcolm III in the 11th century. His wife was Margaret, who was later canonised, and she swept away the old monastic Celtic church and placed it under the jurisdiction of Rome. The castle as you see it now is not a thing of great beauty, though the years have given it a quiet dignity. It dates from all periods, with the earliest building being the tiny **St. Margaret's Chapel**, dating from the 12th century. It was most probably founded by Margaret's son, David I, in her memory.

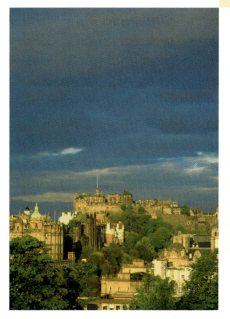
Edinburgh Castle

The castle is the second most visited historic attraction in Britain after the Tower of London, helped no doubt by the yearly **Edinburgh Military Tattoo**, an extravaganza of military bands, marching and spectacle which takes place on the **Castle Esplanade** every year in August. On the Esplanade is the **Tomb of Ensign Ewart** of the Royal Scots Greys, now called the Royal Scots Dragoon Guards. Charles Ewart was a sergeant serving with the regiment at the Battle of Waterloo in 1815 who captured the Imperial Eagle Standard of the French 45th Regiment, and who was promoted to ensign for his bravery. He died in Manchester in 1846, but his remains were brought back to Edinburgh in 1938 and reinterred on the Esplanade.

Overlooking the esplanade is the **Half Moon Battery**, built by Regent Morton in the 16th century. Behind it is the **National War Memorial**, designed by

Robert Lorimer, which lists the names of all Scottish soldiers killed in the 20th century. The **King's Lodgings** are opposite, and it was here that Scottish monarchs had their apartments. They date from the 15th century and later, and it was here, in 1566, that Mary Stuart gave birth to James VI of Scotland and I of England. A curious legend grew up about the birth which stated that Mary's child had been stillborn, and that another baby was substituted. When the birth room was being refurbished at a later date, the bones of a new born child were found entombed in the walls.

The Scottish crown jewels, known as the **Honours of Scotland**, can be seen in the **Crown Chamber**, along with the **Stone of Destiny**. It was supposed to have been the pillow on which the Biblical Jacob slept, and numerous Irish and Scottish kings up until the late 13th century were crowned sitting on it.

Then, in 1297, Edward I of England took it from Scone Abbey near Perth, and it lay in Westminster Abbey for 700 years. Some people claim, however, that the monks of Scone Abbey fooled Edward by giving him a worthless drain cover and hiding the real stone. Others claim that when the stone was "liberated" from Westminster Abbey by Scottish Nationalists in 1953, another stone was substituted by the perpetrators when it was returned, and the the real stone still lies hidden in Scotland somewhere. Also within the castle is the **National War Museum of Scotland**, which explores military service in Scotland for the last 400 years.

The **Royal Mile** is a long thoroughfare that leads down a narrow ridge from the castle towards the **Palace of Holyroodhouse**. In reality, it is a number of streets, starting off with Castlehill, then passing through the Lawnmarket,

Mr Wood's Fossils

5 Cowgatehead, Grassmarket, Edinburgh EH1 1JY
Tel: 0131 220 1344
e-mail: mwfossils@blueyonder.co.uk
website: www.mrwoodsfossils.co.uk

If you're looking for an unusual gift or souvenir, then **Mr Wood's Fossils** is the shop for you. It sits just off Grassmarket in Edinburgh, and is a fascinating place, full of fossils of every size and shape. The shop has an international reputation, and if you buy a specimen, you can be sure you are getting the real thing! They come from all over the world, and as a bonus there is also an extensive array of sparkling minerals and crystals. Browse to your heart's content, as there is absolutely no obligation to buy. Admire such treasures as dinosaur and shark teeth, fossil leaves and wood, amethyst geodes and meteorites. Feast your eyes on beautifully preserved fish, ammonites and 540 million year old trilobites.

The shop's manager, Matthew Dale, has a degree in geology, and worked in museums before taking up his post here. He and his staff, who all have geological backgrounds, can offer friendly and knowledgeable advice. Mr Wood himself is Stan Wood, who has been a professional fossil hunter since 1983, and in 1988 public demand for the beautiful objects pushed him into opening this fascinating shop. Over the years he has made many important discoveries, including 30 entirely new species from key evolutionary periods. All the fossils in the shop come with information cards detailing their name, age and location where they were found. The shop is open Monday to Saturday from 10 am to 5.30 pm. There is also a mail order service.

Highland Games, Edinburgh

made - and there is a tasting every Sunday afternoon. Further down is The Hub, the offices of the **Edinburgh International Festival**. The building, which dates from 1842 to 1844, is a former church known as the Tolbooth Kirk, and it has, at 240 feet, the tallest spire in the city.

The whole stretch of the Royal Mile becomes one big street theatre during the Festival and its younger, more rebellious offspring, the **Edinburgh Fringe Festival**. Every inch of space is taken up by jugglers, actors playing out scenes from the plays they are presenting in halls across the city, string quartets, magicians, jazz bands, bagpipers, folk musicians, fire eaters and more. It all looks splendidly chaotic, but in fact it is highly organised, with spaces on the pavements being strictly allocated and timed to the second.

the High Street and Canongate before reaching a short stretch close to the gates of Holyroodhouse known as Abbey Strand. This is the heart of old Edinburgh, usually known as the **Old Town**. Off it are many old "closes" (narrow alleyways) where the people of the city lived in days gone by. It was an egalitarian place in many ways, as rich and poor intermingled in a way not seen anywhere in Europe. Within the high tenements, the wealthy lived on the lower floors, the middle classes lived on the middle floors, and the poor lived on the floors at the top of the building.

One of the most popular attractions on the Royal Mile is the **Scotch Whisky Heritage Centre** in Castlehill. It tells the story of Scotland's national drink over the last 300 years - including how it is

Edinburgh has sometimes been called the "medieval Manhattan", due to the number of 16th and 17th century high rise tenement blocks lining the Royal Mile. But their height isn't apparent from the street. You have to go behind the tenements to see that the lower floors tumble down the steep slope towards Princes Street Gardens and the railway line. **Gladstone's Land** (National Trust for Scotland), in the Lawnmarket,

is typical of such a tenement. The whole building was built about 1620 for Thomas Gledstone, a prosperous merchant, and has painted ceilings. It has been furnished in the way it would have been in the 17th century. In Lady Stair's House, off the Lawnmarket, is the **Writers' Museum**, dedicated to Robert Burns, Sir Walter Scott and Robert Louis Stevenson. The house is named after Lady Stair, who owned it in the 18th century.

St. Gile's Cathedral is undoubtedly the most glorious building on the Royal Mile. Edinburgh, for all its history and importance, was not a cathedral city in medieval times, and it wasn't until the Church of Scotland embraced Episcopalianism that St. Giles got a bishop. Now the bishop has gone, and the Church of Scotland is Presbyterian.

Monks from Lindisfarne built the first church on the site in the 9th century.

St Giles Cathedral, Edinburgh

THE TOWN HOUSE

65 Gilmore Place, Edinburgh EH3 9NU
Tel: 0131 229 1985
e-mail: susan@thetownhouse.com website: www.thetownhouse.com

Owned and managed by Sue Virtue, **The Town House** is an elegant but extremely comfortable B&B establishment just a few minutes walk from the historic Old Town. It was built as a Victorian town house in 1876, and since Sue started offering the very best in Scottish hospitality over 23 years ago, it has earned an enviable reputation as one of the best B&Bs in Edinburgh. This is one place where you will want to come back to, and indeed many guests do just that, so good are the standards of service. This four star establishment has five fully en suite rooms, all with TVs, and all decorated to an exceptionally high standard. There is also a self-catering property and a guest room available which is separate from the guest house. There is private parking available and Princes Street is just a ten minute walk away.

The breakfasts are hearty and filling, just right to set you up when you want to explore the historic and fascinating city of Edinburgh. There is a choice of full Scottish breakfast as well as lighter options, and both use the finest and freshest of local produce wherever possible. The residents' lounge is extremely well decorated and furnished, and with its warm, red walls makes the ideal place where you can relax over a book or newspaper. Sue is a mine of friendly and useful information about where to eat, what to see and do in Edinburgh. For the comfort of the guests, this is a no smoking establishment.

The present building dates mainly from the 15th century, and has a magnificent crown steeple which is one of the icons of the city. At one time, in the Preston Aisle, an arm bone of St. Giles was kept as a holy relic. Attached to the cathedral is a later building - the ornate Thistle Chapel, built in 1911 to designs by Sir Robert Lorimer. Here the **Most Ancient and Noble Order of the Thistle**, founded by James III in the 15th century, has its home. The wood carvings are famous, with one showing an angel playing the bagpipes.

Parliament House is now the home of the Scottish legal system. It sits behind the cathedral, and was, up until the Treaty of Union of 1707, where the Scottish parliament met. The building itself dates from the late 17th century, though it has been altered over the years, and a new, elegant facade was added in 1829. **Edinburgh City Chambers** sits on the other side of the cathedral. At one time it was the Royal Exchange, built between 1753-61. This building gives a good idea of the height of the buildings on the northern side of the Royal Mile. As seen from the street, it is only a few storeys high, but it actually plunges for twelve storeys down the hillside. It was built over old alleyways, and one of them, Mary King's Close, has conducted tours. It was closed off in the 17th century when the bubonic plague swept through the city, and now it is said to be the most haunted spot in Edinburgh.

Further down the Royal Mile is the **Museum of Childhood**, featuring toys, books and games of yesteryear. It even has old medicines, such as the dreaded castor oil. **John Knox's House** stands in the Canongate, and dates from the 15th century. There is no proof that Scotland's stern religious reformer actually lived here, though he may well have died in

---

PATCHWORKS

1-3 Millar Crescent, Edinburgh EH10 5HN
Tel: 0131 477 3555 Fax: 0131 477 3558
e-mail: patchworks01@hotmail.com
website: www.patchworks-edinburgh.com

In Edinburgh's bustling area of Morningside, you'll find a wonderful shop called **Patchworks**. Owned and run by Sue Simpson and Lydia Porteous, it is an exciting quilt shop that offers everything for the quilter, experienced or beginner. There is a stunning range of hundreds of fabrics on sale (even non quilters will be dazzled by all the patterns and bright colours), as well as a carefully selected range of threads, ribbons, kits, cushion packs, books, pamphlets and all the ancillary accoutrements associated with the fascinating hobby of quilting. The shop has been open now for over three years, and so successful has it become that it has doubled its size, testimony to the service and astonishingly reasonable prices for all the goods on display.

Both Sue and Lydia are experienced and highly skilled quilters, so they can offer their customers friendly advice and help. The shop also offers classes in quilting for up to ten students at a time and some of the best quilting teachers in the country regularly hold classes here. There is plenty of parking nearby, and there is wheelchair access. Groups can visit by arrangement, and in the past it has had visitors from Dubai, Iceland, the United States, Europe and Australia. It is indeed a Scottish Mecca for anyone interested in quilting, and if you visit Edinburgh, and are a quilter, you cannot afford to miss this wonderful shop.

Photo: Courtesy of Norman Porter

the building on November 24th, 1572. At one time Canongate was a separate burgh, with its own town council and provost. It was granted its charter in 1587, and it was only in 1865 that it was absorbed into Edinburgh. The **Canongate Tolbooth**, where the courtroom and jail for the burgh was located, dates from 1591. It has a clock that juts out over the pavement, and inside is now the **Museum of Edinburgh**, which tells the story of the city and its colourful and historic past.

The Canongate Church was built in 1688, and has been influenced by Dutch architecture. This is probably because Edinburgh's port, Leith, traded with the Netherlands in the 16th, 17th and 18th centuries. The kirkyard has the graves of many famous people. **Adam Smith**, the economist and author of *The Wealth of Nations*, is buried here, as it Agnes McLehose, for whom Burns wrote one of

his loveliest poems, *Ae Fond Kiss*. Burns is also connected with the grave of **Robert Fergusson** the poet, who died in a madhouse aged only 24. When Burns visited Edinburgh, he paid a visit to the grave of his hero, and was astounded to find that there was no stone erected above it so he bought and paid for one himself. **White Horse Close**, further down the Canongate, is one of the most picturesque of the city's old closes, and it was here, in days gone by, that the coach for London and York left. James Boswell used it on many occasions.

At the foot of the mile is the Palace of Holyroodhouse. It is the Queen's official residence in Scotland, and grew out of the Abbey of Holyrood, founded by David I in 1128 for Augustinian canons (which is why part of the royal Mile is called "The Canongate", meaning the street of the canons). It is said that David was hunting in the area, and when he

ART ET FACTS

19 Roseburn Terrace, Edinburgh EH12 5NG
Tel: 0131 346 7730
website: www.picturesonnet.com

Art et Facts has been trading in this area of Edinburgh since 1989, and during that time has earned an enviable reputation as one of the best galleries in the city. It shows paintings and prints from a range of artists, with the subjects as diverse as sport, portraiture, landscapes, wildlife, boats, music and books. It has a special interest in the work of Macintosh Patrick, and normally carries many of his originals and prints. The gallery is owned and managed by George Rendall, who took on the business 14 years ago, after working for some time in an Edinburgh disco. He had absolutely no experience of running this kind of business, but since then he has become an acknowledged expert on many Scottish artists. He is now planning to run a series of regular exhibitions in the future, each one covering a particular artist or theme.

Though the shop has a deceptively small front, the inside is full of colour and surprises, with the walls covered in watercolours, prints and oil paintings from many artists. George is always on hand to offer friendly, impartial and knowledgeable advice, and the prices range form a few pounds to many thousands, depending on what you're after. The gallery also offers a skilled framing service, and has a wide range of mouldings to suit your every need. It sits about a 20 minute walk to the west of Princes Street, beyond Haymarket Station, and it is well worth seeking out. If you are after an unusual gift, or a souvenir of your stay in one of Britain's loveliest cities, then Art et Facts is for you.

fell from his horse, was injured by a cornered stag. As he grappled with its antlers, they miraculously turned into a holy cross, or "rood".

The abbey's guest quarters soon became a favourite with the Scottish kings, as they were more comfortable and less draughty than Edinburgh Castle up the hill. Gradually, the quarters were enlarged and beautified, and by the time of the Reformation they had been turned into a palace. Perhaps the most famous person to live there was Mary Stuart, better known as Mary Queen of Scots. She set up court here after her return from France as a young widow in 1561, and it was here that her Italian secretary **Rizzio** was murdered. The picture gallery has portraits, most of them fanciful, of over 100 Scottish kings. In the Abbey Strand, next to the entrance to Holyroodhouse, is the new **Queen's Gallery**, housed in a former church, where there are changing exhibitions of works of art from the royal collection.

The **Scottish Parliament Building** is close to Holyroodhouse. Many opening dates have been set for it, the latest being some time in 2004. It was designed by the late Catalan architect Enric Miralles, and there has been much criticism in Scotland about the ever increasing cost of the place.

In Holyrood Road is **Our Dynamic Earth**, an exhibition and visitors centre

MUSEUM OF SCOTLAND

Chambers Street, Edinburgh
Tel: 0131 247 4422
website: www.nms.ac.uk

The Museum of Scotland tells the remarkable story of a remarkable country. From the geological dawn of time to modern day life in Scotland, you'll discover the roots of a nation - a land steeped in fascinating cultures and terrible wars, passionate religion and scientific invention. A land of creative struggle - and occasionally of glorious failure. In a unique and purpose-built new museum, are gathered together the treasured inheritance and cultural icons which tell Scotland's many stories. The people, the land, the events that have shaped the way we live now. And very probably the way you do too.

If you weren't aware of the extraordinary history and impressive achievements of this small country, then it's time to find out. Because after more than 3,000 million years of Scotland's story, we now have the perfect place in which to celebrate it - the Museum of Scotland. The exhibits include the earliest known fossil reptile found in Bathgate, dating back to 338 million years BC, artifacts from around 8,000 BC when the first settlers arrived and a tiny shrine thought to date from AD750.

The museum shop sells a wide variety of souvenirs and a cafe and restaurant ensure that all appetites are catered for. Guides are available and there is a rooftop garden with spectacular views. Open Monday to Saturday 10am-5pm and Sunday 12 noon-5pm. Disabled access.

that takes you on a journey from the beginning of time right up until the present day. It features dinosaurs, lava flows, earthquakes and tropical rainstorms. To the south of the Royal Mile, in Queen street, is the Royal Museum, with the new **Museum of Scotland** (see panel above) next door. The Royal Museum is one of the most important places of its kind in Europe, with many important international collections on geology, natural history, science, the arts, archaeology and history, while the Museum of Scotland concentrates on Scotland itself.

One of the hidden gems of Edinburgh sits in the Cowgate. This is the **Magdalen**

Chapel, built in 1547 by the Guild of Hammermen. It contains some of the best pre-Reformation stained glass in Scotland as well as the tomb of its founder. The **Church of the Greyfriars** is also to the south of the Royal Mile. As it's name suggests, it was built in 1612 on the site of the former Greyfriars' Monastery, and it was here, in 1638, that the Solemn League and Covenant - which rejected bishops in the Church of Scotland - was signed. From this one act grew what became known as the "Killing Times", when "Covenantors" were hounded, prosecuted and killed by the troops of Charles II for adhering to their religious principles. It was the Killing Times that gave Scottish Lowlanders a hearty dislike of the Stuart dynasty, and they never flocked to support the Jacobite Uprising.

In nearby Candlemaker Row is the famous statue of **Greyfriar's Bobby**, which commemorates a faithful terrier who stood guard over his master's grave in the Greyfriar's kirkyard in the 19th century. Walt Disney's famous film was totally inaccurate, though it did reflect

THE GEORGIAN HOUSE

7 Charlotte Square,
Edinburgh EH2 4DR
Tel/Fax: 0131 226 3318
or Tel: 0131 225 2160
e-mail: thegeorgianhouse@nts.org.uk
website: www.nts.org.uk

The Georgian House is part of Robert Adam's masterpiece of urban design, Charlotte Square. It dates from 1796, when those who could afford it began to escape from the cramped, squalid conditions of Edinburgh's Old Town to settle in the fashionable New Town. The house's beautiful china, shining silver, exquisite paintings and furniture all reflect the domestic surroundings and social conditions of the times. Video programme. New touchscreen programme featuring a virtual tour of the house.

the fascination people have felt about the story over the years.

In the 18th century, Edinburgh was a crowded, bustling, insanitary place, centred on the Royal Mile. The then Lord Provost, James Drummond, proposed a competition whereby architects would submit plans for an elegant, new area of housing to the north of the medieval city. The competition was won by James Craig's imaginative plan for an area of broad streets, tree-lined squares and solid, elegant houses. This became the New Town, the most imaginatively designed urban area in the whole of Europe at the time.

Princes Street was one of the streets. It was decided to build on the north side of the street only, leaving the south side

ROSEBERY HOTEL

13 Rosebery Crescent, Edinburgh EH12 5JY
Tel: 0131 337 1085

The **Rosebery Hotel** is a charming and extremely comfortable small hotel in Edinburgh's exclusive West End. It has two coveted stars from VisitScotland, and situated within in an elegant town house that is friendly and warm. Here, where the bedrooms are spacious yet cosy and decorated to the highest standards, you'll get a good Scottish welcome. The breakfasts are hearty and filing, and use only the finest and freshest Scottish produce wherever possible. If you're looking for a base from which to explore Edinburgh, then this is the place for you!

clear to give a superb view of Edinburgh Castle. At that time, a shallow stretch of water called the Nor' Loch was located between the new development and the castle, and this was subsequently drained to create the present day **Princes Street Gardens**. In Charlotte Square is the **Georgian House** (National Trust for Scotland - see panel opposite), in which late 18th century interiors have been recreated using period furniture, fittings and hangings. At **28 Charlotte Square** is the National Trust for Scotland's headquarters, plus an art gallery. The central gardens of the Square is one of the venues for the yearly Edinburgh Book Festival, when a great marquee is erected.

St. Mary's Cathedral is Edinburgh's biggest church, and sits at the west end of the New Town. It is an immense structure built in Victorian times for the Episcopalian diocese of the city, and rivals a medieval Gothic cathedral in scale. It has three spires, which have become Edinburgh landmarks.

Edinburgh's art galleries are dotted all over the New Town and beyond, and contain internationally important collections of painting and sculpture. **The National Gallery of Scotland** is on the Mound, behind the **Royal Scottish Academy** and next to Princes Street Gardens, while the **Scottish National Portrait Gallery** is in Queen Street.

THE ROYAL YACHT BRITANNIA

Ocean Terminal, Leith, Edinburgh, Scotland
Tel: 0131 555 5566
e-mail: enquiries@tryb.co.uk
website: www.royalyachtbritannia.co.uk

For over 40 years **The Royal Yacht *Britannia*** served the Royal Family, travelling over one million miles to become the most famous ship in the world. Travelling to every corner of the globe, in a career spanning 968 royal and official visits, she played a leading role in some of the defining moments of recent history. To Her Majesty The Queen and the Royal Family, *Britannia* proved to be the perfect royal residence for glittering State Visits, official receptions, honeymoons and relaxing family holidays. Since her decommissioning *Britannia* has now made Edinburgh's historic Port of Leith her final home and is open to the public throughout the year. Now owned by The Royal Yacht *Britannia* Trust, a non-profit making charity, any proceeds go towards *Britannia's* maintenance.

Your tour of *Britannia* starts in the Visitor Centre on the second floor of Ocean Terminal. Here you can learn about *Britannia's* fascinating history through exhibits and photographs before you collect your complimentary audio handset and step on board *Britannia,* a privilege previously reserved for guests of Her Majesty The Queen and the Royal Family. Starting at the Bridge and finishing at the gleaming Engine Room, come and discover the reality behind life and work on board this Royal Yacht. Viewing five decks, using the lift or stairs for easy access, you will tour *Britannia* at your own pace and enjoy highlights that include the State Dining Room, the Drawing Room, the Sun Lounge, the Wardroom and the Chief Petty Officers' Mess. *Britannia* is furnished with artefacts from The Royal Collection, which are on loan from Her Majesty The Queen.

Further out are the Dean Gallery and the **Scottish National Gallery of Modern Art**. All are connected by a dedicated, frequent bus service.

The **Scott Monument** dominates Princes Street. It is over 200 feet high, and looks for all the world like a huge Gothic spaceship about to take off. From the top there are some marvellous views. Register House, at the east end of Princes Street, houses the National Archives of Scotland, including the famous **Declaration of Arbroath**, sent by Robert I to the Pope. It was designed by Robert Adam, with work beginning on it in 1774. Close to it is an Edinburgh institution - the **Café Royal**, which is actually a pub full of atmosphere. West Register House, which also stores Scotland's archives, is on Charlotte Square, within what was St George's Church, built in the early 19th century.

The **Royal Botanic Gardens** are situated off Inverleith Row, well north of the New Town. There are 70 acres of gardens here, and a wealth of plants, trees and shrubs form all over the world. They were founded in 1670 as "physic gardens" close to Holyrood, but transferred to Inverleith in 1823. Further north is Leith, Edinburgh's port. Up until 1920 it was a separate burgh, but in that year was absorbed into the city. The **Royal Yacht Britannia** (see panel on page 157) is moored at Leith, outside the Ocean Terminal Shopping Mall. Guided tours round it are available to see how the other half lived when they were on the high seas. It is worth exploring some of the older parts of the port, as in recent times it has become a desirable place to live.

Further west is the former fishing village of Newhaven, with its distinctive rows of old fishermens' houses. The **Newhaven Heritage Museum** is next to the old harbour, and explains the history and heritage of the area. Within it you will see a model of the greatest fighting ship of its day, the Great Michael. It was built at Newhaven, the keel being laid in 1507, and was the pride of James IV's Scottish navy. It took four years to build, and was the envy of England and France, as none of their ships could match it in size or firing power. However, in 1513 it was laid up in Brest in France, where it quietly rotted away. Travelling further west, you arrive at Granton. **Granton Harbour** was once a bustling, busy place, full of ships from all over the world. Now it is given over to yachts, and the great days have gone. There are plans to redevelop this whole area, thanks to an organisation called Waterfront Edinburgh. One of the proposals is to link it to the centre of the city with a new tram service - the first trams in the city since they were withdrawn in the 1950s. Another proposal is to build Scotland's first World Trade Centre.

Edinburgh Zoological Gardens are located in Corstorphine, a western suburb of the city. They cover 80 acres, and are famous for their "Penguin Parade", when the zoo's collection of penguins go walkabout. But beware - it is entirely up to the penguins whether this parade takes place or not, and on some days, they can't be bothered.

The extensive ruins of **Craigmiller Castle** (Historic Scotland) are on the south eastern outskirts of the city. They date mainly from the 14th century, with many later additions. It was built by the Preston family, who gave a relic of St. Giles to St. Giles Cathedral, and after which the church's Preston Aisle is named. Mary Stuart stayed here twice, with her 1566 visit being just before the baptism of her son, who would later become James VI. Three months later, her husband Darnley was murdered.

AROUND EDINBURGH

MUSSELBURGH

6 miles E of Edinburgh city centre on the A199

The town was named after the extensive mussel beds at the entrance to the River Esk, on which the town stands. It now forms part of the Edinburgh conurbation, and has many commuters living in it. The **Tolbooth** dates from the late 16th century, and was built from masonry taken from the former Chapel of our Lady of Loretto. **Inveresk Lodge Gardens** (National trust for Scotland) is a fine terraced garden with an Edwardian conservatory surrounding Inveresk Lodge (not open to the public). The gardening methods used here have been deliberately chosen so that they can be used in your own garden. The **Battle of Pinkie**, the last battle to have been fought between Scottish and English armies, took place near Musselburgh in 1547.

PRESTONPANS

7 miles E of Edinburgh city centre on the B1348

The **Battle of Prestonpans** took place in 1745 between a Jacobite army headed by Charles Edward Stuart and a Hanovarian one commanded by Sir John Cope. It was a resounding victory for the Jacobites, and the fighting was all over in 15 minutes. Many of the Hanovarian troops, who had been caught unawares by the Jacobites early in the morning, became trapped against the high wall of **Prestongrange House**, which can still be seen. The troops, who were terrified for their lives, tried to scale the wall and drop into the comparative safety of the house grounds. Ever since the battle, Sir

EILDON

109 Newbigging, Musselburgh, Edinburgh EH21 7AS
Tel/Fax: 0131 665 3981
e-mail: eve@stayinscotland.net
website: www.stayinscotland.net

Eildon is a beautifully restored Georgian townhouse seven km east of Edinburgh city centre, and close to the city bypass. Owned by Eve Campbell Roach, it is a three star B&B establishment that offers three well-decorated and comfortable rooms - a master en suite bedroom, with double and single bed, the garden room. with a double bed, and the blue room, which has twin beds. All rooms have colour TVs, hair dryers, radio and hospitality trays, and assistance with laundry and ironing is available if required. This is one of the best and friendliest B&Bs in the area, and is highly recommended by previous guests.

ARDEN HOUSE

26 Linkfield Road, Musselburgh EH21 7LL
Tel/Fax: 0131 665 0663 website: www.ardenhouse-guesthouse.co.uk
e-mail: accommodation@ardenhouse-guesthouse.co.uk

Only 15 minutes from the centre of Edinburgh, **Arden House** is an imposing Victorian villa offering superior three star accommodation. Many of the building's original features have been retained , giving a feeling of elegance and the rooms are comfortable and well furnished, most with en suite facilities, and all with TV and tea/coffee making facilities. Breakfast is served in the elegant and spacious dining room, where the menu includes full Scottish, Continental and vegetarian.

INVERESK HOUSE

3 Inveresk Village, Musselburgh EH21 7QA
Tel: 0131 665 5855
e-mail: chute.inveresk@btinternet.com

Inveresk House is a family run, award winning B&B that sits on the site of a Roman settlement. The house dates from 1592, and is owned and managed by Alice and John Chute, who have created a spacious and welcoming interior with period furnishings and oil paintings. There are three fully en suite, king sized rooms which are adaptable for family groups, and most have king sized beds. Full Scottish breakfasts (or lighter options) are served in a dining room with an ornate plaster ceiling. There is ample parking, and it is ideally placed for East Lothian's 27 superb golf courses.

John Cope has been ridiculed for the defeat, and a famous Jacobite song called *Hie, Johnnie Cope* was written which questioned whether he and his troops were awake early enough to defend themselves. The criticism was not wholly justified, as Sir John was not wholly to blame, and went on to have a distinguished military career.

PORT SETON AND COCKENZIE

9 miles E of Edinburgh city centre on the B1348

Seton Church (Historic Scotland) was built in the 15th and 16th centuries as a collegiate foundation. The chancel and delightful apse are 15th century, while the curiously truncated steeple and the transepts were added by the widow of Lord Seton, who was killed at the Battle of Flodden in 1513. It is dedicated to St. Mary and the Holy Cross, and has some Seton tombs, as well as some good vaulting. In 1544 it was looted by the troops of the Earl of Hertford during that period known as the Rough Wooing.

Seton Castle dates from 1790, and was designed by Robert Adam. It replaced the former Seton Palace, one of the grandest buildings in Scotland at the time. Mary Stuart visited the palace after Lord Darnley had murdered her Italian secretary, Rizzio.

Cockenzie is a former fishing port, whose name probably derived from Cul Choinnich, meaning "Kenneth's Corner". As well as fishing, the small harbour traded in coal and salt. The **Cockenzie Power Station**, which overshadows the two villages, is a coal fired poser station which officially opened in May 1968.

DALKEITH

7 miles SE of Edinburgh city centre on the A68

Dalkeith was at one time an important stopping place on the A68, once the main road south from Edinburgh. It is a fairly large town which has become industrial in character ever since coal was mined on a commercial basis in the area. **Dalkeith Palace** was built round the former Dalkeith Castle for Anne, Duchess of Buccleuch, and wife of James Scott, the Duke of Monmouth, who was Charles II's illegitimate son.

Monmouth plotted against his father, and in 1685 he landed at Lyme Regis after exile on the continent, declaring himself "head and captain-general of Protestant forces of the kingdom". He was eventually defeated at Sedgemoor in the same year, and was executed in the Tower of London ten days later.

DALKEITH COUNTRY PARK

The Ranger's Office, Dalkeith, Midlothian EH22 2NA
Tel: 0131 654 1666 Fax: 0131 654 2111
e-mail: cmonson@buccleuch.com
website: www.dalkeithcountrypark.com

Dalkeith Country Park offers a wonderful family day out. There
is just so much to do in its 1000 acres, from strolling along its
lovely woodland walks, admiring its many architectural gems
and watching children playing in the adventure play areas, to
studying the ancient oak woods (a site of special scientific interest) and having a cup of coffee or a
light snack in the café. It belongs to the Buccleuch Estates, headed by the Duke of Buccleuch, which
manages estates both in Scotland and England, and which has an international reputation for
conservation and land management. Dalkeith has the reputation of being one of the best country
parks in the country, a reputation it guards jealously by offering the very best in everything it does!

It sits close to the town of Dalkeith and has been open to the public since the 1940s for informal

recreation. In 1984 a large and exciting woodland adventure
play area was added, and proved so popular that it has been
added to every year since. The parkland surrounds the old
Dalkeith House, which has many historical associations.
Since it was built it has seen the hand of famous architects
such as Adam, Vanbrugh, Playfair, Bryce and Burns. A ranger
service operates throughout the year to help people
appreciate and enjoy all that the park offers. It organises
guided walks and talks, as well as special school activities
on such themes as forestry, wildlife and landscape history.
There is also an estate shop, where you are free to browse.

St Nicholas Parish Church has an
old, ruined apse attached to it, and in it
is the tomb of Anne, Duchess of
Buccleuch and Monmouth.

NEWTONGRANGE

8 miles SE of Edinburgh city centre on the A7

Coal mines were first sunk in the area by
the monks of Newbattle Abbey in the
13th century. By the 19th century, the
Midlothian coalfields were among the
biggest in Scotland, and employed many
people. All have disappeared now,
though the **Scottish Mining Museum**, at
the former Lady Victoria Mine, tells the
story of the industry and its people.
There is a recreated coal face, as well as
winding engines and a visitors centre.

ARNISTON

10 miles SE of Edinburgh city centre off the A7

For 400 years, the Dundas family has
lived at **Arniston House**. It was built in

the early part of the 18th century to
designs by William and John Adam on
the site of an earlier tower house. The
interiors are fine and detailed, and there
is also a collection of paintings by artists
such as Raeburn and Ramsay.

BORTHWICK

11 miles SE of Edinburgh city centre off the A7

The ruins of **Borthwick Castle** are both
large and impressive. They date from
about 1430, and it was to Borthwick that
Mary Stuart came after her marriage to
the Earl of Bothwell in 1566. Over 1,000
Scottish nobles, who objected to the
marriage, cornered the couple in the
castle, demanding that Bothwell be
executed for his part in the murder of
Darnley, Mary's first husband. Bothwell
escaped to Dunbar, leaving Mary to deal
with her nobles. When the nobles heard
of Mary's predicament, they assumed
that she would see through his treachery.

EDINBURGH CRYSTAL

Penicuik, Midlothian EH26 8HB
Tel: 01968 675128 Fax: 01968 674847
e-mail: kmeldrum@edinburgh-crystal.co.uk

Edinburgh Crystal sits in the small Midlothian town of Penicuik, south of Edinburgh, and is undoubtedly one of the best visitor attractions in the east of Scotland û one of only a handful with a five star rating. For this reason, you just can't afford to miss what is an enjoyable and rewarding day out. Here, in this modern factory, exquisite objects are fashioned in crystal by craftsmen and women who are skilled in the art of glassblowing, cutting and engraving. Glass has been produced in the Edinburgh area for at least four centuries, so Edinburgh Crystal is continuing an age old tradition, while at the same time developing new techniques that enhance the efficiency of the manufacturing processes and the quality of the finished objects.

Shopping within the Edinburgh Crystal's Visitor Centre has always been a fantastic experience,

but it has now got even better, with a major refurbishment that shows off the largest collection of Edinburgh Crystal in the world to perfection! There is a First Quality Shop, which sells the full range of crystal objects, and a Factory Shop, which sells second quality objects and discontinued lines at fantastic prices. This is retail therapy at its best, and you are free to browse to your heart's content. Friendly, knowledgeable staff are always on hand to offer advice, and there is no pressure to buy. And the centre doesn't just sell crystal - it also offers a wide range of other brands, such as Border Fine Arts, Royal Worcester Giftware, Portmeirion, Dartington, Arran Aromatics, Highland Stoneware, and so much more.

Within the Heritage Centre are cabinets which display the most significant and beautiful pieces produced by the company over the years. There are also attractive, colourful presentation boards that explain the history of the company, as well as glass making in Edinburgh through the centuries. If you want to see the craftsmen at work transforming molten crystal into beautiful finished pieces, factory tours are available. You will see molten glass being blown at over 1000 degrees Celsius into lovely decanters and sparkling glasses. Their movements seem choreographed as craftsmen pass hot glass from one to another to complete the process. You then move on to the cutters, who cut the patterns for which Edinburgh Crystal is renowned into the glass. Lastly, you will see the engravers, who add intricate decoration using only a copper wheel. And during all of this you are able to ask the craftsmen questions, and find out about the skills involved.

A 'hands-on' tour is also available for groups, where you yourself can have a go at glassblowing, using the same 'irons' as the craftsmen as you attempt to blow a glass bubble. Next you will try cutting a pattern into a crystal tumbler, and lastly the tumbler is taken to the engravers, who will engrave your name on it. The finished tumbler is then polished, boxed and presented to you as a totally unique memento of your visit to one of the most fascinating factories in Scotland.

But Mary was besotted with the man, and as soon as the nobles left, she dressed up as a pageboy and escaped, later joining up with Bothwell again. Borthwick Parish Church is modern, though it has a 15th century aisle containing the tombs of the first Lord and Lady Borthwick.

ROSSLYN

7 miles W of Edinburgh city centre on the B7006

If you love mysteries, you'll love **Rosslyn Chapel**, which is dedicated to St. Matthew. To some people, it is the most important place in Christendom, as it provides a direct link to Jesus. But even if you can't believe the legends, you can certainly appreciate one of the loveliest and most exuberant churches in the whole of Britain. It was founded by Sir William St. Clair, the last Prince of Orkney, in 1446 as a collegiate church, though only the choir was finished. Sir William lived at nearby **Rosslyn Castle**, and had the church interior decorated with stone carvings that are unique, and which includes both Masonic and Templar symbolism.

The carvings show plants that only grow in the New World, even though Columbus hadn't yet sailed the Atlantic when the church was built. There are also pagan symbols, such as the "Green Man", as well as the famous **Apprentice Pillar**. This was said to have been carved by an apprentice mason when his master was away. When the master returned and saw the intricacy and detail in the carving, he killed the apprentice in a fit of jealousy. Whether the story is true or not, of course, is another matter.

Much has been written about the church lately. One theory says that Jesus himself is buried in the crypt (which has never been opened), another says that his writings are buried there, while yet another says that the crypt contains the uncorrupted bodies of several Knights Templar, still in their armour. And in a recent book, it was claimed that the church was a recreation of Solomon's Temple in Jerusalem. Perhaps the most famous story is that the church contains the **Holy Grail** - the cup form which Christ drank at the Last Supper. It is supposed to be embedded in one of the pillars.

If the body of Jesus lies in Rosslyn Chapel, then of course, the Resurrection never took place, and the whole fabric of Christianity falls apart. For that reason, most people have dismissed the legends as nonsense, while others - equally as intelligent - say that Rosslyn truly has some hidden significance for Christians. Whatever your views, it is a place well worth visiting just to see the wonderful interior. However, it is still a working church, so entry on a Sunday may be restricted.

The **Rosslyn Glen Country Park** has wooded walks that go past an old gunpowder works.

PENICUIK

9 miles S of Edinburgh city centre on the A701

The Pentland Hills rise to the immediate west of the town, with their highest peak being **Scald Law** at 1,899 feet. **Flotterstone Visitors Centre**, just off the A702, can provide maps as well as arrange walks and tours of the hills. The **Alan Ramsay Obelisk**, dedicated to the memory of Alan Ramsay the poet (who was born in Leadhills in Lanarkshire) stands in the grounds of Penicuik House. **St Mungo's Parish Church** dates from 1771, and has a detached belfry from an older church. The **Edinburgh Crystal Visitors Centre** (see panel opposite) is at Eastfield, and explains about glass making. There is also a shop.

EASTSIDE FARM COTTAGES

Eastside, Penicuik, Midlothian EH26 9LN
Tel/Fax: 01968 677842
e-mail: eastsidecottages@aol.com website: http://travel.to/eastside

Enjoy peace and tranquillity in the heart of the Pentland Hills Regional Park.
The four star **Eastside Farm Cottages** are within Eastside Farm, and offer self
catering accommodation of the highest standard. There are three beautifully
converted cottages situated around a courtyard which combine old world
charm with all modern conveniences. They sleep from two to six, and have
TVs, hi fis and well equipped kitchens. They make the ideal hideaway locations
where you can unwind and enjoy rural living on a 3000 acre farm. All bed
linen, towels, electricity and logs are included in the price.

CRICHTON

11 Miles SE of Edinburgh city centre on the B6367

The ruins of **Crichton Castle** (Historic
Scotland) date from the 14th century,
with later additions. It was built by the
Crichton family, and later occupied by
the Earl of Bothwell, Mary Stuart's
husband. It has a range of Italian-style
Renaissance stonework added by the Earl
after his visit to Italy in the late 16th
century. **Crichton Collegiate Church**
was built in 1449 by Lord Crichton,
Chancellor of Scotland, for a college of
priests who would say daily mass for him
and his family. **Vogrie Country Park** is
centred on Vogrie House, and has a golf
course, picnic areas and walks.

SOUTRA

16 Miles S of Edinburgh city centre on the A68

Soutra Aisle is all that remains of a
medieval hospital that once stood here,
looked after by Augustinian monks. This
was the main road south from
Edinburgh in those days, so it catered for
travellers and pilgrims as well. An
archaeological dig uncovered evidence of
surgery during medieval times, and even
some pieces of bandage were uncovered
with human tissue still attached to them.

Soutra is one of the best vantage
points in the Lowlands, and from here
you get a wonderful view over Central
Scotland and Edinburgh to the

Highlands. On a clear day, over 60
Highland peaks can easily be seen.

CRAMOND

**5 miles W of Edinburgh city centre on a minor road
off the A90**

Though it forms part of the Edinburgh
conurbation, the village of Cramond
seems quiet and isolated on the banks of
the River Almond where it enters the
Firth of Forth. It has many picturesque,
whitewashed cottages, and a Parish
Church that dates from 1656, with a
medieval tower. It sits within the ruins of
a **Roman Fort**. The Rev'd Robert Walker,
who was immortalised by the painter
Raeburn as he skated on Duddingston
Loch, was the minister here in the 18th
century. At one time the village was a
centre for the manufacture of nails. A
small pedestrian ferry connects the
village with the west bank of the river.

INGLISTON

7 miles W of Edinburgh city centre off the A8

Edinburgh International Airport is to
be found here. Every year **The Royal
Showground** hosts the Royal Highland
Show, Scotland's premier country,
farming and outdoor fair.

BALERNO

7 miles SW of Edinburgh city centre off the A70

Balerno is mainly visited to see **Malleny
Garden** (National Trust for Scotland). It

Malleny Gardens, Balerno

covers three acres, and is dominated by
400 year old yew trees. It houses the
National Bonsi Collection for Scotland,
and has a fine collection of roses.

RATHO

**8 miles W of Edinburgh city centre on a minor road
off the A8**

From the **Edinburgh Canal Centre**
cruises are available along the Union
Canal, which connects the Forth and
Clyde Canal with Edinburgh. **St. Mary's
Parish Church** was founded in the 13th
century, though it has been altered over
the years, and little now remains of the
original fabric apart from an arch at the
west end. There is a Templar grave slab
just inside the main door of the church.

SOUTH QUEENSFERRY

9 miles W of Edinburgh city centre off the A90

South Queensferry is an ancient
town, having been granted its burgh
charter in the 1570s. Dominating
the town are the two bridges which
span the Firth of Forth at this point -
the **Forth Rail Bridge** and the **Forth
Road Bridge**. The rail bridge was
built between 1883 and 1890, and
represents the zenith of Victorian
civil engineering. It is a structure
which is recognised world wide. The

road bridge was completed in
1964. This part of the Firth of
Forth, where the water narrows
to no more than a mile wide, has
been a favourite crossing point
for over 1,000 years. In the 11th
century, St. Margaret of Scotland,
wife of Malcolm III, established a
ferry here to take pilgrims to
both Dunfermline and St.
Andrews, and it is from her that
the name "Queensferry" derives.
Before the road bridge was built,
there was a car ferry which took
passengers to North Queensferry in Fife.
In the shadow of the rail bridge is the
Hawes Inn, built in 1683. It features in
R.L. Stevenson's Kidnapped. Opposite it,
on the shore, is the slipway for the old
car ferry.

The town's buildings date from the
16th century onwards. **Plewlands House**
(National Trust for Scotland) dates from
1643, and has been converted into
private flats. The church of the former
Carmelite Friary in Rose Lane was built
in the 15th century, and is now an
Episcopalian church. The **Queensferry
Museum** in the High Street tells the story
of the town and its people.

Dalmeny House is to the east of the
town, and overlooks the Firth of Forth. It
is the home of the Primrose family, Earls

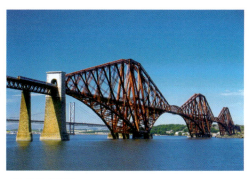

Forth Rail Bridge

of Rosebery, and was built in the 1830s. There are excellent collections of paintings and furniture. **Dalmeny Church** is one of the best preserved Norman churches in Britain. It has a richly carved south doorway, chancel and apse.

HADDINGTON

The former county town of East Lothian is one of the most historic in Scotland, and has preserved a lot of its ancient character. It became a royal burgh in the 12th century, when David I granted its charter. At one time it was the fourth largest town in Scotland, but the rapid expansions of the late 18th and 19th centuries passed it by. It is strategically placed just off the A1, but even the Edinburgh-London rail line never came near.

This has been the town's gain, and it is now a much sought after place for Edinburgh commuters to live. Its parish church, the cathedralesque **Church of St. Mary**, is one of the largest parish churches in Scotland, and some people still wrongly refer to it as an abbey. It was formerly collegiate, and dates from the 15th century. It's ruined choir was restored in the 20th century, and now that the church is complete again, it forms the western end of the annual **Haddington to Whitekirk Pilgrimage**, an ecumenical event that attracts people from all the main Christian religions. This ecumenicalism is underlined by the **Lauderdale Aisle** within the church. It is, in fact, a small Episcopalian chapel within a Presbyterian church, and is maintained by the Earls of Lauderdale. In the church's choir is buried **Jane Welsh**, Thomas Carlyle's wife, who was born in a

PETER POTTER GALLERY

10 The Sands, Haddington, East Lothian EH41 3EY
Tel: 01620 822080 e-mail: laura.framebo@dial.pipex.com

Haddington is one of the most historic towns in Scotland, with its roots deep in history. Situated in the former fire station (which is a listed building), the **Peter Potter Gallery** has played a significant role in the life, not just of the town, but of the whole area of East Lothian. Since the death of its founder in 1982, it has been run by a charitable trust, and now offers displays and exhibitions of art and craft work that can be bought and admired for ages to come. The gallery has a varied programme of exhibitions, featuring works from artists from the immediate area and from further afield, both professional and amateur, established and new to the art world. There are wonderful paintings, prints, jewellery, glassware, ceramics and wood carving, representing the work of over 100 people at any one time. Prices range from as little as £2 up to £2,000, so this is the perfect place to buy a souvenir of Scotland that is tasteful, lasting and unusual.

The gallery also sells quality, well-designed cards and a wide and substantial range of art and craft

materials, with a ten per cent discount for members of local art clubs on production of their membership cards. One of the gallery's most popular features is its coffee shop gallery, which has wonderful views of the medieval St. Mary's Church (one of the biggest parish churches in Scotland) and the Nungate Bridge over the River Tyne. Here visitors can enjoy light lunches, home baking and tea and coffee in a comfortable and welcoming setting, while enjoying the artwork and craft items surrounding them. Children are also very welcome.

J.S. MAIN AND SONS

87/89 High Street, Haddington, East Lothian EH41 3ET
Tel: 01620 822148 Fax: 01620 824662
e-mail: saddler.haddington@ukonline.co.uk

For over 100 years, **J.S. Main and Sons** have been saddlers and retailers
of riding equipment and also sell a wide range of wonderful, sturdy
outdoor clothing including Barbour. In addition, the shop has a great
range of quality general hardware and leather goods. If you're holidaying
in the area, then this is where you can get your local shooting supplies
and fishing permits. Tom and John Main, the present owners, offer the
best in friendly, knowledgeable service, so why not call in and see for
yourself? You won't be disappointed!

house in the town which can still be
seen, but which is not open to the
public. St Mary's is one of the few
churches in Scotland to have a full peel
of bells, and the changes are rung
regularly. They were installed in 1999.

Nearby are the ruins of the small St.
Martin's Church, which was founded in
the 12th century. The 16th century
Nungate Bridge over the Tyne is behind
St Mary's, and is named after a medieval
nunnery that used to stand near it. The
writer Samuel Smiles was born in the
town in 1812, and though he wrote
many things, he is mainly remembered
for his book *Self Help*.

It was in Haddington that John Knox
was supposed to have been born in 1505,
and it is likely that both Alexander II
and William the Lion were born in the
town as well. The Scottish parliament
met here in the 16th century to agree to

the marriage of Mary Stuart to the young
Dauphin of France - something which
angered Henry VIII of England. He had
wanted Mary to marry his own son, and
thus unite Scotland and England. In fact,
up until the parliament met in
Haddington, he had tried to persuade
the reluctant Scots to agree to the union
by sending the Earl of Hertford north
with an army to terrorise the
countryside. Haddington was one of the
towns that suffered during what became
known as the "Rough Wooing", and it
must have pleased its inhabitants to see
that it played a part in snubbing the
English king.

The **Town House** is a graceful building
with a tall spire, and dates from the late
1740s. it was designed by William Adam,
though the spire was added later. Close
to the town is the mansion of
Lennoxlove, home to the Dukes of

ABBEY MAINS

Haddington, East Lothian EH41 3SB
Tel: 01620 823286 Fax: 01620 826348
e-mail: joyce.abbeymains@farmersweekly.net

This comfortable and cosy B&B is within the old
farmhouse at **Abbey Mains**, which dates from 1745.
Joyce and David Playfair have been extending a warm
Scottish welcome to guests for over ten years, and have
earned a reputation that is second to none. There are

three guest bedrooms, two of which are en suite and one which has a private bathroom. In this no
smoking establishment, the breakfasts are prepared from the freshest produce possible (most of it
from the farm itself) and are always filling. Guests have their own private lounge to relax in, and tea
and coffee is always available.

THE OLD BOTHY

Begbie, Haddington, East Lothian EH41 4HQ
Tel: 01620 823017 Fax: 01620 829306

If you're looking for comfortable B&B accommodation near Haddington, then **The Old Bothy** is for you! Owned and run for over 12 years by Anita Husband, it has two beautifully decorated rooms, one en suite, and both furnished by Laura Ashley, there is also a hospitality tray and TV. The home cooked breakfasts are delicious, and cooked on an Aga. Anita also has a dried flower business, and offers wreaths, and garlands for sale. This is a warm, friendly establishment that you will want to come back to again and again!

Hamilton since 1946. It has many treasures, not least of which is the death mask of Mary Stuart. It shows that she was, as many contemporary commentators noted at the time, an extremely beautiful woman, even if she was 45 years old when she was beheaded in 1587. The origins of the house are to be found in the 13th century, when it was known as Lethington Hall, home to the Maitland family.

AROUND HADDINGTON

GULLANE

6 miles N of Haddington on the A198

Gullane is a small golfing resort just inland from the Firth of Forth. The **Muirfield Course** is home to the Honourable Company of Edinburgh Golfers, and the course itself has hosted

GULLANE DELICATESSEN

40c Main Street, Gullane, East Lothian EH31 2AL
Tel: 01620 842134 Fax: 01620 843461
website: www.gullanedeli.co.uk

Anyone who is on a self-catering or camping holiday in the East Lothian area should head for the **Gullane Delicatessen**, one of the best delis, not just in East Lothian, but in the south of Scotland. Owned and run by Mark Cervi, who has been in the trade for over 15 years, it is the ideal place to stock up with fine foods, wines, liqueurs and spirits. There are mouth watering displays of cheeses, (including local brands), cold meats, hams, pates, dressings, preserves, pickles, sausages, fresh truffles, speciality cakes, oatcakes and biscuits from such places as Britain, France and Italy, and a fine range of honeys from as far afield as New Zealand.

The range of wines is equally outstanding, with the shop specialising in wines from the south of France and the south of Italy. And, being in Scotland, there is also a range of single malts, as well as rums and grappa. The shop is large and airy, with an eye catching outside colour scheme of red and

black. It sits across from Gullane's historic old church, and has been open for four years. Such is the quality of the produce that Mark sells, he has attracted a faithful clientele that is both demanding and knowledgeable about fine foods. This isn't just a place to shop - it is a place to browse, and you could happily spend an hour or two just going round looking at the marvellous displays on the shelves and chilled cabinets. Mark is always happy to advise. If you shop here, you're sure to find quality, freshness and flavour at prices you can really afford.

the British Open on many occasions. On the West Links Road is the **Heritage of Golf** exhibition, tracing the history of the sport in the area.

DIRLETON

6 miles N of Haddington on off A198

Dominating this small village are the impressive ruins of **Dirleton Castle** (Historic Scotland). They date back to at least the 13th century, though some of what you see now is older. The castle

Dirleton Castle

was originally built by the Vaux family, which was Norman, and which was invited to settle in Scotland by David I. It was also owned by the Halyburtons and the Ruthvens. A member of the Ruthven family was involved in the murder of Rizzio, Mary Stuart's Italian secretary. During the Wars of Independence it was taken by Edward I of England, but by 1311 it was back in the hands of the Scots.

The castle also has some magnificent gardens. They probably existed in the 16th century, when the centrepiece was a knot garden surrounded by yew hedges, later converted to a bowling green. There were also lawns, terraces, walks and a dovecot. Today's gardens have more more modern plantings, and Victorian and 20th century Arts and Crafts gardens have been created. They also have the longest herbaceous border in the world.

ABERLADY

6 miles N of Haddington on the A198

Aberlady was formerly the port for Haddington, but now it is a quiet village sitting on the shores of the Firth of Forth. The village was the home of one

of Scotland's most famous writers, **Nigel Tranter**, who died in the year 2000. His historical romances were meticulously researched, and covered every period of Scottish history. There is a small cairn to his memory near Quarry House, where he lived.

The **Aberlady Bay Nature Reserve** covers 1,439 acres of foreshore and sand dunes, and is popular with bird watchers and walkers. The **Myreton Motor Museum** has over 50 mainly pre-war vehicles on display (the earliest one being from 1896). All are well maintained and in good running order. The Parish Church was rebuilt in the 19th century, though it has a 16th century tower attached. **Luffness Castle**, now a hotel, stands to the east of the village. It was once the ancestral home of the Hepburns.

ATHELSTANEFORD

2 miles NE of Haddington on the B1343

This pleasant little village sits at the heart of Scotland's history. It was here, in AD832, that the **Battle of Athelstaneford** took place between a Pictish and Scottish army under the command of Angus mac Fergus and a Northumbrian one under King Athelstane. On the day before the battle, Angus mac Fergus saw a great vision in the sky - a huge white cross made up of clouds. He took it as a great omen, and on the following day he led his troops to victory. A white cross on a blue background was then adopted as his flag, and it eventually became the Saltire, or St. Andrew's Cross - Scotland's national flag. If the story is true, then it is the oldest national flag in Europe. That is why the background colour for the Saltire should always be sky blue, and not the dark blue as seen in the Union Jack. The **National Flag Centre** in the village tells the full story.

NORTH BERWICK

7 miles NE of Haddington on the A198

The town was granted royal burgh status in 1373 by Robert II, making it one of the oldest towns in Scotland. It is a holiday and golfing resort, and behind it is the immense **Berwick Law**, an old volcanic plug which rises to a height of 613 feet. Another volcanic plug is the 350 feet high **Bass Rock**, which sits three miles north east of North Berwick in the Firth of Forth. Over 150,000 seabirds nest there annually, and on other, smaller islands such as Craigleith and Fidra. The **Scottish Seabird Centre** next to the town's old harbour has displays and exhibitions about Scotland's seabirds. You can even manoeuvre remote cameras mounted on the islands to get a good look at the nesting birds without disturbing them. There are also powerful telescopes and binoculars on a viewing platform. In the 8th century the Bass Rock was home to a hermit called **St. Baldred**. In later times it served as a prison for Covenantors and Jacobites, and traces of the old fortifications can still be seen.

WESTGATE GALLERY

39-41 Westgate, North Berwick, East Lothian EH39 4AG
Tel:01620 894976
e-mail: info@westfategallery.co.uk
website: www.westgategallery.co.uk

The **Westgate Gallery** sells a wide range of paintings, prints, ceramics, glassware, gift ware and candles, all at reasonable prices. The owner, Stewart Muirhead, offers friendly and knowledgeable advice about what is on offer in the shop, which is mainly the work of Scottish artists. There is also a gallery café where you can have a refreshing cup of tea or coffee while admiring the colourful paintings, prints and crafts that surround you. Stewart also offers a framing service, and supplies works of art to businesses both large and small.

THISTLES

82 High Street, North Berwick, East Lothian EH 39 4HF
Tel: 01620 893606 Fax: 01620 893614

Thistles is an Alladin's cave of goods ranged over 2,000 square feet of space on two levels, with prices ranging from under £1 to over £2,000. It is owned and run by Ewan and Maggie Capperauld, who offer a superb range of antiques, gift items, microscopes and telescopes, antique and reproduction furniture, Wemyss and Dunmore pottery, original and reproduction paintings, cookware, cards and candles. You could spend a whole day here and still not see all that is on offer. And in addition, there are classic wedding cars available for hire. You can't afford to miss such a fascinating place when you visit East Lothian.

Beside the Seabird Centre are the scant remains of North Berwick's **Auld Kirk**. It dates from the 12th century onwards, though it was finally abandoned in the 17th century due to coastal erosion. Over 30 well-preserved skeletons were excavated during the building of the centre, the earliest one dating from the 7th century, showing that this site may have had a Celtic monastery of some kind on it at the time. The **North Berwick Museum** is housed in a former school in School Road, and tells the history of the church and the town.

A curious tale of witchcraft and bloodshed is told about North Berwick. In the 16th century, it was supposed to have been the home of a **Witches Coven**. The witches were put on trial in 1595, and it was soon being talked about throughout the country. One of the accusations made against it was that it caused a great storm to rise up when James VI was returning to Scotland from Denmark with his Danish bride.

It all began with a girl galled Gellie Duncan. She seemed to have the power to heal, which immediately aroused suspicions, and her master, David Seton, tried to extract a confession of witchcraft from her using thumbscrews. He then had her body examined for "marks of the devil", and these were duly found on her throat. She confessed and was put in jail. She further confessed, however, that she was one of 200 witches and warlocks in the area, who, egged on by Seton's enemy, the Earl of Bothwell, were trying to harm James VI. She told her captors that at Hallowe'en in 1590, they all convened at the Auld Kirk, where Satan appeared to them and preached a

Bass Rock, North Berwick

blasphemous sermon. James VI had all the witches and warlocks executed. Gellie herself perished in the flames on the Esplanade before Edinburgh Castle.

There is no doubt that Gellie made up the story about the coven in a vain attempt to save herself, but some people have speculated that perhaps the Earl of Bothwell himself had dressed up as Satan to take part in the coven. Whatever the true story, many innocent people perished because of superstition and a fear of the unknown.

DUNBAR
11 miles E of Haddington on the A1087

Dunbar is a small royal burgh that was granted its charter in 1445. A former fishing and whaling port, it is now a holiday resort, and has the famous Belhaven Brewery to the north of the town. The **Battle of Dunbar** took place in 1650 between a Cromwellian army and a Covenanting army under the command of General Leslie. A stone commemorates the event.

The ruins of **Dunbar Castle** date from the 12th century, and were originally built for the Cospatrick family, which later changed its name to Dunbar. It was to this castle that Edward II came after his defeat at Bannockburn. He then boarded a ship for Berwick-upon-Tweed. The Countess of Dunbar, known as "Black Agnes", held the castle for five months against the English before she was relieved by a Scottish force in 1338. After Mary Stuart abdicated in the 16th century, the castle was dismantled on the orders of the Scottish Parliament.

The **Old Town House** dates from 1620, and has a small museum and interpretation centre on local history and archaeology. A newer attraction - if that is what it can be called - is the **Torness Nuclear Power Station**, which was built in the early 1980s about five miles south of the town. There is a visitor centre that explains the processes

involved in generating electricity from nuclear power.

In 1838, John Muir was born in the town. He was the founder of the American national parks movement, and his birthplace in the High Street, is now the John Muir Centre. The 170 acre **John Muir Country Park** lies to the north west of the town, and was opened in the late 70s. It was the first park of its kind in Scotland.

TANTALLON CASTLE

8 miles NE of Haddington off the A198

The ruins of Tantallon Castle (Historic Scotland) stand on a cliff top above the Firth of Forth. It was at one time the seat of the powerful Douglases, Earls of Angus, with the castle as you see it now being built for William, 1st Earl of Douglas. It sits opposite the Bass Rock, and these two mighty structures make a powerful picture. Cromwell ordered

WILLIAM MASON

70-80 High Street, Dunbar EH12 1JH
Tel/Fax: 01368 862747
e-mail: wmmasons@aol.com
website: www.masons-shoes.co.uk

If you are looking for quality footwear while in East Lothian, then look no further that **William Mason** of Dunbar. It is an independent family business that only sells boots and shoes of the highest quality, and was founded in 1873. The present owners, Sarah and Hamish Mason, have been in charge for over 15 years, and therefore have extensive experience. In addition to the Dunbar shop, there is also one in North Berwick and two in Haddington - one for adult footwear and one ("Wee Masons"), for children. The staff in all the shops have the same commitment to friendly and courteous service, and can offer advice that will help you choose boots or shoes that are just right for you. They are also trained in fitting children's shoes, and can advise on specialist children's footwear.

All the shops are bright and airy, with wonderful displays of footwear for all occasions. All the big names are here - Gabor, Barkers, Van Dal, Elephanten and so on, and all at competitive prices. Susan

is president of the Independent Footwear Retailers Association, and "Wee Masons" won a Best Children's Shoe Shop Award in 2001 - guarantees that when you shop in a Mason's shop, you will be dealing with people who know what they're talking about. So if you're looking for sturdy boots, footwear for formal occasions, sandals for the beach, or just comfortable yet hard-wearing shoes to wear while driving around and exploring Scotland, then one of the William Mason shops is sure to have just what you want.

General Monk to besiege the castle, and after 12 days he took and destroyed it.

WHITEKIRK

7 miles NE of Haddington off the A198

St. Mary's Parish Church in this small, pleasant village is the eastern end of the Haddington and Whitekirk Pilgrimage, held every year in May. The village, however, had been a place of pilgrimage since medieval times. Before the Reformation, people used to come to the village to be cured at the Well of Our Holy Lady, which has long been lost. In 1413, it is said that over 15,000 people of many nationalities made the trip.

The church dates from the 12th century and later, and close to it is the **Tithe Barn**, built in the mid-16th century. In medieval times, the church claimed one tenth ("tithe" is another word for "tenth part") of its parishioner's produce, and this is where it was stored.

A pilgrim of a very unusual kind visited the church in 1435. His name was Aeneas Sylvius Piccolomini, and he was a young Italian sent from Rome to be an envoy at the court of James I in Edinburgh. However, during the winter sea crossing from the Continent, his ship was blown off course by a raging gale and blizzard. Fearing for his life, the young Aeneas vowed that if he made it to dry land, he would give thanksgiving at the nearest church dedicated to Our Lady. The ship was wrecked off the coast of East Lothian, between Dunbar and North Berwick, and the young nobleman walked ten miles in a blinding snowstorm to Whitekirk, where prayers were duly said. Twenty years later, Aeneas Sylvius Piccolomini became Pope Pious II.

Tantallon Castle

TRAPRAIN LAW

4 miles E of Haddington on a minor road off the A1

Traprain Law makes a good climb if you are reasonably fit. From the top are are some wonderful views out over the farmlands of East Lothian, and it's worth the climb for this alone. But there is another reason to climb it, and that's the hill fort that occupies the summit. It was occupied from Neolithic times right up until the Dark Ages, and its outlines can easily be seen. It was the capital of a tribe called by the Romans the Votadini, which means "the farmers". Many Roman remains have been found here, including a horde of Roman silver, showing that there was a lot of trade between the tribesmen and the Roman occupiers.

EAST LINTON

6 miles E of Haddington off the A1

This small village sits just off the AI, the main road from Edinburgh to Berwick-upon-Tweed. A small detour is amply repaid, as the houses and cottages make a charming scene. The 16th century **East Linton Bridge** once carried the AI before the village was bypassed.

John Rennie the civil engineer was born at the mansion house of Phantassie, to the east of the village. **Phantassie Doocot** (National Trust for Scotland) had space for over 500 birds, and it was here that "doos" (pigeons) nested, providing a supply of fresh meat over the winter months to people in the area. If you want to have a look inside, the key is available at **Preston Mill** (also National Trust for Scotland), a short distance away. This is a picturesque building sitting in an idyllic rural spot, and dates from the 17th and 18th centuries. It is still in working order, and with its conical roof and red pantiles, it is a popular subject for artists and photographers.

Preston Kirk dates mainly from the 1770s, though the chancel is 13th century. It was used as a mausoleum by the Smeaton family who lived locally. The ruins of **Hailes Castle** lie to the west of East Linton, and was acquired by the Hepburn family in the 14th century, who altered it in later years. The most famous member of the family was James Hepburn, the Earl of Bothwell, who married Mary Queen of Scots in 1567.

MUSEUM OF FLIGHT

East Fortune Airfield,
East Lothian EH39 5LF
Tel: 01620 880308
Fax: 01620 880355
website: nms.ac.uk/flight

The **Museum of Flight** is based at East Fortune Airfield, a Scheduled Ancient Monument and one of the most famous sites in world aviation history. It tells the history of East Fortune (established in 1915 as a fighter base to protect Scotland from Zeppelin attacks) and of the Scottish built airship R34 which left East Fortune and flew to Long Island, New York, becoming the first return Transatlantic flight. The Museum collection is housed in the original hangars and restoration work can be seen in progress. A large selection of models, toys and books is on sale in the shop and the Parachute Cafe serves light refreshments.

EAST FORTUNE
4 miles NE of Haddington on the B1377

The **Scottish Museum of Flight** (see panel below) is situated in a former World War II airfield. It is a marvellous collection of aircraft, rockets, photographs, memorabilia and models. One of the exhibits is a Prestwick Pioneer, the only aircraft ever to have been wholly designed and built in Scotland. You can also see a Soviet MIG, a Lightning and a Blue Streak rocket.

STENTON
7 miles E of Haddington on the A6370

This is one of the prettiest villages in a county noted for its villages. Its name means "stone town", and it was given conservation status in 1969. The T-plan Parish Church dates from 1829, and has some good stained glass. The tower of the **Old Parish Church**, which was built in medieval times, can still be seen. Stenton, from the 17th until the 19th century, had an important agricultural fair, and it was on the **Tron** that the wool was weighed.

Pressmennan Lake lies to the south of the village. This is one of the few "lakes" in Scotland (as opposed to lochs), though it is entirely artificial, having been created by the local landowner in the 19th century. The **Pressmennan Forest Trail** lies along its southern edge, and from its highest point you can see Arthur's Seat in Edinburgh 22 miles away, and the Bass Rock in the Firth of Forth, nine miles away.

GARVALD
6 miles SE of Haddington off the B6370

Lying snugly on the northern slopes of the Lammermuir Hills, Garvald is a small community with a Parish Church that dates partly from the 12th century. South east of the village is Nunraw, with the **Abbey of Sancta Maria** in its grounds. It is a Cistercian foundation, with the monks arriving in 1946 from Tipperary in Ireland. The abbey buildings date form 1952, and it was the first Cistercian abbey built in Scotland since the Reformation. However, a Cistercian nunnery, founded in 1158, had once stood on the site, though nothing of it now remains. Nunraw House is now the abbey guest house.

GIFFORD

4 miles S of Haddington on the B6369

Gifford is a planned village, laid out in the 18th century by the local laird. The **Mercat Cross** Dates from 1780, and the **Town Hall** from 1887. **Yester Parish Church** was built in the early 18th century, and has a medieval bell. Within the church is a memorial to John Witherspoon, who was born in the village in 1723. He was the only Scotsman to put his name to the American Declaration of Independence.

Yester House was designed by Adam in 1745, and stands to the south east of the village. The ruins of 13th century Yester Castle are close by, and within them is an underground chamber known as **Goblin Ha'**. The narrow road from Gifford south into the Lammermuir Hills is a fine drive through some wonderful countryside. It takes you past the Whiteadder Reservoir and down into the rich farmlands of Berwickshire.

PENCAITLAND

6 miles SW of Haddington on the A6093

Winton House was built for the Seton family over 500 years ago, though it has many later additions. It was designed by the king's master mason, and is famous

EAGLESCAIRNIE MAINS

by Gifford, Haddington, East Lothian EH41 4HN
Tel/Fax: 01620 810491
e-mail: williams.eagles@btinternet.com
website: www.eaglescairnie.com

Eaglescairnie Mains is a handsome Georgian house set in a 350 acre working farm, among the glorious scenery of East Lothian. Owners Barbara and Michael Williams have been offering excellent four star B&B accommodation in the farmhouse for over 13 years, and they now invite you to experience the very best in Scottish hospitality. There are three extremely comfortable no smoking rooms on offer - doubles/twin or singles - either fully en suite or with private bathrooms. The rooms have been decorated with imagination and flare, and each has central heating and views over a garden and hills. Guests can relax in the well appointed coral drawing room, with its deep chintz sofas and open log fire, or they can explore the farm, for which a small leaflet is provided.

This is a working farm, and it places great emphasis on good husbandry, with landscape and wildlife conservation very much to the fore. There is a tennis court if you feel like some hectic activity

before dinner, but if you prefer something more peaceful, there are board games, a small library of guidebooks and history books, brochures and TV available in the drawing room. A full Scottish breakfast, using only the freshest of local produce, is served in the breakfast room or in the lovely geranium-filled conservatory. Lighter options are available but all will be beautifully cooked and prepared to your satisfaction. This is an establishment where children and well behaved dogs are more than welcome, and there is unlimited private and safe parking.

for its "twisted chimneys". It overlooks the Tyne, and has lovely terraced gardens. **Pencaitland Parish Church** has the 13th century Winton Aisle.

The **Glenkinchie Distillery** is to the south of the village, and has a small exhibition and display area. There are tours showing how malt whisky is distilled.

Linlithgow Palace

LINLITHGOW

This old royal burgh lies at the heart of Scottish history. It has many old buildings, but none has as much history as **Linlithgow Palace** (Historic Scotland). The ruins sit on the shores of **Linlithgow Loch**, and date from the time of James I in the 15th century. It replaced an older castle - possibly a simple tower house - where Edward I once stayed when he invaded Scotland in support of his puppet king John Ballioll. The present castle was a favourite of Scottish kings, and James V was born here in 1512. It was also the birthplace in 1542 of his more famous daughter, Mary Stuart, better known as Mary Queen of Scots. She was probably born in James V's own chamber, now known as the **Queen's Bedchamber**, in the north west tower. She stayed at the Palace for seven months before she was taken to Stirling by her mother, Mary of Guise. When Mary returned from France after her husband King Francis died, she stayed briefly at the castle before moving to Edinburgh.

It was then allowed to decay, though Cromwell stayed briefly in the Palace in 1650 when he invaded Scotland after it had declared Charles II king. Then, in

1745, Charles Edward Stuart himself stayed in the Palace. A year later, it was the turn of the Duke of Cumberland - known as "Butcher Cumberland" - and the Hanovarian troops. However, the troops slept too close to the palace fires, and when they finally moved out, the straw from their mattresses caught fire, and the whole building was soon ablaze. Today it is roofless and uninhabitable, but it still gives an idea of the comparative opulence that the Scottish monarchs lived in. The **Outer Gateway** to the palace grounds still stands, and on it are the coats-of-arms of the four orders of chivalry to which James V belonged - the Thistle of Scotland, the Garter of England, the Golden Fleece of Burgundy and St. Michael of France.

St. Michael's Parish Church is one of the largest and most complete medieval parish churches in Scotland. It stands opposite the Palace, and dates mainly from the 15th century, though a church stood on the site long before that. The church was especially dear to James IV, and he used to worship there regularly. In 1513, he decided to invade England in support of France, which had been invaded by Henry VIII. The Scottish court, including his wife Margaret, who was Henry VIII's sister, opposed the idea, but James wouldn't change his mind.

A few days before he set out he was at mass in the church, and a strange man with long, fair hair suddenly entered the church and strode right up to the king, who was kneeling in prayer. Before the king's bodyguard had time to react, the man, who was dressed in a sky blue gown tied at the waist with a white band and carried a pikestaff, started to harangue the startled king. He said he had been sent by "his mother" to tell James that the invasion would end in disaster, and that he must call it off. He also added, almost as an afterthought, that he shouldn't consort with other women.

The bodyguard and some of the courtiers tried to grab the man, but before they could do so he appeared to vanish into thin air. Confusion reigned, and people were soon saying that the man was a ghost. The reference to "his mother" was a reference to Our Lady, to whom James was particularly devoted. James ignored it all, however, and eventually invaded England. He was killed at Flodden, and the Scottish army and nobility were all but wiped out by Henry VIII's troops.

One of the courtiers who witnessed the incident was Sir David Lyndsay (Lord Lyon and a noted playwright) and he committed the details to paper. Because of this, the ghost theory was believed for a long while, though nowadays more prosaic explanations are given, all of them involving trickery. One says that Queen Margaret was put up to it by her brother to try and stop James's invasion plans, as Henry could not afford to deploy troops on his northern border at that time. Another says that Margaret was just fearful for her husband's life, and wanted the venture stopped. Yet another says it was the courtiers themselves.

It was almost certainly a trick carried out by Margaret and some of the courtiers, though it is doubtful if Henry was involved. The old man got close to the king, something that would not have happened if the courtiers had not allowed it to happen, and he just as quickly melted away, no doubt aided by those self same courtiers. The blue gown and white cord are significant, as they are associated not just with Scotland's national flag, but also with The Virgin, to whom James was particularly devoted. And the reference to not consorting with other women was Margaret's own contribution to the whole proceedings, as James was notorious for his womanising. Sir David Lyndsay, having theatrical experience, may have "produced" the entire thing, and written about it after Flodden as evidence of the king's folly.

A plaque on the old **County Buildings** marks the spot where the Earl of Moray,

Union Canal, Linlithgow

Regent of Scotland during James VI's minority, was assassinated by the Hamiltons in 1570. In Annet House in the High Street is the **Linlithgow Story**, which explains the history of the town, and the story of the assassination is told there.

The Union Canal, linking the Forth and Clyde Canal with Edinburgh, runs through Linlithgow, and at the **Linlithgow Canal Centre** in Manse Road is a small museum dedicated to the waterway. Trips along the canal are available. **Beecraigs Country Park** sits to the south of the town, and is set in 913 acres of land near the Bathgate Hills. It has a loch where fishing is allowed.

The **House of the Binns** (National Trust for Scotland) is the ancestral home of the Dalyell (pronounced ("Dee-yell") family, and sits to the north east of the town. In 1601 an Edinburgh butter merchant called Thomas Dalyell married Janet, daughter of the first Baron Kinloss. In 1630 he bought the lands of Binns, and enlarged the small mansion that stood on it. What you see today is essentially that house.

Thomas's son was also called Thomas, though he has gone down in history as "Bloody Tam Dalyell", a king's man who was the scourge of Covenantors. In 1649, when Charles I was executed, he vowed never to cut his hair until there was a king on the throne once more. A portrait in the house shows Tam with long, flowing locks. He also went to Russia, where he advised the Tsar on reorganising the Russian army. For this he was made a Russian nobleman, which earned him yet another nickname - the "Bloody Muscovite".

Hopetoun House also sits north east of the town. It is home to the Marquis of Linlithgow, and designed by Sir William Bruce, with enlargements by William Adam, who introduced the sweeping

curves. The inside is rich and opulent, with spectacular plasterwork, tapestries, furnishings and paintings. The parkland extends to 1,000 acres, with a deer park and spring garden.

The main approach to the house is by a grand Royal Drive, which is used exclusively by royalty. George IV used it in 1822, as did Queen Elizabeth in 1988.

AROUND LINLITHGOW

BO'NESS
3 miles N of Linlithgow on the A904

Bo'ness is short for Borrowstoneness, a name that is no longer used. It was formerly one of Scotland's leading whaling ports, and used to export coal from the Lothian coalfields. The Antonine Wall, which stretches across Scotland from the Clyde, has its eastern end close to the town.

The **Bo'ness and Kinneil Railway** has been developed since 1979 by the Scottish Railway Preservation Society. Trips are available on steam trains which run between Bo'ness Station and Birkhill Station south west of the town. At Birkhill the **Birkhill Fireclay Mine** can be visited.

Kinneil House was built by the Hamiltons in the 16th and 17th centuries, and sits within the Kinneil Estate. Though it isn't open to the public, it can be viewed from the outside. Within the stables block is the **Kinneil Museum**, with displays and artifacts illustrating Bo'ness's history from Roman times.

BLACKNESS
4 miles NE of Linlithgow on the B903

Blackness Castle (Historic Scotland) is shaped like a huge ship, and sits on a promontory that juts out into the Firth of Forth. It was built by Sir George Crichton, Sheriff of Linlithgow and Admiral of Scotland, in about 1449. There is an intriguing but completely untrue story about how the castle came to be built. It passed to the Douglases in the early 1500s, and at about the same time James V appointed Archibald Douglas as Lord High Admiral of Scotland. However, it soon transpired that when Archibald went to sea, he invariably became seasick.

The young James was angry, and threatened to remove Archibald from a post which was extremely lucrative, as Archibald could sell commissions. Archibald promised to build a ship on which he would never be seasick, and James was placated. So he had Blackness rebuilt in the shape of a ship, and from there he commanded the Scottish navy. The story, however, is completely untrue. The real reason for the castle's shape is the restricted site on which the castle is built.

TORPHICHEN

3 miles S of Linlithgow on the B792

In 1124, the Knights of the Order of St. John of Jerusalem, otherwise known as the Knights Hospitallers, founded a monastery at Torphichen, which later became known as **Torphichen Preceptory** (Historic Scotland). The knights were an order of military monks which had originally been founded in the 11th century to protect St. John's Hospital in Jerusalem, and look after pilgrims travelling to the Holy Land.

All that remains of the Preceptory (so called because the abbot of the monastery was called the "preceptor") today are the crossing and transepts of the church. Above the crossing is a tower which looks more like a castle than a church tower (no doubt because of the monk's military set up). There is a small

display within it about the monks, and about the modern Order of St. John, founded in Scotland as a separate order in 1947 by George VI. This new order runs old folk's homes, hospitals and mountain rescue units in the country.

Where the nave of the monastic church once stood is now **Torphichen Parish Church**, partly built from the masonry of the old preceptory in 1756.

LIVINGSTON

6 miles S of Linlithgow off the M8

Livingston is one of the five new towns created in Scotland in the 1940s, 1950s and 1960s (the others being Glenrothes, East Kilbride, Cumbernauld and Irvine), and now has a population of about 50,000. It was built round a historic village where sits the **Livingston Parish Church** of 1732, and is now one of the main shopping centres in West Lothian, with undercover malls that offer all-weather shopping.

The **Almond Valley Heritage Centre** in Millfield has displays and exhibitions about the area's local history and natural history, and features the shale industry, which once flourished in West Lothian. The **Almondell and Calderwood Country Park** is three miles west of the town centre, and has riverside and woodland walks. It was originally a private estate belonging to the Erskine family, and an area has been left undeveloped to encourage wildlife. The Oakbank Shale Bings - spoil heaps of red shale-like rocks - remind the visitor of the shale industry that once dominated West Lothian. A good view, which takes in Fife on a clear day, can be had from their tops.

MID CALDER

8 miles SE of Linlithgow off the A71

The apse of the parish church, the **Kirk of Calder**, dates from the 16th century. In 1848 the Polish pianist and composer

Chopin stayed at **Calder House** (not open to the public), and in the 16th century John Knox first administered Holy Communion using the new reformed liturgy in a previous house which stood on the site.

BATHGATE

6 miles S of Linlithgow on the A89

Bathgate is a substantial industrial town, and was formerly centre for the shale oil industry. In 1811 **James Young** (also known as "Paraffin" Young) was born here. It was he who established the shale industry in West Lothian, and opened the world's first oil refinery in 1850, extracting the oil from the local shale, a red, slate-like mineral. Also born in the town was **Sir James Young Simpson**. At the incredibly early age of 28, he was appointed to Edinburgh University's Chair of Midwifery. He was the seventh son of the local baker, and pioneered the use of chloroform into midwifery to dull the pain of childbirth. His efforts, incredibly enough, were at first opposed by many eminent doctors and clerics of the time, who believed that eliminating pain from childbirth was contrary to God's will.

The 1,071 feet high **Cairnpapple Hill** (Historic Scotland) lies north of the town, and was the site of a fort or temple built about 4,000 to 4,500 years ago. Fragments of bone and pottery have been found during various archaeological digs. The view from the top on a clear day is magnificent, and the climb is not all that difficult if you are reasonably fit. The mountains of Arran, an island in the Firth of Clyde, and the Bass Rock in the Firth of Forth can be seen.

In Mansfield Street is the small **Bennie Museum**, which has collections of objects connected with the history of Bathgate. **Polkemmet Country Park** lies four miles west of the town, and has a golf course, a driving range, bowling green and picnic areas.

6 FIFE AND KINROSS

The Kingdom of Fife is steeped in Scottish history. James II once said that it had "a fringe of gold on a beggar's mantle", meaning that in his day it had a poor interior but many prosperous ports and towns on its coastline. It is a peninsula that is bounded on the north by the Firth of Tay and on the south by the Firth of Forth, and for all its importance in Scottish history it was never the easiest place to get to by land. But it did have these ports, and they traded with France, the Baltic countries, the Netherlands and England, and ferries criss crossed both firths.

This trade with the Continent meant that the county was heavily influenced by Europe, and even today you see houses roofed with red pantiles rather than slates, the pantiles originally having been brought into the ports as ships' ballast from the Netherlands. The ports that traded with Europe - Crail, Anstruther, St. Andrews, Pittenweem, Elie are still there, though now they rely in tourism for their living. They are all picturesque places, and with their small harbours, old cottages and cobbled alleyways, they must have been photographed over and over again for cards and calenders.

The town of Dunfermline is in Fife. It was Scotland's capital before Edinburgh assumed the mantle, and it was in Dunfermline that Margaret, Malcolm III's queen, first began modernising Scotland in the 11th century, turning it from a backward kingdom on the edge of things into a truly European monarchy with links to many other countries. Scotland's great hero of the Wars of Independence, Robert the Bruce, afterwards Robert I, King of Scotland, is buried within the town's abbey.

St. Andrews is also in Fife. Before the Reformation, it was Scotland's ecclesiastical capital, with the country's largest cathedral (in fact, it was Scotland's largest and most complex building of any kind until well after the Reformation). In a country where cathedrals were not normally large, ornate affairs, it rivalled most of the English cathedrals in size and architecture. The town was also where Scotland's first university was founded in 1413. The university is still there, as are the students, who can be seen in the town during term time, some in the traditional red gowns. At

Pittenweem Village

LOCATOR MAP

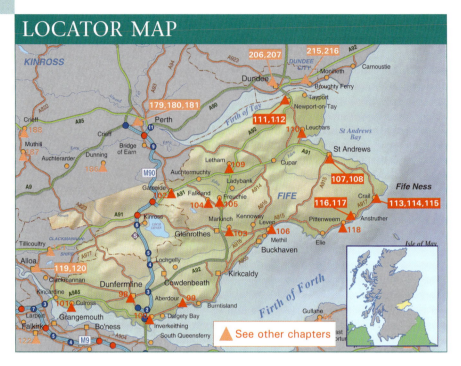

▲ See other chapters

ADVERTISERS AND PLACES OF INTEREST

one time, it was a place of pilgrimage, and seen from a distance today it seems to shimmer with spires and church towers. The town still attracts pilgrims, but nowadays they come with a set of golf clubs and a suitcase full of Pringle sweaters and tasselled brogues. For this is the world home of golf, and the golf course is a regular venue for the British Open.

Elie Beach

The county's largest town is Kirkcaldy (pronounced "Kir-coddy"), famous as a centre of linoleum manufacture. So much so that people could always tell when they were approaching the town by the "queer-like smell", produced by the manufacturing processes, and indeed there is a song about Kirkcaldy with those exact words in it. But there is so much more to Kirkcaldy than industry. It is a royal burgh, and has many historical associations. It's nickname is the "Lang Toun". At one time it consisted of one long street along the coastline, though it has spread inland nowadays.

To the west of the county coal mining was king. The Fife coal fields used to employ thousands of men, but it has all but gone, leaving in its wake many small mining communities, like Cowdenbeath and Cardenden. They are not picturesque places, but they have a sense of community that has been lost in many other towns and villages in Scotland. Just outside Dunfermline is one of the hidden gems of the county - Culross, an ancient burgh that hasn't changed all that much since the 17th century.

Kinross-shire sits to the west of Fife. Before local government reorganisation in 1975 it was Scotland's second smallest county, and though it now comes under a local government area called "Perth and Kinross-shire", it still has many links with Fife. It sits in a saucer-shaped depression with, at its centre, Loch Leven. It's an agricultural county, and its soft, gentle countryside, ringed by low hills, is well worth exploring. But even in such a small place as Kinross-shire events took place that shaped Scotland's history. Mary Stuart was held captive in Loch Leven Castle, on an island in Loch Leven, and made a daring escape from it. At Crook of Devon, in 1662, a coven of witches was uncovered, with the witches later being put on trial and executed. And Scotlandwell was yet another place of pilgrimage. A friary and a holy well once stood in the village, and pilgrims came from all over seeking cures for their illnesses. The well is still there, and the waters can still be drunk, though whether they actually offer a cure for anything is another matter.

DUNFERMLINE

Dunfermline was at one time the capital of Scotland, and it was here that the Scottish kings held court until Malcolm III (known as "Malcolm Canmore") moved to Edinburgh. His queen was Margaret, who later became **St. Margaret of Scotland**, and their reign, from 1057 to 1093, was a turning point in the Scotland's history. Margaret was Malcolm's second wife (his first wife being Queen Ingibiord, widow of the Earl of Orkney), and she was the sister of Edgar Aetheling, heir to the English throne. She was half Anglo Saxon and half Hungarian, and was an accomplished and refined woman.

The story goes that her brother at first paid homage to William the Conqueror. But Edgar eventually led a revolt, which was crushed. He fled with his mother and sister, and eventually arrived by ship on the Fife coast. They made their way to Dunfermline, where Malcolm instantly fell in love with Margaret and they married. No doubt it was a love match, but he also surely recognised in Margaret a woman who could help him realise his ambition to make Scotland a modern country that was fully integrated into Europe.

Margaret was scandalised by what she found. The Roman Catholic Church (and she was a devout Catholic) held no sway in the country, though it was supposed to be subservient to Rome. Instead the priests observed the old Celtic rites when celebrating mass. They were called Culdees (from the Irish "céli dé", meaning "servants of God". She banished the priests and founded

---

TOWN HOUSE

48 East Port, Dunfermline KY12 7JB
Tel: 01383 432382 Fax: 01383 432381
e-mail: info@townhouserestaurant.co.uk
website: www.townhouserestaurant.co.uk

At the **Town House** in the historic town of Dunfermline (once Scotland's capital), only the finest and freshest local produce is used wherever possible to create the fine dishes on its menu. There is also a hint of European influence in the cuisine in this spacious restaurant - one of the best and most visited in Fife. Relax with good food and fine wines, and take in the decor, which is modern, chic yet comfortable. It has a style all of its own, featuring bare stonework, designer furniture and local artwork which has been specially commissioned to create a superb space for eating and being with friends.

Before you dine, enjoy a drink in the bar, which is stocked with a fine range of malt whiskies, brandies and liqueurs. Or perhaps it is just a coffee you want, a lazy lunch during a shopping trip or a quick bite? The Town House can provide that as well, with the same care and attention to detail being shown. The prices are all surprisingly reasonable, considering the high standards set by Paul Brown, who runs and owns

the establishment. Private functions, exclusive dinner parties, corporate events, presentation lunches and even wine tastings can also be accommodated within the bar and mezzanine dining area. As the restaurant's brochure says: "While we do the work, you do the business"! So if you're in the attractive town of Dunfermline, with its magnificent abbey church, why not pay the Town House a visit? You won't be disappointed!

Dunfermline Abbey

Dunfermline Abbey, inviting monks from Durham to serve in it.

She also made the Scottish court more refined and in tune with European manners, and one of her lasting innovations was placing buttons on the sleeves of gentlemen's garments. Throughout Europe, and not just in Scotland, it had always been the custom for men to blow their noses on their sleeves, and Margaret wanted to stamp out the habit.

She could not have done it alone, of course. She had Malcolm's help all along the way. Though he could neither read nor write, he longed to bring Scotland into the mainstream of European thinking. He had even been at the English court of Edward the Confessor for a short while, and may have originally met Margaret there. He saw the refinement of the court, and the embracing of new, exciting ideas. Only a few years previously, he had moved Scotland's capital from Scone in Perthshire to Dunfermline so that it could be nearer the influence of the ports that traded with the Continent. But for all this, there was a cruel, wayward streak in Malcolm, and no

matter what his wife did, he always seemed intent on waging war. And he didn't embrace his queen's new ideas out of a love of God or the Roman Catholic Church - he saw that a structured, Roman Catholic hierarchy would give the country stability and make it easier to rule.

Margaret died four days after her husband, who was killed, along with his son, while invading Northern England in 1093. She was canonised in 1250, and her tomb in Dunfermline Abbey became a place of pilgrimage. Today she is still revered in Scotland. Her shrine was destroyed at the Reformation, though parts of it can still be seen.

Today's Dunfermline Abbey is a mixture of styles. The nave is obviously Norman, as can be seen from its round arches and stout pillars, and owes a lot to Durham Cathedral. Beneath the floor are the remains of the original, smaller church founded by St. Margaret. The choir and tower were rebuilt in the early 19th century as the parish church for the town, and it was during its construction that workmen came upon a peculiar stone coffin. It contained the skeleton of a man, wrapped in lead and a gold cloth. Some of the skeleton's ribs had been sawed and removed, and it was immediately recognised as the skeleton of Robert I, better known as Robert the Bruce. His body had been buried in the abbey in 1329 when he died of leprosy, though his heart had been removed beforehand to be taken to the Holy Land for burial.

The bones were reburied with reverence, and a brass plate was erected over the spot beneath the church's pulpit. And around the abbey tower the words "King Robert The Bruce" were carved in stone.

The **Dunfermline Abbey and Palace Visitors Centre** (Historic Scotland) tells the complete story of the abbey, and of the royal palace that was later built where the monastic buildings once stood. A magnificent 200 feet long wall is all that remains of the palace, where Charles I was born in 1600.

Andrew Carnegie was born in Dunfermline in 1835. He emigrated to America in 1848 with his parents, and by the 1880s he was the richest man in the world, thanks to his iron and steel making interests. He retired in 1901, and set about distributing his wealth. His birthplace, a humble weaver's cottage in Moodie Street, is still there, and is now the focal point of the **Andrew Carnegie Birthplace Museum**. It tells the full story of his life from his birth to his death in 1919. Close to the Louise Carnegie Gates (named after Andrew's wife), at the entrance to Pittencreiff Park. is a statue of the great man. And New York is not the only place to have a **Carnegie Hall**. Dunfermline has one as well, in East Port, and it houses a theatre and concert hall.

To the west of the abbey is a great mound called **Malcolm's Tower**, all that remains of Malcolm's castle. The old burgh coat-of-arms has the tower as an important feature. It sits within **Pittencrieff Park**, which is famous for its peacocks. The park was gifted to the town by Carnegie in 1908. The place had always fascinated him when he was young, and was privately owned. Access was always denied him, so when he had the money he bought it and threw it open to the people of his home town. **Pittencrieff House Museum**, housed in a 17th century mansion, has an art gallery and displays on local history.

In Maygate, north of the abbey, is the **Abbot House Heritage Centre**, within a 14th to 16th century house. It was formerly the Abbot's Lodging, and poets, kings and bishops often stayed here. Over 1,000 years of history can be seen, from Pictish times right up until the present day. St. Margaret's Shrine has been reconstructed within it, and it shows just how rich the interior of the abbey was before the Reformation. Near Chalmers Street car park, some way north of the Heritage Centre, is **St. Margaret's Cave**. It was here that Margaret use to come to pray in solitude. A story tells of Malcolm becoming suspicious when his wife disappeared for hours at a time, and he became convinced that she had taken a lover. So he followed her one day, and discovered her within the cave on her knees deep in prayer.

To the north of the town, at Lathalmond, is the **Scottish Vintage Bus Museum**, housed in a former Royal Navy stores depot. Opened in 1995, it has possibly the largest collection of vintage buses in Britain.

AROUND DUNFERMLINE

COWDENBEATH
5 miles NE of Dunfermline off the A909

Though mining has long since gone from this part of Fife, there are still many small mining villages and towns in the area. Cowdenbeath is one of them, and it still retains its "small town" community spirit. The **Cowdenbeath Racewall** hosts stock car racing every Saturday evening from March to November. Even though the town only has a population of about 11,000, it has a football team which plays in the Scottish League, the nickname of which is the "Blue Brazils".

LOCHGELLY

7 miles NE of Dunfermline on the B981

At one time, the name "Lochgelly" struck terror in every Scottish schoolboy's heart, as it was here that the ubiquitous leather straps known as "Lochgellys", which were used for corporal punishment in schools, were made. The **Lochore Meadows Country Park** covers 919 acres of reclaimed industrial land north of the town, and is now it is a haven for wildlife. Loch Ore, which was created as a result of mining subsidence, is stocked with brown trout.

ABERDOUR

6 miles E of Dunfermline on the A921

The restored **St. Fillans Parish Church** is partly Norman, and has a "leper's window" so that, in olden times, lepers could observe the mass while remaining isolated from the rest of the congregation. The substantial ruins of **Aberdour Castle** (Historic Scotland) are close to the church. They date from the 14th century and later. The castle was originally built in the 12th century by the de Mortimer family, but passed to the Douglases in 1342, and became home to the Earls of Morton. Since 1790, when the Douglases moved out, the castle has had many uses - a school, a Masonic lodge and housing for soldiers. In 1924 it was taken into state care.

DALGETY BAY

4 miles SE of Dunfermline off the A921

The ruins of **St. Bridget's Church** (Historic Scotland) date from the 12th century, and have many interesting features. There is a piscina (a shallow stone basin for rinsing the communion chalice) near where the altar stood, and the lofts (small galleries) can still be seen. The graveyard, with some interesting old gravestones, faces the shore, and makes an attractive picture. The church must have been in existence before 1178, because in that year it is mentioned in a Papal Bull of Pope Alexander III. Every year in June an open air service is held within its walls.

It was near Dalgety Bay that the famous murder of James Stewart, 2nd Earl of Moray, took place in 1592. He was married to the daughter of Regent Moray, and was a dashing and handsome man. However, he was forever feuding with the Gordons, who were Earls of Huntly and one of the great Catholic families of the time. He was falsely accused of being involved in a plot to overthrow James VI, and the then Earl of Huntly saw a way of permanently ridding himself of the Earl. Armed with a King's Warrant, he set out to seize him. He eventually found Moray staying at Donibristle Castle, the home of his mother, near Dalgety Bay, and had his

SHORELINE STUDIO

2 Shore Road, Aberdour, Fife KY3 0TR
Tel/Fax: 01383 860705
e-mail: ianmcc@shoreline.demon.co.uk
website: www.shoreline.sco.fm/www.architects.sco.fm

In the picturesque seaside village of Aberdour you'll find the **Shoreline Studio**, a gallery which exhibits works of art from artists and craftpersons working and living mainly in Scotland. Owned and managed by Judith and Ian McCrorie, you are free to browse among the oils, watercolours, prints, cards, ceramics, stained glass, sculpture and jewellery. This is a colourful, fascinating place, full of great works of art that would adorn any wall or shelf. Judith herself is an artist and Ian is an architect, and they can offer friendly, knowledgeable advice on any purchase you wish to make.

INVERKEITHING MUSEUM

The Friary, Queen Street,
Inverkeithing, Fife
Tel: 01383 313838 (Fife Council
Museums West, Dunfermline)

Inverkeithing Museum is housed in the upper floor of a wonderful 14th century Friary guest house, standing amidst well-tended gardens. The gallery is small but has a lovely collection of local photographs, paintings and artefacts, illustrating the history of the area. Admiral Greig, Inverkeithing's most famous son - the "Father of the Russian Navy", is featured. Open Thursday, Friday, Saturday and Sunday 11am to 12.30pm and 1pm to 4pm. Admission is free but access is by stairs only and so is not suitable for the disabled.

troops surround it. Moray, however, refused to surrender, and the castle was set on fire.

Some men ran out the front of the castle as a diversion while Moray himself ran out the back, hoping to hide among the dunes on the shore. Unfortunately, and unbeknown to him, his bonnet had caught fire, and the smoke gave his hiding place away. He was hacked to death, with some people claiming that Huntly struck the fatal blow.

When James VI found out about the assassination, he at first appeared angry, but later said he was unconcerned, something which outraged the people of Edinburgh. Moray had been a popular figure at court and with the common people, and when they further found out Huntly had been armed with a King's Warrant, James VI and his Privy Council wisely decided to move to Glasgow until tempers had died down. A famous ballad was later written about the incident.

It may have been one death among many at the time, but it still touched the hearts of the common people. The Protestant religion had officially been embraced by the Scottish Parliament 32 years previously, but it was still uncertain

whether it would last, and the country was in turmoil, with Catholic and Protestant families feuding and jockeying for power. To placate his subjects, James VI eventually had Huntly imprisoned in Blackness Castle, but within a few weeks he was free.

INCHCOLM

6 miles SE of Dunfermline, in the Firth of Forth

On this small island stands the substantial remains of **Inchcolm Abbey** (Historic Scotland), dedicated to St. Columba, and this is the reason why the island is sometimes called the "Iona of the East". The story goes that Alexander I, son of Malcolm III and his wife Margaret, were crossing the Forth in 1123 when a storm blew up. The royal ship dropped anchor close to the shore of Inchcolm, and the royal party sought refuge there. For many years, it had been the home of a succession of hermits, and the hermit at the time shared his meagre supplies with the king and his men, and offered them shelter.

The storm lasted three days, and when the king eventually continued on his way, he vowed to found a monastery on the island dedicated to St. Columba. Before he could do so, however, he died, and it was his younger brother, David I, who eventually founded a priory for Augustinian canons, known as "black canons", which eventually became Inchcolm Abbey. A small stone building to the west of the present abbey buildings may have been the original hermit's "cell", though it has been much altered over the years. The abbey buildings themselves, as we see them today, date mainly from the 15th century, and are the most complete in Scotland, though the church choir has all but gone.

In the 18th century a hospital for wounded Russian sailors was established on the island, when part of the Russian fleet was based on the Forth, and in the 20th century it was fortified as part of the country's sea defences. Some of the fortifications can still be seen. The first air raid of World War II took place close by in September 1939 at Rosyth and the Forth Rail Bridge, and 500 troops were then stationed there to man the anti-aircraft guns that were set up.

NORTH QUEENSFERRY

3 miles S of Dunfermline off the A90

For many years, this small royal burgh was the northern terminus of a ferry founded by St. Margaret of Scotland in the 11th century. When the Forth Road Bridge opened in 1964 the ferry stopped operating.

The town sits on a small peninsula which juts out into the Forth, which explains why it was always popular as a crossing point - it was the river's narrowest point. The **Forth Bridges**

Visitor Centre is within the Queensferry Lodge Hotel, and explains about both the Forth Rail Bridge and the Road Bridge. There is a scale model of the Forth, as well as documents and photographs.

Deep Sea World is also at North Queensferry. It takes you on a walk across the "ocean floor", in reality a long underwater tunnel made of glass, and fish swim above and beside you as you walk along it. You can see piranha fish, stingrays and electric eels, and even stroke a shark.

North Queensferry is the start of the **Fife Coastal Path**, which stretches the 78 miles round the coast towards the Tay Bridge, passing many small fishing villages and towns on the way.

CHARLESTOWN

3 miles SW of Dunfermline on a minor road off the A985

There are large deposits of limestone in the area surrounding Charlestown, and in 1756 Charles Bruce, the 5th Earl of Elgin, built the village to exploit them. At one time 14 kilns produced lime for agriculture, building and iron and glass making. It was a model community for its day, with a school, good housing, and a harbour.

The works finally closed in 1956, having produced, it is estimated, over 11 million tons of quicklime. Guided tours are sometimes available through the industrial remains. The adjoining village of **Limekilns** was at one time the port for the monks of Dunfermline Abbey.

Forth Railway Bridge

CULROSS

7 miles W of Dunfermline on a minor road off the A985

No one should miss Culross. It is a perfect example of what a 16th, 17th and 18th century Scottish burgh looked like. Though it is more of a village than a town, it is actually a proud royal burgh, having been granted its charter from James VI in 1592. Up until local government reorganisation in 1975, it even had its own town council and provost. Walk down the cobbled streets, and you walk through history. The cottages and houses that form its core have been perfectly preserved, though most of them are still lived in. The reason for this picturesqueness and sense of history is not an enlightened council that wanted to preserve the town's history, but the town's relative poverty in later years. There wasn't the money to sweep away the old buildings and build new ones.

Now much of the town is owned by the National Trust for Scotland, and it is a thriving and lively community once more. Some of the streets, especially those round the **Mercat Cross**, dating from 1588, have a feature called the "crown o' the causie" - a raised portion in the middle of the road where the gentry and well off could walk without getting their shoes wet or muddy. The common people, of course, had to walk at the side of the road, where the water and dirt accumulated.

At the top of the village are the remains of **Culross Abbey**. Most of the monastic buildings are now in ruins, but the choir of the abbey church was restored in 1625 and now serves as the parish church. It was founded in 1215 by

CULROSS POTTERY AND GALLERY

Sandhaven, Culross, Fife KY12 8JG
Tel/Fax: 01383 882176
e-mail: camilla@culrosspottery.demon.co.uk
website: www.culrosspottery.com

Culross is a small, quaint mediaeval burgh caught in time. The architecture is mainly 16th and 17th century, and many of the houses are owned by the National Trust for Scotland. Here, in a former 17th century granary in a cobbled street, you will find one of the best places in Fife to buy that special gift. **Culross Pottery and Gallery** is owned and managed by Camilla Garrett-Jones. Downstairs is a working pottery, where you can see items being hand built or thrown, and upstairs is a colourful, airy gallery , where a wide range of hand-made pottery, jewellery, glassware, cards and paintings can be seen, mostly from local artists. A recent exhibition area is a contemporary garden where artwork is displayed. You can browse to your heart's content and there is always friendly, impartial advice on hand.

Camilla herself is an accomplished potter, and studied at the Glasgow School of Art. Also working at the pottery is Val Burns, and both have their own styles. Camilla mostly 'builds' her pots using local plants to impress into the clay, creating fascinating and individual organic shapes. She smoke fires her coiled pots, and is the maker of the unique mediaeval watering pot. Val

mainly throws her pots on a wheel, creating objects equally beautiful. She also makes individual 'tiger skin' coiled pots. Both fire using a gas kiln, and decorate and glaze in a style that combines tradition with modern methods. Camilla is determined to uphold the highest of standards and originality in the objects she chooses to display and sell. And she is equally determined to offer great value for money. So if you're looking for a gift that is just that wee bit different, then you have to visit the Culross Pottery and Gallery.

Culross Palace

Malcolm, Earl of Fife, for Cistercian monks. Off the north transept is the Bruce Vault, where an impressive monument marks the spot where Sir George Bruce, his wife, and their eight children are buried.

The main industries here were once coal mining, salt panning and the making of baking girdles. Coal mining had been introduced by the monks of the abbey, who, for all their piety, were always on the lookout for money making schemes. Sir George Bruce took over the mines after the Reformation, and even dug a tunnel beneath the Firth of Forth. It came up to sea level about a mile from the coast, where a wall prevented water getting in. James VI once paid a visit to the mine, and when he walked along the tunnel and found himself surrounded by water when he emerged into daylight, he immediately panicked and started shouting "Treason!"

The coal led to another industry - salt panning. The coal was used to heat huge pans of sea water, and at one time there were 50 such pans along the coastline. Yet another industry was the manufacture of girdles - round flat implements for making scones and bread. Robert the Bruce ordered that each one of his troops be issued with

a Culross girdle to cook oatcakes.

Nothing is left of Sir George's mining operations, though his house, now called **Culross Palace**, still stands. Building work started in 1597, and it is a typically late 16th and early 17th century dwelling. Along from it is the **Town House**, once Culross's town hall. It was gifted to the National Trust for Scotland when the local town council was wound up in 1975, and now houses a tourist centre. It was built in 1625, and at one time the attic was used as a prison for witches, while the ground floor was a debtor's prison.

The Study stands beside the old Mercat Cross. It dates from about 1610, and after Culross Palace, it is the town's grandest building. When Scotland had an Episcopalian church, this was where Bishop Leighton of Dunblane stayed when visiting the area. His study (hence the name of the house) was in the Outlook Tower.

In AD514 St. Kentigern, patron saint of Glasgow, was supposed to have been born near the town, and small chapel was erected in 1503 by Bishop Blackadder to mark the spot. The story of his birth is a well known one in Scotland. King Loth was the king of the Lothians in the 6th century, and had a daughter called Thenew (better known as Enoch). She became pregnant, and so outraged was her father that he cast her adrift on a boat in the Firth of Forth. She eventually came ashore at Culross, where a holy man named Serf had founded a small monastery. When Thenew gave birth to a son, St. Serf took him and his mother into his care. The boy was Kentigern, and when he achieved manhood he set off west and founded a monastery at Glasgow. It is a romantic story, but it may not be true, as it is now known that St. Serf lived in the 7th century.

Stretching from Longannet past Culross to Combie Point on the Firth of Forth is the **Torry Bay Local Nature Reserve**, which has many species of birds, such as shelduck, greenshank and great crested grebe.

KINCARDINE ON FORTH
10 miles W of Dunfermline on the A985

Kincardine sits at the northern end of the Kincardine Bridge, which up until the Forth Road Bridge was opened in 1964, was the only vehicle crossing point on the river below Stirling. It dates from 1936, with a middle section that once swung round to allow ships to pass. The town is a jumble of old cottages and houses, and there are the ruins of the **Tulliallan Church**, dating from the 17th century. The burgh's Mercat Cross is also from the 17th century. To the west of the town is **Tulliallan Training College**, the main training college in Scotland for policemen. It was in Kincardine, in 1842, that Sir James Dewar, inventor of the vacuum flask, was born.

KINROSS

Once the county town of the second smallest county in Scotland, Kinross now sits quietly on the shores of Loch Leven. The M90 passes close by, and this has meant that it has become a commuting town for Edinburgh. The Tolbooth dates from the 17th century, and on the **Mercat Cross** are the "joups", an iron collar placed round the neck of criminals as a punishment.

Kinross House dates from the 17th century, and was built for Sir William

Bruce, Charles II's surveyor. He was responsible for Holyroodhouse in Edinburgh. It is built in the Palladian style, and has gardens that are sometimes open to the public. The story goes that the house was intended for James VII, (II of England) then Duke of York..

Loch Leven covers about 3,250 acres, and is famous for its trout fishing, though this has diminished of late. The trout are highly prized for their delicate pink flesh, due to the small fresh water shellfish on which they feed. The whole loch is a National Nature Reserve, with the **Vane Farm Nature Reserve** on its southern shore. It is owned and looked after by the Royal Society for the Protection of Birds, and was the first educational reserve in Europe. The loch has two islands. On **St. Serf's Island** are the remains of a small priory and chapel, and on the other are the ruins of **Loch Leven Castle** (Historic Scotland). From June 1567 until May 1568 Mary Stuart was held captive here, having been seized in Edinburgh for her supposed part in the murder of her husband Darnley. At the time she was married to Bothwell, who was also implicated in the plot. While being held prisoner, she was instructed to divorce Bothwell and renounce the throne, but resisted, as she was already pregnant by him. She gave birth to stillborn twins, but even then she refused to abdicate or divorce Bothwell.

Eventually she managed to escape in a daring manner. The castle was owned by the dowager Lady Douglas, mother of Mary's half brother the Earl of Morton, who subsequently became Regent when Mary at last abdicated some time later. She, and her two other sons, Sir George and Sir William, looked after her. However, George soon fell in love with the queen, and hatched various plots for her escape. All of them failed, and he was eventually banished. But someone else had fallen in love with Mary, and this was Willie Douglas, a 16 year-old page boy who was thought to be Sir William's illegitimate son.

Mary was normally held in the third floor of the tower, and one evening, while the Douglases dined below, young William dropped a napkin over the castle keys, which his father had placed on the table. He then picked up the napkin and the keys at the same time. Mary and her personal servants later crept out of her room and went downstairs to the main doorway, where Willie was waiting. He unlocked the door, and they slipped out and into a waiting boat carrying George Douglas, Lord Seton. They sailed to the shore where a troop of loyal soldiers waited for them. They all then went to the safety of Niddrie Castle.

When they left Loch Leven Castle,

young Willie is supposed to have locked the stout doors behind him and dropped the keys in the water. Over the years, the water level of the loch has dropped about four feet, and indeed a set of stout keys was discovered buried in the ground next to the castle some years ago, lending credence to the story. People can now visit the castle by a small ferry that leaves from the pier at Kinross.

The **Cashmere at Loch Leven Exhibition** is within the premises of Todd and Duncan, and traces the history of this luxury fabric. And at the **Scottish Gliding Centre** at Portmoak people can try an "air experience flight". An experience of a different - and much louder - sort is to visit the annual **T in the Park** rock festival, Scotland's largest, which takes place near Kinross every year in July.

THE LOMONDS GALLERY

The Gateside Mills, Gateside, Fife KY14 7ST
Tel: 01337 860860
e-mail: nev@thelomondsgallery.co.uk
website: www.thelomondsgallery.co.uk

The **Lomonds Gallery** is twinned with Trinity Arts in Pittenweem, and is located on the first floor of the Gateside Mills on the outskirts of Gateside Village. It is a fine showcase for Scottish artists, and exhibits paintings, sculpture, ceramics, jewellery and a selection of prints of works associated with the artists who exhibit here. This is the ideal place to have a browse, or buy an extra special reminder of your holiday in this wonderful part of Scotland. There are two exhibition rooms, and the exhibitions themselves change on a regular basis, meaning there is always something new and interesting to see and admire.

The owner, Neville Storer, is himself an artist of renown, and has his studio within the gallery. He will be more than pleased to offer advice and information, and answer any questions you may have. The atmosphere is friendly and welcoming, and there is never any pressure to buy anything. Why not

relax with a cup of coffee as you view what is on offer? The gallery also carries a range of Royal Talens art supplies, which are manufactured in The Netherlands, and reckoned to be the finest in Europe. As part of the service, Neville has a nationwide mailing service, and prides himself on offering "quality at affordable prices". Why not take advantage of the value bulk/group/student user plan and get more for your money. Neville can supply details. Plus he offers art courses, demonstration evenings and art therapy classes. If you're ever in this area of Fife, you can't afford to miss the Lomonds Galleries.

AROUND KINROSS

MILNATHORT
2 miles N of Kinross off the M90

The ruins of **Burleigh Castle** can be seen to the east of the town. It was a stronghold of the Balfour family, with the head of the family being raised to the peerage in 1606. However, the 5th Lord Balfour forfeited the title and lands for his part in the Jacobite Uprising in 1745. The castle then passed to the Irwins and finally the Grahams of Kinross.

SCOTLANDWELL
5 miles E of Kinross on the A911

Scotlandwell sits on the western slopes of the Lomond Hills, where mineral springs bubble up to the surface. The Bishop of St. Andrews set up a small hospice here, with a later bishop giving it to the Trinitarians, or "Red Friars", a monastic order which had originally been founded to raise money for the release of captives in the Holy Land during the Crusades. They established a Holy Well , which soon became a place of pilgrimage, and brought in lots of money. However, the local landowners, the Arnots of **Arnot Tower** (the ruins of which can still be seen) coveted the wealth that the monks were accumulating, and decided to take over. They introduced younger sons to the order of monks, and when enough were in place, occupied the friary. Archibald Arnot, the Laird of Arnot's second son, was elected "minister" (the name given to the head of a Trinitarian house), and he began creaming off the money. At the Reformation, the friary and its lands passed directly to the Arnots, but by then pilgrimages were a thing of the past.

The Holy Well is still there, and is now a memorial to Henrietta, a former Laird of Arnot's wife. Within the graveyard of the church is a plaque which marks the spot where the friary once stood.

CROOK OF DEVON
5 miles W of Kinross on the A977

There is nothing much to see in this small, quiet village. However, there is a gruesome story attached to it. A coven of witches was discovered in the village, and in 1662 three women were strangled to death and their bodies burnt at a "place called Lamblaires". A few weeks later four men and one woman were executed in the same way, and soon after another two women were sentenced to death. One, however, was spared because of her age.

By this time the other members of the so-called coven had fled from the area. But two further women were put on trial. One was executed and one, unusually, was acquitted. Her name was Christian Grieve, and so incensed were the local clergy that she had escaped execution that she was re-tried and eventually burnt at the stake.

The trials, of course, were a travesty, and people used them to settle old scores and grievances. Women whose only "crime" was to be old and confused would admit to devil worship, while others, in a futile attempt to escape death, would implicate others. Still more of the accused turned the tables on their accusers by naming them as witches and warlocks as well, and many a minister or priest suddenly found himself on the receiving end of the justice they had formerly handed out. In this way, it appeared that Scotland was awash with devil worship, when in fact it was almost non-existent.

Today the area called Lamblaires is a grassy knoll in a field adjoining the village. It looks peaceful enough, and nothing reminds you of the events that took place there all these years ago.

KIRKCALDY

This old royal burgh was granted its charter in 1644. At one time it was known as the "Lang Toon", as the town appeared to stretch out along one main street. The **Links Market**, reckoned to be the longest street fair in Europe, takes place here every April. The streets are cordoned off from traffic and given over to swings, roundabouts and all the fun of the fair.

Kirkcaldy Museum and Art Gallery has exhibits devoted to **Wemyss Ware**, which, from 1882 until 1930, was manufactured in the town by Robert Heron and Son. This earthenware pottery is possibly the most sought after pottery ever to have been manufactured in Scotland. Its decoration is bold, simple and direct, and such was the methods used in its firing that there was a lot of wastage. For this reason it was always expensive to buy, which adds to its appeal today. The museum also has exhibits on local history, plus a collection of paintings.

Ravenscraig Castle was built by James II in the 15th century for his queen,

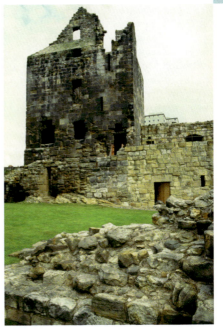

Ravenscraig Castle

Mary of Gueldres, and the extensive ruins now sit on a promontory adjacent to the public park. It was later occupied by the Sinclairs, who were Earls of Orkney. Overlooking the harbour is **Sailor's Walk**, the town's oldest house. The **Old Parish Kirk** sits at the top of Kirk Wynd, and dates from 1808, though its tower is medieval.

At one time **Dysart** was a separate burgh, but in 1930 it was absorbed into Kirkcaldy. Its harbour area is very picturesque, with whitewashed houses dating from the 16th, 17th and 18th centuries. At one time this was a salt panning area, and **Pan Ha'**, a group of 17th century buildings, reminds us of that time. **St. Serf's Tower** dates from the 15th century, and is all that is left of the old parish kirk. It looks more

Dysart Harbour

like a castle than a church tower, which reflects the fact that this area used to be attacked regularly by ships of the English navy. In Rectory Lane is the **John McDouall Stuart Museum**, dedicated to the life of the locally born explorer who made the first two-way journey across the Australian continent in 1861-62.

Adam Smith, the founder of the science of economics, was also born in Kirkcaldy in 1723, and his famous book, *The Wealth of Nations*, was partly written in his mother's house in High Street, which is now gone. William Adam was also born in Kirkcaldy in 1689, as was his son, Robert, in 1728.

In the Abbotshill Kirkyard stands a memorial to an unusual local writer. Her name was Marjory Fleming, though she is more commonly known as "Pet Marjory". She died in 1811 aged only eight, and yet people have been delighted and surprised by her writings down through the years. She kept a journal, in which she jotted down all her thoughts and observations on her short life. She was considered to be unruly, and when her mother gave birth to another child in 1809, she was packed off to live with her aunt and cousin Isa in Edinburgh. Encouraged by Isa, she eventually filled three notebooks. Had she not died of meningitis one day short of her ninth birthday, who knows what

she might have accomplished. Her last work was a short, poignant piece to her cousin. After her death, her work was published, and was an instant hit, though some Victorians tut-tutted at her honesty when describing her own tantrums and sulks.

AROUND KIRKCALDY

GLENROTHES
6 miles N of Kirkcaldy on the A92

Glenrothes was one of the new towns established in Scotland after World War II. **Balbirnie Park** extends to 416 acres, and has a late Neolithic site which dates from about 2900BC.

FALKLAND
10 miles N of Kirkcaldy on the A912

This little royal burgh (no bigger than a village) in the shadow of the **Lomond Hills** was granted its charter in 1458, though it was one of four Fife royal burghs which never functioned as such, the others being Earlsferry, Auchtermuchty and Newburgh. There are two distinct peaks peaks in the Lomond Hills - West Lomond at 1,713 feet (the highest point in Fife) and East Lomond at 1,471 feet.

Falkland has old cottages and houses dating from the 17th, 18th and 19th

ALISON AND ROY MURRAY

4 Balbirnie Craft Centre, Balbirnie Park, Markinch, Fife KY7 6NE
Tel/Fax: 01592 753743

Alison and Roy Murray are renowned designers and creators of fine modern jewellery, in gold, platinum and silver, and incorporating a vast selection of precious and semi precious stones. Each piece is fashioned with care, and they make ideal gifts or reminders of your holiday in Scotland. Why not have a piece made that incorporates a Scottish river pearl? Or have an old piece re-modelled? A collection of Alison and Roy's work is always on display in their workshop, and you are welcome to come along and browse. Someone is always on hand to offer courteous, expert advice, and the prices are always competitive.

centuries, and quaint cobbled streets. The Town Hall dates from 1805, and has a small exhibition about the town. In the square is a house which has a small plaque commemorating Richard Cameron, a local schoolmaster. He was a leading Covenantor, and was killed at the Battle of Airds Moss in Ayrshire in 1680.

Falkland was a favourite retreat and hunting spot for the Scottish kings, who had a hunting lodge here. **Falkland Palace** (National Trust for Scotland - see panel below) was built in the 15th century on the site of this lodge, which was an old tower at one time owned by the Earls of Fife. In the 16th century James V had the tower enlarged into a magnificent Renaissance palace. It was never like Edinburgh or Stirling, which featured strongly in the politics and running of the country. Rather it was a country retreat where the Stuart monarchs could escape the pressures of government and indulge in a sport they all enjoyed - hunting stags and boars. It was in Falkland Palace that James V, father of Mary Stuart, died in 1542, and it was also a place, it is said, much loved by Mary herself.

Mary was born a few days before her father died, and on his deathbed, on being told of the birth of a female heir to the Scottish throne, exclaimed, "It cam' wi' a lass, and it'll gang wi' a lass." ("It came with a girl, and it will go with a girl."). He imagined that the Stuart line, which had started with Marjory Bruce, daughter of Robert I, would end with his daughter Mary. However, he was wrong in one respect. Mary was not the last Stuart monarch. This was Queen Anne, who died in 1714. So James's prophecy came true after all. Falkland Palace is nominally the property of the monarch, and its chapel, housed in what was the Banqueting Hall, is the only Roman Catholic chapel within royal property in the country.

FALKLAND PALACE AND GARDENS

Falkland, Cupar, Fife KY15 713U
Tel: 01337 857397 Fax: 01337 857980
Shop: 01337 857918
website: www.nts.org.uk

The Royal Palace of Falkland was the country residence of Stuart kings and queens when they hunted deer and wild boar in the Fife forest. Mary, Queen of Scots spent some of the happiest days of her tragic life here, "playing the country girl in the woods and parks". The Palace was built between 1501 and 1541 by James IV and James V, replacing an earlier castle and palace buildings dating from the 12th century, traces of which can still be seen in the grounds. The roofed South Range contains the Chapel Royal, and the East Range the King's Bedchamber and the Queen's Room, both restored by the Trust. The Keeper's Apartments in the Gatehouse are now also on display. The palace contains fine portraits of the Stuart monarchs and two sets of 17th century tapestry hangings.

The garden, designed and built by Percy Cane between 1947 and 1952, contains three herbaceous borders enclosing a wide lawn with many varieties of shrubs and trees. Here also is the original Royal Tennis Court the oldest in Britain still in use built in 1539. There is also a small herb garden border featuring quotations from John Gerard's book *Herball* (1597). Exhibitions at Royal Tennis Court and at Town Hall.

LOMOND HILLS HOTEL & LEISURE CENTRE

Freuchie, Fife KY15 7EY
Tel: 01337 857329/857498
Fax: 01337 857329/858180
e-mail: reception@lomondhillshotel.net
website: www.lomondhillshotel.net

The **Lomond Hills Hotel & Leisure Centre** proudly offers three star comfort at two star prices. The original building was a coaching inn dating from 1753, and sits in the small, picturesque village of Freuchie. It has 24 well equipped en suite bedrooms (two of which are honeymoon suites with four poster beds), a smart restaurant serving wonderful food, bars, lounges, function suites, sauna, Jacuzzi, gym and swimming pool. The whole hotel speaks of style and comfort, and it makes the ideal base form which to explore the Kingdom of Fife.

Charles I and Charles II both visited Falkland, and indeed, in 1650, Charles II founded the **Scots Guards** here. His father had previously founded a regiment in 1642 called "Argyll's Regiment" to act as his bodyguard in Ireland, and this had merged with nine other regiments to form a regiment called the Irish Companies. Charles II renamed it The King's Lyfeguard of Foot while at Falkland, and proclaimed it to be his personal bodyguard. It was later renamed the Scots Guards.

The King's Bedchamber is in the East Range, as is the Queen's Room, and within the Gatehouse are the Keeper's Apartments. The gardens are modern, dating from the mid-20th century, and have lovely herbaceous borders. Within the gardens is the **Royal Tennis Court**, which dates from the early 16th century, making it the oldest court still in use. "Real tennis" is played using the roofs of "lean tos" on either side of the court, a relic of the game's origins within castle courtyards, and there is still a thriving club at Falkland today.

WEMYSS

4 miles NE of Kirkcaldy on the A955

The substantial ruins of 14th century **Macduff Castle** stand on the cliffs above the shoreline. A previous castle which stood here since the 12th century was the home of the Earls of Fife, also known as the Thanes of Fife. The present ruins were built by the powerful Wemyss family, and then passed through various

DUNCLUTHA GUEST HOUSE

16 Victoria Road, Leven, Fife KY8 4EX
Tel: 01333 425515 Fax: 01333 422311
e-mail: pam.leven@dunclutha-accomm.demon.co.uk
website: www.dunclutha-accomm.demon.co.uk

Dunclutha Guest House is a well-appointed and friendly establishment within a former Victorian manse. There are three full en suite rooms and one with private bathroom, and all are extremely comfortable, with TVs, tea/coffee making facilities and built in wardrobes. Why not relax or watch TV in the cosy lounge? The breakfast room is spacious and inviting, and here you can have a traditional full Scottish breakfast or, if you prefer, a light Continental breakfast. Either way, it will you set you up beautifully so that you can explore an area of Scotland that is rich in heritage and lovely scenery!

families before passing back to the Wemyss family. In 1666 the Countess of Sutherland and her children lived here during an outbreak of the plague in Edinburgh. Parts of the tower were dismantled in the 1960s, as it was considered unsafe. It is said to be haunted by the ghost of a grey lady.

Below the castle, in the cliffs facing the shoreline, are some caves with curious carvings within them. They are said to date form Pictish times, though this part of the coast has suffered so much erosion that they have become dangerous, and can no longer be entered. However, they can be viewed from the shore.

LARGO

11 miles NE of Kirkcaldy on the A915

Lower Largo sits on the shores of the Firth of Forth, while Upper Largo sits about half a mile inland, where the early 17th century Parish Church stands. It was here that **Sir Andrew Wood**, Scotland's greatest seafarer, had his castle. He died in 1515, and was buried in the kirkyard. He commanded the largest and most magnificent fighting ship of its day, the Great Michael, built in Newhaven near Edinburgh between 1507 and 1511. Nothing now remains of Wood's castle but a tower.

Lower Largo was also the birthplace of Alexander Selkirk in 1676. He was the seafaring son of a shoemaker, and while on board a ship called the Cinque Ports in 1704 , quarrelled with the captain. He was put ashore on Juan Fernadez Island in the Pacific Ocean as a punishment. He remained marooned there for five years until he was rescued. Daniel Defoe based his book *Robinson Crusoe* on Alexander's adventures, though the two men never met. There is a statue of Selkirk near the harbour.

KINGHORN

4 miles SW of Kirkcaldy on the A921

One of the most decisive events in Scottish history took place at the **Pettycur Crags** to the west of the town. In 1286, Alexander III of Scotland was returning from Edinburgh to be with his new consort, Queen Yolande, daughter of the Count of Dreux. He had previously been married to Princess Margaret, daughter of Henry III of England, However, she and their sons had died, so he had no male heir.

His nobles had tried to dissuade Alexander from travelling from Edinburgh to Kinghorn, where his new queen awaited him, as there was a storm blowing, and the Firth of Forth was dangerous. Alexander, however, was adamant, and the party set out. Miraculously, they made it across the Forth, but when they reached the top of Pettycur Crags, Alexander got detached from the main party. His horse stumbled and threw him over some cliffs, where he was killed.

The heir to the Scottish throne was Margaret, Alexander's three year-old granddaughter. She was the daughter of Eric II of Norway, and as she was being brought back to Scotland she died on board ship. Therefore there was no legitimate heir to the throne, creating a power vacuum which was soon filled by warring noblemen, all jockeying to seize power. Edward I of England was asked to intercede, and he saw his chance. He had always coveted Scotland, and now installed a puppet king, John Balliol, on the Scottish throne, hoping eventually to absorb Scotland into England.

Many Scotsmen, including William Wallace, refused to accept the puppet king, and Edward began a campaign of quelling resistance in the country. Thus were born the Wars of Independence, which culminated in the crowning of Robert the Bruce as King of Scotland in 1306 and the Battle of Bannockburn in 1314. A monument, erected in 1886, marks the spot where Alexander was killed.

BURNTISLAND

6 miles SW of Kirkcaldy on the A921

This small royal burgh was granted its royal charter in 1541. It was known as Portus Gratiae by the monks of Dunfermline Abbey before the Reformation. **The Binn**, a 632 feet high hill, overlooks the town. For many years it was a port for exporting the coal from the Fife coalfields, though its history goes back well before this.

St. Columba's Parish Church is one of the most important churches in Scotland. After the Reformation, Scotland was a poor country, and it was decided to retain as many of the former Roman Catholic churches as possible and convert them for the new, reformed liturgy. However, some new churches had to be built, and St. Columba's was one of them. It is now the first church still in use to be built in Scotland after the Reformation. It dates from 1592, and is a four square building possibly based on a Dutch design. The Holy Table (the word "altar" was not allowed in those days) sits in the centre of the church, with the pews facing it on four sides, thus emphasising the "equality of all believers". However, things were not as equal as all that, as elaborate lofts and pews were built for the local gentry, and they can still be seen.

This church is the birthplace of the **Authorised Version of the Bible**, as James VI attended a General Assembly of the Church of Scotland there in 1601, and put forward a proposal for a new translation of the bible into English. The suggestion was accepted by the ministers, though it was not until James ascended the throne of England as well that work started on the translation in London.

The **Burntisland Edwardian Fair Museum** is in the town's High Street, and has displays about Edwardian fairgrounds and local history. In 1633 Charles I's baggage ship, the **Blessing of Burntisland**, sank in the Forth just off Burntisland, taking all his treasure with it. Since then there have been many attempts to trace and salvage the treasure.

ST ANDREWS

St. Andrews, up until the Reformation, was one of the most important towns, not just in Scotland, but in the whole of the British Isles. Perhaps one should call it a city, as it was the ecclesiastical capital of the country, and had a huge cathedral, which nowadays is in ruins. It is also a university town and the world home of golf.

St. Andrews Cathedral was Scotland's largest building in pre-Reformation times. It was founded by Bishop Arnold in 1160, though the ruins as you see them today date from many periods. In the late 13th century the great nave was built, though its west front was later blown down in a great storm and had to be rebuilt. The whole building was finally consecrated in 1318 in the presence of Robert I. The cathedral has a **Cathedral Visitor Centre** adjacent to the ruins.

However, St. Andrews' history as an ecclesiastical centre goes back long before the present cathedral. **St. Rule's Tower** and its attached chancel is all that remains of an earlier cathedral which was built about 1127. You can climb to the top of the tower and get a magnificent view out over the town. Even when this cathedral was built, there was already a monastery of Culdees of the old Celtic Church, and in the 13th century they built the church of **St. Mary on the Rock** for themselves, the ruins of which can be seen at the east end of the cathedral and outside its precincts. It was the first collegiate church in Scotland, so called because the services were conducted by a college of priests. But gradually the Culdee monks converted to Roman Catholicism, and were allowed to become part of the cathedral chapter.

St. Andrews Castle

The town gets its name from Scotland's patron saint, St. Andrew. Legend tells us that St. Rule (also known as St. Regulus) came from Patras in Greece in the 4th century, bringing with him the holy relics of St. Andrew. He set up a shrine for them on the Fife coast, at what was then called Kilrimont, and is now St. Andrews. Another, more likely story, is that the relics were brought by Bishop Acca from the monastery of Hexham in Northumberland in 732. A church was built to house them, and this grew into

St. Andrews Cathedral, where the relics were kept in a shrine behind the high altar. This made St. Andrews one of the great European places of pilgrimage, and people came from all over to worship at the shrine.

St. Andrews Castle was the residence of the cathedral's bishop, and later archbishop. Its ruins sit on the coast to the north of the cathedral. It was here that the bloody murder of **Cardinal David Beaton**, Archbishop of St. Andrews, took place in 1546. In March of the same year, **George Wishart** the Protestant martyr had been burnt at the stake in front of the castle on Beaton's orders, which made him many enemies.

In May a group of Fife lairds broke into the castle and murdered him in his bedroom. They then hung the body from the window. A long siege of the castle ensued, with the Earl of Arran employing sappers to dig a tunnel deep under the castle in an attempt to undermine it. The tunnel is still there, and it can be visited. The **St. Andrews Castle Visitor Centre** is on The Scores, and tells the story of the castle.

One other Archbishop of St. Andrews was murdered. This was the Protestant **Archbishop James Sharp**, and the foul deed took place in 1679. The Church of Scotland was Episcopalian at the time, and government troops were persecuting Covenantors, a huge group of people who opposed bishops in the church. Sharp was one of the main instigators, and he was a hated man. He was returning to St. Andrews from Edinburgh with his daughter, and was waylaid by Covenantors at Magus Moor, near the town. Not averse to acts of cruelty themselves, the Covenantors stabbed him to death in front of his daughter.

Nor was Wishart the only Protestant to have been martyred in St. Andrews. Patrick Hamilton was burnt at the stake in 1528 outside St. Salvator's Church in North Street, which forms part of **St. Salvator's College**, founded by Bishop Kennedy in 1450, and now part of the university.

It was at the beginning of the 15th century that Pope Benedict XIII issued a Papal Bull which founded the university. In the 16th century a further two colleges were added - St. Leonard's College and **St. Mary's College**. St. Leonard's was eventually incorporated into St. Salvator's, and a girls' school now occupies its site. However, its chapel, **St. Leonard's Chapel**, still exists, the earliest parts dating from the 12th

century, which shows it was in existence long before the university was founded.

St. Mary's College lies off South Street, and is undoubtedly the most beautiful of the colleges. You reach it by a stepping through a graceful arch into a grassy quadrangle surrounded by mellow old buildings which date from the 16th century and later. At the foot of Stair Tower is **Queen Mary's Thorn**, said to have been planted by Queen Mary (Mary Queen of Scots) in 1565 on one of her many visits to the town. She possibly lodged at what is now known as **Queen Mary's House** in South Street, which dates from about 1525. It was once the lodgings of a cathedral canon, and Charles II also stayed there in 1650.

In front of Madras College in South Street, the town's main school, is all that remains of a **Dominican Friary**, founded by Bishop Wishart in the 13th century. This is the north transept of the friary church, and it dates from the 16th century. It has some lovely tracery in its glassless windows. Nearly across from it is the town's church - **Holy Trinity Parish Church**. It was founded in the 15th century, though the present building is largely a rebuilding of the early 20th century. It contains a memorial to Archbishop Sharp, killed in 1679. However, after the Church of Scotland finally became Presbyterian, his bones were removed from the tomb, as he was a hated man.

The **West Port** sits at the west end of South Street. It was one of the original gates of the town, and was built about 1589 on the site of an earlier gate. In North Street, at the cathedral end, is the **St. Andrews Preservation Trust Museum and Garden**, housed in a charming old building dating from the 16th century. And in Kinburn Park, on Double Dykes Road, is the **St. Andrews Museum**. The

Botanic Gardens are in the Canongate, and sit in 18 acres of land. There are glasshouses containing plants from all over the world, as well as rock and peat gardens and a lake.

The **St. Andrews Aquarium**, on The Scores, has a collection of fish and marine animals, and nearby is the **Martyr's Monument** of 1842, which commemorates the Protestant martyrs who were executed in St. Andrews. The **British Golf Museum** is close by, and traces the history of the game. It has many exhibits covering the 500 years since the game was invented in Scotland.

Old Course, Royal and Ancient Golf Club

St. Andrews is still a place of pilgrimage, only now pilgrims come for the golf courses. The **Royal and Ancient Golf Club** is the ruling body for world golf apart from the United States and Mexico. It formulates and classifies the rules (and new ones are added every year as new situations arise) as well as organises the annual British Open, which takes place at coastal golf courses all over Britain. The most famous course in St. Andrews is the Old Course, and next to the 18th green is the Royal and Ancient's clubhouse.

Both Tom Morris and his son (also called Tom) were born in St. Andrews.

They were the greatest golfers of their time (some say of all time, considering the primitive equipment they used), and they now lie buried in the Cathedral graveyard, where there is a striking memorial. Old Tom was greenkeeper at St. Andrews, having been appointed in 1865, and his son won the Open Championship three times in a row while still a teenager. However, this early promise was cut cruelly short when he died in 1875 aged only 24. Some people say the cause of death was a broken heart after his young wife died in childbirth.

About three miles outside the town is **Craigton Country Park**. It has a "Rio Grande" railway, a boating lake, crazy golf, putting and a host of other attractions and activities. In the summer months there is an admission charge.

FERNIE CASTLE HOTEL

Letham, near Cupar, Fife KY15 7RU
Tel: 01337 810381 e-mail: mail@ferniecastle.demon.co.uk
Fax: 01337 810422 website: www.ferniecastle.demon.co.uk

Fernie Castle was first recorded in 1353, with the present building being over 450 years old. Now it is the four star **Fernie Castle Hotel** that offers all the romance and character of Scotland's turbulent past coupled with modern amenities. There are 20 individually designed en suite rooms equipped to the highest standards. Dining can take place in the vaulted Keep Bar or in the elegant Auld Alliance Room. The food is superb, and afterwards guests can relax over a quiet drink or coffee in the Wallace Lounge, with its turret snuggery. Weddings or corporate events can be held in the Balfour Suite, and private dinner rooms are also available.

HILLPARK HOUSE

96 Main Street, Leuchars, St Andrews, Fife KY16 0HF
Tel: 01334 839280 e-mail: enquiries@hillparkhouse.com
website: www.hillparkhouse.com

Owned and run by Nick and Sandy Stilwell, **Hillpark House** extends a warm welcome to their five star B&B establishment. Here you can experience the very best in hospitality, and relax in a Victorian house that has authentic country decor and antiques. There are three spacious and comfortable rooms, each with colour TV, hospitality tray, phones, electric blankets and ironing facilities, and each has an en suite shower room or adjoining private bathroom. Use it as a base from which to explore an area that is rich in history, or spend a couple of nights here as you travel round. Either way, you won't be disappointed

STARRS

24 High Street, Newport-on-Tay, Fife DD6 8AD
Tel: 01382 540055 Fax: 01382 543064
e-mail: GPL@darstra.co.uk
website: www.darstra.co.uk/starrs

Treat yourself at **Starrs**! This friendly gift and coffee shop has something for everyone. Choose from a wide range of unique, high quality gifts carefully sourced and expertly gift wrapped free of charge. Sample one of the many selections of hot and cold drinks, fresh filled rolls and homebakes. There is a range of up to the minute newspapers and magazines to browse through at your leisure in light airy surroundings.

KM ARTS

Ploughman's Cottage, Naughton Estate,
Newport-on-Tay, Fife DD6 8RN
Tel/Fax: +44(0)1382 330444
e-mail: karin@muhlert.fsnet.co.uk

Karin Muhlert finds the inspiration for her fabulous contemporary three-dimensional paper art on the beaches of nearby St. Andrews. Born in Sweden, she has lived in Scotland for over 20 years, and is a highly respected artist who trained at Duncan of Jordanstone College of Art in Dundee. She has exhibited throughout the United Kingdom (notably at the Chelsea Craft Fair) and on the Continent, and regularly sells her work nationally and internationally. Karin can be visited by appointment only, and accepts commissions.

AROUND ST. ANDREWS

CUPAR

8 miles W of St. Andrews on the A91

This small, pleasant town sits on the River Eden, and was once the administrative centre for the old county of Fife. The **Mercat Cross**, topped with a unicorn, was moved from Tarvit Hill to its present location in 1897 to commemorate Queen Victoria's Diamond Jubilee. The **Douglas Bader Garden** in Duffus Park was laid out for the benefit of the disabled.

The Old Parish Church dates from 1785, though the tower is medieval. **Hill of Tarvit Mansionhouse** (National Trust for Scotland) is a fine Edwardian mansion lying two miles south of the town. It was designed by Sir Robert Lorimer in 1906, and has French, Scottish and Chippendale furniture. There is also a collection of paintings, an Edwardian laundry and lovely gardens.

Nearby is **Scotstarvit Tower** (Historic Scotland), which was built by the Inglis family soon after 1487, when they were granted the Lands of Tarvit from James III. In 1612 it was bought by Sir John Scott, a lawyer. Having been deprived of the posts of judge and Director of Chancery by Cromwell, he retired to Scotstarvit which was visited by the most liberal and learned eminent Scotsman of the time.

West of Cupar, at Rankeilor Park, is the **Scottish Deer Centre** and **Raptor World**. At the Deer Centre are examples of Scotland's two native deer species, the red deer and the roe deer, plus other species from around the world. At the Raptor Centre you can learn about birds of prey such as owls, hawks and falcons. There are also flying displays.

LEUCHARS

4 miles NW of St. Andrews, on the A919

The **Leuchars Air Show**, organised by the Royal Air Force, takes place here every September, in one of Scotland's largest RAF bases. Perhaps the village is most famous for its church, the **Parish Church of St. Athernase**. It is one of the finest Norman churches in the country, and was founded in about 1187 by one Saier de Quince, a crusader knight. Much of the exterior, it is said, remains exactly as the masons built it. No one really knows who St. Athernase was. An obscure reference calls him "Ithernaisce, who spoke not", suggesting that he might have been a mute.

NEWPORT-ON-TAY

9 miles NW of St. Andrews on the A92

Newport-on-Tay sits at the southern end of the Tay Road Bridge. A mile away is the strangely named **Wormit**, which sits at the southern end of the Tay Rail Bridge. The ruins of **Balmerino Abbey** (National Trust for Scotland) sit about five miles to the west. It was founded in 1229. The ruins are undergoing stabilisation work and are not open to the public, though they can viewed from a distance.

NEWBURGH

16 miles W of St. Andrews on the A913

Newburgh was granted its royal burgh status in 1631. Before that, it was dependent on the monks of **Lindores Abbey**, the scant ruins of which are nearby. This was a Tironensian house founded in 1178, and it was the first abbey in Scotland to be sacked by Protestants during the Scottish Reformation. The **Lang Museum** in the High Street traces the history of the town and its people.

AUCHTERMUCHTY

16 miles W of St. Andrews on the A91

This small, compact town sits in a fertile area known as the Howe of Fife, and has a **Tolbooth** dating from 1728. It is an ancient place, having been granted royal burgh status in 1517. The TV series *Dr Finlay* was filmed here, a small area of the town centre being turned into a typical Scottish town of the 1930s.

CRAIL

8 miles SE of St. Andrews on the A917

Crail is an old port in that area of Fife known as the East Neuk. It is possibly the most picturesque of the villages in an area that is renowned for its picturesque villages. The small harbour must be one of the most photographed and painted harbours in Scotland, and features on calendars, postcards and in books of photographs. The village is a magnet for

Crail Harbour

THE BEEHIVE

28 High Street South, Crail, nr Anstruther, Fife KY10 3TE
Tel: 101333 450330

While in this lovely part of Scotland, with its picturesque fishing villages, why not visit **The Beehive** in Crail? This gift shop and tearoom is one of the best in Fife, and you are always assured of a warm welcome, wonderful food, and souvenirs at affordable prices. You could try one of their Jannetta's ice creams - they are renowned in the area, and the shop's owner, Linda Lockhart, often finds herself running out. Or how about those Scottish delicacies, clootie dumplings and shortbread? The shop also sells a range of confectionery such as rock, fudge and Scottish tablet. So make your way to The Beehive when you're in Crail.

MARINE HOTEL

54 Nethergate South, Crail, Fife KY10 3TZ
Tel: 01333 450207

The East Neuk of Fife is a charming area of Scotland, full of picturesque fishing towns. In one of them, Crail, you'll find the **Marine Hotel**, a friendly, family-run hotel that offers the very best in Scottish hospitality. The bedrooms are spacious and tastefully decorated, and have private bathrooms. The atmosphere is relaxed and informal, and the owners are always willing to offer advice and help on what to see and where to go. Try their full Scottish breakfast - it sets you up beautifully for a day's holidaying in this wonderful part of Scotland.

THE HONEYPOT

6 High Street South, Crail, Fife KY10 3TD
Tel./Fax: 01333 450935
e-mail: info@honeypotcrail.net

The Honeypot is a traditional guest house and tearoom run by the husband and wife team of Aileen and Ruary Muirhead. It sits in the picturesque fishing village of Crail, and offers Scottish hospitality at its best. On the tearoom's menu are delicious teas, coffees, home baking and snacks, while the guest house offers single, double, family and twin accommodation in comfortable, spotlessly clean rooms. There is also a self-contained annex for families or golf groups up to four, and there is ample car parking. Evening meals are available by prior appointment, and dogs are welcome by arrangement.

painters, and you can see many of them seated in front of their easels painting and drawing the quaint old cottages. The Tolbooth dates from the 16th century, with a design that owes a lot to Dutch architecture. In the Marketgate is the **Crail Museum and Heritage Centre**, which tells the story of the town, its people and its industries.

The **Secret Bunker** lies about three miles west of Crail, in some unremarkable farmland. It was Scotland's secret command centre in the days of the Cold War, and lies 100 feet underground encased in 15 feet thick concrete walls. It was from here that Scotland would have been run in the event of a nuclear attack. It is entered by an innocent looking farmhouse, and guarded by three tons of blast proof doors. Now that the Cold war is over, you can enter it and see the operating theatres, the two cinemas, and the café for yourself. Similar bunkers were built all over Britain, and they were all taken off the secret list in 1993.

ANSTRUTHER

9 miles S of St. Andrews off the A917

The name of this former herring fishing port is sometimes pronounced "Ainster". It is actually two small royal burghs called Anstruther Easter and Anstruther Wester, with the dates of their charters

being, respectively, 1583 and 1587. It is yet another picturesque village in this part of Fife, and has many old cottages with crow step gables, whitewashed walls and red pantiles.

Just after the Spanish Armada was defeated in 1588, one of the Spanish ships is said to have put in at Anstruther harbour. The ship's commander, Jan Gomez de Midini and his crew stayed there and were offered hospitality by the people of the town. This, of course, was at a time when Scotland and England were still separate countries, and the Scots had a hearty dislike of their southern neighbours. A few years later the commander repaid the hospitality when he discovered fishermen from the village marooned in a foreign port after their boat had been shipwrecked. He re-equipped them and sent them home at his own expense.

The **Scottish Fisheries Museum** (see panel below) is housed in a group of attractive buildings around three sides of a cobbled courtyard. One of the buildings stands on the site of St. Ayle's Chapel, owned by the monks of Balmerino Abbey, which stood close to the shores of the Firth of Tay in North Fife. In the museum, you can follow the fleet with the "herring lassies", explore a fisherman's cottage and see skilled

THE SPINDRIFT

Pittenweem Road, Anstruther, Fife KY10 3DT
Tel/Fax: 01333 310573
e-mail: info@the spindrift.co.uk
website: www.thespindrift.co.uk

In the picturesque fishing village of Anstruther you'll find one of
the best guest houses in Fife - **The Spindrift**. Owned and run by
Christine and Kenneth Lawson, it offers comfortable, superbly
furnished rooms and an ambience that speaks of friendly service, a warm welcome and value for
money. Prepare yourself to be pampered - the breakfasts and the evening meals are superb, and there
is a small but select wine list. Why not relax in one of the elegant public rooms over a drink from the
honesty bar? This is one place you're sure to come back to.

SCOTTISH FISHERIES MUSEUM

St. Ayles, Harbourhead, Anstruther, Fife KY10 3AB
Tel/Fax: 01333 310628
e-mail: info@scottish-fisheries-museum.org
website: www.scottish-fisheries-museum.org

Fishing has always been important to the small villages that
fringe the East Neuk of Fife and in the **Scottish Fisheries
Museum** you can learn all about the industry, not just in
Fife, but throughout Scotland. It is a truly fascinating place,
and is housed in buildings dating from the 16th to the
19th centuries. There are displays on many facets of the industry, and a trip round makes a great day
out for children and adults alike. It begins by examining a replica dug-out canoe dating from AD500,
created in the museum workshop to illustrate that fishing in Scotland goes back to ancient times.
After it was made in 1991, it was tested in Anstruther Harbour, and performed beautifully!

There are many galleries, each one highlighting a facet of the industry. There is an area on whaling,
for example, plus a gallery called 'The Herring Market', with a net-loft where nets were repaired, a fish
merchant's office, and lively herring lassies gutting and packing the catch. There are also, of course,
fishing boats, and you can see and touch the craft that took hardy fishermen out into the seas round

Britain in days gone by. One of the most fascinating galleries
is the one dedicated to Zulu fishing boats. How did they get
their name? What key role did they play in the industry? There
is also a tearoom, a room which you can book to enjoy your
packed lunch, and a shop, where you can pick up well-crafted
souvenirs to remind you of your trip to one of the most
interesting and enjoyable museums in Scotland. It is wheelchair
friendly, and special themed visits can also be arranged. It makes
a memorable day out.

craftsmen at work. The museum also
has the Memorial to Scottish Fishermen
Lost at Sea.

Six miles SE of Anstruther, out in the
Firth of Forth, is the **Isle of May**, where
there are ruins of an old priory.

In 1635, Scotland's first lighthouse was
built here, though it was no more that a

coal-burning brazier on top of a stone
tower. Trips to the island can be made
from Anstruther.

PITTENWEEM
9 miles S of St. Andrews on the A917

Like most fishing villages in the East
Neuk of Fife, Pittenweem is an attractive

FISHER STUDIO & GALLERY

11-13 High Street, Pittenweem, Fife KY10 2LA
Tel: 01333 312255
e-mail: fishergallery@btconnect.com
website: www.fishergallery.co.uk

The East Neuk of Fife is famed for its quaint fishing villages and the artists who have settled there to take advantage of the wonderful light and scenery. Pittenweem is one of the most picturesque of the villages with a working harbour, little galleries and shops, spectacular views, and hosts the famous Pittenweem Arts Festival every August.

In the year 2000 Jan and John Fisher and their daughter Anna, moved into one of the old town houses in the High Street, and opened the **Fisher Studio and Gallery**. Accomplished artists themselves who have exhibited throughout Britain, they bring a wealth of experience to running a gallery.

The exhibitions change four times a year, showing paintings, sculpture, ceramics, glass and craft by selected artists working in Scotland. All exhibitions feature new work by the resident artists, and visitors are most welcome. There is also a selection of cards and prints.

The Fisher Gallery is open every day from 10am-6pm in summer, 10am-5pm in winter with a closed period early in the year. For information about the current or forthcoming exhibitions, phone the gallery or check out the website.

*Pittenweem Harbour
by Jan Fisher*

place full of quaint cottages grouped round an old harbour. Most are whitewashed, with red pantiles, showing the connection this area once had with the Low Countries. The original pantiles were brought across from the Netherlands as ballast, and the locals liked them so much that they started making their own.

Parts of **Pittenweem Priory** can still be seen. It moved here from the Isle of May to offer better protection from pirates. Guided tours round the remains can be arranged through the local minister. The **Parish Church** has a substantial tower dating from the 16th century, while the rest is Victorian. St.

Fillan's Cave is suppose to be where the 8th century saint and missionary to the Picts, St. Fillan, used to go for private prayer. It was renovated and re-dedicated in 1935.

Kellie Castle (National Trust for

Pittenweem Harbour

WALK 5

Elie, St Monans and Kilconquhar

Start	Victoria Hotel, Elie
Distance	10 miles (16.1km)
Approximate time	5 hours
Parking	Public Parking in High Street, Elie
Refreshments	Elie, St Monans and Kilconquhar
Ordnance Survey maps	Landranger 59 (St Andrews) and Pathfinder 374, NO40/50 (Anstruther)

The East Neuk of Fife is one of the most scenic areas in the Scottish lowlands, famed for its lovely coastline and charming villages. This walk links the three picturesque villages of Elie, St Monans and Kilconquhar, and explores several miles of beautiful coastal scenery. This is a long and varied walk with many points of interest and you should allow a full day, planning to break for lunch at either St Monans or Kilconquhar.

From the Victoria Hotel, head down School Wynd towards the sea, and turn left at the foot of the hill. Follow this street (The Toft) as it curves around Elie Bay, and continues to the end of the harbour breakwater. The harbour dates from the late 16th century, and the large building that dominates the pier-head is an old granary.

Return towards the village, and turn right through a gap in the wall to follow the path that curves around the shore of Wood Haven to Elie Ness, where a small footbridge over a tidal channel leads to a white-washed and crenellated light-tower built in 1908. Elie Ness is made of a volcanic rock known as tuff, which comprises blocks of basalt embedded in layers of volcanic ash. The rocks also contain rare crystals of garnet, known locally as "Elie rubies". The next headland to the east bears a circular folly known as the Lady's Tower. It was built in the 1760s as a bathing-house for Lady Janet, wife of the local laird, Sir John Anstruther.

Continue along the coastal path towards St Monans, passing the ruins of two castles. The first, Ardross Castle (dating from 1370), is little more than a pile of overgrown rubble to the right of the path, but the second, Newark Castle, is more substantial. Newark was acquired in 1649 by General David Leslie, the Covenanter commander who defeated the Marquis of Montrose at Philiphaugh in 1645. Nearby stands a beehive-shaped dovecot. Up ahead lies the attractive fishing village of St Monans, with the square tower of its famous fishermen's church. The Church of St Monan was built by David II in the 1360s and restored in the 19th century; its spare but dignified interior is graced by a model full-rigged ship dating from 1800.

Pass the church Ⓐ and turn left up the narrow street beside the burn. At the bridge that leads leftwards into the church car park, keep straight on along the path between the burn and the houses to reach the main road (A917), and turn left along the pavement.

WALK 5

After ½ mile (800m), turn right at two solitary trees **B** on to a minor road and follow it towards the village of Kilconquhar. As the road crosses the slopes of Scuddie Hill, about ½ mile (800m) before Kilconquhar, there is a beautiful view of Kilconquhar Loch surrounded by woods and overlooked by the spire of the village church.

Turn left at the T-junction in the village. Kilconquhar (pronounced 'Kinneucher') is one of Scotland's prettiest villages, set on a hillock overlooking the loch. It is dominated by the 80ft (24m) spire of its parish kirk, built in 1821 on the site of a 12th-century church. Continue through the village past the ancient Kinneucher Inn, which dates from the early 18th century. Where the main road bends 90° to the left, keep straight on. Cross the main road (A917) and go down the road towards Shell Bay Caravan park; where the road forks, bear left.

At the end of the woods you reach the entrance to the caravan park **C**; keep left along the road heading towards Kincraig Hill. At a crossroads, go straight on past a barrier and signs reading "Keep your dog on a lead" and "No unauthorised vehicles". The road bends to the right up the hill and along a terrace, from the far end of which is a grand

view over Shell Bay and the Firth of Forth. From the end of the terrace **D**, cut back left and then right, then left again up to the crest of Kincraig Hill. Follow a path across the summit of the hill, past the triangulation pillar and radio mast, and the ruins of wartime concrete buildings. The hill is composed of columnar basalt and volcanic tuff, which outcrop on the cliffs to the south. At low tide the cliffs and caves can be explored via the "Chain Walk", a path that leads west from the golf course and negotiates several steep sections by means of chain handrails and steps cut into the rock.

The path continues along the top of the steep southern face of Kincraig Hill, then drops down diagonally across the slope to the corner of Earlsferry Golf Course. Pass right of the green and follow a sandy path along the crest of the dunes above the bay. At the far end of the bay, signed "Danger – golf course", go round the point behind the 11th tee, and keep right of the crag beyond the 10th green. The path keeps close to the sea and leads across two rocky ridges to a couple of benches that enjoy a lovely view across Elie Bay. Head along the road to the left of the white house, and continue along Earlsferry High Street to return to the Victoria Hotel. ●

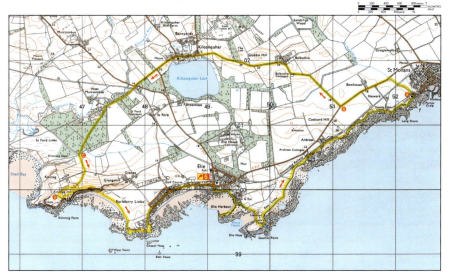

Parish Church of St Monans

Scotland) dates from the 14th century, and lies a few miles inland. It is one of the best examples in Scotland of Lowland domestic architecture, and contains superb plaster ceilings, murals, panelling and furniture designed by Sir Robert Lorimer, who refurbished the whole place in the 19th century. There are also lovely gardens.

St. Monans

10 miles S of St. Andrews on the A917

The motto of this fishing village is "mare vivemus", which means "we have life

Elie Harbour

from the sea". It is famous for the **Parish Church of St Monans**, which stands almost on the shoreline. It was founded by David II, son of Robert the Bruce, after he had survived a shipwreck on the Forth, and is a substantial building of nave, transepts and a stumpy spire. The building was never completed, and today is is still without a chancel. Salt panning was once an important industry here, and the 18th century **St. Monans Windmill** at one time formed part of the salt panning complex.

Elie and Earlsferry

10 miles S of St. Andrews off the A917

These two villages surround a sandy bay, and form one continuous settlement. Earlsferry is, in fact, a small royal burgh, and was at one time the northern terminus for a ferry that crossed the Forth (hence its name). The "Earl" in its name is the Earl of Fife, and a story is told that MacDuff, who was a thane of the Earl, took refuge in a cave near Earlsferry after having escaped from King Macbeth. He was then ferried across the forth to Dunbar. An old pathway called the **Cadger's Road** once ran from Earlsferry to Falkland, and along it the "cadgers" took fish to supply the royal table.

Elie is a small holiday resort with a fine sandy beach and golf courses. **Elie Parish Church** is in High Street, and dates from 1639. **Gillespie House** dates from the 17th century, and has a fine carved doorway. The town's most famous citizen was James Braid, who won the British Open Gold championship five times between 1901 and 1910.

7 CENTRAL SCOTLAND

The area between the Firths of Clyde and Forth is often referred to as Scotland's "waist", as it sits where the country is at its narrowest. Before the Kincardine Bridge was built in 1936, the lowest road bridging point of the Forth was at Stirling, which meant that it was at the very core of Scottish history. To the north west of the town are the Campsie and Kilsyth hills, so any army marching north had to come through the narrow strip of land at Stirling. That's why so many decisive battles have been fought around here - two at least near Stirling (Bannockburn and Stirling Bridge) and two in Falkirk (both called the Battle of Falkirk).

Loch Ard Autumn Scene

It is also why Stirling Castle was built on a rocky outcrop. It overlooks the whole area, and marching armies could be seen approaching. Whoever took Stirling Castle controlled the whole area north of the Forth and Clyde.

Both Stirlingshire and Clackmannanshire have seen great changes in their boundaries over recent years due to local government organisation. Dunblane, just north of Stirling, was at one time in Perthshire, as was Callander and Port of Menteith. For a while, Clackmannanshire ceased to exist as a county, though it is now a county once more. It still proudly proclaims itself to be Scotland's smallest, with an area of 55 square miles. It sits in the shelter of the Ochil Hills, bounded on the south by the River Forth, which at this point is still tidal. It was once a centre for textiles and woollens, due to the swift streams that tumbled down from the hills and powered the mills. A string of quaint villages called the "hillfoot villages" sit along the Ochils, and are well worth visiting.

Travel to the north west of the area and you come to one of the most attractive parts of Scotland - the Trossachs. It's not a range of hills, nor is it a county. It's simply a geographical area full of natural beauty. The hills are not as grand as those in the Grampians or the Cairngorms, and there is no

Walking on Ben Lomond

brooding majesty. But it is lovely, with stretches of water such as Loch Katrine, Loch Venachan and Loch Drunkie.

Stirling is one of Scotland's most historical places, and this was recognised in 2002 when it was granted city status. The castle has been fought over for centuries, and was always a favourite with the Scottish monarchy. Mary Stuart stayed here, and her son James VI was crowned king of Scotland in the Church of the Holy Rood. Falkirk, too, is an ancient town, though it is more industrial in nature. Alloa is Clackmannanshire's largest town, and at one time was the centre of Scotland's brewing industry.

The whole area also has many architectural gems, which are well worth seeking out. There's Stirling Castle, of course, the Wallace Tower, Alloa Tower, Dunblane Cathedral, the scant ruins of Cambuskeneth Abbey, Doune Castle and Castle Campbell.

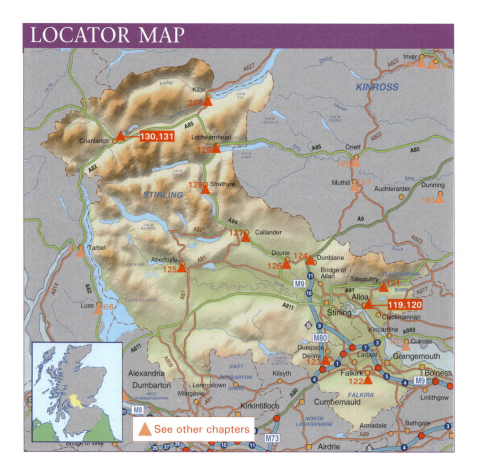

LOCATOR MAP

See other chapters

CENTRAL SCOTLAND

CLACKMANNAN

In the centre of this small town - once the county town of Clackmannanshire - is the belfry of the old **Tolbooth**, which was built to take prisoners in the late 16th century. It was built by William Menteith, the sheriff of the town, who objected to holding the prisoners in his own house. Beside it stands the **Mannau Stone**. When St. Serf came to this area in the 7th century to convert it to Christianity, he found the locals worshipping the sea god Mannau, or Mannan, in the form of this stone, which was called at the time the "clach mannau", hence the name of the town. Another story says the town got its name when Robert the Bruce rested in the town, and on leaving it discovered that he had left a glove (or "mannan") lying next to the stone (or "clach").

Clackmannan Tower (Historic Scotland), built on the site of a royal hunting lodge, dates mainly from the 14th century and later, and was once owned by Robert I. It is not open to the public, but can be viewed from the outside. Robert Burns visited Clackmannan in 1787, and his fame

must have gone before him, as he was "knighted" by a descendant of Robert I, a Mrs Bruce, who lived in a mansion house which once stood near the tower. She was in her nineties at the time, and was described as a woman of "hospitality and urbanity". She still had her ancestor's helmet and sword, and used the sword for the knighting ceremony. She declared that she had a better right to offer knighthoods than "some people", meaning the Hanovarian kings in London, whom she viewed as common and vulgar.

The **Parish Church** dates from 1815, and is built on the site of a much older one. In fact, St. Serf may have founded a small chapel here in the 7th century. There is one thing well worth seeing inside it - the Coronation Window, gifted to the church by its congregation in 1953 on the occasion of Elizabeth II's coronation. In 1997 the Queen visited the church especially to see it.

The Gartmorn Dam Country Park and Nature Reserve lies two miles north of the town. At its centre is the 170-acre Gartmorn Reservoir, originally built by John Erskine, 6th Earl of Mar, to power the pumps which pumped water out of his coal mines. It is therefore the oldest man made reservoir in Scotland. The park is popular with walkers and nature lovers, and the waters of the reservoir are stocked with brown trout.

AROUND CLACKMANNAN

ALLOA
2 miles W of Clackmannan on the A907

Alloa is the largest town in Scotland's smallest county. It sits on the banks of the Forth, and its name is supposed to mean "the way to the sea". It is an industrial town, with its traditional industries being brewing, glass making and engineering. Most of these have gone now, though one brewery remains. **St. Mungo's Parish Church** dates from 1817, though it incorporates the 17th century tower of an earlier church. **Alloa Tower** (National Trust for Scotland - see panel opposite) is all that is left of the ancestral home of the Erskines, at one time one of the most important Scottish families. It was built for Alexander Erskine, the 3rd Lord Erskine, in the late 15th century. They eventually were elevated to the peerage as the Earls of Mar (later to become the Earls of Mar and Kellie) and became Hereditary Keepers of Stirling Castle.

The Erskines were custodians of Mary

Alloa Tower

Stuart when she was a child, and she lived in Alloa Tower for a time. James VI also stayed here when young. The 6th Earl was devoted to the Stuart cause, and after the 1715 Jacobite Uprising was sent into exile. The family's story is told within the tower, and the present Earl of Mar and Kellie has loaned it many exhibits.

THE ROYAL OAK

7 Bedford Place, Alloa, Clackmannanshire FK10 1LJ
Tel: 01259 722423 Fax: 01259 215523
e-mail: ahilton@theroyaloakhotelfreeserve.co.uk

The **Royal Oak** is situated in the conservation area of Alloa, and dates originally from the 19th century. It is now an extremely comfortable family owned hotel that boasts eleven fully en suite rooms (one with a four poster bed), a popular restaurant and a function suite. It appeals to both holidaymakers and locals, who flock to sample the hotel's high teas. The food is superb, as are the beers, wines and spirits served in the cosy Oak Pub. This is the ideal base from which to explore the region.

ALLOA TOWER

Alloa Park, Alloa, Clackmannanshire FK10 1PP
Tel: 01259 211701
Fax: 01259 218744

Alloa Tower, the largest surviving keep in Scotland, dates from the 14th century. It was home to successive generations of the Earls of Mar, who played host to, and were guardians of, many Scots monarchs. Here, so legend has it, Mary, Queen of Scots was reconciled with Darnley and shortly thereafter granted the 5th Lord Erskine the much coveted earldom in 1565. One tradition holds that Mary's infant son, later James VI and I, died shortly after his birth and was replaced by the baby son of the Earl of Mar.

The Tower has seen six major alterations, the most dramatic being the sweeping Italianate staircase and dome added in the early 1700s by the 6th Earl of Mar. But it still retains original medieval features such as the dungeon, first floor well and magnificent oak roof timbers. Fully restored and furnished to a high standard, the Tower contains a unique collection of family portraits and silver on loan from the present Earl of Mar and Kellie.

Alloa Museum and Gallery is in the Speirs Centre in Primrose Street, and explains the history of the town.

TULLIBODY

4 miles W of Clackmannan on the B9140

According to an old legend, Tullibody was founded by Kenneth McAlpine, the first truly Scottish king, in the 9th century. He called it "Tirlbothy", meaning the "oath of crofts", as he made an oath there not to lay down his arms until his enemies were all killed. A stone once marked the spot where the supposed oath was taken. **Tullibody Auld Brig** spanning the River Devon was built in 1535 by James Spittal, tailor to the Scottish royal family. In 1559 the eastern arch was dismantled to impede the progress of the French army which had been sent in support of Mary of Guise, Mary Stuart's mother. However, the French in turn dismantled the roof of St. Serf's church and built an entirely new bridge. Robert Dick, the self taught but eminent biologist, was born in Tullibody in 1811.

BLAIRLOGIE

6 miles NW of Clackmannan on the A91

Blairlogie is possibly the most attractive of the "hillfoot villages" of Clackmannanshire. It was the first conservation village in Scotland, and sits in the shadow of **Dumyat**, a hill which has the remains of a hilltop fort at its summit. The name comes from "Dun Maetae", meaning the "fort of the Maetae", an old Pictish tribe.

MENSTRIE

4 miles NW of Clackmannan on the A91

Menstrie Castle is where **Sir William Alexander** was born in 1567. He was the 1st Earl of Stirling, and founder of Nova Scotia, Scotland's only North American colony. The only part of the castle open to the public is the **Nova Scotia Commemoration Room**, which has displays about Sir Alexander and the colony. There are the armorial bearings of 109 Nova Scotia baronetcies created in Scotland, each one of which went on sale at 3,000 Scottish merks each. **Sir Ralph Abercromby** was also born in the village. He commanded the British troops at the Battle of Alexandria in 1734, and died there of wounds he had received during the battle.

ALVA

3 miles NW of Clackmannan on the A91

Sitting at the foot of the Ochil Hills, Alva is one of the "hillfoot villages" which once relied on spinning and weaving. The Ochil's highest peak, **Ben Cleuch** (2,363 feet) is to the north east. At the **Mill Trail Visitors Centre** you can see what life was like in the mills over the last 150 years. The Mill Trail is a signposted route taking you to many of the mills with retail outlets. The **Ochil Hills Woodland Park** has woodland walks and a visitor centre.

Alva Glen is called the "Silver Glen", as silver was once mined there. **St. Serf's Parish Church**, which was built in 1815, has some communion plate made of the local silver. It was the Erskine family who mined it, and it seems to have been a hit or miss affair. Sir John Erskine once showed two mines to a friend, saying than out of one mine he earned £50,000, which he immediately lost in the second one.

STIRLING

Stirling is one of the most important places in Scotland. It sits astride the main route north from the Lowlands to the Highlands, and whoever occupied Stirling Castle controlled Central Scotland. It was this strategic position, of course, which ensured its place in Scottish history. The huge volcanic plug dominating the area was ideal as a defensive position, and a castle or fortification has stood on it for thousands of years. A town gradually established itself on the eastern slopes, and thus Stirling was born. It became a royal burgh in 1226, and in 2002 it officially became a city, something which the citizens look on with pride, even

though in Scotland city status is not viewed with the same importance as it is in England.

Stirling Castle (Historic Scotland) dominates the town. It covers a mixture of styles and dates, and, like Edinburgh Castle, is not one building but a number of buildings atop a volcanic plug. There's no doubt that a fortress of some kind has stood here since before the Dark Ages, though it is only in the 12th century that it enters recorded history, when Alexander I dedicated a chapel there. In 1174, William I of Scotland ("William the Lion") handed it over the English.

By the Wars of Independence in the late 13th and early 14th centuries, it was back in Scottish hands, and was the only Lowland castle that wasn't held by the English. It was also making it difficult for the English to conquer the north, so in 1304 Edward made a determined effort to capture it, and it eventually fell. It was held by them for the next ten years, until, in 1313, Edward Bruce, brother of Robert I, laid siege to it. Its commander, Sir Philip Mowbray, agreed to surrender if the castle if wasn't relieved by the English by June 24th 1314.

By this time Edward I's son, Edward II, was on the English throne, though he wasn't half the man his father had been. However, as he didn't want to lose Stirling, he sent out a huge army to relieve it. The Scots met this army at Bannockburn, and won the day, thus securing Scotland's independence from England.

All traces of the 14th century castle have gone, and most of what you see now dates from the 15th and 16th centuries. James III built the Great Hall as a meeting place for the Scottish Parliament and to house great ceremonial occasions. James IV then built a Renaissance style palace to make Scotland a country at the heart of new

Stirling Castle

European thinking. His son James V finished the work. James VI then added the final touch to the castle - the Chapel Royal. These three elements - the hall, palace and chapel remain the historical core of the castle to this day.

But for all the pomp associated with the Scottish court, life at the castle still had its lighter moments. When James IV was staying there, one of the members of his court was an Italian monk called John Damien. He was the abbot of Tongland Abbey in Dumfriesshire, and took a great interest in science. In 1507 he announced to a startled king that, with the right equipment, man could fly. James was intrigued, and asked John to prove it. The monk eagerly accepted the challenge, and said that he would jump from the castle walls and soar like a bird.

A date for this flight was set, and John

Damien started making his preparations. He told his servants to amass a large collection of feathers, but only from birds which could fly, and from these he built a huge pair of wings. On the allotted day, James IV and his court assembled on the battlements of the castle, and were no doubt astonished and amused to see John crouching on the parapet, the wings strapped to his arms and back, and his arms flapping in imitation of a bird.

After making a short speech, Damien started flapping his wings again, and launched himself off the parapet. He dropped like a stone onto the castle midden, where more than just kitchen waste was deposited. He could not have fallen a great distance, as the only damage he did to himself was break a leg. He later discovered that his servants had not been able to collect enough "flying bird" feathers in time, so had added some hens' feathers. John blamed his failure on this, though from then on his nickname became the **Frenzied Friar of Tongland**, and he never regained his formal standing in court as a man of science.

In St. John Street you'll find the **Church of the Holy Rood**, which dates form the 14th century. It was built on the orders of James IV, who, legend has it, actually worked alongside the masons when it was being built. It is one of the most beautiful churches in Scotland, and it still has its original oak roof. The young Mary Stuart was crowned Queen of Scots here in 1543 when she was one year old, and in 1567 her son James VI (later to be James I of England) was crowned here also. The kirkyard was once the jousting yard for the castle, and great tournaments were held here. One of the monuments in the kirkyard is the **Martyr's Monument**, commemorating two women who were drowned at Wigtown for their religious beliefs.

Lady's Rock is next to the kirkyard, and it was here that the ladies of the court used to sit and watch royal extravaganzas and events taking place in the fields below. **Cowane's Hospital**, dating from 1629, is close by. It is named after John Cowane, who left money in his will for the building of an almshouse for unsuccessful Stirling craftsmen and merchants, which he called "decayed guildsmen". It later became a school, then an epidemic hospital, and is now a venue for concerts.

The **King's Knot** sits beneath the south side of the castle and the church. It is all that is left of a formal garden planned and laid out in the 1490s. It has a large, octagonal mound (now grassed over) where once colourful flowers and shrubs bloomed. The King's Park (now covered by housing and a modern municipal park) was once a favourite hunting ground for the Scottish kings.

The **Old Town Jail** is at the top of St. John Street, and dates from 1847. For 400 years before that, prisoners were held in the Tolbooth, which was overcrowded and filthy. From 1888 until 1935 it was used as a military prison, as the castle up the hill was garrisoned by troops. Now it is a visitors centre that shows what life was like for prisoners and wardens in the 19th century. You'll meet a character called Jock Rankin, who was the town's hangman, and if a prisoner should try to escape while you're visiting, do exactly as the warden tells you and you will come to no harm.

Mar's Wark is close to the church, and gets its name form the Earl of Mar, whose "wark" ("work") it was. He was the Regent of Scotland and guardian of the young James VI in the 16th century, and to announce this status and power he began building a fine new town house and palace in 1570. Mar's Wark was the result, though all that remains of it is a stunning Renaissance facade with nothing behind. On the opposite side of the road is **Argyll's Lodging** (Historic Scotland), another Renaissance-style mansion, this time built in 1630 by Sir William Alexander, the founder of Nova Scotia. It was subsequently acquired by the Dukes of Argyll, and in the 1670s the 9th Duke enlarged it. It is now the best example in Scotland of an 17th century aristocratic town house. Most of the rooms have been restored, and you can see how a gentleman and his family lived in the 17th century.

Very few Scottish towns still have their town walls standing. In Stirling, however, parts of the **Town Wall** can still be seen. They date from the 1540s, when Henry VIII was trying to force a marriage between his son Edward and Mary Stuart, a period known as the "Rough Wooing". They stretch along the south side of the town, from the Old Town Jail to about Dumbarton Road. There was never a wall to the north of the town, as attacks always came form the south. However, people whose houses were on the northern edge of the town were obliged to build thick, impregnable walls at the backs of their gardens as a means of defence. Incorporated into the Thistle Shopping Mall is **The Bastion**, which dates from the 16th century. It is one of the wall's original defensive towers, and contains a vaulted guardroom and an underground chamber. Within it is a display about Stirling's history.

To the north of the castle is the **Beheading Stone**, a grim reminder of just how bloody times were in the early 15th century. While James I was held captive by the English, Scotland was ruled for 18 years by the Duke of Albany, his two sons and the Earl of Lennox. They nearly bankrupted the country with their greed, and committed acts of

unspeakable cruelty to remain in power. When James was released in 1426, he had the four men beheaded on the Beheading Stone.

The heart of the old town is the **Tolbooth**, built by Sir William Bruce in 1704. It was the centre of municipal life, being where the baillies and councillors met to decide on the business of the town. A courthouse and jail was added in 1809. It is now an intimate concert venue. Near the Tolbooth is the Mercat Cross, with a unicorn on top of it. It is known locally, for some reason, as the "puggy".

Two famous battles have been fought in and around the city. William Wallace defeated the English in 1297 at the **Battle of Stirling Bridge**. The English were under the command of John de Warenne, Earl of Surrey, and Hugh de Cressingham. They were supremely confident of victory, considering the Scots to be an ill-equipped rabble. However, Wallace was a master tactician, and used the bridge to divide the English army, leaving half on one bank and half on the other, before going in for the kill. It more or less put paid to Edward I's plans to conquer the country, and he had to start his campaign all over again. The present Old Stirling Bridge dates from the late 15th century. Up until 1831, when the New Stirling Bridge was built, it was the lowest crossing point of the Forth. Up until 1936, when Kincardine Bridge was built, the new bridge was the lowest crossing point for vehicles.

The date of the Battle of Bannockburn - 1314 - is engraved on every Scot's heart. It finally ended England's expansionist plans northwards, and from then until the Union of Parliaments in 1707, Scotland was recognised as an independent, sovereign nation. Henry VIII and one or two other kings may have raised the issue now and again of Scotland being subservient to England, but it was always done in a half-hearted manner, as if they knew the battle had been lost.

But for such an important battle, it is interesting to note that no one actually knows where it took place. It was certainly to the south of Stirling, close to the Bannock Burn, and several sites have been pointed out as possible ones. What is certain, however, is that it didn't take place where the **Bannockburn Heritage Centre** (National Trust for Scotland) now stands. It sits two miles south of the city, on the A872, and has exhibitions, an audio visual display and the famous statute of Bruce astride a horse (a Scottish icon) by Pilkington Jackson. It was unveiled by the Queen in 1964.

Scotland's other national hero is William Wallace, and at the **National Wallace Monument** on Abbey Craig, across the Forth to the east of the city he is remembered. It is 200 feet high, has 246 steps, and from the top you get a panoramic view that takes in the Forth Bridges to the east and Ben Lomond to the west. The Battle of Stirling Bridge is explained here, as is Wallace's travesty of a trial at Westminster and his subsequent execution for treason against England in1305, even though he was Scottish. The monument also contains Wallace's great two-handed sword. He has been given the nickname "Braveheart", though in truth he was rarely called this before Mel Gibson's film was released in 1995.

On the banks of the Forth, to the east of the city, are the remains of **Cambuskenneth Abbey** (Historic Scotland). David I founded it in 1140 for Augustinian canons, and in 1326 Robert the Bruce held a parliament here, three years before he died of leprosy. The abbey's detached bell tower is complete, though only the foundations remain. James III and his queen, Margaret of Denmark, were buried before the abbey's high altar in 1488, and a monument now marks the spot.

On Dumbarton Road is the Smith Art Gallery and Museum. It was founded in 1874 from a bequest of artist Thomas Stuart Smith, and features displays on the history of the city, as well a collection of important paintings by artists such as Naysmith and Sir George Harvey.

AROUND STIRLING

FALKIRK
9 miles SE of Stirling on the A803

For all its industry and bustle, Falkirk is an ancient town that received its burgh charter in 1600. It sits at an important point on the main route from Edinburgh through Stirling and on into Northern Scotland. **Stenhousemuir**, close to the town, was once the meeting place of drove roads that came down from the Highlands. Great herds of cattle were kept here before being driven south to the markets of the Borders and Northern England. At the three "trysts" held each year, over 24,000 head of cattle were sold.

Falkirk means the "kirk of the mottled stones", which refers to the medieval kirk that once stood here. The present **Old Parish Church** dates from 1810, and incorporates masonry from an earlier church, including the old tower of 1734. Within its kirkyard was buried Sir John de Graeme, who fought alongside Wallace at the Battle of Falkirk in 1298, and was killed.

The **Town Steeple** dates from 1814, and was designed by the famous architect David Hamilton. It replaced an earlier, 17th century building. In 1927 it

OAKLANDS

32 Polmont Road, Laurieston,
Falkirk FK2 9QT
Tel/Fax: 01324 610671.
e-mail: andrew@bruce.net

Close to the spectacular Falkirk Wheel you'll find a wonderful B&B called **Oaklands**, which is owned and run by Helen and Andrew Bruce. This warm, friendly establishment was built in 1910, and sits just five minutes from Junction 5 of the M9 motorway. It has three extremely comfortable double rooms, two with en suite shower rooms and the third with an adjacent bathroom. Each has a TV, clock radio and hospitality tray, and children are most welcome in the shared family room. The breakfasts are beautifully cooked, and there is a choice of full Scottish or Continental. You'll be made very welcome at Oaklands.

was struck by lightning, and had to be rebuilt.

The two great Lowland canals of Scotland, the Forth and Clyde and the Union Canal meet at Falkirk. They were linked at one time with a great series of locks, but this has been replaced by the magnificent **Falkirk Wheel**, the world's only rotating boat lift. It is 120 feet high, and carries boats from one canal to the other in "gondolas" suspended from rotating arms.

There have been two battles fought at Falkirk. One was in 1298, when Wallace's Scottish army was defeated by the army of Edward I of England, which had superior horsemen and archers. Wallace had to flee, and remained a fugitive until his capture and execution in 1305. The other was in 1746, when Charles Edward Stuart's Jacobite army defeated a Hanovarian army when fleeing north from Derby.

The Antonine Wall was a great structure of turf erected by the Romans soon after AD138 on the orders of Emperor Antonius Pius. It stretched the 38 miles from the Firth of Clyde to the Firth of Forth, and was designed to keep out the wild northern tribes when the Romans briefly occupied Southern Scotland. **Rough Castle** (National Trust for Scotland), five miles form Falkirk, is one of the wall's best preserved fortifications. Parts of the wall can be seen in **Callendar Park**, where sits Callendar House, a magnificent mansion house modelled on a French chateau. In 1293 Alexander III granted land to a Malcolm de Kalynter, a Norman, and he built a wooden castle on the site. A descendant of Malcolm forfeited the lands in 1345 after plotting against the king, and they then passed to Sir William Livingstone.

The Livingtones were supporters of

Mary Stuart, and indeed one of the Livinsgtone family, Mary Livingstone, became one of the famous "Four Marys" who attended the queen. However, if you count up the number of Marys, you find that there were a lot more than four, as in those days a "mary" was another name for a high born servant or attendant. In 1600 the head of the family was created Earl of Linlithgow by James VI.

In the 18th century, however, they weren't so lucky. They were Episcopalians, and ardent Jacobites. The then Earl of Linlithgow had to flee to the Continent after the failure of the 1715, and his daughter Anne married the ill-fated Earl of Kilmarnock, who was later beheaded for his part in the Battle of Culloden. On the evening before the Battle of Falkirk, the Hanovarian commander stayed at Callendar House, and not knowing that she had Jacobite

sympathies, had dinner with Anne. So captivated was he by her looks and good manners that he ignored all entreaties to prepare for the battle which was to take place the following morning. In consequence, he was soundly defeated.

In 1783 the house was bought by William Forbes, a merchant, and his descendants lived there for just under 200 years. It now belongs to the local council, and is a heritage centre with a museum attached. You can explore a Georgian kitchen, a printer's and a clockmaker's workroom and a general store. The great Victorian library has been converted into an archive of books, documents and photographs of the area and its families, and the **Major William Forbes Falkirk Exhibition** traces the history of the town. Also in Callendar Park is the **Park Gallery**, which hosts exhibitions and workshops.

CARRONBRIDGE HOTEL

Denny, Stirlingshire FK6 5JG
Tel: 01324 823454

Jackie and John Bisset will give you a real Scottish welcome if you stay at their splendid hotel on the banks of the River Carron - the **Carronbridge Hotel**. This picturesque old hostelry has been around since at least 1659, so the traditions of good food, comfortable rooms and hospitality have been around here for over 300 years! There are three rooms on offer - one family and two twin, and all are fully en suite and scrupulously clean. There are hospitality trays and colour TVs in each room, and as well as bed and breakfast, evening meals are also available. It is ideally placed for country pursuits, as a great base from which to explore an area rich in history, or as an overnight stop as you head north or south.

Delicious pub grub is served all day to order, and Jackie, who does the cooking, is proud of the fact that she uses only the freshest of local produce wherever possible. Try the wonderful steak pie, or the chicken curry, or even the sizzling steaks with all the trimmings. And why not have a drink with your

meal? The Carronbridge Hotel has a wide range of beers and spirits, including a range of single malts, and there is a small but select cellar of fine wines. If you're driving, of course, there is also a range of soft drinks. The hotel offers full Scottish breakfasts - just right to set you up for a hard day's sightseeing. - or lighter options such as Continental breakfasts should you prefer. The prices are remarkably reasonable, and the place has a friendly feel about it that will ensure you feel right at home. Jackie and John are a mine of information about the attractions in the area, and the places to visit.

BONNYBRIDGE

8 miles S of Stirling on the B815

Bonnybridge is a quiet, unassuming industrial village with nothing much of interest to see. However, it does claim to lie at the centre of an area of central Scotland that has earned the nickname of the **Bonnybridge Triangle**. For there are more sightings of UFOs and unexplained

The Pineapple

phenomena here than anywhere else in Scotland. It all started in 1992, when a cross-shaped cluster of lights was seen hovering above a road, and since then the sightings have intensified, with mysterious football-sized lights, triangular-shaped craft and spaceships with doors that open and close.

GRANGEMOUTH

12 miles SE of Stirling on the A904

Grangemouth makes no pretence towards history or quaintness. It is a modern town, and the centre of Scotland's petrochemical industry. It was laid out in the 18th century by Sir Laurence Dundas at the same time as the Forth and Clyde Canal was being dug, and indeed the canal enters the Forth here.

The **Grangemouth Museum** sits on Bo'ness Road, and there are displays about the history of the town. The **Jupiter Urban Wildlife Garden** is off Wood street, and was established in 1990 on a piece of land that was formerly a railway goods yard. It is owned by both the Scottish Wildlife Trust and Zeneca (formerly ICI), and is surrounded by industrial buildings, smoke stacks and busy roads. It shows how industrial land can be reclaimed and cleaned up and

given over once more to nature. It has four ponds, an area of scrub known as the Wilderness, a wildlife plant nursery and a formal wildlife garden. In addition, the area has been colonised by foxes, and deer have been seen.

AIRTH

8 miles SE of Stirling on the A905

This small, unassuming village was once the site of a huge royal dockyard in the 15th and 16th centuries. Now tourists visit it to see one of the most unusual buildings in Scotland - **The Pineapple** (National Trust for Scotland) in Dunmore Park. It was built in 1761 as a summer house, and has on top of it a huge 45 feet high pineapple made out of stone. Now it can be rented as a holiday home.

Airth Castle (now a hotel) has parts dating from the 14th century. Within an earlier castle on the site William Wallace's uncle was held captive by the English. Wallace eventually freed him.

BRIDGE OF ALLAN

2 miles N of Stirling off the M9

On the **Airthrie Estate** is the campus of Stirling University. James VI had first suggested a college of university in the town in 1617, but it wasn't until 1967 that one was finally founded. It began with 180 undergraduates, and now has a student population of over 3,500.

The Airthrie Estate, with its picturesque lake, was owned by Sir Robert Abercrombie, who first saw Bridge of Allan's potential as a health spa when he had the waters of a local well analysed. The estate was then bought in 1844 by a Major Henderson, who developed the spa even further. So popular did the place become in Victorian times that it had a pump room, baths and many hotels and guest houses which catered for people coming to "take the waters".

The **Fountain of Ninevah** on Fountain Road was built by Major Henderson in 1851 to commemorate the archaeological excavations going on at that time in Ninevah, on the banks of the Tigris. Drink of another kind is made at the **Bridge of Allan Brewery** on Queens Lane. Tours round this micro brewery are available, with tastings.

Within **Holy Trinity Church**, which was built in 1860, are some furnishings designed by Glasgow architect Charles Rennie Mackintosh.

DUNBLANE
5 miles N of Stirling off the M9

The **Cathedral Church of St. Blane and St. Laurence** (Historic Scotland) dominates this small city. It dates mainly from the 13th century, when the 8th Bishop of Dunblane, Clement, decided to demolish the small, poorly maintained Norman building and replace it with something more dignified. He retained the Norman tower, however, though it was heightened in the 15th century. However, this is not a cathedral in the Gothic tradition of Elgin, St. Andrews or the great cathedrals of England. It is an intimate place, with neither side aisles or transepts.

But the history of the town goes back long before Norman times. It was founded in the 7th century by a Celtic monk called St. Blane, or Blan, who was born on the island of Bute in 602. Here he founded a Celtic monastery, which would have been a series of chapels, churches, cells and storerooms of wood and wattle enclosed within a "rath" or low turf wall. So sacred did the place become that in about 1150 it was decided to make the place the seat of a bishop when Scotland was gradually adopting the Roman Catholic Church. However, it was always a poor diocese, and at one point the Pope ordered the dioceses of Glasgow and Dunkeld to contribute to its income as a way of making it viable. With this money, Clement was able to rebuild the church in the 13th century.

With the arrival of the Reformation in the 16th century, the church became the town's parish church. Only the choir was used, as the reformed church had no need for ceremonial or elaborate liturgies. Gradually the nave fell into disrepair, and became ruinous. However, in 1898 it was restored and re-roofed, and the church returned to its former size. In 1914 Sir Robert Lorimer did further work on the choir, and designed the choir stalls as you see them today. They are one of the glories of the church.

When the Reformation came to Scotland, Dunblane's importance waned, and it became a weaving centre, with the weavers working from their small weaving cottages. But in Victorian times, when its train station opened, the town enjoyed something of a revival as a small holiday resort for prosperous merchants from Glasgow and Edinburgh. **Dunblane Hydro** was built in 1875 to take advantage of the tourists, and it is still a luxury hotel today.

KIPPENROSS

Dunblane, Perthshire FK15 0LQ
Tel: 01786 824048 Fax: 01786 824482
website: www.aboutscotland.com/stirling/kippenross
e-mail:kippenross@hotmail.com

Kippenross is the perfect place to stay overnight if you visit the Stirling area. Sue and Patrick Stirling-Aird offer a warm welcome and excellent Scottish hospitality in their historic house, which sits within a small estate on the banks of the river Allan. The extremely comfortable rooms are all en suite, and are elegantly furnished with antiques. The breakfasts - whether full Scottish or continental - use only the finest local produce wherever possible. The grounds were laid out by Thomas White, a well known landscape designer, and R.L. Stevenson loved to walk along the banks of the river. Visit Kippenross, and you will love it too.

The **Dean's House** was built in 1624, and was lived in by Dean James Pearson at a time when the Church of Scotland was Episcopalian. It now houses a small museum highlighting the history of the town and cathedral. **Bishop Leighton's Library** dates from 1681, also a time when the Church of Scotland had bishops. It contains over 4,000 books, some of them priceless.

The site of the **Battle of Sheriffmuir** is about three miles north east of the town. It took place in 1715, and was one of the deciding battles in the first Jacobite Uprising. However, it was unusual in that it was a battle without a victor, the result being a stalemate. The Jacobite forces were led by John Erskine, 11th Earl of Mar, while the government army was led by John Campbell, 2nd Duke of Argyll.

FINTRY

12 miles SW of Stirling on the B818

This village sits below the northern slopes of the **Campsies**, a range of hills that forms the northern backdrop for the city of Glasgow, 14 miles away. The hills are renowned for their fine walks and views, with the highest peak, **Earl's Seat** (1,878 feet) giving views north across the Endrick glen and southwards towards Glasgow. North of Fintry are the **Fintry Hills**, where there is also some good walking to be had.

Fintry regularly wins awards in the "Best Kept Small Village in Britain" and "Britain in Bloom" competitions. To the east is the **Loup of Fintry**, a 94-feet high cascade on the Endrick Water. **Culcreuch Castle** is a 700 year old tower house within an estate that is now a hotel. It was a seat of the Galbraiths, with the last chieftain living there being Robert Galbraith, who fled to Ireland in 1630 after killing a guest in his home - an unforgivable breach of Scottish etiquette. The **Carron Valley Reservoir**, four miles east of the village, dates from the 19th century, and supplies water to Falkirk and Grangemouth. Trout fishing is available, though a permit is needed.

KIPPEN

9 miles W of Stirling on the B822

This attractive little village sits north of Fintry, on the other side of the Fintry Hills. To its north is a large expanse of flat land called **Flanders Moss**. **Kippen Parish Church** is reckoned to be one of the finest post-Reformation churches in Scotland, and dates from 1825. The ruins of the former church, built in 1691, still survive, surrounded by an old graveyard.

It was in 1891 that Duncan Buchanan planted a vineyard within glasshouses in the village. One of the vines later grew to be the largest in the world, and was known as the **Kippen Vine**. It had an annual crop of over 2,000 bunches of table grapes, with 1959 being a bumper year, when 2,956 bunches were harvested. It covered an area of 5,000 square feet, and stretched for 300 feet along four connected glasshouses. People eventually came from all over Scotland - and even abroad - to gaze at it. The vinery closed down in 1964, when it could boast not only the world's largest vine, but also the second and third largest as well. The vines were all chopped down, and the land was later used for housing.

ARNPRIOR

12 miles W of Stirling on the A811

The area surrounding Arnprior is Clan Buchanan country. In the 16th century a man called John Buchanan lived in a tower house, or castle, in Arnprior. He styled himself the **King of Kippen**, even though the king of Scotland - who would have taken a dim view of his title - lived close by in Stirling.

He gave himself the nickname in an unusual way. One day a party of hunters, returning from a deer hunting trip, passed by the castle, carrying prime venison for James V's court. John waylaid them, and took the venison. The hunters told him the venison was from the royal hunting grounds, and therefore reserved for the king, but John refused to hand it back, saying that if James was the King of Scotland, then he was the King of Kippen.

The king was told of John's impudence, and was advised to take revenge. However, for some reason James found the incident amusing, and he and some courtiers rode out to Arnprior to meet the self-styled "king". When he reached the castle, he demanded admission. This was refused, because, a guard advised the party, John Buchanan was at dinner. One of James V's more

unusual habits was to dress up as a peasant and travel the countryside surrounding Stirling, talking to the common people and gauging their opinions. When he did this, he called himself the "Guidman of Ballengeich", "guidman" meaning simply "good man".

However, most of the court and the Scottish nobility knew of this habit. So the king asked the guard to tell his master that the "Guidman of Ballengeich" wished to see him. On being informed of this, John immediately knew who his visitor was, and rushed to the main gate, fully expecting to be arrested for disobeying a royal command, or worse, treason. He was met, however, by a party of laughing courtiers, with James laughing the loudest.

Buchanan invited them all into his home to dine on the venison that he had taken from the hunters. During the dinner, the king told Buchanan that he could take as much venison as he liked from the royal hunting grounds, as long as he would entertain the king whenever he passed by. He also invited his "brother monarch" to dine with him at Stirling Castle any time he liked, and the pair of them became firm friends.

GARGUNNOCK

6 miles W of Stirling off the A811

This pleasant little village sits about a mile south of the River Forth, which, before 1975, was the boundary between Perthshire and Stirlingshire. The Parish Church is a pleasant building which was rebuilt in 1774. At the top of nearby **Keir Hill** once stood an ancient fort, excavated in 1957.

PORT OF MENTEITH

15 miles W of Stirling on the B8034

This little village sits on the shores of the **Lake of Menteith**, sometimes called the "only lake on Scotland" (as opposed to loch). It's a claim that can't stand up to much scrutiny, as there are many stretches of water in the country - some natural, some artificially created - that have the name "lake" instead of "loch".

The name probably comes from the "laigh of Menteith", meaning the expanse of flatlands to the south of the lake called Flanders Moss, and indeed at one time the stretch of water was called the Loch of Mentieth. There is no doubting its beauty, however, and it must be one of the loveliest stretches of water in Scotland. **Inchmahome Priory** (Historic Scotland) sits on one of the lake's small islands, and is where Mary Stuart was kept after the Battle of Pinkie in 1547. It was founded in 1238 by Walter Comyn, Earl of Menteith, for Augustinian canons. Within the chapter house are some fine examples of carved medieval effigies and tombstones.

On the nearby **Inchtulla** ("inch" means island) the Menteiths had their home, and on **Dog Island** they kept their hunting dogs.

ABERFOYLE

17 miles W of Stirling on the A821

Aberfoyle has been called the "Gateway to the Trossachs", and sits on the River Forth about three miles after it flows through beautiful **Loch Ard**. A narrow road heads westward from Aberfoyle and hugs the northern shore of the loch for part of the way before turning north for Stronachlachar, going through some wonderful scenery as it does so.

And heading north form the village is the Duke's Road, named after the Duke of Montrose. It takes you into the Trossachs proper, where you'll find **Loch Achrie** and the wonderfully named **Loch Drunkie**. The **Scottish Wool Centre** lies just behind the village main street, and as its name implies, is dedicated to Scottish wool. The story takes you from the sheep to the products made from wool. You can visit the Spinner's Cottage, and have a go at spinning yarn from newly sheared wool, and there are also occasional vsitis from local shepherds, who put on sheepdog demonstrations. The place also sells a large range of woollen goods, from skirts and jumpers to jackets, scarves and blankets.

It was in Aberfoyle that the famous disappearance of the **Rev'd Robert Kirk**, minister of Aberfoyle Parish Church, took place in the 17th century. It is a curious tale, and well worth retelling. Robert Kirk was born in 1644, and throughout his life had, for some reason, an abiding interest in fairies, believing them to be real entities who inhabited the same world as us. He even wrote a book about it called *The Secret*

GREEN GALLERY

Main Street, Aberfoyle FK8 3UG
Tel: 01877 382873
e-mail: greengallery@sol.co.uk website: www.greengallery.co.uk

The **Green Gallery** specialises in the very best in contemporary Scottish arts and crafts. Painting - ceramics - wood - metal work - textiles - all are represented here. Over the ten years since it was founded, it has gained an enviable reputation in showcasing not only established artists, but young, upcoming artists as well. Owned and run by Rebecca Walker, it has plenty of natural light in its galleries, which shows off the items to perfection. If you're looking for something just that wee bit out of the ordinary to remind you of your holiday, then this is the place for you.

Commonwealth of Elves, Fauns and Fairies.

However, the story goes that the fairies were displeased with Robert for revealing all their secrets, and one day in 1692, while walking on Doon Hill, he disappeared. It was well known in the area that Doon Hill was the site of one of the magical entrances to the fairy kingdom. A search was mounted, but nothing was found. People, not unnaturally, claimed he had been taken by the little folk, and that one day he would return from the fairy kingdom looking not a day older than when he was taken.

However, there is a curious addition to the story. Robert's wife, some people claim, was visited by the fairy folk long after he disappeared, and told that her husband would be returned. He would reappear during a Sunday service in his old church, and she had to throw a knife at him, piercing his flesh, so that he would not be taken back again.

On the appointed day Robert, looking not a day older, did indeed enter the church, but his wife could not bring herself to throw the knife. Before the astonished eyes of the new minister and congregation, he disappeared once more.

Curiously, there was indeed a Rev'd Robert Kirk who was a minister at Aberfoyle in the 17th century, and he really did disappear while walking on Doon Hill. But perhaps the credulous villagers, knowing his interest in fairies, added the "explanation" to account for the disappearance, while all the time he was the victim of more down to earth crimes such as of robbery and murder. We will never know - unless he reappears one day in 17th century dress and gives an account of his stay with the fairies.

At **Gartmore**, a conservation village two miles south of Aberfoyle off the A81, is the **Cunninghame Graham Memorial**

Queen Elizabeth Forest Park, Aberfoyle

(National Trust for Scotland), which commemorates Robert Cunninghame Graham of Ardoch. He was a Scottish writer and politician who died in 1936. The memorial was moved here in 1980 from Castlehill in Dumbarton.

DRYMEN

20 miles W of Stirling off the A811

Buchanan Castle was, during World War II, a military hospital, and its most famous patient was Rudolph Hess, who, unknown to Hitler, parachuted into Scotland in 1941 on a secret mission to see the Duke of Hamilton. The castle as we see it now dates from 1855, though it is partly ruinous. It was built by the 4th Duke of Montrose after a former castle which stood on the site was destroyed by fire in 1852.

Drymen is one of the stops on the West Highland Way, the long-distance footpath that stretches from Milngavie in the south to Fort William in the north. It also sits close to the less busy eastern shores of Loch Lomond, and the quiet village of **Balmaha**, on the shores of the loch and also on the West Highland Way, is only three miles to the north west. The views out over Britain's largest sheet of water are very pretty, though to get really superb views you should climb **Ben Lomond**, eight miles to the north. It's a steep climb, as the mountain is a Munro, which means it is over 3,000 high. But it well worth the effort, and thousands of Glaswegians have made the same climb over the years.

Loch Lomond, nr Balmaha

BALFRON

16 miles W of Stirling on the A875

One of Scotland's most famous architects, **Alexander "Greek" Thomson**, was born in Balfron in 1817. He worked mainly in Glasgow, and many of his buildings are now showpieces for his work, which showed influences from ancient Greece and Egypt.The village was at one time a spinning and weaving centre, and has a Parish Church dating from 1832.

BLAIR DRUMMOND

5 miles NW of Stirling on the A84

The **Blair Drummond Safari and Adventure Park** is one of Scotland's most visited tourist attractions. You can tour by car or coach, and see animals from all over the world in conditions that allow them plenty of freedom. You can take a trip round Chimp Island by boat or watch a sea lion show as you glide above the lake on the "Flying Fox".

DOUNE

7 miles NW of Stirling on the A820

Doune Castle (Historic Scotland) was one of the seat of the Earls of Moray, and is now one of the best preserved 14th century castles in Scotland. It was originally built for the Dukes of Albany, who were Regents of Scotland during the minority of James I. However, when James took control of the kingdom, he executed the Duke for plotting against his brother, and took possession of the castle himself. It remained a royal residence until the Morays acquired it. It consists of two main towers connected by a great hall which has a high, wooden ceiling. In 1883 it was restored by the 14th Earl of Moray, and is now open to the public.

Though it is only a small village, Doune was granted burgh status in 1611, and originally stood close to the castle. In the early 1700s, to improve the view from the castle, it was moved to its present position. The 17th century **Mercat Cross** comes from the original village.

WOODLANE CRAFTS

Clandon House, The Cross, Doune FK16 6BE
Tel/Fax: 01786 841000
e-mail: woodlanecrafts@onetel.net.uk

Woodlane Crafts offers the very best in a wide range of quality handmade Scottish crafts which are sure to become unique and treasured possessions. Owned and managed by Cheryl Sivewright, Woodlane Crafts highly individual selection of items include handmade mosaics, silk art, copper and pewter mirrors, ceramics, knitwear, jewellery, handbags and accessories and greetings cards- all at competitive prices. Nothing that is here can be found in a chain store making it unique and wonderful. Though not an art gallery, Woodlane Crafts does sell some artwork and arranges commissions. Cheryl has created an inviting environment where friendly, knowledgeable advice is always available.

Two doors along Cheryl also runs **Wood 'n' Tots**, a dream of a shop, specialising in children's clothing, beautifully crafted traditional wooden toys and accessories. It is a veritable Aladdin's cave of colour and fun, with well-constructed, well-designed toys which are sure to awaken every child's imagination. There are tumbling toys, teddies and pull along trucks and a host of other toys we all used to play with as kids-bringing back happy childhood memories. The clothing is funky, fun and sure to appeal to any doting parent, as well as representing amazing value for money.

It was once a centre for the manufacture of high quality pistols. The industry was started in 1646 by a man named Thomas Cadell, and so well made were his pistols that they soon became prized possessions. It is said that the first gun fired in the American War of Independence was made in the village.

Doune Bridge across the Teith dates from the late 16th century, and was commissioned by James Spittal, tailor to James VI. Before that, a ferry had plied the waters, and it is said that James once arrived at the crossing without any money. The ferryman refused to take him across, even though James promised to pay him later. So, to gain revenge, he had the bridge built, putting the ferryman out of business.

DEANSTON

8 miles NW of Stirling on the B8032

Deanston was built round a cotton mill founded in 1785 on the banks of the River Teith. The owners were four brothers, one of whom was associated with Sir Richard Arkwright. It eventually closed in 1965. It now houses the **Deanston Distillery**, which makes a range of single malt whiskies, using the same water source that once powered the mill.

CALLANDER

13 miles NW of Stirling on the A84

Callander stands just to the east of the Trossachs, and is the main town for visitors exploring one of the most picturesque and delightful areas of Scotland. It is also home to the **Rob Roy and Trossachs Visitor Centre**, housed in a former church in Ancaster Square. Here the story of the area and its most famous son, Rob Roy, is told. His real name was Robert McGregor, the "Roy" signifying his red hair, and he lived from 1671 to 1734. Even today, people cannot agree about the character of the man. Was he a crook and brigand or was he a sort of Scottish Robin Hood? The probability is that he was a bit of both - a doughty defender of people's freedoms while at the same time looking after his own interests whenever possible. His lands were confiscated by the Duke of Montrose in 1712, and he was eventually imprisoned by the English in 1712.

He would probably have remained an obscure figure in Scottish history had it not been for Daniel Defoe's book *Highland Rogue*, and the later *Rob Roy* by Sir Walter Scott. A recent film - which, like most films about Scottish heroes, is not historically accurate, made him more famous than ever. The truth is that he was not a rough, uncouth Highlander with a penchant for bloodshed and battle, though he got involved in much of that from time to time. He was an educated man with a huge library who could read and write English and Gaelic - and this at a time when reading and

writing in any language was a rarity. It was Sir Walter Scott who made him act dishonourably at the Battle of Sheriffmuir in 1715, when in fact he acquitted himself with valour and honesty fighting on the Jacobite side. His funeral was on New Year's Day 1735, and people came from all over Scotland to attend.

Hamilton Toy Museum in Main Street has rooms full of toys from all eras, including modern collectables such as Thunderbirds, Star Wars and Star Trek figures.

Loch Katrine
23 miles NW of Stirling near the A821

Loch Katrine is not only one of the most beautiful lochs in Scotland, it is also the city of Glasgow's water supply. In the mid 19th century, a forward thinking city council decided that Glasgow should have an endless supply of clear, untainted water - one of the first cities to do so. The level of Loch Katrine was raised considerably, and tunnels and aqueducts were constructed between the loch and the city, 30 miles away, to carry the water southwards using only gravity. In 1859 Queen Victoria declared the scheme open during a grand ceremony, and 90 million gallons of water a day started to flow towards Glasgow.

Abbotsford Lodge

Stirling Road, Callander, Perthshire FK17 8DA
Tel: 01877 330066 Fax: 01877 339363
e-mail: sam@abbotsfordlodge.fsnet.co.uk
website: www.abbotsfordlodge.co.uk

Standing in its own grounds in the lovely small town of Callander, **Abbotsford Lodge** is a superior hotel with 17 comfortable bedrooms, most of which are en suite, and all of which have tea/coffee making facilities. Guests are pampered here, and the friendly owners go out of their way to make sure your stay is as enjoyable as possible. There is a spacious lounge with TV and an attractive sun lounge where you can enjoy a quiet drink. The food is superb, and the hotel has earned an enviable reputation in the area for the standards and quality of its cuisine. You can't afford to miss the Abbotsford.

ARDOCH LODGE

Strathyre, Perthshire FK18 8NF
Tel: 01877 384666 e-mail: ardoch@btinternet.com
website: www. ardochlodge.co.uk

Ardoch Lodge, an early Victorian Scottish country house set
in 12 acres, is an idyllic retreat from which to explore an area of
Scotland rich in history, heritage, sport and wildlife. It lies close
to the picturesque village of Strathyre, within the Loch Lomond
and Trossachs National Park. This superior guest house is owned and run by Yvonne and John Howes,
who bring the highest standards of hospitality to one of the best guest houses in Perthshire. The
comfortable bedrooms are decorated to an extremely high standard, and are spacious and welcoming.
All have private bathrooms, refreshment facilities, hair dryers, radios and alarm clocks. The beds are
comfortable and there are splendid views from the windows.

The food is outstanding, with only the freshest of local produce being used in the kitchen. The
breakfasts can be as light as you like, though the traditional Scottish breakfasts, which are hearty and
filling, come highly recommended! The dinner menu changes daily, and has three courses with a
choice in each. Loin of lamb with apricot and almond stuffing served with Madeira wine gravy, or

breast of chicken with a whisky and grain mustard sauce are typical
dishes. The guest house is not licensed, but guests can bring their
own drinks, which Yvonne and John will willingly serve at no extra
charge. Ardoch Lodge welcomes well behaved pets but you are
requested to bring your own bedding for them, not allow them onto
beds or other furniture and clean up after them. Within the grounds
of the Lodge is a small range of comfortable self catering cottages
and cabins, and you are invited to request information about them.

CLACHAN COTTAGE HOTEL

Lochside, Lochearnhead, Perthshire FK19 8PU
Tel: 01567 830247
website: clachancottagehotel.co.uk

The **Clachan Cottage Hotel** sits right on the lochside
at Lochearnhead, with beautiful views out over the
water, and is one of the best hotels of its kind in the
area. The rooms are spacious and well-equipped, with
most of them being fully en suite and having
hospitality trays. Most of them look out over the loch.

The warm, cheerful restaurant is open all day, and has an enviable reputation for its food, with the
cuisine being Scottish with a hint of French. In fact, the restaurant is featured in Scotland's "Food
Bible" - *the Taste of Scotland* Yearbook. Try the succulent, juicy sirloin steaks with a rich pepper sauce
sweetened with brandy and red wine, or the crispy Barbarie duck roasted with a sweet and sour sauce
flavoured with a basmati perfumed rice. Or even the Scottish salmon steak poached in a Chianti wine
masked in lemon scented cream dotted with shrimps and snipped chives. Delicious!

There is also a great selection of wines, and you're sure to find something to accompany your meal
to perfection. Or why not enjoys a quiet drink in the cosy bar? There is a wide range of single malts, as
well as wines, beers, liqueurs and of course, soft drinks, should you be driving. Here you can meet the
locals and get to know a bit about an area that is particularly rich in history and heritage. Should the
weather turn chilly, there is always a log fire burning in the grate. Loch Earn is famous for watersports
such as water skiing, and the hotel has its own shop selling and hiring a wide range of equipment,
with prices to suit most pockets. Whether you want to spend a few days in the area, or whether you're
looking for B&B accommodation as you pass through, then you can't go far wrong with the Clachan
Cottage Hotel.

Loch Katrine

The engineering that made this happen was the most advanced in the world at the time, and it was the largest engineering project of its kind. Between Lochs Katrine and Lomond was a small loch called **Loch Arklet**, and its waters flowed westwards into Loch Lomond. By a series of dams, this was reversed so that the water flowed eastwards into Loch Katrine, ensuring that the water levels remained high. Even today, the system of dams and aqueducts works well, and Glasgow still gets its water from this source.

But the loch was famous even before this. Sir Walter Scott set his poem *The Lady of the Lake* here, and at **Glengyle** (which cannot be reached by car), near the western end of the loch, Rob Roy McGregor was born in 1671. The **SS Sir Walter Scott**, a steamship, has been plying the waters of the loch from the beginning of the 20th century, giving pleasure cruises to thousands of people over the years. It takes you from the pier at the east end of the loch towards **Stronachlachar**, some six miles to the west. At Stronachlachar is a small island known as the **Factor's Island**, so called because of one of Rob Roy's escapades. He captured the Duke of Montrose's factor, who was collecting rents in the area, and took him to the island, where

he was imprisoned He then sent a ransom note to the Duke, who ignored it. So Rob Roy relieved the factor of the £3,000 worth of rent money he was carrying and sent him back to the Duke.

Loch Katrine sits at the heart of the Trossachs, a name which means "prickly", no doubt referring to the wooded and heather clad hills. There are other lochs as well, and they are equally as beautiful as Loch Katrine. **Loch Lubnaig** is a long, narrow loch to the east which can be reached via the A821 and the A84. At the southern tip are are picturesque **Falls of Leny**. On the way you pass Loch Achray and Loch Venachar. Loch Drunkie can only be reached by foot through some woodland, but it is a well marked path, and the resultant views make it worth while.

BALQUIDDER
24 miles NW of Stirling off the A84

If you continue north along the A84 past Loch Lubnaig, you will come to a narrow road leading west which takes you to Balquidder. It sits near the eastern end of **Loch Voil**, in an area known as **Breadalbane**, which translates from the Gaelic as "the uplands of Alba", Alba being the old name for Scotland. This is Clan McGregor Country, and here, in the kirkyard of the roofless kirk, is the grave of Rob Roy and some of his family.

KILLIN
30 miles NW of Stirling on the A827

The Rivers Dochart and Lochay spill into **Loch Tay** at its western end, where sits the village of Killin. The loch itself stretches eastwards deep into Perthshire, with the best views being from the narrow, unmarked road that runs along the whole of its southern shore.

The **Breadalbane Folk Centre** is

PORTNELLAN HIGHLAND LODGES

Glen Dochart, Crianlarich, Perthshire FK20 8QS
Tel.: 01838 300284
e-mail: relax@portnellan.co.uk
website: www.portnellan.co.uk

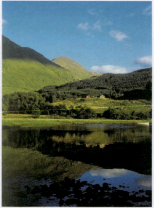

Winner of the **Best Self Catering Holiday Homes Award** and the **Most Enjoyable Self Catering Property Award**, this family

run business since 1980 has 21 exclusive lodges and cottages able to sleep 2 - 8 people.

Nestled in a stunning private estate of 70 acres, each property has been awarded the highest accolade for quality of 4 or 5 stars by the Scottish Tourist Board. Enjoy the romantic tranquillity of the Scottish Heartlands, on the northern edge of the **Loch Lomond National Park**.

Each lodge and cottage has panoramic views over our lochs, mountains and glen. Easy access to many visitor attractions including castles, distilleries, museums, highland games, outdoor activities, quality restaurants and pubs. Warm, pine interiors with thoughtful touches, en-suite luxury bathrooms, sauna, spa-bath, DVD player, telephone, bathrobes, towels, Molton & Brown bath and shower products compliment the 5 star quality. **Full details on the website.**

INVERARDRAN HOUSE

Crianlarich, Perthshire FK20 8QS
Tel: 01838 300240
e-mail: john@inverardran.demon.co.uk
website: www.inverardran.demon.co.uk

Owned and run by Janice and John Christie, **Inverardran House** is a great B&B that offers three fully en suite bedrooms and one room with private bathroom to discerning guests. All are spacious, comfortable and well-furnished, with hospitality trays in each one. The house, which is well proportioned and elegant, has been whitewashed with red trim on doors and windows, giving a warm and cosy feel to it. It sits in an idyllic location close to the West Highland Way, the long distance footpath connecting the central belt of Scotland with Fort William, and is a former hunting lodge which is ideally situated for exploring Loch Lomondside, Perthshire, the Trossachs and Stirlingshire. It also makes the ideal stopping off point should you be heading north or south along the A82 or A85.

Janice and John pride themselves on the warmth of their welcome, and strive to make your stay as enjoyable as possible in their family home. Janice prepares hearty breakfasts using the finest and freshest of local produce, or you can have something lighter if you prefer. By prior arrangement, she can also cook evening meals which are delicious and filling. The house is set in open grounds, and there is a large garden where children can play in absolute safety. A self-catering cottage is also available for hire, and it is beautifully appointed. Arrangements can be made with the village shop in Crianlarich for delivery of groceries and newspapers if your requirements are sent one week in advance. The countryside around Crianlarich is ideal for walking, birdwatching or studying nature.

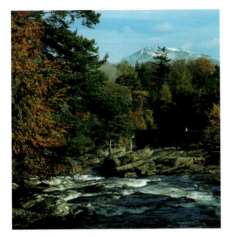

View from Killin towards Ben Lawers

within the village, and it has displays and exhibits about the history of the area. Beside it are the **Falls of Dochart**, a series of cascades on the River Dochart, and three miles north west, reached by a minor road, are the **Falls of Lochay**, on the River Lochay. After you park your car, care should be taken when approaching them on foot. On the Glen Lochay road sits the **Moirlanich Longhouse** (National Trust for Scotland). This small 19th century building is a rare surviving example of a surviving cruck-frame cottage and byre which was once common throughout the Highlands. It has been little altered, and retains many original features. It was home to three generations of the Robertson family, the last member moving out in 1968. The cottage is furnished in typical 19th century style, and in an outbuilding is a display of working and "Sunday best" clothing which was actually found in the longhouse when the NTS took it over.

One mile to the north of Killin are the ruins of 16th century **Finlarig Castle**, once a Campbell stronghold. It is said to have been built by Black Duncan of Glen Orchy, one of the most feared of the Campbells. In the grounds are the remains of a gruesome beheading pit, as well as a mausoleum, built in 1829 on the site of an earlier mausoleum.

CRIANLARICH
32 miles NW of Stirling on the A82

There is some marvellous walking and climbing country surrounding this busy village. The West Highland Way passes close by, bringing with it hikers and walkers in search of food and shelter. The twin peaks of **Ben More** (3,843 feet) and **Stobinian** (3,821 feet) are to the south east, while the **Falls of Falloch** are four miles south west on the A82, with a small car park close by.

TYNDRUM
40 miles NW of Stirling on the A82

Even though it has a population of about 100, this otherwise unimportant village has two railway stations. This is because the line north from Glasgow divides a few miles south of the village, one going to Fort William and one to Oban. Both lines pass through Tyndrum, and there is a station on each. It sits at the northern end of **Strath Fillan**, through which snakes the West Highland Way. At **Dalrigh** ("the field of the king") Robert the Bruce was defeated in battle in 1306, and close by was where **Strathfillan Priory** once stood, founded by Bruce in 1318 for Augustinian canons.

St Fillan was an Irish monk who lived during the 8th century, and who preached and worked in the area. He founded a small monastery, which may have been where the later priory stood. It is said that when he was supervising the building work on his monastery, a wolf attacked and killed one of the oxen used to bring building materials to the site. St. Fillan, instead of killing the wolf, prayed that it might take the ox's place, and it duly became a beast of burden.

LOCATOR MAP

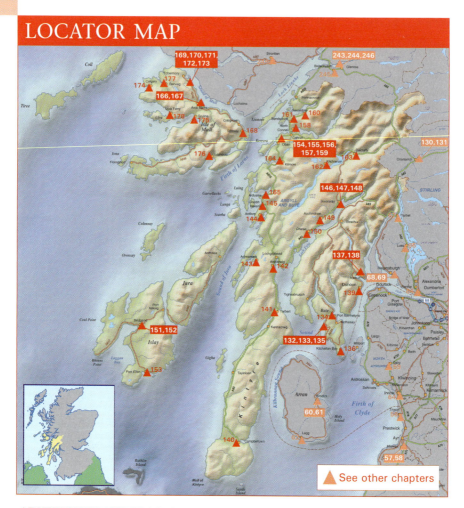

169,170,171, 172,173

243,244,246

246

Coll

Tobermory
177
174 Calgary Dervaig

166,167

Tiree

Lismore Ferry Aros Mains
178 Salen
175 Isle of Mull

168

161 160

158

Kerrera

154,155,156, 157,159

130,131

Iona
176

93

164

162

146,147,148

STIRLING

ARGYLL AND BUTE

165

145
149

144

150

137,138

143
142

68,69

139

141

134

151,152

Islay

132,133,135

136

153

Arran

140

60,61

Firth of Clyde

57,58

△ See other chapters

ADVERTISERS AND PLACES OF INTEREST

8 ARGYLLSHIRE & THE INNER HEBRIDES

Argyllshire sits on the western seaboard of Scotland, where long sea lochs penetrate the landscape and high, misty mountains tumble down into fertile Glens. Most of the Inner Hebrides - islands such as Mull, Jura and Islay (pronounced "Eye-lah") - are within Argyllshire as well, making for a diverse and beautiful landscape. The word "Argyll" comes from the Gaelic *Earraghaidheal*, meaning the "coastline of the Gaels".

Most of the county was, at one time, within the ancient kingdom of Dalriada,

Oban Bay

Argyllshire in Winter

founded by the "Scotti" in the 6th century as a colony. They emigrated from Northern Ireland, where there was already a "Kingdom of Dalriada" centred on Antrim, and it is from them that we get the name "Scotland". Their kingdom, which had its capital at the great hill fort of Dunadd, was one of the most powerful in the land, and eventually the Dalriadan king, Kenneth McAlpin, also ascended the throne of the Picts in AD843, thus creating the embryonic kingdom of Scotland, which in those days was wholly north of the Firths of Forth and Clyde. It wasn't until the 11th century that the kingdom of the Lothians and Strathclyde were taken into Scotland to create the country as we know it today.

The other great Dalriadan centre was Dunstaffnage, north of Oban, where a large medieval castle now stands, one of the most magnificent on Scotland's western seaboard. The religious capital was on the small island of Iona, off the coast of Mull, where St. Columba had founded his great monastery. This was a place of learning, piety and study, and it's fame spread, not just throughout Scotland, but throughout Britain and even parts of the Continent. It was Columba, when he declared Aidan king of Dalriada in AD574, who instituted the first Christian "coronation" in Britain, and invented part of the ceremony that is still used today - the shouting out of "God Save the King!" by the assembled dignitaries. Iona is still a place of pilgrimage. People who visit the island talk of the calmness they experience there, and the great feeling of peace. Of course, it also has the great abbey, plus the ruins of a nunnery and a burial ground that is supposed to contain the graves of many Scottish kings.

Argyllshire is a county of castles, most of them, alas, now ruined. Castle Sween, on the shores of Loch Sween, is the oldest stone-built castle on the Scottish mainland, and to the immediate north of Oban are the brooding remains of Dunolly Castle, a former MacDonald stronghold that seem to stand sentinel over the sea.

The towns are also attractive. Oban, Lochgilphead, Campbeltown, Inveraray and Tobermory are all by the sea, and all are now holiday resorts.

The rest of the land is sparsely populated, and there is some fine walking country. The roads rarely get clogged up (though Oban itself can get busy during the summer months), and as you turn a corner new vistas of land, sea and sky seem to open up all the time. Rain is common here, though the warm waters of the Gulf Stream mean that there is very rarely snow

Duart Castle, Isle of Mull

on the low ground on the coast. They also mean wonderful gardens, and places like Ardkinglas, Crarae and Arduaine must be visited to see the exotic species that flourish there.

Man has lived in Argyllshire for centuries, and the place is abundant with standing stones, burial cairns, stone circles and henges. This is most evident around Kilmartin, where you can hardly walk across a field without tripping over something from pre-history. Some of the cairns - beautifully built from stone - date from long before the pyramids. And there are intriguing legends here as well. When the Knights Templar, an order of monastic soldiers, was suppressed by Pope Clement V in 1307, they didn't disband, legend tells us. Instead they set sail from La Rochelle in France with their fabulous treasure and made for the western seaboard of Scotland. At that time, Robert I had been excommunicated by the Pope, so Papal authority didn't extend this far.

Argyllshire's coastline is rugged and rocky, with many sea lochs, promontories and islands. Mull is the largest island, with Jura and Islay a close second. But there are other hidden gems which are not visited as much as the larger islands, but which deserved to be better known. These include Colonsay, Coll, Tiree, Bute and Lismore, the last one meaning "great garden" in Gaelic, reflecting its flat terrain and fertile soil.

The Mull of Kintyre, that great arm-like peninsula hanging down and enclosing the western side of the Firth of Clyde, is also in Argyllshire. Though part of the mainland, it is in some ways more remote that many of the islands, as there are no direct flights to major airports. A car trip from Campbeltown to Glasgow - no more that 60 miles as the crow flies - can take four hours over twisting roads. This is the area made famous by Sir Paul McCartney when he wrote his hit song *Mull of Kintyre*.

BUTE

This small island sits in the Firth of Clyde, and its main town, **Rothesay**, was once a favourite holiday resort for Glaswegians, who called it "Scotland's Madeira", not just because it was on an island, but because of its mild weather.

Rothesay Castle

Fine Victorian mansions line the front, built by prosperous Glasgow merchants as holiday homes. Here their families and servants would stay for a couple of months in the summer, while the head of the household commuted by ferry and train to Glasgow each day. A lot of them are now guest houses or been converted into flats. But working class Glaswegians also holidayed in Rothesay. Every year, thousands of them descended on the town for a fortnight's holiday during the "Glasgow Fair" - the last two weeks in July. They caught the train to Wemys Bay on the Renfrewshire coast and took the ferry across.

The town became a royal burgh in 1401, and in the 14th, 15th and 16th centuries **Rothesay Castle** (Historic Castle) was a favourite retreat for Scottish kings. In fact, Robert III died there. It dates from at least the 13th century, when it was besieged by the Vikings. King Haakan of Norway took it in 1263, but was later defeated at the Battle of Largs. The castle was in a ruinous state until 1816, when the 2nd Marquis of Bute had it partly rebuilt.

The title "Duke of Rothesay" was bestowed by Robert III on his eldest son in the 15th century, making it the first

CANNON HOUSE HOTEL

5 Battery Place, Rothesay, Isle of Bute PA20 9DP
Tel: 01700 502819   e-mail: cannon.house@btinternet.com
Fax: 01700 505725   website: www.cannon.househotel.co.uk

On the waterfront in the historic town of Rothesay, the **Cannon House Hotel** calls itself the "country house hotel in town". It is a handsome Georgian building with the ambience of an elegant, quiet and welcoming country hotel. It has seven en suite rooms - two twin and five double - that are individually styled, and come complete with TV and tea/coffee making facilities. A delicious and different dinner menu is available each evening which takes advantage of local produce accompanied by a moderately priced wine list. This is the ideal base to explore the island.

Scottish dukedom. Before that, the highest title was "earl". Nowadays the title is borne by the heir to the throne of Britain.

The **Bute Museum** is close to the castle in Stuart Street, and has exhibits and displays about the history of the town, island and Firth of Clyde. On the southern outskirts of the town, near the present High Kirk, is the ruined **Church of St. Mary**. It dates from the 13th and 14th centuries, and has two magnificent canopied tombs. One contains the effigy of a woman and child, and the other the effigy of a man, possibly that of Walter, High Steward of Scotland (and ancestor of the Stewart kings), who died in 1326. The church, because of the magnificence of the tombs, is sometimes erroneously called the "abbey church", though no abbey was ever built on Bute.

The **Isle of Bute Discovery Centre** is housed in the town's Winter Garden on the front. There are interactive displays and plasma screens that give a "hands-on" story of the town. There is also a cinema and theatre, and an "anibod", a robot lookalike, this one being of Johnnie Beattie, one of Scotland's best loved comedians who used to appear here during the summer season. One of the most unusual attractions of the island - if indeed they are attractions -

are the **Victorian Gents' Toilets** at the end of the pier. They date from 1899, and are still functioning. They are full of ornate design, and were voted the second most enjoyable place in the world to spend a penny in. To find the most enjoyable, unfortunately, you will have to go to Hong Kong.

St. Blane's Chapel stands about seven miles south of Rothesay. It is a Norman structure, and is within the "rath" or low, boundary wall, of a Celtic monastery founded by St. Blane in the 6th century. The whole area shows how a Celtic monastery would have been laid out at the time, as the foundations of the round beehive cells lived in by the monks can still clearly be seen. The Norman chapel stands where the monastery's wooden church would have been. In keeping with such ancient foundations, there are two graveyards at St. Blane's - one for men and one for women.

At Straad (a name which tells you that Vikings once lived on the island) there are scant remains of **St. Ninian's Chapel**, which may date from before Norman times, and at Kilmichael there are the ruins of **St. Macaille's Chapel**, from the same period.

Mount Stuart House, near the lovely village of **Kerrycroy**, is the ancestral

CRAIGMORE PIER RESTAURANT

Mountstuart Road, Rothesay,
Isle of Bute PA20 9LD
Tel/Fax: 01700 502867

Housed in what were Victorian pier buildings, with its huge, stone archway, the **Craigmore Pier Restaurant** is a traditional tearoom and licensed restaurant that offers the very best in Scottish food. It is open seven days, and is renowned for its home baking and home cooked food, which is served in a warm, relaxed atmosphere, with an old world interior with exposed beams. Anne and Kenneth Ruthven own and run the restaurant, and offer a special a la carte candle lit dinner each Saturday evening where only the finest and freshest of local produce is used wherever possible.

KAMES CASTLE

Port Bannatyne, Isle of Bute,
Argyll and Bute PA20 0QP
Tel: 01700 504500 Fax: 01700 504554
e-mail: kames-castle@fsmail.net
website: www.kames-castle.com

Set on the lovely island of Bute, known as "Scotland's Madeira" because of its mild weather, **Kames Castle** is a historic castle built by the Bannatyne family in the 14th century. It is a majestic tower house, and looks exactly as you would imagine a Scottish castle to be - strong, impregnable and romantic. It is one of the oldest continuously inhabited houses in Scotland, and now offers five three star self-catering cottages within the 20 acres of beautiful grounds that surround it. The estate sits close to the scenic Kames Bay, north of the island's largest town, the royal

burgh of Rothesay. There is an unusual selection of mature trees and shrubs within the estate, thanks to the warming influence of the Gulf Stream, which flows by the island. The cottages are of varying sizes, and sleep between four and nine in absolute comfort. They are normally let from Saturday to Saturday, on a weekly or fortnightly basis, and come with all bed linen, towels, and so on, as well as electricity and heating costs.

Each of the cottages has been modernised, making the accommodation extremely comfortable and welcoming. All are centrally heated, with a well-equipped kitchen (including washing facilities), and a traditionally furnished lounge with colour TV and video. Three of the cottages (Ninian, Catan and Marnoc) sleeps five, four and four, and form part of the picturesque castle courtyard, whereas the two larger cottages (Clutha and Colmac) sleep nine and six, and stand separately, close to the two acre, 18th century walled garden. All are extremely picturesque, and made from the local stone. The estate is divided into three parts - parkland, woodland and the walled garden, with guests being free to explore and enjoy all of it. The walled garden has recently been restored, and supplies the estate with fruit and vegetables. Guests are free to pick and use the produce as well. Within the small village of Port Bannatyne there are one or two shops, and Rothesay itself, with its big shops and supermarkets, is only a few miles away.

The island of Bute is easily accessible from the mainland by a frequent carry ferry running to and from Wemyss Bay. The beautiful Kames Bay is close by, and there are many activities available on the island, from golf, sailing and wind surfing to sea and fresh water fishing, bird-watching and exploring the island's rich historical heritage. The world's last ocean going paddle steamer, the PS Waverley, often calls at Rothesay, and a cruise on her is one of the undoubted pleasures of the Firth of Clyde. But if it's just a quiet, unstrenuous, relaxing holiday you want, then Kames Castle is the place for you as well.

THE CRAIGMORE

48-49 Crichton Road, Rothesay, Isle of Bute PA20 9JT
Tel/Fax: 01700 503533
e-mail: craigmore@cairncross.org website: www.cairncross.org

The Craigmore prides itself on being one of the oldest privately owned hotels on Bute. The Victorian mansion house is situated in a quiet area of Rothesay with uninterrupted views of Firth of Clyde, Loch Striven, Rothesay Bay and Kyles of Bute. The hotel has 16 comfortable and well appointed rooms, all with en suite facilities. The restaurant is noted for the fresh, local produce it uses in its cuisine, and it has a selection of fine wines to choose from. The stylish lounge bar is the ideal place for pre-dinner drinks or a relaxing malt whisky after your meal. Special breaks available for three and seven night stays.

home of the Marquesses of Bute. It dates from 1877, when it was completely rebuilt after a disastrous fire. The architect was Robert Rowand Anderson, who came up with designs for a magnificent Victorian Gothic house. It was then filled with treasures that reflected the importance of the owners. At the same time, however, it encompassed every modern convenience, and was the first Scottish house to be be lit by electricity, and the first private house to have a heated indoor swimming pool. It stands in 300 acres of gardens, and is open to the public.

Near Port Bannatyne, north of Rothesay, is **Kames Castle**, which dates from the 14th century. It, too, stands in some beautiful gardens, but neither it nor the gardens are open to the public. One place which can be visited is the **Ascog Hall Fernery and Garden**, three miles south of the town. It was built in 1870, and has a sunken fern house with over 80 species of sub-tropical ferns. It was awarded the first-ever Scottish prize by the Historic Gardens Foundation, a world wide organisation which promotes historic gardens and gardening.

Ardencraig Gardens is accessed via Ardencraig Lane in Rothesay. They were bought by the local town council in 1968, and in summer are a riot of colour. **Canada Hill** stands to the south of the town, and from it there are magnificent views out over the Firth of Clyde to the mainland. It is so called because people used to congregate here to watch ships full of emigrants leaving Scotland bound for North America.

Today the main access to the island is still by the car ferry which plies between Wemyss Bay and Rothesay. However, a smaller, and in some ways more intriguing, car ferry plies in the summer months between Ardentraive on the Cowal peninsula and Rhubodach on Bute. The distance is no more that a

Rothesay Harbour

ST. BLANE'S HOTEL

Kilchattan Bay, Isle of Bute PA20 9NW
Tel: 01700 831224 Fax: 01700 831381
website: www.isleofbute.com

The **St. Blane's Hotel** takes its name from the Island of Bute's own saint, St. Blane, who was born on the island in the 6th century and gave his name to the small cathedral city of Dunblane. He also founded a small Celtic monastery on the island, and the fascinating ruins can still be seen to this day.

The hotel was built in 1881, within the seclusion of a sandy bay, and has one of the most serene and breath taking locations on Bute. It is the ideal place to stay, especially for those people who appreciate walking, fishing, golf, sailing, sightseeing, or just relaxing in a warm friendly and informal atmosphere after the hectic bustle of modern life.

It is a traditional, family run hotel whose rooms are all fully en suite, with colour TVs, tea and coffee making facilities and individual decors. There is also a four-poster room which has a luxurious feel to it, just right for newly weds or an extra special stay. The dining room is spacious and bright, and in the fully licensed bar both dinners and tasty lunches are served daily, with only the freshest of local produce being used in the kitchens. Why not relax with a single malt in the bar in the evenings, and let the worries of the world wash away? The hotel's owners, Allison and Paul Harley, take great pride in the standards they have set, and if you visit Bute, they will offer you a warm welcome.

quarter of a mile, though to get to the Cowal side takes two hours by car from Glasgow.

The Highland Boundary Fault, that great geological fault that separates the Scottish Highlands from the Lowlands, passes through Bute, the exact spot being marked by **Loch Fad**. This means that the northern part of the island is in the Highlands, and the southern part is in the Lowlands. The scenery reflects this - the north part of the island has high moorland, whereas the southern part is rich farmland.

DUNOON

Like Rothesay, Dunoon was once one of the Clyde's leading holiday resorts. It sits on the Cowal Peninsula, which juts southwards from Argyllshire, and though it's on the mainland, the best way to get to it is by ferry, which leaves from

Gourock. Each year in August the town hosts the **Cowal Games**, one of the most famous and important gatherings in Scotland. Here such activities as tossing the caber, throwing the hammer and sword dancing are carried on in a tartan-rich atmosphere.

The **Castle House Museum** sits in Castle Gardens, and has a permanent exhibition called "Dunoon and Cowal Past and Present". As well as photographs, artifacts and models which bring the area to life, there are also furnished Victorian rooms and a shop. Close by is a statue to **Highland Mary** (real name Mary Campbell), Robert Burns's lover, who had agreed to emigrate with him to Jamaica. She was born in Dunoon, and while on her way home from Ayrshire to prepare for her trip, she died and was buried at Greenock.

In Hamilton Street is the factory of

Power Boat Racing, Dunoon Harbour

of the year, making satellite photography impossible. The Americans abandoned it in 1992, leaving a large hole in the local economy. With them they took their shiny American cars and their accents, which at one time were common in the streets of Dunoon.

AROUND DUNOON

KILMUN

3 miles N of Dunoon on the A880

Dunoon Ceramics, which makes mugs, plates and other items. There is a shop, and guided tours of the factory are available. To the north of the town is the **Holy Loch,** once an American nuclear submarine base. It was chosen not just because of its deep water, but because Argyllshire has a cloud covering for most

Kilmun Church was founded in 1442 by Sir Duncan Campbell, ancestor of the present Dukes of Argyll. Close to the present Church of St. Munn is a Campbell mausoleum dating from 1794, and in its kirkyard is the grave of **Elizabeth Blackwell,** who, in 1842, was the first woman in Britain to graduate as

COT HOUSE HOTEL

near Sandbank, Kilmun, Dunoon, Argyll PA23 8QS
Tel: 01369 840260 Fax: 01369 840689
e-mail: cothousehotel@ talk21.com
website: www.cothousehotel.co.uk

The **Cot House Hotel** occupies a superb position close to the shores of the Holy Loch, among some of the best scenery in Argyll. It is an attractive, white-washed old building with crow step gables, and takes its name from "coite", an old Gaelic word for a boat, as this was the former home of a ferryman that took people across the local river. It is owned and run by Rita Gillespie and Russell Buchanan, who have created a haven for fishermen on the nearby River Eckaig and people who enjoy warm Scottish hospitality, comfortable accommodation and fine food and drink. Over the years, the Cot House Hotel has earned many plaudits for the quality of its cuisine, which is based on the "Natural Cooking of Scotland" scheme, and which uses fresh, local produce from the lochs, rivers, farms and glens of Argyll.

Choices on the menu include fish, game and meat, with vegetarian and vegan options should you require them, all served in the cosy dining room that boasts a welcoming log fire when the weather gets chilly. There is also a children's menu. The bar has a great range of single malts, and in good weather guests can take advantage of the patio and beer garden, which overlooks a popular children's play area. The guest bedrooms are all tastefully decorated and equipped, and all are, of course, en suite. An indication of the hotel's standing is the fact that it has won the Licensed Trade News Award for the family Welcome of the Year, and has been a runner up in the Independent Hotel Caterer of the Year Award. The hotel makes the ideal base from which to explore this part of historic Argyll .

WHITE HEATHER HOLIDAYS

Auld Kirk, Shore Road, Kilmun, Dunoon,
Argyllshire PA23 8SO
Tel: 01369 706709 e-mail: grogans4@aow.com

Kilmun is a small, attractive village that sits on the shores of
the Holy Loch, a few miles north of Dunoon. Here you will
find **White Heather Holidays**, a select development of five
superb self catering lodges set among some of the most
spectacular scenery in Argyllshire. The lodges are extremely
comfortable, and beautifully equipped throughout, with
spacious rooms and many labour saving devices in the kitchens. They are also furnished to an
exceptional standard, so that holidaymakers can have a relaxing and enjoyable holiday. Each lodge is
ideally placed for touring, or as the perfect retreat to recharge the batteries and refresh the mind. Well
behaved children and pets are more than welcome.

While you're staying in one of the lodges, why
not pay a visit to the olde worlde complex of
shops? **Sweet Memories** is a traditional sweet
shop - the kind we all remember from our
childhood - selling a wide range of sweets, all
made in Scotland. There's a vast array of jars filled
with confections of all colours and sizes, and it is
a joy for both adults and children alike to browse
through the many delicious items on offer. Just
the place if you have a sweet tooth!

Above Sweet Memories you'll find the **Tudor
Tearoom**, which is open daily and on Sundays
in the holiday season. You can have tea, coffee
and soft drinks, as well as light lunches, afternoon
teas and delicious home baking, all made on the premises. Try the tempting scones, cakes and pastries!
There are open fires during the winter months, and children are more than welcome.

Toys Toys Toys is another superb shop. It is really two shops in one, with one part selling everything
you need for the baby and toddler, from equipment and prams to clothes and teething rings. The
other part sells a wide range of good quality toys, from the latest favourites featuring modern technology
to olde style dolls, doll's clothes, jigsaws, toy soldiers and aeroplanes.

Presents of Mind is just right for browsing through. It sells traditional Scottish gifts and souvenirs,
all made in Scotland, such as candles and candle burners, glass ornaments, glassware, pottery and
cards. It is full of nooks and crannies, and you are sure to find the right present or souvenir here to take
home with you after a perfect holiday in this beautiful part of the world.

Curiosity Jewellers carries a wide range of lovely, well designed jewellery in gold and silver, such
as chains, bracelets, earrings and rings. It also has
a magnificent selection of smart ladies' and gents'
watches, either with genuine leather or expanding
metal straps. This is the place to come to treat
yourself, or to buy that extra special present for a
loved one!

A short walk will then bring you to **Changing
Rooms**, within a large, airy building where you
will find modern furniture, lamps, rugs, carpets
a, kitchen accessories, glasses, towels and soft
furnishings. The whole place is full of vibrant
colour, giving it a really modern feel.

a doctor of medicine. Also in the kirkyard is the grave of a former minister of the church, the Rev'd Alexander Robinson, who was deposed because of heresy in 1897. He had written a book called *The Saviour in the New Light*, in which he criticised some aspects of the Gospels.

BENMORE BOTANIC GARDEN

Dunoon, Argyll PA23 8QU
Tel: 01369 706261
website: www.rbge.org.uk

A member of the National Botanic Gardens of Scotland, **Benmore Botanic Garden** is famous for its collection of trees and shrubs. Set amid dramatic scenery, the west coast climate provides ideal growing conditions for some of the finest Himalayan rhododendrons. Guided walks are available to discover the secrets of this sensational garden, including the historic formal garden with Puck's Hut and established conifers. There is something of interest all year round and autumn provides a beautiful array of colours. There is a cafe for refreshments and a shop to buy gifts and plants, whilst various exhibitions and events take place in the Courtyard Gallery. Phone for details.

The **Kilmun Arboretum** sits on a hillside, and covers almost 180 acres. It was first planted in 1930, and has trees from all over the world. It is owned and maintained by the Forestry Commission, which does research work here.

BENMORE
6 miles N of Dunoon off the A815

The **Benmore Botanic Garden** (see panel above) is part of the Royal Botanic Garden in Edinburgh, and covers about 140 acres. There is a wide collection of trees and shrubs from all over the world, including 250 species of rhododendron, an avenue of giant redwoods and a formal garden. Some of the tallest trees in Scotland are to be found in the Glen Massan Arboretum, including a Douglas fir that is over 178 feet high. From the top of Benmore Hill, within the gardens, there is a magnificent view across Holy Loch to the Firth of Clyde and the Renfrewshire coast.

TOWARD
6 miles S of Dunoon on the A815

Toward Point is the southernmost tip of the Cowal Peninsula. **Toward Castle**, now in ruins, dates from the 15th century, and was a Lamont stronghold.

They were forever fighting with their neighbours the Campbells, and things came to a head in 1646, when the Campbells laid siege to Toward Castle. After trying unsuccessfully to blow it up, they offered the Lamonts safe passage as far as Dunoon if they surrendered. The Lamonts took them at their word, and left the castle.

However, the Campbells immediately rounded them all up and took them to Tom a Moid ("The Hill of Justice") in Dunoon, where 36 of them were hung. There had always been religious differences between the Lamonts and the Campbells (the Lamonts favoured an episcopal Church of Scotland, while the Campbells had Covenanting sympathies), but it was not this which prompted the executions. Previous to this, the Lamonts themselves had massacred Campbells at Strachur, and also massacred some villagers at Kilmun while they hid in the church.

CAMPBELTOWN

This small settlement must be the most isolated town on mainland Britain. Though only 60 miles from Glasgow as the crow flies, it takes at least four hours

THE OYSTERCATCHER

10 Hall Street, Campbeltown, Argyllshire PA28 6BU
Tel: 01586 550334
e-mail: george@oystercatcher.abelgratis.co.uk

The Oystercatcher is right on the harbour front, and is a gallery
and shop owned and run by George and Gill Stewart. Here you
will see a wide selection of wonderful artists' materials, original
paintings, prints plus a framing service. Gill opened the gallery
14 years ago to display George's watercolours, and, thanks to
demand, has now diversified into crafts and gifts that make the ideal souvenir of your stay on the
Mull of Kintyre. George is knowledgeable about everything he sells, and will offer friendly advice. He
also undertakes commissions at amazingly reasonable prices.

to get there by car, as the twisting route
is 140 miles long, and takes you along
the Mull of Kintyre, up into Argyllshire
proper, round Lochs Long and Fyne, and
finally down the shores of Loch Lomond
or the Gare Loch to Dumbarton, and
from there into Glasgow. It is the second
youngest royal burgh in Scotland,
having received its charter in 1700
(Dunkeld in Perthshire is the youngest,
having been granted its charter in 1704).
It is only 12 miles from the Irish
mainland, and though it sits in the
highalnds, it is 25 miles further south
that Berwick-upon-Tweed.

The main industries used to be fishing
and distilling, but now the fishing has
gone and only three distilleries remain
out of the 30 that once were situated

here, and which produced two million
gallons of spirit a year. For this reason it
relies more and more on tourism.

It sits on the small Campbeltown
Loch, guarded by the island of **Davaar**.
Within a cave on the island is a famous
painting of the Crucifixion painted by
local artist David MacKinnon in 1887.
The island can be reached on foot at
low tide via a shingle beach known as
The Doirlinn.

Campbeltown Cross sits near the
harbour, and dates from the 14th
century. It was used as the "mercat cross"
(market cross) after the town achieved
royal burgh status. **Campbeltown
Museum** in the High Street has exhibits
and artifacts which tell the history of
both the town and the Mull of Kintyre.
There are many standing stones
and old chambered cairns in the
surrounding countryside.

AROUND CAMPBELTOWN

SOUTHEND
8 miles S of Campbeltown on the B842

The most southerly village in
Argyllshire sits at the very tip of
the Mull of Kintyre. It was at
Keil, near the village, that St.
Columba is supposed to have

Campbeltown Harbour

first set foot in Scotland after his sea crossing from Ireland. Almost immediately he set of northwards again, until he finally reached Iona, where he set up his monastery. In Keil's ancient churchyard are footprints on a rock which are said to be those of St. Columba. It was near here also that 300 MacDonald clansmen led by Sir Alasdair MacDonald were massacred in 1647 after surrendering honourably. **St. Ciaran's Cave** is close by, with a stone altar and a water basin still within it. Some people have claimed that this is Scotland's very first church.

SADDELL

8 miles N of Campbeltown on the B842

Saddell Abbey (Historic Scotland) was founded in 1148 by Somerled, Lord of the Isles. It was completed by his son Reginald - who also founded Iona Abbey and Nunnery - and handed over to the Cistercians.

Nothing much remains of the abbey nowadays, apart from the presbytery and the north transept. As at other places in Argyllshire, stone carving flourished here, and 11 beautiful graveslabs can be seen, each one showing either a monk or a knight in full armour. **Saddell Castle** (not open to the public) was built in 1508 for the Bishop of Argyll when he visited.

SKIPNESS

26 miles N of Campbeltown on the B8001

Skipness Castle (Historic Scotland) was originally built in the 13th century, though it has been much altered over the years. It is first mentioned in 1261, when it was owned by the McSweens, though it later came into the

hands of the Earls of Menteith. Finally it was acquired by the Campbells, and was abandoned in the 17th century, when a newer house was built close by.

The ruins of **Kilbrannan Chapel**, near the shore, date from the 13th century, and are all that is left of a chapel dedicated to St. Brendan. Look out for five medieval graveslabs in the kirkyard and within the shell of the church itself.

Claonaig, three miles south west of the village, is a ferry port for a small summer-only ferry that connects the Mull of Kintyre with Arran.

TARBERT

31 miles N of Campbeltown on the A83

At this point, the Mull of Kintyre is no more than a mile wide. To the east is East Loch Tarbert, and to the west is West Loch Tarbert, where, at **Kennacraig**, the Calmac ferries leave for Islay and Jura. In 1093 King Magnus Barelegs of Norway dragged his longships across the narrow strip of land from one loch to the other. This was at a time when the Western Isles formed part of the Norse kingdom, and the king had now "proved" that the Mull of Kintyre was an island, and therefore belonged to him.

An Tairbearth sits to the south of the

Kintyre from Tarbert

village, and is a heritage centre that relates the area's and people's history. Also south of the village is Stonefield Castle, where you will find **Stonefield Castle Garden**, which is open to the public. As with so many gardens in Argyllshire, it has a good collection of rhododendrons, as well as plants from Chile and New Zealand and conifers such as sierra redwoods.

GLENBARR

10 miles NW of Campbeltown on the A83

The **Clan Macalister Centre** (see panel below) is housed within Glennbarr Abbey, a large mansion house. It traces the history of the clan as far back as Somerled, Lord of the Isles, nearly 900 years ago.

GIGHA

17 miles NW of Campbeltown off the west coast of Kintyre

This small island (no more than six miles long by two miles wide at its widest) is reached by a ferry from Tayinloan on the A83. The name means "God's island", and it is not a bad description of a place that seems to have its own micro climate. When the rest of Argyllshire is misty, Gigha is sometimes bathed in sunshine. Near the ferry port at Ardminish are the 50-acre **Achamore Gardens**, testimony to the effects of the Gulf Stream on the west coast of Scotland. They were founded by Sir James Horlick, of bedtime drink fame, after he bought the island in 1944. They

---

GLENBARR ABBEY MACALISTER CLAN VISITOR CENTRE

Glenbarr, by Tarbert,
Argyllshire PA29 6UT
Tel: 01583 421247

Set amid the stunning scenery of the Mull of Kintyre, Glenbarr Abbey is a magnificent house whose early 19th century Gothic Revival wing houses the **Glenbarr Abbey Macalister Clan Visitor Centre**, dedicated to the history and traditions of one of Scotland's proudest clans - the Macalisters. Under the personal care of Angus Macalister, 5th Laird of Glenbarr, it features memorabilia of the clan, some of it donated by clan members from all over the world. However, it goes much further than that. Here you also get a fascinating picture of Scottish family life in a beautiful country house in the 18th and 19th centuries. There are displays of family jewellery, patchworks, a beautiful thimble collection, a Spode dinner service, Sevres and Derby porcelain, antique toys and 19th century fashions, including military uniforms. The roots of Clan Macalister goes deep into the history of Scotland.

It takes its name from one Alister Mor, younger son of Donald of the Isles, a grandson of Somerled, who was killed in Ireland in 1299. Some of the clan emigrated to the Cape Fear area of North Carolina in 1739, creating a strong bond between America and Scotland. This sense of history and continuity gives the visitor to Glenbarr Abbey a rare glimpse into how the clan systems of old worked in Scotland, and how a chief rallied his clan around him in times of peace and times of war. There is also a tearoom, forest walks, a gift shop, nature trails and picnic areas. Truly, there's something for everyone at Glenbarr Abbey.

are famous for their rhododendrons and camelias. Since 2001, the island has been wholly owned by its inhabitants.

LOCHGILPHEAD

This small, neat town sits at the head of Loch Gilp, and is the main shopping centre for a vast area of Argyllshire. It sits in an area known as Knapdale, which roughly corresponds to that area of the Mull of Kintyre north of Tarbert.

Like most of Argyllshire, it seems on the edge of things nowadays. However, this was not always the case. At one time, this whole area was at the centre of a great trade and communications network that took in Ireland, Southern Scotland, Norway, the Hebrides, the Isle of Man and Northern England. Travel was easy by boat, and trade flourished. It came within the old Celtic kingdom of Dalriada, which flourished between the 5th and 9th centuries. The Dalriadans had originally emigrated from an Irish kingdom (also called Dalriada) to set up a colony in what is now Argyllshire, and soon the colony was more important than the original kingdom. It gave us St. Columba, the Gaelic language and even the name "Scotland", as the Dalriadans were called "Scotti".

Kilmory Woodland Park sits off the A83 to the south east of the town, and contains rare trees plus a garden and woodland walks. The park surrounds Kilmory House, which has been converted into local government offices. The **Crinan Canal** (often called "Scotland's most beautiful shortcut") connects Loch Fyne with the Sound of Jura, thus eliminating the need for fishing boats and small crafts to head south and go round the Mull of Kintyre. Its eastern terminus is at **Ardrishaig**, just south of Lochgilphead, and its western

GREY GULL INN

Ardrishaig, Argyllshire PA30 8EU
Tel: 01546 606017 Fax: 01546 606167
e-mail: bp@greygull.fsnet.co.uk website: www.greygull.co.uk

Set in the small village of Ardrishaig, the **Grey Gull Inn** is warm and welcoming and offers the very best in Scottish hospitality. It is family owned and run, meaning personal attention at all times, in an atmosphere that is informal and yet efficient. The building is well proportioned and attractive, with whitewashed walls that lend an air of elegance. There are 24 rooms on offer, all fully en suite, five of which are family rooms. Some of the rooms are on the ground floor, which make them ideal for the disabled visitor. Some have wonderful views out over Loch Gilp and Loch Fyne towards the hills on the Cowal Peninsula.

This is the ideal location for family holidays or short breaks away from the bustle of modern life, and the ferries to and from Arran and Islay are only 40 minutes away by car. Ardrishaig sits next to the picturesque town of Lochgilphead and the Crinan Canal, and there is so much to do and see in the

area, such as hill walking, fishing, mountain biking and of course, golf. If it's just a relaxing, unhurried holiday you are after, of course, you can explore the area's historical links, such as Dunadd to the north or the Mull of Kintyre to the south. The Grey Gull's food is superb, and uses only the freshest of local produce wherever possible. You can eat at any time of the day in the smart yet relaxed restaurant and wash it down with one of the inn's wonderful selection of wines, or one of the local ales. The inn is under the personal supervision of Bruce Potter, who is knowledgeable about the area, and can advise on the many things to see and do.

terminus is at the village of Crinan itself, on the tiny Loch Crinan. In 1795 an Act of Parliament had authorised the building of a canal between Ardrishaig and Crinan, and work got under way in 1794. It finally opened in 1801, though it still wasn't complete. By 1804 work still hadn't finished, and its debts had risen to £14,000.

In 1805, some of the banks collapsed and had to be rebuilt. It opened again in 1809, though when Thomas Telford the civil engineer inspected it in 1815, he declared that even more work was needed. Finally, it reopened in 1817, and everyone was at last pleased with it.

For all this work, the canal is only nine miles long, However, it has 15 locks, and the geology through which it was cut was complex and difficult. Queen Victoria passed through it in 1847 as she was making a tour of the Highlands, and it soon became a popular route for yachts as well as fishing boats and puffers. Perhaps the most unusual craft to pass through the canal were midget submarines during World War II.

AROUND LOCHGILPHEAD

DUNADD
4 miles N of Lochgilphead off the A816

Dunadd (Historic Scotland) is undoubtedly the cradle of the county. It is a great rocky outcrop that rises sheer from the flat area of land called Crinan Moss, with, on one side, the River Add curling round its base. It was here that the great kingdom of **Dalriada** - which corresponds to modern day Argyllshire - had its capital. In those days this rather lonely looking place had an entirely different aspect. It was covered in stone ramparts, palaces, wooden and stone buildings, pathways and fortifications.

Great banners would have hung from its walls - especially when the king was in residence - and ships would have been anchored in the River Add, which in those days would have been navigable right up to the rock. It, and the kingdom of Dalriada itself, was founded in the 5th century by immigrants from what is now County Antrim in Northern Ireland, where there was already a great kingdom called Dalriada. Gradually the Scottish Dalriada grew more important than its Irish equivalent, and became a separate and more powerful nation. With them when they came, the Irish brought the Stone of Destiny, upon which the ancient Irish kings sat when they were crowned or anointed.

In AD843, the King of Dalriada, Kenneth MacAlpin, also ascended the throne of the Pictish kingdom, situated to the east of Dalriada, which he had inherited through his mother. Thus an embryonic Scottish kingdom was born, though at this time there were still two independent kingdoms in the Lowlands. When they were assimilated into the country in the 11th century, the modern kingdom of Scotland as we know it today came into being. Kenneth moved his capital to Scone (taking the Stone of Destiny with him), which more central, and the glory days of Dunadd as a centre of royal power came to an end.

There is a car park at the foot of the rock, and the climb up to the top is quite difficult in places. Some of the ramparts can still be seen, though all of the buildings have long since gone. The view from the top is quite spectacular, and on a small rocky outcrop can be seen some ancient carvings. One is of a boar, another has ogham writing, and a third is a carved footprint. There is also a small, shallow depression. All, it is surmised, were used in the coronation ceremonies of the Dalriadan kings, though only the footprint and the bowl's purposes are known for certain. The king placed his foot in the footprint, and was anointed with oil from the bowl-like depression.

The kings of Dalriada were special. At this time, kingship was not as it is now. Kings were looked upon as great leaders or chieftains, and had no mystical role. St. Columba, who was a Dalriadan, changed all this when he organised the first true British coronation ceremony. He crowned and anointed Aidan as king of Dalriada in AD574. It was a ceremony that relied on Biblical precedent, and set the king apart as someone with almost super-human powers given to him by God.

Excavations have shown that Dunadd traded with England and the Continent, and that at the foot of the rock there were workshops that made jewellery, weapons and iron goods. No doubt a small township grew up there as well, at a time when townships in Scotland were almost unknown. It was at the crossroads of great trading routes, and must have been quite prosperous and powerful, receiving ships from many nations, and dignitaries who had come to pay their respects to the king.

KILMARTIN
8 miles N of Lochgilphead on the A816

The area surrounding the small village of Kilmartin is said to be the richest in Scotland for historical remains. Within a six mile radius of the village over 150 prehistoric and 200 later monuments are to be found. There are such things as standing stones, stone circles, cairns, graves, chambered tombs, henges, medieval castles, crosses, carved graveslabs and old kirks.

The present **Kilmartin Parish Church**

dates from 1835, though a church of some kind has stood here for centuries. Within it is a decorated cross dating from the 9th century, and within the kirkyard are three further crosses, also dating from the 9th century. Crosses of this kind were used by the old Celtic church as preaching stations, and later small churches were built on the spot.

Also within the kirkyard is the finest collection of carved medieval graveslabs in Western Scotland. They date from the 14th and 15th centuries, though one or two might be older. They might come as a surprise to those people who have a romantic idea of the Scottish fighting man as being a wild Highlander in a kilt and tammie waving a broadsword as he dashes across the heather. These knights are in conventional armour, and surrounding the carvings on the graveslabs are coats-of-arms, swords and crosses, showing that the knights came from the aristocratic classes, and would not have looked out of place anywhere else in Europe.

They add fuel to the theory that it was to this part of Scotland that the **Knights Templar** came when they were suppressed by Pope Clement V in 1307, egged on by Philip le Bel, King of France. There are many sites in the area which have medieval graveslabs similar to the Kilmartin ones, such as Kilmarie, Kilmory and Kirkmichael Glassary, and all have what appear to be Masonic and Templar symbolism on them. The great Templar fleet left La Rochelle in France, supposedly carrying the Templar treasure, and were never heard from again. Could they have headed for this part of Scotland? Did they bring their treasure? At the time Robert I was excommunicated from the Catholic church for murdering his rival the Red Comyn within a friary church in

Dumfries, so the Pope's jurisdiction didn't extend to Scotland. Some people certainly think they settled here. Edward I, during the Wars of Independence, bemoaned the fact that the Scots - who were a poor nation compared to England - always seemed to have more than enough money to defend themselves.

There is even a theory that the Templar treasure was something more than money - it was a great secret to do with Jesus. Whatever the truth, many books have been written about it, linking this part of Argyllshire with events that were happening on the mainland of Europe.

However, there are no doubts about the importance of Kilmartin's historical monuments. In a field behind the church is the **Glebe Cairn**, dating from about 1500-2000BC. Nowadays it is no more than a large, round pile of stones, though it formed part of a collection of such cairns known as the linear cemetery

which stretches for a mile southwards along the floor of Kilmartin Glen. The others are the Nether Largie North Cairn, the Nether Largie Mid Cairn, the Nether Largie South Cairn and Ri Cruin Cairn.

All are accessible by foot, as is the **Dunchraigaig Cairn** (which doesn't form part of the linear cemetery), just off the A816. The **Temple Wood Circles** date from about 3,500BC, making them much older than the Egyptian pyramids. There are two circles, with the northern one possibly being a solar observatory for the early agriculturalists who came into the area. Burials were introduced at a later date. The **Nether Largie Standing Stones** stand close to the circles, with the **Ballymeanoch Standing Stones** to the south of them. Of the original seven stones, only six survive.

The ruins of **Carnassarie Castle** (Historic Scotland) are to the north of

---

ASHFIELD ESTATE COTTAGES

Ashfield Farm, Achnamara, near Lochgilphead, Argyllshire PA31 8PT
Tel: 01546 850242 e-mail: ashfield@aol.com
Fax: 01546 850331 website: www.scotland2000.com/ashfield

Ashfield is a 500-acre family estate on the shores of beautiful Loch Sween in mid-Argyllshire. Here you will find the **Ashfield Estate Cottages**, which offer superior self catering accommodation to discerning tourists. The whole area is a tourists' paradise, with plenty of hill walking, climbing, bird watching, cycling, golf, sailing and fishing to be had. There are many historical attractions to seek out and the town of Lochgilphead, with its leisure facilities, is just ten miles away.

Millstone Cottage has recently been renovated to an extremely high standard and downstairs has a comfortable, open plan living room, fully fitted kitchen, a shower room and WC. Upstairs has a double and a twin bedroom, with a folding bed and cot on request. Heating and electricity is included in the rent, as are duvets, linen and towels. It is available for short, out of season breaks, and a deposit secures your booking. There are also two logs cabins on offer situated within 45 acres of mixed woodland

which has 1.5 km of coastline, private jetty, slip and boathouse suitable for small boats. The Bothy is attractive, warm and cosy, with two bedrooms, an open plan living room/kitchen and a bathroom. Lighting is by a 12 volt battery and wind turbine. The Boathouse is for small groups, with a team leader's room with stove, wash basin and twin beds, and six wall bunks in the main room. There is no electricity or telephone, but there is a basic kitchen, gas cooker and BBQ. Both cabins have wood burning stoves which supply hot water.

the village. They date from the 16th century, when the castle was built for John Carswell, Protestant Bishop of the Isles, who translated John Knox's reformed liturgy, the Book of Common Order, into Gaelic. It was the first book ever to be printed in that language.

Such is the complexity of the antiquities in the area that anyone wishing to visit and examine them should first head for the **Kilmartin House Museum** in the village, where the history and significance of the whole area is explained from after the last Ice Age until the 11th century, when Dunadd was finally abandoned.

KIRKMICHAEL GLASSARY

4 miles N of Lochgilphead on a minor road off the A816

The old kirkyard of Kirkmichael Glassary, surrounding the present 19th century

Parish Church, has another fine collection of carved graveslabs from medieval times and later.

KILMARIE

10 miles NW of Lochgilphead on the B8002

The Craignish Peninsula lies to the north of Kilmartin, and juts south westwards into the sea, opposite the island of Scarba.

Beyond the attractive village of **Ardfern**, where many yachts bob in the sheltered waters of Loch Craignish, is **Kilmorie Old Parish Church**. This roofless ruin was dedicated to St. Maelrubha, an Irish saint who lived in the 7th and 8th centuries. He was, after St. Columba, probably the most popular saint on Scotland's western seaboard. Within the church is another marvellous collection of carved graveslabs, this time dating from the 14th and 15th centuries.

COLLAIG POTTERY

Ardfern, near Lochgilphead, Argyllshire PA31 8QN
Tel: 01852 500310
e-mail: antonia@collaig.co.uk website: www.collaig.co.uk

For a unique gift from Argyll, why not walk up the pretty wooded lane from the coastal village of Ardfern to the rural pottery at Collaig? Here you can admire a wide range of hand thrown earthenware, all beautifully displayed and presented in the shop upstairs. Downstairs in the workshop you will find Antonia on the potter's wheel, or meticulously

decorating each piece with a broad palette of coloured slips. She produces both traditional and contemporary designs, ranging from the bold swirl of "Corrievreckan" to a detailed representation of "Argyll", where little tin-roofed crofts nestle in the hills and yachts scud amongst islands in the sun.

"Jazz" is a bold design of red and blue stripes and "Illyria" allows blowsy blue flowers to curl sumptuously over the rims and across each surface of the ware. There are more ranges and a full range of tableware, so whether you just want a mug for a friend, or you need a salt-pig for the kitchen, you are sure to find something to suit at a very reasonable price. Home of the annual Ardfern and Craobh Arts Festival, you will often find exhibitions here too, as well as in other venues throughout the villages. When you have finished browsing you can walk back down to the friendly village pub with its roaring log fires, or enjoy a coffee at the "Crafty Kitchen".

LUNGA ESTATE

Craobh Haven, by Lochgilphead, Argyllshire PA31 8QR
Tel: 01852 500237 Fax: 01852 500639
e-mail: colin@lunga.demon.co.uk
website: www.lunga.com

Lunga is a lovely Scottish estate on the Craignish
Peninsula in Argyllshire, and has views out over the water
to the islands of Shuna, Scarba and Luing. Here you will
find warm comfortable traditional country house rooms
for B&B and a range of self catering cottages and flats for
2-8 people, just right for a holiday in one of the most picturesque and historic areas of Scotland. They
have fully equipped kitchens with hobs, ovens, fridge freezer, dishwasher, microwave and a range of
utensils, crockery and cutlery. Each unit has a colour TV, video or DVD, radiators or storage heaters, an
open log fire and a telephone.

The B&B accommodation is within Lunga House itself, and is old world and comfortable, with
either private bathrooms or private shower rooms. Full Scottish breakfasts are served, with lighter

options if required. Dinners can be arranged, with most meals
served in the wood panelled morning room or the dining room.
Guests can also make use of the hall , which has a cosy seating
area and a selection of history and reference books, stagheads,
tigers and maps for you to peruse. And in the great drawing room
there are games such as shove ha'penny, ping pong and snooker,
as well as a grand piano. Lunga Estate therefore makes the ideal
base from which to explore this area of Argyllshire, or as a
stopping off point as you head north or south on your travels.
Stay here, and you won't be disappointed.

KILMORY

**13 miles SW of Lochgilphead on a minor road off
the B8025**

On the shores of Loch Sween, north of
Kilmory, stand the substantial ruins of
Castle Sween, said to be the oldest
stone-built castle on the Scottish
mainland. It's founder was a man called
Suibhne, ancestor of the MacSweens,
who lived in the 13th century. The area
surrounding the castle later became a
centre for superb stone carving, and at
the 700 year old **Kilmory Knap Chapel**
you can see the **Kilmory Sculptured
Stones**. This is a superb collection of
carved graveslabs, all contained within
the old chapel, and all collected from the
kirkyard. Some go back at last 1,000
years, while others are later. The carvings
include armoured knights, blacksmithing
and woodworking tools, swords and
crosses. The theory is that surrounding

Castle Sween was a small township
serving the castle, and that these stones
marked the graves of soldiers and
craftsmen who lived there and serviced
the people living in the castle.

MacMillan's Cross is the most
spectacular of the carved stones, though
it is one of the later ones, dating from
the 15th century. On one side it shows
the Crucifixion, and on the other a
hunting scene. Some words in Latin are
also carved, and these translate as "This
is the cross of Alexander MacMillan". No
one knows who this Alexander
MacMillan was, or whether the cross
marked the site of his grave. Whoever he
was, he must have had enough power
and money to have had such a
magnificent piece of carving carried out.
On a small peninsula across Loch Sween
is **Keils Chapel**, which has another good
collection of graveslabs.

INVERARAY

Inveraray is a perfect example if an 18th century planned town. It sits on the western shores of Loch Fyne, and is, for all its size, a proud royal burgh, having been granted its royal charter in 1648. It formerly stood between Inveraray Castle and the loch, but when the 3rd Duke of Argyll decided to pull down his old, decaying castle and build a new one, he moved the township further south. The town is now an elegant burgh with wide streets and finely proportioned Georgian houses and tenements, all whitewashed. In the summer months, when tourists flock to it, it feels like a busy metropolis, though in fact it is no larger than a village.

Inveraray Town

Inveraray Castle (see panel below) sits to the north, and it can easily be seen from the road. It is a four-square building with good proportions and a fairy tale turret at each corner, giving it the look of a French chateau. It was designed by Roger Morris and Robert

INVERARAY CASTLE

Castle Estate Office, Inveraray, Argyllshire PA32 8XE
Tel: 01499 302203 Fax: 01499 302421
e-mail: enquire@inveraray-castle.com
website: www.inveraray-castle.com

Inveraray Castle is the ancestral home of the chief of Clan Campbell. It is situated on the shores of picturesque Loch Fyne and close to Inveraray, surely one of the most interesting small towns in Scotland. Though it is first and foremost the well loved family home of the 13th Duke and Duchess of Argyll, it is also a treasure house of fine furniture, paintings, tapestries, porcelain and other *objets d'art* that recall a more elegant time. It is open to the public, and you can marvel at the weapons in the armoury, the family portraits, the ornate plasterwork, the four poster beds, the old kitchen and so on. Or you can explore the gardens and grounds, and admire the outside of a castle that was built in the 18th century, and owes more than a little to the elegance of the great French châteaux of the Loire Valley.

The Campbells have been at the heart of Scottish history for centuries, and are descended from solid British stock that once lived in the ancient Kingdom of Strathclyde, arriving in Argyllshire as part of a royal expedition in about 1220. The 11th Earl of Argyll became a duke in 1701, and each duke since has been a loyal king's man - supporting the House of Hanover during the Jacobite Uprisings of 1715 and 1745 and sometimes serving with distinction in the British Army. There is a fascinating "Clan Room", where Campbells from all over the world come to learn about the family. But even if you're not a Campbell, Inveraray Castle is still worth visiting.

Mylne, and contains a famous armoury, French tapestries, Scottish and European furniture and a genealogy room that traces the history of Clan Campbell.

There are two churches in the town. The parish church dates from 1794, and sits in the centre of the town, right in the middle of the main street. It, too, was designed by Robert Mylne, and is divided into two separate churches - one where the services were conducted in English and one where they were conducted in Gaelic, though this rarely happens nowadays. The **Church of All Saints** dates from 1886, and has a fine bell tower from which there is a good view of the town and loch. It also has a peel of ten bells - in fact, it is the heaviest peel of ten bells in the world, and one of the few Scottish churches where bell ringing

is popular. Each bell is named after a saint, and has the name inscribed on it. Ringers can sometimes be watched in action, and visiting bell ringers can participate by appointment.

Inveraray was the town from which justice was dispensed for this part of Argyllshire. **Inveraray Jail** (see panel opposite) dates from the early 19th century, and is now a museum showing what conditions were like in a prison at that time. You can see the cells that housed murderers, thieves and madmen, housed in two cell blocks built in 1820 and 1848. The 1848 one illustrates the more "enlightened" conditions under which prisoners lived, though there are still branding irons, thumbscrews, and whips on display. Another section of the jail has a mock up of an early 19th

NATURAL ELEMENTS CRAFTS GALLERY

Church Square, Inveraray, Argyllshire PA32 8TX
Tel/Fax: 01499 302379
e-mail: natural.elements@chsq.freeserve.co.uk

Inveraray is one of the most picturesque and charming towns in Scotland. Its whitewashed buildings sit on the shores of Loch Fyne, and attract many tourists each year, who come to see the elegant Georgian architecture and the magnificent Inveraray Castle. It is here, in the town's Church Square, that you will find **Natural Elements**, an art and craft gallery that displays and sells some of the best luxury hand crafted goods in the west of Scotland. It is owned and managed by Alison Burnett who trained in Glasgow and

London and, since opening in the year 2000, has earned a reputation as a place where you will experience efficient, friendly service and value for money.

The gallery stocks the work of 40 Scottish crafts people- with 70 per cent coming from Argyllshire itself - and here you can see woodwork, basketry, pottery, jewellery, textiles, metalwork, mosaics and mixed media, all combining the elegance and beauty of good Scottish design. Alison also stocks a fine range of pewter panels, mirrors, greetings cards, notelets and candles. All the products are made from natural materials, which helps to sustain the environment, and all are unique and individually crafted. This is the ideal place to buy a souvenir of your visit to the area, or a special gift for a loved one. Feel free to browse and Alison is always on hand to offer friendly, expert advice on a gift or souvenir that is just right for you. The interior is colourful and inviting, and it may be a cliché to call it an Aladdin's cave or a treasure trove of colour and texture, but that is exactly what it is. Opening times: 10am-1pm, and 2pm-5pm, closed on Tuesdays.

century courtroom, complete with sounds and High Court judge.

A three masted schooner of 1911, the Arctic Penguin, sits by the pier, and inside is the **Inveraray Maritime Museum**. There's an onboard cinema showing films about what conditions were like for Scotland's west coast sailors. The 60-acre **Argyll Wildlife Park** is situated two miles south of the town, on the A83, and you can see fallow deer, badgers, wild goats, wallabies and foxes. There are also quiet woodland paths. It was close to Inveraray, at Camus, that Neil Munro, one of Scotland's most famous authors, was born. He was a journalist who worked for a Glasgow paper, and his most famous books are the tales about Para Handy, the skipper of a west coast puffer. Over the years, various TV series have been made, based on the books. On the A819 through Glen Aray, which runs northwards from Inveraray, is a memorial to the man, close to where he was born.

INVERARAY JAIL

Church Square, Inveraray, Argyll
Tel: 01499 302381
Fax: 01499 302195

Inveraray Jail, the former County Courthouse and prison for Argyll, tells the story of the men, women and children who were tried and served their sentences here. Fascinating displays give an insight into the harshness of prison life in the 19th century, including cells where murderers, madmen and children were crammed in together, the courtroom where trials took place and the airing yards where prisoners were allowed to take an hour of exercise each day. An exhibition of items such as branding irons and thumb screws illustrates the punishments inflicted. There is an excellent range of gifts and souvenirs available at the Jail Shop. Ring for details.

AROUND INVERARAY

CAIRNDOW

6 miles NE of Inveraray, on the A83.

This little village sits on the opposite shores of Loch Fyne from Inveraray. It stands at the end of **Glen Kinglas**, which goes eastwards from the village towards Arrochar, passing the wonderfully named **Rest and be Thankful**, high above Glen Croe, which lies several hundred feet below. It is a spectacular drive in the summer months, though the road sometimes gets blocked in winter.

Within the Ardkinglas Estate at Cairndow, on the edge of the loch, is the **Ardkinglas Woodland Garden**. A combination of frequent rain, mild weather and light, sandy soil has created the right conditions for the growing of coniferous trees, and the gardens have plenty. It was established in 1875 by the Callander family, and it has several champion trees that are either the tallest or widest in Britain. As with other gardens in Argyllshire, there is also a collection of rhododendrons.

At Clachan Farm is the **Clachan Farm Woodland Walks**, which allow you to see many species of native tree as you walk along, such as oak, hazel and birch. The walks vary in length from a few hundred yards to a mile and a half.

ARROCHAR

13 miles E of Inveraray on the A83

This pleasant village sits at the head of Loch Long, which is a sea loch. Two miles to the east is the small settlement of Tarbert, which sits on the shores of Loch Lomond, a fresh water loch. It sometimes surprises people to learn that Britain's largest sheet of water lies so close to the sea in parts - and indeed Loch Lomond may at one time have been a sea loch. From the jetty at Tarbert small craft leave for cruises on the waters of Loch Lomond.

There is some superb walking and climbing country around Arrochar. **Ben Narnain** (3,036 feet) is three miles to the west, as is **Ben Ime** (3,318 feet). Perhaps the best known mountain in the area, even though it isn't the highest, is **The Cobbler**, also known as Ben Arthur (2,891 feet). This area is the home of mountaineering in Scotland, and the country's first club, the Cobbler Club, was formed here in 1865.

Near the **Jubilee Well** in Arrochar are the **Cruach Tairbeirt Walks**, footpaths which give some lovely views out over Lochs Lomond and Long. They total over one and a half miles in length, and though they are well-surfaced, some can be quite steep.

AUCHINDRAIN

5 miles S of Inveraray on the A83

There was once a West Highland village at Auchindrain, and it has now been brought back to life as the **Auchindrain**

Township (see panel below), an outdoor museum and interpretation centre. Many similar settlements were abandoned in the 19th century during the Highland Clearances, when landlords removed people from the land and replaced them with the much more profitable sheep. Queen Victoria visited the village when it was inhabited, and now, once more, you can see what she saw. Most of the cottages have been restored and furnished in period style, and there are also displays and exhibits illustrating life in a West Highland village in the 18th and 19th centuries.

STRACHUR

4 miles S of Inveraray, across Loch Fyne on the A815

Strachur Smithy has been restored as a small museum and craft shop, and still has some of the original tools used by a blacksmith in the 19th and early 20th centuries. **Lachlan Castle** is the ancestral home of Clan McLachlan, and lies six miles south of the village, on the B8000. This is now the Cowal Peninsula, and if you continue south along the B8000, you will eventually arrive at a turn-off to the west for **Portavadie**, the eastern terminus for the Partavadie/Tarbert car ferry. It runs during the summer months only, and takes you onto the Mull of Kintyre. If you turn east instead of west at the junction, you will eventually arrive at **Tighnabruaich** on the picturesque Kyles of Bute. The road continues northwards to Glendaruel, hugging the shoreline on the way, and giving some marvellous views over the narrow **Loch Riddon**. Near

AUCHINDRAIN TOWNSHIP

Auchindrain, Inveraray, Argyll PA32 8XN
Tel: 01499 500235

Auchindrain is an original West Highland township, or village, of great antiquity and the only communal tenancy township in Scotland to have survived on its centuries old site much in its original form. The township buildings, which have been restored and preserved, are furnished and equipped in the style of various

periods to give the visitor a fascinating experience of what life was really like for the Highlander in past centuries. Also on site is a visitor centre with displays on West Highland life, a gift shop, refreshments, picnic area and free parking.

Glendaruel, in the kirkyard of the church, built in 1610, there are the **Kilmodan Sculptured Stones**.

CRARAE

10 miles S of Inveraray on the A83

Crarae Gardens (see panel) is one of the best known woodland gardens in Scotland. Because of the mild climate in this part of the country, and the high rainfall, rare trees and exotic shrubs thrive. There are over 400 species of rhododendron and azaleas which give a brave and colourful display in late spring and summer. In the autumn the deciduous trees come into their own, with their warm, fiery colours. There are sheltered woodland walks and a spectacular gorge. The Scottish Clan Garden features plants associated with various Argyllshire clans.

ISLAY

44 miles SW of Inveraray in the Atlantic Ocean

It was from Islay (pronounced "Eye-lay") that the MacDonalds ruled the whole of the Western Isles at a time when they were almost a separate kingdom, and beyond the reach of the king in Dunfermline or Edinburgh. It is one of the

CRARAE GARDEN

Crarae, Inveraray, Argyll PA32 8YA
Tel/Fax: (Visitor Centre) 01546 886614
or Tel: 01852 200366

The main garden at Crarae is unique, with a strong "sense of place". Set on a hillside down which tumbles the Crarae Burn, the scene is reminiscent of a Himalayan gorge. The surrounding tree and shrub collections are rich and diverse, planted for artistic and naturalistic effect. The garden contains one of the best collections of the genus Rhododendron in Scotland, unusually rich in cultivars, as well as part of the National Collection of Nothofagus and particularly good representations of Acer, Eucalyptus, Eucryphia and Sorbus. The autumn colours of the leaves and berries are a perfect balance to the earlier blooming rhododendrons and azaleas.

Extending to around 25 hectares, the garden was traditionally accessed by a network of paths that criss crossed the burn via a series of footbridges. The Trust intends to reinstate these routes as part of a phased programme of repairs to allow visitors full access once again.

most beautiful of the Inner Hebrides, with lofty mountains to the east which rise to over 1,500 feet, and low moorland and farmland to the west. It is famous for its malt whisky distilleries, and indeed distilling is the the island's major industry. Most of the distilleries have conducted tours and visitor centres

Loch Indaal, Isle of Islay

ISLAY WOOLLEN MILL COMPANY

Bridgend, Islay, Argyllshire PA44 7PG
Tel: 01496 810563 e-mail: weave1@btopenworld.com
Fax: 01496 810677 website: www.islaywoollenmill.co.uk

Sheila and Gordon Covell worked in the textile industry all their working lives before fulfilling a dream and setting up the **Islay Woollen Mill Company** at the Old Mill at Bridgend in Islay, Britain's oldest, still working woollen mill. It was built in 1883, replacing an earlier building and produces an excellent range of top quality woven fabrics much in demand by the Hollywood film industry. Islay Woollen Mill designs featured, for instance, in *Braveheart* starring Mel Gibson and *Forrest Gump* starring Tom Hanks. But you can also buy garments made from Islay Woollen Mill fabrics. All are at keen prices, and they make lovely gifts or souvenirs of a holiday spent on the Inner Hebrides.

The range of scarves, for instance, includes the *Braveheart*, which is exclusive to the mill and the Finlaggan reflects Islay's heritage, as it was where the Lords of the Isles had their seat of power in medieval times. You can, of course, just buy the cloth, and there is a wide range of over 30 tartans

available, from Royal Stuart to Dress MacLeod. All the fabrics are woven on three looms, said by the British Museum to be the "most unique collection of antique machinery". You can actually watch Gordon at work as he weaves the cloth. This is a shop where browsing is welcome. There is absolutely no obligation to buy, and friendly advice is always available. For two years running the mill was even voted "best place to shop in Argyllshire and the Islands". There is ample parking space and picnic facilities, and there is disabled access to the hand weaving workshop.

ELIZABETH SYKES BATIKS

Studio and Gallery, Islay House Square, Bridgend, Islay PA44 7NZ
Tel/Fax: 01496 810147 e-mail: ehs@islatran.demon.co.uk
website: www.islatran.demon.co.uk

Liz Sykes has lived and worked on Islay for over 25 years, practising the ancient craft of batik. Her studio and gallery, are housed within an old joinery dating from 1748; this forms part of the beautiful Georgian Islay House Square. She draws pictures on white silk, then paints hot wax over the parts to remain white. The silk is then immersed in a dye bath, and only the unwaxed parts take up the colour. This is repeated over and over, using different coloured dyes, until a full colour picture is built up. Original silk batiks are hung on the old stone walls of the gallery, and there are also prints taken from them, either framed or unframed, as well as greetings cards. Plus there are original scarves and ties, together with other batik products that are both colourful and elegant.

If you want to make sure that you can see original batik being made when you visit, please phone in advance. In addition to batik, the gallery contains beautiful silver and pewter scarf brooches, by

Scottish jewellers, paperweights and CDs by local musicians. Gift vouchers are available, as are really good cups of tea or coffee. All the picture framing is done on the premises and indeed Liz offers a general bespoke picture framing service. She also offers one-day introductory workshops at very reasonable prices. These are great fun, and at the end of the day you will be taking home work you will be proud of. The gallery/studio is open Monday to Saturday from 10am - 5pm.

where you can sample a dram that is unlike the whiskies produced on the mainland. This is because the grain is dried over peat fires, imparting a rich, peaty flavour to the spirit.

At Port Askaig are the **Bunnahabhain** and **Caol Ila** distilleries, and to the east of **Port Ellen** are the distilleries of Lagavulin, Laphroaig and Ardbeg. **Bowmore** is possibly the most famous on the island, and is in the village of the same name. Across the loch is the **Bruichladdich** distillery. A ferry connects Port Ellen to the mainland at West Loch Tarbert on the Mull of Kintyre.

On islands in **Loch Finlaggan**, west of **Port Askaig** (which has a ferry to Feolin Ferry on Jura and Tarbert on the Mull of Kintyre) there are the ruins, dating from

Bowmore Round Church

medieval times, of the complex from which of the Lords of the Isles once ruled. A visitor centre is close by which explains the history of the Lordship plus the ruins. Ancient burial slabs can be seen, though they mark the graves of women and children. The chiefs were usually buried on Iona.

Near Lagavulin are the ruins of

GLENMACHRIE

Port Ellen, Islay, Argyllshire PA42 7AQ
Tel/Fax: 01496 302560
e-mail: glenmachrie@lineone.net website: www.glenmachrie.com

Glenmachrie is a picturesque, whitewashed four star guest house in Port Ellen, on the lovely Isle of Islay. It is pat of a 450-acre working farm, and is run and managed by Rachel and Alastair Whyte, who bring many year's experience to the task of creating a friendly, informal guest house that offers extremely high standards and excellent value for money. Rachel herself is a trained chef, and teaches other chefs in the natural cuisine of Scotland. Upon arrival, you will be made welcome by Rachel, who will offer you complimentary tea/coffee and home baking in her elegant sitting room. The guest house is beautifully furnished, and has many family antiques on display.

There are five extremely comfortable bedrooms - a family room, two doubles and two twins with colour TVs, radios, hair dryers, electric blankets, hospitality trays, irons and ironing boards. The food is outstanding as Rachel uses only the finest and freshest of local produce wherever possible. The full Scottish is filling and hearty, though lighter options are always available. Evening meals are available by arrangement, with the cuisine showing imagination and flair. Venison, local lamb and beef, salmon,

free range eggs, poultry and pheasant regularly appear on the menus. Rachel will also make you packed lunches by prior arrangement. Glenmachrie has repeatedly been selected to appear in *Taste of Scotland* publications, and has been awarded the coveted four medallions from the VisitScotland Food Grading Company, so you know you are getting the very best. One of the joys of Glenmachrie is sitting in the front sunroom and watching the glorious sunsets for which the Hebrides are justly famous.

Dunyveg Castle, a stronghold of the MacDonalds. At one time its owner was a man called Coll Ciotach, or "left-handed Coll". While he was away on business, the castle was captured by his enemies, and his men held prisoner. They then lay in wait for Coll's return so that they could also overpower him. However, Coll's personal piper alerted him when he was approaching the castle by playing a warning tune on his pipes, and Coll turned and fled. The piper got his right hand cut off for this act, and never again could he play his beloved pipes.

The **Kildalton Cross and Chapel** is at Ardbeg. The cross dates from the 9th century, and is richly carved with religious motifs. Bowmore is on the A874 beside the waters of Loch Indaal, and the **Bowmore Parish Church** is one of only two round churches in Scotland. It was founded in 1767 by Daniel Campbell, and the reason for its shape is simple - the Devil cannot hide in any of its corners. **Port Charlotte**, also on Loch Indaal, is where you'll find the **Islay Natural History Trust**. Its information centre has lots of details of on the natural history and wildlife of the island. Also in Port Charlotte is the **Museum of Islay Life**, which tells of everyday life on

the island through the ages.
Portnahaven sits at the tip of the Rhinns of Islay, beyond Port Charlotte. About four miles from it, on the moorland, is the **Cultoon Stone Circle**, no doubt used in ancient times to predict the seasons so that farming could be carried out effectively. Three of the stones have survived, and 12 lie at the point where they once stood.

JURA
42 miles SW of Inveraray in the Atlantic Ocean

Jura is a romantic island of peat bogs, mist and lofty mountains. The **Paps of Jura**, to the south of the island, is the best known range, with Ben an Oir, at over 2,500 feet, being the highest peak.

The island's only road takes you from **Feolin Ferry** (where there is a ferry to Islay) north along the east coast. On the way you'll see the **Jura House Garden**, with its collection of Australian and New Zealand plants, which thrive in the mild climate. **Craighouse**, with its distillery, is the main settlement on the island, and behind the parish church is a room with a small display about life on Jura down through the ages. A mile or so north is the ruined **Chapel of St. Earnadail**. This obscure Celtic saint was a disciple of St. Columba, and a story is told that when he died, he wished to be buried on his beloved Jura. When asked exactly where, he told his followers that a cloud of mist would rise up and guide them to the right spot. When he died, a cloud of mist duly guided them to this spot.

If you follow the road further north, you'll come to **Ardlussa**, where it peters out into a track. Within the old burial ground is the grave of

Craighouse towards the Small Isles

Towards the Isle of Jura

Mary MacCrain, marked by a tombstone. She died in 1856 at the ripe old age of 128. The people of Jura must have had the secret of longevity, as the stone says she was a descendant of Gillouir MacCrain, who "kept one hundred and eighty Christmases in his own house, and died during the reign of Charles I".

Between Jura and the island of Scarba is the notorious **Corryvreckan** whirlpool. The name comes from the Gaelic *coire bhreacain*, which means "speckled cauldron", and it is best viewed from the cliff tops above it on Jura, even though it is a three mile walk to get there. It is caused by a tidal race in the Gulf of Corryvreckan between the two islands, and the best time to see it is when a spring tide is running westwards against a west wind. It has in its time taken many ships to the bottom, and the sound of it, they say, can be heard at Ardfern on the mainland, over seven miles away.

But there is a much better story about how the whirlpool got its name. A Norwegian prince called Breachkan once visited the Scottish islands, where he fell in love with a beautiful princess who was a daughter of the Lord of the Isles. The two of them wished to marry, though the Lord of the Isles was against the union. However, he finally relented, provided Breachkan could moor his boat in the middle of the Corryvreckan for three days. Such was his love for the princess that the prince took up the dangerous challenge. He had three stout cables made - one from hemp, one from wool and one from the hair of a virgin. He then sailed into the whirlpool, where he dropped anchor, the anchor being tied to the boat by the three cables. Suddenly a great storm blew up, and the tide started racing. The whirlpool became a raging monster, but Breachkan wasn't worried, because he knew that if the first two cables snapped, the third made from hair would hold firm. But on the third day it too snapped, sending the prince to a watery grave. The woman from whom the hair came had not been a virgin after all.

OBAN

It is hard to imagine that in the 18th century Oban was no more than a collection of humble cottages grouped round a small bay. It only got its burgh charter in 1820, one of the last in Scotland to do so. Even then, however, it was an unimportant place, and it wasn't until the railway reached the town in 1880 that it prospered. People soon discovered its charms, however, and began building holiday villas, homes,

BARRIEMORE HOTEL

Corran Esplanade, Oban, Argyllshire PA34 5AQ
Tel/Fax: 01631 566356 e-mail: reception@barriemore-hotel.co.uk
website: www.barriemore-hotel.co.uk

The four star **Barriemore Hotel** sits on the Corran Esplanade, to the
north of the town, and has beautiful views of the islands of Kerrera,
Lismore and Mull. The house itself is a magnificent Victorian villa,
built in 1895 for a wealthy local banker called John Stuart McCaig.
Many original features have been retained by the owners, Ina and
Haemish Dawson, making this an elegant yet informal place to stay,
with an emphasis on comfort, service and value for money.

There are thirteen fully en suite rooms, all non smoking, and all
either double or twin. Each one is individually furnished, and has a
colour TV and hospitality tray. Some even command magnificent views out over the bay towards
Mull. There is a lounge with a fabulous stained glass window, and a separate bar, which is just right for
a quiet drink after exploring this part of Argyllshire. The traditional Scottish breakfasts are served in
the dining room, though lighter options are available. In the evening the dining room becomes a

stylish restaurant where resident chef Mark (with over 17 years
experience working in top Scottish hotels) creates imaginative dishes
using fresh, local produce wherever possible. The Barrymore has a
table license, and carries a select range of wines for your meal.
Beautiful gardens surround the hotel, and there is a patio where you
can sit and relax in the evenings. Ina and Haemish are local people,
so know Oban and its surrounding countryside intimately, and can
offer advice on where to go and what to see.

SWEETIES

100 George Street, Oban, Argyllshire PA34 5NR
Tel: 01631 566699 Fax: 01631 570470

Sweeties is based on an old fashioned Scottish sweet shop of
the 1930s, and sells over 350 different kinds of mouth watering
sweets, hand made in Scotland in the old fashioned way. To
enter the shop is to step back in time and experience olde worlde
service and courtesy. The sweets are arranged in jars on wooden
shelves, and there are no modern shop fittings, just an old style counter. Suitable antiques such as old
sweet tins and furniture complete a picture that takes you back to your childhood. 1930s music even
plays from an old wireless set. You are sure to find something to satisfy the sweetest tooth in this shop
full of memories.

JOHN STREET STUDIO

John Street, Oban, Argyllshire PA34 5NS
Tel: 01631 570470 Fax: 01631 570470
website: www.obanart.com

If you are looking for an usual gift when in Oban, why not head
for the **John Street Studio**, and treat yourself or a loved one to
an original oil painting or water colour? There is a wide range to
choose from in this light and airy gallery, as well as pottery,
textiles, prints and sculpture. It prides itself in being a showcase
for talented local artists, and there are lots of local landscapes on show. There is also a framing service,
and art classes can be arranged. This is a friendly gallery that highlights affordable and colourful
works of art, and someone is always on hand to offer experienced advice.

hotels and guest houses.

Now it is a bustling holiday resort, known as the "Gateway to the Western Isles". Dominating it is what must be the most unusual building in Argyllshire, **McCaig's Folly**. And though it looks exactly like the shell of a great Roman coliseum, it is anything but a folly. It was built by an Oban banker called John Stuart McCaig, with work starting in 1897. He wanted to establish a great museum and art gallery inside it, and at the same time create work for unemployed men in the town. However, he died before it was completed. In his will he left sums of money for the erection of large statues of himself and his family around the parapet, but they were never built.

Dunollie Castle sits to the north of the town beyond the Corran Esplanade. The site has been fortified since the Dark Ages, though the present castle was built by the McDougalls in the 12th century and later. There are two cathedrals in Oban - the Roman Catholic **Cathedral of St. Columba**, a 20th century granite building, and the **Cathedral Church of St. John the Divine**, dating from the 19th century.

Hebridean Ferry, Oban

Oban Pier is the departure point for ferries to many of the Western Isles, including Lismore, Mull, Coll, Tiree, Colonsay, Barra and South Uist, and it is enjoyable just spending some time watching the ferries come and go. A **World in Miniature** is on the Old Pier, and it has over 60 tableaux filled with miniature objects of furnishings and furniture, all hand made by craftsmen. Even the paintings are faithful copies of well known works of art. In Stafford Street is the **Oban Distillery**, which produces one of the six "classic malts" of Scotland. Tours are available.

Sheltering Oban is the small island of **Kerrera**, which can be reached by passenger ferry from a point two miles

BLAIR VILLA SOUTH

Rockfield Road, Oban, Argyllshire PA34 5DQ
Tel: 01631 564813
e-mail:blair.villa.south.oban.argyll@onmail.co.uk

A warm welcome awaits you at the three star **Blair Villa South**, a lovely old Victorian villa with gorgeous views towards the islands of Kerrera and Mull. There are three comfortable rooms on offer - two double which are fully en suite, and a single with private facilities. All have colour TVs and tea/coffee making facilities. Delicious cooked breakfasts are served in the spacious dining room, though lighter options are available if required. The house sits five minutes from the centre of the town, and is convenient for the train station, ferry terminal and shops.

Isle of Kerrera

Start	Kerrera Jetty
Distance	6 miles (9.7km)
Approximate time	3½ hours
Parking	Kerrera ferry slipway, GAllanch road, 2 miles (3.2km) south west of Oban
Refreshments	None
Ordnance Survey maps	Landranger 49 (Oban and East Mull), Pathfinders 343, NM62/72 (Firth of Lorn (North)) and 344, NM 82/92 (Oban (south) and Kilninver)

The earliest ferry to the isle of Kerrera departs on the dot of nine o'clock in season and the next is at 10.30am. Thereafter there is a regular service (every hour or so), with intending passengers being asked to turn a board to show the ferryman that he is in fact wanted at the advertised times (in any event it would be as well to check with Oban Tourist Information Centre first – see the list of useful organisations on pages 94 and 95). Kerrera has the air of romance about it common to all the islands off this coast. It is an intensely beautiful place, well worth the small effort involved in getting there.

On landing turn left at the telephone box along the track which follows the eastern shore of the island. There are lovely coastal views across the Horse Shoe to the Sound of Kerrera and the mainland beyond. The track goes through a gate before the first farm (Ardchoirc): fork left here to continue along the coast. The field on the left is called Dail Righ, the "King's Field", where Alexander II of Scotland died in 1249. The crofts of Gallanach are well seen on the other side of the Sound, below steep crags, while Oban is to the north-east.

The Little Horse Shoe is a tiny bay which appears to be a graveyard of

fishing boats. The track passes in front of the lovely whitewashed cottages overlooking the bay, which is sheltered by a steep, tree-covered hill. The track continues, snaking uphill to lose the view of the sea, though mainland peaks are just visible to the south-east.

Fork to the left **A** before the white cottage (Upper Gylen), going through a gate by a sheepfold to climb the hill in front of the white cottage, with a wall to the right.

After a very short distance a wonderful view is revealed below – the ruins of Gylen Castle **B** provide an atmospheric foreground to the prospect of the Firth of Lorn. The castle had a short history, being built in 1582 by the MacDougalls of Dunollie and lasting only until 1647 when it was left a ruin by Covenanters.

From the castle follow the cliffs west, crossing a stream and taking a path at the foot of a steep crag to turn north. This path joins a track **C** on to which you turn left to pass two cottages, the second one (Ardmore) derelict. The narrow path which is followed uphill from the remains of the second cottage was once a drove road. Cattle from Mull were landed on Kerrera at Barr-nam-boc Bay and driven south to be shipped to the mainland from the tiny haven of Port Dubh. (Alternatively they would be swum to the mainland from the east coast of the island.)

Level ground is soon reached above Ardmore and the views to Mull and Lismore improve as the path heads northwards. Morvern lies beyond the lighthouse on Lismore.

The going is easy on this smooth grassy path, which descends to another deserted croft – Barnabuck **D**. Presumably it is the shelter offered by Mull which allows trees to grow in this enchantingly beautiful spot.

Take the zigzag track up the hill from Barnabuck. There is a fine view when the crest of the hill is reached, and Oban will soon be seen ahead, with the distinctive shape of Ben Cruachan in the distance (on a clear day you will see Ben Nevis too). When the track meets with the one from Slaterich turn right to return to the ferry. ●

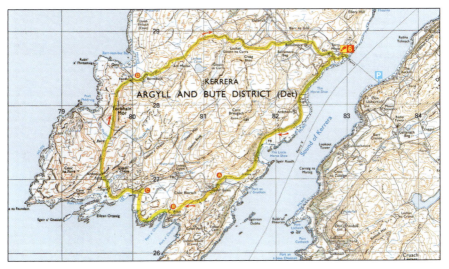

CRUACHAN CRAFTS

North Connel, Near Oban, Argyllshire PA37 1RA
Tel: 01631 710833

Cruachan Crafts is in a lovely rural setting north of Oban and over the Connel Bridge which spans the entrance to Loch Etive, where the waters of the Falls of Lora (Europe's only sea falls) tumble over the sea bed at certain times of the day. The craft shop sits one mile east of the A828, and along a minor road signposted to Bonawe. This is an enchanting shop, housed in a picturesque whitewashed country cottage, and is owned by Norman Asher, who is dedicated to bringing only the finest crafts to the attention of discerning customers and tourists. Norman himself is a craftsman of the highest standards, bringing high levels of artistry and skills to his own wooden furniture, figures and *objets d'arts*.

In fact, since he opened his large shop and workshop in 1999, it has grown in popularity, and it now carries a wide stock of items from around the world. If you're looking for a souvenir of your time in Scotland, then this is the perfect place to buy it. And if it's a bigger piece you're looking for - say a

nest of coffee tables, a table, a set of seats or a garden bench - then Cruachan Crafts is the place for you. Everything is keenly priced, and you'll be buying something which is unique, as everything is specially hand crafted to exacting standards. Norman can even arrange for larger pieces to be sent on to you, or if your car is big enough, and its in stock, you can take it with you. And he accepts one-off commissions, so if you don't see anything in wood that takes your fancy, then he will gladly craft something to your own specification. There is plenty of car parking space, and Norman will go out of his way to give you a warm welcome.

LERAGS HOUSE

Oban, Argyllshire PA34 4SE
Tel: 01631 563381
e-mail: stay@leragshouse.com website: www.leragshouse.com

Situated south of the town of Oban, **Lerags House** is one of the finest guest houses in Argyllshire. This no-smoking establishment is owned and managed by Charlie and Bella Miller, and has a relaxed informal atmosphere, though it refuses to compromise on service and all round value for money. There are six guest rooms and a suite on offer, all individually decorated and furnished to exacting standards, and all with a warm and comfortable ambience. The Loch View suite is on the first floor, and features a super king sized bed and a fully en suite bathroom with shower over the bath. The views out across the garden and loch to the hills beyond are superb.

The six rooms vary from a single room with en suite shower, ideal for someone travelling alone, to double rooms and twins. All have en suite facilities, and most have colour TVs. Tariffs are usually on a bed, breakfast and evening meal basis, and the guest house features in the *Taste of Scotland* scheme. This, coupled with three coveted medallions from VisitScotland, means that the food is consistently

superb. Bella creates dishes that show real imagination and respect for the ingredients. There is a three course, fixed price menu combining Australian flair with fresh, local Scottish produce, and of course, there is also a choice at breakfast, where you can have a full Scottish breakfast or lighter options.

Lerags House is also licensed for civil weddings, which can be organised for you and which can be carried out in the old, stone courtyard close to a 100 year old magnolia tree, or in the elegant sitting room.

Oban Harbour

miles north of the bridge, near Barcaldine, is the **Oban Seal and Marine Centre**. It is Scotland's leading marine animal rescue centre, and looks after many injured seal pups that have been orphaned or abandoned by their parents.

AROUND OBAN

DUNSTAFFNAGE
3 miles N of Oban off the A85

south of Oban on a minor road. At its south end are the gaunt ruins of **Gylen Castle**, another former MacDougall stronghold. **Armaddy Castle Garden** lies eight miles south of the town, off the B844, and is yet another of the superb gardens in the area.

Connell Bridge straddles the entrance to **Loch Etive**, about four miles north east of Oban. It was once a rail bridge, but now carries the A828 north towards Fort William. Beneath the bridge are the **Falls of Lora**, a natural rocky outcrop on the bed of the loch. When the tide is ebbing the water seems to rush from the loch towards the sea, tumbling over the rocks in imitation of a waterfall. A few

On a promontory sticking out into Firth of Lorne stands **Dunstaffnage Castle** (Historic Scotland), one of the most romantically situated castles in Scotland. Seen from the east, its setting is glorious, with the island of Lismore behind it, and beyond the mountains of Morvern. It was originally built in the 13th century by Ewan MacDougall, though there has been a fortification here since the days of the Dalriadan kings. When the king of the ancient Celtic kingdom was not at Dunadd, the capital of the country, he was staying here in some splendour.

The building as you see it now dates form the 13th to the 19th centuries. In 1309 it was taken by Robert the Bruce, who gave it to the Stewarts, who, when

---

ARGYLL POTTERY

Barcaldine, by Oban, Argyll PA 37 1SQ
Tel: 01631 720503
website: www.scottishpotters.org

Alan Gaff is a member of The Guild of Master Craftsmen and a superb potter who owns the **Argyll Pottery**. The showroom is a treasure trove of wonderful pots, plates, cups lamps etc, all subtly decorated and fired in a wood burning kiln. All pots are made on the premises using a stoneware clay to produce a wide range of domestic ware and some individual pieces. His prices are both keen and competitive. Why not get a souvenir of your visit to Argyllshire here? If you pay him a visit, you won't be disappointed.

they mounted the throne, turned it into a great royal castle. In 1470 the first Earl of Argyll, Colin Campbell, was made hereditary "captain", or keeper of the castle.

It was the scene of a gruesome incident which took place in 1363. The then Stewart owner was set upon in the castle grounds and murdered by a band of local MacDougalls, who still laid claim to the building. They then took the castle, though a few months later David II sent an army of men to oust the MacDougalls. This was duly done with great loss of life.

The castle has its own ghost, a lady called the **Ell Maid**. Sometimes, on stormy nights, she can be heard wandering through the castle, her footsteps echoing off the stone floors as if she were wearing armour. If she shrieks and sobs, it means bad news for the castle. But if she laughs, then all will be well. Nowadays she invariably laughs.

Dunstaffnage Chapel is outside the castle, and dates from the 13th century as well. Chapels were usually placed within the defensive walls of castles, so this is unusual. A small burial aisle for the Campbells of Dunstaffnage is tagged on to the east end.

KINLOCHLAICH GARDENS

19 miles N of Oban off the A828

Kinlochlaich Gardens were created in 1790 by John Campbell. It sits on the shores of Loch Linnhe, in an area known as Appin.

ARDCHATTAN

8 miles NE of Oban on a minor road on the N shore of Loch Etive

Duncan MacDougall built **Ardchattan Priory** in the 13th century for the Valliscaulian order of monks. The ruins of the church can still be seen, though the other buildings were incorporated

KINTALINE PLANT AND POULTRY CENTRE

Benderloch, Oban, Argyll PA37 1QS
Tel: 01631 720223 e-mail: ctg@kintaline.co.uk
website: www.kintaline.co.uk / www.obanfarmpark.co.uk

Kintaline Plant and Poultry Centre is a fascinating place that you can't afford to miss. Jill and Tim Bowis run a 24 acre farm, producing some of the best domestic poultry and waterfowl in the country. Productive pure breeds are now very rare, and this centre is one of the few places where efforts are made to improve the egg numbers, colours and qualities of each generation. It is open to the public all year round, and you can see over 30 breeds, with their histories and peculiarities explained. For those who want chickens or ducks in the garden, you can buy everything you need here, from the birds themselves to housing, books and feed. You'll also get lots of useful advice both at the farm and online from their very comprehensive websites. For those self-catering in the area they sell great eggs for your breakfast.

Jill also runs a plant nursery, growing thousands of interesting, easy and unusual perennials, herbs and alpines. She also brings in rhododendrons, clematis and bedding plants from personally selected nurseries in the area. There are always new plants being propagated, and Jill and Tim intend to plant out more of the park. Tim's passion is trains, and you and your children can help him run his G scale narrow gauge steam and American diesel trains on sundays. There is a shop with four public internet access points, lots of books and magazines on gardening and keeping poultry to browse and buy. For the more adventurous, both Jill and Tim offer week long working holidays, where you get to experience life on this fascinating farm in its myriad facets.

ROINEABHAL COUNTRY HOUSE

Kilchrenan, near Taynuilt, Argyll PA35 1HD
Tel: 01866 833207 Fax: 01866 833477
e-mail: maria@roineabhal.com website: www.roineabhal.com

This luxury four star guest house has a superb location among the glens of western Argyll and has three rooms that have been lovingly furnished with pieces collected by the owners, Roger and Maria Soep. Each has colour TV and hospitality tray, and the downstairs room has been designed for disabled guests. At **Roineabhal Country House.** Maria places great emphasis on natural cooking and langoustines, scallops, wild venison and salmon feature regularly on the dinner menus. The breakfasts are traditional and hearty, though lighter options are always available.

into Ardchattan House in the 17th century by John Campbell, who took over the priory at the Reformation. **Ardchattan Priory Garden** is open to the public and has herbaceous borders, roses, a rockery and a wild flower meadow.

TAYNUILT

9 miles E of Oban on the A85

Taynuilt lies on the A85, near the shores of Loch Etive. Near Inverawe is the **Bonawe Furnace**, which was built in 1753. The working of iron was carried

Loch Etive

out here for over 10 years, and the furnace made many of the cannonballs used by Nelson against the French. In fact, in 1805 the iron workers erected **Nelson's Statue**, the first such statue in Britain, and it can still be seen near Muchairn Church. **Barguillean Angus Garden**, established in 1957, extends to nine acres, and is on the shores of the tiny Loch Angus three miles south of the village. The loch is a sanctuary for injured swans. The garden was created in memory of Angus MacDonald, a journalist who was killed in Cyprus in 1956.

LOCH AWE

16 miles E of Oban on the A85

If you travel east along the A85 from Dunstaffnage, and go through the Pass of Brander, you will reach Loch Awe, Scotland's longest loch. This is its northern shore, though it stretches south west towards Kilmartin for over 25 miles. The village of Lochawe sits on the shore, with the magnificent runs of **Kilchurn Castle** (Historic Scotland) nearby. It was the seat of a minor branch of Clan Campbell who eventually became the Earls of Breadalbane. It was built in the 15th century, though what you see nowadays dates from later periods also.

St. Conan's Kirk is a gem of a church that sits on the banks of the loch. It is reckoned to be one of the most beautiful in Scotland, though it dates only from 1880. It was built by Walter Douglas Campbell, brother of the Earl of Breadalbane, who lived nearby. Not only did he commission it, he designed it and did some of the woodwork as well. The church as it was originally built was small, so in 1907 Walter began extending it. He died in 1914, however, before it was finished. World War I interrupted the work, and it was only finished in 1930. Now it has all the feel of an English church rather than a Scottish one. There is a lovely chancel, an ambulatory, a superb nave with a south aisle and various chapels and cloisters.

To the west of the village of Lochawe is the **Cruachan Power Station** (see panel above), one of the many hydroelectric stations in Scotland. The waters of Loch Cruachan, high above Loch Awe, have been harnessed by the station as they tumble down through pipes and turbines and then into the loch. The turbine hall is a huge artificial cave carved out of the mountain, and is one of the wonders of Scottish civil engineering.

However the turbines can actually act as pumps if they go into reverse, and they can lift 120 tons of water a second from Loch Awe back up into Loch Cruachan. It does this at night, using

CRUACHAN VISITOR CENTRE

Dalmally, Argyll PA33 1AN
Tel: 01866 822618 Fax: 01866 822509
e-mail: visit.cruachan@scottishpower.com
website: www.scottishpower.com/cruachan/

Hidden deep within the mountain of Ben Cruachan on the shores of Loch Awe is Cruachan Power Station. Here, a short distance from Oban, you can discover one of the hidden wonders of the Highlands. A power station buried one kilometre below ground. At its centre lies a massive cavern, high enough to house the Tower of London. Here enormous turbines convert the power of water into electricity, available to you in your home at the flick of a switch. Take an unforgettable journey into Ben Cruachan and find out how power is generated. Experienced guides will lead you along a tunnel cut from solid rock. A coach will transport you into a different world, a place so warm that sub-tropical plants grow.

Find the nerve centre of the station and understand how the power of water from Loch Awe is harnessed to provide a rapid response to sharp rises in demand for electricity. A generator can go from standstill to an output of 100,000 kilowatts in two minutes to provide as much electricity as necessary.

Back on the surface, the visitor centre has many things to see and do. The Exhibition includes touch screens and demonstrates the way in which power will continue to be generated in the future. To finish off, there is a lochside cafeteria and gift shop. Open Easter to mid-November 9.30am-5pm; August 9.30am-6pm.

electricity produced by conventional power stations that would otherwise go to waste, and in this way it is actually "storing" electricity in the form of water for when demand is heavy. The station can produce enough electricity to power a city the size of Edinburgh. Tours are available.

KILMELFORD
11 miles S of Oban on the A816

Though no more than a group of cottages with an old church and a hotel, Kilmelford was once an important place. To the west, near the shores of Loch Melfort, was one of the biggest

CORRYVRECKAN

Dal an Eas, Kilmore, Oban, Argyllshire PA34 4XU
Tel/Fax: 01631 770246 e-mail: yacht.corryvreckan@virgin.net
website: www.corryvreckan.co.uk

Beginner or expert, you're sure to enjoy a sailing holiday aboard the
Corryvreckan, a yacht that sails among the sheltered lochs and
remote islands of the west coast of Scotland. It's an experience not
to be missed. Laze in the sun - go beachcombing, bird watching or whale spotting - learn how to hoist
and set the sails - learn about navigation - in an exciting but safe environment. The yacht is big, blue,
and beautiful, and owned and run by Douglas and Mary Lindsay, who have a wealth of yachting
experience. In addition, Mary is a first class cook, and your on-board dinners will be long remembered.

gunpowder mills in Scotland. Many
small industries like this dotted
Argyllshire at one time, and it is a happy
hunting ground for the industrial
archaeologist. In the kirkyard of the
small **Parish Church** of 1785 are some
gravestones marking the graves of
workmen killed in the mill as they
helped to make the "black porridge".

Most of the mill buildings are still

there, though they have now been
converted into cottages in a time share
development.

ARDUAINE

13 miles S of Oban on the A816

On south facing slopes overlooking
Asknish Bay is the 50-acre **Arduaine
Gardens** (National Trust for Scotland).
Like most of the gardens in this area, it

LOCH MELFORT HOTEL AND RESTAURANT

Arduaine, by Oban, Argyllshire PA34 4XG
Tel: 01852 200233 e-mail: reception@lochmelfort.co.uk
Fax: 01852 200214 website: www.lochmelfort.co.uk

One of the finest hotels and restaurants in Scotland is
complemented by one of the finest locations. For the **Loch
Melfort Hotel and Restaurant** sits on the shores of Asknish
Bay, on Argyllshire's beautiful coastline. In 2002/2003 it
won the coveted Les Routiers "Scottish Hotel of the Year" award, and is a member of that select band
of establishments known as "Scotland's Hotels of Distinction". So its reputation as a place that offers
comfortable accommodation and fine cuisine is second to none.

The 26 guest rooms are spotlessly clean, as you would expect, and all have been lavishly decorated,
with private bathrooms, colour TV, radio and direct dial telephones. Most also have stunning views
across Asknish Bay to the mountains of Jura, Shuna and Scarba, where the sunsets are sometimes
stunning. Some are contained within the main body of the house, while the majority are located
within the Cedar Wing, a more modern building attached to the house by a covered walkway. Two of
the rooms boast king-sized beds.The hotel's award-winning restaurant has large panoramic windows

that look out across Asknish Bay, and serves food that has won
two AA rosettes. The food is outstanding, and justly famous
throughout Scotland. The kitchen uses only the finest and freshest
local produce in season, and the menu is thoughtful and
imaginative. The hotel has a select wine list that complements the
food, and in the lounge bar you can relax with a glass of one of its
many single malts. The Loch Melfort Hotel is the ideal base from
which to explore the area surrounding Oban. It is warm, friendly
and welcoming, and an ideal place to relax.

Arduaine Gardens

has a wonderful collection of rhododendrons, as well as herbaceous borders and trees from all over the world.

DALAVICH

13 miles SE of Oban on a minor road on the banks of Loch Awe

The **Dalavich Oakwood Trail** is a two-mile long trail laid out by the Forestry Commission. It is situated on a minor road off the B845 near Kilchrenan, on the shores of Loch Awe, and you can also see alder, hazel, birch and juniper as well. You can also see various sites where charcoal burners produced charcoal for the Bonawe Ironworks.

SEIL ISLAND AND LUING

8 miles S of Oban on the B844

These two islands are known as the "slate islands" because of the many slate quarries that were once situated here. Seil is a genuine island, though it is separated from the mainland by Seil Sound, which is only a few yards wide. Clachan Bridge, nicknamed the **Bridge Across the Atlantic**, connects it to the mainland. It is a high arched bridge to allow fishing boats to pass underneath at high tide, though very few boats now use it. It got its name because at one time it was the only bridge in Scotland to connect an island to the mainland,

though the more recent Skye Bridge now dwarfs it.

On the island side of the bridge is a late-17th century inn called the Tigh na Truish, or "House of Trousers". This recalls the aftermath of the Jacobite Uprising, when the wearing of the kilt was forbidden. The men of Seil Island paid no attention whatsoever to this edict when they were on the island, and kept wearing the kilt. When they crossed to the mainland by the then ferry, they changed into trousers at the inn.

The village of **Ellenabeich** lies on the west coast of the island, and facing it is the small island of Easdale. Ellenabeich was at one time an island, but the narrow channel separating it from Seil Island proper was filled in with spoil from the local slate quarries. The biggest quarry was situated right on the coastline at Ellenabeich. Its floor was 80 feet below the water line, and during a great storm, its sea wall was breached and the waters came flooding in. Fortunately, this happened during the night, and no one was killed or injured. But it was the end of the quarry, and now it has become a small harbour - albeit a deep one.

An Cala Garden dates from the 1930s, and is behind a row of cottages that have now been turned into one home. There are meandering streams, slate terraces, and wide lawns. A 15-feet high wall protects the garden from the Atlantic winds. One of the small slate worker's cottages in the village has been turned into a **Heritage Centre**, and has displays, exhibitions and artifacts concerning the slate industry and the life of the slate workers. The island of Easdale is no more than a few yards offshore, and is connected to Ellenabeich by a small passenger ferry. Here, too, slate quarrying

View from Seil towards Mull

was carried out, and one of the cottages has been converted into the **Easdale Island Folk Museum**.

Cuan sits at the southern tip of the island, and is the northern terminus for the Luing Ferry. Luing is a larger island than Seil, though it is sparsely populated. As with Seil, slate quarrying was the main industry.

LISMORE

7 miles NW of Oban, in Loch Linnhe.

The name Lismore comes from Gaelic, and means "great garden". The island is no more that nine miles long by half a mile wide at its widest, and is low lying and fertile. In fact, the highest point, **Barr Mór**, is only 412 feet high, though there are some wonderful panoramic views from the top. A car ferry connects the island to Oban, and there is a small passenger ferry in the summer months which connects the island to the mainland at Port Appin. The main village is **Achnacroish**, on the eastern coast, and it also the terminus for the Oban ferry.

Lismore was the seat of the Bishops of Argyll, and **Lismore**

Cathedral stood at Kilmoluaig, near the small village of Clachan. It was damaged just after the Reformation, though it became a cathedral once more when the Church of Scotland embraced bishops. The choir walls were lowered and incorporated into the present parish church in 1749.

The site of the cathedral has been a centre of Christian worship for many years before the medieval cathedral was built. St. Moluag set up a small monastery there in AD564, and even then the place was popular, due to its fertile soil and flat land. A story is told of St. Moluag and another Celtic saint, St. Mulhac, who were arguing about who should found a monastery there. They finally agreed to a race across from the mainland, with the first one whose flesh touched the soil of Lismore being the one who could build the monastery. They duly set out, and when the two boats were approaching the shore it was evident that St. Mulhac was going to win. However, St. Moluag took out his dagger and chopped off his hand, which he threw with his other hand onto the shore. St. Mulhag, when he realised just

Lismore Lighthouse

how much the other saint wanted the island, withdrew from the contest. This was supposed to have taken place at Tirefour, where there are the remains of a broch now called **Tirefour Castle**.

On the west coast of the island are the ruins of **Achadun Castle**, home to the bishops of Argyll, and further up the coast are the ruins of **Coeffin Castle**, a MacDougall stronghold built in the 13th century.

MULL
8 miles W of Oban in the Atlantic Ocean

Mull is the largest and most beautiful of the Inner Hebridean islands that lie within Argyllshire. A car ferry plies back and forwards from Oban to the pier at **Craignure** all day, so it is also one of the most accessible.

Its name comes from the Gaelic Meall, meaning "rounded hill", and it is an island of hills and mountains. Even the

AROS MAINS AND COTTAGE

Aros Mains, Aros, Mull, Argyllshire PA72 6JP
Tel: 01680 300307 website: www.arosmains.co.uk
e-mail: Maggie.Thomson1@btinternet.com

Aros Mains is a comfortable 18th century Georgian house on the island of Mull, built by the Chamberlain to the Duke of Argyll in the 1790s. A superb self catering apartment is available on its first floor that overlooks Salen Bay and the romantic ruins of Aros Castle, once a stronghold of the Lord of the Isles. The accommodation consists of a large lounge, a fully equipped kitchen/dining room, three bedrooms (two large doubles, one with a double bed and two singles, and one with a double bed and a single, plus a compact bunkroom with two adult sized bunks) and two bathrooms.

The apartment is exceedingly well appointed, with cooker, fridge, microwave, dishwasher, washing machine, hi fi, TV and high chair. Heating is night storage heaters, and electricity, linen and towels are all included. In addition, a self catering cottage is available, sleeping four, with a single fouton for a fifth guest. It is very spacious and comfortable, and comes equipped with cooker, microwave, washing

machine, TV and hi fi. Electricity, linen and towels are included in the price. The beach is only 100 yards away from these properties, there is ample parking, and there is a relaxing lawn garden from which to view some marvellous scenery, and see a variety of wildlife such as otters, golden eagles, sea eagles and deer. Owner Margaret Thomson is proud of the standards she has set with these properties, and will offer you a warm Highland welcome. The properties make the ideal base from which to explore beautiful Mull, and Tobermory, with its restaurants and shops, is only ten miles away.

THE PUFFER AGROUND

Aros, Isle of Mull, Argyllshire PA72 6JP
Tel: 01680 300389 e-mail: graham@ellis389.fs.net.co
Fax: 01680 300595 website: www.scotland.selfcatering.net

The **Puffer Aground** was once a blacksmith's house, and from 1975 until 1995 it was a restaurant. Now it is a self catering establishment that offers a comfortable bedroom with a king size double bed that separates to form twin beds, a very well equipped kitchen and a bathroom with bath, shower and WC. The sitting/dining room is partially panelled, with beamed ceiling and portholes from the old Lochfyne, the first diesel electric ship ever built. A cot and high chair are available, and all linen is supplied. Heating is by night storage heaters, and in the summer months electricity is included in the rent.

Romans knew about it, with Ptolemy calling it Maleus. Ben More is the highest peak, at 3,140 feet, and it is the only "Munro" (a Scottish peak above 3,000 feet) in any of the Scottish islands.

Torosay Castle (see panel) lies close to Craignure, and can be reached by the narrow gauge **Mull and West Highland Railway**, a one and a quarter mile railway line which was opened in June 1984. Along the way, you can see plenty of wildlife, such as deer, songbirds, gulls and sometimes even sea otters. The railway has six locomotives. both steam and diesel, from the sleek steam engine "Waverley" to the "Glen Auldyn", a no-nonsense diesel

TOROSAY CASTLE & GARDENS

Torosay, Isle of Mull
Tel: 01680 812421

Torosay Castle and Gardens is a beautiful Victorian house surrounded by 12 acres of spectacular gardens. You are free to wander around the principal rooms of the house and browse through family scrapbooks and memorabilia. Outside is an important collection of Italian statues, formal terraces and a variety of plant collections and garden

settings, including a Japanese Garden with an impressive sea view. As this is a working farm, children will be fascinated with the herd of Highland Cattle and you can round off with a visit to Mull Weavers to see a demonstration on traditional dobby looms. Tearoom, shop and free parking available. Open April to mid October 10.30am-5pm. Gardens open all year.

ISLE OF MULL SILVER AND GOLDSMITHS

Main Street, Tobermory, Isle of Mull, Argyllshire PA75 6AT
Tel/Fax: 01688 302345
e-mail: mullsilver@btinternet.com website: www.mullsilver.co.uk

When you are on the beautiful island of Mull, and you are looking for an unusual gift or souvenir, why not head for the **Isle of Mull Silver and Goldsmiths**? Their distinctive blue-fronted shop is on Main Street, and here you will find a wide range of jewellery and other objects made on the premises from gold and silver. The craftspeople here concentrated on making products in the traditions of silver making that have been practised for centuries in Scotland. They use clean, simple lines and shapes, sometimes incorporating intricate motifs from the Celtic past. They started trading from a remote farmhouse in the centre of the island, then from a small industrial estate in Tobermory and now from the town's colourful main street, overlooking the bay.

The shop stocks Christening spoons, 9 and 18 carat gold rings, traditional quaiches (two handled Scottish drinking vessels) as well as a fine range of jewellery by other manufacturers both Scottish and from further afield. The shop draws a lot of its inspiration

from the sacred island of Iona, and one of the most popular items for sale is a St. Columba's Cross. There are also St. Ronan's Spoons, based on four silver spoons found beneath the floor of St. Ronan's Chapel. Or why not treat yourself or a loved one to a Highland ring brooch? They have traditional motifs, and are based on actual stone carved motifs found on the island. The business is owned and run by Phil Campbell, a local man who graduated from Edinburgh Collage of Art, and Shiona Finlayson from Edinburgh, who joined the company in 1987.

GLENGORM ESTATE

Tobermory, Isle of Mull, Argyllshire PA75 6QE
Tel: 01688 302321 Fax: 01688 302738
e-mail: enquiries@glengormcastle.co.uk
website: www.glengormcastle.co.uk

Situated on the northern tip of the beautiful Isle of Mull, Glengorm Castle overlooks the Atlantic Ocean, and has magnificent views out over the waves to the Outer Hebrides and the islands of Rum, Skye and Canna. The castle was built in 1860, and sits at the headland of Glengorm's vast area of coastline, forests, lochs and hills. **Glengorm Estate** truly stands apart from the surrounding Western Isles, already known for their dramatic scenery, due to its tranquillity and sheer natural beauty.

The Estate has some wonderful holiday accommodation to enable you to take advantage of the area's outstanding features and have a relaxing and memorable holiday. Within the castle itself, for instance, are five sumptuously furnished bedrooms that are offered on a B&B basis, with four being fully en suite and the fifth having a private bathroom. To sit in the library enjoying a dram as the sun sets over the magical island of Coll must be one of the most pleasurable experiences there is. The

breakfasts, as you would expect, are hearty and filling, and prepared from only the finest and freshest of local produce. The estate is the island's main supplier of fresh food, so some of the produce is locally grown. Just right to set you up for a day's sightseeing, walking, fishing or birdwatching.

In addition the estate offers some of the best self catering accommodation in the west of Scotland. The Terrace and the Turret flats are within the castle itself, and sleep six and five respectively. They are beautifully furnished, and come with TVs, a fully equipped kitchen and comfortable, well-decorated bedrooms. The Terrace has a separate entrance, and unfortunately young children and pets are not allowed in the Turret. Other self catering accommodation is dotted around the estate, within old, stone cottages. The Sorne cottages sleep six, and have sitting/dining rooms, kitchen, bathroom and shower, and three bedrooms - a double and two twins. The Lodge and Cnoc Fuar sleep four, with The Lodge having a double and a twin, while Cnoc Fuar has a double and a twin with bunk beds. Each one has a sitting/dining room, bathroom and kitchen. Lephin sleeps five, and has two double bedrooms and a single, plus kitchen/dining room, sitting room and bathroom. Dunara Cottage is the smallest of the cottages, and sleeps two. It has a double bedroom. a sitting/dining room, kitchen and bathroom. All the properties have colour TVs, and bed linen, towels and tea towels are supplied. All self catering accommodation has electric convertor heaters in the rooms, and the estate will provide firewood for open fires when required.

Within Glengorm there is a coffee shop and farm shop, where you can buy fresh produce grown on the estate and a variety of plants and shrubs. Tobermory, which has shops and a supermarket, is only a few miles away. Visitors are welcome to enjoy the estate's lawns, gardens and woodland walks while staying here. The whole place speaks of comfort, relaxation and good, old fashioned value for money. A holiday at Glengorm is a real pleasure, and will leave you with many happy memories to cherish in the future.

Tobermory Harbour

and the clan chief still lives there. The MacLeans fought on the side of Charles Edward Stuart during the Jacobite Uprising, and the castle was confiscated by the government soon after the uprising was crushed. In 1911 the 26th McLean chief, Sir Fitzroy MacLean, bought it back and had it fully restored.

However, not all McLean chiefs were dashing and chivalrous. The 11th chief was an unsavoury character, and, the story goes, detested his wife, whom he had married for money. He had her tied up and marooned on a rocky island offshore that flooded at high tide, hoping she would drown. Eventually the waters rose and she was washed away, with the "distraught" chief reporting his sad loss to her brother, the Earl of Argyll.

The Earl then invited the chief to his

hydraulic, and the beautiful "Lady of the Isles". The gardens at Torosay are particularly fine, and the castle is sometimes open to the public. Much older is **Duart Castle**, perched above the cliffs at Duart Point, about two miles south of Craignure as the crow flies. It is the ancestral home of Clan MacLean,

BROOMHILL

Breadalbane Street, Tobermory, Isle of Mull, Argyllshire PA75 6PX
Tel: 01688 302349
e-mail: jpawle@amserve.net

Broomhill is a substantial, whitewashed house set in its own grounds a few minutes from the colourful waterfront area of Tobermory, Mull's capital. It was formerly a manse and is now a B&B owned and run by Jane Pawle. She is proud of the high standards of hospitality she has achieved, and the reputation she has gained for running one of the best B&B establishments in Tobermory. She has two rooms on offer - a fully en suite double and a single, both of which are extremely comfortable and decorated to a high standard. The overall ambience is relaxed and informal, with a distinctly country feel to everything and just a hint of luxury.

Jane is an accomplished cook, and the breakfasts at Broomhill are hearty and filling - just right to set you up for a hard day's sightseeing on this most beautiful of islands. She uses only the finest and freshest of local produce wherever possible. The views from the garden out over Tobermory towards

Calve Island, Morvern and Ardnamurchan are stunning, and a peaceful summer evening spent in the garden is a very enjoyable experience. And don't forget - in the bay lies a sunken Spanish galleon, which alas has never given up any treasure. There is private parking, and lots to do in the surrounding area. You can explore Tobermory itself, or head for the small theatre at Dervaig. Or how about a day spent on the beautiful island of Iona? The wildlife is outstanding, and there is good fishing, sailing and hill walking to be had.

SGRIOB-RUADH FARM

Tobermory, Isle of Mull, Argyllshire PA75 6QD
Tel: 01688 302235
e-mail: mull.cheese@btinternet.com
website: www.isleofmullcheese.co.uk

Sgriob-Ruadh Farm, on the beautiful island of Mull, is the home of Isle of Mull Cheese, a winner in the BBC Food and Farming Awards 2002 as the 'Best Food Producer'. It is owned and run by Christine and Jeffrey Reade, who together bought the farm in 1980 when it was derelict. Together they have brought it back to life, creating a business that has gone from strength to strength because of their commitment to quality and value for money. It is a truly fascinating place, and cannot be missed if you visit Mull. Here you can not only see the cheeses being made, you can watch the animals being milked and can buy some of the cheese, which has earned a world wide reputation for its quality and taste.

ISLAND BAKERY ORGANICS

Tobermory, Isle of Mull, Argyllshire PA75 6PY
Tel: 01688 302223
e-mail: organics@islandbakery.co.uk
website: islandbakery.co.uk

While you're on the island, why not visit **Island Bakery Organics**, a busy harbour-side deli in Tobermory, the island's capital? It is owned and run by Joe Reade, Christine and Jeffrey's son, and his wife Dawn. It stocks the full range of Isle of Mull Cheeses, of course, and its' experienced in-house chefs and bakers also produce a stunning range of mouth-watering delicatessen fare, including fresh, hand-baked bread every morning, home made pates, fresh salads, cooked and cured meats, game pies, pastries, tarts and cakes. The shop's range of organic biscuits is rapidly gaining fame, and was the UK winners of the Organic Food Award 2002. The shop has also been the Country Living Baker of the year in 1999 and won Great Taste Awards in 2001 and 2002.

THE CALGARY HOTEL

Calgary, by Dervaig, Isle of Mull,
Argyllshire PA75 6QW
Tel: 01688 400256
website: www.calgary.co.uk

Just uphill from the beautiful white sands of Calgary Beach is the three star **Calgary Hotel**, one of the best hotels on the lovely Isle of Mull. It is in an idyllic spot, within a small, green glen banked with mature trees. It was converted from old farm steadings, and still retains that friendly farmhouse atmosphere, while having all the modern conveniences you would expect from a top quality hotel. It is the ideal base from which to explore Mull, with one of its features being the Dovecote Restaurant (open Tuesday-Sunday), which is famous for its good food and fine wines. The Carthouse Art Gallery and Tearoom is open 11am-4pm from Easter to October, and displays local artwork and serves lunches and home baking. There is also four star self catering accommodation.

castle at Inveraray so that they could commiserate together. The chief accepted the invitation, but when he got to Inveraray castle and sat down to dinner, in walked his wife alive and well. She had been rescued by a passing fishing boat. Nothing was said by the wife or the Earl, and the chief eventually brought his wife home to Duart Castle. Still nothing was said by either the wife or her brother, and the chief grew terrified, knowing that retribution would eventually come.

Macquarie's Mausoleum

But before anything could happen, the wife died of natural causes, and the chief felt a great burden lift from his shoulders. He married again, and this second wife also died. Eventually he married a third time - a marriage which lasted 30 years, and which produced a fine son and heir. The chief slept easy in his bed every night, knowing he had got away with his crime. However, one year he had to attend to business in Edinburgh and there he was brutally murdered in mysterious circumstances at the same time as the Earl of Argyll was staying in the city. There was no apparent motive for the crime - nothing was stolen, and the chief had not quarreled with anyone. His wife had been avenged.

TORLOCHAN

Gruline, Isle of Mull, Argyllshire PA71 6HR
Tel/Fax: 01680 300221
e-mail: sam@duffy4152freeserve.co.uk

Situated in the heart of the beautiful island of Mull, **Torlochan** is a small working croft with two extremely comfortable three star self catering cottages that are just right for a quiet and relaxing holiday among beautiful scenery. Dairidh sleeps four in two double bedrooms, while Claghaig sleeps two in one double bedroom. Both are well appointed, with open plan kitchen/dining area, lounge with TV and music centre, and bathroom/shower. There are also open fires and electric heating. Logs and coal are available, and there is ample car parking.

BARRACHANDROMAN

Lochbuie, Isle of Mull, Argyll PA62 6AA
Tel/Fax: 01680 814220/247
e-mail: edwards@barrachandroman.co.uk
website: www.barrachandroman.co.uk

Barrachandroman offers self catering accommodation in **The Farmhouse** (sleeping up to eight people) and bed & breakfast in **The Barn** with two double and one twin bedded rooms. Both are graded four star standard by Visit Scotland. Situated 12 miles from the ferry terminal at Craignure and near the shore at the West end of Loch Spelve this is the ideal base from which to explore the island, for walking or wildlife watching, or just to wind down and relax.

Fishnish Pier, on the A849 about six miles west of Craignure on the island's northern coast, is the southern terminus of a ferry that connects the island to Lochaline on the mainland. It crosses the Sound of Mull, the stretch of water between the island and Morvern. At **Salen** the A849 road becomes the A848. Not far away is **Macquarie's Mausoleum**, where Major General Lachlan Macquarie, Governor General of New South Wales and sometimes called the "father off Australia" lies buried. Eight miles further west is the island's capital - **Tobermory**. It's name means "Mary's well", and it is an attractive small town famous for the many brightly painted houses facing the sea. **Mull Museum** is in Glengorm Road,

ACHNACRAIG

Dervaig, Isle of Mull, Argyllshire PA75 6QW
Tel: 01688 400309
website: www.holidaymull.org/achnacraig/index.html

Achnacraig offers superb bed & breakfast in this delightful stone

farmhouse, set in the peaceful Glen Bellart with its winding river and buzzards circling overhead. It has oak beams, modern plumbing and a huge guest lounge to relax in. There is a choice of three comfortable bedrooms (a double, a twin or a single) and a hearty Scottish breakfast awaits in the morning. A self catering cottage sleeping up to six is also available.

NAUST

Ulva Ferry, Isle of Mull, Argyllshire PA73 6LY
Tel: 01688 500239
e-mail: sally@naust.fsnet.co.uk

Naust is a cottage that stands in two acres of rock and heather, high above the road on the beautiful Isle of Mull. There are wonderful, uninterrupted views of Loch na Keal and Loch Tuath from the south facing cottage garden and terrace, and the island of Ulva is just offshore. Beyond it you can see the small island of Inch Kenneth, with its early Christian associations, and on a clear day you can even see Iona. Here, in this tranquil spot, you will find all the peace and relaxation you could ever wish for, away from the stresses of modern life. Craignure, the island's ferry port for the Oban/ Mull ferry, is a 45 minute car journey away, though there are also car ferries at Fishnish and Tobermory.

The cottage boasts a pretty, twin-bedded room with en suite facilities which is beautifully furnished and decorated. Breakfast is served in the garden room, where guests can enjoy fine open views that take the breath away. The cottage is owned and run by Sally and Laurie, who make every effort to

make sure that your stay is an enjoyable one. A simple supper on the evening of your arrival can be prepared by arrangement, as the nearest pub or restaurant is nine miles away, and special diets can usually be catered for, and the home cooking is excellent, using fresh local produce wherever possible. Sally and Laurie are extremely knowledgeable about the area, and can help you plan your stay on Mull. This is a great area for birdwatching, and has one of the largest concentrations of golden eagles in Europe. You may even choose to join a wildlife safari, with local guides who know the finest viewpoints.

and explains the history of the town and island.

At the bottom of the bay on which the town sits is the famous wreck of the **San Juan de Sicilia**, part of the Spanish Armada fleet, which took this route round Scotland after defeat by the English. Scotland was an independent country at the time, and had no quarrel with Spain, so the ship weighed anchor in the bay to take on supplies. A mysterious explosion blew her up, and she sank to the bottom. Soon rumours were circulating that she had 30 million ducats aboard her at the time, and though some items were eventually recovered, successive dives to the wreck failed to find any ducats. She now lies completely covered in silt, and it is unlikely that anything else will ever be recovered from the wreck.

From Tobermory the narrow B8073 heads south west to **Dervaig** and then **Calgary**. The **Mull Little Theatre** is in Dervaig, and though it only seats 38, it is a proper theatre that puts on a season of professional productions every year.

Calgary gave its name to the great Canadian city in Alberta. In 1883 a member of the Royal Canadian Mounted Police visited the area, and was so impressed with the scenery that he name the Canadian city after it. The road continues along the shores of **Loch Tuath**, where there are views of the island of **Ulva**, visited by Boswell and Johnson in 1773. It then joins the B8035, and if you turn south you will skirt the shores of the beautiful **Loch na Keal**. This minor road rejoins the A849 once more. Turn south again and head for **Bunessan** on the shores of the small Loch na Lathaich, where there is the **Ross of Mull Historical Centre**. This explains

the local history of the area. At the end of the A849 is **Fionnphort**, where the ferry for Iona leaves. Before crossing to the island, you should visit the **Columba Centre** to prepare you. But please note: tourist cars are not allowed on Iona.

IONA

36 miles W of Oban in the Atlantic Ocean

Iona is no more than three miles long and a mile and a half wide, and yet it is one of the most sacred places in Europe. Unfortunately, in the summer months, it is also one of the busiest. Here, in AD563, St. Columba, newly arrived from Ireland, set up a famous monastery and began converting the Picts of the Highlands to Christianity. This monastery would have been built of wood and wattle, with many small cells for the monks to live in as well as chapels, storerooms and workshops. Nothing of it now survives, apart form part of the rath, or boundary wall. The present **Iona Abbey** sits on the site of the monastery, and was founded in 1203 by Reginald, son of Somerled, Lord of the Isles. It was largely rebuilt in the 16th century, and what you now see dates from that time. It housed Benedictine monks, and in later years became a cathedral.

Iona Abbey

After the Reformation, however, it was abandoned and became roofless. Then, in the 20th century, the Rev'd George MacLeod, a Church of Scotland minister, set about restoring it, and founded the ecumenical Iona Community, who still use it today. Beside the cathedral is the **Relig Odhrain**, or St. Oran's Cemetery, and within it is the **Ridge of the Chiefs**, which is supposed to contain the bodies of many West Highland clan chiefs. Close by is the **Ridge of the Kings**, where, it is said, 48 Scottish, eight Norwegian and four Irish kings lie buried, including Macbeth. However, modern historians doubt if any kings are buried there at all. One person who is buried there, however, is John Smith, Leader of the Labour Party, who died in 1994.

Fingal's Cave, Isle of Staffa

St. Oran's Chapel sits next to it, and was built as a funerary chapel in the 12th century. Near the jetty are the substantial ruins of **St. Mary's Nunnery**, again founded by Reginald. It housed Benedictine nuns, and Reginald offered the position of prioress to his sister Beatrice. Within the Chapel of St. Ronan, next to the priory, is a small museum.

Iona has many old preaching crosses. Perhaps the best are the 10th century **St. Martin's Cross**, near the abbey, and MacLean's Cross, from the same date. Along the front of the abbey church is part of the old **Road of the Dead**, leading to St. Oran's Cemetery, and just west of the abbey is **Tor Ab**, a low rocky mound on which St. Columba's own cell may have stood.

The former manse of the parish church was designed by Sir Thomas Telford, and within it you'll find the **Iona Heritage Centre**, which tells of the lives of the people who have lived in the island down through the years.

STAFFA
34 miles W of Oban in the Atlantic Ocean

Staffa (National Trust for Scotland) is a small, uninhabited rocky island that sits about six miles north of Iona, and which can be reached by special excursion boat from Oban. Its most spectacular feature is **Fingal's Cave**, in the high cliffs surrounding the island, which inspired Felix Mendelssohn to write his overture of the same name. The cliffs are formed from hexagonal columns of basalt rock, and look almost man-made. They resemble staves of wood, some over 50 feet high, and because of this the Vikings name the island Stav Y, or "Stave Island".

COLL AND TIREE
50 miles W of Oban in the Atlantic Ocean

The twin islands of Coll and Tiree can be reached by car ferry from Oban. The ferry first unloads and loads at **Arinagour** on Coll then goes on to **Scarinish** on Tiree, so it can be used to sail between the two islands as well. Low lying, they can be explored by car in a few hours, with the roads being narrow and winding. Robert I granted Coll to Angus Og of Islay, who built the now ruined **Breachacha Castle** to the south of the island. In 1856 an incident took place on Coll which came to be known as the **Great Exodus**. The southernmost part of the island is the most fertile, and in that year it was sold to one John Lorne Stewart. He immediately raised the rents of his tenants to a level they couldn't afford, and despite protests, he refused to negotiate. So, one night, all his tenants left their crofts and moved north to the less fertile lands owned by the Campbells, where the rents were considered reasonable. Thus Lorne Stewart was left with no rent at all.

Tiree, the southernmost of the two islands, means the "land of corn" in Gaelic, and is one of the most fertile in the Inner Hebrides. It is relatively flat, and has the nickname Tir fo Thuinn, meaning the "land beneath the waves". The highest peaks are **Ben Hynish** (460 feet) and **Ben Hough** (387 feet). It also has the reputation of being the sunniest place in Britain, though it also has the less enviable reputation of being the windiest. Near Vaul in the north east of the island is the **Ringing Stone**, which, when struck, makes a clanging noise. Legend says if it ever shatters Tiree will be flooded and disappear under the sea. The small **Sandaig Museum** at Sandaig is within a restored thatched cottage.

COLONSAY AND ORONSAY
40 miles W of Oban in the Atlantic Ocean

Separating these two small islands is an expanse of sand called **The Strand**. At high tide, it is completely covered by water, and at low tide you can walk from one island to the other. Ferries service the islands from both Oban and West Loch Tarbert, calling at **Scalasaig** on Colonsay.

Colonsay is the bigger of the islands, and is full of sandy coves, fertile land

and rock strewn beaches. **Kiloran Valley** is sheltered and warmer than the rest of the island, and in 1722 **Colonsay House** (not open to the public) was built here by Malcolm Macneil, using stones from an old chapel which stood close by.

Oronsay lies to the south of Colonsay, and is famous for the well preserved ruins of **Oronsay Priory**, the most important monastic establishment after Iona in the Western Isles. History gives us two founders - St. Oran, Columba's companion who gave his name to the cemetery on Iona, and St. Columba himself. When he left Ireland, the story goes, he first set foot on Colonsay, the crossed over to Oronsay, where he established a small monastery. However, he had made a vow that he would never set foot in Ireland again, and would not look on its shores. He could see Ireland from Oronsay on a clear day, so moved on to Iona.

Oran or Columba may indeed have founded a monastery on Oronsay, but the bit about Columba not wanting to see Ireland, or set foot on it ever again, is not true. He actually returned to Ireland on several occasions.

The present priory was founded by John, Lord of the Aisles, in the early 13th century. He invited canons from Holyrood Abbey to live within it, and they duly arrived. The church as you see it now is 15th century, with the cloisters being built a hundred years later. Some carved slabs can bee seen within the former Prior's House, and in the graveyard is the 16th century **Oronsay Cross**. It is intricately carved, and carries the words "Colinus, son of Christinus MacDuffie". St. John's Cross sits east of the Prior's chapel, and has a carving of St. John the Evangelist.

LOCATOR MAP

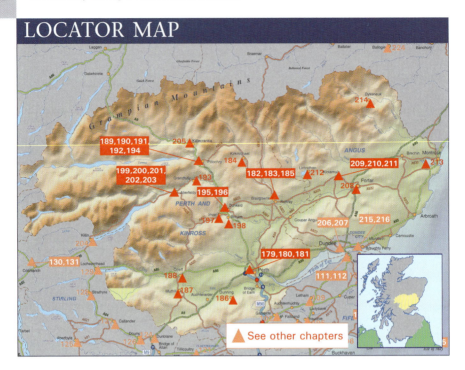

189,190,191,192,194

199,200,201,202,203

205

184

193

195,196

197

198

182,183,185

212

209,210,211

213

208

206,207

215,216

214

130,131

129

128

126

129

179,180,181

188

187

186

111,112

204

▲ See other chapters

ADVERTISERS AND PLACES OF INTEREST

9 PERTHSHIRE AND ANGUS

The popular conception is that Scotland is divided into two areas: the Lowlands to the south and the Highlands to the north. However, in reality the split is more east/west, with what is called the Highland Boundary Fault running from Helensburgh on the Clyde north east to Stonehaven on the North Sea. And in Aberdeenshire, beyond the boundary fault, there are still areas of rich low, farmland.

Perthshire and Angus are two counties that straddle the Highland Boundary Fault. Even though Scotland is a stable country geologically, the fault is still active, with many small earthquakes being recorded. So, within the two former counties, there is a rich divergence of scenery, from mountains and moorland to rich farmland, busy

Loch Lubnaig

towns and sandy beaches. The glens of Angus, such as Clova, Doll and Prosen, which wind their way into the foothills of the Grampians, are particularly attractive, even though they are not as rugged as some glens in the Highlands proper. And the A9 road north from Perth towards Inverness passes through some wonderfully wooded glens, taking in historic towns and villages such as Dunkeld, Pitlochry and Blair Atholl. In fact, Perthshire is marketed by the local tourist board as the "big tree country".

Perthshire is a wholly inland county, a place of agriculture, high hills, glens and lochs. Here you will find Loch Tummel and Loch Rannoch, which are sung about in the song *The Road to the Isles*, and the loneliest railway station in Britain at Rannoch Moor. It is also the county of the Gleneagles Hotel, and, of course Perth, which is one of the most prosperous cities in Britain.

Angus, to the east of Perthshire, has a coastline with cliffs and sandy beaches. Dundee, Scotland's fourth largest city, is here. It used to be famous for what was called "the three Js" - jam, jute and journalism. Now only journalism remains, in the guise of D.C. Thomson, whose comics gave birth to such folk legends as Denis the Menace, Lord Snooty, Oor Wullie and the Bash Street Kids. The British Open is sometimes held at Carnoustie, and at Arbroath Abbey the Declaration of Arbroath was signed. This is possibly the most important document in Scotland's history, and it was sent to the Pope. In it, Scotland reaffirmed its independence from England, and stated that the country was fighting not for gain or conquest, but for freedom.

Before local government reorganisation, Perth was a city, with a Lord Provost rather than a Provost - one of only six places in Scotland that had that honour, the others being Glasgow, Dundee, Edinburgh, Aberdeen and Elgin. And technically it still is a city, as no document has ever taken the honour away from it.

It is often referred to as the "Fair City of Perth", and this is no idle description. It sits on the Tay, many miles from the sea, and was at one time an important inland port. However, it may be in the Lowlands, but it has never been scarred by industry in the way that some other towns and cities have. It is the main shopping centre for a huge area, and is one of those places where "town meets country". Dundee, on the other hand, prospered through industry, even though it is an ancient place with its roots deep in Scottish history. It sits on the north bank of the Firth of Tay, and is connected to Fife by a rail and road bridge.

When John Graham of Claverhouse was elevated to the peerage, he took the title Viscount Dundee. He is that rarity in history - a "goodie" and a "baddie" at the same time. As Bonnie Dundee, he was the dashing Jacobite, brave and chivalrous; to others he was Bloody Clavers, a man who killed and maimed cruelly and indiscriminately as he suppressed the Covenantors, who objected to the imposition of bishops on the Church of Scotland by Charles II.

Everywhere in Perthshire and Angus, there is history and heritage aplenty. In AD685 the Northumbrians were defeated by the Picts under King Nechtan at the Battle of Nechtansmere. The Battle of Killiecrankie in 1689 was the first Jacobite battle in Britain. Dunkeld and Brechin have medieval cathedrals. Arbroath has the ruins of its abbey, and at Blair Atholl, the Duke of Atholl has the only private army in Britain. And Glamis Castle was the ancestral home of the late Queen Elizabeth the Queen Mother.

Then there are the literary associations. D.C. Thomson's cartoon characters have already been mentioned, and they appeared in such famous comics as the *Dandy* and *Beano*. J.M. Barry was born at Kirriemuir, and Violet Jacob was born near Montrose.

PERTH

Perth is one of the loveliest cities in Scotland. It sits on the Tay, and though you might not realise it, at one time it was an important inland port. It has a population of about 45,000, which is large by Scottish standards, and the fact that it is far from the Central Belt, where industry proliferated, has meant that it never succumbed to the ravages experienced by many other historic Scottish towns of a similar size .

The city centre is compact, and sits between two large open spaces, the **North Inch** and the **South Inch**. Many of the truly historic buildings have gone, but at least they were replaced in Victorian times with elegant buildings that speak of prosperity and continuity. One of the most famous incidents in Scottish history took place in Perth in 1437. James I had decided to move his court to the city, and it was here he was murdered. He was an unpopular ruler, and the deed was not unexpected. The facts are simple, though they have been embellished over the years.

He was staying in the city's Dominican friary (now gone) and was attacked by some noblemen led by the Earl of Atholl, who claimed the crown. They tried to get into James's room, but a version of the story says that one of the Queen's ladies-in-waiting bravely stuck her arm through the bolt holes on the inside of the door, preventing them from entering. This gave James time to climb out the window and try to make his escape by going down into the sewer beneath the friary. However, he wasn't quick enough, and within the sewer his pursuers stabbed him to death.

In the centre of the city is **St. John's Kirk**, one of the finest medieval churches in Scotland. It was from this church that

LOOSE THREADS

10 South St Johns Place, Perth, Perthshire PH1 5SU
Tel/Fax: 01738 628879
e-mail: info@loose-threads.com website: www.loose-threads.com

Perth is one of Scotland's loveliest cities. Situated on the River Tay, it has played a leading role in Scotland's stirring and sometimes turbulent history. Near to the main high street, you'll find one of the best haberdashery and fabric specialists in Scotland, if not Britain - **Loose Threads**, owned and run by Irene Munro. This is a colourful and inviting shop that sells a wide range of craft fabrics and haberdashery items, including 100 per cent cottons, plains and prints, silks, lame and voiles. In the craft department you'll find a full range of Pebeo and Anita paints, stencils, rubber stamps, appliqué and rug kits - in fact, too many items to mention separately. As you would expect, there are also threads and knitting wools, and for quilters there are over 1,000 bales of 100 per cent cotton in stock.

The shop also stocks John Deere and Case cushion and wall hangings, as well as cot panels and soft toys. Loose Threads offers a mail order service for all the goods it sells. If you visit the premises, however, you're in for a treat, as the colours and textures that greet you as you pass through the door will take your breath away. There's just so much on offer that you could spend a couple of hours here, just admiring the stocked shelves and displays. The staff are friendly and knowledgeable, and can guide the novice as well as cater for the more experienced person. So if you're in Perth, or even just passing through, make your way to Loose Threads and be prepared to be dazzled by what's on offer.

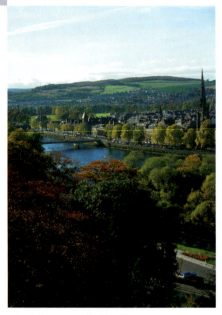

Perth from across the River Tay

the town took its former name, St. Johnstoune, which is now carried by the town's football team. It was founded in about 1243, though the church as it stands today dates from the 15th century. It still has Renaissance glass in some of the windows, and it was here that John Knox first preached after returning to Scotland from his exile in Europe.

A later church is the Gothic **St. Ninian's Cathedral**, which dates from the 19th century, and is the seat of the Episcopalian bishop of St. Andrews, Dunkeld and Dunblane. It was designed by William Butterfield, who also designed Keble College, Oxford.

Balhousie Castle in Hay Street houses the **Black Watch Regimental Museum**. The regiment was raised in 1725 to patrol or "watch" the Highlands after the suppression of the 1745 Jacobite Uprising. The **Perth Museum and Art**

FRAMES CONTEMPORARY GALLERY

10 Victoria street, Perth PH1 5SL
Tel/Fax: 01738 631085 e-mail: hugh.goring@btinternet.com
website: www.framesgallery.co.uk

Owned and managed by Hugh Goring, **Frames Gallery** is situated in the heart of the beautiful city of Perth. It was founded in 1991 with the clear commitment to show the very best of contemporary Scottish art, and has been doing so ever since. In 1997 a purpose built extension was added which now houses larger exhibitions. The whole place is spacious, light and restful, showing off the many objects and paintings to perfection. Throughout the year many exhibitions take place, and visitors will be delighted with the range and style of paintings - both oil and watercolour - that are hung. There is an eclectic mix of semi-abstract, still life and landscape, and there is sure to be something that captures the imagination.

The artists range from the established and highly respected to the new, exciting talent of the up and coming, and because Hugh and his friendly staff know the Scottish art scene intimately, they can

always advise on a painting or other work of art that is just right for you. The paintings on show invariably include the exciting, abstracts oils of Marj Bond, and the oils and watercolours of Malcolm Cheape, who is famous for his boat paintings. The gallery also shows sculpture, craft work, pottery and sometimes photography, and you are more than welcome to browse. Hugh also offers a framing service which specialises in hand made frames, and indeed it was selected for the Harpers & Queens 'A List' of best framers in the United Kingdom. The gallery is open Monday to Friday from 9 am - 5.30 pm and on Saturday from 9 am to 5 pm.

Gallery is on George Street, and is one of the oldest of its kind in Britain. It has a fine collection of objects and paintings that go beyond the history of the city itself. The **Ferguson Gallery** in Marshall Place is dedicated to the painter J.D. Ferguson, a member of a group of painters called "The Scottish Colourists". He lived from 1874 until 1961. The gallery was opened in 1929 in a former early 19th century waterworks.

Catherine Glover is the heroine of Sir Walter Scott's novel *The Fair Maid of Perth*. She was the daughter of Simon Glover of Curfew Row, and reputedly lived in the 14th century. She was noted for both her beauty and piety, and was courted by all the young men of Perth. She also came to the attention of the Duke of Rothesay, son of Robert III. However, she rebuffed his advances, and eventually the Duke assembled a few men, and together they tried to enter Catherine's house at the dead of night. However, his plans were thwarted by a young man called Hal Gow, who sent the Duke and his men packing, having first hacked of one of the intruder's hands. Amazingly, Catherine slept through it all, though Hal awakened her father and showed him the severed hand. The story ends happily when Hal himself woos and wins Catherine and marries her.

The present **Fair Maid's House** only dates from the 17th century, though it does incorporate some medieval walls which may have belonged to the original house. Scott's book, though based on fact, greatly embroiders the story, and in 1867 the French composer Bizet took it as the basis for his opera *The Fair Maid of Perth*, making it more popular than ever.

Bells Cherrybank Centre is an 18-acre garden next to the headquarters of the Bell's whisky distilling company. It incorporates the **National Heather Collection**, which has over 900 varieties

of the plant. **Kinnoull Hill**, to the east of the city, rises to a height of 729 feet above the Tay, and is a wonderful vantage point, giving marvellous views of the Carse of Gowrie. The **Fairways Heavy Horse Centre** is close by, and here you can see Clydesdale horses.

AROUND PERTH

HUNTINGTOWER

2 miles west of Perth off the A85

Huntingtower (Historic Scotland) has no connection with John Buchan's novel of the same name, which is set in Ayrshire. However, it does have plenty of history attached to it. It was once owned by the Ruthven family, Earls of Gowrie, and in 1582 the famous "Raid of Ruthven" took place here, when the then Earl of Gowrie and his friend the Earl of Mar tried to kidnap the young James VI.

ELCHO

3 miles E of Perth on a minor road near the River Tay

Elcho Castle (Historic Scotland) was the ancient seat of the Earls of Wemyss, and is a fine example of a 16th century tower house. It sits on the banks of the Tay, and its windows have the original wrought iron grills.

ERROL

9 miles E of Perth on a minor road off the A90

The **Carse of Gowrie** is a narrow stretch of fertile land bordering the northern shore of the Firth of Tay. **Errol** is a peaceful, picturesque village within it, which has a large **Parish Church** dating form 1831. Such is its size that it is sometimes called the "cathedral of the Carse". The village gives its name to an earldom, with the earl being known, appropriately enough, as the "Earl of Errol".

ABERNETHY

6 miles SE of Perth on the A913

The picturesque village of Abernethy is not only a place which gave its name to a biscuit. It is famous as the home of the **Abernethy Tower** (Historic Scotland). One of only two such towers in Scotland (the other one is in Brechin), it dates from the end of the 11th century, and was used as a place of refuge for priests during times of trouble or attack.

SCONE

2 miles N of Perth off the A93

Scone Palace is the home of the Earls of Mansfield, and dates from the early 19th century. It is open to the public, and has fine collections of furniture, needlework and porcelain. Historically and culturally, the palace is one of the most important places in Scotland. It was built near the site of **Scone Abbey**, and close to it was the **Moot Hill** (which can still be seen) where the kings of Scotland used to be crowned. They sat on the Stone of Destiny during the coronation, and a replica of it can still be seen on the summit. The original was kept within the abbey itself, and when Edward I of England sacked the abbey in 1296, he carried it off to London as the spoils of war. The last king to be crowned at Scone was Charles II in 1651.

Scone Palace

STANLEY

6 miles N of Perth on the B9099

The small village of Stanley sits on the River Tay, and is a former mill village. Sir Richard Arkwright had an interest in the mills, the first of which was built in 1786. Three further mills were built in the 1820s, powered by seven water

CHINA GALORE

Tel: 01250 886351

China Galore is Scotland's leading china matching register. It specialises in finding, supplying and buying dinner, tea and coffee services that are obsolete or discontinued. Over the years it has built up many contacts, and if you are looking for items to complete a service, or you have a service you wish to sell, then this is the place for you. All the famous names are covered - Royal Doulton, Wedgwood, Spode, Minton, Meakin and so on. Registering with the service is free of charge, and the small group of dedicated staff regularly scour Scotland and Ireland for the choicest items.

wheels. Four miles away are the ruins of **Kinclaven Castle**, which was a favourite residence of Alexander II in the 13th century.

MEIKLEOUR

10 miles N of Perth on the A984

The **Meikleour Hedge**, on the outskirts of the village, is supposed to be the world's tallest hedge. It borders the A93 for 600 yards, and is now over 100 feet high. It is made up of beech trees, and was planted in 1746 as a memorial to those who fell at Culloden.

BLAIRGOWRIE

14 miles N of Perth on the A93

Blairgowrie, and the adjacent village of **Rattray**, is the centre of Scotland's raspberry and strawberry growing area. **Cargill's Visitor Centre** is within an old corn mill sitting on the banks of the Ericht, a tributary of the Tay, and at **Keithbank Mill** there is a small heraldic museum. The waterwheel at Keithbank is said to be Scotland's largest.

The **Cateran Trail** gets its name from a band of brigands who used to descend

PIOB MHOR OF SCOTLAND

37-43 High Street, Blairgowrie, Perthshire PH10 6DA
Tel: 01250 872131 e-mail: piobmhor@dircon.co.uk
Fax: 01250 873649 website: www.piobmhor.dircon.co.uk

If it's items of traditional Scottish Highland dress wear you are after, then **Piob Mhor of Scotland** is the place for you. Located in the "Heart of Scotland", on the route to Braemar and Royal Deeside, Piob Mhor (Gaelic for "Great Pipes") has everything that you could ever want; kilts, plaids, Highland dancer's outfits, kilted skirts, even bagpipes and feather bonnets are all made locally using only the finest materials.

Over the years, Piob Mhor has gained an international reputation for the manufacture of championship Highland dancer's outfits and supplies Scottish pipe band, military and regimental dress wear to customers throughout the world. The shop itself is an Aladdin's Cave for everything connected with Scotland; from Scottish antiques and collectables to tartans and tweeds. You could spend the whole day just browsing through the wonderful variety of items on display. As you would expect, the shop stocks an impressive range of traditional Highland dress wear: kilts, plaids, Highlander shirts, Prince Charlie and Argyll jackets, doublets, sporrans, hose, brogues, ties, sgian dubh, dirks, plaid brooches, kilt pins, belts, buckles and clan accessories.

Alternatively, if its a Souvenir or Gift you are after, then Piob Mhor of Scotland offers an impressive

selection of quality crystal, celtic and Rennie MacKintosh jewellery, clocks, watches, silver, pewter, ceramics, fine fragrances, CD's, tapes, Scottish whiskies, wines, ales and liqueurs. Without doubt, this is definitely the place to savour the real atmosphere of Scotland.

Whether you are looking for a complete Highland outfit or a gift for that special occasion, Piob Mhor's friendly and knowledgable staff will be more than happy to assist. Why not spend an afternoon here? You will be made most welcome.

RIVERSIDE GRANARY

Lower Mill Street, Blairgowrie, Perthshire PH10 6AQ
Tel: 01250 873032 Fax: 01250 873032
e-mail: colinsbarron@hotmail.com
website: www.segima-fine-art.co.uk

When you're in Blairgowrie you can't afford to miss the **Riverside Granary**, situated beside the River Ericht. It is a gallery which is an Aladdin's cave of colour, with nooks and crannies that house a wide range of arts and crafts products. The walls are hung with wonderful pieces of artwork, including oil paintings, watercolours and prints, and shelves full of hand-thrown ceramics, such as bowls, plates, cups and saucers.

The artists represented include Drönma, Jonathan Burns, Claire Ryan, Beverley Black and Audrey Mackie, and there is a fine range of signed limited prints by James McIntosh Patrick, Neil Barlow, Steven Townsend and Pam Carter. There is also a framing service, and there are some unique and unusual artifacts from Papua New Guinea, such as masks and shields. The Riverside Granary is also a café where you can relax over a cup of tea or coffee. Everything from a light snack to a full lunch is always available, with the food being cooked on the premises from the freshest of local produce. There is also mouth watering home baking and a range of soft drinks. This is the perfect place to have a break while sightseeing in the area, and you could also buy an unusual gift or souvenir here. Everything is keenly priced, and the owners, Colin and Jane Barron, are always on hand to offer friendly advice on your purchases.

STRATHARDLE INN

Kirkmichael, Near Blairgowrie, Perthshire
Tel: 01250 881224
e-mail: bookings@strathardle.co.uk

Situated within the village of Kirkmichael, in beautiful Strathardle, the **Strathardle Inn** is one of the best and most comfortable hostelries in Perthshire. It is a handsome building of warm stone dating from Victorian times, which is fitting, as Queen Victoria was known to love this area. There are five bedrooms on offer, all extremely comfortable and well appointed with colour TV and hospitality tray, and all fully en suite. The proprietor and his wife take a great pride in the standards they have set here, and will offer you a warm Scottish welcome.

They also take a pride in their prices, which offer wonderful value for money, whether you're staying in the hotel or stopping for a meal. The food is outstanding, the cuisine being traditional Scottish, using only the best and freshest local produce wherever possible, and the breakfasts are hearty and filling. The restaurant area is spacious, and there is a bar and lounge. The cosy bar has an

open fire that is just right for those chilly nights, and serves a wide range of real ales, beers, lagers, spirits wines and liqueurs. And, should you be driving, soft drinks are always on offer. The lounge is smart and comfortable, with inviting sofas, settees and easy chairs where you can relax over a quiet drink. The whole area surrounding Kirkmichael offers much to the visitor. Fishing, golf and shooting are available, as well as walking on the Cateran Trail, a 60-mile circular route using existing footpaths and minor roads which takes you on a tour of the area.

IVYBANK GUEST HOUSE

Boat Brae, Blairgowrie, Perthshire PH10 7BH
Tel: 01250 873056 Fax: 01250 873056
e-mail: Ivybankhouse@hotmail.com
website: www.ivybank-guest-house.co.uk

Near the banks of the River Ericht in Blairgowrie is the **Ivybank Guest House**, an extremely comfortable and well-appointed B&B establishment. This superb sandstone Victorian villa has three guest rooms, two doubles with four poster beds and a twin. They are all fully en suite, and have colour TVs and hospitality trays, ensuring an enjoyable stay. The breakfasts are traditional Scottish, and are beautifully cooked using fresh local produce wherever possible, though lighter options are on offer should you require them. The Ivybank is right at the centre of Perthshire, so is a great base from which to explore the area.

on Perthshire from Deeside in olden times and steal cattle. It is a 60-mile circular route using existing footpaths and minor roads, and takes you on a tour of the area. It has been designed to take five or six days to complete, and has stops every 12 or 13 miles.

COUPAR ANGUS

12 miles NE of Perth on the A94

Coupar Angus is a small burgh which received its burgh charter in 1607. It is situated in an area known as Strathmore, and has the scant ruins of **Coupar Angus Abbey**, founded for Cistercians, in the old kirkyard.

FORTEVIOT

6 miles SW of Perth on the A935

Forteviot was once the capital of a small Pictish kingdom. In a field to the north of the River Earn used to stand the **Dupplin Cross**, erected in the 9th century by King Kenneth MacAlpin in memory of King Constantine of the Picts. It was taken to the Museum of Scotland for restoration in 1998, and in 2002 was brought back to Forteviot, where it was erected within the **Parish Church of St. Serf**.

DUNNING

8 miles SW of Perth on the B934

St. Serf's Parish Church has a good 12th

century tower. The church itself was founded in 1219 by Earl Gilbert of Strathearn, though it has been much altered and rebuilt over the years. Near the village is a monument topped with a cross which marks the spot where **Maggie Wall**, a witch, was burnt to death in 1657.

AUCHTERARDER

12 miles SW of Perth on the A824

This small royal burgh is to be found two miles north of Gleneagles Hotel. It is now bypassed by the A90, and has a long main street full of buildings from Victorian times and earlier. The **Auchterarder Heritage Centre**, within the tourist office, has displays telling the history of the town.

The cruciform **Tullibardine Chapel** (Historic Scotland) sits about three miles west of the town, off the A823. It is a collegiate foundation, and is one of the few such churches in Scotland to have survived almost unaltered since it was founded in 1446 by David Murray of Dumbarton, ancestor of the Dukes of Atholl.

MUTHIL

15 miles SW of Perth on the A822

The ruins of the former **Muthill Parish Church** (Historic Scotland) lie within the village, and date from the 15th century.

DUNCRUB HOLIDAYS

Dalreoch, Dunning, Perthshire PH2 0QJ
Tel: 01764 684368 Fax: 01764 684633
e-mail: reservations@duncrub-holidays.com
website: www.duncrub-holidays.com

The former private chapel of Duncrub Park is set in 180 acres of well maintained parkland, a ten minute stroll form the quiet conservation village of Dunning. Once the chapel of a 19th century mansion house pulled down in the 1950s, it is now the centrepiece for the five star **Duncrub Holidays**, with two luxurious self catering apartments created within the church itself and the former chapel house. Many original features have been retained, and it now offers what must be the most unusual and delightful holiday accommodation in Scotland. The Chapel House boasts an entrance hall, galley-style kitchen with stained glass window, dining room with original panelling, tiles and French windows leading out onto a private patio and enclosed garden. There is a sumptuously furnished sitting room, two bedrooms and a bathroom.

The Tower House is immediately below the spire and has many original features, such as stained glass windows and beautifully carved angels. It has a kitchen/dining area and sitting room on the ground floor, and upstairs (reached by a stone spiral staircase) is a bathroom and a double bedroom with painted cherubs on the ceiling. Both apartments come with TV, video, hi fi and central heating. The development is owned and run by Wilma Marshall, whose dream it was to convert the church into possibly the most unusual yet comfortable self catering accommodation in Scotland.

The tower, however, is Norman, and was once free standing. A Culdee church, staffed by Celtic monks, stood here before the Norman church was built.

Three miles east of Muthill, off the B8062 is the **Innerpeffray Library**, one of the oldest libraries in Scotland. It was founded in 1691 by David Drummond, and is housed in a building specially built for it in 1750. It contains many rare books, including a copy of the Treacle Bible, so called because chapter 8, verse 22 of the Book of Jeremiah is translated as " Is there not triacle (treacle) at Gilead", instead of "balm". Before moving to its present building

it was housed in **Innerpeffray Chapel** (Historic Scotland), dating from 1508 and founded by Sir John Drummond of Innerpeffray as a collegiate church.

Drummond Castle Gardens (see panel) lie two miles west of the village. They were first laid out in the 17th century, improved in the 19th and

DRUMMOND CASTLE GARDENS

Muthill, Crieff, Perthshire PH5 2AA
Tel: 01764 681257 Fax: 01764 681550
e-mail: thegardens@drummondcastle.sol.co.uk

Described as one of the finest formal gardens in Europe, **Drummond Castle Gardens** were first laid out in the early 17th century by John Drummond, the 2nd Earl of Perth and include a John Mylne sundial erected in 1630. The gardens were renewed in the 1950s by Phyllis Astor, preserving features such as the ancient yew hedges and the copper beech trees planted by Queen Victoria to commemorate her visit in 1842. Open Easter weekend and then May to October 2pm-6pm. Castle not open to the public.

replanted in the 20th. When Queen Victoria visited the gardens in 1842, she planted some copper beeches which can still be seen.

To the east of Muthill are the sites of two 1st century Roman signal stations. The **Ardunie Signal Station** and the **Muir O'Fauld Signal Station** were two of a series running between Ardoch and the Tay.

FOWLIS WESTER
12 miles W of Perth on a minor road off the A85

A church has stood on the site of the **Parish Church of St. Bean** since at least the 8th century. The present church dates from the 15th century, and within it are two cross slabs, one being ten feet high with Pictish markings on it. A replica of the larger one also stands on the village green. Also in the church is a fragment of Clan McBean tartan, taken to the moon by American astronaut Alan Bean in November 1969.

CRIEFF
14 miles W of Perth on the A85

Crieff is the capital of Strathearn, and sits at the entrance to Loch Turret, where you will find the picturesque **Falls of Turret**.

At the **Crieff Visitor Centre** on Muthill Road you can see paperweights, pottery and miniature animal sculptures.

The **Glenturret Distillery** at The Hosh is Scotland's oldest, and tours are available, where you can see what is involved in the distilling industry. A "dram" is always available at the end of it.

COMRIE
21 miles W of Perth on the A85

Comrie is the "earthquake capital of Scotland", as it sits right on the **Highland Boundary Fault**, the geological fault that marks the border between the Highland and the Lowlands. The first recorded tremor took place over 200 years ago, and in 1839 a major one took place which did a lot of damage. The **Earthquake House** was built in 1869, and houses instruments that measure the many earthquakes that take place here (though most of them pass unnoticed by the general public).

North of the village, in Glen Lednock, is the **De'ils Cauldron Waterfall**, overlooked by a monument to Henry Dundas, 1st Viscount Melville, who lived between 1742 and 1811.

ST. FILLANS
26 miles W of Perth on the A85

St. Fillans stands at the eastern end of **Loch Earn**, at the point where the River Earn, a tributary of the Tay. leaves the loch. It is named after St. Fillan, and two of his relics, a bell and pastoral staff, are

THE CERAMIC EXPERIENCE

Bennybeg, Muthill Road, Crieff, Perthshire PH7 4HN
Tel: 01764 655788
e-mail: ceramicx.crieff@virgin.net
website: www.ceramicx.biz.

Come and paint your own designs on a plate or mug, decorate anything from a tile to a teapot, let your imagination run wild. Have your child's hand or footprint recorded on a plate forever as a unique gift. Paint an item in acrylics and you can take it with you that day or have it glazed and fired to be picked up a day or so later or sent by post. Enjoy a coffee and cake in the café while your children play in the soft play area. Voted "the most enjoyable visitor attraction" in Perthshire. Suitable for ages from seven days to seventy, this is one place you just can't afford to miss.

CELTIC COUNTRY - THE SHEEP SHOP

69 Atholl Road, Pitlochry, Perthshire PH16 5BL
Tel/Fax: 01796 473559
e-mail: sheepshop@supanet.com
website:www.thesheepshop.uk.com

The **Sheep Shop** is famous for its unique character and huge stock
of all things to do with sheep. Shopping here is a remarkable
experience. You'll find a breathtaking display of slippers, toys,
novelties, household wares, pottery, models, children's clothing,
cards, soap, clocks, key rings, pencils and mobile phone covers
(the list goes on and on) that takes the sheep as its inspiration. There are also sheepskins, of course,
and a range of adult fashions derived from our woolly friends. In addition, the shop carries a range of
keenly priced Celtic gifts and music, mostly hand crafted carefully in Scotland, as well as books, hand-
painted silk scarves and so much more.

And what about Scottish thistles? They form part of the superb range of flowers and blooms carried
by the shop that are so real looking that you almost feel like popping them in water. But, unlike real
blooms, they last forever, adding an elegant touch of colour to any design scheme. Have the sheep

ties, sheep socks, hot water bottle covers, Wellington boots and
draught excluders been mentioned? Or the sheep confectionery,
baseball caps, purses and bird hangers? The only real way to
appreciate the fabulous range of goods on offer is to visit the
place. The sheep has featured so much in Scotland's social history,
and in this shop you'll find the remarkable animal in all its facets.
There's sure to be something here to take your fancy as a souvenir
to take home or gift for a loved one. From the practical to the
decorative, the Sheep Shop has got it all.

MACDONALD BROS

6/8 Bonnethill Road, Pitlochry, Perthshire
Tel: 01796 472047 Fax: 01796 472267
e-mail: rory-macdonalds@msn.com
website: www.macdonalds-bros.co.uk

Just off Pitlochry's main street are the premises of **Macdonald Bros**,
one of the best butcher's shops in the area. It is owned and managed
by Tom and Lilias Macdonald and their son Rory, who are the third
generation to run this traditional family business, founded in 1928. It specialises in quality Aberdeen
Angus beef reared on local farms, which has been the shop's hallmark since it first started trading. The
Macdonalds know the farms well, and can even trace the beef back to particular animals, so you know
you are getting prime quality here. The shop also sells local Scottish lamb and pork, as well as wild
venison. The shop's own sausages, pies and lasagnes are famous throughout the area, as is the home
made haggis, black pudding and white pudding. People come from far and wide to buy the succulent
home made steak pies, with their large chunks of juicy beef and crisp pastry topping.

But Macdonald Bros is so much more that a butcher's shop. In
1997 it expanded into the premises next door, and now sells a
wide range of delicatessen foods, such as cheeses, pates, Loch Fyne
salmon, ready meals, cooked meats, sausages (including their
famous steak and ale sausages, made from local beer), milk, sauces,
bread, morning rolls and so much more. And it also sells a select
range of beers, wines and spirits, so is fast earning the reputation
of being Pitlochry's one stop shop! All the friendly staff are trained
to at least Elementary Hygiene level, so you know the shop has
stringent standards of hygiene and cleanliness.

housed within the Museum of Scotland. St. Fillan was one of Scotland's premier saints, and the Abbot of Inchaffray carried the saint's relics into battle at Bannockburn. The Scots partly attributed their victory to this. At the top of the 600-feet high **Dunfillan Hill** is a rock known as **St. Fillan's Chair**. To the south west, overlooking Loch Earn, is **Ben Vorlich**, which rises to a height of 3,224 feet, making it a Munro.

PITLOCHRY

Pitlochry must be one of the best touring bases in Scotland. It claims to be the geographical centre of Scotland, and as far away from the sea as you can get in the country. Though not a large town, it, it has many hotels, B&Bs and guest houses, as tourism is the main industryhere, and it makes a good overnight stop on the way north to Inverness.

But the town has its own attractions, not least of which is the marvellous scenery that surrounds it. The B8019 west towards **Loch Tummel**, which leaves the A9 about three miles north of Pitlochry, is very beautiful, and at the **Forestry Commission Visitor Centre** there are displays about the wildlife of the area. From the **Queen's View** you get a magnificent view of Loch Tummel and beyond. The queen in question is said to be Victoria, who stopped at this

point during her Highland tour in 1866. However, others claim it was named after Mary Stuart, who visited in 1564.

Loch Faskally, just to the north of the town, is man-made, and forms part of a huge hydroelectric scheme. At the **Pitlochry Visitor Centre**, near the dam which holds back the waters of the loch, is the famous **Salmon Ladder**, which allows salmon to climb up to the loch from the River Tummel below. There is a viewing gallery where you can see the fish as they pass. There are also displays about how electricity is produced from water power. Beside the loch is a picnic area with an archway called the **Clunie Arch**, and it is the exact dimensions of

Pitlochry Railway Station

DUNDARAVE HOUSE

Strathview Terrace, Pitlochry, Perthshire
Tel /Fax: 01796 473109
e-mail: dundarave.guesthouse@virgin.net
website: www.theaa.com/hotels/11251.html

Dundarave House is an elegant stone-built villa which sits in an elevated position, giving superb views of Pitlochry and the Tummel Valley. Owned and managed by Barbara and David Braine, it offers the very best in Scottish hospitality on a B&B basis. There are seven comfortable rooms, each with colour TV, hairdryer and hospitality tray, and all have central heating. Pitlochry is set among some of the best scenery in Scotland, and Dundarave House makes an ideal base from which to explore it.

LOCH TUMMEL INN

Strathtummel, by Pitlochry, Perthshire PH16 5RP
Tel: 01882 634272

The three star **Loch Tummel Inn** overlooks the lovely waters of Loch Tummel, a few miles north west of Pitlochry. It is an old coaching inn built originally by the Duke of Atholl, and throughout the years since then has been offering good food, good drink and great accommodation. The interior, with its country-style furniture and fittings, speaks of tradition coupled with modern conveniences. All the bedrooms are comfortable and superbly appointed, with tea and coffee making facilities, colour TVs, private bathroom, central heating and even electric blankets. The restaurant is housed in what was a hayloft, and here fine food is served. All the produce used in the kitchens is local wherever possible, and is always fresh. The food is traditional Scottish, with Continental influences, and the menu has a superb range of dishes that have been cooked with imagination and flare. The hotel even smokes its own salmon.

A good selection of quality wines is on offer, and there is sure to be something that complements

your meal admirably. Why not have a drink in the relaxing bar, housed in what were the stables? As you would expect, there is a wide range of single malts to choose from, as well as Scottish beers, real ales, spirits and liqueurs. Meals are also served. And the hotel lounge is a cosy place, with, in the colder months, a real coal fire. There is also a garden terrace, with a wonderfully smelling herb garden next to it.

MALCOLM APPLEBY

Designer/Goldsmith/Engraver, Aultbeag, Grandtully,
by Aberfeldy, Perthshire PH15 2QU
Tel: 01887 840484 Fax: 01887 840785

Fabulous jewellery and stunning silver are to be found in abundance at **Malcolm Appleby**. People come from all over the world to see him delicately engrave many items of silverware and jewellery in his workshop, and buy the finished products. Known locally as the "yellow house", Malcolm's idiosyncratic home and workshop nestle in a quiet corner of Grandtully, a picturesque village situated by the River Tay. He is a member of the Association of British Designer Silversmiths, and is considered to be one of the most original and highly skilled craftsmen working in Britain today. Known primarily as an engraver, he has been commissioned on many occasions by private companies, public bodies and individuals to produce wonderful pieces of silverware that in themselves are works of art.

His designs are drawn from a wealth of inspiration - the natural world, myths, elemental ideas and personal experience, sometimes laced with a mischievous sense of humour. His output ranges from

bangles, belt buckles and brooches to cufflinks, necklaces and bowls. New pieces are being completed all the time, and visitors are welcome to watch him in his workshop by appointment. And despite the high levels of craftsmanship, prices are surprisingly reasonable. A silver button (which is sure to become a family heirloom) will only cost you about £12 And from mid-October to early January he has a "Christmas shop" where people can buy a present for a loved one. Be sure to phone in advance to make arrangements.

BURNSIDE APARTMENT HOTEL

19 West Moulin Road, Pitlochry, Perthshire PH16 5EA
Tel: 01796 472203 Fax: 01796 473586
e-mail: reception@burnsideapartments.co.uk
website: www.burnsideapartments.co.uk

If you're looking for new-style holiday accommodation in Scotland, then the **Burnside Apartments** in Pitlochry are for you. It's the town's first apartment hotel, where you can experience the luxury of hotel living with the comfort and privacy of your own apartment. The apartments are individually designed and exceptionally well-appointed, with spacious living/dining areas, kitchens, bath/shower rooms and cosy bedrooms. They sleep two to six people, can be rented daily, house keeping included, and the attractive Bistro is not to be missed. The Burnside Apartment Hotel can accommodate and welcomes disabled visitors.

the tunnel that brings the water from Loch Tummel, to the west, to the Clunie Power Station.

To the east of the town is the **Edradour Distillery**, situated among the hills. It is Scotland's smallest distillery, and was established in 1825 and produces a malt whisky using only local barley. Conducted tours, finishing off with a thirst-quenching dram, are available. Also not to be missed is the **Pitlochry Festival Theatre**, which sits beside the waters of the Tummel. It is a purpose-built theatre, and presents a varied programme of professional drama during the summer months. It is one of Scotland's most popular venues, and advance booking is advisable.

The A924 climbs up east from Pitlochry, taking you through some marvellous scenery. It reaches a height of 1,260 feet before dropping down into Kirkmichael and then on to Bridge of Cally. **Kindrogan** is a Victorian country house where the Scottish Field Studies Association offer residential courses on Scotland's natural history.

There are many guided walks available round Pitlochry, organised by such organisations as Scottish Natural Heritage, the Scottish Wildlife Trust and the Forestry Commission. A booklet on them is available from local tourist offices.

AROUND PITLOCHRY

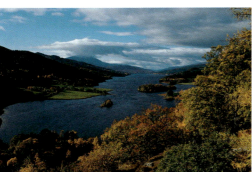

Loch Tummel

SPITTAL OF GLENSHEE
13 miles NE of Pitlochry on the A93

A small medieval hostelry once stood near this village, which lies 1,125 feet above sea level at the heart of the Grampian Mountains. The main road north from Perth to Braemar passes through it, and five miles north of the village, near the Aberdeenshire border, is a combination of steep inclines and double bends known as the **Devil's Elbow**. At Cairnwell the

A93 reaches a height of 2,199 feet above sea level, making it the highest public road in Britain. It can be blocked for weeks on end with snow during the winter.

DUNKELD

11 miles S of Pitlochry off the A9

Dunkeld, though no bigger than a village, is in fact a small cathedral city. On a picturesque spot on the banks of the Tay sits **Dunkeld Cathedral**, with its restored chancel now used as the parish church.

After Kenneth MacAlpin, king of Dalriada, ascended the throne of Scotland in the 9th century, he made his capital at Scone. Dunkeld already had an important Celtic monastery, so Kenneth made his ecclesiastical capital there, and placed relics of St. Columba within it, safe from marauding Vikings. In AD865 records show that the Abbot of Dunkeld

The Hermitage, Dunkeld

THE PEND

5 Brae Street, Dunkeld, Perthshire PH8 0BA
Tel: 01350 727586 Fax: 01350 727173
e-mail: molly@the pend.sol.co.uk website: www.thepend.com

The Pend offers four star guest house accommodation, with three extremely comfortable rooms, comprising two family and one double room, each with TV, wash hand basin and hospitality tray. There are also two large, well-appointed bathrooms. It was awarded as the best B&B in Scotland in the 2003 *Which Hotel Guide* and is *Taste of Scotland* accredited. Superb food is served in the combined dining/sitting room and the table d'hôte dinner reflects the wonderful produce available in Perthshire. The breakfast menu is tailored to suit any palate and there is also a select wine list.

ZIGZAGS

18 Atholl Street, Dunkeld, Perthshire PH8 0AR
Tel:01350 728666

For unusual and appealing gifts and wonderful paintings, visit **Zigzags** in Dunkeld, one of the best craft shops in all of Perthshire. Owned and run by David Amos, the rear of the shop has been converted into a small gallery to exhibit the paintings of David's wife and other artists. The front of the shop has a wonderful range of craft ware such as pottery, jewellery, glass, cards and colourful fabrics. It sits close to the centre of town, and if you ever travelling up or down the A9, which bypasses Dunkeld, why not make a small detour to view this colourful and unusual shop?

was the chief Scottish bishop long before St. Andrews took over.

The present cathedral dates from many periods. The chancel (now the parish church) was built in in the early 14th century, while the ruined nave is 16th century. Within the chancel is the tomb of Alexander Stewart, son of Robert II of Scotland and brother of Robert III. His nickname was the **Wolf of Badenoch**, and he sacked the great cathedral at Elgin in the 14th century.

In 1689 the **Battle of Dunkeld** was fought in the small town, when Jacobite troops were defeated by a force of Cameronians under **William Cleland**. It was an unusual battle, in that the town itself was the battlefield, with soldiers running up and down the streets and using the town's buildings as cover. Cleland was mortally wounded during the battle, and now lies buried in the ruined nave of the cathedral. In the

grave next to him, curiously enough, lies the grandson of Prince Charles Edward Stuart, the greatest Jacobite of them all. The Prince's illegitimate daughter had an affair with the Archbishop of Rouen, and subsequently gave birth to Count Rohenstart, a name made up from "Rouen" and "Stuart". He was what is nowadays called a "playboy" and on a trip to Scotland in 1854 he was killed in a carriage accident.

Most of the "little houses" in the town date from a rebuilding after the battle was over. The National Trust for Scotland looks after many of them nowadays, and rents them out. One of the buildings is called the **Ell Shop**, as an old Scottish measure called an "ell" is displayed on its wall. It approximates to 37 inches. In the square is the **Atholl Memorial Fountain**, erected in 1866 in memory of the 6th Duke of Atholl.

The **Beatrix Potter Exhibition and**

JEAN BURHOUSE

The Old Sawmill, Inver, Dunkeld, Perthshire PH8 0JR
Tel: 01350 727723 Fax: 01350 727261
e-mail: sales@jeanburhouse website: www.jeanburhouse.com

Jean Burhouse is Scotland's leading supplier of craft materials. Whether you're into wood working, turning or carving, picture framing, moulding, glassware or ceramic painting, then the shop probably has just the thing for you. There's a truly stunning range of supplies and materials, including brushes, craft lathes, chucks, waxes, gilding materials, books and polishes, and over 100 species of hardwood timber. The staff are friendly and knowledgeable, so you can shop here in complete confidence, knowing that you are getting the very best materials and tools at prices to suit your pocket.

KATIE'S TEA ROOM

Perth Road, Birnam, by Dunkeld, Perthshire PH8 0AA
Tel: 01350 727223 e-mail: birnamauto@btopenworld.com
Fax: 01350 727154 website: www.birnamautopoint.co.uk

When driving along the A9, or exploring the beautiful little cathedral city of Dunkeld, why not stop at **Katie's Tea Room** in Birnam for a welcome break? You can have teas, coffees and soft drinks, accompanied by delicious home baking, biscuits and confections. Or you can have a light lunch or snack, including tasty home-made soups, sandwiches or crispy salads. Everything is cooked on the premises, the decor is light and airy, with the dining area seating up to 40 in perfect comfort. Colourful prints and paintings adorn the walls, giving a warm, relaxing atmosphere as you eat.

TOMBUIE SMOKEHOUSE

Aberfeldy, Perthshire PH15 2JS
Tel: 01887 820127; Fax: 01887 829625

For Scottish food at its best, there's no beating the **Tombuie Smokehouse**, set within an attractive hill farm on the outskirts the lovely town of Aberfeldy. It has earned itself an enviable reputation for its award winning smoked produce including venison, ham, lamb and cheeses. The shop is situated at the east end of Aberfeldy (closed Jan/Feb) or you can visit on line at www.tombuie.com.

MAINS OF MURTHLY FARM COTTAGES

Mains of Murthly, Aberfeldy, Perthshire PH15 2EA
Tel/ Fax: 01887 820427

Set among some truly beautiful scenery in a 550-acre working farm, the **Mains of Murthly Farm Cottages** offer the very best in self-catering accommodation. Donald's Cottage has two bedrooms, a double room with en-suite bathroom and a family room which enjoys a private bathroom with bath and walk in shower. It also has a dining/sitting room with open fire and TV, and a fully fitted kitchen. Hill Cottage has a double and single bedroom, a sitting/dining room, an upstairs bathroom and a fully fitted kitchen. Both properties are extremely comfortable, offering great value for money. There is a large garden area and ample parking.

GATEHOUSE NURSERY

Gatehouse, near Aberfeldy, Scotland PH15 2EL
Tel: 01887 820472 Fax: 01887 829827
website: www.gatehousenursery.net

Gatehouse Nursery is a family run garden plant nursery that sells a large selection of home grown summer bedding and basket plants, as well as ornamental trees, fruit trees, shrubs and herbaceous perennials for the garden. You can't afford to miss this wonderful place if you're in the area, as it is full of colour and fragrances, and is arguably the highest nursery in Scotland, at 1,000 feet above sea level. It is owned and run by Bridget and Neil Black, who are committed to great service, sound advice and value for money. It lies two miles south of Aberfeldy on the A826 Aberfeldy - Crieff road.

INNERWICK ESTATE

Glen Lyon, Aberfeldy, Perthshire PH15 2PP
Tel: 01887 866222 Fax: 01887 866301
e-mail:innerwickcott@hotmail.com website: www.innerwick.com

If you are looking for self catering accommodation in beautiful Glen Lyon, look no further than **Innerwick Estate**. It has a range of stone built cottages and houses set in the idyllic, rural surroundings of an organic sheep farm. Ballinloan cottage sleeps four people, the Farm House sleeps six and Innerwick Cottage sleeps four to six. All are superbly appointed, with TVs, well equipped kitchens, pillows and duvets, central heating, open fires and pay phones. If you're looking for a property that is larger, then Ballinloan House offers five star accommodation for eight in a substantial stone built house that is comfortable and cosy.

Gardens at the Birnham Institute commemorates the fact that Beatrix Potter regularly holidayed in the area when she was a child, and took much of her inspiration from the surrounding countryside. The **Loch of the Lowes**, to the east of the town, has a wildlife centre owned by the Scottish Wildlife trust.

ABERFELDY
8 miles SW of Pitlochry on the A827

This small, attractive town has enduring fame due to a song written by Robert Burns called *The Birks o' Aberfeldy*, "birks" being birch trees. It was written in 1787, and while it is a well known song, it is by no means certain that Burns was writing about this place. Some Burns scholars say that the poet was writing about Abergeldie in

General Wade's Bridge

Aberdeenshire.

General Wade's Bridge crosses the Tay here. It was built in 1733 as part of a road building programme in the Highlands which would ensure that the area was "policed" during Jacobite unrest. Six regiments were raised to do

---

KELTNEYBURN SMITHY

by Aberfeldy, Perthshire PH15 2LF
Tel: 01887830267
e-mail: scottishironfairy@hotmail.com website: www.ironfairy.co.uk

Keltneyburn Smithy near Aberfeldy has been a working smithy for the last 200 years, producing implements and tools used by the local agricultural community. Now it is the base for two businesses working out of the same establishment. For the last 30 years the smithy has been run by John and Morag Cumming, with John designing and manufacturing a wide range of ornamental gates, railings and other ironwork, all beautifully crafted to the highest standards. His wife Morag also works in iron, though her works are on a more intimate scale. She produces a range of iron work that ranges from the elegant to the downright wacky, and they are sometimes bold, sometimes intricate and sometimes functional, but they are always sturdy and well-crafted.

Their daughter Heather is now following in her parents' footsteps, and produces a wide range of furniture and garden sculpture. This is metalwork as true art, all created by an exciting young artist. Her imaginative spirit and lively sense of humour combine to make each piece a highly original work of art. Fairies, wizards, frogs, chairs, candelabra, figures from mythology and birds have all featured in her repertoire of pieces. Each work is a one-off, and she also undertakes individual commissions for anything from an ostrich or a fairy to a giraffe or horse. The showroom beside the smithy highlights the work of these three crafts people, and prices range from a few pounds to several hundred depending on the size and complexity of the piece. This is the ideal place to buy a highly unusual, hand crafted gift or souvenir that is sure to be prized and admired for many years.

WALK 7

Birks of Aberfeldy

Start	Birks signpost beside Crieff Road, Aberfeldy
Distance	4 miles (6.4km)
Approximate time	2½ hours
Parking	Birks of Aberfeldy car park, Crieff Road
Refreshments	Hotels, pubs and café in Aberfeldy
Ordnance Survey maps	Landranger 52 (Pitlochry to Crieff), Pathfinder 323, NN84/94 (Aberfeldy), Explorer 21 (Pitlochry and Loch Tummel)

This is an extension of a popular 200-year-old walk through the steep, wooded gorge of the Moness Den, with its sheer rockfaces and noisy waterfalls. The extension takes in wide, high-level views over Strath Tay and the town of Aberfeldy. The paths along the edges of rock precipices have been made easier and safer, with hand-rails and walkways bridging awkward places. However, it is still quite a steep walk, ascending some 600ft (183m) in a mile (1.6km). The Birks of Aberfeldy are the subject of a Burns poem of the same name.

Soon after the footpath leaves the car park at the foot of the glen it splits into two. Take the left fork **A** over a footbridge above a small waterfall. After a stand of beech trees, the path starts climbing through the natural woodland of the glen – a mix of wych-elm, ash and willow, rowan, guelder rose, oak and hazel. Ferns of many varieties are prolific. Wintergreen and wood vetch prosper in the wet ground and flower from June to August. The Moness Burn is chock-a-block with huge boulders, many of which must weigh two or three tons. The glen was formed by the gouging action of the retreating glaciers about 10,000 years ago, and the numerous waterfalls are formed by streams tumbling down the side of the glen and by the main burn flowing over bands of hard rock. However hard rock is, it will, little by little, be eroded by the action of water, especially when water freezes in a fissure, expands and cracks the rock. Chunks fall off and clutter the floor of the valley.

The wee burns falling down the rockside have been bridged, making the going easier and drier, and they provide pretty sights,

especially where steps and bridges take the path higher in a spiral-staircase configuration round the falling water. Nearing the top of the glen, the path follows a hairpin bend **B** to climb suddenly much higher, but there is another path that keeps straight ahead for a few yards to a fenced rock platform overlooking a flight of five cascades, each falling into a pill. Take the hairpin bend. The path goes by steps and bridges to the top edge of the glen, where the trees give way to fields. Ahead now, well below the path, are the Falls of Moness, dropping 80ft (24m) over a stone sill. Continue along the path and then go up on to the opposite flank of the glen, where there is a closer view from a bridge spanning the top of the falls. From here there is a straightforward, unspectacular forest path leading downhill back to the car park.

Ignore this route back. At the top of the short slope up from the bridge, turn off left on to a narrow footpath **C**, little more than a rabbit-run, which takes you uphill a bit through a broadleaf wood and on to the farm road from Urlar. Turn right on this road and go downhill about 100 yds (91m) and through a gate on the left  **D**. You are then on another farm road that is mostly grass and, judging by its appearance, little used. This descends gently through thinly spaced trees for nearly 1 mile (1.6km) to Dunskiag **E**, a fairly large farmhouse with outbuildings, all empty and forlorn on the hillside overlooking the River Tay. The farm road from Farrochill to the west passes Dunskiag and takes you all the way back into Aberfeldy. It is a road with uninterrupted views to the north and provides plenty to look at. The tip of Ben Lawers can be glimpsed to the west and, panning a little to its right, one sees the top of Schiehallion. Immediately across the strath is Castle Menzies, a 16th-century fortified tower-house now in the care of the clan society and open to the public. Next to it is seen the tiny village of Weem, with The Weem – a whitewashed old inn – clearly visible. It was there that General Wade lodged while building his military roads and bridges hereabouts. There is a portrait of him on the outside wall. There is no public bar, only a cocktail bar for residents and those using the restaurant. However, it may be possible for walkers to be served sitting outside in summer.

Aberfeldy is seen complete in the embrace of a curve of the Tay. The river is crossed by Wade's bridge, which was built in 1733 to a design by William Adam, who was the father of Robert Adam, Scotland's most famous architect. It was the most ambitious of 35 major bridges along a 250-mile (400km) network

of new roads, and it is the only one that still survives as a functioning highway. There is a strange obelisk at each of the four corners of the central arch, and the stone parapet is so high that it cannot be looked over. Its strategic importance in Scotland's first proper road system is obvious when viewed from the high level of the farm road. To the right of Wade's bridge, on the edge of the golf-course, is a white pedestrian suspension bridge – the first in the world to be constructed of glass fibre.

The farm road drops down into the outskirts of the town to become a street, ending at the junction with Crieff Road **F**, the A826, running south from the town centre. Turn right at this junction. The car park is 200 yds (183m) on the right. Incidentally, water from the Moness Burn flows for 500 yds (457m) from the bottom of the glen through a tunnel under the houses to power a water mill. ●

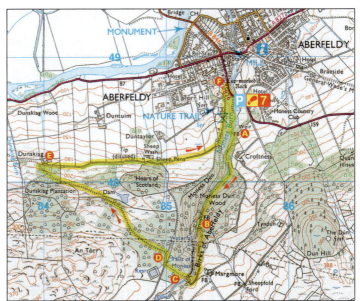

the policing, and in 1739 they amalgamated to form the 43rd Highland Regiment of Foot. The regiment's first parade was at Aberfeldy in May 1740. Its name was later changed to The Black Watch, and the **Black Watch Memorial**, built in 1887, commemorates the event.

Dewar's World of Whisky is right on the A827. It celebrates one of Scotland's most famous whisky firms, and in Mill Street is the **Aberfeldy Water Mill**, which was built in 1825 and restored in 1987. It has a visitor centre which tells the story of milling in Scotland. A mile or so north of Aberfeldy, near Weem, is **Castle Menzies** (pronounced "Ming-iz"), home to Clan Menzies. It is a 16th century building, built by James Menzies of Menzies, son-in-law of the Duke of Atholl. The last descendant of the main line died in 1910, and it is now owned by the Menzies Charitable Trust, who run a small museum within it. Charles Edward Stuart spent two night here in 1746.

KENMORE

13 miles SW of Pitlochry on the A827

Killin, which is dealt with in the Central Scotland section of this book, is at the western end of Loch Tay, while Kenmore is at the eastern end. It was founded by the Earl of Breadalbane in the 16th century, and is now one of the most popular villages in the Highlands for watersports.

Loch Tay is the source of the River Tay, which flows down past Dunkeld to Perth,

---

BEN LAWERS NATIONAL NATURE RESERVE

Lynecloch, Main Street, Killin FK21 8UW
Tel: 01567 820397 (Information Centre)
or Tel/Fax: 01567 820988 (office; Mon - Fri, 9 - 3)

The central Highlands' highest mountain, **Ben Lawers** is 1,214 m (3,984 ft), with views from the Atlantic to the North Sea. In the Trust's care are 3,374 ha (8,339 a) of the southern slopes of the Lawers range and 1,348 ha (3,33 1a) of the Tarmachan range, noted for a rich variety of mountain plants and including Meall nan Tarmachan (1,044 m, 3,425 ft). Birds include raven, ring ouzel, red grouse, ptarmigan, dipper and curlew. Nature trail and other areas are fenced to exclude sheep and deer and to allow the restoration of trees, shrubs and herbaceous plants; projects include pioneering work to restore treeline woodland habitats. Audio visual programmes with special version for children.

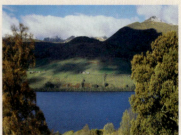

---

and forms the Firth of Tay before entering the North Sea. It is 14 miles long by less than a mile wide, and has a maximum depth of about 500 feet, making it one of Scotland's deepest lochs. Overlooking it from the north is Ben Lawers (3,984 feet high), with the **Ben Lawers Mountain Visitor Centre** (see panel above) on a minor road off the A827.

The **Scottish Crannog Centre** is at Acharn, two miles west of Kenmore on the southern shore of Loch Tay. It is run by the Scottish Trust for Underwater Archaeology, and explains all about crannogs - man-made islands built in in shallow water connected to the shore by an artificial causeway. From 2500BC up until the 17th century people lived on them in Scotland, as they were easily defendable. Off the north shore of the loch is an island called **Eileen nan Bannoamh**, which means "Isle of the Holy Women", where a small Augustinian nunnery was founded in the 13th century.

FORTINGALL

15 miles SW of Pitlochry on a minor road off the B846

Fortingall sits at the entrance to **Glen Lyon,** said to be the most beautiful glen in Scotland. It is 25 miles long, and running through it is the River Lyon, which rises in remote Loch Lyon, part of a hydroelectric scheme. At **Bridge of Balgie,** 10 miles west of Fortingall, a minor road strikes south over the hills towards Loch Tay, passing **Meall Luaidhe** (2,535 feet high). It makes a lovely car journey in the summer months. Bridge of Balgie is where well known wildlife artist Alan Hayman has a studio and gallery. Four miles north of Fortingall on the B846 is the delightfully named **Glengoulandie Deer Park,** where you can see herds of red deer, Highland cattle, goats and sheep.

The village was laid out in the 19th century by Sir Donald Currie the shipping magnate, and it has some picturesque thatched cottages that look as if they should be in England. In the kirkyard is the 3,000 year old **Fortingall Yew,** said to be the oldest living thing in Europe. The tree looks its age unfortunately, but it has every right to.

Fortingall, however, has one unique claim to fame which links it with the Bible. It is said that **Pontius Pilate,** governor of Judea during the time of Christ, was born here. His father was supposed to have been a Roman officer who was sent to Scotland by the Emperor, though the status of his mother has never been recorded. She may have been the Roman officer's wife, who accompanied her husband from Rome, or she may have been the daughter of a local tribal chief. No one knows if the story is true or not, but there was certainly a Roman camp nearby.

KINLOCH RANNOCH

17 miles W of Pitlochry on the B846

This small, picturesque village sits on the River Tummel at the point where it leaves **Loch Rannoch.** At **Dalchosnie,** south east of the village, Robert the Bruce is said to have had a skirmish with English troops in 1306. Also to the south east is one of Scotland's best known mountains, **Schiehallion,** a Munro which is 3,547 feet high. From the top there are views as far as the Lowlands. This whole area was ravaged by Government troops after the Jacobite Uprising, with cottages and houses being put to the torch as local people looked on helplessly.

Within the village is a monument to **Dugald Buchanan,** who wrote religious poetry. He was born in the early 18th century in the parish of Balquidder, and was offered the position of schoolmaster and preacher in Kinloch Rannoch. The story goes that in those days the local minister was only able to attend to the Kinloch Rannoch part of his parish every three or four weeks, and consequently the parishioners stopped observing the Sabbath. Instead they played football

Loch Rannoch

KILLIECRANKIE

Pitlochry, Perth & Kinross PH16 51G
Tel/fax: 01796 473233 (Visitor Centre)
or 01350 728641 (Ranger Office)
e-mail killiecrankie@nts.org.uk
website: www.nts.org.uk

On 27th July 1689, the Pass of Killiecrankie echoed with the sound of battle cries and gunfire when, nearby, a Jacobite army led by "Bonnie Dundee" defeated the government forces. One soldier evaded capture by making a spectacular jump across the River Garry at Soldier's Leap. The magnificent wooded gorge, much admired by Queen Victoria in 1844, is tranquil now, and is designated a Site of Special Scientific Interest because it is a fine example of an oak and mixed deciduous woodland. The Visitor Centre exhibition features the battle, natural history and ranger services. In the Centre, visitors can now watch birds nesting, via a remote camera in the woodlands.

and other sports. Rather than antagonise them, Buchanan invited the villagers to attend one of his own "sports" on a Sunday, and when they turned up, he began gently preaching to them about the wickedness of breaking the Sabbath. Soon he converted most of the village, and when he died in 1768 he was a much respected man.

Two roads lead west from Kinloch Rannoch, one hugging the northern shore of the loch (the B846) and one the southern shore. They meet at the western end of the loch, and the B846 goes on towards **Rannoch Station**, said to be the most isolated railway station in Britain. Beyond the station is **Rannoch Moor**, called "Europe's last great wilderness". It featured in *Kidnapped* by Robert Louis Stevenson.

But even here the landscape is man-made, as at one time the whole area was covered by trees - the so-called "Caledonian Forest" that blanketed most of the Highlands. As man encroached on it, he gradually felled all the trees, creating the moorland we see today. At **The Black Wood of Rannoch**, however, some of the original forest can still be seen.

KILLIECRANKIE
3 miles N of Pitlochry off the A9

The famous **Battle of Killiecrankie** took place in 1689 between Jacobite and Government troops. The government troops were led by General Mackay, and as they were making their way through the narrow Pass of Killiecrankie they were attacked from above by the Jacobite army of Viscount Dundee (also known as "Bonnie Dundee"). The Jacobites claimed

Soldier's Leap

victory, but Dundee himself was mortally wounded. The **Killiecrankie Visitor Centre** (National Trust for Scotland - see panel) has displays and exhibits illustrating the battle. At the northern end of the Pass is the **Soldier's Leap**, high above the River Garry. A government trooper called Donald McBean leapt across the 18-feet wide gap to escape some Jacobites who were chasing him.

BLAIR ATHOLL

6 miles NW of Pitlochry off the A9

Sitting above the village is **Blair Castle**, ancestral seat of the Dukes of Atholl. It originally dates from 1269, though over the years it has been considerably altered and added to, and it was completely refurbished in the 18th and 19th centuries. About 30 furnished rooms can

be seen by the public, and they have fine collections of furniture, paintings, china and armour.

The Duke is the only person in Britain who is allowed to have his own private army, the **Atholl Highlanders**. A small museum explains its history, and has displays of costumes and weapons. In the kirkyard of **St. Bride's Church** in Old Blair is the grave of Viscount Dundee, known as "Bonnie Dundee". He was killed in the Battle of Killiecrankie in 1689.

The **Clan Donachaidh Museum** is at Bruar, four miles north of Blair Atholl, and celebrates the history of Clan Robertson. Close by are the beautiful **Falls of Bruar**, which can bee seen from footbridges which span it.

DUNDEE

Scotland's fourth largest city sometimes has the unfortunate reputation of being dull and largely industrial. While the city's fortunes were built on trade and industry, there is still much to see and admire here, as its roots go deep into Scottish history. In the 12th century, it was one of the largest and wealthiest towns in Scotland, and in the middle of 14th century it became a proud royal burgh.

It sits on the north bank of the Firth of Tay, and two bridges connect it to Fife - the **Tay Road Bridge** and the much more famous **Tay Rail Bridge**. The road bridge was opened in 1966, while the rail bridge dates originally from 1878.

On the evening of December 28th, 1879 the original rail bridge collapsed during a violent storm while a train was crossing it, with all 75 passengers perishing in the waters of the Tay. One of Dundee's best known citizens, **William Topaz McGonagall**, wrote a poem about

Blair Castle

it which not only immortalised the disaster, but immortalised himself as well:

> Beautiful Railway Bridge of the Silv'ry Tay,
> Alas! I am very sorry for to say
> That ninety lives have been taken away
> On the last Sabbath Day of 1879,
> Which will be remember'd for a very long time.

It has been called "the worst poem in the world", and McGonagall himself has been called the "world's worst poet", but perhaps critics are being unfair. He was a simple hand loom weaver whose education ended when he was seven years old, and he was trying to make sense of a tragedy that undoubtedly touched him. Who knows what he might have achieved had he been given the educational advantages we take for granted today.

He was born in Edinburgh in 1830, the son of Irish immigrants, and came to Dundee with his parents after having lived in Paisley and Glasgow. When he was 47 years old, he felt "a strange kind of feeling" to write, and that's exactly what he did - he wrote. When he died in September 1902 he was still writing.

The **Old Steeple** - the steeple of St. Mary's Church - dates from the 15th century. The rest of the church dates from rebuildings in the 18th and 19th centuries, and was at one time divided into four separate parish churches. In the 1980s there were still three congregations within it - the Steeple Church, Old St. Paul's and St. David's, but they eventually combined. It has a peel of eight bells, and you can climb the tower to see them. From the top there is a good view of the city and the Tay, and in an antiquities room there is a small display of carved stones from old Dundee buildings that have disappeared over the years.

The **Wishart Arch** in the Cowgate is one of the city's old gateways, and gets its name from George Wishart the reformer who preached from its top during the plague of 1544. The RSS Discovery was Scott of the Antarctic's ship, and was built in Dundee in 1901. Now it forms the focal point for the **Discovery Point & RSS Discovery**, at Discovery Quay. You can "travel" to Antarctica in the Polarama Gallery and find out about Dundee's maritime history. Another famous ship is moored at Dundee - the **HM Frigate Unicorn**. It lies at City Quay, and is the oldest British-built ship still afloat. It was built at Chatham outside London in 1824 for the Royal Navy, and carried 46 guns. The conditions aboard a wooden sailing ship during the time of Nelson have been recreated, including officers' quarters and the

UNIVERSITY OF DUNDEE BOTANIC GARDEN

Riverside Drive, Dundee DD2 1QH
Tel: 01382 647190   Fax: 01382 640574

Described as the jewel in the crown of the University, the Garden is open for public enjoyment as well as its

principal function of education, conservation and supplying plant material for teaching and research within the University of Dundee. The Garden, set on south facing land near the banks of the River Tay, has a wide range of trees and shrubs, tropical and temperate glasshouses, water-garden and herb garden, as well as collections of indigenous British plants and others from all over the world. Guided tours are available by arrangement and to round off, why not enjoy refreshments in the coffee shop or a browse in the gift shop. Free parking. Disabled amenities.

Maritime Discovery Centre, Dundee

cramped conditions lived in below deck by the crew.

Dundee was famous at one time for the "three Js" - jute, jam and journalism. Now only journalism remains, in the guise of D.C. Thomson Ltd., and Dundee is home to such comic characters as Denis the Menace, the Bash Street Kids, Little Plum and Lord Snooty. At the corner of Reform Street and High Street there are statues to two of the most famous characters - **Desperate Dan** and Minnie the Minx.

Jute is remembered at the **Verdant Works**, in West Henderson Wynd, voted Europe's best industrial museum in 1999. The industry at one time employed over 40,000 people in the city, and here, in a former jute mill, you can learn all about the trade, from its beginnings in India right through to the finished product. Original machinery is on display, and you can see the living conditions of the people who worked in the industry.

Dundee

Contemporary Arts Centre (known as the "DCA") is at 152 Nethergate. It specialises in contemporary art and film, and has galleries, two cinemas, print workshops, shop and research facilities. And in the Greenmarket is **Sensation**, Dundee's science centre. It uses specially designed exhibitions and displays to bring science to life, and here you can discover how a dog sees the world, how to use your senses to discover where you are, and why things taste good or bad. The **Mills Observatory** (see panel below) also deals with scientific matters, and is Britain's only full time public observatory. It is within Balgray Park, west of the city centre, and is accessed from Glamis Road. It has a Cooke 25mm telescope plus a small planetarium and several displays about astronomy. At Albert Square are the **McManus Galleries** which contain Scottish paintings of the 18th and 19th centuries. It also has a museum with a particularly fine collection of ancient Egyptian objects.

Dudhope Castle in Dudhope Park dates from the 13th century, and was

---

MILLS OBSERVATORY

Glamis Road, Balgay Park, Dundee DD2 2UB
Tel: 01382 435846 Fax: 01382 435962
e-mail: jeff.lashley@dundeecity.gov.uk
website: www.mills-observatory.co.uk

Mills Observatory, housed in a classically styled sandstone building, is the UK's only full time public observatory. Here you can see the stars and planets for yourself through an impressive Victorian telescope and look at safe projected images of the sun. The planetarium has an artificial night sky giving you the chance to view constellations and planets. More can be learnt through the changing displays, audio and visual presentations and an interactive computer. The shop offers a range of gifts and educational items. Admission to the observatory is free.

once the base for the Hereditary Constables of Dundee. In its time it has been a woollen mill and a barracks. Though not open to the public, it can be viewed from the outside. **Dundee Law** looms 571 feet above the city, and from its summit there is a superb view of the city, the Firth of Tay and the Fife coast.

Broughty Ferry was once described as "the richest square mile in Europe" on account of the fine mansions built there by the Dundee jute barons. It sits to the east of the city, and at Castle Green is the **Broughty Ferry Museum**, housed in a 15th century castle built by the Earls of Angus. It highlights the area's military history and Dundee's long connections with the whaling industry. Annually, on New Year's Day, the **Ne'erday Dook** ("New Year's Day Plunge") takes place at Broughty Ferry, when hardy souls try to swim across the Firth of Tay to Fife. At the junction of Arbroath Road and Claypotts Road is the wonderfully named **Claypotts Castle**, built by John Strachan in the 16th century.

The **Carse of Gowrie** is to the west of the city, and is a flat expanse of very fertile land bordering the north bank of the Tay. The **Camperdown Wildlife Centre** is on the A923 Coupar Angus Road, and here you can see Scottish and European wildlife, including brown bears, Scottish wildcats, wolves and bats.

AROUND DUNDEE

BALGRAY
4 miles N of Dundee on a minor road west of the A90

The **Tealing Souterrain** is an ancient underground dwelling dating from about 100AD. It was accidentally discovered in 1871, and consists of a curved passage 78 feet long and seven feet wide, with a paved floor.

FOWLIS EASTER
6 miles W of Dundee on a minor road off the A923

The **Parish Church of St. Marnan** dates from 1453, and is one of the finest small churches in Scotland. Unusually for a Scottish church, it still has parts of its old rood screen, as well as medieval paintings and the finest sacrament house in Scotland.

GLAMIS
10 miles N of Dundee on the A94

Glamis Castle was the childhood home of the late Queen Elizabeth the Queen Mother. It is one of the most substantial and historic castles in Scotland, and is open to the public. The lands of Glamis (pronounced "Glams") were given to Sir John Lyon in 1372 by Robert II, the first Stewart king, and still belongs to the same family to this day, though they are now the Earls of Strathmore and Kinghorne. In 1376 Sir John married Princess Joanna, the king's daughter, and Glamis has had royal connections ever since.

Glamis Castle

The present castle was built in the French chateau style in the 17th century round the original tower house, and has been added to over the years. Shakespeare used the old tower as the setting for Macbeth, and Duncan's Hall, in the oldest part of the present castle, is said to have been built on the actual spot where Macbeth murdered Duncan. It's a good tale, but history tells us that Duncan was probably killed in battle near Elgin. During the reign of Elizabeth of England, Shakespeare and his company of players went to Aberdeen to perform before James VI, and he may have visited Glamis on the way.

Drama and Glamis seem inextricably linked. In 1540 Lady Glamis was burnt to death in Edinburgh for plotting against James V, and for being a witch. All her lands were seized, and when she was later found to have been innocent of all charges (much too late for her, of course), the lands were restored to her son.

It also has the reputation of being one of the most haunted places in Scotland. The ghosts include a White Lady, a Grey Lady, a servant boy and a man in armour. And. of course, there is the famous story of the secret room which has no door from the inside. Legend has it that within this room, which still exists supposedly, and whose exact location is only known to the earl and his heir, one of the early Lords of Glamis and his friend the Earl of Crawford played cards with the devil, and were sealed up as a punishment.

At Kirkwynd, in the village of Glamis, is the **Angus Folk Museum** (National Trust for Scotland - see panel above). It is

---

ANGUS FOLK MUSEUM

Kirkwynd, Glarnis, Forfar,
Angus DD8 I RT
Tel: 01307 840288
website: www.nts.org.uk

Housing one of Scotland's finest folk collections, this museum presents a vivid insight into how the rural workforce used to live. Six charming 18th century cottages contain the domestic section, and the agricultural collection is in the farm steading opposite, illustrating changes in the Angus countryside over the last 200 years. One of the most dramatic artifacts is the restored 19th century black horse drawn "Glenisla" hearse.

---

housed in a row of picturesque 18th century cottages, and contains one of the finest collections in Scotland. One of the exhibits is, rather appropriately for Glamis castle's reputation, a 19th century hearse.

FORFAR

13 miles N of Dundee on the A932

Forfar is a royal burgh, and was once the county town of Angus. One of Scotland's favourite foods is named after it, the **Forfar Bridie**, which is a bit like a Cornish pastie, with meat and vegetables contained within a pastry crust. It used to be a popular meal among farm workers, as it was light, easily carried about, and contained everything you would find in a main meal.

The town's history is explained in the **Meffan Museum and Art Gallery** in West High Street. It was built in 1898 after a bequest from the daughter of a provost of the town. This part of Scotland was inhabited by the Picts in ancient times, and, as far as we know, they had no alphabet or written language. However, they were expert stone carvers, and in the museum there are many examples of their work. You can also walk down an old cobbled street and see old shops and workshops. There is also a small display about witchcraft.

BARBARA BURT DESIGN

7 St Malcolm's Wynd, Kirriemuir, Angus DD8 4HB
Tel/Fax: 01575 574445   e-mail: kinloch@tesco.net

Scotland has a language all of its own. Do you know what "glaikit" means? Or "crabbit"? If you visit the **Barbara Burt Design** shop in Kirriemuir you'll soon find out. Barbara Burt has created a range of hand finished sewn goods and gifts that explain many of the country's fascinating and colourful words. There's also a fine range inspired by Celtic and Scottish designs, which come in vibrant colours. In fact, this is the shop for that extra special souvenir, and all at keen prices. Not only have the items been designed and made in Scotland, they reflect the customs and legends of a country rich in history and heritage. In a range from scented coasters to hand sewn patchwork quilts, one speciality that is always popular is the "Quillow", a comfortable cushion which contains a cosy fold-out blanket and is available in quilted or fleece fabric. And a child sized one has now been launched.

Barbara has been well-established in the sewn gift and fabrics business for many years, and her goods are sold in Scotland and many countries abroad. From tea cosies and cafetiere cosies, from cushions to wall hangings, Barbara Burt has them all, at surprisingly reasonable prices. She also undertakes individual commissions, and details are available when you visit the shop. And the words "glaikit" and "crabbit"? Well - the former means untidy or dishevelled, and is usually applied to a person, and the latter means short-tempered. If you buy one of her products with the words on it, you'll be able to remember them and use them at every opportunity.

VISOCCHI'S

37 High Street, Kirriemuir, Angus DD8 4EG
Tel: 01575 572115

Some of the best ice cream in Scotland is made in **Visocchi's**, a family run shop in Kirriemuir, birthplace of J.M. Barrie, who created Peter Pan. It is a family run business, and has been in existence since 1930. The third generation of Visocchis, Elena and Michael, now run it, adding even further to its fine reputation. An ultra-modern ice cream plant has recently been added to the premises, catering for the many people who come from far and wide to buy and sample it. The recipe, of course, is a jealously guarded family secret, but it is no secret that only the finest natural ingredients go into it. Not only that, each batch has to pass the demanding eye - and taste buds - of Michael himself, ensuring a product that tastes heavenly time after time. And many of the ways you can eat the ice cream are openly on display. Cones - wafers - chocolate wafers - oysters - snowball - can all be bought here.

There is ice cream in many tempting flavours and colours, and many diplomas and awards adorn

the shop's walls, a testament to the skill that goes into making the ice cream. But it is so much more than an ice cream parlour. There is a fine café as well that can seat up to 80, sells wonderful coffee and snacks at extremely competitive prices. There's a fine range of confectionery, and visitor's shouldn't miss the old-style ice cream vendor's tricycle that adorns the seating area. The shop's modern front sits opposite Kirriemuir's Peter Pan Fountain, and if the boy who never grows up were to step into Visocchi's today, he would be spoiled for choice, and wouldn't want to leave until he had tasted every flavour.

Balgavies Loch lies five miles east of the town, and is a Scottish Wildlife Trust reserve where you can see goldeneyes, cormorants and great crested grebes. Keys to the hide are available from the ranger at the Montrose Wildlife Centre (see page 327), ten miles away. Also to the east of the town, on the B9113, are the ruins of **Restenneth Priory** (Historic Scotland). It was founded by David I, and has some of the earliest Norman work in Scotland. It was later sacked by Edward I of England, then rebuilt on the orders of Robert I, whose son, also called Robert, was buried there.

KIRRIEMUIR

15 miles N of Dundee on the A926

The playwright J.M. Barrie was born in this village in 1860, and now the **J.M. Barrie Birthplace** (National Trust for Scotland) at 9 Brechin Road is open to the public as a museum dedicated to the man who wrote *Peter Pan*. Barrie was a clever child, and attended both Glasgow Academy and Dumfries Academy before entering Edinburgh University. He wrote many things besides *Peter Pan*, one of them being a book called *A Window in Thrums*, "Thrums" being a thinly disguised Kirriemuir. In the centre of the town is another reminder of its most famous son - the **Peter Pan Statute**.

In 1930 he donated a **Camera Obscura** (National Trust for Scotland) to his home town, one of only three such cameras in the country (the other two being in Edinburgh and Dumfries). It is situated within the cricket pavilion on Kirriemuir Hill, and is open to the public. The **Kirriemuir Aviation Museum** on Bellies Brae has a private collection of World War II aircraft.

The town is one of the gateways to the beautiful Angus glens, situated among the foothills of the Grampians. You can get a taste of them at the **Gateway to the Glens Museum** in the High Street. The B955 will take you up and into **Glen Clova**, and by taking a minor road at the Clova Hotel you will come to the lonely **Glen Doll** before it peters out among the peaks of the Grampians. If you turn west at Dykehead you'll enter **Glen Prosen**, which also winds up into the Grampians. Near Dykehead there is a cairn which commemorates Robert Scott and Edward Adrian Wilson the Antarctic explorers. Wilson lived in Glen Prosen, and some of the Antarctic expedition was planned here. You can follow Glen Isla along the B951 until you reach the A93. On the way, you will pass the **Loch of Lintrathan**, which is noted for its wildlife. If you turn up a minor road just after Dykends you will come to the lonely but beautiful **Backwater Reservoir** and its dam.

THRUMS HOTEL

Bank street, Kirriemuir, Angus DD8 4BE
Tel/Fax: 01575 572758

A picturesque, stone-built, whitewashed building in a lovely old Scottish town – that's the **Thrums Hotel** in Kirriemuir. Named after J.M. Barrie's book *A Window in Thrums*, it is a family run establishment with 11 extremely comfortable and well-appointed en suite guest rooms, which are a combination of singles, twins and doubles. Each one has a TV and tea and coffee making facilities. Beautifully cooked lunches and evening meals are available seven days a week, served either in the spacious dining room or lounge bar. Thrums is a hotel with a warm, friendly and inviting atmosphere, and your stay here is sure to be enjoyable and relaxing.

PEEL FARM

Lintrathen, by Kirriemuir, Angus DD8 5JJ
Tel: 01575 560205
e-mail: frances.flemingl@btopenworld.com
website: www.peelfarm.com

Peel Farm is located six miles west of the lovely town of Kirriemuir, birthplace of J.M. Barrie, the author of *Peter Pan*. It sits on the site of the castle once owned by Sir Alan Durward, and a stone seat nearby is a reminder of Durward's Dyke, a turf fence built to keep deer on the estate. Nothing of the castle now remains, though the red deer are still there. These days they are shot only through the lens of a camera.Owned and managed by Frances Fleming, Peel Farm offers local Scottish crafts such as pottery, jewellery, glassware, sewn items, greetings cards and a host of other items that make perfect gifts or souvenirs of your stay in Angus. In the new Courtyard at Peel Farm you will find antiques, local designer knitwear, tartan gifts, metal crafted items, furnishing and patchwork fabrics etc.

The friendly coffee shop, open 10am-5pm daily, serves soup and snack lunches, home baking and award winning jams. All the food is made from local fresh produce and the jam from raspberries grown in the Strathmore valley, an area famous in Scotland for its soft fruit production. Parties are catered for and evening opening is possible by arrangement. Peel Farm organises Saturday afternoon craft demonstrations and a programme of workshops. Residential workshops can also be organised and tailored to suit. When you visit why not take a walk to the scenic gorge past the deer park to the waterfall. Peel Farm is one attraction you should not miss when you are exploring Angus. Peel Farm is closed January and February.

DUNNICHEN

13 miles NE of Dundee on a minor road off the B9128

One of the most important battles in Scottish history was fought near this small village, though even some Scots themselves have never heard of it. In AD685 the **Battle of Nechtansmer**e was fought between an army of the Picts and a Northumbrian army under the command of the Northumbrian king, Ecgfrith. It marked a turning point in history, as the Northumbrians had embarked on a campaign to extend the boundaries of their kingdom. They had already taken the Lothians and Fife, and now they wanted to push north deep into Pictish territory and eventually take North East Scotland. However, the Northumbrians were soundly beaten, and King Ecgfrith himself was killed, thus halting the Northumbrian

campaign in its tracks. In Dunnichen, at the crossroads, is a cairn which commemorates the battle.

LETHAM

14 miles NE of Dundee on a minor road off the A932

This small, picturesque village was founded in 1788 by a man called George Dempster, who was the local landowner. Here, farm workers who had been forced off the land by new agricultural improvements were housed, and it became a centre for spinning and weaving. However, when power looms were introduced into the mills of the local towns the cottage industry died.

ARBROATH

16 miles NE of Dundee on the A92

Arbroath has a special place in the hearts of all Scots. It was here, in 1320, that

Scotland's nobility declared, in unequivocal terms, that Scotland was a sovereign, independent nation, and unanswerable to England. The document was called the **Declaration of Arbroath**, and was sent to the Pope in Rome. In it, they declared that they were fighting not for glory, nor riches, nor honours, but for freedom, "for that alone, which no honest man gives up but with life itself". And the document goes further than that - it says that the Scots would only support their king (in this case Robert I) if he fought for that ideal. If he didn't, then ordinary Scots would have the right to depose him. No English document would ever dared to have said that a king could be deposed if his subjects disagreed with him, and it clearly showed the difference between kingship in Scotland and England. Whereas an English king ruled a country with boundaries, a Scots king ruled a people, to whom he was answerable. This is why Queen Mary was called "Mary Queen of Scots" and not "Mary Queen of Scotland".

The Declaration was drawn up, most probably, by Abbot Bernard de Linton, a Norman Scot who was also the Chancellor of Scotland, in **Arbroath Abbey**, the ruins of which still dominate the town. A Visitor Centre in the abbey precincts explains the significance of the document, and how Scots still view it with pride.

The abbey was founded in 1176 by William the Lion, and dedicated to St. Thomas a Becket, and the red sandstone ruins you see today date from the 12th century and later. It was one of the few Tironensian abbeys in the country. Portions of the abbey church still survive, including the south transept, which has a great rose window, symbol of Arbroath today. In 1951, when the Stone of Destiny was "appropriated" from Westminster Abbey by some

Scottish Nationalist students, the abbey ruins became its temporary home.

Arbroath Museum is in Ladyloan, housed within the signal tower for the Bellrock Lighthouse. It charts the history of the town and its associations with the sea through a series of models, sounds and even smells.

The town has had a harbour at the "Fit o' the Toon"("Foot of the Town") since the 14th century at least, and it supported a great fishing fleet at one time. **Arbroath Smokies** (smoked haddocks) are a great Scottish delicacy, though their origins are actually to be found in a small fishing village four miles north of Arbroath called **Auchmithie**. The story goes that the villagers stored fish in the lofts of their cottages, and one day one of them caught fire. The smoke penetrated the fish, preserving and flavouring them, and soon the villagers were smoking the fish commercially.

The Cliff Nature Trail is well worth exploring. It winds for one and a half miles northwards along the red sandstone cliffs as far as Carlinheugh Bay, and there is plenty of bird life and rock formations to see. The town is also a favourite holiday spot, and in West Links Park is **Kerr's Miniature Railway**. Open during the summer, it is Scotland's oldest miniature railway, and runs for over 400 yards along the main Aberdeen to Dundee railway line.

St. Vigeans

18 miles NE of Dundee on a minor road off the A92

This little village gets its name from the dedication of its church, which was originally founded in the 11th century. It was dedicated to St. Fechan the Confessor, who died in 1012. Over the years, his name was Latinised to St. Vigianus, and then simplified to St. Vigeans. The term "confessor" is used to describe someone that suffered for his beliefs but did not die because of them. When the church was being rebuilt in the 19th century, over 32 Pictish stones were discovered, and they are now housed in **St. Vigeans Museum**, close to the small hill on which the church stands.

ABERLEMNO

18 miles NE of Dundee off the B9134

The **Aberlemno Pictish Stones** (Historic Scotland) date from the Dark Ages. Most of them are within an enclosure north of the kirkyard, while one is within the kirkyard itself. It shows a finely carved cross on one side surrounded by serpents, and a hunting scene on the other.

BRECHIN

22 miles N of Dundee off the A90

This small town's football team has the name "Brechin City", as it looks upon itself as a city because of the medieval **Brechin Cathedral**. It was founded in the 12th century (though what you see nowadays dates from later centuries), on the site of a Celtic church which had been endowed by the queen of Kenneth II, king of Scots between AD971 and AD995. It soon became Angus's main church, though when the the medieval cathedral was built, Roman Catholic priests replaced the Culdee clergy.

In 1806 the nave, aisles and west front were completely refurbished, though in the early part of the 20th century the church was restored to its original design. **The Brechin Museum**, in St. Ninian's Square, has displays and artifacts about the cathedral and the town. Attached to the cathedral is an 11th century **Round Tower**. Only two of these towers have survived in Scotland, though they are common in Ireland.

They were used by the local clergy as a place of refuge during troubled times. There are only scant ruins of a **Maison Dieu Chapel**, founded in 1267 by Lord William de Brechin as part of an almshouse.

Brechin Castle (not open to the public) is the ancestral home of the Earls of Dalhousie, and within the Brechin Castle Centre is a garden centre, model farm and walks. **Pictavia** is a living museum and interpretation centre which tells about that enigmatic people who occupied this part of Scotland for centuries, the Picts. Their name means "painted people", due to their habit of tattooing themselves, and they fought the Romans, the Vikings and the Anglo Saxons. In later times, when they had formed themselves into a powerful kingdom, they also fought with the people of Dalriada, a kingdom in what is now Argyllshire. But in 843 King Kenneth MacAlpine, king of Dalriada, also ascended the throne of the Picts, and Scotland was formed.

At Menmuir are the **White Caterthun** and the **Brown Caterthun**, hills on which are the well preserved remains of old Iorn Age forts. They give good views out over the Angus countryside. The Caledonian Railway runs on Sundays during the summer. Passengers can travel between Brechin Station on Park road and nearby Bridge of Dun, about five miles away. The railway has seven steam engines and eight diesel, and is run by the Brechin Railway Preservation Society.

Brechin is the gateway to one of the most beautiful of the Angus glens - **Glen Lethnot**. Near the head of the glen is an old trail (unsuitable for vehicles) that takes you over the Clash of Wirren to Glen Esk, where there is the **Glenesk Folk Museum**, with displays and artifacts about rural life in this part of Scotland.

The trail is sometimes called the **Whisky Trail**, as the route was at one time used by illicit distillers, who had their stills up here in the hills, and who hid their filled casks in the corries and caves of the area.

MONTROSE

25 miles N of Dundee on the A92

Montrose sits on a small spit of land between the North Sea and the tidal Montrose Basin, where you will find the **Montrose Basin Wildlife Centre** (see panel below). The basin is famous for its bird life, and thousands of bird watchers come here every year.

Montrose Basin

Some of the Battle of Britain pilots were trained at the old Montrose Air Station. In 1912 12 such stations were planned by the government, to be operated by what was then called the Royal Flying Corps, and now called the Royal Air Force. Montrose was the first to be built, and was opened in 1913. Now it houses the **Montrose Air Station Museum**, where there is a small collection of aircraft, documents, mementos and photographs relating to military aviation.

Montrose is an ancient town, having been granted royal burgh status in the 12th century. It is not so strategically important nowadays, though the name was adopted by the Graham family when it was ennobled. Perhaps the most famous member of the family was James Graham, 5th Earl and 1st Marquis of Montrose. Born in 1612, he succeeded to the earldom in 1625, and first supported the Covenantors in their struggle to keep the Scottish church Presbyterian. He then changed sides, and was made Lieutenant-General of Scotland by Charles I, and unsuccessfully tried to invade Scotland with an army. He later tried to raise

---

MONTROSE BASIN WILDLIFE CENTRE

Rossie Braes, Montrose, Angus DD10 9TJ
Tel: 01674 676336 Fax: 01674 678773

Montrose Basin is the 750-hectare enclosed estuary of the South Esk river. Virtually untouched by industrial development and pollution, the Basin provides a rich feeding ground for thousands of resident and migrant birds. The daily tidal cycle and passing seasons, each with its own characteristic pattern of birds - winter and summer visitors and passage migrants - ensure something new and different every month of the year. From here you might see eider ducks, pink footed and greylag geese, otters and much more.

Magnificent views of the wildlife can be seen through high powered telescopes and binoculars, whilst television cameras bring

the wildlife right into the centre. Unique displays show how a tidal basin works and the routes taken by the migrating birds. There are lots of buttons to press, boxes to open, touch tables and microscopes - ideal for children - and there is a fully equipped classromm for children to enjoy a range of educational activities. A nearby hide provides a closer view of the wildlife and the shop is stocked with a range of unusual and exciting gifts. Open 1st April to 31st October, daily 10.30am-5pm and 1st November to 31st March, daily 10.30am-4pm.

a Royalist army in the Highlands, travelling in disguise. He was a brilliant leader, and defeated Covenanting armies in many skirmishes. Charles's defeat at Naseby in England however, left him vulnerable, and his army was eventually trounced at Philiphaugh in 1645. He fled to the Continent, but later returned in 1650 in support of Charles II. Charles, however, would have nothing to do with him and he was hanged in the same year.

To the west of the town is the magnificent **House of Dun** (National Trust for Scotland), designed by William Adam, father of the more famous Robert, in 1730 for David Erskine, Lord Dun. Its plasterwork is magnificent, and there are also furnishings and a collection of embroidery and woolwork by Lady Augusta Kennedy-Erskine, illegitimate daughter of William IV and his mistress Mrs Jordan.

EDZELL

27 miles NE of Dundee on the B966

Edzell Castle (Historic Scotland) dates from the 15th century. Now a ruin, it was a seat of the Lindsay family, and one of the finest and most elegant castles in Angus. The gardens were especially beautiful, and were laid out in 1604 by Sir David Lindsay, though he died before they could be completed. They illustrate the fact that life in a Scottish castle could be comfortable and refined, and nothing like the harsh, draughty conditions people now imagine. The walled garden was called an "Italian Renaissance garden in Scotland", and featured carved panels showing heraldry, the "liberal arts", deities and the "cardinal virtues". The summer house contains surviving examples of the carved panels.

The Lindsays were Jacobites, and in

DALHOUSIE ESTATES HOLIDAY COTTAGES

Dykeneuk, Glenesk, Angus DD9 7YY
Tel: 01356 670273
e-mail: gleneskcottages@aol.com
website: dalhousieestates.co.uk

In Glenesk, at the foot of the Grampian Mountains in Angus, is the Dalhousie Estate, where you will find the **Dalhousie Estates Holiday Cottages**. There are four self catering cottages on offer in this unspoilt and undeveloped part of Scotland, all well placed to explore the surrounding countryside, which is rich in history and scenery. The picturesque cottages are all stone built and extremely cosy, and offer superior accommodation for the discerning holiday maker. Glenmark Cottage is the most remote, and sleeps four plus a baby in a double and a twin room. The comfortable living room has an open fire, and there is a bathroom/WC and kitchen. There is no electricity, though there is a Calor gas water heater, lamps, cooker and portable gas heaters. Sorry, no pets are allowed at Glenmark.

Heatherbank is within the hamlet of Tarfside, and sleeps six plus a baby in one double room and two twins. There is also a sitting room/kitchen which is well-appointed, and a bathroom/WC. Two well behaved pets can be accommodated. Milton Cottage is about two miles from Tarfside, in the depths of the country and has a double and single room. There is also a sitting room/kitchen and a bathroom/WC. Two dogs are allowed, but only between August 1 and April 15. Woodheaugh is within a large garden, and sleeps up to six in a double room and two twins. It has central heating plus an open fire. There is also storage for bicycles. All the cottage rents include fuel and linen. These cottages are the perfect retreat for those wishing a relaxing holiday, or for those wishing to climb, walk, fish or shoot.

1715 sold the castle to the Earl of Panmure, also a Jacobite sympathiser. After the Jacobites were defeated, the castle was forfeited and sold to an English company which went bankrupt in 1732. The castle became ruinous, though in the 1930s the gardens were restored to their former glory.

Within Edzell village is the **Dalhousie Arch**, built in 1887 over one of the roads leading into the village as a memorial to the 13th Earl of Dalhousie and his wife, who died within a few hours of each other.

MONIFIETH

6 miles E of Dundee on the A930

Monifieth is a former holiday resort, and has some good sandy beaches. At **St. Rule's Church** some carved Pictish stones were discovered that are now within the Museum of Scotland in Edinburgh.

The local golf course was used for the qualifying rounds of the British Open when it came to Carnoustie, to the east of the town.

THE OLD ANCHOR

48 Grey Street, Broughty Ferry, Angus
Tel: 01382 737899

Lee Cooney is the host at the **Old Anchor**, one of the most popular pubs in Broughty Ferry. He offers a warm welcome to patrons old and new, and invites them to come along and share in its unique and friendly atmosphere. The food and drink, of course, are outstanding, with a fine range of wines, spirits, liqueurs, lagers, beers and cask conditioned real ales, and, should you be driving, soft drinks. Why not try one of the hostelry's famous pub meals? They are reasonably priced and always tasty, with fresh local produce being used in the kitchens wherever possible.

The Old Anchor has been welcoming guests for over 100 years, and has seen off the trend to update and modernise, which invariably means losing a character and ambience that has been built up over many years. That's not to say that the pub doesn't offer efficient service and high hygienic standards. It does, and it takes a great pride in them. But, uniquely, it has managed to combine them with all the traditions of good, old fashioned Scottish hospitality and warmth. The decor is bright and open, with freshly upholstered seating and plenty of natural light. You can have a bit of "craik" with the regulars over a refreshing pint, play dominoes or darts, or you can just sit and read the paper in a bar that invariably has an open fire burning when the weather turns cold. Broughty Ferry is on the doorstep of Dundee, the "City of Discovery", and here you will be spoiled for choice when it comes to guest houses and B&Bs. Why not make the town your base when exploring the area? And why not end each day with a drink at one of the friendliest pubs in the area? You won't be disappointed!

KINGENNIE FISHING AND HOLIDAY LODGES

Broughty Ferry, Dundee, Angus DD5 3RD
Tel: 01382 350777 e-mail: kingennie@easynet.co.uk
Fax: 01382 350400 website: www.kingennie-fishings.com

Why not enjoy a relaxing break at the **Kingennie Fishing and Holiday Lodges**? Even if you don't fish, this small holiday development is the ideal place to unwind after the stresses of modern life. For those who just want to fish, permits are available for whole day, half day or evening and those staying at the lodges receive a 20 per cent discount on permits. There are four modern luxurious four star lodges, each one superbly equipped and extremely comfortable. There are four pools, three for trout and one new coarse lake. There's also a tackle and accessories shop.

LOCATOR MAP

▲ See other chapters

ADVERTISERS AND PLACES OF INTEREST

10 THE NORTH EAST

Of all the areas of Scotland, perhaps the North East has the most varied landscapes. From the high, windswept mountains of the Grampians and Cairngorms to the rich pastoral lands of Buchan; from tiny, picturesque villages to the cityscape of Aberdeen, and from historic towns like Elgin to high, wild sea cliffs at Dunnottar Castle near Stonehaven, the area has got the lot. It also has the

Brig O Dee, nr Braemar

largest concentration of castles in Europe (over 1,000), and a trail that takes you round the best of them. There's also a whisky trail that takes you to many of Scotland's distilleries, as Banffshire and Moray are famous for the production of fine malt whiskies. It is amazing that two distilleries only a few miles from each other can make whiskies with entirely different characteristics. This is a remarkably quiet part of Scotland, though it is steeped in history, with country lanes that sometimes take you up wooded glens into the mountains, and clean beaches with not another soul in sight.

The Grampians form a chain which goes diagonally across Scotland, taking in the Cairngorms, and the whole area is popular with climbers and walkers. Queen Victoria, when she bought Balmoral, popularised Deeside, a glen which strikes deep into the heart of the mountains.

ADVERTISERS AND PLACES OF INTEREST

The area encompasses the former counties of Aberdeenshire, Kincardineshire to the south, and Banffshire and Moray to the west. So much of the area remains unknown and unvisited by tourists, who head for Aberdeen, Royal Deeside, possibly the Strathspey distilleries, and give the rest a miss. The agricultural lands of Buchan, for instance, deserve to be explored. They lie above the Highland line, and yet they owe more to the Lowlands than the Highlands.Kincardineshire has literary connections and small fishing villages. It was here that Lewis Grassic Gibbon set his bleak novels of rural Scottish life. He came from the same mould as Ayrshire novelist George Douglas Brown, and rejected the couthy and comfortable images of Scotland's countryside that earlier novels had presented - the so-called "Kailyard School" - where people were happy, contented and wanted for nothing.

And in Moray there is Elgin, once one of the most important ecclesiastical centres in Scotland. It's huge cathedral is a ruin now, but at one time it was one of the grandest in Scotland, and could compare to the great cathedrals of England and the Continent. Surrounding the town is the Laigh of Moray, an area of flat, fertile land that is intensely cultivated.

Unlike the Lowlands, none of the inland towns, such as Huntly or Inverurie, have been industrialised to any great extent, and the villages generally remain quaint and picturesque. The coastline is as dramatic as anywhere in Britain, and the Coastal Trail takes you from St. Cyrus in the south to Findhorn in the west. The ruins of Dunnottar Castle are perched dramatically above the sea, while the Ythan Estuary is a Site of Scientific Interest, rich in aquatic life and birdlife.

Slains Castle, south of Peterhead, was one of the inspirations for Bram Stoker's *Dracula*, and the fishing port of Fraserburgh was, for a very short while, a university town. And for all its crowds, Royal Deeside cannot be missed. The glen winds up into the Grampians, and Braemar has the reputation of being the coldest place in Britain in winter, which is unbelievable when you see it on a warm summer's day. The names of the places associated with Royal Deeside are all well known; Aboyne, Balmoral and Crathie have featured in newsreels charting the progress of the Royal Family on holiday, and seeing these places for real explains why Queen Victoria fell in love with this place.

Aberdeen is Europe's oil capital, and a great place of learning. It is Scotland's third largest city, and though there is industry here, it is still a place of elegant buildings, museums and theatres. And it is cosmopolitan as well, thanks to oil money, and has bars, nightclubs, boutiques, grand hotels and restaurants. It is an ancient place, and was granted its royal burgh crater by William the Lion in 1175. Old Aberdeen, once a proud, separate burgh, was granted its charter in 1489, though it never achieved the status of being a royal burgh.

ABERDEEN

Aberdeen Harbour

Aberdeen is Scotland's third largest city. It sits at he mouth of two rivers - the Dee and the Don, and indeed the name Aberdeen means "at the mouth of the Dee and Don". It is known as the Granite City, as most of its old buildings are made of this local building stone. This has made it a stylish and attractive place, as the stone seems to sparkle in the sunshine. It is certainly Scotland's most prosperous city, on account of the North Sea oil fields, which have attracted workers from all over the world. Its docks and harbours, where there were once fishing boats, is now full of ships servicing the oil rigs out in the North Sea.

But it is also a centre of learning, administration, shopping and culture. It does not have the industrial landscapes that have marred many of Scotland's industrial areas, yet it still manages to earn huge amounts of money from the world's most important industry - oil. It has an enviable quality of life, and while it may be far to the north of Glasgow and Edinburgh, it still enjoys a relatively

mild, and certainly drier, climate than the West Central Scotland, thanks to the mountains that protect it. It is an ancient city, having been made a royal burgh in 1175, and even then it was a busy port, trading with the Baltic ports and increasing its wealth even then. It was sacked three times by the English during the Wars of Independence, and in 1337 Edward III finally managed to raze it to the ground. But for all that, it grew again, with Aberdeen University being founded in 1494.

There are two Aberdeens - the original one, and another, called perversely Old Aberdeen. Both were separate burghs at one time, with their own magistrates, baillies and provost. Now they have joined together to form the city as we know it today. Old Aberdeen, however, still exists as a well defined district, and it is here you will find **St. Machar's Cathedral**. It was founded in about 1131 and dedicated to a saint who was one of St. Columba's companions. Legend says that St. Machar came to the area and was commanded by God to build a monastery and a church at a point where a river bends in the shape of a bishop's

River Dee Suspension Bridge, Aberdeen

crozier close to where it enters the sea. He eventually found what he was looking for on the banks of the Don, and established his religious settlement there. Gradually it grew in importance, until in the 12th century the diocese of Aberdeen was formed, and the site of the monastery was chosen for its cathedral. The present church dates from the 14th century and later, and though it is substantial, it is only the nave and the two west towers that have survived. They were built by Bishop Gavin Dunbar, who was also responsible for the magnificent heraldic ceiling.

William Elphinstone, Lord High Chancellor of Scotland, was its bishop between 1488 and 1514. He printed the first book of liturgy in Scotland, called the Aberdeen Breviary, and indeed introduced printing into the country. He also founded Aberdeen University in 1494. **King's College Chape**l, part of this original university, was built in 1505, and a monument to Elphinstone can be found in the quadrangle in front of it. The chapel's distinctive crown steeple was built in honour of James VI in the early 17th century, and when it was blown down in a great storm in 1633 people blamed witchcraft. The King's

College Centre explains the college's history.

In 1593 another college was founded - **Marischal College**. The man behind it was George Keith, Earl Marischal of Scotland, and to begin with it was a separate university. Therefore the city had two universities, the same number as the whole of England at the time. The present Marischal College buildings date from the 19th century. In 1860 the two colleges merged to form Aberdeen University. The Marischal College Museum has a collection of classical and Egyptian artifacts, as well as collections of local interest.

The **Brig o' Balgownie** over the Don, close to St. Machar's, dates from the 14th century, and has a fine single arch. To the south of the city is the **Bridge of Dee**, built in the early 1500s by Bishop Dunbar. At Bridge of Don is **Glover House**, where a a very unusual Scotsman, Thomas Blake Glover, lived. He was born in Fraserburgh in 1838, and went to Japan 19 years later. Japanese society was still feudal in those days, but Glover managed to sell Scottish-built warships and arms to Japanese rebels who were fighting a civil war. He was also sending young Japanese men to Britain to be educated at university, and soon earned the nickname the "Scottish Samurai". He helped found the Mitsubishi shipyards, which set Japan on its way to being a manufacturing nation, and also helped found the famous Kirin Brewery. To this day his picture adorns Kirin labels. For a short while he had an affair with a Japanese woman, and when Puccini came across a short story based on the affair, he embroidered it and wrote the opera *Madam Butterfly*.

Seaton Park, Aberdeen

Aberdeen's main parish church is the grandiose **Church of St. Nicholas,** which stands in St. Nicholas Street. After the Reformation it was too big for reformed services, so was divided into two churches, called the East Church and the West Church. These were reunited in the late 18th and early 19th centuries, when the church was largely rebuilt. Of the original medieval church only the transepts and the crypt now survive. It has a carillon of 48 bells, the largest in Britain.

Union Street is the city's main street. It is over a mile long, and is full of shops, most of them nowadays branches of chain stores. It was laid out in the early 1800s to celebrate the union of Britain and Ireland. At one end, in Castle Street, is the 17th century Merkat Cross, standing close to where the city's castle once stood. **Provost Skene's House** near St. Nicholas Church dates from the 16th century. It is named after a former Lord Provost, and has painted ceilings and period furniture. **Provost Ross' House** is on Ship Row, the oldest street in Aberdeen still in use. It was built in 1593,

and named after its most prominent owner, John Ross, who was Lord Provost in the 18th century. It is now the **Aberdeen Maritime Museum**, with displays and exhibits on Aberdeen's seafaring history. It even has a simulation of a helicopter ride out to an offshore drilling platform.

At Schoolhill is the **Aberdeen Art Gallery and Museum**, which has paintings and sculpture by Reynolds, Degas and Epstein. In the museum section there are exhibits and displays about Aberdeen's history. The museum incorporates James Dun's House, which was built in the 18th century. The **Planetarium** at Aberdeen College shows the stars as they "move" through the heavens. They are projected onto an overhead dome. Military history is dealt with at the **Gordon Highlanders Museum** (see panel below) on Viewfield Road. This famous regiment, which Sir Winston Churchill called "the finest regiment in the world", was amalgamated with the Queen's Own Highlanders in September 1994 to form a new regiment called The Highlanders.

GORDON HIGHLANDERS MUSEUM

St Lukes, Viewfield Road, Aberdeen AB15 7XH
Tel: 01224 311200 Fax: 01224 319323
e-mail: museum@gordonhighlanders.com
website: www.gordonhighlanders.com

The story of The Gordon Highlanders spans 200 years of world history and is packed with tales of courage and tenacity on the field of battle. At the museum you can re-live the compelling and dramatic story of one of the British Army's most famous regiments, through the lives of its outstanding personalities and of the soldiers of the North East of Scotland who filled its ranks.

The spectacular exhibition includes a unique collection of the finest of the regiments treasures, including a remarkable display of Victoria Crosses; strikingly detailed life size and scale reproductions of some of the Regiment's finest moments in battle; state of the art touch screens to let you explore the deeds and values that made the Regiment great, and stunning film presentations which convey the story of the "Gordons".

A stroll in the delightful museum gardens can be rounded off with light refreshments in The Duchess Jean Tea Room. A range of souvenirs are available at The Gordon Gift Shop. Open April to October, Tuesday to Saturday 10.30am-4.30pm and Sunday 1.30pm-4.30pm.

South Pier Lighthouse, Aberdeen

Aberdeen is a city built of granite. And the city developers of old didn't have to look far for the building material. At one time over 100 granite quarries were located in and around the city. **Rubislaw Quarry**, near the Queen's Own Highlanders Museum, was one of the largest. It was still being worked up until 1971, when it had reached a depth of 480 feet. Now it has been partially filled with water and fenced off. However, some of it can still be seen from Queen's Road.

Footdee (or "Fittie" as it is known by Aberdonians) sits on the north bank of the Dee, and it is where the city's original fishing community lived. Their small cottages have all been smartened up, and it is a desirable place to live.

On the outskirts of the city, on the B9077 road that follows the Dee, is the **Blairs Museum**. Up until 1986 a Catholic seminary was located here, training young men for the priesthood. Now the museum holds the Scottish Catholic Heritage Collection, and you can see objects associated with Bonnie Prince Charlie, his Jacobite followers and Mary Stuart. There are also

rich vestments, communion vessels and paintings.

AROUND ABERDEEN

STONEHAVEN

15 miles S of Aberdeen off the A90

Near the town's harbour stands the town's 18th century Mercat Cross. From the **Steeple**, close by, James VII of Scotland and II of England was declared king in 1715. The oldest building in the town is the Tolbooth, which dates from the 16th century. It stands beside the picturesque harbour, and was used for a time as a storehouse by the Earl Marischal of Scotland, George Keith. Within it is now the Tolbooth Museum, where you can find out about the history of Stonehaven, including its fishing fleet.

The traditional **Fireball Festival** is held every Hogmanay in the "Auld Toon" area of the town, near the harbour. At midnight, men march along the streets swinging wire mesh balls stuffed with burning rags, wood and coal. It dates from pre-Christian times, and the light from the fireballs was

Stonehaven Harbour

supposed to attract the light of the sun, ensuring that it would return after the dark days of winter.

Dunnottar Castle stands on a promontory two miles south of Stonehaven, protected on three sides by steep cliffs and on the fourth by St. Ninian's Den, a deep ravine. It was originally built in the 13th century, though the ruins you see now are later. During the Wars of Independence it was held by the English, and in 1297 William Wallace set it alight, burning to death every English soldier within it. During the English Commonwealth, Scotland's crown jewels (called the"Honours of Scotland") were hidden in the castle. When Cromwell's troops laid siege to the place in 1652, they were smuggled out by the wife of the minister at Kinneff, six miles south, and hidden in the church.

Dunnottar Castle

LAIRHILLOCK INN & CRYNOCH RESTAURANT

Netherley, by Stonehaven, Kincardineshire AB39 3QS
Tel: 0800 074 1095 Fax: 01569 731175
e-mail:lairhillock@breathemail.net
website: www.lairhillock.co.uk

"Quality is everything" is the motto of the **Lairhillock Inn and Crynoch Restaurant**, which is set in beautiful Deeside, just 15 minutes drive from Aberdeen. It is no idle boast, as this former coaching inn, which dates back 200 years, has a cosy snug bar, a lounge and conservatory, the Crynoch Restaurant and the Ostlers function suite. Wherever you dine in the Lairhillock, you will be greeted warmly and served appreciatively. The inn's real ales and real fires are renowned in the area, and the Crynoch Restaurant has been voted "No 1 in the North East of Scotland". It is featured in 11 good food guides, and dishes are based on fresh local produce such as Aberdeen Angus beef, Scottish lamb and fish and shellfish from the North Sea.

In 2001/2002 the inn itself was awarded the coveted "Independent Pub Caterer of the Year" award for Scotland, and the owner Roger Thorne strives to maintain high standards of quality and service coupled with good value for money. The lunches and dinners served here, and in the conservatory are prepared with the same care and expertise as the ones served in the Crynoch, and the menu is both innovative and imaginative. The Ostlers is a tastefully decorated and furnished function suite that once formed the inn's barn and stables. Here you can hold a private celebration, or business function secure in the knowledge that the food and service is second to none.

INVERBERVIE

22 miles S of Aberdeen on the A92

This small village is, in fact, a royal burgh, which shows that at one time it was an important place. David II was shipwrecked off the coast when he was returning from exile in France, and was "kindly received" by the inhabitants of the village. In gratitude, in 1341, he granted it a royal charter. This was no empty gesture - it allowed the village certain lucrative privileges. It could hold a market and charge for the buying and selling of produce, for instance, and being a king's burgh, was not answerable to local landowners. John Coutts, whose son Thomas Coutts founded the famous London bank, was born here in 1699. **Hallgreen Castle** (not open to the public) was built by the Dunnets in the 14th century.

The **Hercules Linton Memorial and Garden** was opened in 1997. Hercules was born in Inverbervie in 1837, and designed the *Cutty Sark* tea clipper, which was built in 1869 at Dumbarton.

KINNEFF

19 miles S of Aberdeen on the A92

In 1651 the Scottish crown jewels were used at the coronation of Charles II at Scone. They were then hidden in Dunnottar Castle to keep them safe from Cromwell's Parliamentarian troops, but when the secret leaked out they were smuggled out by the wife of the minister at Kinneff, six miles to the south. There the minister, the Rev'd James Grainger, hid them under the floor of **Kinneff Parish Church**. Every three months they were secretly dug up and placed before a fire in an attempt to keep them in good condition. At the Restoration in 1660 they were taken to Edinburgh Castle. Though the church is no longer used for worship, it can still be visited.

ARBUTHNOTT

19 miles S of Aberdeen on the B967

In the kirkyard of Arbuthnott Church lie the ashes of Lewis Grassic Gibbon, the Scottish novelist. His real name was James Leslie Mitchell, and he was born in Aberdeenshire in 1901. When he was seven years old, he moved to Kincardineshire, and lived close to Arbuthnott. In 1929 he decided to become a professional writer, and with his wife Rebecca moved to Welwyn Garden City near London. There he wrote the trilogy *A Scot's Quair*, set in the North East of Scotland. The three books are dark and brooding, painting a picture of rural life that was miles away from the happy, idyllic books on country life in Scotland written by writers who belonged to the "kailyard" school. The **Lewis Grassic Gibbon Centre** in the village was opened in 1991, and celebrates the life of one of Scotland's most talented writers.

Arbuthnott Church dates from the 13th century onwards, and was, before the Reformation, collegiate, i.e. served by a college of priests. In 1491 one of the priests, James Sibbald, wrote what became known as the **Arbuthnott Breviary**, which set out the form of service to be used within the church. It can now be seen in the museum at Paisley, outside Glasgow.

MARYCULTER

7 miles SW of Aberdeen on the B9077

The Knights Templar, an order of monastic monks which was suppressed in 1312 by Pope Clement V, owned lands at Maryculter, and established a preceptory and church here. In 1319 the last preceptor of the monastery, William de Middleton "of the tempill house of Culther" was tried at Edinburgh by the church authorities. Maryculter sits on the south bank of the Dee, in Kincardineshire, and when a church was erected on the north bank, in Aberdeenshire, the surrounding parish became known as Peterculter.

Drum Castle (National Trust for Scotland) sits four miles west of the village. The tower house is one of the oldest in Scotland, and was the work of Richard Cementarius, first Provost of Aberdeen. Robert I later gave it to the Irwyn family, and for 653 years it was owned by this family, which over the years changed its name to Irvine. In 1619 it was enlarged by the addition of a grand Jacobean mansion. The grounds contain the **Old Wood of Drum**, a woodland of ancient oak. There is also a walled garden and walks within the grounds.

FETTERCAIRN

27 miles SW of Aberdeen on the B974

This village sits on the western edge of that fertile expanse of land known as the Howe of the Mearns. At its heart is the **Kincardine Cross**, which once stood in the township of Kincardine, which gave Kincardineshire its name.

The **Fettercairn Arch** commemorates a visit to Fettercairn by Queen Victoria and Prince Albert in 1861. The B974 winds north from Fettercairn and enters **Glen Dye** before reaching Strachan and eventually Banchory. It's a wonderful run in the summer months, with many fine views.

A mile north of the town, off the B974 is **Fasque**, where William Gladstone the 19th century prime minister, had his home. It is open during the summer months.

GARLOGIE

10 miles W of Aberdeen on the B9119

The **Garlogie Power Mill** has the only beam engine to have survived intact in its original location in Scotland. The mill made woollens, and is now open to the public, with displays about its history.

BANCHORY

17 miles W of Aberdeen on the A93

As befits a town which is known as the "Gateway to Royal Deeside", the **Banchory Museum** in Bridge Street has a collection or royal commemorative china, as well as displays on tartans and the natural history of the area. A further display celebrates the life of Banchory's most famous son, **J. Scott Skinner**, the musician and composer known as the"Strathspey King". He was born here in 1843.

Three miles east of the town is **Crathes Castle** (National Trust for Scotland - see panel on page 341). It was built by the Burnetts of Ley after Robert I had granted them the Lands of Ley in 1323,

CONTINENTAL CREAM

14 Dee Street, Banchory, Kincardineshire AB31 5ST
Tel: 01330 825733

If it's high quality confectionery of distinction you're after when visiting Royal Deeside, then **Continental Cream** is the shop for you. Sweets from all over the world is stocked here, with hand-made Belgian and Scottish chocolates being the shop's speciality, as well as boxed sweets, chocolate, candy bars and superb toffees. Delicious Mackie's ice cream is also sold - just right to cool you down after a hectic time sightseeing in one of the most historic areas in the country. Why not call in and see for yourself the wide range of quality confectionery on offer?

INVERGLEN GIFTS

20 Dee Street, Banchory, Aberdeenshire AB31 5ST
Tel/Fax: 01330 820222

We all like to browse before we buy a gift or souvenir to take home from holiday and if you are exploring beautiful Royal Deeside, with its stunning scenery, then one of the best places to go is **Inverglen Gifts**, right in the heart of Banchory. It is owned and managed by Ellie Rattenbury, who takes a great pride in the quality of the many gifts she sells. Her background is in design education, so you know that everything on offer has been carefully chosen by someone with an eye for good design and value for money. The shelves and display areas in the spacious, colourful shop are crammed with eye-catching goods, any one of which would make the perfect gift.

There is one off designer jewellery, stained glass wall hangings and candle holders, small sculptures, Scottish toiletries, local craft products, pottery, prints of local scenes, greetings cards, wrapping paper, silk scarves, decorative and scented candles, Scottish preserves, and much more. It is the sort of place where you will want to browse and take your time, and Ellie is always on hand to offer friendly, knowledgeable advice. Nearly everything in the shop has been made in Scotland, so you know you will be buying a gift that is both stylish and appropriate. Royal Deeside is one of the most beautiful areas in the Highlands, and is full of history and heritage. When you visit, make sure you stop at Banchory (there is plenty of parking nearby) and call in at Inverglen Gifts.

BANCHORY LODGE HOTEL

Banchory, Kincardineshire AB31 5HS
Tel: 01330 822625 e-mail: enquiries@banchorylodge.co.uk
Fax: 01330 825107 website: www.banchorylodge.co.uk

Set amid the glorious scenery and heritage of Royal Deeside, the **Banchory Lodge Hotel** is Scottish hospitality at its very best. Originally built in the 16th century as a coaching inn, it now blends this sense of continuity with high standards of service and value for money. There is ample scope for sport here (including angling, as the River Dee passes through the grounds of the hotel) as well as for just taking it easy in beautiful surroundings. The cuisine is superb, and the 22 bedrooms (which are all en suite) are comfortable yet elegant.

though the present castle dates from the 16th century. The **Horn of Ley** hangs in the Great Hall, and was presented to Robert I by the Burnetts when he gave the family the land. Six nature trails are laid out within the grounds, and there is a walled garden with a herbaceous border and topiary dating from 1702.

KINCARDINE O'NEILL

23 miles W of Aberdeen on the A93

This village with the Irish sounding name claims to be the oldest on Deeside.

And though it is no larger than a village, it is in fact a small burgh which was granted its charter in 1511. In 1220 the first bridge across the Dee beyond Aberdeen was built here, so it became an important settlement. The ruins of **St. Mary's Kirk** date from the 14th century, and it may have been built as the chapel of a small medieval hospital that stood here before the Reformation. Up until 1733 it was thatched (which wasn't unusual in those days), but in that year it is said that someone shot at a pigeon perched on the thatch, and it caught fire. The **Old Smiddy Centre** explains about the workings of a blacksmith's workshop, and has a display about the area's history.

ALFORD

23 miles W of Aberdeen on the A944

Alford sits in a fertile area called the Howe of Alford. The **Alford Valley Railway and Railroad Museum** is at Haughton House, where there is a two mile long narrow gauge passenger railway with steam and diesel engines. It runs between April and September.

The **Grampian Transport Museum** sits close to the golf course, and there are working exhibits explaining the history of transport in the area. Four miles south of the village is one of the area's finest castles, **Craigievar Castle**. It looks exactly like a castle from a fairy tale, with its pepper pot turrets and towers. It was built in about 1626 by William Forbes, a rich Aberdeen merchant. He was also known as "Danziger Willie", because of his many trading links with Baltic ports. It has a fine collection of 17th and 18th century furniture, as well as family portraits.

CRATHES CASTLE AND GARDENS

Banchory, Aberdeenshire AB31 5QJ
Castle: Tel: 01330 844525
Fax: 01330 844797
Ranger service: Tel: 01330 844651
e-mail crathes@nts.org.uk
website: www.nts.org.uk

King Robert the Bruce granted the lands of Leys to the Burnett family in 1323: the ancient Horn of Leys, which can be seen today in the Great Hall, marks his gift. The castle, built in the second half of the 16th century, is a superb example of a tower house of the period. Some of the rooms retain their original painted ceilings and collections of family portraits and furniture.

A visit is enhanced by the 1.5 hectares (3.75 acres) of walled garden, which incorporates herbaceous borders and many unusual plants, providing a wonderful display at all times of the year. The great yew hedges, fascinating examples of the art of topiary, date from as early as 1702. Explore the estate on the seven waymarked trails (including one suitable for wheelchairs) that lead through the mixed woodlands, along the Coy Bum and past the millpond. In the Visitor Centre a new exhibition, *A Walk on the Wild Side*, explores the wildlife on the Crathes Estate.

ABOYNE

27 miles W of Aberdeen off the A93

Every year, in this small Royal Deeside town, the **Aboyne Highland Games** are held in late summer. The town prospered after the railways came to Deeside in the 19th century, and it soon became a small resort. There is a lovely, but in some places difficult, walk up **Glen Tanar** two miles west of Aboyne. Five miles north is the **Culsh Earth House**, which is at least 2,000 years old. It is a long, dog legged

THE SIGN OF THE BLACK FACED SHEEP

Ballatar Old Road, Aboyne, Aberdeenshire AB34 5HJ
Tel: 01339 887311 Fax: 01339 887301
e-mail: blackfacedsheep@talk21.com

One of the best known shops in Aboyne is **The Sign Of The Black Faced Sheep**, a name you won't forget in a hurry. Nor will you forget the wonderful service and value for money in the gift and tea room. Much of the merchandise is made in Scotland, so it is the perfect place to pick up those souvenirs of your holiday. The food is outstanding, and includes freshly baked rolls, platters of smoked salmon, venison and roast beef. You just can't go wrong at The Sign Of The Black Faced Sheep.

SPECIALITY SHOWCASE

Ballogie Shop, Ballogie, Aboyne,
Aberdeenshire AB34 5DP
(B976 South Deeside Rd - between Banchory and Aboyne)
Tel/Fax: 01339 886104 website: www. butterworthpaintings.co.uk

The **Speciality Showcase** in Aboyne is managed by Sarah Harker, daughter of renowned artist Howard Butterworth, who paints the exquisite landscapes of the area. Here, in this converted post office and village shop, you will find his lovely paintings on sale, plus cards and prints based on them. Also on sale are genuine Black Forest cuckoo clocks and a select range of quality Scottish gifts. This is a place you cannot afford to miss if you're touring Royal Deeside.

BARCLAY'S OF BALLATER

24 Bridge Street, Ballater, Aberdeenshire AB35 5QP
Tel: 01339 755521
Email: barclayballater@aol.com
Website: www.barclaysofballater.co.uk

From table lamps to teddy bears, prints to place mats, **Barclay's of Ballater** has got it all. This lovely shop is an Aladdin's cave of items that make the ideal souvenir of your holiday on Royal Deeside. There's Moorcroft , Spode, and Royal Crown Derby pottery as well as cards, candlesticks and solid oak furniture that speaks of craftsmanship and tradition. But be warned - once you enter this fascinating shop, you won't want to leave.

THE MCEWAN GALLERY

Ballater, Royal Deeside, Aberdeenshire AB35 5UB
Tel: 01339 755429   e-mail: art@mcewangallery.com
Fax: 01339 755995 website: www.mcewangallery.com

The **McEwan Gallery** was established over 40 years ago, and specialises in fine Scottish paintings of the 17th to the 20th centuries and Dutch and English paintings of the 19th and 20th centuries. Here you can browse at your leisure and view wonderful pictures that speak of artistry and craftsmanship. The gallery is owned by Dorothy and Peter McEwan, who are more than willing to offer help and advice. Peter is the author of the definitive *Dictionary of Scottish Art and Architecture*. There is also a wide range of old sporting books, especially those to do with golf.

underground tunnel which was probably not a dwelling but a store house. A torch is recommended when exploring it.

BALLATER

34 miles W of Aberdeen on the A93

Ballater is a small village surrounded by the birch and pine woodland of Royal Deeside. It is not an old settlement, having been founded just before the railways came to the area. The Deeside line from Aberdeen stopped here, about seven miles short of Balmoral Castle. Prince Albert, while not averse to using the railway line to get to Balmoral, objected to it going any further, as it might upset the tranquillity of Queen Victoria's Highland retreat.

Royal Deeside has some good country drives, and one of he best is along **Glen Muick**, to the south of the village. A narrow, unmarked road takes you as far as the small village of Spittal of Glenmuick, though the road is inclined to get busy in the summer months. You can leave your car in the car park there, and walk the short distance to **Loch Muick**, or you can head off into the hills. To the west of the loch is **Lochnagar**, which, despite its name, is not a loch but a mountain. It is one of Scotland's Munros, and rises to a height of 3,786 feet. Prince Charles once had a story published called *The Old Man of Lochnagar*.

As you drive out of Ballater towards Glen Muick, you pass **Birkhall** (not open to the public). It was bought by Edward VII before he became king.

BALMORAL

42 miles W of Aberdeen on the A93

When Queen Victoria fell in love with Scotland, she and her husband Prince Albert looked at many properties which could be converted into a holiday home. In 1852 Prince Albert bought Balmoral, as the queen had visited Deeside four years earlier and fallen in love with it.

The castle as you see it today dates from that time, though it has been the site of a castle for centuries. The first recorded reference to it is in 1484, when it was called "Bouchmorale". The grounds stay open all year, closing only when the Royal Family is in residence. Close to the castle is **Crathes Church**, where the Royal Family worships. A church has stood here since the 14th century, and its ruins can be seen in the kirkyard of the present church, which dates from 1855. Within the kirkyard is the grave of **John Brown**, Queen Victoria's ghillie, whom people claim had an affair with the widowed queen. The **Royal Lochnagar Distillery** stands near the church, and has a visitors centre. It was given a Royal warrant in 1864 by Queen Victoria. A **Victorian Heritage Trail**, which traces Queen Victoria's footsteps

Balmoral

through the entire area, has been laid out. A leaflet is available from most tourist offices.

BRAEMAR

50 miles W of Aberdeen on the A93

Braemar sits high in the Cairngorms at an altitude of 1,100 feet, and is supposed to be Britains's coldest place. Between 1941 and 1970 its average temperature was only 6.4 degrees Celsius, and on two occasions, in 1895 and 1982, it experienced temperatures of minus 28.2 degrees Celsius, the lowest temperatures ever officially recorded in Britain. For all that, in the winter of 2003 it also recorded temperatures of

The River Dee, Braemar

about 18 degrees Celsius, which had people walking about in short-sleeved shirts. A week later, however, the weather returned to normal and it snowed.

The **Braemar Highland Games** is held annually in September, with the Royal Family in attendance. **Braemar Castle** is the ancestral seat of the Farquharsons (pronounced "Far-kwarsons") of Invercauld, and was built in 1628 by the Earl of Mar on the site of an earlier castle. It was used as a base by Government troops during the Jacobite Uprising. It contains the world's largest example of a semi-precious stone called a Cairngorm, weighing in at 52 pounds.

The **Mar Lodge Estate** (National Trust for Scotland) is five miles west of Braemar on a minor road. It extends to 72,598 acres, and has been described as the most important nature conservation landscape in Britain. It opens daily, and the Lodge itself is occasionally open to the public as well.

Braemar Highland Games

To the south of Braemar is **Glenshee**,

one of Scotland's most popular winter sports areas. The snowfields stretch over three valleys and four Munros, with 25 miles of marked pistes as well as off-piste skiing.

INVERURIE
14 miles NW of Aberdeen off he A96

Inverurie is a large royal burgh sitting on the river Don. It's name, according to legend, comes from an incident when the Romans were advancing into the area. One soldier, when he first saw the settlement, exclaimed "urbe in rure!", meaning "a city in the countryside!". It's an extremely unlikely tale, though the town later incorporated the words into its coat-of-arms.

Mar Lodge Estate, Braemar

Mary Stuart visited the town in 1562, and stayed in the now gone royal castle which stood on the mound known as the **Bass**. In 1411 the **Battle of Harelaw** was fought nearby. Donald, Lord of the Isles, led a force of Highlanders against a

LETHENTY MILL

Inverurie, Aberdeenshire AB51 0HQ
Tel: 01467 622489 Fax: 01467 629631
e-mail: info@lethentymill.com
website: www.info@lethenty-mill.com
 and www.woodshop.co.uk

Set in the beautiful Aberdeenshire countryside, **Lethenty Mill** is a traditionally run, family owned business that specialises in high quality hardwood furniture, fitted kitchens and other items. It is owned and managed by Allan Fyfe who in 1977, decided to pursue his dream making and restoring furniture.

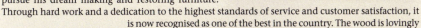

Through hard work and a dedication to the highest standards of service and customer satisfaction, it is now recognised as one of the best in the country. The wood is lovingly cut, shaped and assembled in the workshops on the premises.

All of Lethenty Mill's products are special, and unlike anything you'll find in a DIY showroom of furniture store. This is craftsmanship of the highest standard, and Allan prides himself on his in-depth knowledge of what wood can do, and how it can be used to make something that is both practical and beautiful. He also tutors on cabinet making, and his courses on hardwoods and how to work them are both inspiring and practical. The Letherty Mill showrooms have a wonderful range of fitted kitchens and kitchen furniture, and you will be fascinated by the styles on display. On display are examples of furniture designs, some new, some old based on the local vernacular which can be purchased in kit form as part of a home study course. The mill is open Monday to Friday from 9 am to 5 pm, and on Saturdays 10 am to 5 pm, or by appointment.

TORRYBURN HOTEL

School Road, Kintore,
Aberdeenshire AB51 0XP
Tel: 01467 632269 Fax: 01407 632271
website: www.guesthousesonline.co.uk

The **Torryburn Hotel** is an immaculate, well patronised hotel situated in three acres of ground on the edge of Kintore, a historic royal burgh which can trace its history back to the 13th century, when it was granted its royal charter by King William the Lion. It is an elegant, Georgian building of local granite that has been converted into an extremely comfortable and popular hotel that boasts three stars from Visit Scotland. It has 12 extremely comfortable fully en suite rooms, all sumptuously furnished and decorated to a high standard, and all having tea and coffee making facilities, colour TV, direct dial telephone, trouser press and a range of toiletries. The rest of the hotel is equally as sumptuous, with leather

Chesterfields in the lounge, deep piled carpets and prints on the walls. In the lounge, with its open fire, you can relax and read your paper.

The food, as you would expect from such an establishment, is outstanding, and the menu boasts a range of imaginative and beautifully prepared dishes that use only the finest and freshest of local produce wherever possible. Why not start with a bowl of Cullen skink - a traditional Scottish fish soup made from smoked haddock, potatoes, onions and cream? It will set you up for your main course, which could be roast beef with Yorkshire pudding, oven baked breast of chicken stuffed with haggis and served with a mushroom, shallot and whisky cream sauce, or even a deep fried fillet of haddock served with the best and crispest chips in the area. And to finish you could have the ever-popular sticky toffee pudding, the hotel's own Torryburn trifle, or a dairy ice with toffee sauce? There is a select wine list, and you are sure to find something that will complement your meal. After your coffee, head for the lounge for a single malt from the wide choice on offer. The hotel is open to non residents, who can enjoy a drink in the lounge, or have a meal in the 30 seat Conservatory Restaurant and Poppies Coffee Shop.

There is so much to do in the area. The hotel has the fishing rights for a length of the River Don, which runs nearby. There are also several challenging golf courses in the area, as well as good walking countryside, birdwatching and many historical attractions and gardens to visit. It is only 12 miles from the lively city of Aberdeen, so great restaurants, night clubs, cinemas and theatres are all within half an hour. The Torryburn Hotel is also the ideal base from which to explore two of the North East of Scotland's best known and most fascinating tourist attractions - the Castles Trail, which takes you to some grand houses and castles, and offers a marvellous insight into how the great and good of the

area lived all these years ago - and the Whisky Trail, which takes you to some of the best known distilleries in Scotland where you can see how Scotland's greatest export is made, and possibly sample a few drams.

The hotel is owned and managed by Alex Cunningham, who is proud of the high standards he has set. The staff will always be pleased to offer advice on where to go in the area, and Alex himself is keen to welcome you to one of the finest hotels in Aberdeenshire.

Lowland army, and while the outcome was indecisive, it helped secure the supremacy of the Lowlands over the Highlands for a while. A monument now marks the spot.

In 1805 work began on digging the **Aberdeenshire Canal** between Inverurie and Aberdeen. Never a financial success, it was sold to the Great North of Scotland Railway who drained it and used part of the route to build a railway line. **Port Elphinstone**, to the south east of the town, recalls the canal, and part of it can still be seen there today. It was the only canal in Britain that closed every winter due to it freezing over. To the west of the town is **Bennachie**, a hill that has been called "Aberdeenshire's Mount Fuji". Though not particularly high (1,600 feet), it gained some fame through the song *The Back o' Bennachie*. The **Bennachie Visitor Centre** at Chapel of Garrion explains the social and natural history of the hill.

Castle Fraser (National Trust or Scotland) sits six miles south of the town. It was built by Michael Fraser, with work starting on it in 1575, though it wasn't completed until 1632.

KINTORE

10 miles NW of Aberdeen off the A96

This small royal burgh, which is no bigger than a village, was granted royal burgh status in the 13th century by William the Lion of Scotland. The **Parish Church** dates from 1819, and it has some masonry from the sacrament house of the medieval Kirk of Kinkell incorporated into the west staircase. The **Kintore Tolbooth** dates from 1740.

MONYMUSK

17 miles NW of Aberdeen off the B993

The **Parish Church of St. Mary** is one of the finest medieval parish churches in Scotland. It was built in the early years of

the 12th century, and sensitively restored in 1929. The **Monymusk Reliquary**, a small 8th century wooden box covered in bronze and silver at one time contained a bone of St. Columba, and was paraded in front of Robert I's troops before the Battle of Bannockburn in 1314. It was kept in the priory church at Monymusk, but is now in the Museum of Scotland.

OYNE

21 miles NW of Aberdeen on the B9002

The **Archaeolink Pre-History Park** tells the story of archaeology in Aberdeenshire, where over 700 ancient sites have so far been identified, from old Pictish carvings to stone circles and cairns. It's aim is to bridge he gap between ancient history and modern times by way of interactive exhibits and displays.

FYVIE

23 miles NW of Aberdeen off the A947

Fyvie Castle (National Trust for Scotland - see panel on page 348) was once a royal

Fyvie Castle

stronghold, one of a chain of such fortresses throughout Scotland. The oldest part dates from the 13th century, and over the years five successive families have created what is probably the finest example of baronial architecture in Scotland. Legend states that these five families - Preston, Meldrum, Seton, Gordon and Leith - were each responsible for one of the castle's five towers. Panelling and plasterwork dating from the 17th century can be seen in the Morning Room, and there is a fine collection of paintings by Raeburn, Romney, Gainsborough and so on.

Huntly

33 miles NW of Aberdeen on the A96

Huntly is a small, historic town that sits in that area of Aberdeenshire called Strathbogie. It is dominated by the ruins of **Huntly Castle** (Historic Scotland), an

old Gordon stronghold dating originally from the 12th century. The Gordons were a powerful Borders family from around the village of Gordon. They moved north in the 14th century and settled in the Huntly area, where they soon became one of its most powerful families. In the 16th century George, the 4th Earl of Huntly, rebuilt the castle in grand style, though James VI later demolished it once more when the 6th Earl rebelled against the king in 1594.

The 6th Earl found favour with James VI again, and became a marquis in 1599. He rebuilt the castle over the next few years, and the ruins we see today date from that rebuilding. The castle fell into decay in the 18th century, but even now you can see that it was not just a fortress, but an elegant and stately home where people like Mary Stuart and Perkin Warbeck, pretender to the English throne

Fyvie Castle

Fyvie, Turriff, Aberdeenshire, AB53 8JS
Tel: 01651 891266
Fax: 01651 891107
Ranger service: Tel: 01330 844651
website: www.nts.org.uk

Fyvie was once a royal stronghold, one of a chain of fortresses throughout medieval Scotland. From 1390, following the Battle of Otterburn, five successive families created probably the finest example of Scottish Baronial architecture. An old tradition claims that these families

Preston, Meldrum, Seton, Gordon and Leith each built one of Fyvie's five towers. An air of mystery is

created by the ghosts and legends associated with this castle. The oldest part dates from the 13th century, and within its ancient walls is a great wheel stair, the finest in Scotland. Contemporary panelling and plaster ceilings survive in the 17th century Morning Room and the opulence of the Edwardian era is reflected in the interiors created by the first Lord Leith of Fyvie. A rich portrait collection includes works by Batoni, Raeburn, Romney, Gainsborough, Opie and Hopprier, and there is a fine collection of arms and armour, and 17th century tapestries.

The grounds and loch were designed as landscaped parkland in the early 19th century. The 18th century walled garden, has been redeveloped as a celebration of Scottish fruits and vegetables. Visitors can also enjoy the restored racquets court, ice house, bird hide, restored earth closet and beautiful lochside walks.

of Henry VII of England, were once entertained.

In the town square is the **Brander Museum**, where there are displays and artifacts covering local history, arms and armour, and the life of local author George MacDonald, who died in 1905. He mainly wrote stories about fairies and fantasy which had a strong religious message.

RHYNIE

33 miles W of Aberdeen on the A914

Rhynie is a small agricultural village mainly visited for the **Anderson Bey Museum**. George Anderson was a major in the Seaforth Highlanders who later became a colonel in the Egyptian army. There are photographs, mementos and documents relating to his life.

KENNETHMONT

31 miles W of Aberdeen on the B9002

Just outside the village is **Leith Hall** (National Trust for Scotland), home of the Leith (and later Leith-Hay) family from 1650 onwards. They had a tradition of military service and the exhibition "For Crown and Country: the Military Lairds of Leith Hall" has memorabilia relating to the lives of the many family members who served in the army. The most famous laird of them all, Andrew Hay, was a Jacobite, and fought for Charles Edward Stuart at Culloden. After the battle he became a fugitive, though, being over seven feet tall, he found hiding difficult. In the exhibition you can see his hose, which measure three feet from knee to heel.

There is also a six-acre garden with herbaceous borders and a collection of Alpines and primulas. A Chinese moon gate sits at the top of the garden, and from it there are good views of the surrounding hills.

ELLON

15 miles N of Aberdeen on the A948

Ellon is a small town sitting on the River Ythan, in that area known as the Formartine. Though over four miles from the sea, it was once a small, thriving port with a steamer that took people up and down the river.

The **Formartine Way** is a walkway based on old railway tracks in the area, and runs from Dyce, just outside Aberdeen, to Fraserburgh on the northern coast. **Pitmedden Garden** (National Trust for Scotland) sits five miles west of the town on the A920. Its central feature is the Great Garden, laid out by Sir Alexander Seton, 1st Baron of Pitmedden, in 1675. It was recreated in the 1950s using elaborate floral designs, with four parterres, three of them being inspired by designs at the Palace of Holyroodhouse in Edinburgh, and the fourth by Sir Alexander's coat of arms. There is also a visitor centre and a **Museum of Farming Life**.

The ruins of **Tolquhon Castle** lie a mile north west of Pitmedden. It was built in the 1580s by William Forbes, 7th Lord Tolquhon, and in 1588 James VI visited it. To commemorate the event, his coat of arms, plus that of the Forbes, were carved over the doorway. At Tarves, two miles north, Forbes and his wife were later buried in an elaborate tomb within the parish church. The church is now gone, but the **Forbes Tomb** still remains.

HADDO HOUSE

17 miles NW of Aberdeen near the B9005

Haddo House (National Trust for Scotland) is undoubtedly the grandest stately home in Aberdeenshire. It was designed by William Adam for the 2nd Earl of Aberdeen in 1732, and then refurbished in the 1880s. It is noted for its fine furniture, paintings and objects d'art. The grounds were landscaped in the 19th century, and the **Kelly Lake** is one of the few natural "lakes" (as opposed to "lochs") in Scotland.

ELGIN

This small town - or should it be city? - is noted for the ruins of **Elgin Cathedral**, one of the most magnificent pre-Reformation churches in Scotland, one which could compare with the great cathedrals of England or Europe. Before local government reorganisation in 1975, it certainly was a city, as it was one of only six places in Scotland that had a Lord Provost as opposed to a Provost, the others being Glasgow, Edinburgh, Dundee, Aberdeen and Perth.

The cathedral was dedicated to the

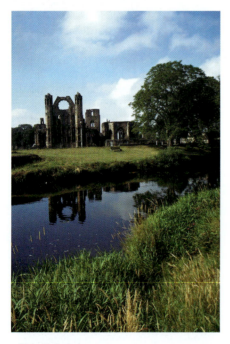

Elgin Cathedral

Holy Trinity, and work started on it in about 1224. There had been three cathedrals within the diocese before this one was built, at Birnie, Spynie and Kinneder. By the end of the 13th century the main work on the cathedral was complete, though 90 years later Alexander Stewart, son of Robert II, set fire to it after he quarrelled with the Bishop of Moray. Repair work on the fabric of the church went on right up until the Reformation. After the Reformation the cathedral fell into disrepair, and it became a quarry for the citizen's of Elgin. But people's perception of the ruins gradually changed, and in 1807 a keeper was appointed to preserve them. The **Panns Port** was the eastern gateway to the cathedral precincts, and it still stands. So too does the the **Old Mills**, in Old Mills Road. It is the last remaining meal mill on the River Lossie, and was founded in the 13th century by the monks of Pluscarden Abbey, six miles south west of Elgin.

St. Giles Parish Church is a graceful building with Doric Columns in the city's main street, giving it the appearance of a Greek temple. It dates from the 1820s, when the old medieval parish church, known as the "Muckle Church of Elgin" was demolished. **Elgin Museum** is in the High Street, and has important collections covering local history, natural history and archeology. **The Moray Motor Museum** is in Bridge Street, and has a small collection of cars and motor bikes. Another place worth visiting is the **Johnston's Cashmere Visitors Centre**, where there are displays about how cashmere is made. There is also a shop. North of the city are the substantial remains of **Spynie Palace** (Historic Scotland), where the bishops of Moray lived. It sits next to the tiny Loch Spynie, and dates mainly from the 14th century.

HOPEMAN LODGE

Hopeman, Elgin, Morayshire IV30 5YA
Tel: 01343 830245
e-mail:mcul@hopemanlodge.co.uk
website: www.hopemanlodge.co.uk

The village of Hopeman sits on the Moray Firth coast, and it is there
you will find **Hopeman Lodge**, sitting in eight acres of land close to
a safe, clean sandy beach. Part of the lodge date back over 200 years,
and it has now been converted into four stunning, all-electric holiday
flats, furnished to a high standard yet retaining a simplicity that
ensures a trouble free holiday. All flats have a living room, bedroom, kitchenette and bathroom, and
all bed linen and towels are provided. Extra foldaway beds and cots are provided at no extra cost.

DUFFUS

4 miles NW of Elgin on the B9012

The ruins of the **Church of St.
Peter** (Historic Scotland) stand
close to the village. Though
mainly built in the 1700s, the
base of the tower is 14th century
and the porch is 16th century.
Opposite the porch is the old **St.
Peter's Cross**, a typical example
of a medieval mercat cross.
Markets were sometimes held in
churchyards in Scotland.

Lossiemouth Beach

Duffus Castle, now in ruins,
was the original seat of the de
Moravia family, which gave its name to
the district. It dates form the 13th
century and later, and has a particularly
fine motte and bailey. **Gordonstoun**, the
private school attended by both Prince
Philip and Prince Charles, is housed in
an 18th century mansion which sits
close to Duffus.

LOSSIEMOUTH

5 miles N of Elgin on the A941

Originally established in the early 18th
century as the port for Elgin,
Lossiemouth is now a small holiday
resort with a fine sandy beach. The
**Lossiemouth Fisheries and Community
Museum** concentrates on the history of
the town and its fishing fleet. There is
also a reconstruction of the study of

James Ramsay MacDonald, Britain's
first Labour prime minister, who was
born in a humble fisherman's cottage in
Lossiemouth in 1866.

FOCHABERS

8 miles E of Elgin on the A96

Fochabers was founded in the 18th
century, when the then Duke of Gordon,
to improve his view, moved a huddle of
cottages within his parkland to a better
site. It has a large, spacious square, with,
at one side, the elegant **Bellie Church**,
with grand a porticoed front. Within the
former Pringle Church is the **Fochabers
Folk Museum**, with exhibits on local
history. The imposing **Milne High
School** was built in 1844, the gift of a
local man who made his money in New

Orleans in the United States.

West of the village is **Baxter's Highland Village**, built next to the factory of what is undoubtedly Scotland's most famous food firm. The business started in 1868, when George Baxter, one of the Duke of Gordon's employees, opened a small grocery shop in Fochabers. George's wife began making a range of bottled jams and preserves in the back shop, using produce from the rich fertile lands surrounding the village. Now the firm sells to countries all over the world, and is a regular target for takeovers from foreign companies who imagine they have discovered an unsophisticated, little known, but extremely successful business. The village has a reconstruction of what the original village shop looked like, plus it sells most of the items in the Baxter range.

BUCKIE

13 miles E of Elgin on the A990

The **Buckie Drifter** on Freuchnie Road is a small museum and interpretation centre that tells the story of this small town and the Moray Firth fishing fleet. The **Peter Anson Gallery** within the local library, exhibits the maritime paintings of Peter Anson (1889 - 1975). Born in Portsmouth, he settled on the

Buckie Harbour

Moray coast in 1938, first at Portsoy, then at Macduff, where he was to stay for over 14 years.

The mouth of the River Spey is situated five miles west of the town, and though it is half a mile wide when it enters the sea, no great port was ever established here. The village of **Kingston** was founded in 1784 by William Osbourne and Ralph Dodworth, who came from Kingston-upon-Hull in Yorkshire. It was close to the mouth of the Spey that Charles II came ashore in 1650 after his stay in Holland. His ship ran aground in shallow water, and he was taken ashore on the back of a villager.

CULLEN

18 miles E of Elgin on the A98

Cullen is a picturesque royal burgh and former fishing port. The 16th century **St. Mary's Church** was collegiate. It dates originally from the 13th century. There is an imposing lairds's loft, the Seafield Loft, added in 1602. There is a monument to James, First Earl of Findlater and Seafield and Chancellor of Scotland. The dramatic ruins of **Findlater Castle** sit dramatically on the sea cliffs about a mile east the village.

DESKFORD

17 miles E of Elgin on the B9018

The ruins of **Deskford Church** date from the mid-16th century. The church was founded by Alexander Ogilvy of Deskford, and has a richly carved sacrament house, one of the best in the country.

FORDYCE

21 miles E of Elgin on a minor road off the A98

Fordyce Castle was built in 1592 for Thomas Menzies of Dun, an Aberdeen merchant who became provost of the city. It is not open to the public, but can be viewed from the outside. The **Fordyce Joiner's Workshop and Visitor Centre** has a range of woodworking tools and exhibitions about joinery in the north east of Scotland.

CRAIGELLACHIE

12 miles S of Elgin on the A95

Craigellachie Bridge, designed by Thomas Telford, spans the Spey in one graceful arch. It was built in 1814, and is Scotland's oldest iron bridge. The village is at the heart of the **Malt Whisky Trail**, and most of the distilleries in Speyside have tours round the distillery and a visitor centre where you can sample the product. The **Speyside Cooperage** sits close to Craigellachie, and here you can see whisky casks being manufactured and repaired. The **Glen Grant Distillery** is three miles north of the village at

Glenliver Distillery

HIGHLANDER INN

10 Victoria Street, Craigellachie, Speyside, Banffshire AB38 9SR
Tel: 01340 881446 Fax: 01340 881520
e-mail: highinn@aol.com
website: www.milford.co.uk/go/highlanderinn.html

Set in beautiful Speyside, on the Speyside Whisky Trail, the three star **Highlander Inn** is the ideal base from which to explore this beautiful area of Scotland. There are five extremely comfortable guest bedrooms, all fully en suite, and all with colour TVs and hospitality trays. The standards of service here are excellent, and the whole place speaks of high quality, friendly service and real value for money. Meals are served in the quaint dining room or lounge bar, and all the food is prepared from only the finest and freshest of local produce wherever possible.

The chef has devised a menu that concentrates on the natural cooking of such specialities as game, beef, salmon and seafood from the Moray Firth. The Highlander Inn has been accorded *Taste of Scotland* status, and the place is popular with both locals and visitors alike for tasty lunches and romantic evening meals. As befits a hostelry on the Speyside Whisky Trail, the bar stocks over 80 kinds of malts. Also available is a good range of wines to accompany you meal, as well as cognacs, real ale, lager and liqueurs. If you are driving, then there is also a wide range of soft drinks. At the weekend, the lounge hosts live, traditional music. The whole Speyside area is a tourist's paradise, and the Speyside Way, a long distance pathway, passes close by the inn. You can visit many of the distilleries, and at the end of the tour sample a wee dram. There is also good walking and many historic sites to visit.

THE WHISKY SHOP

Fife Street, Dufftown, Banffshire AB55 4AL
Tel/Fax: 01340 821097 website: www.dufftown.co.uk
e-mail: whiskyshop.dufftown@virgin.net

Dufftown proudly calls itself "Scotland's Whisky Capital", as it sits
in the heart of Speyside and its whisky trail. And in this small,
delightful town you will find a shop dedicated to the area's main
product - **The Whisky Shop**. With over 300 varieties of single malt
on its shelves, it is a place not to be missed. It was opened in 1997 by Fiona Murdoch, a whisky
connoisseur whose family have been in the wine and spirit trade for generations, and it now attracts
customers from all over the world, many of whom have their favourite brands sent to them by mail
order. But this place is more that a whisky shop: it is also a whisky information centre.

Here you can get helpful advice about Scotland's favourite tipple - which
malts to buy, where to try them and which distilleries to visit. It has maps
showing all Scotland's distilleries, and details of those you can visit in the
immediate area. And the shop also stocks liqueurs, Scottish fruit wines and a
fine selection of real ales from all over the country. There are regular talk and
taste sessions during the summer months, but groups or individuals can book
tutored tastings at any time, and it's a great way to find out about the subtle
differences in single malts. If you wish to browse, there will be no pressure put
upon you, and if you wish to buy friendly, helpful advice is always on hand.
The shop is open seven days a week from Easter to October, and late into the
evenings during the long summer nights. At other times it closes on Sunday.
This is the place to come to learn about single malts, or to purchase a bottle to
take home with you.

BOOGIE WOOGIE GIFT AND COFFEE SHOP

2 Regent Street, Keith, Banffshire AB55 5DX
Tel: 01542 888077 Fax: 01542 888037
e-mail: info@boogiewoogieshop.com
website: boogiewoogieshop.com

Boogie Woogie, in the heart of the small town of Keith,
sells "imaginative gifts for imaginative people", and this is
no idle boast. There is a wide range of gift ware from all
over the world - clothing from California, pottery from
Poland, toys from the Czech Republic, jewellery from Afghanistan and Ibiza and, at Christmas,
decorations from Scandinavia and Germany. You are free to browse the marvellous collections on
display, and no one will disturb you or hurry you along. The china and jewellery are especially attractive,
and the fashion clothing on the first floor is sure to have something for everyone. The range of woollens
is especially good, as are the scarves and leather goods. The shop also stocks smart suits, skirts and

tops, as well as bags and accessories.

There is also a small café where you can relax over a tea or
a cup of cappuccino while reading the daily papers that are
always available. Why not have one of the home-baked cakes
and scones, or a slice of the Boogie Woogie's famous carrot
cake? Snacks are also available, as are light lunches and
afternoon teas. The place is owned and run by Jane
Macpherson, a local girl who, after working for some time in
London, came home to open up this shop. She and her staff,
both in the café and the gift shop, are friendly and
knowledgeable, and will give you a warm welcome.

Rothes, and four miles south, at Dufftown, is the Glenfiddich Distillery.

The Keith and Dufftown Railway runs the nine miles between Dufftown and Keith, and is known as the "Whisky Line". It is Britain's most northerly heritage railway.

Balvenie Castle (Historic Scotland) is in Dufftown. It was once a Comyn stronghold, and the ruins as you see them today date form the 13th century

and later. Another castle, this time intact, sits nine miles SW of Craigellachie. Ballindalloch Castle dates from the 16th century, though it has been added to over the years. It is home to the MacPherson-Grant family, who have lived here since it was built, and it is open to the public in summer. Near the castle is the Glenfarclas Distillery, and the Glenlivit Distillery sits four miles further south off the B9008.

EASTER CORRIE

Tomnavoulin, Glenlivet, Ballindalloch AB37 9JB
Tel: 01807 590241 website: www.eastercorrie.com
e-mail: bookings@ eastercorrie.com

Situated midway between Aviemore and Royal Deeside, Easter Corrie comprises four comfortable and attractive self catering cottages that make an ideal base for exploring the historic North East of Scotland. All the cottages, which sleep either four or six, are equipped to an extremely high standard. Electricity, duvets, bed linen and towels are included in the rental, and there is parking for two cars at each cottage. Well behaved dogs are welcome by prior arrangement. The cottages nestle in a secluded glen within the Glenlivet Estate, where there are some of the finest landscapes in Scotland.

MINMORE HOUSE HOTEL

Glenlivet, Banffshire AB37 9DB
Tel: 01807 590378 Fax: 01807 590472
e-mail: enquiries@minmorehousehotel.com

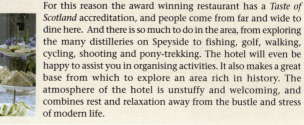

Minmore is an elegant stone built country house standing amid the magnificent scenery of the Glenlivet Crown Estate in the heart of Speyside. Now it has been tastefully converted into one of the best hotels in the area - the four star Minmore House Hotel. It stands in four acres of landscaped gardens, where croquet and tennis can be played during the day or in the long summer evenings for which this part of Scotland is famous. The hotel has one suite and ten spacious and extremely comfortable rooms, all fully en suite and all beautifully furnished and individually decorated.

The hotel takes a great pride in its cuisine, and the General Manager, Mr Janssen, is a famous chef who brings the highest of standards to the hotel's kitchen. He prepares everything on the menu from the finest and freshest of local produce, including vegetables and herbs from the hotel's own gardens.

For this reason the award winning restaurant has a *Taste of Scotland* accreditation, and people come from far and wide to dine here. And there is so much to do in the area, from exploring the many distilleries on Speyside to fishing, golf, walking, cycling, shooting and pony-trekking. The hotel will even be happy to assist you in organising activities. It also makes a great base from which to explore an area rich in history. The atmosphere of the hotel is unstuffy and welcoming, and combines rest and relaxation away from the bustle and stress of modern life.

OLD PANTRY RESTAURANT AND GIFT SHOP

The Square, Aberlour, Banffshire AB38 9NY
Tel./fax: 01340 871617

The **Old Pantry Restaurant and Gift Shop** is on a corner setting in the heart of the old village of Aberlour, on the Speyside Whisky Trail. Here you will find a spacious restaurant on the ground floor and a marvellous and colourful gift shop above it, crammed full with gifts and souvenirs of all kinds. The restaurant can seat up to 40 people in absolute comfort, and has a varied menu that ranges from light snacks such as filled baguettes, toasties and baked potatoes to salads, fish, chips and peas, macaroni cheese, chicken curry, home made pie and pasta with tomato and basil sauce. If it's just a refreshing cup of tea or coffee with cakes or scones you are after, then this is available as well.

The food is all beautifully cooked using local fresh produce wherever possible, and the prices are remarkably reasonable considering the high quality. There is also a small selection of wines to

accompany your meal, and a range of beers and spirits. The upstairs gift shop is reached by a separate entrance, and is an Aladdin's cave full of jewellery, pottery, glassware, brass, ornaments, prints, cards and so on, and there is sure to be something that would make that ideal gift or souvenir. Feel free to browse - no one will disturb you as you look round. However, if you do need help, the staff is friendly and knowledgeable, and will guide you to the perfect purchase. Aberlour is set among some lovely scenery, and the Old Pantry Restaurant and Gift Shop is the ideal place to stop for a break or lunch as you explore.

A'ANSIDE STUDIOS

5 Main Street, Tomintoul, Ballindalloch, Banffshire AB37 9EX
Tel: 01479 872074 e-mail: info@aanside.co.uk
 Fax: 01479 872094 website: www.aanside.co.uk

High in the Cairngorm Mountains, at the gateway to the Cairngorm National Park, lies the village of Tomintoul, where you will find the fascinating **A'anside Studios.** Here Jacqui and Barry Horning have been designing and crafting the finest in wood and stained glass since 1992. A professional cabinet maker, Barry uses the very best native hardwoods to create furniture and exquisite boxes in modern and traditional styles. Jacqui is an artist who works in stained glass, and creates a myriad of designs for lamps, mirrors, windows and decorative panels in Victorian, Art Deco and late 20th century styles.

Visiting the Studios you can watch the ancient craft of stained glass construction where traditional cathedral glass and modern handmade opalescent and art glass are combined with lead and copper foil techniques to produce artefacts of stunning brilliance. Personal tuition in stained glass design, with classes limited to a maximum of four, is available. Located within the same premises are a shop and gallery where the work of artist-craftsmen from throughout Scotland are displayed and available

for purchase. The collection is rightly named "Scotlands Finest" and would make ideal gifts or souvenirs of your visit to this dramatic Highland location. The studio shop, rated four stars by Visit Scotland, is bright and colourful, and if you should wish to browse, no one will pressure you, though knowledgeable advice is always at hand should you need it. Should you wish to commission something in wood or stained glass for your business or home, then both Jacqui and Barry will be pleased to dicuss your requirements and provide a competitive quotation for the work.

TOMINTOUL

27 miles S of Elgin on the A939

Tomintoul is the highest village in the Highlands. Surprisingly, it is not the highest village in Scotland, that honour going to Wanlockhead in Dumfriesshire. The A939 road south from the village towards Cockbridge is called **The Lecht**, and is famous for the number of times it is blocked by snow in the winter months. The ski area called The Lecht sits six miles south east of the village. **Tomintoul Museum** explores the local history of the area.

COCKBRIDGE

31 miles S of Elgin on the A939

Colgarff Castle (Historic Scotland) sits in a lonely moorland setting, and is a 16th century tower house within an unusual star-shaped enclosing wall. It was garrisoned by Jacobite troops during the 1715 and 1745 Jacobite Uprisings, but was taken by government troops after the Battle of Culloden. The troops remained in the castle right up until 1831, helping the local revenue men stamp out illegal distilling.

PLUSCARDEN

6 miles SW of Elgin on a minor road well off the B9010

Pluscarden Priory was founded in 1230 for Valliscaulian monks, though it was later taken over by the Benedictines. It has the distinction of being the only medieval monastery in Britain that still has monks living and worshipping within its walls. In the 19th century the Bute family acquired the medieval ruins and in 1948 presented them to the monks of Prinknash Abbey in England. They set about restoring some of the buildings, and though it started out life as a priory, it became a fully fledged

CARDEN SELF CATERING

The Old Steading, Alves, Elgin, Moray IV30 8UP
Tel: 01343 850222 Fax: 01343 850626

Within Carden Farm, west of the historic city of Elgin with its magnificent ruined cathedral, you will find **Carden Self Catering**, a series of eight lovingly cared for self-catering holiday cottages. Pleasantly situated on the fertile coastal plain of Moray, they enjoy views of open, picturesque countryside, with the hills of distant Sutherland visible across the Moray Firth. The properties consist of two detached cottages and six courtyard cottages created from the original 18th century farm steading. There are three cottages which sleep two, three which sleep four and two which sleep six. All are furnished and maintained to an extremely high standard to ensure that guests have an enjoyable and relaxing holiday at any time of the year.

The kitchens are fully fitted with electric cooker, microwave oven, fridge/freezer, dishwasher, washing machine and tumble dryer, and the cozy living rooms all have colour TVs with Teletext, video and hi-fi. The bathrooms and shower rooms all have WC and wash hand basins. All the cottages are inspected

each year by Visit Scotland, and continue to be awarded the coveted four star grading. The cottages are owned and managed by Suzanne and Gavin MacKessack-Leitch, who pride themselves on their value for money approach plus the attention to detail that makes every cottage a "home from home". The beach is only a few miles away, and the city of Inverness is only an hour away by car. The cottages are open throughout the year, and Suzanne and Gavin invite you to take a short break, or a week or a fortnight, here, among the superb scenery, history and heritage of Moray.

WALK 8

Findhorn Gorge

Start	Sluie Walk car park on A940, 5 miles (8km) south of Forres
Distance	2½ miles (4km)
Approximate time	1½ hours
Parking	Sluie Walk car park
Refreshments	None
Ordnance Survey maps	Landranger 27 (Nairn & Forres), Pathfinder 162, NJ05/15 (Forres and Dallas)

The Findhorn is one of Scotland's most scenic rivers, rising deep in the heart of the Monadhliath Mountains between Kingussie and Loch Ness, and foaming through a succession of remote valleys and wooded defiles to reach the sea at Findhorn Bay. The gorge at Sluie has been a tourist attraction since Victorian times, and this walk follows a traditional route along a well-made path on the eastern side of the river.

Sluie Wood is part of the Moray Estates, and the walk is waymarked throughout its length. Start along the path behind the notice-board in the car park, then turn right and continue downhill on a farm road towards the abandoned farm buildings at Mains of Sluie **Ⓐ**. This was once a salmon-fishing station, and Sluie Pool used to yield a rich harvest of fish, but gone are the days of the 17th century when the Earl of Moray could boast that his fishermen had caught "at one draught, six and twenty scores" of fish – that is, 520 salmon in a single haul of the net.

Pass to the left of the buildings and follow a delightful path along the edge of the Findhorn Gorge. Mixed woodland of

beech and oak, larch, fir and Scots pine borders the crags, which tower above foaming rapids and peaty brown pools. The path clings to the lip of the ravine, where the forest floor is carpeted with heather and moss, and dotted with primrose, wood anemone and forget-me-not; on the far side is the great forest of Darnaway, planted by Francis, Earl of Moray at the beginning of the 19th century. The gorge becomes deeper and more precipitous as you go further upstream, and the bedrock changes from reddish-brown sandstone to more resistant schists and gneisses.

After ½ mile (800m) you come to a wooden barrier, where a sign directs walkers to cut back left up the hillside **Ⓑ**

The path soon widens to a forestry road. Fork right at a junction, and right again at the next, to reach the edge of a clearing with an abandoned cottage in the middle **C** . The route now bends round to the left, and follows a farm track past a few more ruined cottages to rejoin the outward route just below the car park.

There is another spectacular section of gorge three miles (4.8km) further south (fork right at Logie on the B9007) at Randolph's Leap, a short distance upstream from where the River Divie joins the Findhorn. Steps lead down from the road to a narrow rocky defile, at one point only 10ft (3m) across. A stone marks the height reached by the water during the catastrophic Moray floods of August 1829 – an astonishing 50ft (15m) above normal level.

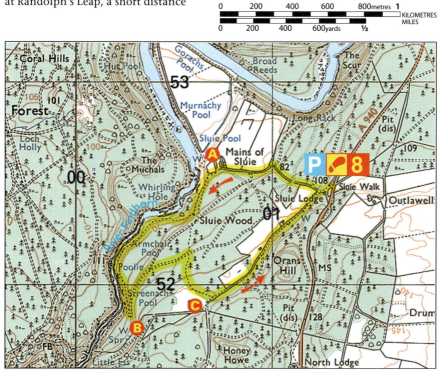

abbey in 1974. It is open to the public, and there is a small gift shop.

FORRES

12 miles W of Elgin on the A96

Forres is an ancient town, having become a royal burgh in the 12th century. It's medieval layout can still be discerned today among its more modern buildings, though it is more open and green that it was then. **Sueno's Stone** (Historic Scotland) is one of Scotland's largest carved Pictish stones, and dates from the 9th century. One side shows a cross, while another shows battle scenes. The **Falconer Museum** in Tolbooth Street was founded in 1871, and has collections on local history. Dominating the town is the **Nelson Tower**, built in 1821 to commemorate Nelson's victory at Trafalgar. There are 96 steps to the top, and if you manage the climb, you will be rewarded by some spectacular views out over the town and countryside towards the Moray Firth.

Four miles west of Forres is **Brodie Castle** (National Trust for Scotland - see panel above). It is a fine 16th century Z-plan tower house with later additions, and has associations with the Brodie family going back possibly to 1160, when they were given the surrounding lands by Malcolm IV. The grounds have a unique collection of daffodils in spring, a lake and woodland walks. North east of Forres are the scant remains of **Kinloss**

BRODIE CASTLE

Brodie, Forres, Moray IV36 2TE
Tel: 01309 641371 Fax: 0 1309 641600
e-mail brodiecastle@nts.org.uk

Brodie Castle is a fine 16th century Z-plan tower house with 17th and 19th century additions, set in peaceful parkland. The family association with the area predates the castle, going back at least to Malcolm, Thane of Brodie, who died in 1285, and possibly to 1160, when it is believed Malcolm IV endowed the Brodies with their lands. The castle was damaged in an attack in 1645 by Montrose's army, but survived. It contains fine French furniture, English, Continental and Chinese porcelain, and a major collection of paintings, including 17th century Dutch art, 19th century English watercolours, Scottish Colourists and early 20th-century works. The magnificent library contains some 6,000 volumes.

The grounds are famous for their unique daffodil collection in spring. Explore them along the woodland walks, one by the edge of a 1.6 hectares (4 acres) pond with access to wildlife observation hides.

Abbey, with an RFA base close by. **The Dallas Dhu Distillery** (Historic Scotland) lies south of the town, and is a working distillery that explains the processes involved in the distilling of malt whisky.

Culbin Sands is one of the most unusual landscapes in Scotland. It had been a fertile stretch of land along the shores of the Moray Firth until a great storm in 1694 blew great drifts of sand - some as high as 100 feet - over the whole area, burying everything and causing people to flee their homes. Eventually an eight square miles area of "desert" was created, and it became known as "Scotland's Sahara". Over the years further storms exposed the foundations of the original cottages, and they would then be covered over when the winds blew again. The landscape continued to shift and expand until the 1920s, when trees were planted which managed to stabilise the area.

Findhorn Bay is a small "lagoon" lying to the north of Forres. At its seaward side is the small village of **Findhorn**, where you will find the **Findhorn Foundation**. It is one of Britain's most successful centres for promoting alternative lifestyles, and was founded in 1962 in a caravan park by Dorothy MacLean and Peter and Eileen Caddy. The **Findhorn Heritage Centre and Museum** explores the history of the area.

FRASERBURGH

Fraserburgh Beach

This large fishing port sits on the northern coastline of that large farming area known as Buchan. It was founded in the 16th century by Alexander Fraser, the eighth laird of Philorth. In 1546 he built a new harbour for the fishermen of Broadsea, a settlement that stood on Kinnaird Head, and it soon prospered. Alexander's plans for the town also included a university, and he even obtained permission from James VI to found one. And for a short while the university actually functioned, with the principal being a Church of Scotland minister called Ferme. However, Ferme was later arrested on the orders of the king for attending a general assembly of the church in Edinburgh without his permission, and the embryonic university soon folded. **College Bounds**, one of Fraserburgh's streets, recalls the days when the town had a seat of learning.

The **Old Kirk** in Saltoun Square, for all its name, was only built in 1803 to replace the original church built by Alexander between 1570 and 1571. The **Fraser Burial Aisle** from this 16th century church still survives.

Kinnaird Lighthouse (Historic Scotland) is now a museum dedicated to Scottish lighthouses. It is unusual in that it is built onto a 16th century castle, created by Alexander Fraser as his home

at the same time as he was developing the town. Next to the lighthouse is the **Wine Tower**, possibly built as Fraser's personal chapel. It has three floors, but curiously, no connecting stairways.

At Sandhead, to the east of the town, is the 19th century **Sandhead Meal Mill**, which shows how oatmeal was ground in Scotland. The **Memsie Burial Cairn** is at Memsie, three miles south of Fraserburgh. It dates from about 1500BC.

AROUND FRASERBURGH

PETERHEAD
15 miles SE of Fraserburgh on the A982

Peterhead is one of the main fishing ports in the North East, and was founded by George Keith, the 5th earl Marischal of Scotland, in 1593. The fishing industry is now in decline, but the port still services the North Sea oil industry. The **Arbuthnott Museum** in St. Peter Street explains the history of the town, and has a large collection of Inuit, or Eskimo, artifacts. In a purpose built building to the south of the town is the **Peterhead Maritime Heritage**, which tells of the town's long associations with the sea, its fishing fleet and the modern oil and gas industry.

At Cruden Bay, on the A975 seven

BUCHAN EMBROIDERY

Unit 2, Glenogie Business Centre, King Street, Peterhead AB24 2HU
Tel/Fax: 01779 480900

After you've visited the fascinating Arbuthnott Museum or Peterhead Maritime Heritage in the large fishing town of Peterhead, why not visit **Buchan Embroidery**, which sells a wide range of beautiful embroidery by Kathryn Buchan, whose husband and daughter work alongside her. The shop is in a former school building, which has been converted into a small crafts centre close to the main shopping area of this attractive town, and you are more than welcome to come along and browse at your leisure. Kathryn and her family are very knowledgeable about the goods they offer for sale, and can offer friendly advice should you wish to buy a gift or a unique souvenir of your holiday in this part of Scotland.

The business was set up in the year 2000, and has now become established as one of the main craft outlets in the area. It sells knitwear, embroidery, towelling, children's wear, sports wear and so much more, all individually embroidered to your specification. There is a smart, colourful display area and a workshop where you can see Kathryn working. Choose your embroidery design and see it coming to life before your eyes as Kathryn works - it's so fascinating you'll want to come back again and again. Kathryn offers a speedy and accomplished design service, and commissions are undertaken. You can be sure of efficient service and keen prices, with the finished goods being posted to anywhere in the world. Buchan Embroidery is *the* embroidery place in the North East of Scotland.

miles south of the town, are the ruins of **Slains Castle**, built by the Earls of Errol in the 16th century. The ruins as you see there date from the 19th century, after several rebuildings. While staying at an inn at Cruden Bay in 1895, **Bram Stoker** began writing his famous horror novel Dracula, and he must have been inspired by Slains Castle, as he originally wanted the Count to arrive in Britain close to their ruins, rather than at Whitby.

OLD DEER

12 miles S of Fraserburgh on the B9030

On the banks of the River Ugie are the remains of **Deer Abbey** (Historic Scotland). It was founded in 1219 by William Comyn, Earl of Buchan, for the Cistercians, and though little remains of the church, the walls of some of the other buildings are well preserved. The **Aden Farming Museum** sits within a

country park, and has exhibits and displays about the farming industry in Buchan. There are three separate themes in the museum - the Aden Estate Story, the Weel Vrocht Grun ("well worked ground") and the country park itself.

MAUD

12 miles S of Fraserburgh on the B9029

Maud, for all its rural setting, grew up in the 19th century around a stop in the railway line connecting Fraserburgh with Aberdeen. In the village's former station is the **Maud Railway Museum**, and here you can see exhibits and displays connected with the Great North of Scotland Railway.

TURRIFF

20 miles SW of Fraserburgh on the A947

Turriff is an old town set in the rich farmlands of Buchan. The Knights

FORGLEN ESTATE

Home Farm Office, Forglen Estate, Turriff,
Aberdeenshire AB53 4JP
Tel: 01888 562918 Fax: 01888 562252
e-mail: holidaycottages@easicom.com

In the beautiful Deveron Valley you will
find the ancient **Forglen Estate**, lying on
the banks of the river. It offers 10
comfortable secluded stone built self-
catering cottages, each one attractive and
picturesque, and well equipped. They blend
beautifully into the countryside, and are
havens of peace in a busy world. Here you
can enjoy the woodland walks, the

tumbling stream in the "Glen Garden" and the varied wildlife. The cottages are available throughout
year, each season having its own particular charms. You will be sure of a warm welcome, as will obedient
dogs, who will relish all the walks available!

Templar once owned land hereabouts,
and built a Templar church (now gone).
The town's **Parish Church** was built in
1794, though remnants of the former
church were incorporated into it.

Turriff was the scene of a famous
incident which came to be known as the
"Turra Coo" ("Turriff Cow"). Through it
Turriff became famous, and newspapers
latched on the story with glee. In 1911
and 1913 new National Insurance Acts
were passed by the government which
required employers to pay 3d per week
per employee. Britain's farming
community objected to this, as they
reckoned that farm workers had a
healthy lifestyle and didn't need
insurance. And curiously enough, the
farmers were supported by the farm
workers in this.

Robert Paterson, a Turriff farmer,
refused to pay, so one of his cows was
seized to be auctioned off. The auction
was held in Turriff, and turned into a
fiasco when the cow, which had slogans
painted all over it, took fright and
bolted. The auctioneer, who was trying
to bring some gravitas into the situation,
was then pelted with eggs and flour, and

the whole thing was abandoned.

Three days later the auction took place
again, this time in Aberdeen, and the
cow fetched £7. At first the government
expressed satisfaction with the outcome.
However, when it was explained to them
that Robert Paterson's friends had
clubbed together and bought the cow,
and then returned it to Robert, they were
furious. The authorities had paid £12 to
recover the unpaid National Insurance,
while Robert had paid nothing. Seven
miles south west of the town, on the
B9001, is the **Glendronach Distillery**,
with distillery tours and a visitor centre.

BANFF

20 miles W of Fraserburgh on the A98

This small fishing port at the mouth of
the River Deveron was once the county
town of Banffshire, a county which
disappeared at local government
reorganisation in 1975. It is one of
Scotland's oldest royal burghs, having
been granted its charter in 1163 by
Malcolm IV.

The **Banff Museum** in the High Street
is one of the oldest in Scotland, and was
founded in 1823. It has an important

collection of Banff silver. **Duff House** (Historic Scotland) was built between 1735 and 1737 for William Duff of Braco, who later became the Earl of Fife. It was designed by William Adam, and after an argument between Adam and Duff, Duff abandoned the house, and it was left to James, the 2nd Earl, to complete both it and the grounds. It is now a satellite gallery of the National Galleries of Scotland, and has paintings by such artists as Raeburn and El Greco.

Six miles west of Banff is the old fishing village of **Portsoy**, which is worth visiting just to see the quaint harbour and the buildings which surround it.

MACDUFF

19 miles W of Fraserburgh on the A98

Macduff sits next to Banff, on the opposite bank of the Deveron. It was founded in 1783 by James, the 2nd Earl of Fife, who also completed Duff House. The **Macduff Marine Museum** has a large tank surrounded by viewing areas, and gives you a good view of marine animals and fish from all angles. It also has a wave making machine which allows you to see underwater life as it is lived in the shallow waters around Scotland.

11 THE HIGHLANDS

Ask anyone to describe typical Scottish scenery, and they'll talk of high, mountains, dark, brooding lochs and misty, romantic glens. And though other areas of Scotland have this kind of scenery, it is the Highlands that has most of it.

It is an area with no recognised boundaries. Some people talk of the Highlands as being that area north of the Highland Boundary Fault, which follows a line drawn from Helensburgh on the banks of the Clyde to Stonehaven on the North Sea. This would take in areas described elsewhere in this book, such as Argyllshire and the Grampians. Others would exclude the lowlands of Aberdeenshire and that long strip of rich farmland stretching right along the southern shores of the Moray Firth.

Loch Quoich at Sunrise

The area described in this chapter could be called the heart of the Highlands. It occupies the western half of the country, from Nairnshire in the east to the rugged Atlantic coast in the west, and from the boundaries of modern Argyllshire and Perthshire in the south to the coastline far to the north. It is mostly wild country, though it is penetrated by some amazingly beautiful and fertile glens. Some bits of it are totally inaccessible unless you are prepared to don sturdy outdoor gear and go walking over the hills. But if you wish to do this, you are strongly advised to tell someone of your intended route, and your estimated time of arrival at your destination. This also applies in the summer months.

Inverness is the capital of the Highlands. It is a city with the most rapid development in Britain, and it has been described as having an enviable quality of life. Certainly the weather here is remarkable, as it gets less rain than most other parts of Britain, due to the mountains to the west. If you travel up the A9 from the south and pass over the Beauly Firth by way of the Kessock Bridge, its sprawling suburbs give the impression of a large city, butits population is no more than 45,000. Some of the countryside surrounding it

LOCATOR MAP

See other chapters

ADVERTISERS AND PLACES OF INTEREST

even looks like the Lowlands, with rich fertile farmland, though if you head south west on the A82 towards Loch Ness this impression is soon dispelled.

Ben Nevis is within the Highland area, and it is Britain's highest mountain. So, too, is Loch Morar, Scotland's deepest loch. Loch Ness, possibly Europe's most famous stretch of water, begins only a few miles from the centre of Inverness. And there was bloodshed aplenty in the area. The last true battle fought on British soil was fought at Culloden, and at Glencoe the massacre of the MacDonalds by the Campbells took place.

The west coast is rugged, with sea lochs penetrating deep into the mountains. On Loch Carron you will find Plockton, the setting for *Hamish Macbeth*, and even here the weather is surprising. Palm trees flourish due to the warm waters of the Gulf Stream, though the rainfall is much higher than the British average. Towns and villages are few, and mostly on the coast. Some grew as settlements fairly recently, when landowners cleared the inland glens of people to make way for the more profitable sheep, and settled them on the coast. It was a time known as The Clearances, and it happened all over the Highlands. Many Scots emigrated, mostly to the United States and Canada.

The east coast, from John O' Groats in the north to Nairn in the south, is altogether gentler, with many ancient villages and towns. Dornoch has a medieval cathedral, as has Fortrose. Tain was a place of pilgrimage in medieval times, and Strathpeffer, in the 19th century, became one of Britain's most popular spa towns, with a regular train service to and from London.

And, as ever, there are the rugged mountains in the central part of the area. The scenery is austere and gaunt in places, while elsewhere there is a majesty that cannot be matched anywhere else in Britain. The Gulf Stream has little effect here, and snow can still fall in May. Glencoe and Aviemore are ski resorts, though the season stops long before May.

Scotland's two northernmost counties are Caithness and Sutherland. Here you will find what is called the Flow Country, an area of low peaks, moorland and lochans. The scenery isn't as dramatic as the Western Highlands, but it has a ruggedness all of its own.

The Highlands are an area that amaze people who have never visited. The scenery is wild and untamed, through some of the sheltered glens have rich woodlands and farmland. The weather isn't always rainy or cold, and during the summer, when the sun shines the quality of the light is startling. Mountains that are many miles away are sharp and clear, and you almost feel you could reach out and touch them. But there are lonely places as well. Walking over a high ridge, or trampling over heather moorland is an experience not to be missed if you are reasonably fit. You may meet not another soul for hours, and you feel the world is yours.

FORT WILLIAM

Fort William lies at the western end of Glen More - the "Great Glen", in an area known as Lochaber. The West Highland Way stops here, on the banks of **Loch Linnhe**. The "fort" in the name refers to a fort built in the 1650s by General Monk, and which was rebuilt in the days of William and Mary to house 6,000 troops. It was called Maryburgh in honour of the queen. It was dismantled in the 19th century to make way for the Fort William railway line, and only parts of a wall now survive.

Ben Nevis and Fort William

After the railway came to Fort William, the place burgeoned as a holiday resort and centre for exploring the West Highlands. Its main industry is still tourism, and in the summer months the town is full of climbers and walkers. A few miles east is **Ben Nevis**. At 4,406 feet, it is Britain's highest mountain, and a fairly easy five mile walk will take you to the summit. It is reached by way of **Glen Nevis**, said to be one of Scotland's most beautiful glens. However, even on fine days, you should still dress appropriately

THE GRANGE

Grange Road, Fort William, Inverness-shire PH33 6JF
Tel: 01397 705516   Fax: 01397 701595
e-mail: jcampbell@grangefortwilliam.com
website: www.thegrange.scotland.co.uk

The Grange is one of the most luxurious B&Bs in Inverness-shire, and is to be found in the picturesque town of Fort William. In fact, so highly regarded is it that it has been awarded a coveted five stars by Visit Scotland. This typically Scottish turreted and whitewashed house dates from 1884, and overlooks the placid waters of one of Scotland's loveliest sea lochs, Loch Linnhe. There are four luxurious and sumptuous rooms, all en suite, and all individually decorated and furnished. In addition, there are complementary flowers and sherry in each room. One of them - the Rob Roy Room, was favoured by film actress Jessica Lange during the filming of *Rob Roy* in the local countryside.

This is a truly charming B&B, with antiques, log fires in the colder months, crystal and colourful flowers everywhere. Upon your arrival, tea is always served in the comfortable lounge to make you feel right at home. It is owned and run by Joan Campbell, who offers the highest standards of Scottish

hospitality to all her guests. There is a large and varied breakfast menu, which is served in the Grange's spacious dining room overlooking Loch Linnhe, with the produce being sourced locally wherever possible. Try their locally smoked haddock, the traditional full Scottish breakfast of sausage, bacon, egg, black pudding and tomato, or a lighter option, such as oatcakes with honey and banana. This is the perfect place to use as a base while exploring this historic and beautiful part of Scotland, or to spend one or two nights in as you pass through.

Loch Linnhe

(layers are ideal) and let someone know where you are going and when you are due back. From the top you can see the Cairngorms, the Cuillins on Skye, and the peaks of Argyllshire to the south. On exceptionally clear days it is said you can even see the coast of Northern Ireland. The **Glen Nevis Visitor Centre** has exhibits about wildlife and local history, and, importantly, information about the weather conditions on the mountain.

A mile to the east are **Aonach Beag** and **Aonach Mor**, Ben Nevis's little brothers. This is a winter sports area, though it is busy in the summer as well. Britain's only mountain gondola - a modern six seater "Doppelmayr" - takes you half way up Aonach Mor if you don't feel like walking. There's a restaurant and bar at the top, and plenty of good walking country. The area is reached from the A82.

The **West Highland Museum** is in Cameron Square in Fort William. The most famous exhibit is the 18th century "Secret Portrait of Charles Edward Stuart". When first seen, it is a meaningless swirl of colours and patterns, but when placed on a polished surface a likeness of the prince appears as if by magic. There is also a small exhibition about the Queen's Own Cameron Highlanders, a regiment which is no more. In 1961 it merged with the Seaforth Highlanders to form the Queen's Own Highlanders.

North west of the town, at Corpach, is the award winning **Treasures of the Earth**, one of Europe's finest collections of gemstones and crystals. The ruins of **Inverlochy Castle** (Historic Scotland) date from the 13th century and later, and sit one and a half miles north east of Fort William. Montrose beat an army of Covenanting Campbells here in 1645. Though not open to the public, the ruins can be viewed from the outside. On the A82 is the **Ben Nevis Distillery and Whisky Centre**, where there are conducted tours and a tasting.

The **Caledonian Canal** begins it long journey towards Inverness at Fort William. It is, in fact, not one canal, but several, each one connecting the lochs of the Great Glen, such as Lochy, Oich and Ness. **Neptune's Staircase** is a series of eight locks rising up a hillside which raises the canal over 60 feet. It is situated at Banavie, and was designed by Thomas Telford in the early 1800s.

Eight miles north east of the town is Spean Bridge, where commandos trained during World War II. The **Spean Bridge Commando Memorial** commemorates the men who trained here, and was designed by Scott Sutherland. It shows three commandos, and was unveiled by the late Queen Mother in 1952. The **Spean Bridge Mill** has a tartan centre

Caledonian Canal, nr Fort William

AROUND FORT WILLIAM

KINLOCHLEVEN

9 miles SE of Fort William on the B863

Kinlochleven sits at the head of Loch Leven, and is on the West Highland Way. Up until the year 2000 an aluminium smelting works stood here, and in the **Aluminium Story Visitor Centre** you can see how hydroelectric power from the Blackwater Reservoir, high in the hills, was used to power the works.

and demonstrations of tartan weaving.

During the summer the **Jacobite Steam Train** takes you along the famous Fort William to Mallaig line, one of the most beautiful in Britain.

BALLACHULISH

10 miles S of Fort William on the A82

Ballachulish sits on the southern shores of Loch Leven, close to where a bridge carries the A82 across the mouth of the

RIVER COE BISTRO AND LODGE

Inveriggan, Glencoe PH49 4HP
Tel/Fax: 01855 811248
e-mail: rivercoe@visitglencoe.co.uk
website: www.visitglencoe.co.uk

Glencoe is known for its majestic beauty and is a name that echoes down through the years because of the massacre of the Clan MacDonald by the Campbells that took place there in 1692. Near the village of Glencoe, and on the banks of the River Coe, you will find the **River Coe Bistro and Lodge**, a wonderful new restaurant and Bed & Breakfast establishment that was built to the highest standards in 2003. It is built with warm pine logs, and fits snugly into the surrounding countryside.

A warm welcome awaits you by Peter and Paulette Weir at the River Coe Bistro. Here you will find gourmet dining, with a menu of many imaginative dishes using fresh local produce wherever possible.

The Bistro specialises in seafood and also has a good selection of meat and vegetarian dishes Daily specials include homemade pasta. There is a small but select wine list to complement your meal and a good selection of after dinner drinks including Scottish whiskies and liqueurs.The 24-seat dining area is conservatory style, with magnificent views of the mountains and river. The Lodge rooms are luxurious and spacious with large ensuite bathrooms with showers. Each room has a veranda with views towards the mountains and river, where guests can enjoy a complementary drink on arrival.

GLENCOE & DALNESS

The National Trust for Scotland Visitor Centre,
Glencoe, Argyll PH49 41A
Tel: 01855 811307 or 01855 811729
Fax: 01855 812010
e-mail: glencoe@nts.org.uk
website: www.nts.org.uk

Some of the finest climbing and walking country in
the Highlands is to be found within the 5,680
hectares (14,035 acres) in the Trust's care, in an area
of dramatic landscapes and historical fact and
legend. The infamous massacre of 1692 took place
at many sites throughout the glen, but one of the
main locations is just a short walk from the Trust's new eco friendly Visitor Centre at Inverrigan.

Geologically, the Glencoe hills are significant as
an example of a volcano collapsing in on itself during
a series of violent eruptions. This is also an area of
international botanical importance, particularly for
the woodlands and Arctic alpine flora. In the lower
part of Glen Coe the Trust owns a flock of sheep and
fold of Highland cattle, part of a unique project to
manage an area of internationally important
grassland. The property includes a large Special Area
of Conservation.

The A82 Glasgow to Fort William road runs
through this spectacular glen and the Visitor Centre
is a perfect stopping place for the traveller going north
or south. Enjoy *Living on the Edge*, an interactive exhibition exploring the landscape, wildlife and
history of this special place. Find out what it feels like to climb on ice; discover how the glen was
formed; and try your hand at solving the conservation problems faced by the Trust.

FERN VILLA GUEST HOUSE & COTTAGES

Loanfern, Ballachulish, Highland PH49 4JE
Tel: 01855 811393 Fax: 01855 811727
e-mail: cli@fernvilla.com website: www.fernvilla.com

The three star **Fern Villa Guest House and Cottages** sit in a truly beautiful part of Scotland. Owned and run by June and Kenneth Chandler, the licensed guest house offers five extremely comfortable en suite guest bedrooms, three of which are doubles and the other two twins. The Natural Cooking of Scotland forms the basis of the cuisine, with only the finest and freshest of local produce being used wherever possible. The delicious dinners consist of three courses , with a small selection of wines, and the breakfasts are filling and hearty. Self Catering Cottages also available.

loch. A cairn marks the spot where Jacobite sympathiser **James of the Glen** was hanged for a murder he almost certainly did not commit. He was found guilty of murdering **Colin Campbell**, a government agent whose nickname was the "Red Fox", by a judge and jury that were all from Clan Campbell. Another cairn marks the site of the murder itself. The **Information and Interpretation Centre** in the village has displays on the local wildlife and history.

To the east of the village is one of the most evocative places in Scotland - Glencoe. It was in 1691 that the **Massacre of Glencoe** took place. Due to bad weather, McIan of Clan MacDonald had failed to take the Oath of Allegiance to William and Mary in time, and a party of Campbells were sent to Glencoe to massacre his people. They pretended to come in peace, and were shown great

GLEANN LEAC NA MUIDHE B&B AND GLENCOE MOUNTAIN COTTAGES

Gleann Leac na Muidhe, Glencoe, Argyllshire PH49 4LA
Tel/Fax: 01855 811598
e-mail: cl@glencoemountaincottages.co.uk website: www.glencoemountaincottages.co.uk

"We invite you to do your own thing - or let us look after you." That's the motto of the four star **Glencoe Mountain Cottages & B&B**, set in beautiful, majestic Glencoe. It is situated one mile up a private farm track, and has a peaceful setting, surrounded by mountains. It is an ideal base for both climbers and walkers, or as a restful hideaway from the stresses of modern living. Here you can either stay in one of two beautiful self catering cottages, or enjoy the very best in B&B in Anna and Jeff Amis's home.

The B&B accommodation consists of two double bedrooms, one en suite and one with private facilities. They are comfortable and spacious with colour TV, hospitality tray and hair dryer. The guests' sitting room is relaxing and cosy, and the breakfasts are hearty and filling, using fresh local produce wherever possible. Anna and Jeff regret that no pets are accepted in the no smoking B&B establishment, though well behaved pets (maximum two) are welcome in the self catering cottages.

The cottages each have three bedrooms, are comfortably furnished with spacious living rooms

with TV sets, and the kitchens are fully equipped. Heating and hot water comes from off peak electricity, and is billed at the end of your stay. Bed linen and towels are included in the rent, as are outdoor furniture and barbecue equipment. A cot and high chair are available on request.

Nevis Gorge and Steall Falls

Start	Head of Glen Nevis Road
Distance	3 miles (4.75km)
Approximate time	2½ hours
Parking	Car park at end of Glen Nevis road
Refreshments	None
Ordnance Survey maps	Landranger 41 (Ben Nevis and Fort William), Outdoor Leisure 38 (Ben Nevis and Glen Coe)

This popular short walk goes through a gorge, often described as Himalayan in character, to reach a verdant meadow backed by one of the country's most scenic waterfalls, the 'bridal veil' of An Steall Ban. The path is rough, traverses steep, wooded slopes, and is fortunately not over-tidied, so the atmosphere of grandeur is unspoilt.

The drive up Glen Nevis from Fort William is full of character. Travel early, as the car park is often full later on. Stop briefly where the road swings left to cross the River Nevis. Below the bridge are the Lower Falls, and above lies the climbers' playground of the Polldubh Crags. Further on, the road squeezes between two arching Scots pines, where big boulders bear the scratch marks of passing glaciers. At the car park a remarkable long waterslide comes down the hill. In summer (though not on Sundays) a mobile refreshment kiosk may be present.

The gorge footpath leaves from the car park where a signpost indicates that it is 15 miles (24km) to Corrour Station – which you see on Walks 14, 18 and 20. (The remoteness of this station emphasises the wildness of the region.) The gorge is steeply wooded and the path rough in places with a touch of 'exposure' to it (the term climbers use for

the sense of having nothing beneath them!) – all the more to impress the visitor. The water boils through and the rocks are worn into many pots and cauldrons, some of which can be seen well up the crags, a clear indication of how the waters have carved their way down in the past.

The path suddenly comes out from the confines of the gorge Ⓐ (one steps down over a low wall) on to a big green meadow backed by the distant falls. Note the large crag, up to the left, which has clear water-channel marks on it, way above the present river level!

Follow the path up the edge of the meadow to gain a closer view of the falls, which at about 300ft (90m) are surpassed in height only by the Eas a' Chual Aluinn and the Falls of Glomach, neither of which can be seen so easily. The name *An Steall Ban* means 'the white spout'. A bridge of just three strands of wire leads over to a cosy cottage which is a local climbing club's 'hut' **B**. There is no necessity to cross (which will be a relief to the timid) unless you are determined to stand right below the falls.

A ten-minute walk up the glen brings you to a ruin (also called Steall) **C** which is a good place to picnic and explore the river, the Allt Coire Guibhsachan, which comes down in a series of falls and clear pools – perfection on a midge-free, sunny day.

On the return look out for a track zigzagging up the spur above the gorge entrance **A**. Very few walkers notice this alternative route out. (Those not sound of wind and limb are advised to return by the main path.) Turn right at the wall at the gorge mouth and along by some big boulders. After the fifth

boulder turn left and you are on the clearly defined path which corkscrews up with sturdy determination till it comes level with the top of the gorge. Here a cairn marks this superb viewpoint **D**. The name *Mam Cumhann* means 'narrow pass' and is clearly appropriate.

Continuing, take care on approaching the trees to follow the correct route. After the viewpoint the path swings right and is marked by a small cairn on a boulder. (Straight on is a false trail leading to difficulties.) It soon crosses a gully bed, wends on and, after another gully **E**, descends steadily to rejoin the outward track. ●

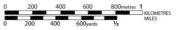

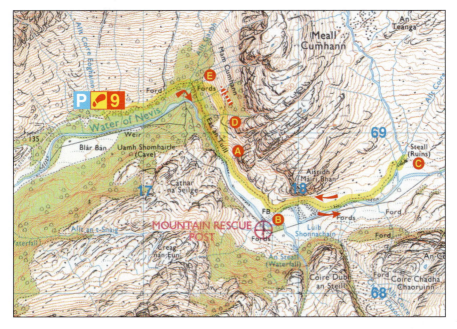

hospitality. However, on the morning of February 13th they set about systematically killing every member of McIan's people, including women and children, with only a few escaping. A monument in the shape of a tall Celtic cross commemorates the event, and a new **Glencoe Visitor Centre** (National Trust for Scotland - see panel on page 370) at Inverrigan explains what happened on the fateful morning.

Glencoe

The surrounding countryside is also owned and maintained by the National Trust for Scotland, and there are some marvellous walks. Further east is the Glencoe skiing area with a chair lift that remains open in the summer months.

ACHNACARRY

9 miles NE of Fort William on a minor road off the B8005

Achnacarry Castle was the home of Cameron of Locheil, known as "Gentle Locheil", one of Charles Edward Stuart's

DISTANT HILLS GUEST HOUSE

Spean Bridge, Inverness-shire PH34 4EU
Tel/Fax: 01397 712452
e-mail: enquiry@distanthills.com website: www.distanthills.com

Owned and run by Margaret and Derek Pratt, **Distant Hills** is a four star guest house that offers the very best in Scottish hospitality in an area of outstanding beauty and history. There are seven beautifully furnished and decorated en suite rooms, three doubles and four twins, with TVs and tea/coffee making facilities. The spacious guest lounge has a TV and video, as well as games and pastimes. Full Scottish breakfasts are served (with lighter options available) , and evening meals can be served by prior arrangement. Distant Hills makes a comfortable and friendly base from which to explore the Western Highlands.

FOREST LODGE

South Laggan, Invergarry, by Spean Bridge, Inverness-shire PH34 4EA
Tel: 01809 501219 Fax: 01809 501476
e-mail: info@flgh.co.uk website: www.flgh.co.uk

Janet and Ian Shearer run **Forest Lodge**, creating a relaxed and friendly atmosphere for the comfort of their guests. The accommodation consists of seven rooms all of which are en suite. There are also hospitality trays, and each room is centrally heated. Disabled access is via a ramp, and there are two extremely comfortable guest lounges, with TV, tourist material and games. Dinner is available by prior arrangement, and everything is home cooked using fresh local produce wherever possible. Details are available on the website.

most ardent supporters. After Culloden, the castle was completely destroyed by Government troops, and now only a column of masonry remains. The Camerons forfeited their estates and were banished from Britain, though they were allowed back in the early 19th century. In the **Cameron Museum** you can see displays and exhibits connected with Clan Cameron. A minor road goes past the castle and takes you along the shores of **Loch Arcaig**.

FORT AUGUSTUS

28 miles NE of Fort William on the A82

Fort Augustus was one of the government forts built in the early 18th century to keep those Highland clans who were sympathetic to the Jacobite cause in check. It was built on the orders of General Wade between 1729 and 1742, though it was actually taken by the Jacobites in 1745. In 1876 **Fort Augustus Abbey** was built on the site of the fort for Benedictine monks, but it closed in 1998, with many of its valuable books and manuscripts being donated to the National Library of Scotland. The **Caledonian Canal Heritage Centre** is within an old lock keeper's cottage, and tells of the canal's history over the years.

ARDNAMURCHAN PENINSULA

10 miles W of Fort William

If you travel north from Salen on the

A861, then turn off just north of Acheracle onto a minor road, you will come to the ruins of **Castle Tioram** (pronounced "Chirrum"), on the shores of Loch Moidart. It was originally built by Lady Anne MacRuari, whose son gave his name to Clan Ranald, in the mid 14th century. At the head of the loch is a line of five beech trees. Originally there were seven, and they commemorate the **Seven Men of Moidart**, who landed with Charles Edward Stuart and sailed with him up Loch Shiel towards Glenfinnan.

If you leave the A861 at Salen and travel west along the B8007, you will skirt the southern shores of the Ardnamurchan Peninsula and eventually land up at Ardnamurchan Point, mainland Britain's most westerly point. It is a wonderful run, full of majestic scenery. At Glenborrodale, on Loch Sunart, there is the late Victorian **Glenborrodale Castle** (not open to the public), once the home of Jesse Boot, founder of the Boots the Chemists chain. At **Kilchoan** there are the remains of **Mingary Castle**, once a stronghold of Clan McIan. It was visited by James IV in the 1490s, and later passed to the Campbells.

STRONTIAN

20 miles SW of Fort William on the A861

This little village sits in an area known as

ARIUNDLE CENTRE

Strathview, Strontian, Argyllshire PH36 4JA
Tel: 01967 402279

Set in the heart of romatic Argyllshire, the **Ariundle Centre** is a licensed restaurant, tearoom and workshop that specialises in dying yarns, spinning and knitting, with the wool coming from the Centre's own goats and sheep. This is a fascinating place where great food and snacks are served, and where you are sure of great value for money and a warm welcome at all  times. Why not try one of their candlelit suppers? There are also centres at Lochaber Siding, Fort William, Steam Train and Glenfinnan.

Sunart, which lies to the south of Loch Shiel. The village gave its name to the metal strontium, which was discovered in the local lead mines in 1791.

MORVERN
24 miles SW of Fort William

Morvern is that area that sits across the Sound of Mull from Mull itself. If you leave the A861 just east of Strontian and head south along the A884, you will pass through it. At the southern end of the road is Lochaline, which has a small ferry to Mull. **Lochaline Castle** sits at the head of Loch Aline, and was the ancestral home of Clan MacInnes. It is one of the few clans in Scotland without a chief, and clan members now take great pride in this. The last chief was murdered by John, Lord of the Isles, in 1354.

GLENFINNAN
14 miles W of Fort William on the A830

Glenfinnan sits at the head of Loch Shiel, and it was here that Charles Edward Stuart raised his standard in 1745. It was not here, however, that the Prince first set foot on Scottish soil, for Loch Shiel is a fresh water loch. He landed at first on Eriskay, in the Western

Charles Edward Stuart Monument

Isles, and from there sailed to the mainland at Loch nan Uamh. He then rode inland to Loch Shiel, where he stayed at a MacDonald household on the western banks. From there he sailed to the head of the loch at Glenfinnan. The **Charles Edward Stuart Monument** (National Trust for Scotland) was erected in 1815, and there is a visitor centre nearby that tells the story of his landing.

ARISAIG
29 miles W of Fort William on the A830

From Arisaig there are good views across to the islands of Rum and Eigg. South east of the village is **Loch Nan Uamh**, where Charles Edward Stuart first set foot on the Scottish mainland. A cairn marks

CAMUSDARACH

Arisaig, Inverness-shire PH39 4NT
Tel/Fax: 01687 450221
e-mail: camdarach@aol.com website: camusdarach.com

On Scotland's north west coast you will find **Camusdarach**, a small estate offering B&B, self catering accommodation and camping. There are two extremely comfortable south facing B&B rooms in the main house which share a bathroom, and in Camusdarach Farmhouse are two self catering apartments with fully equipped kitchens, both sleeping 4-6 people. Millburn Cottage is situated within its own gardens on the beautiful Rhu peninsula, and sleeps 6-8 people. The 42-pitch campsite was recently voted one of the best beach-side sites in the UK, with an immaculate toilet and shower block and electric hook up points.

Ben Nevis from Mallaig

Western Scotland. South east of the town is Scotland's deepest fresh water loch, **Loch Morar**. Its maximum depth is 1,077 feet, which is 90 feet more than the height of the Eiffell Tower. A minor road two miles south of Mallaig takes you to its shores. Like Loch Ness, this loch is also supposed to have a monster, this time nicknamed "Morag".

the spot. When his campaign to have the Stuarts restored to the British throne failed, he sailed for France from the same place.

MALLAIG

31 miles NW of Fort William on the A830

Mallaig is a fishing port and ferry terminal for Skye, South Uist and some smaller islands. The **Mallaig Heritage Centre** on Station Road explains the history of Morar, Knoydart and Arisaig. The **Mallaig Marine World Aquarium and Fishing Exhibition**, near the harbour, tells the story of Mallaig's fishing industry and explains about the marine life found in the waters off

KYLE OF LOCHALSH

40 miles NW of Fort William on the A87

The ferry that once ran between Skye and Kyle of Lochalsh has now been replaced by the graceful **Skye Bridge**. The **Lochalsh Woodland** (National Trust for Scotland - see panel on page 381) lies three miles east of the village along the A87, and has sheltered walks on the shores of Loch Alsh, as well as shrubs, trees and flowers. Further east you come to one of the most photographed castles, not just in Scotland, but in the world. **Eileen Donan Castle** sits on a small tidal island, connected to the mainland by a bridge, at the entrance to Loch Duich.

SPRINGBANK GUEST HOUSE

Eastbay, Mallaig, Inverness-shire PH41 4QF
Tel/Fax: 01687 462459 e-mail: susan@giles5050.fslife.co.uk

Mallaig is a small, attractive fishing port and holiday resort with views across to the misty isle of Skye. Here, within a picturesque, whitewashed cottage you will find the **Springbank Guest House**, offering good accommodation with a homely atmosphere. It is owned and run by Sue and Tony Giles, and has eight extremely comfortable and well appointed rooms, with a wash hand basin and tea/coffee making facilities in each. The guest lounge/dining room has marvellous open views. The breakfasts are traditional Scottish, though lighter options are available if required. Evening meals and packed lunches are available by prior arrangement.

KYLE HOTEL

Main Street, Kyle of Lochalsh, Ross-shire IV40 8AB
Tel: 01599 534204 Fax: 01599 534932
e-mail:thekylehotel@btinternet.com website: www.kylehotel.co.uk

An inn has stood on the site of the **Kyle Hotel** since the early 1700s
and the traditions of fine Scottish hospitality still continue, as the
hotel is one of the best in the area. All the bedrooms are en suite, with
hospitality tray, TV, telephone and hair dryer. The food is remarkable, with only the finest local produce
being used wherever possible, and the menus show flair and imagination. Kyle of Lochalsh is the
gateway to Skye, and you can visit Eileen Donan Castle, one of the most photographed castles in
Scotland. Hill walking, golf, sailing and many other activities are available.

TIGH-NAN-SAOR

39 Harbour Street, Plockton, Ross-shire IV52 8TN
Tel: 01599 544241 e-mail: martin@tigh-nan-saor.co.uk
Fax: 0870 7052547 website: www.tigh-nan-saor.co.uk

Set in the beautiful village of Plockton, where *Hamish Macbeth* was
filmed, **Tigh-nan-Saor** is a B&B that offers three en suite guest rooms.
They are all extremely comfortable, with TVs, hospitality trays and
two have magnificent sea views. To the front is the garden overlooking
Loch Carron, with tables and chairs where you can relax and take in the scenery. The spacious guest
lounge/dining room is on the ground floor, where your full Scottish breakfast is served, or something
lighter if you choose. Tigh-nan-Saor is full of books, which are shared with guests, and many paintings
by the house's owner, a professional artist. Long stays are available.

CONCHRA HOUSE

Sallachy Road, Aldelve, Kyle of Lochalsh,
Ross-shire IV40 8DZ
Tel: 01599 555233 Fax: 01599 555433
e-mail: sue@conchrahouse.co.uk
website: www.conchrahouse.co.uk

Conchra House was built in about 1760 as the seat of the
local Constable, and later became the ancestral home of the
McRae's of Eilean Donan Castle. "Conchra" means "sheltered
haven" in Gaelic, and it is an apt name, as it now offers a welcoming haven for visitors enjoying the
majestic beauty of the Kintail landscape. The hotel has six conveniently sized, cosy bedrooms, five
fully en suite and one enjoying private facilities, with two rooms on the second floor that double up
to make an excellent family suite, allowing guests that extra degree of privacy. Downstairs, the spacious
and tastefully appointed lounge provides the perfect environment for relaxing before a crackling log
fire, reading a book or newspaper, or planning the next day's activities.

Food is served in the inviting dining room, and all the produce is sourced locally wherever feasible
so that it is as fresh as possible. The breakfasts are traditional Scottish (or you can have something
lighter if you prefer), and the evening meals are all prepared on the premises, with menus that are
imaginative and varied. Special diets can be catered for by arrangement. The house is owned by Sue
and David Holland, who are proud of the high standards they maintain, and it has an unstuffy,
informal family atmosphere that will put you at your ease as you relax and recharge your batteries.
There is so much to do and see in the area as well, from birdwatching (you might see a golden eagle)
to hill walking and golf. Skye is only ten minutes away by car, as is Eilean Donan Castle, one of the
loveliest in Scotland, where part of the movie *Highlander* was filmed. A small function suite is also
available at Conchra House, and it can be used for small conferences, seminars and parties.

Originally built in 1220 by Alexander II, it is now the home of Clan MacRae, and has a small museum. Continue eastwards along the A87 and you come to Shiel Bridge, where Glen Shiel strikes inland. The **Five Sisters of Kintail** (National Trust for Scotland) overlook it, and a battle was fought here in 1719, where a Jacobite army was defeated. Legend says that ghostly, fighting figures can still be seen at the battle site.

BALMACARA ESTATE & LOCHALSH WOODLAND GARDEN

Lochalsh House (INITS), Balmacara, Kyle, Ross-shire IV40 8DN
Tel: 01599 566325 Fax: 01599 566359
e-mail balmacara@nts.org.uk
Ranger/naturalist:
Tel: 01599 511231 Fax: 01599 511417

A crofting estate of 2,750 ha (6,795 a) with outstanding views of Skye and Applecross, and including the village of Plockton, an

Outstanding Conservation Area. The estate also includes the Coille Mhor oakwood Special Area of Conservation (SAC). The neighbouring Loch Alsh is part of the Loch Alsh & Loch Duish marine SAC. Visitors can discover more about this secluded, fascinating area at the small Visitor Centre at Balmacara Square, where an interactive CD ROM, guides to the extensive footpath network and other local information are available. The Visitor Centre is located within the recently restored farm steadings beside the old millpond. There are also

craft workshops and a small delicatessen within the Square complex, an excellent spot for a picnic. Lochalsh Woodland Garden offers quiet sheltered walks by the lochside among mature Scots pine, oalks and beeches with developing collections of rhododendrons, fuchsias, bamboos, hydrangeas and ferns. Interpretation provided at the reception kiosk in the garden.

The village of **Plockton** sits on Loch Carron, and was the setting for the popular BBC drama series *Hamish Macbeth*, based on the popular books. In the series the village was called Lochdhub, and people were surprised to see palm trees growing this far north - testimony to the effects of the Gulf Stream. The ruins of **Strome Castle** (National Trust for Scotland) sits east of

LOCH DUICH PLANTS

Forester's Bungalow, Inverinate, near Kyle of Lochalsh, Ross-shire IV40 8HE
Tel/Fax: 01599 511407 e-mail: donald.macintosh@tesco.net
website: www.lochalsh.com/duichplants

Set amid superb scenery, **Loch Duich Plants** is a colourful garden centre sitting close to the beautiful Loch Duich. Here you will find shrubs, trees, plants, alpine heathers, garden sundries, cut flowers, gift tokens, ceramics and a host of other garden supplies. It even sells pet food, and bouquets and wedding flowers can be made up at extremely competitive prices. The staff are friendly and knowledgeable, and are always on hand to offer skilled advice. You can send flowers to any part of the world, as it is part of the teleflorist network.

VISIT KINTAIL

Beinn Fhada, Inverinate, near Kyle of Lochalsh, Ross-shire IV40 84F
Tel /Fax: 01599 511407
e-mail: donald@visitkintail.co.ukwebsite: www.visitkintail.co.uk

Kintail is a rugged, unspoilt area of the Western Highlands that offers
some of the best and most dramatic scenery in Scotland.One of the
country's last great wildernesses, it is easily reached from Edinburgh,
Glasgow and further south. The new Skye Bridge is the gateway to that lovely island. Eilean Donan
Castle, one of the most beautiful and famous castles in Scotland, is in Kintail, and there are plenty of
opportunities for hill walking, bird watching, fishing and sea angling. Watch a golden eagle soar, sea
otters play, deer, badgers, pine martins and wild goats. Eat in spotless tearooms and pubs and stay in
one of the hotels, guest houses and B&Bs, and experience real Scottish hospitality.

SOLUIS MU THUATH

Braeintra, by Achmore, Lochalsh, Ross-shire IV53 8UP
Tel/Fax: 01599 577219
e-mail: soluismuthuath@btopenworld.com
website: highlands accommodation.co.uk

Soluis Mu Thuath is a five bedroom, family run, non-smoking guest
house in one of the loveliest parts of the Western Highlands. All the
rooms (a family room, a double and three twins) are spacious, beautifully furnished, and fully en
suite, with TVs and hospitality trays. Two of them are on the ground floor, and are suitable for the
accompanied disabled. The guest lounge is warm and welcoming, with log fire, a range of games and
stunning views. The breakfasts are hearty and filling, and there is a table license for evening meals.
Everything is home cooked to perfection, using fresh local produce wherever possible.

WEST HIGHLAND DAIRY

Achmore, Stromeferry, Ross-shire IV53 8UW
Tel: 01599 577203 e-mail: info@westhighlanddairy.co.uk
Fax: 01599 577331 website: www.westhighlanddairy.co.uk

Situated down a quiet lane leading to the shores of beautiful Loch
Carron, the **West Highland Dairy** is the one of Scotland's small band
of artisan cheese makers. The dairy also manufactures yogurt, crème
fraiche and delicious ice cream, not to mention traditional dairy
desserts. It is a family run business that makes up to 12 different types of cheese from both cow and
sheep milk. The range includes hard and soft cheese, along with blue and surface ripened cheeses. All
the products are available from the dairy shop along with oat cakes, honey and a selection of home
made jams and marmalade. Most of the fruit for the jam is grown in the dairy garden.

　　　Katherine and David Biss, who have had many years experience within the industry in a production
and teaching role, opened the Dairy in 1987, and with hard work and an eye for quality, have created
a range of products which are popular with locals and tourists alike.

　　　An unusual aspect of the dairy business is its training role. Once a month a three-day cheese

making course is offered to aspiring cheese makers. The course participants
are accommodated in local B&B and spend the three days learning the basics
of cheese manufacture. Practical skills teaching are combined with the
theoretical aspects of the process. Katherine's book *Practical Cheesemaking* is
good introductory reading. Come and try some cheese and buy a picnic of
oat cakes, cheese and a dairy dessert. There is a beach at the bottom of the
lane where you can sit and eat your picnic and enjoy the peace. You might be
fortunate enough to see an otter.

GRAMARYE STUDIO

An Cuilionn, Achmore, Stromeferry, Ross and Cromarty IV 53 8UU
Tel/Fax: 01599 577264
e-mail: sales@gramaryestudio.co.uk
website: www.gramaryestudio.co.uk

Gramarye Studio is a small, friendly working studio that exhibits the
work of Annie Coomber, who produces offbeat linocut prints and
colourful papier maché items finished in fine papers. The studio is situated in a particularly beautiful
part of Scotland and here you are bound to find the perfect souvenir or gift. Also on display are cards,
tags and notelets, all designed by Annie. It is open on Wednesday, Thursday and Friday, Easter -
October 10.30 to 5.30 (Monday to Friday in May). A mail order service is also available.

Plockton, on the opposite
side of the loch. It was a
stronghold of the Lord of the
Isles, and later belonged to
the MacDonnells of
Glengarry. After a siege in
1602, it was blown up.

Portree, Isle of Skye

SKYE

40 miles NW of Fort William

Though the Skye Bridge has
in some ways robbed Skye of
its island status, it is still one
of the most beautiful places
in Scotland. The most famous
natural features are the
Cuillins (or more properly, Cuillin
Mountiains), a range of hills to the south
east of the island. Though not high, they
are spectacular, and present a challenge
to any climber. The highest peak is the
3,309 feet **Shgurr Alasdair**.

Broadford is one of the island's main
settlements, and lies on the A87, west of
the Skye Bridge. The road then follows
the coast, and at Sconser is a ferry that
takes you to the small offshore island of
Raasay, once visited by Johnson and
Boswell as they made their Highland
tour. Skye's main settlement is **Portree**,

ISLE OF SKYE CRAFTS/THISTLE STITCHES

Torr Park, Torvaig, Isle of Skye, Inverness-shire IV51 9HU
Tel/Fax: 01478 612361 e-mail: info@isleofskyecrafts.com
website: www.isleofskyecrafts.com

About two miles out of Portree is the **Isle of Skye Crafts/Thistle Stitches**,
a wonderful company that sells a wide range of truly beautiful cross
stitch kits for the amateur and the more advanced. There is a working
studio that offers various designs, plus a fine selection of wools and other
items associated with the craft. There are many designs on show, though
it specialises in uniquely Scottish themes, such as birds and animals,
Scottish scenes and clans and tartans. This is a great place to pick up a unique Scottish souvenir.

ISLE OF SKYE SOAP CO. LTD.

(The Shop off the Square), Somerled Square, Portree, Isle of Skye,
Inverness-shire IV51 9EH
Tel/Fax: 01478 611350
e-mail: sales@skye-soap.co.uk website: www.skye-soap.co.uk

If you're looking for an unusual and thoughtful gift, or a souvenir of
your stay on the misty Isle of Skye., then look no further than the **Isle of
Skye Soap Company**. It supplies unique, hand-crafted aromatherapy
soap, without colouring, using only the purest essential oils, plus a range
of other products. Soaps like this are far better for your skin and it is far
better for the environment as well. The shop carries a huge range of items
from the company's extensive catalogue, and the smells and textures of the products are out of this
world. Ginger and cinnamon - seaweed and cedarwood - orange and oatmeal - rosewood, almond and
thistle - myrtle and heather - the range and combinations of essences and fragrances just go on and

on. Plus there is bath oil, drawer sachets, hand cream, lip balm, pillow
sachets and even soft cosy dressing gowns embroidered with the Isle of
Skye Soap Company name.

The company was established in 2000, and opened their showroom
two years later in an old weaving shed with wonderfully coloured
stained glass windows. All the soaps - and there are over 17 unique
varieties - are carefully handcrafted, as are the bath bombs, and they
are all carefully wrapped to make them as fresh and fragrant as possible.
The natural colours of the Isle of Skye throughout the year are used as
the inspiration for the Cuillin range of products, named after the island's
Cuillin Mountains, one of the most beautiful areas of Scotland.

GLENVIEW HOTEL

Culnacnoc, by Staffin, Isle of Skye, Inverness-shire IV51 9JH
Tel: 01470 562248 Fax: 01470 562211
e-mail: doreen@theglenviewhotel.fsnet.co.uk
website: www.glenview-skye.co.uk

Set on the Trotternish Peninsula on the lovely Isle of Skye, the
pet-friendly **Glenview Hotel** offers five extremely comfortable
bedrooms - two doubles with four poster bed, one double and two twin/doubles. Four are fully en
suite, while the fifth has its own private bathroom. The building was constructed in 1903, and was
once a local merchant's house, and it has lost none of it's Edwardian charm. It has lovely views over
the Old Man of Storr, and there is nothing better than sitting at a table or bench in the garden in the
still of the evening with a quiet drink as you relax after a hard day's sightseeing.

The spacious and welcoming guest lounge has an open fire, TV and video, and in the dining room
the very best of gourmet food is served. Doreen Harben and Ian Stratton have owned and run the
hotel since 2002, and since then have earned a wonderful reputation for its cuisine. They are extremely
proud of the food they serve, and use only the freshest local produce wherever possible. They boast

that their seafood is "fresh from the boat to the table". The
restaurant is open to non residents. The ambience is informal
and friendly, and the prices very reasonable. The whole area
surrounding the hotel is rich in history, and river and loch
fishing is available. Charter boats can also be hired for sea fishing
excursions into the Minch. This is a warm, inviting
establishment, and should you visit, Doreen and Ian will go
out of their way to make your stay both pleasurable and
rewarding.

ISLE OF SKYE FALCONRY

Kirklee, Kensaleyre, Isle of Skye, Inverness-shire IV51 9XE
Tel: 01470 532489
e-mail: skyefalconry@hotmail.com website: isleofskye-falconry.co.uk

Falconry is an exciting and fascinating activity, and now you too can
have a go at it. **Isle of Skye Falconry** will let you experience the beauty
and grace of birds of prey from around the world. There is a range of
courses varying from a full day Introduction to a birds of prey course and a raptor management
course. There are also "Hawk Walks", where you get a basic introduction followed by a walk where a
Harris hawk will follow and fly to you through the trees, this is a two hour session. All by appointment
only. There are also displays which can be booked for your own event.The business is run by Jenny
Sandiford and Euan Naylor, who have had years of experience. Open all year round.

about ten miles north of Scorser. It is the
gateway to the **Trotternish Peninsula**,
which thrusts out into the Little Minch,
that expanse of water between Skye and
the Outer Hebrides. A road goes in a
circular route round the peninsula,

bringing you back at Portree, and it
makes a good run with many views. **Uig**
is a small ferry port connecting Skye to
Harris and North Uist. At Kilmuir is the
grave of **Flora Macdonald**, who helped
Charles Edward Stuart escape from South
Uist after his defeat at
Culloden.

Loch Dunvegan

The **Waternish Peninsula**
lies west of Trotternish. Near
Stein, along the B886, you
will find **Skyeskins**,
Scotland's only traditional
tannery, which makes hand-
combed fleeces. There is a
shop and a visitor centre,
where you can see the
traditional implements used
by the tanner, as well as the
hand finishing process that
gives the fleeces their
luxurious feel.

STEIN INN

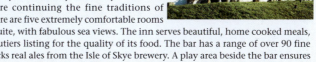

Waternish, by Dunvegan, Isle of Skye, Inverness-shire IV55 8GA
Tel: 01470 592362 e-mail: angus.teresa@steininn.co.uk
website: www.steininn.co.uk

The three star **Stein Inn** is proud of the fact that it is the oldest
inn on the lovely Isle of Skye. It is family owned by Teresa and
Angus MacGhie, who are continuing the fine traditions of
Highland hospitality. There are five extremely comfortable rooms
on offer, all are fully en suite, with fabulous sea views. The inn serves beautiful, home cooked meals,
and has a coveted Les Routiers listing for the quality of its food. The bar has a range of over 90 fine
single malts, and also stocks real ales from the Isle of Skye brewery. A play area beside the bar ensures
that parents can relax in peace over a quiet drink.

SKYESKYNS

17 Loch Bay, Waternish, Isle of Skye IV55 8GD
Tel/Fax: 01470 592237
e-mail: clive@skyeskyns.co.uk website: www.skyeskyns.co.uk

Set amid the dramatic scenery of the Waternish Peninsula, **Skyeskyns** is Scotland's only traditional exhibition tannery. Here you can see the age-old processes involved in producing sheepskins. There is a free guided tour, where you will see all the traditional implements used by the tanner. These help to create the world famous Highland hand-combed fleece, which is exclusive to Skyeskyns. After the tour, you can browse in the fascinating showroom, where a wide range of soft, fleecy sheepskins are on display. They make the perfect souvenir of a visit to the "misty isle".

KILMUIR PARK

Dunvegan, Isle of Skye, Inverness-shire IV 55 8GU
Tel/Fax: 01470 521586
e-mail: info@kilmuirpark.co.uk website: milford.co.uk/go/kilmuir.html

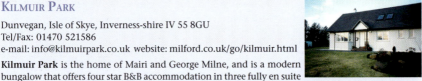

Kilmuir Park is the home of Mairi and George Milne, and is a modern bungalow that offers four star B&B accommodation in three fully en suite bedrooms. The rooms have TV/radios, hair dryers and tea/coffee making facilities. The furnishings are comfortable and colour coordinated to make your stay restful and relaxing. The beautifully cooked breakfasts are full Scottish, though something lighter is also available. Mairi will also cook delicious evening meals by prior arrangement, using local produce wherever possible. There is plenty of parking space, and the guest lounge has a TV, video player, small library and a selection of games.

OLD SCHOOL RESTAURANT

Dunvegan, Isle of Skye, Inverness-shire IV55 8GU
Tel/Fax: 01470 521421

For great food on the lovely Isle of Skye, head for the **Old School Restaurant** in Dunvegan. As the name suggests, it is housed in Dunvegan's old school building, which was erected in 1870. Owned and managed by Mary Ann MacKenzie since 1985, it has earned an enviable reputation as one of the best eating places on the island. Now her son John has joined her as manager/chef, and she invites you to sample traditional Scottish food at its very best. The kitchen uses only the finest freshest local produce wherever possible, including locally caught fish and shellfish, game, poultry, beef and vegetables.

The dishes are imaginatively prepared, and always cooked to perfection. For starters, why not try the langoustines, or the Talisker haggis – Scotland's national dish with a dash of malt whisky served with "mashed tatties and neeps"? For your main course you could have venison fillet served with a honey, whisky and English mustard sauce, or prime Aberdeen Angus steaks with all the trimmings. The main courses also include fish dishes, and vegetarian options are available as well. The restaurant

carries a select range of wines to accompany your meal, as well as a range of single malt whiskies. There is plenty of parking space, and on warm summer evenings you can even eat outside while admiring the lovely views. The restaurant can seat 50 people in absolute comfort, and there is plenty of wheelchair access plus disabled toilets. So for a culinary experience that combines the best of food, the finest of wines and an ambience that speaks of traditional Scottish hospitality, you can't do better than pay a visit to the Old School Restaurant.

THE HIGHLANDS

A mile north of the village of Dunvegan is **Dunvegan Castle**, ancestral home of Clan MacLeod. Much of the castle is Victorian, though parts date back to the 13th century. In the Drawing Room is the famous "Fairy Flag", which is supposed to bring success to MacLeods in battle. But it's magic only works three times, and it has already been used twice. There are many legends associated with it, ranging from a fairy mother giving birth to the son of a clan chief and using it to cover the son, to it being brought back from the Holy Land or it being an old Norse battle standard.

Uig Ferry, Isle of Skye

The **Angus Macaskill Museum**, close to Dunvegan, is dedicated to Scotland's only true giant, Angus MacAskill, who lived between 1825 and 1863, and was 7ft 9in tall. When three years old, he and his family emigrated to Cape Breton. At Colbost, on the B884, is the Colbost Croft Museum, based on an old "black house", a traditional cottage of turf or stone with a thatched roof.

To the south east of the island, on the

ORBOST GALLERY

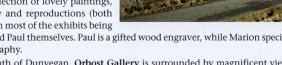

nr Dunvegan, Isle of Skye,
Inverness-shire IV55 8ZB
Tel:01470 521207 Fax: 01470 521613
website: www.orbostgallery.co.uk

This purpose built art gallery is jointly owned by Marion Roberts and Paul Kershaw, and was opened in 1977. Here you can see a wide selection of lovely paintings, original prints, calligraphy and reproductions (both framed and unframed), with most of the exhibits being the work of both Marion and Paul themselves. Paul is a gifted wood engraver, while Marion specialises in water colours and calligraphy.

Situated a few miles south of Dunvegan, **Orbost Gallery** is surrounded by magnificent views of the sea, cliffs and mountains. Most of the works on exhibition celebrate the varied, rugged scenery of the Highlands and the Isle of Skye in particular. Besides Marion and Paul's work, there are paintings by

Jill Aldersley, Andrew McMorrine, Angus Stewart, Helen Robertson and other talented artists who are invited to exhibit their work. A selection of antique prints is usually on show, and the gallery offers a picture framing service and sells a range of artists' materials. As well as the large gallery area, there is a working studio with an iron handpress. Commissions are undertaken and the prices, like those of the exhibits in the gallery, are remarkably reasonable. Expert advice is always on hand if you wish to buy something to remind you of your visit to Skye

KINLOCHFOLLART

by Dunvegan, Isle of Skye, Inverness-shire IV55 8WQ
Tel: 01470 521470 Fax: 01470 521740
e-mail: klfskye@tiscali.co.uk website: www.klfskye.co.uk

Kinlochfollart is a welcoming family home owned and run by
Rosemary and Donald MacLeod who are introducing four-day
breaks-with all meals included and laundry-based on
individually arranged itineraries to make the most of the size
and diversity of Skye, the island. In an informal house-party
atmosphere guests are able to enjoy superb food, log fires, library and conservatory.. There are spectacular
views from all the rooms including the two double bedrooms with en-suite facilities, and a third with
nearby private bathroom. A non-smoking house..

RAVEN PRESS GALLERY

Colbost, by Dunvegan, Isle of Skye, IV55 8ZS
Tel: 01470 511748
e-mail:raven@kathleenlindsley.co.uk
website: www.kathleenlindsley.co.uk

At the lochside Raven Press Gallery
you can see the fine skills of wood
engraving, and printing on an
Albion handpress of c1845. A
selling exhibition of meticulously
framed and exquisite images of birds, beasts and landscape is
complemented by handbound books, vibrant resist-dyed and
painted silks and handknit design.

Sleat Peninsula, is the **Armadale Castle
Gardens and Museum of the Isles**. It
sits within a 20,000 acre estate, once
owned by the MacDonald's of Sleat.

CANNA

57 miles NW of Fort William

Canna comes from Gaelic for
"porpoise island", and is owned
by the National Trust for
Scotland (see panel opposite). It
is one of the smaller of the Inner
Hebrides, being 5 miles long by
about a mile wide. It is reached
by ferry from Mallaig.

EIGG

40 miles W of Fort William

The Isle of Eigg Heritage Trust
bought the island in 1997 on

behalf of its inhabitants. It's most
famous feature is the 1,277 feet high **An
Sgurr**, which slopes up gently from one
side and plunges almost vertically on the
other. The main settlement is at
Cleadale, on the north west shore,

Eigg

CANNA

Inner Hebrides
Tel: 01687 462466
website: www.nts.org.uk

The most westerly of the Small Isles, **Canna** is five miles long and one mile wide. Its cultural background, archaeology and ornithology make it one of the most interesting islands in the Hebrides. Sustainable farming and crofting systems are carried out on the island, which is a Special Protection Area for its large population of seabirds, especially shags, which nest in the cliffs of its dramatic shoreline. Canna is also a Special Area of Conservation. Pony trekking is available.

though the ferry main pier is at Galmisdale to the south east. Near Galmisdale are two caves, The **Massacre Cave**, also known as St. Francis's Cave, and **MacDonald's Cave**, also known as Cathedral Cave. MacDonald's Cave has held Catholic church services in it since the Jacobite Uprising, and occasionally still does. Massacre Cave got its name from a bloody incident in 1577, when 395 MacDonalds, who were hiding from a MacLeod raid, were suffocated to death when the MacLeods tried to smoke them out.

MUCK

46 miles W of Fort William

The name "Muck" comes from the Gaelic "eilean nam muc", meaning island of pigs. It is a low lying island, easily reached by ferry from Mallaig, and has some good beaches. **Port Mor** is the main village and harbour, and close to it are the remains of

a prehistoric fort called **Dun Ban**. The highest point on the island is the 445 feet high **Beinn Airein**, from which you get some wonderful views of the whole of the island.

RUM

47 miles W of Fort William

Sir George Bullough bought Rum in 1888, and immediately changed its name to "Rhum", as he objected to it sharing a name with an alcoholic drink. However, in 1957 the Nature Conservancy Council took over the island, and in 1991 gave it back its real name. It has nothing to do with drink, and though no one knows for certain, the name may derive from the Norse meaning "wide island".

Nowadays it is an Area of Special Scientific Interest, as it has some plant life that has remained unchanged since the Ice Age. The main settlement is at Kinloch, where Sir George Bullough built **Kinloch Castle** as his island home. **The Bullough Mausoleum** sits in Glen Harris, to the south of the island, and is where

Isle of Muck

MILLWOOD HOUSE

36 Old Mill Road, Inverness, Inverness-shire IV2 3HR
Tel: 01463 237245 Fax: 08704 296806
website: www.millwoodhouse.co.uk

Millwood House stands in a beautiful secluded garden in a quiet, exclusive area of Inverness, with the city centre being a short walk away. It has been given the much coveted five star status from Visit Scotland, which means that it offers all that is best in Scottish hospitality. The house is a picturesque, two-storied cottage built about 60 years ago, surrounded by conifers and lavender, with a terrace that is a profusion of colour in the summer months. The three double rooms on offer are all fully en suite, and beautifully furnished to an extremely high standard. Each has a colour TV, cottage charm and a view of the garden. The guests' sitting room has been furnished with antiques and flowers, and has an open fire, just right for autumn evenings, when you can curl up on one of the cozy chairs and browse through the many books.

The breakfasts at Millwood House are all beautifully cooked using only the freshest of local produce wherever possible. Choose from a wide range of dishes, from a delicious traditional Scottish breakfast

of home cured bacon, eggs, sausage, tomatoes etc., Scottish smoked salmon with scrambled egg or Scottish kippers with tomatoes. These are served in the handsome dining room, where there is a striking display of beautiful dishes. Within the extensive gardens, where you are free to stroll, there is a hammock for lazy, summer days, a wheelbarrow filled with flowers and other interesting features. The owner, Gillian Lee, has a wealth of information on what to see in and around Inverness (including Loch Ness), and offers tea or coffee with biscuits when you first arrive.

CASTLE GALLERY

43 Castle Street, Inverness, Inverness-shire IV2 3DU
Tel: 01463 729512 Fax: 01463 729513
e-mail: info@castlegallery.co.uk website: www.castlegallery.co.uk

One of Scotland's leading art galleries is set in Inverness, capital of the Highlands of Scotland. Run and owned by Denise Collins, who has a degree in fine art, **The Castle Gallery** has an unrivalled reputation for the quality of its artists, the innovation of its shows and the range of services to collectors. It is housed in a sympathetically restored 18th century building (with exposed wattle and daub) in the lee of Inverness Castle, and offers space on two floors for paintings, prints, sculpture, ceramics, glass, wood, textiles and jewellery. Figurative and abstract works from both Scottish and British artists are on show, and with works by established and rising artists, there is something for everyone here.

Prices range from £20 to over £5,000, and the gallery accepts all major credit and debit cards, and can arrange interest free credit on purchases over £400. The staff are friendly and welcoming, and always on hand to offer expert advice on anything you may wish to purchase. The gallery can also pack, export and arrange VAT refunds for people from outside the European Community, and can provide personal and expert advice on framing, using museum quality, acid-free materials. The gallery has been commended for the quality of its exhibits and exhibitions by the Crafts Council, which is an honour in its own right. If it's an original painting you're after, or a piece of craftwork that will remind you of your trip to Scotland, then the Castle Gallery is the place for you.

Sir George, his wife Monica and his father John now lie.

INVERNESS

This small city is the capital of the Highlands. It is said to be one of the most rapidly expanding places in Europe, and though it only has a population of about 45,000, its hinterland supports a further 20,000 people.

It has all the feel and bustle of a much larger place, however,

Bridge over the River Ness

and has many shops - more than you would imagine for a place its size. It stands at the north eastern end of Glen More ("Great Glen"), at the point where the River Ness enters the Moray Firth. It was once the capital of the kingdom of the Picts, and it was to Inverness that St. Columba came in the 6th century to convert Brude, King of the Picts, to Christianity. The doors of the king's fortress were slammed shut on him but when he marked them with the sign of the cross, they were supposed to have flown open again of their own accord.

People have suggested that the fortress may have stood on **Craig Phadraig**, two miles west of the place where the river Ness enters the firth, while others have suggested **Torvean**, just outside the city. The present **Inverness Castle** dates from the early 19th century, and stands on a

site where a castle has stood since the 12th century. This is not the site, however, of Macbeth's castle, where Shakespeare set part of his play. General Wade enlarged the castle after the Jacobite Uprising of 1715, and was held by government troops up until they surrendered in 1745. The present building is now the local courtroom, and close to it is the **Flora MacDonald Statue**.

The **Town House** is in Bridge Street, and its building was completed in 1882. It was here, in 1921, that the only cabinet meeting ever to have taken place outside London in modern times was held. Across from it is the **Tolbooth Steeple**, dating from the late 18th century. It is all that is left of the former courtrooms and jail. In Castle Wynd is the **Inverness Museum and Art Gallery**,

St Andrews Cathedral

where there are extensive collections relating to the town and the surrounding area.

Abertaff House (National Trust for Scotland) is situated in Church Street, and is the town's oldest secular building. It dates from 1593, and was the town house of the Frasers of Lovat, whose main home was in Strathglass. However, it is not open to the public. Also in Church Street **Dunbar's Hospital**, which dates from 1668, and was founded as a hospital for the poor by a former provost. It has now been converted into flats.

Balnain House (National Trust for Scotland) is on the western side of the River Ness, in Huntly Street. It dates from 1726, and is now the NTS's regional offices. **Inverness Cathedral** also stands on the western bank. It was designed by Alexander Ross, and built between 1866 and 1869 in Gothic style. The two large towers at the western end were supposed to have had tall spires, but these were never built. The **Old High Church**, Inverness's parish church, is dedicated to St. Mary, and is in Church Street. It dates from the mid 1700s,

RIVERSIDE GALLERY

11 Bank Street, Inverness IV1 1RB
Tel/Fax: 01463 224781
e-mail: riversidegallery@tiscali.co.uk
website: www.riversidegallery.info

Pleasantly situated on the banks of the River Ness, the **Riverside Gallery** is the place to buy a piece of contemporary Scottish art while in the Highlands. It is owned and managed by Hugh Nicol, and has oil paintings, watercolours and prints that range from wonderful landscapes and still life through to colourful wildlife, sporting subjects and natural history. The gallery is spacious and light, covering two floors in a 19th century building, and the work on show changes continuously to reflect the lively arts scene in and around Inverness.

Hugh has owned the gallery since 1986, and is a walking encyclopaedia on modern Scottish art and artists, so you know that when you buy from the Riverside Gallery, the work is from an artist who is skilful with the brush and highly respected in their field. Hugh is dedicated to bringing contemporary

Scottish art to the people at realistic prices, so you won't have to dig too deep to be the proud owner of a painting or print that will become the centre piece of a room in your home. He also offers a framing service, and through his many contacts in the art word, can arrange for restoration work to be carried out on both oils and watercolours using skilled, local people. The gallery also exhibits locally produced craft work such as glassware, intricate wood carvings and hand painted silk scarves and ties. The gallery is open from Monday to Friday from 9.30 am to 5 pm, and on Saturday from 9.30 am to 4 pm.

though parts may be even older. The former church that stood on the site was used to house Jacobite prisoners after the Jacobite Uprising, and indeed it was the in the kirkyard that many of them were executed. The **Old Gaelic Church** as we see it today dates from 1792, though it incorporates masonry from an earlier church built in the mid 1600s.

But Inverness has more modern structures as well. The **Kessock Bridge** connecting Inverness with the Black Isle was opened in 1982, and carries the A9 across it as it heads north towards Thurso. The bridge spans the Great Glen Fault, so earth tremors had to be taken into account when designing it. At North Kessock is the **Dolphins and Seals of the Moray Firth Visitor and Research Centre**. The Firth is famous for its dolphins, and boats leave from many

ports on its coastline to give you a closer look at them.

AROUND INVERNESS

GOLSPIE
40 miles N E of Inverness on the A9

Above the town, on **Bienn a'Bhragaih**, is a huge statue of the 1st Duke of Sutherland, who died in 1833. It was sculpted by Chantry, and a plaque tells us it was erected by a "mourning and grateful tenantry to a judicious, kind and liberal landlord". The words, however, are not all they seem. The Duke was one of the instigators of the hated Clearances of the 19th century, and there have been repeated calls to have the statue blown up and removed. Others have argued that it should stay where it is as a reminder of those terrible days.

Dunrobin Castle (see panel), the seat of the Dukes of Sutherland, is Scotland's most northerly grand house, and one of the largest in the Highlands. It resembles a magnificent French chateau, though the core is 14th century. It was designed by Sir Charles Barry, the man who designed the Houses of Parliament in London. The castle has 189 rooms, and some are open to the public in the summer. There is also a small museum in a summer house.

DUNROBIN CASTLE & GARDENS
Golspie, Sutherland KW10 6RR
Tel: 01408 633177
e-mail: dunrobin.est@btinternet.com

Dunrobin Castle is the most northerly of Scotland's great houses. It is the largest house in the northern Highlands with 189 rooms and is one of Britain's oldest continuously inhabited houses, dating in part from the early 1300s. The magnificent formal gardens were designed by Barry, the architect of the Houses of Parliament and the Victorian museum contains a fabulous collection of Pictish stones, local history, geology and wildlife specimens. Complete your visit with some light refreshments in the Castle Buffet and browse around the gift shop with its large range of gifts, souvenirs and local craftware. Open 1st April to 31st May and 1st to 15th October, Monday to Saturday 10.30am-4.30pm and Sunday 12 noon-4.30pm; 1st June to 30th September, Monday to Saturday 10.30am-5.30pm and Sunday 12noon(10.30 during July and August)-5.30pm.

LAIRG

40 miles N of Inverness on the A836

Lairg became important in olden times as it sits at the south eastern end of **Loch Shin**, where various Highland roads converge. **Ord Hill**, to the west of the town, has a small archaeological trail which takes you round many sites. Loch Shin itself has been harnessed for hydroelectric power, and five miles south, on the B864, are the **Falls of Shin**, with an accompanying visitor centre.

DORNOCH

30 miles N of Inverness on the A949

Dornoch hit the headlines in December 2000 when pop singer Madonna and Guy Ritchie were married in **Dornoch Cathedral**. The church, which was originally built in the 13th century, was remodelled in Victorian times, though many old features can still be seen. Sixteen Earls of Sutherland are said to be

buried within its walls. In 1722, Dornoch also achieved fame, but for a different reason. In 1722, Scotland's last execution for witchcraft took place here, and a stone on the links commemorates the event. An old woman, Janet Horne, was burned to death for supposedly turning her daughter into a pony. The presiding judge at the trial was later criticised for his handling of the whole thing.

TAIN

23 miles N of Inverness on the A9

Though quiet now, Tain at one time was one of the most famous places in Scotland. Pilgrims came from all over - even from the Continent - to visit the shrine of St. Duthac which was within **St. Duthac's Collegiate Church**. He lived at a time when the Roman Catholic Church was replacing the old Celtic monasticism in Scotland, and though he was called the "Bishop of Ross", this may have been in the old Celtic sense, where

---

MANSFIELD HOUSE HOTEL

Scotsburn Road, Tain, Ross-shire IV19 1PR
Tel: 01862 892052 Fax: 01862 892260
e-mail: info@mansfieldhouse.eu.com
website: www.mansfieldhouse.eu.com

The four star **Mansfield House Hotel** is a luxury country house hotel with a warm and welcoming atmosphere. The building dates from the 1870s and has been substantially extended since then, though it retains many of its original features, such as pine panelling and ornate plaster ceilings. It even claims to have a ghost - albeit one who is as friendly as the staff. All the bedrooms have recently been refurbished to an exceptionally high standard, so that they are fully en suite, with colour TVs, trouser presses, thick towelling robes and so-on. The rooms in the Victorian part of the house have antique furniture, and many bathrooms have Jacuzzis.

The public rooms are spacious and comfortable, and there is a well stocked bar with over 80 single malts on offer. It's the ideal place to relax after a day exploring this part of Scotland, which is steeped in history. Dining at the Mansfield is a civilised affair, with stylish surroundings, crisp linen and, of course, delicious food. You can eat in the bar and grill from 12noon-2.30pm, or in the dining room from 7pm-10pm. The hotel has won many awards for its cuisine, and it has even featured in the *Taste of Scotland* yearbook. Only the finest and freshest of produce is used wherever possible, and the menu has been assembled with imagination and flare. At one time Tain was a place of pilgrimage, due to the shrine of St. Duthac in the local church. Now it is a place of pilgrimage for those people who appreciate a warm, Highland welcome in a luxurious yet comfortable hotel.

SOUTH CORNER

21 Market Street, Tain, Ross & Cromarty IV19 1AR
Tel: 01862 892997 Fax: 01862 810932

South Corner was established in 1998 to provide tourists and local people with a wide range of unusual jewellery, gemstones and gifts. Owned and run by Ulrike Zywietz, it sits within a historic 18th century building, right in the heart of a royal burgh that is in itself historic. Ulrike prides herself on the quality and affordability of the items on display, and is always on hand to offer friendly and expert advice when you wish to buy a unique gift or souvenir of your trip to this part of Scotland. As well as jewellery and gems, there is a wonderful selection of medieval-type plaques that would look great on any wall.

a bishop was a roving holy man. He died in Armagh in Ireland in 1065, though his remains were brought back to Tain in 1253. Another relic brought back was a shirt worn by him, which was supposed to protect the wearer from death or injury. **Tain through Time** is an exhibition that tells the life story of St. Duthac and the pilgrimage.

FORTROSE

8 miles NE of Inverness on the A832

This small royal burgh stands on a small peninsula called, perversely, the **Black Isle**. Very little remains of **Fortrose Cathedral** (Historic Scotland), apart from part of the chapter house and the

TARBAT DISCOVERY CENTRE

Tarbatness Road, Portmahomack, Tain, Ross-shire IV20 1YA
Tel: 01862 871351 Fax: 01862 871361
e-mail: info@tarbat-discovery.co.uk
website: www.tarbat-discovery.co.uk

Tarbat Discovery Centre, housed in a beautifully restored 18th century church, is a major attraction in the Highlands of Scotland. Archaeology has revealed the first Pictish monastery from the early days of Scotland's conversion to Christianity in the 6th - 9th centuries AD and the finds from the important excavations are exhibited here. Visitors can discover the workings of the archaeologists and the unfolding story of the Picts. Some wonderful carved Pictish sculpture is displayed and a gallery is devoted to Tarbat through the centuries. A gift shop offers a unique range of souvenirs.

south aisle of the chancel and nave. It was founded in the 12th century, though the ruins as you see them today date from the 14th. Within it are three canopied tombs, one being of Euphemia Ross, grand-niece of Robert I and wife of the hated Wolf of Badenoch.

To the east of the town is **Rosemarkie**. Within the **Groam House Museum** there are displays and artifacts about the Picts, those mysterious people who once lived in this part of Scotland.

CROMARTY

16 miles NE of Inverness on the A832

The royal burgh of Cromarty sits on a small headland on the Cromarty Firth. It is said to be the best preserved 18th century town in Scotland, and certainly the narrow streets and old cottages and houses have an old world feel about them. But at one time it was also a sad place, as it was from Cromarty that many people left their native Scotland during The Clearances, heading for the New World.

Cromarty's most famous son is Hugh Millar, who was born in 1802. He was the "father of geology", as well as being a writer and editor, and his birthplace, the thatched **Hugh**

ARDIVAL HARPS

Orchard House, Castle Leod, Strathpeffer Ross-shire IV14 9AA
Tel/Fax: 01997 421260
e-mail: info@ardival.com website: www.ardival.com

The imposing gateway of Castle Leod leads you to the home of a small but enterprising business named **Ardival Harps**. The company's designs are based on instruments played in Scotland during the past thousand years, making an Ardival Harp the modern inheritor of a strong and vibrant historical tradition. Sources include the earliest harps in Europe, taken from carvings on Pictish standing stones and brass-strung clarsachs of the sort played in the Scottish Highlands and Ireland for hundreds of years. Renaissance bray harps, with buzzing bray pins, are also a speciality along with more familiar gut-strung lever harps. 2003 sees the 10th anniversary of the company, which now enjoys an international market for its high-quality instruments.

Wood for the harps is sourced and seasoned by Alex Dunn at his sawmill, Cromartie Timber, on the Castle Leod estate. Local wood, mostly sycamore, ash, beech and lime, is used and is carefully chosen for its figure, colour and acoustic properties. Alex's wife Zan coordinates activities and is the person most likely to answer the telephone. George Pirie is the wood worker who actually builds the harps, having honed his skills making wooden toys and custom-made furniture. Finally, Bill Taylor is the teacher-in-residence, who brings a player's point of view to marketing and design.

The Ardival team quickly discovered many people were unfamiliar with historical harps and had difficulty finding sources of music and playing techniques. Four-day courses- Harp Holidays- were devised to give beginners a hand-on introduction to the fascinating world of Scottish harps. Harp Holidays, led by Bill, take place over a long weekend and cater for beginners on harp. Even those with no previous musical experience find these courses both accessible and enjoyable. The teaching is by ear in the traditional manner, and it is not necessary to be able to read music although written music is always provided. Students have travelled to Strathpeffer from all over the world, from Japan, Scandinavia, Europe, South America, Australia and the USA. But of course most students are from Scotland and the rest of the UK.

Bill Taylor has built an international reputation researching and performing the ancient harp music of Scotland, Ireland and Wales. On the courses he shares his extensive practical and theoretical knowledge in a relaxed and convivial atmosphere. Using simple tunes, students play medieval music on Pictish harps, try out Renaissance-style improvisation on bray harps, play Highland tunes on wire-strung clarsachs, and explore traditional decoration and accompaniment. Teaching days are structured to balance learning with plenty of time for relaxation: after all, it is a holiday.

Details and photographs of the harps appear on the Ardival website, along with booking information and course dates.

Millar's Cottage (National Trust for Scotland) is open to the public. Here you will see fossils and rock specimens, as well as some of the great man's personal possessions. To the rear is a garden of colourful, native plants.

DINGWALL

11 miles NW of Inverness on the A862

This small royal burgh was granted its royal charter from Alexander II in 1227. Its name comes from the Norse, and means "the place of the parliament", which shows that even before the 13th century, it was a place of importance. It is sometimes claimed that Macbeth, King of Scotland, was born here, though there is no doubting that it was also the birthplace of **Sir Hector MacDonald**, a soldier who rose through the ranks of the army in Victorian times to become a general and national hero. However, in the early 20th century he was accused of being homosexual, and committed suicide in 1903. On a hill to the south of the town is the **Mitchell Monument**, built to commemorate him.

The **Dingwall Museum** is within the Old Tolbooth of 1730, and has displays and exhibits on local history and wildlife. The **Dingwall Canal**, now abandoned, ran for a mile between the town and the Cromarty Firth, and was Britain's most northerly canal. It was designed by Sir Thomas Telford, and opened in 1817. But by the 1860s, when the railways arrived, the canal was in decline, and it eventually closed. There is a pleasant walk along the canal banks, starting at Tulloch Street in the town.

STRATHPEFFER

14 miles NW of Inverness on the A834

Though no more that a small village, Strathpeffer was at one time one of the most famous spas in Britain. Trains regularly left King's Cross in the evening, arriving the following morning at Strathpeffer Station, carrying the cream of Victorian society. So fashionable was it that the local paper had a page dedicated to nothing else but naming the crowned heads who were taking the waters that week. And though the spa has gone, the place is still full of genteel hotels, guest houses and B&Bs.

The **Spa Pump Room** has recently been restored to recreate the village's great days, and if you're brave enough you can even sample the sulphurous waters. Also restored are the **Victorian Gardens**, where the great and the good promenaded and played croquet. Within the disused railway station is the **Highland Museum of Childhood**, with dolls, games and toys.

On the eastern outskirts of the village is the **Eagle Stone**, covered in Pictish symbols. A famous Highland mystic nicknamed the "Braan Seer" predicted that if the stone ever fell over three times, the waters of the Cromarty Firth, four miles away, would rise and permanently flood the village. The stone has already fallen over twice, so it is now securely set in concrete.

BEAULY

9 miles W of Inverness on the A862

In 1564 Mary Stuart stayed at **Beauly Priory** (Historic Scotland) while on her way to Easter Ross, and was captivated by the whole area. She is reputed to have said "c'est un beau lieu", ("it's a beautiful place") and gradually "beau lieu" became Beauly. The priory, now in ruins, was founded in 1230 by the Bisset family for Valliscaulian monks, though the Cistercians later took it over. The present ruins date from the 14th and 16th centuries, and in one of the transepts is the burial place of the Mackenzies of Kintail. The A831 runs south west from Beauly towards **Strathglass**, one of the

CULLIGRAN COTTAGES

Glen Strathfarrar, Struy, near Beauly, Inverness-shire IV4 7JX
Tel/Fax: 01463 761285
e-mail: juliet@culligran.co.uk

Culligran Cottages are situated west of Beauly at Struy, where beautiful Glen Strathfarrar strikes off westwards from the equally beautiful Strathglass. The scenery round here is among the most majestic and beautiful in Scotland, and one of the cottages makes the ideal base from which to explore the area. They are owned and managed by Juliet and Frank Spenser-Nairn, and sit snugly amid some stunning scenery protected under a National Nature Reserve agreement close to the waters of the River Farrar and within the Culligran Estate. The accommodation comprises a traditional stone-built cottage and four Norwegian style chalets within a naturally wooded area, and all are comfortable and extremely well appointed. The cottage sleeps up to seven people, and has three double bedrooms, a spacious sitting room, a large kitchen, bathroom and shower room.

The chalets boast an open plan living room with kitchen/dining area, a bathroom and either two or three bedrooms. A sofa bed in the living area means that they can sleep either five or seven depending on size. All are furnished to an extremely high standard, and all have double glazing, electric heaters, cooker and fridge. Frank offers regular guided tours by Landrover of Culligran Deer Farm, where you can watch and even feed the deer. A daily permit allows you to fly fish on the Rivers Farrar and Glass. If you prefer something more energetic, you can hire a Culligran bicycle and explore 15 miles of private roads in the glen. The cottages are open between March and mid-November each year.

GLASS RESTAURANT

Struy, by Beauly, Inverness-shire IV4 7JS
Tel: 01463 761219
website: glassrestaurant@supanet.com

Douglas Brown, is a respected chef who has run the **Glass Restaurant** for over fours years. It is housed within the 150-year-old Struy Inn, which offers B&B or dinner, B&B in four lovely rooms, one of which is en suite. The oak bar features an open fire, and there is a homely, comfortable feel to the place, and this, coupled with the superb cuisine in the 20-seat restaurant, makes it an excellent base from which to explore an area that is rich in history and beautiful scenery. Local fishing, golf and walks can be arranged.

KILDRUMMIE CERAMICS

Kildrummie Smithy, Delnies, Nairn, Nairnshire IV12 5NZ
Tel: 01667 455315

Owned and run by Louise Mackintosh for over 12 years, **Kildrummie Ceramics** is a studio and shop that sells exquisite pottery, all made and fired on the premises. There is fine table ware, garden ware, novelty items and figurines on offer, all wonderfully decorated and glazed. The colours have to be seen to be believed. This is the perfect place to buy a souvenir of your holiday in this part of Scotland. Louise also offers pottery classes suited to both beginners and the more advanced.

THE COSE COTTAGE

Highland Boath, Clunas, Nairn, Nairnshire IV12 5UT
Tel: 01667 404703   e-mail: cose_cottage@hotmail.com
website: www.cosecottage.co.uk

At the end of a lovely, sheltered valley on the edge of the
Cawder Estate you'll find **The Cose Cottage**. This superior self
catering cottage offers a cosy, well furnished sitting room with
wood burning stove, TV, video and music centre, as well as a
well appointed kitchen and two bedrooms and a bathroom
upstairs. The master bedroom has a double bed, while the second bedroom has a double and
single bed. In addition, part of the sitting room can be curtained off to form extra sleeping
accommodation of required.

most beautiful glens in the area. It was here, in the 19th century, that the "Sobieski Stuarts" held court. They claimed to be direct descendants of Charles Edward Stuart, and, though they were undoubtedly charlatans, managed to convince many aristocratic families of their royal lineage. To the east of the village is the **Wardlaw Mausoleum**, one of the burial places of Clan Fraser. At Moniak Castle, south east of Beauly, is the **Moniak Winery**, which makes wines from locally grown fruit.

NAIRN

15 miles NE of Inverness on the A86

Nairn is a popular golf and holiday resort sitting at the mouth of the River Nairn. The weather here is surprisingly mild, and locals still insist that the name Nairn comes from the Scottish "nae rain", meaning "no rain". Though there is no truth in this, the town is undoubtedly drier than most areas in Scotland. It has a fine clean beach and views across the Moray Firth to the Black isle and beyond.

The River Nairn at one time marked the boundary between Gaelic speaking and English speaking areas in the Highlands, though most people now speak standard English. In fact, it is said that the purest English in Britain is spoken in and around Inverness. Two

miles east of the town, in the small village of **Auldearn**, is the **Boath Doocot** (National Trust for Scotland). It sits on a small hillock on which once stood Auldearn Castle. The **Battle of Auldearn** took place in 1645, when James Graham, Marquis of Montrose, soundly defeated a Covenanting army.

Cawder Castle stands five miles south west of the town, on the B9090. Shakespeare made it famous in his play Macbeth, set in 11th century Scotland. The present castle, however, is much later, and with its turrets and towers, is one of the most romantic looking of the Scottish castles. It is open to the public during the summer months.

CULLODEN

5 miles E of Inverness on the B9006

The **Battle of Culloden** was the last large-scale battle fought on British soil. On a cold day in April 1746, when flurries of sleet and snow were falling, the Jacobite forces of Charles Edward Stuart faced government troops commanded by the Duke of Cumberland, third son of George II. The result was a crushing defeat for the Jacobites. On that day, the dream of restoring a Stuart to the British throne died.

The battlefield is on Drumossie Moor, and though the surrounding countryside has been drained and enclosed, the

EASTER DALZIEL FARM B&B AND COTTAGES

Easter Dalziel Farm, Dalcross, Inverness, IV2 7JL

Dalziel Farm B&B is set within a 17th century farmhouse which was partially rebuilt in the 19th century. Here you will find three superbly furnished and decorated guest rooms, all with hospitality trays, duvets and wash basins. There are two double rooms and one twin bedded room and bathrobes can be provided for the convenience of the guests. Breakfast times can be arranged to suit your individual requirements, with the actual breakfasts being served at a large oak table in the spacious dining room. You can choose from an extensive menu that includes a traditional Scottish cooked breakfast to lighter options. Dinners are sometimes served as well if arranged beforehand. The gardens are awash with colour for most of the season and you are invited to stroll round them after a hard day sightseeing in an area that is rich in history and heritage.

Also on the farm are the **Dalziel Self Catering Cottages.** There are three such cottages, and all are well appointed and furnished to an extremely high standard. The four star Birch Cottage sleeps six in

two double rooms and one twin room, the three star Rowan Cottage sleeps four in one double and two single rooms, while the three star Pine Cottage sleeps six in two double rooms and a twin. All cottages are fully heated, and have a comfortable and cosy lounge/dining area, bathroom and fully equipped kitchen. They are surrounded by a large grass garden area and attractive heather beds. Fresh linen (sheets and pillow cases) and towels are supplied free of charge, and changed weekly. There is plenty of parking space on this working farm, and well behaved pets (and children!) are more than welcome.

THE LODGE AT DAVIOT MAINS

Daviot Mains Farm, Daviot, Inverness-shire IV2 5ER
Tel: 01463 772215 Fax: 01463 772099
e-mail: margaret@thelodgeatdaviotmains.co.uk
website: www.thelodgeatdaviotmains.co.uk

For over 20 years, Margaret and Alex Hutcheson have been welcoming guests to their warm and friendly home. **The Lodge at Daviot Mains** offers some of the best guest house accommodation in Scotland. It offers the very best in Highland hospitality, and has seven sumptuously comfortable guest bedrooms (all with countryside views), as well as spacious public rooms which have been furnished with deep sofas and original works of art. There are four double rooms, two twin rooms and a single, and all are en suite, with tea and coffee making facilities, colour TV and video, hair dryer and direct dial telephones. The master bedroom has a four poster bed , a large bay window and an original Victorian bathroom, which came from Margaret and Alex's original house. This room is particularly suitable for honeymooners or for a romantic break.

Margaret has recently won the "Landlady of the Year" award from Highlands of Scorland Tourist Board, and her cooking has gained the Lodge an entry in the *Taste of Scotland* guide. For this reason,

the hearty breakfasts and superb dinners (which must be booked in advance) are justly famous. Signature dishes include casserole of local pork with rosy red apples, Aberdeen Angus beef in a red wine gravy and cold poached salmon with seasonal salad. There is also a small but select wine list, to complement your dinner to perfection. For your comfort, the Lodge is a non smoking establishment, and has been awarded Disability Category 1 Accessibility Status by Visit Scotland. This is luxurious Highland hospitality at its very best.

actual battlefield site has been restored to what it was - a poor, infertile area of moss and peat. You can still see the stones that mark the graves of various clans, and there is a huge memorial cairn at the centre of the battlefield. **Leonach Cottage**, even though it stood next to the battlefield, survived, and has been restored. The **Culloden Visitor Centre** (National Trust for Scotland) has displays which explain the deployment of the troops before and during the battle, and explains the aftermath. There is still a sombre air on the battlefield site itself, and it is said that no one who visits comes away unaffected.

Leonach Cottage

The **Clava Cairns** (Historic Scotland) lie close to the battlefield. They are passaged burial cairns from the Neolithic age, and are among the finest of their kind in Britain.

FORT GEORGE

9 miles NE of Inverness on the B9006

Fort George (Historic Scotland) is named after George II, and sits on a headland that guards the inner waters of the Moray Firth. Work started on building it in 1748 as a result of the Jacobite Uprising. Though Charles Edward Stuart's dream of restoring the Stuarts to the British throne were shattered at Culloden two years previously, there was still much unrest in the Highlands. Manned forts were therefore built to police the area, and Fort George is the only example still standing. It is said to be the finest 18th century fortification in Europe, and seen from the air, it resembles a thick dagger pointing into the sea. The surrounding wall is one mile long, and it cost, in today's terms, £1bn to build. Within it is the **Queen's Own Highlanders Museum**, dedicated to a regiment that ceased to exist in 1994, when it merged with the Gordon Highlanders to form a regiment simply known as The Highlanders.

GRANTOWN-ON-SPEY

27 miles SE of Inverness off the A939

Situated in the heart of Strathspey, Grantown-on-Spey sits at a height of 700 feet above sea level, and is a small touring centre. It is a comparatively new town, having been founded in the late 18th century by James Grant of Grant

BROOKLYNN

Alan & Silvia Woodier
Grant Road, Grantown-on-Spey PH26 3LA
Tel: 01479 873113
e-mail: brooklynn@woodier.com website: www.woodier.com

Situated in the newly created Cairngorms National Park, the four star **Brooklynn** licensed Guest House is the ideal base for your Highland holiday. It sits on the Malt Whisky Trail, and is a beautiful Victorian home with spacious and unusually decorated rooms and pretty gardens with a small wood and stream. The meals are delicious, with traditional and international flavours using local and home grown ingredients. It has a Taste of Scotland accreditation and two medallions for home cooking. There is a comfortable lounge with extensive library and games. It is ideally suited for golf, skiing and many outdoor activities.

ARDCONNEL HOUSE

Woodlands Terrace, Grantown-on-Spey, Morayshire PH26 3JU
Tel/Fax: 01479 872104
e-mail: info@ardconnel.com website: www.ardconnel.com

Owned and run by Antoinette and Ian Hallam, **Ardconnel House** is a spacious and elegant guest house situated in Strathspey, famous for its whisky distilleries. It overlooks a glorious pine forest, a lochan (a small loch) and the Cromdale Hills, and is decorated in Victorian style throughout. There are six extremely comfortable rooms, a double with a four poster bed, a double with a king-sized bed, three superking bedrooms and a single. They all come complete with colour TVs, hospitality trays and hair dryers, and all are fully en suite. The full Scottish breakfasts are hearty and filling, or, if you prefer, lighter options are also available. Antoinette is a chef, and creates exciting and delicious evening meals, which are served in the striking dining room, with its red walls and antique style mirrors.

Typical dishes include poached Scottish salmon in a lemon butter sauce or mushroom risotto served with a salad. She uses only the finest and freshest of local produce wherever possible in season, and can cater for a range of special diets, such as gluten-free, if prior notice is given. For 22 years Ian was in the distilling industry, so he knows all about fine malt whiskies and will give talks in the quiet, spacious lounge on the malt whiskies of Scotland with tastings from the extensive collection of fine malts. Ardconnel House also runs The Strathspey Experience, and Ian can take you on tours round areas of Scotland, such as the Strathspey Whisky Trail, in his luxury people carrier. For your comfort, the guest house is a non smoking establishment, and children over eight years old

SKYE OF CURR HOTEL

Tigh-na-Sgiadh, Dulnain Bridge, Inverness-shire PH26 3PA
Tel: 01479 851345 e-mail: aileen@skyehotel.freeserve.co.uk
Fax: 01479 821173 website: skyeofcurr.com

Situated in the Cairngorms National Park with wonderful views of the Cairngorm Mountains, the **Skye of Curr Hotel** (a STB 3 Star Small Hotel and I.I.P Award winner) is an ideal, tranquil retreat, far from the bustle and pressures of modern life, and yet within easy reach of all the leisure activities of Scotland's glorious Speyside, including skiing in the Cairngorms. The house has, in its time, been home to both the Lipton tea family and the Hartley jam family, but is now a magnificent country house hotel set in two and a half acres of matured wooded grounds. It has been tastefully converted while retaining many original features, and has wood panelling and open fires that give it a feeling of elegance. The restaurant is renowned in the area, with the chef using only the finest and freshest of local produce. The menu includes traditional Scottish fayre such as Aberdeen Angus beef, fresh Spey salmon, venison and wild game from the Highlands and Islands.

There is also a comfortable and cosy lounge bar, where evening bar meals are served. It stocks a wide range of single malts, as well as beers, lagers and liqueurs. There are nine en suite rooms, all

beautifully appointed with TV, hair dryer, tea and coffee making facilities and an electric blanket. Speyside offers so much for the tourist. A visit to the distilleries to sample a "wee dram" of single malt, or the newly appointed Cairngorm Mountain Railway, activities which include golf (there are six courses nearby up to championship standard), watersports at Loch Morlich, fishing, walking and winter sports at the Lecht Ski Centre near Tomintouland. The ambience at the Skye of Curr Hotel is inviting and friendly, small weddings are exclusively catered for.

ROSSMOR GUEST HOUSE

Woodlands Terrace, Grantown-on-Spey,
Morayshire PH26 3JU
Tel/Fax: 01479 872201
e-mail: johnsteward.rossmor@lineone.net
website: www.rossmor.co.uk

Rossmor Guest House is a beautiful Victorian house dating
from 1887 and set in half an acre of land. It has retained
many of its original features, and is the ideal base from which
to explore Strathspey, an area rich in history, heritage and
picturesque countryside. This is holiday accommodation of the highest standard, and it has a coveted
four star rating from Visit Scotland, as well as four diamonds from the AA. It sits at the south end of
Grantown-on-Spey, overlooking pine woods and the Cromdale Hills, and is within easy walking distance
of the town centre. This no smoking establishment has six extremely comfortable guest bedrooms (some

with four posters), all en suite, with colour TVs, tea/coffee making facilities
and hair dryers. Each one has been decorated to a high standard, as have
the elegant guests' lounge and the spacious dining room.

The guest house is owned and run by John and Julia Steward, who is
determined to uphold its fine reputation as a place to experience " country
living". The full Scottish breakfasts are excellent, though lighter options
are available if required. If you are making an early start, Julia will be only
to pleased to cater for this by prior arrangement. The River Spey offers
great salmon fishing, and the Speyside Whisky trail takes you to some of
the most famous Scottish distilleries. The Lecht Ski Centre and the
Cairngorm Ski Slopes are a short car journey away, and the city of Inverness
can be reached by car in 45 minutes. Due to new hygiene standards, Julia
regrets that dogs are not allowed on the premises.

GARDEN PARK GUEST HOUSE

Woodside Avenue, Grantown-on-Spey, Morayshire PH26 3JN
Tel: 01479 873235
e-mail: gardenpark@waitrose.com website: www.garden-park.co.uk

Situated in half an acre of attractive gardens, the **Garden Park Guest
House** is a superior establishment that offers five extremely
comfortable and well decorated guest rooms, including in one a four
poster bed. The service is excellent, with hearty Scottish breakfasts
and superbly cooked three-course evening meals, that have won the guest house a Food Excellence
Award from the RAC. It has a license to serve residents, with a small but select range of wines and malt
whiskies. Small dogs and children over 12 are most welcome, and attractively priced off-season mini
breaks can be arranged for a minimum of three nights dinner, bed and breakfast.

Castle. Its streets are laid out in grid
form, and in Mossie Road is **Inverallan
Parish Church**, completed in 1856 as a
memorial to the 7th and 8th Earls of
Seaforth. An ancient sculptured stone is
built into the kirkyard wall. To the south
of the town is the **Revack Country
Estate**, with gardens, woodland walks
and an adventure playground.

KINGUSSIE

28 miles S of Inverness off the A9

Kingussie (pronounced "King- yoosy")
sits in Strathspey, with, to the east, the
Cairngorms, and to the west, the
Monadhliath Mountains, rising to over
3,000 feet. The **Highland Folk Museum**
in Duke Street highlights the lives of the

AULD ALLIANCE RESTAURANT AND VIEWMONT GUEST HOUSE

East Terrace, Kingussie, Inverness-shire PH21 1JS
Tel: 01540 661506 Fax: -1540 662401
e-mail: viewmount@whsmithnet.co.uk

Guests at the **Viewmont Guest House** have the choice of four en suite bedrooms. All have been tastefully restored and furnished as befits the age and elegance of the house, which dates back to Victorian times. It also has a family room which can link directly to one of the main bedrooms, giving parents peace of mind as their children sleep. The house was built by McKenzie-Mcpherson on his return from Brazil in 1880, where he was ennobled by the Brazilian king with the title of "Count de Sierra Largo". It is owned and run today by Lydie Bocquillon, who comes from Provence, and sets great store by high standards of comfort and value for money. There is a cosy lounge, which, on chilly evenings, has a blazing log fire to warm you.

The **Auld Alliance Restaurant** is on the ground floor, with its name reflecting the historic links between Scotland and France. Lydie does the cooking, and being from Provence, it is traditionally French. It marries the great cuisine of that country with the fresh, traditional produce of Scotland, such as venison, scallops, fresh lobsters, langoustines and prime beef. The table d'hôte menu has a choice of four dishes per course, and all are cooked to perfection. There is a fine selection of wines, and there is sure to be one which will suit your palate. After dinner, you can relax in the lounge with one of the malts or cognacs that are on offer. There is full disabled access and facilities, and smoking is allowed in the lounge.

SHIRAK

38 High Street, Kingussie, Inverness-shire PH21 1HX
Tel: 01540 662280
e-mail: aliette@uk2.net website: www.kingussie.co.uk

Shirak prides itself in being the Highland's only oriental carpet souk. It is located within the McIntosh Gallery in Kingussie, with carpets straight from the markets of the Hindu Kush. There are new and antique rugs direct from Central Asia. Afghanistan and the Caucasus have one of the oldest weaving cultures in the world, and their carpets and rugs, with their traditional designs and bold, striking colours have been prized all over the world since the days of the Mongol Empire. When you're on holiday in Strathspey, why not treat yourself to a rug or carpet?

THE MCINTOSH GALLERY

38 High Street, Kingussie, Inverness-shire PH21 1HX
Tel: 01540 662280 e-mail: aliette@uk2.net

Local artist Simon Cook opened **The McIntosh Gallery** in 1996 as a showcase for his own work. Now, several years later, the works on show are an eclectic mix of contemporary and traditional craftsmanship, plus works of art from landscape to abstract. Etchings by the well known Flemish artist Freddy Theys, for instance, show his exquisite draughtsmanship in his drawings of Orkney and Edinburgh, while the narrative paintings of Dundee born Michael McVeigh celebrate the humour of Scottish people and places. Handmade furniture by Finlay Mackintosh and wood carvings by John Skelton are also displayed,. This is the ideal place to buy that really special gift or souvenir to remind you of your Scottish holiday.

NETHYBRIDGE POTTERY

Easter Culreach, Grantown-on-Spey, Morayshire PH26 3NH
Tel: 01479 821114 e-mail: penny@nethy-pottery.freeserve.co.uk
website: www.nethybridge.com/pottery
Open all year, Tue-Fri 10am-5pm (phone first if travelling specially)

Come to the heart of Strathspey and see the wide variety of pots made
exclusively by Rob Lawson at **Nethybridge Pottery**. He uses a mixture of
ancient and modern techniques to produce a constantly evolving range of
beautiful plates, bowls, mugs, goblets and serving dishes for the table, decorative lamp bases, etc.
Colourful glazing effects are his speciality, with stunning natural patterns in blues, greens, reds and
purples. You can watch Rob at work, and see the skills involved. This is the perfect place to buy a
special gift or souvenir. Commissions are also undertaken.

ordinary people of the Highlands over
the years. And at **Newtonmore**, four
miles south of Kingussie, is another facet
of the museum, where there is a
reconstruction of an 18th century
Highland village.

Ruthven Barracks (Historic Scotland)
lie south east of Kingussie, on the
opposite side of the A9. They were built
in 1719 to house troops who patrolled
the Highlands after the 1715 Jacobite
Uprising. Charles Edward Stuart's
soldiers captured the barracks in 1746
and burnt them.

Four miles north of Kingussie is the
Highland Wildlife Park (see panel on
page 406), which has animals that are
native to the Highlands. There are also
animals which once roamed the area, but
which have now disappeared. To the
west of the village, along the A86, is
Laggan, where the BBC series *Monarch of
the Glen* was filmed.

AVIEMORE

24 miles SE of Inverness off the A9

Once a quiet Inverness-shire village,
Aviemore is now one of the main tourist
and winter sports centres in Scotland.
Though not in itself a particularly
attractive place, it always appears to be
busy, and makes a good stopping off
point as you head north or south on the
A9. The main skiing area lies about seven

miles east of the village, high in the
Cairngorms. Here you will also find the
Cairngorm Funicular Railway (see
panel on page 407), opened in 2001
amid controversy. On the way, you will
pass the **Cairngorm Reindeer Centre** ,
where Britain's only permamant heard of
reindeer can be seen.

The **Rothiemurchus Highland Estate**
contains some of the last remnants of
the great **Caledonian Pine Forest** that

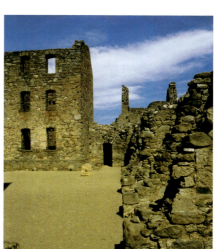

Ruthven Barracks, Kingussie

HIGHLAND WILDLIFE PARK

Kincraig, Kingussie,
Inverness-shire PH21 1NL
Tel: 01540 651270
website: www.highlandwildlifepark.org

Discover the amazing variety of wildlife found in present day Scotland. Then step back in time and meet the creatures that roamed the earth hundreds, even thousands of years ago - the animals of your ancestors. Get closer than you ever thought possible as past meets present in the spectacular setting of the **Highland Wildlife Park**.

Be amazed as you enter the world of the "big bad wolf" which has long been part of myth, fairytale and legend. Find out the truth about these fascinating creatures when you visit the exciting Wolf Territory, where a raised walkway takes you right into the heart of the enclosure. Marvel at the large reserve from the new view point shelter and see herds of beautiful red deer and magnificent Highland cattle, as well as species now extinct in the wild - enormous bison, ancient breeds of sheep and the wild Pzrewalski's horses.

You can explore the rest of the Park on foot and wander around the themed habitats of the capercaillie, polecat, otter, owl, red fox and many more. To make your day complete there is a coffee shop, gift shop, children's trail and play area, free guidebooks and binocular hire. The Park opens daily from 10am (weather permitting in winter) and closes at 4pm November to March and 6pm April to October (7pm June to August).

THE OSPREY HOTEL

Kingussie, Inverness-shire PH21 1EN
Tel/Fax: 01540 661510
e-mail: aileen@ospreyhotel.co.uk website: www.ospreyhotel.co.uk

The Osprey Hotel in *Monarch of the Glen* country is owned and run by Aileen and Robert Burrow, who pride themselves on comfortable accommodation, warm Scottish hospitality and fine food and wines. Surrounded by the Grampian Mountains, it sits in beautiful Strathspey, right next to the Kingussie memorial gardens. The cooking is wonderful, with hearty Scottish breakfasts (or something lighter should you require it) and lavish dinners that use only the finest and freshest produce. Even the bread and the preserves are home made. The Osprey has a coveted AA 5 Diamonds rating, and awards for its dinners and breakfasts.

JUNIPERS GUEST HOUSE

5 Dellmhor, Aviemore, Inverness-shire PH22 1QW
Tel: 01479 810405 Fax: 01479 812850
e-mail: junipers.dellmhor@btopenworld.com

Delmar Harris, who owns and runs **Junipers Guest House**, has been welcoming guests for over 20 years, so you are assured of a warm welcome, a comfortable stay and great value for money. There are four rooms on offer - a family, a triple, a double and a twin, and all are tastefully decorated, with central heating, a colour TV and tea and coffee making facilities. There is ample parking space and the centre of Aviemore is only a short walk away. This is *Monarch of the Glen* country, and the B&B has been awarded three stars by Visit Scotland. Delmar can arrange activities for you such as skiing and sailing.

once covered most of the Highlands. The visitor centre is on the B970 south east of the village, and here mountain biking,

CAIRNGORM MOUNTAIN RAILWAY

Aviemore, Inverness-shire PH22 1RB
Tel: 01479 861261 Fax: 01479 861207
website: www.CairnGormMountain.com

Almost 2km long, Cairngorm's funicular railway is the highest railway in the United Kingdom and takes you up the slopes of Cairngorm, the UK's fifth highest mountain at 1,245metres and one of Scotland's most extreme arctic wilderness environments, valued for its landscape and rare habitats. Travelling up the wind scoured slopes gives a close up view of the northern Cairngorms, created and moulded by over 400 million years of geological drama while, rising above, Cairngorm itself provides a majestic backdrop. Down in the valley below, in Glen More, the panorama is no less dramatic with the ancient Caledonian pine forest and Loch Mortich creating a gentler landscape setting. The Cairngorm Mountain Experience provides an unrivalled opportunity for visitors of all ages and physical ability to relax and enjoy one of Britain's most spectacular mountain areas in safety and comfort.

Nestled just below the summit of Cairngorm the brand new Ptarmigan Station offers spectacular views and is home to the Mountain Exhibition.The story of how the mountains have evolved and how wildlife has adapted to survive in such extreme conditions, climate change, folklore and the human impact on the mountain landscape are all explored. Visitors who want to explore the mountain on foot are encouraged to make use of two, specially created, clearly marked footpaths within the ski area boundary. Both paths start from the railway Base Station. Along each route you'll find information points highlighting topics of interest.

guided tours, hill walking and safari tours in Land Rovers can be booked The estate also has magnificent views, dense forest and winding woodland trails.

Aviemore is one of the termini of the **Strathspey Steam Railway**, that runs the five miles to Boat of Garten. It was once part of the main line running between Aviemore and Forres which was closed in the early 1960s.

CARRBRIDGE

21 miles SE of Inverness on the A938

The arch of the old 18th century bridge after which the village is named still stands, spanning the River Dulnain. The **Landmark Forest Heritage Park** lies to the south of the village, and has a Red Squirrel Trail, Microworld, where you can explore the

DELL OF ABERNETHY COTTAGES

Nethy Bridge, Inverness-shire PH25 3DL
Tel: 01463 224358 Fax: 01479 821643
e-mail: john@holiday-cairngorm.co.uk
website: www.holiday-cairngorm.co.uk

In beautiful Speyside by the Cairngorm Mountains, Dell of
Abernethy has six self-catering cottages one mile from Nethy
Bridge on the edge of the Abernethy Forest nature reserve.
The cottages are all three star inspected by the Scottish
Tourist Board, but differ in size sleeping from 2 to 8 people. They are warm and comfortable with well
equipped kitchens, and set in two and a half acres of lawn and mature woodland. Linen and towels
are included. Visit the web site for more details/vacancies and local information on the area, or contact
John Fleming for a colour brochure.

THE OLD FERRYMAN'S HOUSE

Boat of Garten, Inverness-shire PH24 3BY
Tel/fax: 01479 831370

A warm welcome and comfortable B&B accommodation awaits
you at the former home of "the Boatie", who's ferry used to
cross the River Spey here. There are four rooms, a double, a twin
and two singles. The sitting room has a wood stove, books and
maps but no TV. There is no set time for breakfast, with bread
and preserves all home made and local heather honeycomb. Evening meals may include wild food (
smoked venison, salmon, chanterelles...) with herbs and some vegetables from the cottage garden.
Much of the food is organic. The hospitality of Elizabeth Matthews earned her *Les Routiers* B&B of the
Year 2001(Scotland) award.

FAIRWINDS HOTEL & CHALETS

Carrbridge, Inverness-shire PH23 3AA
Tel/Fax: 01479 841240   e-mail: enquiries@fairwindshotel.com
website: www.fairwindshotel.com

Fairwinds Hotel and Chalets, situated in the heart of the
Highlands, offers a choice of accommodation for discriminating
guests. The hotel is four-star, and set within a Victorian house
which offers an unparalleled standard of comfort with great service
and value for money. The food is outstanding, and the establishment features strongly in the *Taste of
Scotland* scheme. The self catering chalets lie within seven acres of land around a small lochan, and
come fully equipped for the holiday of your dreams. The area is noted for its wildlife, and you can go
for invigorating rambles or relax completely in the comfort of the chalet or hotel.

world of insects, and the Fire Tower, the
tallest timber tower in the country. It's
worth climbing to the top, as it gives
good views over the surrounding
countryside. Six miles east of the village
is the **Speyside Heather Centre**, where
you can learn about a modest plant
which has almost become,•. along with
kilts, sporrans and bagpipes, one of

Scotland's great symbols.

TOMATIN

14 miles SE of Inverness off the A9

Tomatin Distillery, north of the village,
was founded in 1897. It is one of the
highest in Scotland, and has 23 stills. It
has a visitor centre and a tour with a
tasting at the end.

DRUMNADROCHIT

14 miles SW of Inverness on the A82

This attractive village sits on the shores of **Loch Ness**, home to the Loch Ness Monster, or "Nessie", as it is more commonly called. No one has ever proved conclusively that it exists, but tourists and scientists are still attracted to the area in their droves in the hope of catching a glimpse of the elusive monster. The loch is certainly big enough to house a monster, as it is 23 miles long by a mile wide, and contains more water that any other loch in Scotland. The loch is at its deepest (754 feet) just off **Urquhart Castle** (Historic Scotland), near Drumnadrochit, and curiously enough this is where most of the sightings take place.

Urquart Castle

If Adamnan, the biographer of St. Columba, is to be believed, Columba himself encountered the monster in AD565, though in the River Ness and not in the loch. He was making his way along the Great Glen towards Inverness, when he encountered a monster attacking a man in the river. He immediately kneeled down to pray, and the monster released his victim and sunk beneath the water. The man's companions immediately embraced Christianity.

Within Drumnadrochit there are two exhibitions devoted to the monster - the **Original Loch Ness Monster Visitor Centre** and **Loch Ness 2000**. They are more or less in competition with each other, so you can visit whichever one takes your fancy, or you can visit both.

Urquhart Castle was at one time one of the largest castles in Scotland. It sits on a promontory jutting into the loch, and was built in the 16th century. Contrary to what people believe, it was never the ancestral home of Clan Urquhart, but belonged to the Grants. A fortress of some kind has stood here since the Dark Ages, as it occupies a strategic position in

BRIDGEND HOUSE

The Green, Drumnadrochit, Inverness-shire IV63 6TX
Tel/Fax: 01456 450865
e-mail: rluffman.bridgend@amserve.com

Centrally placed in Drumnadrochit, on the banks of Loch Ness, **Bridgend House** is a home-from-home styled B&B with three lovely, comfortable rooms on offer. There is a family/twin room, a double and a single, either en suite or with private bathrooms. This no smoking establishment also offers superbly cooked evening meals, and special dietary needs can be catered for by prior arrangement. The lounge is both elegant and relaxed, with a TV and board games, and, if the weather turns chilly, a warming, open fire. Or you can relax in the sun room or the well tended garden. If you stay here, you're sure to come back again and again!

the Great Glen. In 1689, due to Jacobite unrest, it was blown up by government troops and never rebuilt. There is a small visitor centre which explains the history of the place.

ULLAPOOL

This fishing port and ferry terminal on Loch Broom was founded in 1788 by the British Fisheries Society. By 1792 much of the industrial building work was done, and settlers began moving in, having been given a plot of land and enough stone to build a cottage.

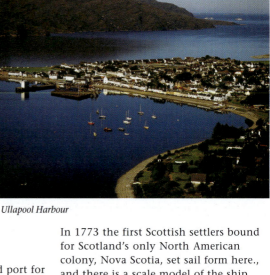

Ullapool Harbour

The town is now the mainland port for the Stornoway ferry, and has embraced tourism. The award winning **Ullapool Museum and Visitor Centre** is housed in a former "parliamentary church" designed by Thomas Telford. These standard-design churches, 32 in all, got their name because they were sanctioned and funded by the British parliament to cater for outlying areas of the Highlands which lacked a place of worship.

Long before this however, the place had been a recognised as a safe harbour.

In 1773 the first Scottish settlers bound for Scotland's only North American colony, Nova Scotia, set sail form here., and there is a scale model of the ship they used in the museum. Close to Ullapool are the **Leckmelm Gardens**, laid out in the 1870s. In 1985 work began on re-establishing them after they had become overgrown, and their former beauty was revealed. Eleven miles north of Ullapool, at Achiltibuie, is the **Hypoponicum**, a garden where plants grow without soil. It calls itself the "garden of the future", and sells kits so that you can also grow plants using only water.

AROUND ULLAPOOL

LOCHINVER

17 miles N of Ullapool on the A837

Sitting on Loch Inver, at the end of the A837, this small village is a fishing port and resort. A narrow, winding road, the B869, strikes out north west from Lochinver, hugging the coastline for most of the way, and eventually joins the A894. It makes a great car run with some wonderful views. The **Assynt Visitor Centre** explains the history and wildlife of the area.

Inland is Loch Assynt, on whose shores you will find the ruins of **Ardvreck Castle**, built in the 1490s by the MacLeods. James Graham, 1st Marquis of Montrose, was kept prisoner here before being taken to Edinburgh to be executed.

CULAG HOTEL

The Pier, Lochinver, Sutherland IV27 4LQ
Tel: 01571 844270 Fax: 01571 844483

Lochinver is within that spectacular area of Scotland called Assynt, and it is here that you will find the **Culag Hotel**, an ideal centre for walkers, ornithologists, or those who just want to relax. Formally the home of the Duke of Sutherland the hotel was originally built as a smokehouse and is over 200 years old. The hotel presently offers 14 comfortable and well appointed en suite rooms, and a renowned cuisine (especially the seafood) that uses only the finest and freshest of local produce. The Wayfarer's bar is disabled friendly and offers a wide selection of single malt whiskies. The owners Ken and Shelia Whalen run this family hotel and offer you a warm welcome and old-fashioned Scottish hospitality.

KYLESKU HOTEL

Kylesku, Lochinver, Sutherland IV27 4HW
Tel: 01971 502231 Fax: 01971 502313
e-mail: kyleskuhotel@lycos.co.uk
website: www.smoothhound.co.uk/hotels/
kylesku.html

Kylesku is a delightful village on the beautiful shores of Locha' Cháirn Bhain in Sutherland, next to the graceful sweep of the modern Kylesku Bridge. All around is breathtaking scenery, and mountains such as Suilven, Quinaig and Ben More Assynt present challenges for serious climbers, while their foothills offer walks for the less adventurous. The unspoilt terrain is home to a host of different species of wildlife. Sightings of deer, badgers, pine martins and wild cats are not uncommon. The **Kylesku Hotel** itself is a picturesque but elegant building dating back to 1680 and is now owned by Imelda and Patrick Gilmour.

There are eight bedrooms, six of which are en suite, and one of which is a family room. Each room has a colour TV and hospitality tray, and some have great views out over the loch to the mountains beyond. The spacious restaurant serves the best food in the area, and, as you would expect, specialises in sea food, though succulent steaks, poultry and vegetarian dishes are also available. Only the freshest of local produce is used wherever possible, and the menu is imaginative and tempting. Meals are also served within the cosy bar, where there is a children's menu as well. The wine list is extensive, and in the bar there is also a wide selection of single malts.

MACKAYS

Durness, Sutherland IV27 4PN
Tel: 01971 511202 Fax: 01971 511321
website: visitmackays.com

Mackays is the premier hotel in this beautiful part of North West Scotland. The building itself is over 250 years old, and was once a village shop and modest hotel. Its new owners, Fiona and Robbie Mackay, have now completely refurbished and renovated it, while still retaining its unique, traditional character. The decor is based on the muted hill and heather tones of the local landscape, giving a restful and pleasing ambience, while the furnishings and furniture, especially in the guest lounge and dining room, are in a pleasing rustic style, with tweed fabrics and warm wood.

It boasts six fully en suite rooms - a family room, two doubles and three twins, all extremely comfortable and spacious. They are individually decorated, with colour TVs and hospitality trays. After a hard day's sightseeing in this lovely part of Scotland you can relax over a welcoming drink in the inviting guest lounge. The restaurant, **Peatstacks**, serves Scottish food with imagination and flair. Being on Scotland's northern coast, seafood is, of course, the speciality and only the finest and freshest of local produce is used wherever possible. The restaurant has earned an enviable reputation in the area as an ideal venue for a celebration dinner or a candlelit meal. There is ample car parking and there are plenty of opportunities for golf, fishing, walking, bird watching and beachcombing.

INNES-MAREE BUNGALOWS

Poolewe, Ross and Cromarty IV22 2JU
Tel/Fax: 01445 781454
e-mail: info@poolewebungalows.com
website: www.poolewebungalows.com

Innes-Maree is situated in magnificent Wester Ross, only a few minutes' walk from the world-famous Inverewe Gardens. It is here that you will find the four star **Innes-Maree Bungalows**, six self-catering cottages, owned by Kenneth Mackenzie MacLean, which are renowned for their comfort and modern amenities. They have been built on a landscaped park, and each one is light and airy, with spacious lounge, dinette/kitchen, two en suite double bedrooms, an adult size twin bunk bedroom, shower rooms and verandah. The kitchen comes fully equipped with cooker, microwave, fridge/freezer and washing machine, while the lounge area has comfortable chairs, occasional tables, colour TV, CD micro system and coal effect fire. Electricity and bed linen are supplied, and both are included in the tariff. Each bungalow has ample parking for two cars, and one bungalow in particular is suitable for the disabled.

A cot and high chair are available on request.

This area of Wester Ross is one of the last great European wildernesses, and is a mixture of mountain glen, loch, forest and safe, sandy beaches. A holiday in one of the cottages is a rare opportunity to explore its beauties, or take part in activities such as angling (both sea and fresh water), climbing, walking, swimming, pony trekking, or just relaxing and unwinding. The village of Gairloch is just six miles away, and there are also shops at Ullapool and Kinlochewe.

DURNESS

50 miles N of Ullapool on the A838

Situated close to Faraid Head, Durness is the most northerly village in the Western Highlands. To the west is **Cape Wrath**, one of only two "capes" in Britain, the other one being Cape Cornwall. A small ferry crosses the Kyle of Durness, and from there you have to walk seven miles to reach it along a minor road. A mile and a half east of the village is the **Smoo Cave**, set into the sea cliffs. It consists of three chambers, and goes right underneath the A838 coast road. The unusual name probably derives from the old Norse "smjugga", meaning "rock".

Cape Wrath, Durness

GAIRLOCH

22 miles SW of Ullapool on the A832

Situated on the shores of Loch Gairloch, this village has one of the most beautiful

THE OLD INN

Gairloch, Ross and Cromarty IV21 2BD
Tel: 01445 712006 Fax: 01445 712445
e-mail: nomadscot@lineone.net
website: www.theoldinn.co.uk

Nestling at the foot of the historic and picturesque Flowerdale Valley, the **The Old Inn** has a magnificent setting among the misty hills of Western Scotland, and with spectacular views across Gairloch harbour to Skye and the Outer Isles. The fact that it was awarded "AA Pub of the Year for Scotland and Northern Ireland 2003", speaks for itself and is well deserved and certainly worth a visit where you will be greeted with a warm welcome and friendly atmosphere. Here you can try pony trekking, fishing, golf or birdwatching, or you can relax and do nothing at all. The inn has three coveted stars, and is a picturesque, whitewashed building that speaks of a long tradition of good, old-fashioned Scottish hospitality. **The Old Inn** has also modern amenities, and offers a high standard of service of which owners Ute and Alastair Pearson are justly proud. The place is renowned for its food, and specialises in Highland game such as venison, and fresh, local seafood, such as crab, langoustine, salmon and lobsters.

The "spit roast" is also popular, and everything is complemented by a comprehensive wine list. The menu is imaginative, and there is sure to be something to appeal to everyone. There is a cosy bar, where you can sit by an open fire and sample a warm, glowing single malt or a thirst-quenching pint of local real ale as you chat to the friendly locals. The rooms are comfortable and spacious, and all have either an en suite bath or shower. In addition, there is a colour TV, tea/coffee making facilities and a direct dial telephone in each room. Family rooms are also available.

AITE NA GEARRA

Croft 25,Diabaig, Torridon, Achnasheen,
Ross & Cromarty IV22 2HE
Tel: 01445 790257
e-mail: sam@gearra.fsnet.co.uk

At **Aite Na Gearra**, among some of the most stunning scenery in
Scotland, you will find two extremely comfortable cottages that offer
the very best in self catering holiday accommodation. Owned and managed by Samantha Wernham,
they offer spectacular views, wonderful sunsets and great opportunities for bird watching, walking,
fishing and climbing. The smaller cottage sleeps two to four people, with wood burning stove, well
equipped kitchen area and toilet/shower room. The larger cottage sleeps three to six people, is beautifully
equipped, and ideal for families. The perfect place for a peaceful holiday.

THE OLD MILL HIGHLAND LODGE

Talladale, Loch Maree, Wester Ross IV22 2HL
Tel: 01445 760271
e-mail: jo.powell@bosinternet.com

The **Old Mill** is a small hotel situated by the island dotted Loch
Maree, among the misty hills and glens of one of the most
majestic and wonderful parts of Scotland. It offers you a warm
welcome, good food and wine, and a chance to enjoy in complete
tranquillity everything that the area has to offer. Surrounding the hotel are two acres of grounds,
where there are flowers, heathers, trees and shrubs, and you are free to wander them at will, taking in
the panoramic vistas of the finest mountain landmark in Wester Ross, Slioch. On one side of the lodge
is a crystal-clear mountain stream, which gives the hotel the cleanest water in the land, and on the
other is a restful summer house beside a burn and quiet pool. The hotel has three twin and three
double guest bedrooms, all en suite and all spacious and well appointed. And in the dining room you
will be served delicious food, made from only the finest and freshest of local produce.

There is a comprehensive wine list to choose from, and after dinner you can relax in the adjacent
sun lounge overlooking the garden, or in the lounge upstairs, and have one of the hotel's single malts.
The hotel is proud of the fact that it doesn't have TV, as reception here is non existent. But if you
choose to put you feet up with a good book, then there's plenty to choose from. But of course, if you

feel a bit more energetic, there is plenty of good hill-walking, bird-watching
and golf at the nine hole Gairloch course, nine miles away. The Gulf Stream
means that this part of Scotland, which is on the same latitude as some
parts of Siberia, has an amazing range of plants and trees. At Plockton,
where *Hamish Macbeth* was filmed, there are even palm trees growing.
The place is owned and run by Joanna and Chris Powell and they will
give you a good Highland welcome.

situations of any village in the Western
Highlands. Within the **Gairloch
Heritage Museum** you can see an
"illicit" still, a traditional village shop
and a lighthouse interior. Other exhibits
explain how life was lived in the Western
Highlands in the olden days.

Five miles north east of the village are
the famous **Inverewe Gardens** (National

Trust for Scotland - see panel opposite).
There are plants here from all over the
world, and they thrive here in the wet,
mild climate.

WICK

Wick is Scotland's most northerly
mainland royal burgh. Once the leading

INVEREWE GARDENS

Poolewe, Ross shire IV22 2LG
Tel: 01445 781200 Fax: 01445 781497
e-mail inverewe@nts.org.uk
website: www.nts.org.uk

The sheer audacity of Osgood Mackenzie's vision in creating this outstanding 20 hectares (50 acres) garden, impressively set on a peninsula on the shore of Loch Ewe, is still astonishing today. The warm currents of the North Atlantic Drift or Gulf Stream help nurture an oasis of colour and fertility, where exotic plants from many countries flourish on a latitude more northerly than Moscow's. Himalayan rhododendrons, Tasmanian eucalypts, a large collection of New Zealand plants (including the National Collection of Oleciria), diverse Chilean and South African introductions combine to give a colourful display throughout the year. Marked footpaths. Visitor Centre. Access to the wider estate.

his son to lay waste to the Sutherland estates. His son refused, and Sinclair had him thrown into a dungeon.

However, the gaoler was sympathetic to John's plight, and agreed to help him escape. John's brother William found out, and betrayed them to his father. The gaoler was executed, and when William went down to the dungeons to gloat, John killed him with his chains. For this, John was starved by his father and denied water. He then fed him salt beef, and John died in agony, his body dehydrated and his tongue swollen. The 4th Earl then had him buried in the local church. Years later, just before he too died, the Earl repented of what he had done, and asked that his heart be placed next to his son's in the same coffin. His wishes were duly carried out.

North of Wick are the the ruins of two castles - 15th century **Girnigoe** and 17th century **Sinclair**, which stand near Noss Head above Sinclair Bay. They were strongholds of the Earls of Caithness, and the older of the two, Girnigoe, was where the 4th earl had his son incarcerated. A mile south of the town, on a commanding site above the sea cliffs, are the ruins of the **Castle of Old Wick**. It is one of the oldest stone castles in Scotland, and was built by Harald Maddason, Earl of Caithness, in the 12th century. In the early 14th century it was

herring port in Europe, it now relies on tourism and industry. Norse influences were strong here at one time, and indeed the town's name comes from the Old Norse word for "bay". James V held a parliament here in 1540 as he toured his kingdom, and **Parliament Square** near the Market Place recalls the event. The **Old Parish Church** dates from 1830, and replaced an older, medieval church. Nothing now remains of it, though in the kirkyard is the **Sinclair Aisle**, ancient burial place of the Earls of Caithness.

The Sinclairs seem to have been a particularly bloodthirsty lot at a time when it was unremarkable to be bloodthirsty. The 4th Earl, George Sinclair, lived in the 16th century, and was suspected of murdering the Earl and Countess of Sutherland so that his daughter could marry their heir, and thus claim the Sutherland lands. However, in 1576 the heir fled the country, and the Earl's plans were thwarted. He was furious, and ordered

Northlands Viking Centre

owned by Sir Reginald de Cheyne, who supported Edward I of England in his attempts to conquer Scotland.

The engineer **James Bremner** was born in Wick in 1784, and died in 1856. He was one of Scotland's most able shipbuilders, establishing a shipyard in the town where over 50 ships were built. He was a colleague of Brunel, and when the SS Great Britain ran aground off Ireland, it was Bremner who salvaged it. To the south of the town, on a hill, is a tall memorial to his memory. Viking influence was strong in this part of Northern Scotland, and the **Northlands Viking Centre** tells the story of the Norsemen and the Vikings who attacked the coastline, and eventually colonised it. The Centre also recounts the life of the local artist John Nicolson.

AROUND WICK

HELMSDALE
30 miles SW of Wick on the A9

Behind this little fishing port is the **Strath of Kildonan**, through which the River Helmsdale flows. In 1868 it was the scene of a famous gold rush after a former Australian prospector called Robert Gilchrist found gold in the river.

Soon people were flocking to the area, and the Duke of Sutherland, seeing a money making opportunity, rented out small parcels of land to the prospectors. At its height, over 500 men were busily digging and panning, and an ugly shanty town soon grew up. The whole thing came to an end two years later, when other landowners in the area complained that the prospecting activities were interfering with their hunting and fishing. The Duke reluctantly put a stop to it all, though today this whole area is still a favourite spot for amateur gold panners.

Timespan is a visitor centre that tells the story of the town and the surrounding area. There are exhibits about the Picts, the Vikings and The Clearances.

LATHERON
15 miles SW of Wick on the A9

The **Clan Gunn Heritage Centre** is within the old 18th century church at Latheron. It traces the history of the clan from its Norse origins right up until the present day. One of the displays gives the story of Henry Sinclair, Earl of Orkney, who is supposed to have crossed the Atlantic in 1398, landing in Newfoundland and what is now Massachusetts, a full 94 years before Columbus's voyage.

Two miles south of Latheron, on the A9, is the **Lhaidhay Caithness Croft Museum**, where you can see a typical Caithness croft of the 18th and 19th centuries, with living quarters, stable and byre all under one roof. And at **Dunbeath**, one mile south, is the **Dunbeath Heritage Centre**, housed in the former village school. Through

tableaux and exhibits, it tells the story of
Dunbeath and its people through the
ages. Neil Gunn, the famous Scottish
author, was born in Dunbeath and
attended the local school.

TONGUE
50 miles W of Wick off the A838

In 1972 a causeway was built across the
shallow Kyle of Tongue to take traffic
westwards on the A838 from this small
village towards Loch Eribol and
eventually Durness. The ruins of **Castle
Bharraich** once belonged to Clan
Mackay, and at Farr, nine miles north
east of the village, is the **Strathaver
Museum**, housed in the old St.
Columba's Church. Its most notable
displays are on The Clearances, which
probably affected this area more than
any other in the Highlands.

ALTNAHARRA
51 miles W of Wick on the A836

Altnaharra sits at the western end of
Loch Naver, and is a centre for game
fishing. The loch is the source of the
River Naver, one of the best salmon
rivers in Sutherland. It flows northwards
from the loch through Strath Naver
until it reaches the sea at Torrisdale Bay.

THURSO
19 miles NW of Wick on the A9

The name Thurso comes from the old
Norse for"river of the god Thor". The
ruins of **St. Peter's Church** within this
fishing village date from medieval times.
It was once a private chapel of the
Bishops of Caithness, whose summer
home was **Scrabster Castle**, now in
ruins. The village of Scrabster itself is the
main ferry port for Stromness in the
Orkneys. The **Thurso Heritage
Museum's** most important exhibit being
the Skinnet Pictish Stone.

JOHN O' GROATS
13 miles N of Wick on the A99

John O' Groats is popularly held to be
the most northerly point on the British
mainland, but in fact this record is held
by **Dunnet Head**, 11 miles to the west.
The place is supposed to be named after a
Dutchman called Jan de Groot, who
lived here. The story goes that, to settle
an argument about precedence within
his family, he built an eight-sided house
with eight doors which gave onto a
room, within which was a table with
eight sides. The house is long gone,
though its site is marked by a mound.
The village sits 873 miles north of Land's
End (which itself is not England's most
southerly mainland point) and 280 miles
north of Kirkmaiden in Wigtownshire,
Scotland's most southerly village.

Stacks near John O' Groats

12 THE WESTERN ISLES

This long string of islands lies off Scotland's north west coast, and from the Butt of Lewis, the most northerly point on the most northerly island, to Berneray, the most southerly island, is about 130 miles. They are the last bastion of true Gaeldom in Scotland, and in some areas Gaelic is still the first language, though the number of native speakers falls each year. But for all that, the Norse influence is strong, and many of the place names owe more to old Norse than they do to Gaelic or English. Up until the Treaty of Perth 1266, the islands belonged to Norway, but in that year Magnus IV surrendered all his Scottish possessions with the exception of Orkney and Shetland.

Norse invasions began in earnest in the late 7th and early 8th centuries. By about AD850 the Norse were firmly in control, and even began settling here in family units. They brought their culture, their language and their racial characteristics, and while some people from the

Drinishader, Isle of Harris

Western Isles still have the dark features and hair of the Celts, just as many have fair hair and a light skin. When they became part of Scotland in 1266, they only paid lip service to the Scottish monarchy, with the Lords of the Isles acting as if they were independent kings. It took much bloodshed before the Norse were finally absorbed fully into the kingdom. Some historians claim that the Norse language was still spoken in some areas of the Western Isles in the 16th century, when it was replaced by Gaelic. Now Gaelic itself is gradually being replaced by English, though there are official programmes in place to preserve the language and its traditions.

The weather in the Western Isles can be harsh, though the effects of the Gulf Stream mean that snow is not as prevalent as in other areas of the country. However, there are between 45 and 50 inches of rain a year, and the winds blowing in from the Atlantic are invariably strong. They don't blow all the time, however, and a summers evening here can be magical, with the sun barely dipping below the horizon, and the quality of light bringing a magical quality to the scenery. At midnight on Lewis it is still light enough on some evenings to read a newspaper.

The people of the Western Isles also takes religion seriously, and Free Presbyterianism has a great influence. The Sabbath is still strictly observed, though planes now fly and boats sail to and from the mainland on a Sunday. Children's playgrounds are chained up, reading a Sunday paper is frowned on, and sometimes it seems as if enjoyment of any kind is strictly forbidden. But this isn't the case. The people of the islands do enjoy their Sundays, which are usually spent in church and then indoors with family and friends.

There are also paradoxes. While Lewis, Harris and some of the other islands are Protestant, South Uist and Barra are staunchly Roman Catholic, not through Irish immigration, as in other areas of Scotland, but because the Reformation passed them by.

The main island is divided into two parts - Harris to the south and Lewis to the north, and both are sometimes referred to as islands in themselves. Before 1975, a county boundary ran right through the island, with Harris being in Inverness-shire and Lewis being in Ross and Cromarty. High mountains and moorland running from Loch Resort in the west to Loch Seaforth on the east

LOCATOR MAP

See other chapters

created the natural boundary, and people from each area did see themselves as different. Now the islands come within a local government area simply called the Western Isles.

Various attempts have been made over the years to introduce industry into the islands, most notably when Lord Leverhulme bought both Lewis and Harris in 1918 and set about promoting the fishing industry, hoping to turn it into the main employer. His efforts ultimately ended in failure, and today the islands rely on crofting, tourism, the weaving of Harris Tweed, and, to some extent, fishing. The Harris Tweed industry is basically a cottage one, with weavers working at looms in their own homes or in special weaving sheds behind the cottages. Some weavers will welcome you into their weaving rooms and explain the processes involved in turning wool into highly prized cloths that find their way all over the world.

The rock of Lewis is gneiss, one of the oldest in the world. It is impermeable, creating a landscape of soggy peat bogs, moorland and shallow lochans, which means that most of the settlements are dotted round the coast. Harris is more mountainous, with some peaks over 2,500 feet high. The rock breaks through onto the surface like old bones in places, giving a bleak but attractive landscape. North Uist, the most northerly of the southern islands, is connected to Harris by ferry, and the other islands (with the exception of Eriskay and Barra further south) are connected to each other by causeway. Though they are close together, each island has its own flavour and clan allegiances.

Nowadays, we tend to think of the Western Isles as being on farthest edge of Europe, away from "civilisation" and the main centres of population. But this was not always the case. Head west from the Western Isles and the next stop might be North America, but at one time they stood on a main trade route, doing business with Norway, Central Scotland, The Isle of Man, Ireland and England. And they have been occupied by man for thousands of years. The Callanish Stone Circle is the second largest stone circle in Britain next to Stonehenge, and is over 4,000 years old. And though we now tend to imbue such circles with mysticism and magic, they had a practical purpose - they predicted the seasons so that farmers knew when to plant, sow and reap. And there are other "mystical" elements on the islands. They are dotted with stone circles, burial cairns, standing stones, old forts, brochs and castles. The local people are proud of them, and each village seems to have its own small museum that records and explains the history of the area.

Ferries for Stornoway, the islands' largest town, leave from Ullapool, and there is a ferry crossing from Oban to South Uist and Barra, as well as one from Uig on Skye to Lochmaddy in South Uist and Tarbert in Harris. And most of the islands have a small airstrip that can take flights from Glasgow Airport.

STORNOWAY

The islands' largest town has a population of about 6,000, with its name coming from the old Norse "stjorna", meaning "anchor bay". It is still a busy port, and is the administrative and shopping capital of both Lewis and Harris. It was founded in the Middle Ages around an old MacLeod castle, and has a large natural harbour and its own airport. On Lewis Street is the **Parish Church of St. Columba**, dating from 1794. The **Free Kirk** in Kenneth Street has been called "the best attended church in Scotland", with the evening service regularly attracting congregations of 1,500. **St. Peter's Episcopal Church** dates from 1839, and has an old font from the Flannan Islands, as well as David Livingstone's Bible. Its bell of 1631 was

Stornoway Harbour

once the town bell which summoned people to important meetings.

Lewis Castle is now a college, and is surrounded by public gardens. It was built in the 1840s and 50s by James Mathieson, a local businessman who earned his money trading in opium and tea in the Far East. In 1843 he had bought Lewis so

---

HEBRIDEAN BREWING COMPANY

18a Bells Road/corner of Rigs Road, Stornoway, Isle of Lewis HS1 2RA
Tel: 01851 700123 Fax: 01851 700234
website: www.hebridean-brewery.co.uk

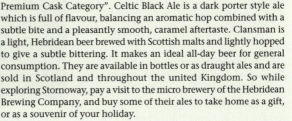

A short distance from the centre of town, and two minutes walk from the ferry terminal you will find the premises of the **Hebridean Brewing Company**, the only brewing company in the Western Isles. It is owned and managed by Andrew Ribbens, who hails from South East England, but whose family originated from Lewis, so he set up the company here in 2001 when he took early retirement. There is small retail outlet on the brewery premises, and tours round the brewery are available by appointment.

The company uses only the finest brewing ingredients. The brands include Islander Strong, Celtic Black Ale and Clansman, each having its own, unique characteristics. The Islander is brewed using special Scots malt, and has a deep ruby colour, and a wonderful flavour that that is predominantly malty. In 2003 it won the bronze medal from the Society of Independent Brewers "Beer of Scotland Premium Cask Category". Celtic Black Ale is a dark porter style ale

which is full of flavour, balancing an aromatic hop combined with a subtle bite and a pleasantly smooth, caramel aftertaste. Clansman is a light, Hebridean beer brewed with Scottish malts and lightly hopped to give a subtle bittering. It makes an ideal all-day beer for general consumption. They are available in bottles or as draught ales and are sold in Scotland and throughout the united Kingdom. So while exploring Stornoway, pay a visit to the micro brewery of the Hebridean Brewing Company, and buy some of their ales to take home as a gift, or as a souvenir of your holiday.

Lewis Castle

carry the famous "orb" symbol, and for it to be genuine it must be made from "virgin wool produced in Scotland", then spun, dyed and finally hand woven in the Outer Hebrides.

West of Stornoway, on the Eye Peninsula, are the ruins of St. Columba's Church, dating from the 14th century. It claims to have 19 MacLeod chiefs buried within it in carved tombs.

that he could "improve" what he saw as a backward island by building new roads and housing, and introducing gas and running water. One of his industrial projects was the extraction of oil from the plentiful peat on the island, and in 1861 he opened the Lewis Chemical Works. However, it was beset by problems, and at one point the works actually blew up, causing fear and panic in the town. It finally folded in 1874.

On Francis Street is the **Museum nan Eilean**, which explains the history of the town and the island. There are some specially good displays on archaeology, and it makes a good starting point if you want to explore the whole island. If you are looking for genuine Gaelic culture, then the **An Lanntair Arts Centre** within the town hall hosts exhibitions of local art, and also has a varied programme of concerts and drama. Sir Alexander MacKenzie, who gave his name to the MacKenzie River, Canada's longest waterway, was born in Stornoway in 1764. In Francis Street, where his house once stood, is the **Martins Memorial**, built in 1885.

Harris Tweed is celebrated at the **Lewis Loom Centre** at Bayhead. Here you can find out all about a cloth that has proved to be one of the most popular in the world. Only genuine Harris Tweed can

AROUND STORNOWAY

RODEL
48 miles S of Stornoway on the A859

Sitting near the Renish Point, the southern tip of Harris, is the famous **St. Clement's Church**, the oldest complete church in the Western Isles. It was built by Alasdair Crotach McLeod in 1500, and from 1540 until his death in 1547 he lived within the church tower. He now lies within a magnificent tomb in the

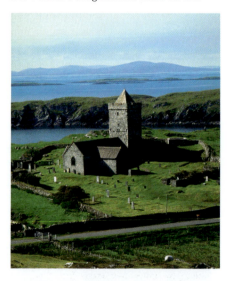

St. Clement's Church

RODEL HOTEL

Rodel, Isle of Harris HS5 3TW
Tel: 01859 520210 e-mail: dmacdonald@rodelhotel.co.uk
Fax: 01859 520219 website: www.rodelhotel.co.uk

The three star **Rodel Hotel** sits above Rodel harbour, and was built as a family home in 1781 by Captain Alexander Macleod of Berneray, who had just bought the Isle of Harris from his cousin. In the early 20th century it became a hotel, and now it has been bought and totally refurbished by the husband and wife team of Donnie and Dena MacDonald, with no expense spared. It embraces both the traditions of the Western Isles and the best of modern craftsmanship, which blends in perfectly with its 18th century exterior. The four bedrooms each have a subtle and individual character of their own, with opulent yet comfortable furniture, soft furnishings and drapes. Each one is fully en suite, and has a hair dryer and tea and coffee making facilities.

Magnificent food is served in the spacious 40-seat restaurant, with only the finest and freshest of local produce being used wherever possible. Here also you can also sample fine wines from the hotel's cellar, and admire the contemporary artwork on the walls, the crisp linen and the sparkling glasses. The lounge bar is fully stocked with a great range of single malts, brandies, real ales, wines and liqueurs, as well as soft drinks. There is plenty to do in the area - Rodel Church is one of the most historic on Harris, and there is also golf, walking, beach combing, nature study, fishing and bird watching. The Rodel Hotel is the perfect place to enjoy a get-away-from-it-all holiday amid some of the most stunning scenery in Scotland!

main body of the church. By the late 18th century the church was ruinous, and it was eventual restored by Alexander MacLeod, a captain with the East India Company.

TARBERT

33 miles S of Stornoway on the A859

This village stands on a narrow neck of land in Harris which is no more than half a mile wide. **Amhuinnsuidhe Castle** (not open to the public) was built in 1868 by the Earl of Dunsmore, who at that time owned Harris. It was the Countess of Dunsmore, his wife, who introduced the Harris Tweed industry to the island. A ferry service connects Tarbert with Uig on Skye.

SCALPAY

33 miles SW of Stornoway

The island of Scalpay is connected to the

5 URGHA

5 Urgha, Harris, Isle of Harris, HS3 3BW
Tel: 01859 502114

5 Urgha is a superior, three star self catering cottage situated on the beautiful Isle of Harris in the Outer Hebrides, set on a clifftop overlooking the sea. It sleeps up to six people in absolute comfort, and comes fully equipped for a relaxing and rewarding holiday. There are three bedrooms - two doubles and a twin, and all linen and crockery are included in the price. There is also a patio and garden for those long, Outer Hebrides evenings. The cottage is heated by is oil fired central heating, and there is a kitchen with cooker, fridge, freezer, washing machine and dishwasher, and a bathroom with shower. Tarbert is two miles away, and close by there is golf as well as good walking country and fishing.

Isle Of Harris Knitwear Co.

Grosebay, Isle of Harris, Outer Hebrides HS3 3EF
Tel: 01859 511240 Fax: 01859 511297
e-mail: harrisknitwear@ hotmail.com
website: www.isleofharrisknitwear.co.uk

From **Isle of Harris Knitwear**, in the romantic Western Isles, comes a look that is the ultimate in high quality, traditional knitwear, using only the "baby soft" yarns used to weave the world famous, lightweight Harris Tweed. Based at the hamlet of Grosebay, near the ferry port of Tarbert, the company was started in the year 2000, turning what was a hobby for two women -Mairi and Katherine - into a thriving business, and it is now established as one of the most progressive on the island. Sweaters, slipovers, scarves and hats are all produced to the highest standards, and you know you are

getting a hard wearing garment at outstanding value for money. Each one is hand stitched and hand washed using established, traditional craft skills, so you also know that they are unique to the island, and nowhere else in Scotland will you find this kind of quality and style.

The company's products are available in all the main clothing and country shops in the Outer Hebrides, and it even offers a reliable and prompt mail order service. (Brochures are available upon request and callers are welcome.) The range of garments is of the highest quality, with many stunning and beautiful patterns that are inspired by age-old Celtic designs. It even undertakes bespoke orders, creating garments that reflect the owners tastes, colours and sizes. Order at one of the many outlets which sell the Isle of Harris range, and you will be measured there and then, and your preferences for colour and design noted also. Then it will be sent to you at any address throughout the world.

The Western Isles know all about high, cold, biting winds during the winter months, and these garments reflect the need for warm, cosy clothing that keeps the elements out. But as well as being practical, they are also stylish, and are just right for both informal indoor wear and for carrying out country pursuits, such as walking, fishing and hiking. The wool used is the very best, and is obtained locally, while the yarns are produced using the traditional carding and ring spinning methods employed throughout the Harris Tweed industry. This makes the finish of the garments unique - they are strong and hard wearing, yet soft, lightweight and extremely comfortable. The long staple and high tensile strength of the wool

allows spinning to a much finer count, at reduced twist, ensuring the finished garment has the softest handle possible. These garments are evocative of the rugged Harris landscape, as soft as a summer evening on the island, and as colourful as one of its famous sunsets. You'll be thrilled if you own one or two of them, and they will find a special place in your wardrobe.

While on holiday, it is always difficult to choose a suitable gift - either for yourself or for a loved one - to bring back with you. Isle of Harris Knitwear garments solve the problem easily. Look out for them while you're in the Western Isles.

SCARISTA HOUSE

Scarista, Isle of Harris HS3 3HX
Tel: 01859 550238 e-mail:timandpatricia@scaristahouse.com
Fax: 01859 550277website: www.scaristahouse.com

Scarista House is one of the best private hotels in the whole of
the beautiful Isle of Harris. It sits on the island's Atlantic coastline,
five minutes north of Northton, where there are some of the best
and cleanest beaches in the whole of Britain. The house itself is
an elegant former Georgian manse dating from 1812, and is one
of the few listed buildings on the island. There are five comfortable en suite bedrooms, three in the
main house and two in the adjacent Glebe Building. All have sea views, and furniture and fabrics have
been carefully chosen to reflect the period of the house. A drawing room and library, both with open
fires, are available to guests.

Scarista's cuisine uses fresh local produce and aims for natural cooking to bring out all the flavours.
The hotel's bread, cakes, jam, marmalade, ice cream and yoghurt are all home made, and special diets
can be catered for. There is a small and select wine list to complement your meal. Scarista House also

has two superior self catering cottages on offer with sea views. Glebe
Cottage sleeps six and Middle Cottage sleeps four. Both cottages
are well equipped and make an ideal base from which to explore
the Isles of Harris and Lewis. There is plenty of fishing, golf, bird
watching, nature study, walking and beach combing. Boat trips
and guided walks can be arranged to take full advantage of the
abundant wildlife, including otters, eagles and dolphins. Being on
the Atlantic coast, the sunsets can be spectacular, and the Northern
lights are sometimes visible.

mainland by the £7m **Scalpay Bridge**,
the biggest ever civil engineering project
in the area, and was opened by Tony
Blair in 1998. The day was especially
memorable for him, as he was attacked
by *culiciodes impunctatus* - the common
midge, which in Scotland is a formidable
foe, flooring stronger men than Mr Blair.

Callanish Standing Stones

SHAWBOST

16 miles W of Stornoway on the A858

Within the former school is the
delightful **Shawbost School Museum**,
which has objects collected by pupils to
illustrate the way people lived and
worked in Lewis, Nearby is a
reconstruction of a Norse
water mill.

CALLANISH

**16 miles W of Stornoway on the
A858**

The **Callanish Standing
Stones** (Historic Scotland) is
the second largest stone
circle in Britain, and dates
back at least 4,000 years,
making it as old as the
pyramids. Four arms made up
of tall monoliths radiate
from it to the cardinal points

THE ORIGINAL CALLANISH BLACKHOUSE TEAROOM

18 Callanish, Isle of Lewis HS2 9DY
Tel: 01851 621373
e-mail: callanishblackhouse@yahoo.com
website: www.callanishblackhouse.com

Blackhouses are small cottages that were once the standard living
accommodation on the Isles of Lewis and Harris, so called to
differentiate them from later cottages, which were built using
lime as a binding agent for the stones, and thus lightened the whole building The roofs were either
thatched or turfed, and had small windows. Warm in winter and cool in summer, they were lived in
up until the middle of the 20th century. Now a typical example has been turned into a warm, welcoming
tearoom and craft shop right next to the Callanish Standing Stones on the island's west coast, often
referred to as "Scotland's Stonehenge". **The Original Callanish Blackhouse Tearoom** is a family
owned establishment which offers the very best in teas, coffees, light meals, soup, snacks and soft

drinks and include Scottish baking, such as scones, cakes
and rolls. The catering area is spacious and welcoming,
with light wood tables and seating.

The crafts for sale represent outstanding value for
money, and the displays are stylish and colourful. You
can choose from pottery, jewellery, Celtic crosses, prints,
and much, much more. This is the ideal place to buy
those gifts or souvenirs for taking home. There is plenty
of parking space and it is open Monday to Saturday
from 10am to 5.30pm. Coach tours are welcome by prior
arrangement.

of the compass, with the northern arm
(which actually veers slightly off true
north) having a double row of stones
enclosing a formal avenue. To modern
eyes, it appears a mysterious place, and
many stories and legends have grown up
about it over the years. One story tells of
a race of giants who met at Callanish to
discuss how to remove the threat of
Christianity from the islands. St. Kieran,
when he heard about this, turned them
all into stone. Another says that the
stones were brought to the island by a
priest king, who employed black men to
erect them. The men who died during
the building were buried within it. A
third story - and for all its modernity,
perhaps the most ridiculous of them all -
says that the stones were erected by
aliens to guide their space ships.

However, though the stones may
eventually have been associated with
primitive ritual, they were erected for a

more practical purpose. By aligning the
stones with heavenly bodies, early
farmers could predict the seasons, and
therefore sow and reap their crops at the
right time. A visitor centre next to them
explains all.

CARLOWAY

17 miles W of Stornoway on the A858

The 1,500 year old **Dun Carloway Broch**
is one of the best preserved brochs in
Scotland. These stone built forts are
common on the mainland and in the
isles, and the one at Carloway is 48 feet
in diameter and has walls are 33 feet
high in places. Stairways are usually
found within the walls, and the ones at
Carloway are among the best preserved
in the country.

GREAT BERNERA

18 miles W of Stornoway off the B8059

The **Great Bernera Bridge**, the first in

the country to be made of pre-stressed concrete girders, connects this small island to the mainland. The local **Community Centre and Museum** has displays about life on the island, and also sells tea, coffee and cakes. An Iron Age village has been excavated on the beach at **Bostadh**, and a reconstruction of an Iron Age house has been built to illustrate what life was like in one of them.

ARNOL

13 miles NW of Stornoway on the A858

At one time most crofters on the Western Isles lived in cottages known as"black houses". These were low cottages with drystone walls (and a central core of earth of clay), turf or thatched roofs, and tiny windows due to the fact that glass was expensive. And though they sound primitive, they worked very well, being warm in winter and cool in summer. The

Arnol Blackhouse (Historic Scotland) shows what conditions were like for those living in them. They got their name in the 19th century to differentiate them from the more modern cottages which used lime as a binding agent.

BALLANTRUSHAL

15 miles NW of Stornoway on the B857

It is said that the **Clach an Trushal** standing stone, which is over 18 feet high, is the tallest in Scotland. A legend states that it marks the site of a great battle, though this has never been confirmed.

SHADER

16 miles NW of Stornoway on the A857

Sitting on a low hill, the **Steinacleit Stone Circle and Standing Stones** date from between 2000 and 3000BC. There is also a burial cairn.

MORVEN GALLERY

Barvas, Isle of Lewis HS2 0QX
Tel: 01851 840216 e-mail: information@morvengallery.com
website: www.morvengallery.com

The **Morven Gallery** lies on the north west coast of the Isle of Lewis, facing the Atlantic Ocean. It is housed in a converted stone steading, and within its spacious, well lit interior, you will find lively, contemporary art that is colourful, accessible and realistically priced. It is owned and run by Janis Scott, herself an accomplished artist and teacher, who is determined to display only the very best creative work from the Hebrides and the mainland. Caroline Bailey's vibrant interpretations of the Hebrides can be seen, as well as the paintings of Kenneth Burns, Pam Carter, David Greenall, Moira Macauley, Ruth O'Dell, Simon Rivett, Vega, Gareth Watson and many more.

Jewellery by silversmith Corinne Curtis and photographs by David Wilson, David Ward and Harry Cory Wright are displayed and it is home to Alice Starmore knitwear designs, Jane Harlington silks, and a range of exclusive "Morven Gallery" garments in silk and wool inspired by the colours and

textures of the Hebrides. In addition to a permanent mixed exhibition, the works of single artists are shown in the main gallery in exhibitions which change monthly during the season. A collection of Morven Gallery Edition Prints which celebrate these paintings is available from the gallery or the website. Janis is knowledgable about all the artists and craftspeople she deals with, and so can offer friendly impartial advice. You are free to browse as much as you like, with no obligation to buy, and you can have a tea or coffee in the attached coffee shop.

GALSON FARM GUEST HOUSE

Galson, Isle of Lewis HS2 0SH
Tel/Fax: 01851 850492
e-mail: galsonfarm@yahoo.com
website: www.galsonfarm.freeserve.co.uk

Situated on the north west coast of the Isle of Lewis, and close to the shores of the Atlantic, the four star **Galson Farm Guest House** offers you all the comforts of home within a fully restored and modernised 18th century farmhouse. It is situated in an 18-acre croft stocked with Hebridean sheep and Highland cattle, and is part of a small village where you can still hear the soft lilt of Gaelic spoken by the people living there. It has three comfortable and beautifully decorated rooms, all with private facilities, central heating, tea and coffee making equipment and hair dryers.

Galson Farm House boasts two residents' lounges, open all day, where tea and coffee are available and open peat fires burn in cooler months. All the food is traditionally cooked on an Aga using the finest and freshest of local produce where possible, and the breakfasts are filling and hearty. The dinners are usually four or five courses, with a varied and imaginative menu each evening. The guest house has a liquor license, and packed lunches can be prepared by prior arrangement. All around there are plenty of opportunities for birdwatching, sailing, fishing, walking, golf and beachcombing. Views of the Butt of Lewis can be seen, and the whole area is rich in history and heritage. Dogs are more than welcome by prior arrangement, and, for your health and comfort, Galson Farm Guest House is a non-smoking establishment.

CALLICVOL QUILTS & 10 CALLICVOL

Port of Ness, Isle of Lewis HS2 0XA
Tel: 01851 810681 e-mail: enquiries@callicvolquilts.com
Fax: 01851 810193 website: www.10callicvol.com

Ness is the most northerly district of the Isle of Lewis, and is a place of history and haunting beauty. And at Port of Ness you'll find **Callicvol Quilts** and **10 Callicvol**. Janet Robson is a self-taught and highly skilled quilter who produces amazing and beautiful patchwork quilts that are works of art in their own right, as well as cushions, bags, tea cosies, cafetiere cosies and potholders. Her studio and shop is a place of light, colour and pattern, and here you can buy examples of her work and see her cutting and stitching the quilts, using traditional cotton, pure wool and some man-made fabrics. She works mainly to commission but there is always a variety of ready-made quilts in stock in a range of sizes.

10 Callicvol is owned and run by her husband, and is an archive that specialises in the history and

traditions of the Highlands, the Western Isles and the Borders. Here you will find thousands of books, maps, documents and photographs relating to the history of these areas. They are preserved in purpose-built accommodation, and are available for public access. Personal attention is assured at all times, and there are occasional displays on aspects of the collection. You can have a free 15 minute consultation, and thereafter the charges for information provided and scanning are extremely reasonable. The collections have been built up over the years by someone who is an authority on the areas mentioned, so you know that the information you are getting is both accurate and reliable.

North Uist

59 miles SW of Stornoway

This mainly low lying island
seems to have more water
than land within its 74,884
acres. The largest loch is
Loch Scadavay, and though
its surface area is only eight
square miles, it has a
coastline 51 miles long. The
island's highest point is the
1,127 feet high **Earval**, to the
south east of the island.

North Uist

Near the south west shore
are the ruins of **Teampall na
Triobad** ("Trinity Temple"). It was, at
one time, a great place of learning, and
may even have been Scotland's first
university. As with most medieval places
of learning, its main aim was to produce
young men for the priesthood, and
scholars came from all over the country
to study here, including, it is thought,
Duns Scotus. It was founded in the 13th
century by Beatrice, prioress of the
nunnery on Iona, and daughter of
Somerled, Lord of the Isles. By the end of
the 15th century, however, its influence
was waning, and during the Reformation
it was attacked, with many valuable

books, manuscripts and works of art
being lost. It is said to have lingered on
until well into the 18th century, when
the last student left. The other building
on the site is **Teampaull MacBhiocar**
(MacVicar's Temple), where the teachers
and lecturers were buried.

The last battle on British soil not to
have been fought with firearms took
place in this area of the island. The
Battle of Carinish was fought in 1601,
when a troop of MacLeods from Harris
were raiding North Uist. They were
attacked by the local MacDonalds, and
hid in Trinity Temple. The MacDonalds,
however, attacked the temple, and only
two MacLeods escaped with
their lives. The **Balranald
Nature Reserve**, run by the
Royal Society for the
protection of Birds, is off the
A865, close to the island's
most westerly point, and
here you can see waders
and seabirds in their
natural habitat.

The island is connected to
Uig in Skye by a car ferry
from **Lochmaddy**, the
island's largest village, and
to An T-Ob on Harris from
Otternish.

Salmon ready for smoking, North Uist

BENBECULA

80 miles SW of Stornoway

Like North Uist, Benbecula is a low lying island dotted with shallow lochans, though its highest point, **Rueval**, is 403 feet high. It's name in Gaelic is Beinn bheag a' bh-faodhla, meaning the mountain of the fords. It is connected to North Uist to the north and South Uist to the south by causeway. The main village is **Balivanich**, on the north west coast, and next to it is the island's airstrip. A short distance south, on the B892, are the ruins of **Nunton Chapel**, supposed to be all that is left of a 14th century nunnery, though it is doubtful if a nunnery ever stood here at all. There is a small visitor centre.

It was from Benbecula that Charles Edward Stuart set sail for Skye in 1746. Lady Clanranald from Nunton House gave him some clothes, and, disguised as Flora MacDonald's maidservant, he went "over the sea to Skye". The MacDonalds of Clan Ranald owned Benbecula up until 1839, when it passed to Colonel Gordon of Cluny. Their main home was the 14th century **Borve Castle**, now in ruins. It sits about three miles south of Balivanich.

SOUTH UIST

87 miles SW of Stornoway

South Uist is a predominantly Roman Catholic island, one of the areas in Scotland which was by-passed by the Reformation. To the north west is the the 30 feet high statute of **Our Lady and the Isles**, sculpted by Hew Lorimer and erected in 1957. The **Loch Druidibeag Nature Reserve** is close to it, and many kinds of wildfowl can be observed here.

A range of hills runs down the east side of the island, with the highest peak being the 2,034 feet high **Beinn Mhor**.

STEPPING STONE RESTAURANT

Balivanich, Isle of Benbecula, Western Isles H57 5DA
Tel: 01870 603377 Fax: 01870 603121

Benbecula, in the Western Isles, is a beautiful island. Balivanich is its main settlement, and it is here that you will find one of the best restaurants in the Outer Hebrides - the **Stepping Stone Restaurant**. Owned and managed by Ewen Maclean, it offers superb food at highly competitive prices in a purpose built and
architecturally designed building of warm, mellow hardwood, piranha pine and large, picture windows. It is spacious and light, and is on two levels, with one level seating 50, and the other seating 30, all in absolute comfort. Glass screens cover the lower windows, adding a touch of elegance and creating a unique ambience.

Ewen trained as a chef in Aberdeen before coming home to Benbecula to open his own eating place. His family own the Hebridean Bakery on the outskirts of the village, where a mouth watering array of traditional oatcakes is baked and then sold all over Scotland. They feature, of course, in the
restaurant's excellent cuisine, which is a mixture of Scottish and international, using only the finest and freshest of local produce wherever possible. The evening menu contains such dishes as local king scallops on a brochette with bacon and tomatoes, pan fried lamb steak with onions, mushrooms and rosemary, and loin of Uist venison in a red wine and rowan jelly sauce with peppers. Plus there is a good selection of fine wines to accompany your meal. During the day, the Stepping Stone also sells lunches, teas, coffees and light snacks.

The west side of the island is a flat area of machair, with fine, white sandy beaches that are among the cleanest in Scotland. The main village is **Lochboisdale**, in the south east corner, and it has a ferry connection with Oban, Mallaig and Castlebay on Barra.

It was at **Milton**, on Loch Kildonan, that Flora MacDonald was born in 1722. Legend has it that that she was a simple Highland peasant lass, devoted to the Jacobite cause and devoted to Charles Edward Stuart. But while she was indeed an ardent Jacobite, she was no simple Highland peasant. She was actually the daughter of a prosperous farmer, and was used to a life of genteel prosperity.

The small **Kildonan Museum** has displays on local history, as well as a tearoom. Further north, on the A865, are the ruins of **Ormiclate Castle**, built in the early 18th century as a sumptuous home for the chief of Clan Ranald. Alas, it was short lived luxury, as the castle was burned down in 1715 after a party to celebrate the Jacobite Uprising got too rowdy.

ERISKAY
110 miles SW of Stornoway

The tiny island of Eriskay sits off the south coast of South Uist, and is connected to it by a causeway. Its main claim to fame is that it gave its name to one of the most beautiful Gaelic songs ever written - the *Eriskay Love Lilt*.

It was in Eriskay, in 1745, that Charles Edward Stuart first set foot on Scottish soil when he stepped off a French ship to begin his campaign to reclaim the British throne for the Stuarts. One of his first actions, legend states, was to plant the sea convolvulus that now thrives in the area. The island found fame of another kind in 1941, when the *S.S, Politician* ran aground on the Sound of Eriskay. It was heading for the United States with 260,000 bottles of whisky, and as soon as the crew were saved, the islanders began removing the cargo "for safe keeping". This lasted for a few weeks until Customs and Excise men arrived on the island. However, they were too late. Some of the cargo had disappeared, and no doubt lay hidden in the peat bogs all over the island. Eventually only 19 people were charged with illegal possession. Sir Compton Mackenzie used the incident as the basis for his comic novel *Whisky Galore*. The wreck is still there, and the last attempt to remove the rest of the cargo - albeit an unsuccessful one - was made in the late 1980s.

South Uist

Isle of Barra

BARRA

115 miles S of Stornoway

Like South Uist, Barra is a Roman Catholic island, and at Heaval, a mile north east of Castlebay, is a statue of the Madonna and Child known as **Our Lady of the Sea**. The island's airstrip is the beach at **Cockle Bay**, a name which is richly deserved, as cockles are still commercially collected there. It is the only "airport" in the world with regular flights where the state of the tides have to be taken into account when compiling timetables.

The island's main settlement is at **Castlebay**, the terminal for the Oban ferry. On an island in the bay is the impressive **Kisimul Castle** (Historic Scotland), the largest fortification in the Western Isles. It was originally built in about 1030 for the then chief of Clan Macneil, a ruthless and bloodthirsty pirate who terrorised the local seas. The present castle dates from the 15th century, though it was extensively restored in the 20th century. It can be reached by a small boat from Castlebay (five minute crossing).

The Macneils were a proud people - especially the clan chiefs. A legend relates that when Noah built his ark, the Macneil chief of the time was invited aboard to escape the flood. He replied haughtily "Macneil already has a boat". This pride continued well into medieval times and even later. After the clan chief had finished dinner, it is said, he employed a man to climb onto the ramparts of Kisimul Castle and announce to the world "Macneil has dined, so other kings and princes of the world may now sit down to dine also".

The burial place of the Macneil chiefs was **Cillebharraidh**, the Church of St. Barr near Castlebay, and the ruins can still be seen. Also buried here is Sir Compton MacKenzie.

13 ORKNEY AND SHETLAND

When James III of Scotland married Margaret, the daughter of Christian I of Denmark, in 1469, the Danish king pledged Orkney and Shetland to Scotland until such time as a dowry was paid. However, the Danish king was too poor to honour his debt, and in 1472 they eventually became part of Scotland.

But Norse influences are still strong. The islanders have never been influenced by Gaelic culture, and Gaelic was never spoken here. All the place names, and some of the family names, have Norse derivations, and indeed some are still pure Norse. The islands are nearer Oslo than they are London, and there have even been isolated calls for the islands' independence from Scotland.

Standing Stones, Stennes, Orkney

Orkney is the southernmost of the archipelagos, with Brough Ness on South Ronaldsay being no more that eight miles form the mainland. The Shetlands lie farther north, with the distance between Sumburgh Head and the mainland being about 100 miles. On road maps, the Shetlands are invariably shown within a small box, and these long distances are never fully appreciated.

Orkney and Shetland may appear isolated nowadays, but in olden times, as with so many of the Scottish islands, they were at the centre of things. They had an importance out of all relation to their size, as they were on the main trading routes between Scandinavia,

Seals at Loch Dunvegan

West Coast of Orkney

Scotland, England and Ireland, and in later times also sat on the main routes between Scandinavia and the New World. Their landscapes have meant that the islands have never been intensely farmed, so archaeological evidence about their past is particularly rich.

Though the two island archipelagos tend to be mentioned in the same breath, they are different. An old saying has it that an Orcadian (a native of the Orkneys) is a farmer with a boat, whereas someone from the Shetlands is a fisherman with a croft. To some extent this is true, as Orkney is the more fertile of the two, though nothing like as fertile as the mainland. The weather on both the Orkneys and Shetlands can best be described as "mixed". The people of the islands have a better description - nine months of winter and three months of bad weather. It is said tongue in cheek, but the wind and rainfall is higher than average.

For all that, the islands are still fairly prosperous, and the reason for this can be summed up in one word - oil. The oil industry has, over the years, transformed their economies, though it has remained relatively unobtrusive, apart form places like Sullam Voe in Shetland, the largest oil port in Europe.

Orkney has about 70 islands, of which 19 are inhabited. Mainland is the largest, and here you will find Kirkwall, Orkney's capital. It is a small royal burgh

St Ninians Isle, Shetlands

and city, as it has a cathedral, the most complete in Scotland. Most of the islands are linked by car ferry, though the best way to explore some of them is on foot. Shetland has about 100 islands, with only 20 being inhabited. It's largest island is again called Mainland, and it is here that Lerwick is situated. It is Britain's most northerly town, and every January the ancient "Up Helly Aa" festival is held here. A Viking ship is paraded through the streets before being ceremonially burnt. It's a custom that goes back to pagan times, when people used fire to attract the sun during the darkest days of winter.

LOCATOR MAPS

ADVERTISERS AND PLACES OF INTEREST

KIRKWALL

This small royal burgh was granted its royal charter in 1486, not long after the Orkneys became part of Scotland. It has a population of about 4,800 people, and sits at the narrowest point on the island of Mainland, dividing it into East and West Mainland. It is a picturesque place, full of old stone buildings, flagged streets and shops that are used by all of the islanders.

Kirkwall Harbour

St. Magnus Cathedral was founded by Rognvald, St. Magnus's nephew, in 1137, though the building as you see it today dates from the 13th to 16th centuries. Magnus was supposed to have been the son of one of the two earls who ruled the islands, and on a raiding expedition to Wales he refused to take part in the usual rape and pillage, deciding instead to sing psalms. This enraged the Norwegian king, also called Magnus, and young Magnus had to flee for his life.

The king eventually died in 1117, and Magnus returned to Orkney, where he

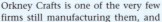

met with Hakon, the ruler of the islands. However, Hakon had him murdered by a blow to the head with an axe.

Most people viewed this story with disbelief, claiming it was an invention to bestow Magnus a certain holiness. However, during some restoration work on the cathedral in 1919, a casket was discovered high up in one of the pillars. Within it were some bones, including a skull which had been split open with an axe.

Earl's Palace, Kirkwall

The **Bishop's Palace** (Historic Scotland) sits close to the cathedral. The earliest parts date from the 12th century, though the substantial round tower dates from about 1550, and was built by Bishop Reid. Further modifications and extensions, now called the Earl's Palace, were made by the tyrant Patrick Stewart, Earl of Orkney between 1600 and 1607. The Stewart earls were hated in the Orkneys, as they exploited the people, impoverishing them and killing and torturing at will. Patrick was eventually arrested for treason in 1615 by James VI, and executed.

Kirkwall comes from the old Norse "kirkjuvagr" meaning "church bay". The church in question is the medieval **St. Olav's Church**. All that is left of it is a doorway in St. Olav's Wynd. Within Tankerness House, a 16th century merchant's house, is the **Tankerness House Museum** containing artifacts and displays about the islands' history. Another museum worth visiting is the **Orkney Wireless Museum** at Kiln Corner. It has examples of radios and wireless sets, both military and domestic, all from the islands.

Kirkwall Castle was dismantled in 1615, and finally demolished completely in 1865. It dated from the 14th century,

ISLAND CRAFTS

8 Quest Buildings, Albert Street, Kirkwall, Orkney KW15 1HL
Tel: 01856 876358

Situated in the centre of the historic town of Kirkwall, **Island Crafts** is a wonderful shop that sells a wide range of hand made goods and gifts that represent the very best in design and craftsmanship. It is owned and managed by Wendy Bews, and has attractive and colourful displays of denim goods such as bags, hats, dresses and cushions, and woollen items such as scarves, jumpers and hats. There is also a great range of pottery, jewellery, natural soaps, hand painted glass, beadware and straw products. This is the perfect place to browse for a gift or souvenir. The prices are very reasonable, and Wendy will offer friendly advice .

and was built by the
Sinclairs of Rosslyn, who
had been created Earls of
Orkney by Hakon of
Norway in 1379. A
plaque on a building in
Castle Street marks
where it once stood.

AROUND KIRKWALL

LAMB HOLM

**7 miles S of Kirkwall on the
A961**

Italian Chapel, Lamb Holm

After a U-boat entered
the islands and sunk the
Royal Oak in 1939, a small string of
islands south of mainland was joined
together by causeways. On Lamb Holm,
one of the islands, is the **Italian Chapel**,
made by Italian prisoners-of-war working
on the causeways. It is a remarkable
building, with its basis being two old
Nissen huts and cast off metal and wood.
In 1960 some of the prisoners returned
and restored it.

AURORA JEWELLERY

The Workshop, Old Finstown Road, St. Ola, Orkney KW15 1TR
Tel/Fax: 01856 871861 e-mail: info@aurora-jewellery.co.uk
website: www.aurora-jewellery.co.uk

Founded in April 1998 by native Orcadians Sara Tait and Steven
Cooper, **Aurora Jewellery** is the sparkling result of a creative fusion
of talent, skill and artistry. The company's philosophy is simple -
to produce design-led, contemporary jewellery of
the highest quality. And it has succeeded admirably.
Their dynamic new collection is designed for people

who enjoy wearing quality jewellery. The company's custom built workshop and
showroom is within walking distance of Kirkwall, and has beautiful views over Scapa
Flow. Here you can admire a range of gold and silver items, all hand finished, and
which are unique in their beauty and craftsmanship.

There are four graduate designers in the company who draw their inspiration from
the Orkneys themselves, especially the islands' natural, botanical, architectural and
mechanical traditions. The collection, which brings a new creative edge to jewellery
making on the islands, is available in silver and nine ct gold, and included is a collection
of exquisite and very special diamond engagement and friendship rings. This is the
place to buy a unique gift or souvenir of the Orkney Islands - one that will be treasured
and admired for many years. Why not browse in the showroom,
or view work in progress? There will be no pressure to buy, and
someone is always on hand to offer friendly, knowledgeable advice.
Prices range from £20 to £1,000. The place is open all day Monday-
Friday and on Saturday 11am-4pm from June to September.

MAESHOWE

9 miles W of Kirkwall off the A965

Here you will find Britain's largest chambered cairn. Maeshowe (Historic Scotland) is 36 feet high and 300 feet in circumference. It was built in about 2,700 BC, and its name translates as "great mound". A long, narrow passage leads into a central chamber surrounded by smaller chambers, each roofed and floored with massive slabs.

The **Stenness Standing Stones** (Historic Scotland) date from around the same time, as does the **Ring of Brodgar** (Historic Scotland), which sits on a narrow neck of land between two lochs. It has been called the most awe inspiring Neolithic site in Scotland. Only four of the Stenness stones still stand, while 27 of the original 67 Brodgar stones still remain.

OPHIR

9 miles W of Kirkwall off the A964

After ordering the murder of Magnus (after whom St. Magnus Cathedral is named) Hakon had **Ophir Church** built in the 12th century. Some people say he did it as an act of penance after a trip to Jerusalem. Only the apse now remains.

STROMNESS

15 miles W of Kirkwall on the A965

This little burgh faces the Orkneys second largest island, Hoy. It was founded in the 17th century, and is a quaint, stone-built place. In Alfred Street is the **Stromness Museum**, which has displays on whaling and the Hudson's Bay Company of Canada, which had a base here at one time, and which employed many men. There are also many displays about **Scapa Flow**, that great bay and natural harbour south of Mainland. After World War I the German fleet was brought to Scapa Flow, and rather than allow it to fall into the hands of the British, the German officers scuttled every one of the ships, sending them to the bottom.

CLICK MILL

13 miles NW of Kirkwall on the B7059

Click Mill (Historic Scotland) is the island's last surviving example of a horizontal water mill, which were once common throughout Scandinavia. At Harray, two miles south of the mill, is **Corrigall Farm Museum**, where there is a working barn and grain kiln.

SKARA BRAE

17 miles NW of Kirkwall on the B9056

In 1850 a storm uncovered the remains of a 5,000 year old village - making it even older than the pyramids. Skara Brae (Historic Scotland) is the oldest known village in Europe, and shows that the people who lived here all these years ago

THIRA

Innertown, Stromness, Orkneys KW16 3JP
Tel: 01856 851181 e-mail: alisonsBBThira@hotmail.com
Fax: 01856 851182 website: www.thiraorkney.com

You are assured of a warm welcome and a restful stay at **Thira**, a purpose built four star B&B establishment two miles from the picturesque, 18th century port of Stromness. Owned and managed by Alison Shearer, it enjoys unrivalled panoramic view of Hoy and Scapa Flow, and has four comfortable, fully en suite rooms with TV and tea/coffee making facilities. There is also an extremely comfortable guest lounge and a spacious dining room where delicious Scottish breakfasts are served, though lighter options are available. There is ample car parking, and is an ideal base from which to explore the Orkney Islands.

CELTIAN JEWELLERY

Rango Cottage, Sandwick, Orkney KW16 3JB
Tel/Fax: 01856 841594
e-mail: info@celtian-jewellery.com website: www.celtian-jewellery.com

Overlooking the beautiful Harray Loch, **Celtian Jewellery** produces mainly gold and silver jewellery, inspired by the wealth of engravings and carvings left behind by the Picts and Vikings. The owner and manager is Ian Kennedy, who set up this business in 1997, and now his exquisite jewellery is much sought after. He also does wood turning and carving, and exhibits work by other craftspersons. His showroom is well worth visiting, as his products make the ideal gift or souvenir. It is open from 10am - 6pm Monday to Friday, and his prices range from a modest £5 to £500.

were surprisingly sophisticated, with comfortable and well appointed houses. A visitor centre shows some of the finds made at the site. Close by is **Skaill House** (Historic Scotland), the finest mansion in Orkney. Work started on building it in about 1628 for George Graham, Protestant Bishop of Orkney. It has been extended over the years, and now houses a collection of furniture, including Graham's bed. On it are carved the words *GEO. GRAHAM ME FIERI FECIT*, which means "George Graham had me made".

BROUGH OF BIRSAY

21 miles NW of Kirkwall on the A966

This little island, which can be reached

on foot at low tide, has the remains of a Norse settlement and a medieval chapel. The ruins of **Earl Stewart's Palace**, once owned by the tyrant who ruled and ruined the Orkneys, overlooks the island. The **Kirbuster Farm Museum** has examples of farm implements used on Orkney farms over the years, plus a Victorian garden.

HOY

17 miles SW of Kirkwall

Hoy is the Orkney's second largest island, and sits to the west of Mainland. A ferry from Linksness to Stromness links it to the larger island, and there is also a small ferry from Lyness to Houton. The **Old Man of Hoy** is a famous stack over 445 feet high off its north west coast, and it is renowned as one of Britain's greatest climbing challenges. On the south west coast is a **Martello Tower**, built between 1813 and 1815 to protect the island from the French. The **Dwarfie Stone** is a unique burial chamber cut into a great block of sandstone. It dates from 3,000 BC.

Earl Stewart's Palace, Birsay

LERWICK

Old Man of Hoy

Lerwick, capital of the Shetlands, has been a burgh since 1818, though its history goes back long before that, as it was originally developed by the Dutch fishing fleet in the 17th century to service their boats. It is Scotland's most northerly town, and with a population of about 7,000 is easily the Shetland's largest settlement. It sits on Mainland, and is so far north that in June there is little or no darkness.

Annually, on the last Tuesday in January, the "Up Helly Aa" festival is held, harking back to the island's pagan Norse days. After being hauled through the streets of the town by men dressed as Vikings, a longboat is set alight, and a rain of lit torches fall onto it from the crowd. It probably harks back to a time when people could not rely on the sun making a reappearance after the dark

THE SPIDERS WEB

51 Commercial Street, Lerwick, Shetland ZE1 0AB
Tel/Fax: 01595 695246
e-mail: info@shetland-knitwear.com
website: www.shetland-knitwear.com

The Spiders Web calls itself an "Aladdin's cave of Shetland knitting", and this is no idle boast. It is situated in Lerwick, in a listed building over 100 years old, and has a wonderful collection of Shetland knitwear all produced by knitters in their own homes, either by hand or on a hand frame. It is owned and run by Barbara Mitchell, who produces her own wide range of jackets, tunics, scarves, hats and gloves. Louise Irvine, who manages the shop in the summer months, is also an experienced knitter and both have a wealth of information about traditional knitting and the range of products stocked in the shop.

The islands are famous for their high quality knitwear and wool, and it is here that you will find the very best that they can offer. Everything is made from hand spun local wool or from commercially

spun coloured Shetland wools, and there are striking and colourful displays of garments by various local craftspeople. There are racks of well designed cardigans, sweaters, tunics, gloves and hats in vibrant colours and both traditional and contempory patterns. You can also buy hand spun wools and a fine range of patterns for your own knitting. Also available is the famous "Prince of Wales" sweater made for Edward VIII to wear while playing golf at St Andrews. There is plenty of parking close to the shop, and it is an ideal place to browse without obligation.

SHETLAND FUDGE/ANOTHER CAT-ASTROPHE

65 Commercial Road, Lerwick, Shetland ZE1 0NL
Tel/Fax: 01595 694324
e-mail: sales@shetlandfudge.com
website: www.shetlandfudge.com

Another Cat-astrophe is a wonderful craft shop selling traditional
and contemporary Shetland arts and crafts. It sits within walking
distance of the centre of Lerwick, and is en route to the ferry
terminal. Owned and managed by Gillian Ramsay, it prides itself
on being Shetlands' only craft shop representing over 50 local producers and craftspeople. This shop
is packed with colourful, well designed goods, all of which would make the perfect gift or souvenir. If
you can't make up your mind, then Gillian will offer you friendly, knowledgeable advice. There are
candles, pottery and porcelain, vases, preserves, prints and paintings, bags, jewellery, cards, teddy
bears, clothing, scarves, and much more.

You must try the well known **Shetland Fudge**, a superb range
of Shetland butter and chocolate fudges that are hand made on
the island, mainly from Scottish produce such as good Scottish
butter and Stewart's rum. It also uses only the finest liqueurs
and extracts, with no artificial colours, preservatives and
flavourings. There are over 25 flavours on offer, and one of the
best known lines is "Puffin Poo", made from white Belgian
chocolate, and you are advised to accept no substitutes - this is
the original and the best. There is ample local parking, and the
double doors means that there is plenty of disabled access. You
can even book your "See Shetland Tour" here as well.

SEE SHETLAND TOURS

10 Hoofields, Lerwick, Shetland ZE1 0NU
Tel: 01595 690777 e-mail: sarah@seeshetland.co.uk
website: www.seeshetland.co.uk

The Shetlands are truly lovely, and to appreciate the islands fully
you need someone to guide you round the sites that highlight
their history, heritage and wildlife. With parties of up to eight
people, **See Shetland Tours** is the perfect way to do this. The
company is owned and run by Sarah McBurnie, who has been a
qualified Shetland Tour Guide since 1999. Whether you are
interested in archaeology, crafts, history, wildlife, geology,
genealogy, photography or local industries, then See Shetland will have something for you. A clean,
modern eight seat minibus will take you round, making sure that you see everything in absolute
comfort. You can book a place on the modern minibus in a small group tour, or book an exclusive
customised tour - whichever you prefer. A full day tour visits a minimum of four attractions and
includes a lunch break.

A half day tour covers the same distance as a full day
one, with all of the sightseeing and two short stops of
interest. There are themed tours available, including two
archaeology tours and a birdwatching tour that takes you
onto the island of Fetlar. Or you can arrange your own
tour, including places of interest you want to see. Sarah
will be glad to take you round them and explain everything
in detail and her fees are surprisingly reasonable. You can
book by phoning the above number.

days of winter, so fire and light was used to attract it. And when the days were seen to be lengthening again, there were great festivities and feasting.

Like the Orkneys, the Shetland Islands are rich in archaeological remains, and many small interpretation centres and museums dot the islands. **Fort Charlotte** was built in about 1653 by Cromwellian troops sent to protect the

"Up Helly Aa" Festival, Lerwick

English fishing grounds, and it is said that it was the first permanent stone building on the islands for centuries. The **Shetland Museum** sits across from the Town Hall in Lower Hillhead, and has some marvellous displays about the islands' archaeology, as well as exhibitions on Shetland life. North of the town is the delightfully named **Bšd of Gremista**. It was the birthplace of

BREIVIEW GUEST HOUSE

43 Kantersted Road, Lerwick, Shetland ZE1 0RJ
Tel/Fax: 01595 695956 e-mail: breiview@btopenworld.com
website: www.breiviewguesthouse.co.uk

Situated on the main bus route, and only 20 minutes walk from the centre of Lerwick, **Breiview Guest House** is situated in a quiet area overlooking Breiwick Bay. Owned and managed by Christine and Dieter Glaser, it is a modern, spacious building, built over 30 years ago, and it has ample car parking.

There is a quiet, sandy beach nearby and the 3,000 year old Clickimin Broch is a few minutes walk away. Breiview makes the ideal base from which to explore the Shetland Islands, which is rich in history and heritage - in fact there seems to be an ancient stone circle, fort or standing stone around every corner.

The guest house, which has a coveted three star rating from Visit Scotland, has six extremely comfortable rooms, all fully en suite, and all having colour TV and tea and coffee making facilities.

The rooms are colour co-ordinated, and well appointed and spacious. Three of them have superb sea views. There is a sumptuously furnished guest lounge and a guests' dining room which again has wonderful sea views. The food is superb, with everything being home cooked from only the finest and freshest of local produce wherever possible. You can have a full Scottish breakfast which is hearty and filling, or something lighter if required. If you require an evening meal, which is always delicious and beautifully cooked, you can order it at breakfast. Both Christine and Dieter take great pride in the

Dis An Dat

Toll Clock Shopping Centre, Lerwick, Shetland ZE1 0DE
Tel: 01595 692665 Fax: 01806 522227
e-mail: sales@disandat.co.uk
website: www.disandat.co.uk

You'll be amazed if you enter **Dis An Dat**, Lerwick's premier gift emporium. This superb gift shop, in Lerwick's town centre, close to the ferry terminal, overflows with dazzling and colourful items, all of the highest quality and all at keenly competitive prices. The displays are bright and stunning, and you are sure to find something that is just right for that special souvenir of your stay on the Shetlands, or as a gift to take to a loved one. Browse the marvellous range of costume jewellery, the silk scarves, ladies' clothing, pot-pourri, essential oils, cruelty-free cosmetics by Bodyline, candles and pottery. There is also a range of woven baskets - everything from sturdy shopping baskets to stylish woven bags that look good with any ensemble. The wonderful smells from the range of home fragrances on offer that penetrate every part of the shop, are pleasant and relaxing, making your visit a pleasure.

The staff have been trained in customer care, and can offer friendly, knowledgeable advice on everything in stock. It is owned and managed by Kathleen Robertson, who brings a wealth of experience to running the shop. She founded it 15 years ago, trading from her home, and since then it has become extremely popular with both locals and visitors alike. She is proud of the range of quality items she sells, and is determined to uphold the high standards she has set, both in the quality of service she offers and value for money.

Herrislea House Hotel

Veensgarth, Tingwall, Shetland ZE2 9SB
Tel: 01595 840208 Fax: 01595 840630
e-mail: herrislea.house@zednet.co.uk
website: www.herrislea-house.shetland.co.uk

The four star **Herrislea House Hotel** is the perfect place to stay while holidaying on the picturesque Shetland Isles. It is situated in the centre of the islands, at Tingwall, where the ancient Shetlands parliament, or "althing", once met long ago and is owned and run by Marjorie and Gordon Williamson. You can feel confident that it offers high standards of service, comfort and value for money. There are 13 beautifully decorated, en suite bedrooms, each having a TV, telephone, computer links and tea and coffee making facilities. At the top of the house is a "family room" which can sleep four, with traditional Shetland box beds in Northern pine that kids always find intriguing.

The food is always prepared from only the freshest and finest of local produce, with the beef and lamb coming from family crofts, and the fish being supplied by local fishermen. Even the vegetables

and fruit are locally grown. You can eat in the spacious and elegant Phoenix Restaurant, or in the more informal atmosphere of the Starboard Tack Cafe Bar, which is filled with memorabilia giving it a special ambience. It also has a children's play area where parents can keep an eye on their children while at the same time enjoying a meal and a drink. And in the hotel's bar you can relax over a drink while listening to music played by Shetland musicians. The "front room" is the ideal venue for small seminars and meetings, and has on line computing, fax, photocopying and telephones.

Arthur Anderson, founder of what is now P&O Ferries, and houses a small museum with displays on his life.

AROUND LERWICK

TANGWICK
35 miles NW of Lerwick on the B 9078

The **Tangwick Haa Museum**, based in Tangwick Haa ("hall") has displays on the history of the northern part of Mainland, The "Haa" itself dates from the 17th century, and was built by the local lairds, Cheyne family. It opened in 1988.

TINGWALL
6 miles NW of Lerwick on the A970

The ancient Shetlands parliament, or "althing", used to meet at **Law Ting Holm** on a small promontory, which at one time was an island, on the Loch of Tingwall. The **Tingwall Agricultural Museum** is housed in an 18th century granary at Veensgarth, and has displays on crofting and fishing.

VOE
17 miles N of Lerwick on the B970

The **Crofthouse Museum** shows what life was like in a 19th century Shetland croft. It comprises a house, steading and water mill, and in earlier times would have housed an extended family of children, parents and grandparents. The men would have earned a living from the sea while the women worked the land.

SCALLOWAY
6 miles W of Lerwick on the A970

It is often said that this small village sits on the Atlantic coast, while Lerwick, its big brother, sits six miles away on the North Sea. It was once the capital of the

THE HOOHEVD STUDIO GALLERY

Hoohevd, Eshaness, Shetland ZE2 9RS
Tel: 01806 503309
website: www.hoohevdstudiogallery.com

The **Hoohevd Studio Gallery** is spacious and welcoming, and is situated in an old croft building dating from the 1750s, and shows a marvellous selection of landscapes, portraits, abstracts, limited edition prints and occasional pieces of quality sculpture. It is owned and run by Paul Whitworth, who is himself an accomplished artist, and who can offer friendly, knowledgeable advice should you wish to purchase a work of art. There is ample car parking, a delightful walled garden and magnificent views over Hamnavoe. Admission is free, and you are welcome to come in and browse without any obligation to buy.

MARY T. DESIGNS

Carsaig Brae, Shetland ZE2 9QT
Tel: 01808 522313
e-mail: mary.eric@lineone.net

At **Mary T. Designs** you will find beautiful, unique designs of hats and scarves made from felted Shetland wool combined with other yarns. These designs give warmth to the wearer, and add a touch of elegance to any outfit. They are designed by Mary Thomson, who has run the business for three years. During that time, they have become extremely popular due to their beauty, their hardiness and their value for money. There is a display of goods, and here you can buy a gift or souvenir to take home with you and remind you of your holiday on Shetland.

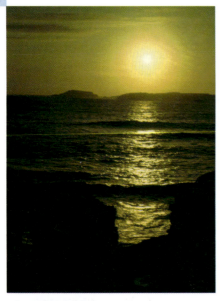

Sunset from Jarlshof

Shetlands, but as Lerwick expanded so the centre of power shifted eastwards. **Scalloway Castle** was built by Patrick Stewart, and dates from about 1600. Patrick, a cruel and bloodthirsty man, was executed 15 years later in Edinburgh on the orders of James VI.

During World War II the village was a secret Norwegian base, and from here Norwegians were ferried across to their homeland to sabotage the German war effort, and resistance fighters who were on the run brought back to Britain. The **Scalloway Museum** tells the story of these brave men.

JARLSHOF
25 miles S of Lerwick on the A970

Jarlshof (Historic Scotland) is one of the most important historical sites in Europe. It sits close to Sumburgh, the Shetland Islands' airport, and was occupied from the Bronze Age right up until the 17th century. There are Bronze Age huts, Iron Age Earth houses, brochs, Pictish wheelhouses, Norse longhouses and medieval dwellings. There is a small museum and interpretation centre attached which unravels the bewildering array of buildings on the site. There is another archaeological site at **Old Scatness**, north of Jarlshof, where you can see brochs, wheelhouses and later dwellings.

BRESSAY
1 mile E of Lerwick

This small island, less than a mile off the Mainland coast, shelters Lerwick's busy harbour, and is connected to it by a small ferry. Close to the ferry terminal is the **Bressay Heritage Centre**, which shows what life was like of the island in former times.

BURRA BEARS

Glenview, Hamnavoe, Burra Isle, Shetland ZE2 9JY
Tel/Fax: 01595 859374
e-mail: wendyinkster@hotmail.com
website: shetlandartsandcrafts.co.uk

Burra Bears is a working studio where Wendy Inkster makes her famous teddy bears. They are made from recycled traditional Fair Isle knitwear, and each bear comes with his own name and personality, making them all individual. These lovable bears are nine inches high, and are stuffed with the leftovers from the sweaters. Wendy also makes the "Yokel Bear", produced from the famous Fair Isle Yoke sweaters. They make a unique gift to take home with you and are available at many outlets all over the islands,

BELTAIN

Lower Wick, Gulberwick, Shetland ZE2 9JX
Tel: 01595 694777
e-mail:beltain@ecosse.net website: www.beltaincandles.co.uk

For candles that fill a room with natural, fresh fragrances, make your way to **Beltain**, in the Shetland Islands. It is owned by Katrina Semple,who hand-makes and sells a wonderful range of fragrant candles that can burn for up to 50 hours. The scents used are of the highest quality, and include such wonderful themes as "winter spice", "tangerine", "rambling rose" and "cinnamon". Beltain also sells scented oils and sachets, aroma rings and "scent pies". Any one of them would make an unusual and welcome gift or souvenir.

Photo by Shannon Tofts,Edinburgh

MOUSA

13 miles S of Lerwick

A broch is an ancient, round, fortified tower made of stone. There are over 70 examples on the Shetlands, with one of the finest being the **Mousa Broch** (Historic Scotland) on this tiny island. It was built sometime between the 1st and 3rd centuries, and is still over 40 feet high. The upper stone courses are gone, but you can still see the stairways embedded in the double walls, which slope inwards as they get higher. The curious thing about brochs such as these is that they are only found in Scotland.

FAIR ISLE

46 miles S of Lerwick

The most southerly of the Shetland Islands lies halfway between Orkney and Shetland. It is owned by the National Trust for Scotland (see panel on page 448), and with a population of about 70, is one of the remotest inhabited islands in the country. The island was once owned by the Scottish director of the Royal Society for the Protection of Birds, George Waterston, and at the **George Waterston Memorial Centre and Museum** there are displays bout the island's history and wildlife.

FETLAR

40 miles NE of Lerwick

This small island is connected to the island of Yell by a ferry. The **Fetlar Interpretive Centre** at Beach of Houble explains the history of the island, and there is a library of films (most transferred to video) and genealogical papers. Though it is locally run and funded, it won the 2000 Museum of the Year Award in the

Cormorants, Fair Isle

Educational Initiative category.

Yell

30 miles N of Lerwick

Yell is the second largest island in the Shetlands archipelago, and is connected to Mainland by a ferry running from Toft to Ulsta. The 17th century **Old Haa of Burravoe** is the oldest complete building on the island, and sits at its south east corner. The **Lumbister Reserve** is owned and managed by the Royal Society for the Protection of Birds, and sits in the middle of the island, between the Whale Firth (Scotland's smallest "firth") and Basta Voe.

Unst

46 miles N of Lerwick

This is the most northerly of the Shetland Islands, and **Hermaness** is the

Fair Isle

Shetland ZE2 9JU
website: www.fairisle.org.uk

One of the most isolated inhabited islands in Britain. In a successful effort to stem depopulation, the Trust has encouraged and initiated various improvements, including a renewable energy project using wind power.

The intricate, colourful knitted patterns, which take their name from the island, are famous and the Fair Isle Knitting Co operative sells island knitwear world wide. Additional crafts now include traditional wooden boat building, spinning, weaving, dyeing, felting, locker hooking, wood-turning and fiddle making, and the manufacture of straw backed chairs, spinning wheels and stained glass windows.

Fair Isle is a bird-watcher's paradise, A warm welcome awaits visitors, with opportunities to observe exceptional flora, fauna, archaeology, spectacular cliff scenery and traditional crofting pr actices. The Trust, in partnership with the islanders and the Bird Observatory, is currently working on marine protection.

most northerly point in the whole of the United Kingdom. The gaunt ruins of **Muness Castle** lie at the south west corner of the island, and mark what was the most northerly castle in Britain. It was built by Lawrence Bruce, a relative of the hated Patrick Stewart, in 1598, and the man was every bit as cruel and bloodthirsty as his more famous relative.

TOURIST INFORMATION CENTRES

ABERDEEN

St Nicholas House,
Broad Street,
AB9 1DE
Tel: 01224 632727
Fax: 01224 620415

ABERFELDY

The Square,
PH15 2DD
Tel: 01887 820276

ABERFOYLE

Trossachs Discovery Centre
Main Street, FK8 3UQ
Tel: 01877 382352

ABINGTON

Welcome Break Service Area
Junction 13, M74
ML12 6RG
Tel: 01864 502436
Fax: 01864 502765

ALFORD

Railway Museum
Station Yard, AB33 8AD
Tel: 019755 62052
Seasonal

ALVA

Mill Trail Visitor Centre,
FK12 5EN
Tel: 01259 769696

ANSTRUTHER

Scottish Fisheries Museum,
KY10 3AB Tel: 01333
311073
Seasonal

ARBROATH

Market Place,
DD11 1HR
Tel: 01241 872609
Fax: 01241 878550

ARDGARTAN

Arrochar, G83 7AR
Tel: 01301 702432
Fax: 01301 702432
Seasonal

AUCHTERARDER

90 High Street,
PH3 IBJ
Tel: 01764 663450
Fax: 01764 664235

AVIEMORE

Grampian Road,
PH22 1PP
Tel: 01479 810363
Fax: 01479 811063

AYR

22 Sandgate
KA7 1BW
Tel: 01292 288688
Fax: 01292 288686

BALLACHULISH

Argyll, PA39 4JB
Tel: 01855 811296
Fax: 01855 811720
Seasonal

BALLATER

Station Square,
AB35 5QB
Tel: 013397 55306
Seasonal

BALLOCH

The Old Station Building
Balloch Road, G83 8LQ
Tel: 01389 753533
Seasonal

BANCHORY

Bridge Street,
AB31 5SX
Tel: 01330 822000
Seasonal

BANFF

Collie Lodge,
AB45 1AU
Tel: 01261 812419
Fax: 01261 815807
Seasonal

BETTYHILL

Clachan,
Sutherland, KW14 7SZ
Tel: 01641 521342
Fax: 01641 521342
Seasonal

BIGGAR

155 High Street,
ML12 6DL
Tel: 01899 221066
Seasonal

BLAIRGOWRIE

26 Wellmeadow,
PH10 6AS
Tel: 01250 872960
Fax: 01250 873701
Ski Line 01250 875800

BO'NESS

Seaview Car Park,
EH51 0AJ
Tel: 01506 826626
Seasonal

BOWMORE

Isle of Islay PA43 7JP
Tel: 01496 810254

BRAEMAR

The Mews,
Mar Road, AB35 5YL
Tel: 013397 41600
Fax: 013397 41643

BRECHIN

Brechin Castle Centre,
Haughmuir, DD9 6RL
Tel: 01356 623050
Seasonal

BROADFORD

Isle of Skye, IV49 9AB
Tel: 01471 822361
Fax: 01471 822141
Seasonal

BRODICK

The Pier,
Isle of Arran, KA27 8AU
Tel: 01770 302140/302401
Fax: 01770 302395

CALLANDER

Rob Roy & Trossachs
Visitor Centre
Ancaster Square, FK17 8ED
Tel: 01877 330342
Fax: 01877 330784

CAMPBELTOWN

Mackinnon House,
The Pier
Argyll, PA28 6EF
Tel: 01586 552056
Fax: 01586 553291

CARNOUSTIE

1B High Street,
DD7 6AN
Tel: 01241 852258
Seasonal

CASTLEBAY

Main Street,
Isle of Barra,
H59 5XD
Tel: 01871 810336
Seasonal

CASTLE DOUGLAS

Markethill Car Park,
DG7 1AE
Tel: 01556 502611
Seasonal

COLDSTREAM

High Street,
TD12 4DH
Tel: 01890 882607
Seasonal

CRAIGNURE

The Pier, Isle of Mull,
PA65 6AY
Tel: 01680 812377
Fax: 01680 812497

CRAIL

Museum & Heritage Centre
62 - 64 Marketgate,
KY10 3TL
Tel: 01333 450869
Seasonal

CRATHIE

Car Park,
Balmoral Castle
AB35 5TB
Tel: 013397 42414
Seasonal

CRIEFF

Town Hall,
High Street,
PA7 3AU
Tel: 01764 652578

DAVIOT WOOD

A9 by Inverness IV2 5XL
Tel: 01463 772203
Fax: 01463 772022
Seasonal

DORNOCH

The Square,
IV25 3SD
Tel: 01862 810400
Fax: 01862 810644

DRYMEN

Drymen Library
The Square, G63 0BL
Tel: 01360 660068
Seasonal

DUFFTOWN

Clock Tower,
The Square, AB55 4AD
Tel: 01340 820501
Seasonal

DUMBARTON

Milton,
A82 Northbound,
G82 2TZ
Tel: 01389 742306

DUMFRIES

Whitesands,
DG1 4TH
Tel: 01387 253862
Fax: 01387 245555

DUNBAR

143 High Street,
EH42 1ES
Tel: 01368 863353
Fax: 01368 864999

DUNBLANE
Stirling Road,
FK15 9EP
Tel: 01786 824428
Seasonal

DUNDEE
7-21 Castle Street,
DD1 3AA
Tel: 01382 527527
Fax: 01382 527550

DUNFERMLINE
13/15 Maygate,
KY12 7NE
Tel: 01383 720999
Fax: 01383 730187
Seasonal

DUNKELD
The Cross,
PH8 0HN
Tel: 01350 727688

DUNOON
7 Alexandra Parade,
PA23 8AB
Tel: 01369 703785
Fax: 01369 706085

DUNVEGAN
2 Lochside,
Dunvegan
Isle of Skye,
IV55 8WB
Tel: 01470 521581
Fax: 01470 521582
Seasonal

DURNESS
Sango,
IV27 4PZ
Tel: 01971 511259
Fax: 01971 511368
Seasonal

EDINBURGH
Edinburgh & Scotland
Information Centre,
3 Princes Street,
EH2 2QP
Tel: 0131 473 3800
Fax: 0131 473 3881

EDINBURGH
Airport Tourist
Information Desk,
EH12 9DN
Counter enquiries only

ELGIN
17 High Street,
IV30 1EG
Tel: 01343 542666/543388
Fax: 01343 552982

EYEMOUTH
Auld Kirk, Manse Road
TD14 5JE
Tel: 018907 50678
Seasonal

FALKIRK
2-4 Glebe Street,
FK1 1HU
Tel: 01324 620244
Fax: 01324 638440

FORFAR
40 East High Street,
DD8 1BA
Tel: 01307 467876
Seasonal

FORRES
116 High Street,
IV36 0NP
Tel: 01309 672938
Seasonal

FORT AUGUSTUS
Car Park,
Inverness-shire,
PH32 4DD
Tel: 01320 366367
Fax: 01320 366779
Seasonal

FORT WILLIAM
Cameron Square,
PH33 6AJ
Tel: 01397 703781
Fax: 01397 705184

FORTH BRIDGES
by North Queensferry,
KY11 IHP
Tel: 01383 417759

FRASERBURGH
Saltoun Square,
AB43 9DA
Tel: 01346 518315
Seasonal

GAIRLOCH
Auchtercairn,
IV21 2DN
Tel: 01445 712130
Fax: 01445 712071
Seasonal

GALASHIELS
St John Street,
TD1 3JX
Tel: 01896 755551
Seasonal

GATEHOUSE OF FLEET
Car Park,
Castle Douglas,
DG7 2HP
Tel: 01557 814212
Seasonal

GIRVAN

Bridge Street, KA26 9HH
Tel: 01465 714950
Seasonal

GLASGOW

11 George Square G2 1DY
Tel: 0141 204 4400
Fax: 0141 221 3524

GLASGOW

Airport Tourist Information
PA3 2PF
Tel: 0141 848 4440
Fax: 0141 849 1444

GLENSHIEL

Kintail, Kyle of Lochalsh,
IV40 8HW
Tel: 01599 511264
Seasonal

GRANTOWN ON SPEY

High Street,
PH26 3EH
Tel /Fax: 01479 872773
Seasonal

GRETNA GREEN

Old Blacksmith's Shop,
DG16 5EA
Tel: 01461 337834
Seasonal

HAMILTON

Road Chef Services,
M74 Northbound
ML3 6JW
Tel: 01698 285590
Fax: 01698 891494

HAWICK

Drumlanrig's Tower,
TD9 9EN
Tel: 01450 372547
Fax: 01450 373993
Seasonal

HELENSBURGH

The Clock Tower,
G84 7PA
Tel: 01436 672642
Seasonal

HELMSDALE

Coupar Park,
Sutherland,
KW8 6HH
Tel: 01431 821640
Fax: 01431 821640
Seasonal

HUNTLY

The Square,
AB54 8BR
Tel: 01466 792255
Seasonal

INVERARAY

Front Street,
PA32 8UY
Tel: 01499 302063
Fax: 01499 302269

INVERNESS

Castle Wynd,
IV2 3BJ
Tel: 01463 234353
Fax: 01463 710609

INVERURIE

18 High Street
AB51 3XQ
Tel: 01467 625800

IRVINE

New Street KA12 8BB
Tel: 01294 313886
Fax: 01294 313339

JEDBURGH

Murray's Green,
TD8 6BE
Tel: 01835 863435/863688
Fax: 01835 864099

JOHN O'GROATS

County Road, Caithness,
KW1 4YR
Tel: 01955 611373
Fax: 01955 611448
Seasonal

KELSO

Town House, The Square,
TD5 7HF
Tel: 01573 223464
Seasonal

KILCHOAN

Argyll,
PH36 4LH
Tel: 01972 510222
Seasonal

KILLIN

Breadalbane Folklore Centre,
Falls of Dochart,
Main Street, FK21 8XE
Tel: 01567 820254
Fax: 01567 820764
Seasonal

KILMARNOCK

62 Bank Street,
KA1 1ER
Tel: 01563 539090
Fax: 01563 572409

KINCARDINE BRIDGE

Pine 'n' Oak,
Kincardine Bridge Road
Airth, by Falkirk,
FK2 8PP
Tel: 01324 831422
Seasonal

KINGUSSIE

King Street
Inverness-shire,
PH21 1HP
Tel: 01540 661297
Seasonal

KINROSS

Kinross Service Area,
off Junction 6, M90,
KY13 7NQ
Tel: 01577 863680
Fax: 01577 863370

KIRKCALDY

19 Whytescauseway,
KY1 1XF
Tel: 01592 267775
Fax: 01592 203154

KIRKCUDBRIGHT

Harbour Square,
DG6 4HY
Tel: 01557 330494
Seasonal

KIRKWALL

6 Broad Street
Orkney, KW15 1DH
Tel: 01856 872856
Fax: 01856 875056

KIRRIEMUIR

Cumberland Close,
DD8 4EF
Tel: 01575 574097
Seasonal

KYLE OF LOCHALSH

Car Park,
IV40 8AG
Tel: 01599 534276
Fax: 01599 534808
Seasonal

LAIRG

Sutherland, IV27 4PZ
Tel: 01549 402160
Fax: 01549 402160
Seasonal

LANARK

Horsemarket
Ladyacre Road, ML11 7LQ
Tel: 01555 661661
Fax: 01555 666143

LARGS

Promenade,
KA30 8BG
Tel: 01475 673765
Fax: 01475 676297

LERWICK

The Market Cross,
Shetland, ZE1 0LU
Tel: 01595 693434

LOCHBOISDALE

Pier Road,
Isle of South Uist,
HS8 5TH
Tel: 01878 700286
Seasonal

LOCHCARRON

Main Street,
IV54 8YB
Tel: 01520 722357
Fax: 01520 722324
Seasonal

LOCHGILPHEAD

Lochnell Street,
PA31 8JL
Tel: 01546 602344
Seasonal

LOCHINVER

Main Street,
IV27 4LT
Tel: 01571 844330
Fax: 01571 844373
Seasonal

LOCHMADDY

Pier Road,
Isle of North Uist,
HS6 5AA
Tel: 01876 500321
Seasonal

MALLAIG

Inverness-shire,
PH41 4QS
Tel: 01687 462170
Fax: 01687 462064
Seasonal

MELROSE

Abbey House,
TD6 9LG
Tel: 01896 822555
Seasonal

MILLPORT

28 Stuart Street,
Isle of Cumbrae,
KA28 0AJ
Tel /Fax: 01475 530753
Seasonal

MILTON SEE ENTRY FOR DUMBARTON

MOFFAT

Churchgate,
DG10 9EG
Tel: 01683 220620
Seasonal

MONTROSE

Bridge Street,
DD10 8AB
Tel: 01674 672000
Seasonal

MUSSELBURGH SEE OLD CRAIGHALL ENTRY

NAIRN

62 King Street,
IV21 4DN
Tel /Fax: 01667 452753
Seasonal

NEWTONGRANGE

Scottish Mining Museum
Lady Victoria Colliery,
EH22 4QN
Tel: 0131 663 4262
Seasonal

NEWTON STEWART

Dashwood Square,
DG8 6GQ
Tel: 01671 402431
Seasonal

NORTH BERWICK

Quality Street,
EH39 4HJ
Tel: 01620 892197
Fax: 01620 893667

NORTH KESSOCK

Ross-shire,
IV1 1XB
Tel: 01463 731505
Fax: 01463 731701
Seasonal

OBAN

Argyll Square,
PA34 4AR
Tel: 01631 563122
Fax: 01631 564273

OLD CRAIGHALL

Granada Service Area A1
Musselburgh,
EH21 8RE
Tel: 0131 653 6172
Fax: 0131 653 2805

PAISLEY

9A Gilmour Street,
PA1 1DD
Tel: 0141 889 0711
Fax: 0141 848 1363

PEEBLES

High Street,
EH45 8AG
Tel: 01721 720138
Fax: 01721 724401

PENICUIK

Edinburgh Crystal
Visitor Centre,
Eastfield, EH26 8HJ
Tel: 01968 673846
Seasonal

PERTH

Lower City Mills,
West Mill Street,
Perth PH1 5QP
Tel: 01738 450600
Fax: 01738 444863

PERTH

Caithness Glass,
Inveralmond A9
Western City Bypass
PH1 3TZ
Tel: 01738 638481

PITLOCHRY

22 Atholl Road,
PH16 5DB
Tel: 01796 472215/472751
Fax: 01796 474046

PORTREE

Bayfield House,
Bayfield Road
Isle of Skye,
IV51 9EL
Tel: 01478 612137
Fax: 01478 612141

RALIA

A9 North by Newtonmore,
PH20 1DD
Tel /Fax: 01540 673253
Seasonal

ROTHESAY

15 Victoria Street
Isle of Bute,
PA20 0AJ
Tel: 01700 502151
Fax: 01700 505156

ST ANDREWS

70 Market Street,
KY16 9NU
Tel: 01334 472021
Fax: 01334 478422

SELKIRK

Halliwell's House,
TD7 4BL
Tel: 01750 20054
Seasonal

SHIEL BRIDGE SEE ENTRY FOR GLENSHIEL

SPEAN BRIDGE

Woolen Mill Car Park,
PH34 4EP
Tel: 01397 712576
Fax: 01397 712675
Seasonal

STIRLING

Dumbarton Road,
FK8 2LQ
Tel: 01786 475019
Fax: 01786 450039

STIRLING - PIRNHALL

Motorway Service Area
Junction 9 M9,
FK7 8ET
Tel: 01786 814111
Seasonal

STIRLING

Royal Burgh of Stirling
Visitor Centre,
FK8 1EH
Tel: 01786 479901

STONEHAVEN

66 Allardice Street,
AB39 2AA
Tel: 01569 762806
Seasonal

STORNOWAY

26 Cromwell Street
Isle of Lewis,
H51 2DD
Tel: 01851 703088
Fax: 01851 705244

STRANRAER

Burns House,
28 Harbour Street,
DG9 7RD
Tel: 01776 702595
Fax: 01776 889156

STRATHPEFFER

The Square,
N14 9DW
Tel: 01997 421415
Fax: 01997 421460
Seasonal

STROMNESS

Ferry Terminal Building
The Pier Head,
Orkney,
KW16 3AA
Tel: 01856 850716
Fax: 01856 850777

STRONTIAN

Argyll,
PH36 4HZ
Tel: 01967 402131
Fax: 01967 402131
Seasonal

TARBERT

Harbour Street,
Argyll, PA29 6UD
Tel: 01880 820429
Seasonal

TARBERT

Pier Road,
Isle of Harris,
HS3 3DG
Tel: 01859 502011
Seasonal

TARBET-LOCH LOMOND

Main Street,
G83 7DE
Tel: 01301 702260
Fax: 01301 702224
Seasonal

THURSO

Riverside,
KW14 8BU
Tel: 01847 892371
Fax: 01847 893155
Seasonal

TOBERMORY

Isle of Mull,
PA75 6NU
Tel: 01688 302182
Fax: 01688 302145
Seasonal

TOMINTOUL

The Square,
AB37 9ET
Tel: 01807 580285
Fax: 01807 580285
Seasonal

TYNDRUM

Main Street,
FK20 8RY
Tel: 01838 400246
Seasonal

UIG

Ferry Terminal,
Isle of Skye,
IV51 9XX
Tel: 01470 542404
Fax: 01470 542404
Seasonal

ULLAPOOL

Argyle Street,
IV26 2UR
Tel: 01854 612135
Fax: 01854 613031
Seasonal

WICK

Whitechapel Road,
KW1 4EA
Tel: 01955 602596
Fax: 01995 604940

INDEX OF ADVERTISERS

Jarrold
Pathfinder Guides

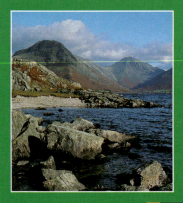

- Ordnance Survey mapping

- 28 walk routes, graded easy, moderate and challenging

- Introduces you to the area and highlights the most scenic routes

- Details useful organisations, refreshment stops and places to leave your car

- Series covers all of the UK

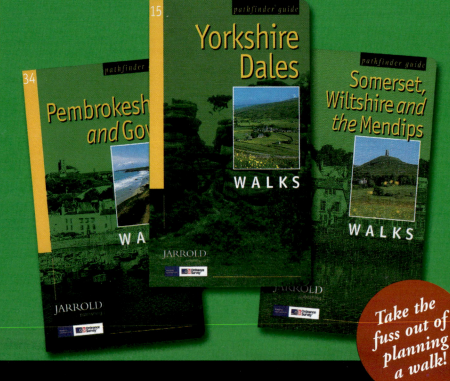

34

pathfinder guide

Pembrokesh
and Gov

W A

JARROLD

15

pathfinder guide

Yorkshire
Dales

W A L K S

JARROLD

pathfinder guide

Somerset,
Wiltshire *and*
***the* Mendips**

W A L K S

JARROLD

Take the fuss out of planning a walk!

Available at tourist outlets,
bookshops and specialist walking outlets

Jarrold
Short Walks

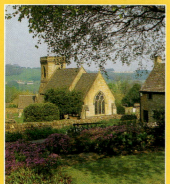

- 20 easy-to-follow walks for the whole family
- Ordnance Survey mapping and colour photography
- Handy pocket-sized format
- Points of interest for children
- Information on refreshment stops, public facilities and transport

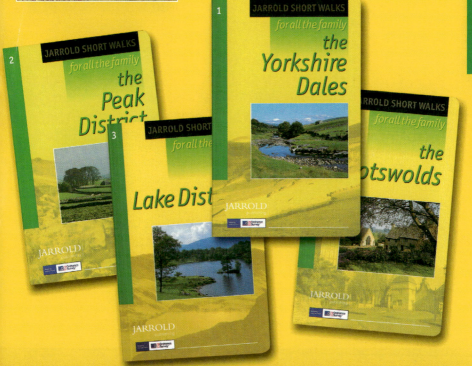

JARROLD SHORT WALKS
for all the family
**the
Peak
District**
2

JARROLD SHORT
for all the
Lake Dist
3

JARROLD SHORT WALKS
for all the family
**the
Yorkshire
Dales**
1
JARROLD

RROLD SHORT WALKS
for all the family
**the
otswolds**
JARROLD

Buy direct: www
Tel: 0126

RROLD
publishing

Travel Publishing

The Hidden Places

Regional and National guides to the less well-known places of interest and places to eat, stay and drink

Hidden Inns

Regional guides to traditional pubs and inns throughout the United Kingdom

Golfers Guides

Regional and National guides to 18 hole golf courses and local places to stay, eat and drink

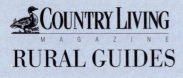

COUNTRY LIVING MAGAZINE
RURAL GUIDES

Regional and National guides to the traditional countryside of Britain and Ireland with easy to read facts on places to visit, stay, eat, drink and shop

For more information:

Phone: 0118 981 7777
e-mail: adam@travelpublishing.co.uk

Fax: 0118 982 0077
website: www.travelpublishing.co.uk

Easy-to-use, Informative
Travel Guides on the British Isles

Travel Publishing Limited

7a Apollo House • Calleva Park • Aldermaston • Berkshire RG7 8TN

ORDER FORM

To order any of our publications just fill in the payment details below and complete the order form. For orders of less than 4 copies please add £1 per book for postage and packing. Orders over 4 copies are P & P free.

Please Complete Either:

I enclose a cheque for £ _____ made payable to Travel Publishing Ltd

Or:

Card No: _____   Expiry Date: _____

Signature: _____

NAME: _____

ADDRESS: _____

TEL NO: _____

Please either send, telephone, fax or e-mail your order to:
Travel Publishing Ltd, 7a Apollo House, Calleva Park, Aldermaston, Berkshire RG7 8TN
Tel: 0118 981 7777   Fax: 0118 982 0077 e-mail: karen@travelpublishing.co.uk

HIDDEN PLACES REGIONAL TITLES	PRICE	QUANTITY
Cambs & Lincolnshire	£8.99	....
Chilterns	£8.99	....
Cornwall	£8.99	....
Derbyshire	£8.99	....
Devon	£8.99	....
Dorset, Hants & Isle of Wight	£8.99	....
East Anglia	£8.99	....
Gloucs, Wiltshire & Somerset	£8.99	....
Heart of England	£8.99	....
Hereford, Worcs & Shropshire	£8.99	....
Highlands & Islands	£8.99	....
Kent	£8.99	....
Lake District & Cumbria	£8.99	....
Lancashire & Cheshire	£8.99	....
Lincolnshire & Nottinghamshire	£8.99	....
Northumberland & Durham	£8.99	....
Sussex	£8.99	....
Yorkshire	£8.99	....

HIDDEN PLACES NATIONAL TITLES	PRICE	QUANTITY
England	£10.99	....
Ireland	£10.99	....
Scotland	£10.99	....
Wales	£9.99	....

HIDDEN INNS TITLES	PRICE	QUANTITY
East Anglia	£5.99	....
Heart of England	£5.99	....
Lancashire & Cheshire	£5.99	....
North of England	£5.99	....
South	£5.99	....
South East	£5.99	....
South and Central Scotland	£5.99	....
Wales	£5.99	....
Welsh Borders	£5.99	....
West Country	£5.99	....

COUNTRY LIVING RURAL GUIDES	PRICE	QUANTITY
East Anglia	£9.99	....
Heart of England	£9.99	....
Ireland	£10.99	....
Scotland	£10.99	....
South of England	£9.99	....
South East of England	£9.99	....
Wales	£10.99	....
West Country	£9.99	....

Total Quantity _____

Total Value _____

READER REACTION FORM

The *Travel Publishing* research team would like to receive reader's comments on any visitor attractions or places reviewed in the book and also recommendations for suitable entries to be included in the next edition. This will help ensure that the *Country Living series of Rural Guides* continues to provide its readers with useful information on the more interesting, unusual or unique features of each attraction or place ensuring that their visit to the local area is an enjoyable and stimulating experience. To provide your comments or recommendations would you please complete the forms below and overleaf as indicated and send to:

The Research Department, Travel Publishing Ltd,

7a Apollo House, Calleva Park, Aldermaston, Reading, RG7 8TN.

Your Name:

Your Address:

Your Telephone Number:

Please tick as appropriate: Comments ☐ Recommendation ☐

Name of Establishment:

Address:

Telephone Number:

Name of Contact:

READER REACTION FORM

Comment or Reason for Recommendation:

....

....

....

....

....

....

....

....

....

....

READER REACTION FORM

The *Travel Publishing* research team would like to receive reader's comments on any visitor attractions or places reviewed in the book and also recommendations for suitable entries to be included in the next edition. This will help ensure that the *Country Living series of Rural Guides* continues to provide its readers with useful information on the more interesting, unusual or unique features of each attraction or place ensuring that their visit to the local area is an enjoyable and stimulating experience. To provide your comments or recommendations would you please complete the forms below and overleaf as indicated and send to:

The Research Department, Travel Publishing Ltd,

7a Apollo House, Calleva Park, Aldermaston, Reading, RG7 8TN.

Your Name:

Your Address:

Your Telephone Number:

Please tick as appropriate: Comments ☐ Recommendation ☐

Name of Establishment:

Address:

Telephone Number:

Name of Contact:

READER REACTION FORM

Comment or Reason for Recommendation:

....

....

....

....

....

....

....

....

....

....

INDEX TO TOWNS & PLACES OF INTEREST